Images of Canada:

The Sociological Tradition

p 9-21   43-66   99-110   133-140
179-184   p 202-218

edited by

James Curtis
University of Waterloo

Lorne Tepperman
University of Toronto

Prentice-Hall Canada Inc., *Scarborough,* **Ontario**

Canadian Cataloguing in Publication Data

Main entry under title:
Images of Canada

Bibliography: p.
ISBN 0-13-453086-1

1. Canada — Social conditions. I. Curtis, James E.,
1943-   . II. Tepperman, Lorne, 1943-

HN103.I53 1989   971   C89-093669-2

Prentice-Hall, Inc., Englewood Cliffs, New Jersey
Prentice-Hall International, Inc., London
Prentice-Hall of Australia, Pty., Ltd., Sydney
Prentice-Hall of India Pvt., Ltd., New Delhi
Prentice-Hall of Japan, Inc., Tokyo
Prentice-Hall of Southeast Asia (Pte.) Ltd., Singapore
Editora Prentice-Hall do Brasil Ltda., Rio de Janeiro
Prentice-Hall Hispanoamericana, S.A., Mexico

ISBN 0-13-453086-1

Production Editor: *Mary de Souza*
Production Coordinator: *Sandra Paige*
Cover and Interior Design: *Denise Marcella*
Typesetting: *Q Composition Inc.*

1 2 3 4 5 AP 94 93 92 91 90

Printed and bound in Canada by The Alger Press Limited

Contents

Acknowledgements

We want to express our appreciation to the scholars, past and present, whose work we present in this volume. This is their book. But, beyond this, these writers deserve our thanks and praise, as we will show, for providing us with windows — "images" or "perspectives" — through which we may observe the basic social processes of Canadian society. Taken together, these images are the defining essentials of a sociology of Canada.

We are also indebted to several people who provided us with valuable assistance of different types in putting this volume together. First, Al Wain, a freelance editor, skillfully shortened almost all of the selections in this volume quite substantially, so that the material would be fast-paced and we could include the work of more authors. Second, Lorraine Thompson, at the University of Waterloo, very ably prepared portions of the manuscript and handled correspondence. Third, four reviewers (B. Blishen, York University; Ellen Gee, Simon Fraser University; L. Laczko, University of Ottawa; David MacLennan, University of Western Ontario) and many colleagues gave us helpful advice on the contents of the book. Finally, at Prentice-Hall, Pat Ferrier, College Acquisitions Editor, gave his strong support to this project from its inception, and Monica Schwalbe, Katherine Mototsune, Jean MacDonald, and Mary de Souza shepherded the manuscript through the editorial and production stages.

Introduction

This book brings together classic readings on Canadian society that have been written from the sociological perspective. Some excerpts are older, groundbreaking or founding articles; others are more recent. The more recent articles develop arguments arising from criticism of founding works on Canadian society. Read together, the articles provide a sense of continuity in discussions about Canadian society. They offer an introduction to a changing Canadian sociology and to the changing society it studies.

Our organizing principle is the **image** of Canada. By image we mean a metaphor, perception or concept that captures a central reality of Canadian history or contemporary social organization. We have identified nine such images in Canadian sociology. There may be others we have not discovered. Moreover, some readers might argue that certain images we discuss are so closely related that they could be merged. So, the fact that we have identified nine images, not eight or ten, is somewhat arbitrary. But the images we discuss are surely central and well known in Canadian sociology.

The nine images we have identified are the following:

Two solitudes: Canada is a society of two quite different cultures, with different ways of thinking and living that have little contact with each other.

A British fragment: English-speaking Canada's culture retains a great deal of British influence over the ways Canadians view tradition and change.

A closed frontier: Canada's geography and terrain have allowed social control to remain firmly in the hands of powerful central interests.

A metropolis and hinterland: Canadian cities, towns and villages are tied together, and to the outside world, through a chain of dominance based on capital.

A fragile federation: Canada's regions are weakly tied together in a confederation; Canadians' sentiments, cultures and allegiances are local, not national.

Accommodating elites: Canada's corporate, state, ideological, and labour elites maintain contact and pursue their often competing interests by means of accommodation and compromise.

A vertical mosaic: In Canada, ethnicity and social class have been historically tied together, with the founding Anglophone group holding the positions of greatest power.

A class society: Social class affects life-chances and loyalties in Canada, and class relations have shaped, and continue to shape, the direction of social change.

The double ghetto: Women in Canadian society suffer additional, unique disadvantages, and have to work twice as hard to get half as much in return.

These images could each be phrased with a question mark following the concept — two solitudes? a British fragment? a closed frontier?, and so on. For many scholars, these images are hypotheses about how Canadian society currently operates or used to operate. While for those who criticize the images or the theories explaining them, the images are followed by question marks because they are not found to be compelling.

Note that these images are not theories; they are concise descriptions of central social patterns in Canada. However, the images come complete with theories explaining how the social patterns of the images occurred and persist. These theories will also be emphasized in our selections. In many instances, the social patterns referred to by one image will also arise in the explanations offered for the patterns of another image.

There has been considerable debate around each of the nine images making up this volume. Such debate may be unsettling for those students of Canadian society who might like to see firm, clear answers about the character of Canadian society. But one will not find pat answers in this book. The debates here yield only clarification and qualification, assisting in the development of a more precise and a deeper understanding of the complex issues involved. Debate makes scholars strive to be more persuasive in their research; the result is a steady, if sometimes slow, accumulation of knowledge in sociology.

The nine images are not mutually exclusive, though in some cases, commitment to one image means a rejection of one or many others. For example, the class society approach, growing out of Marxism, would lead a scholar to expect that Canadian society was ruled by a dominant capitalist class, likely operating through corporate and state elites. This image is not consistent with the idea that there are accommodating elites and that Canadian society is run by a broader set of elites from several institutional areas.

For the most part, the rejection of competing images is rare. Generally, sociologists who have focused on one central image have simply ignored or downplayed the importance of others. For example, John Porter (1965), who characterized Canada as a vertical mosaic easily accepted the notion that Canada had two solitudes, was a British fragment, had accommodating elites and was replete with class inequality. However, Porter more or less ignored the facts of Canada's regionalism — the fragile federation, and its closed frontier, metropolis-hinterland patterns — and the double ghetto.

We do not argue that Canada is the only society that might be characterized by any of these images. For example, many societies display class and gender inequality, competing fragments of earlier colonial cultures, economic dependency and the results of a hard or closed frontier. Moreover, many societies have grown out of British roots and may still be influenced by them. In fact, it would be instructive to study how many of the images discussed in this book might just as validly be applied to other former British colonies (for example, India, South Africa, Australia), to other northern countries or territories (for example, Iceland, Greenland, Norway, Scotland, Siberia), or to other economic dependencies of major powers (for example, Mexico, Rumania, Israel, Korea). The reader can most usefully consider this book a sourcebook for understanding how Canadian society has developed, and how different images of society could be combined for fruitful cross-national comparison.

Although we do not consider each of the nine images uniquely applicable to Canada, we do believe that the details of these images, taken together, uniquely define Canada. That is, no other society — past or present — combines these nine characteristics in the way that Canada does. In this sense, these nine images are central to understanding what Canadian society is about.

Each of the nine images can be studied separately, as is frequently done in research. However, we should remember that they refer to phenomena that occur simultaneously in Canadian society and often affect one another. They are cut from the whole cloth of Canadian society (on this point, see especially Wallace Clement's *Does Class Matter?* in Section VIII of this volume). They should only be "unwoven" from Canadian society for a closer look; a full appreciation of the fabric of Canadian society requires that they be woven back together again. It is for this reason that you will find the materials of different images appearing together both in the selections that follow and in our introductions to the Sections.

One illustration of the inter-connection of the images should suffice for now. Consider the issue of Canadian-American differences in national identity, a question of paramount interest in the literature around Canada as a British fragment. Many researchers wonder why Canadians do not have a more distinctive cultural identity, one that sets Canadians off from Americans more. The British connection has not made Anglophone Canadians as different from Americans as one might expect. Why? As it turns out, all of the other sociological images, with the exception of the double ghetto, have been implicated in scholars' answers to this question. Some scholars have explained the absence of a more distinctive Canadian identity by virtue of the great cultural variations within Canada: by the two solitudes, the frontier, metropolis-hinterland, a fragile federation, and a vertical mosaic. Others have explained it through reference to the strong ties between parts of Canada and parts of the United States. These ties are rooted in the dynamics of class, metropolis-hinterland and accommodating elites.

The first group argues that no single Canadian culture and identity exist largely because of social and economic fragmentation within Canada. They sometimes start with the observation that Canada comprises at least two cultures, French-speaking and English-speaking, and that these two cultures have very different historical roots. Even English-speaking Canada's culture is fragmented. Great differences exist in the world view, art forms, and to some degree, ways of life, in the Maritime provinces, Prairies, and industrial heartland of Ontario. These differences result from a number of historical forces and the geographic realities of frontier-centre and metropolis-hinterland relationships. First, there are great distances between Canadian regions. Until recent times, travel and communication between areas a thousand or more miles apart (as between Toronto and Halifax to the east, or Toronto and Winnipeg to the west) have been limited. The mass media and air travel have played a large part in introducing the

Canadian regions to one another, and so has migration between the hinterlands and the industrial centre. It is likely that regional differences will diminish as travel and communication increase, but at present, the regional distinctiveness still persists.

In addition to the lack of communication is the sheer difference in historical experience. Canada's regions were settled at different times by different kinds of people — for example, the Maritimes by large numbers of Irish and Scottish Catholics, the Prairies by large numbers of Eastern Europeans. Settlers were responding to different economic opportunities: the Maritime settlers to opportunities in fishing, mining, grazing and subsistence farming; the Prairie settlers to opportunities for large-scale wheat farming and cattle raising. They experienced their good times and bad times in different periods of history. The period of Maritime prosperity (the 19th century) had long since ended when Prairie wheat farming became economically secure (in the 20th century), for example.

Not only do past and present experiences differ from region to region, but regions are, to a very large degree, in opposition to one another. A clear sense of exploitation by, and alienation from, the industrial heartland is observable in both the Prairies and Maritimes. A similar feeling once existed in Quebec, but has moderated with the growth of provincial wealth and autonomy in the last 25 years. In the Canadian system of government, many important powers are reserved by the province, making for the fragile federation. The federal government in Ottawa must weigh national interests against regional interests, and one region's interests against another's.

Finally, Canada is also multicultural: it is made up of many large, well established ethnic and linguistic groups. Cultural and linguistic diversity survive in Canada. The many ethnic groups — the Jews, Ukrainians, Italians, Chinese, and dozens of others — do not enjoy formal (i.e., constitutional) recognition as do the founding French, English and Native cultures. But they are being helped and encouraged to avoid assimilation in a way that is absent in the United States. Even if cultural assimilation were desired in Canada, it could not easily be achieved, because of Canada's extremely high rate of immigration. John Porter (1965) characterized Canada as a "great railroad station," with large numbers of people always in transit, both into the country and out of it. This tremendous turnover of population sets severe limits on the development and propagation of a pan-Canadian identity that is as strong or stronger than the ethnic identities which immigrants bring with them. The multiculturalism also maintains a vertical mosaic whereby the British charter group, especially, has a better socio-economic lot than other ethnic groups. This means different lifestyles and experiences, outlooks and identities, for the ethnic groups.

The second group of scholars, who seek to explain the absence of a distinctive Canadian cultural identity, argue that overall similarities in the class structures of Canada and the United States (both are bureaucratized, advanced capitalist societies) have meant that people in the two countries have somewhat similar work lives, and this has functioned to standardize their outlooks and identities. It is argued that this standardization, coupled with increased linkages between the two nations as part of the metropolis-hinterland process (linkages which have been presided over by the accommodating Canadian elites), has tended to homogenize the ways Canadians and Americans think.

So, the phenomenon of the British fragment, like all the images in this volume, has complex relationships with the other phenomena.

In putting together this collection, we do not claim that sociologists have a monopoly on understanding Canadian society. A great many insights are to be found in Canadian history, political science, economics and literature. Indeed it is possible to find most of the same images (and debates) under different names in each of these other disciplines. Sociology does not lay claim to exclusive knowledge, and this book only shows the sociology student from where sociologists have drawn some of these ideas.

Each section contains both older and more recent excerpts. Our purpose is to show how an original insight was either accepted and developed or, as often happened, rejected in favour of an alternate point of view. So for example, recent articles in the Section entitled "A British Fragment" probe whether the British influence on Canadian culture, if it ever existed, still exists today. Similarly, recent articles on the "Metropolis and Hinterland" probe whether Canada is still economically dependent today and, if so, whether the reason is to be found inside Canada's borders.

In selecting pieces, we have tried to represent the most important and well written articles on each image. Some important works and authors had to be left out, otherwise the book could easily have been twice as long. The pieces that have been selected should be considered the first word, not the last word, on the topics we are introducing.

Sections are organized in roughly chronological order, in several senses. What comes earliest in the book is material on issues that (1) influenced Canadian history first, and (2) which sociologists analyzed first. For example, the double ghetto section comes last not because gender inequality is less important in Canadian society than English-French inequality, nor because it is just a recent phenomenon, but because the issues of gender equality have surfaced as central themes in Canadian sociology only in the last two decades.

Is Canada really a vertical mosaic? Does British cultural influence persist? Do elites perform a valuable role, or a harmful role, in Canadian society? Debate continues to surround these and many of the other images discussed in this book. We believe that the evidence is largely complete on many of these questions, and that it is possible to draw conclusions from the mass of sociological research which occupied so many scholars for so long. But rather than press our own views on the research evidence, we will try to leave these questions open. You should ponder them, using the evidence provided here (and elsewhere), and discuss them in class. We hope you find the exercise interesting. Welcome to these debates on the key sociological images of Canadian society!

SECTION I

Two Solitudes

Two Solitudes, a classic Canadian novel by Hugh MacLennan (1945), captures in fiction the way Canada's two main cultures — Francophone and Anglophone — co-existed in post World War I Quebec. The title implies not only the distinctiveness of each culture-group, but also its isolation and the difficulty the two groups have in communicating with each other. Like many images of Canadian society, this goes back a long way. Forty-five years ago, historian Arthur Lower (1943) asked, rhetorically, "who will deny that the deep division between French and English is the greatest, the most arresting, the most difficult" of all the antagonisms on which Canadian society rests. Lower called it the "primary antithesis of Canadian history."

Britain's successful conquest of New France and the subsequent Anglophone domination of French Canadians simply hardened the French Canadian commitment to tradition. As Lower says, every political fight since 1791 has been, at bottom, a fight about the English conquest. He concludes, "If we can understand the reactions of Ecuador or Paraguay to this northern world of Anglo-Saxons, Slavs and Germans in which we live, we shall understand that of Quebec readily enough" (*ibid*.). Accordingly, Lower wonders how the major forces of modern life — chiefly, urbanism and industrialism — will affect Francophone Canadians. "What will be the outcome of the clash of medievalism and modernism, of the regime of the natural law and the acquisitive ethic?" he asks (1943: 7). And this is precisely the question Hugh MacLennan (1945) tried to answer in his novel, *Two Solitudes*. Moreover, the same question motivated Everett Hughes, an American sociologist, to write *French Canada in Transition* (1943), arguably the first important work of Canadian sociology.

Hughes, an American sociologist trained in the United States, was working well within the sociological tradition. From the middle of the nineteenth century onward, social scientists had recorded the changes accompanying what we today call *modernization*. Modernization includes a variety of changes, among them the movement of large numbers of people out of agriculture and into industry, urban residence, mass literacy, a market economy for goods and services, and the unviversal franchise. Many of these changes had begun a century earlier, with the industrial revolution (around 1775) and the American and French revolutions (1776 and 1789, respectively). By 1900, many consequences were in full view, and a backlash had even begun. Some (for example, Robert Nisbet, an American sociologist; see Nisbet, 1966) claim that sociology itself grew out of the conservative backlash against changes which were considered too rapid.

Sociology developed in the late nineteenth and early twentieth centuries as an attempt to understand these enormous transformations. Sociological descriptions of the changes often employed ideal types or polar opposites: *Gemeinschaft-Gesellschaft* (F. Tonnies, [1887] 1963); mechanical solidarity-organic solidarity (E. Durkheim, [1893] 1933); traditional legitimacy-rational legal legitimacy (M. Weber, 1964); feudalism-capitalism (K. Marx and F. Engels, [1848] 1967); folk-urban (R. Redfield, 1953), and so on. In each instance, to be explained was the change from a traditional social order on the left-hand side of the polarity to a modern one on the right-hand side. These typologies shared many similarities. They all dealt with the shift from small, stable, usually rural communities based largely on kinship and emotional ties, to large, fluid, urban communities based on impersonal contract, self-interest and what Marx called "the cash nexus."

This classic issue in social science — the nature of the transformation from the old to new social order, and the problems people have in adapting to the new order — continued to interest social science in the twentieth century: it simply changed locales. Northern and western Europe had already completed the transformation, as had much of North America. To study the transformation in process, one needed an unmodernized enclave: a society in transition. Accordingly, anthropologists studied native contacts with Westerners in Africa, Asia and Latin America. European sociologists focused attention on change in southern and eastern Europe — Sicily, Greece, Turkey, and Spain, for example. American sociologists studied recent immigrants from rural, peasant backgrounds and learned about their adaptation to urban, industrial life. They also focused attention on pre-industrial enclaves in North America: the deep south, the Appalachians, American black populations (whether in the south or newly migrated northward), and in Quebec. These were the nearest examples of what an earlier kind of social order might have looked like.

Countless research projects dealing in some way with modernization share a few common concerns, chiefly: (1) will cultural differences (and antagonisms) disappear with urbanism and industrialism? and (2) will the transformation to modernity be easy, or hard and filled with conflict and misery? Hughes was the first to ask these questions in the Canadian context and specifically about French Canada.

Fifty years later, the world is quite different. In Canada, the two founding cultures communicate more often and more openly than they once did. How did this change come about? Did the Francophones simply modernize, giving up their traditional values along the way? Did both Anglophones and Francophones compromise, each learning from the other? And what part did non-Anglo-Saxon Anglophones, increasingly numerous in Quebec after 1945, play in this transformation?

Implicit in the two solitudes metaphor is a belief that Canadian society is pulled apart by two different ways of thinking. It also implies stability: no one will give up his or her culture unless absolutely forced to do so. Since the Canadian constitution protects both founding cultures, such a renunciation is unlikely. If this theory is correct, the two cultures will probably persist, co-exist and never converge.

However, another hypothesis also makes sense. Bear in mind that the French Canadians have been seriously disadvantaged for most of their history: subject to Roman Catholic Church control over their personal conduct (see the Guindon excerpt in this Section) and to control by English-speaking, typically Protestant, Canadians over matters of earning a living. What if culture is just a shared adaptation to daily experience? If you change that experience, you change the culture. An insular, self-protective French Canadian culture may have been very useful when French Canadians were dominated by Anglo-Saxons and the Catholic Church. Since 1960, they have thrown off both yokes; now they can afford to give up their traditional French Canadian culture. Enjoying new social and economic opportunities, they can change in the direction of the North American cultural norm, because they too now share in the North American lifestyle.

According to this way of thinking, unequal opportunity gives rise to cultural difference. If you equalize opportunity, you eliminate the need for cultural difference. In many ways this image is opposed to the two solitudes image and it implies that Canadians of all backgrounds want the same things but differ in their ability to get them. There are no cultural solitudes, only socially structured differences in opportunity.

The evidence supporting this hypothesis is compelling. Well-educated Francophones have entered fully into the North American lifestyle. Indeed, the Québécois supported the Progressive Conservative party and its free trade deal more staunchly than any other voters in the November 1988 federal election. With economic development and increased clout in confederation, the Québécois have become less politically radical. Moreover, even intermarriage between Anglophones and Francophones — the ultimate measure of social distance — is increasingly frequent, owing to more frequent contact between the two language groups. Greater opportunity (in this case, the opportunity to intermarry) produces social assimilation, just as it produces economic assimilation in other contexts.

Even more dramatic evidence of Francophone modernization is at hand. With increasingly liberal divorce laws, contraception, abortion opportunities, and possibilities for a single life, Francophones have deserted the traditional large French Canadian family in record numbers. Only 25 years ago, sociologist Norman Taylor (1964) was claiming that traditional Francophone loyalties to family life kept modern capitalism from taking root in Quebec. Yet today Francophones have the lowest marriage and fertility rates in the country. Given the chance, they have outdone the traditionally less family-oriented Anglophones in fleeing from family responsibility.

The three papers in this Section offer a variety of views on this issue. In the paper excerpted below, Everett Hughes calls Quebec's rural system "the basis of its culture" and emphasizes that this closed rural system (and Francophone culture) could not have survived without constantly ejecting surplus population. But suddenly, those ejected from the farm were forced to remain in their native region, under Anglo-Saxon industrial authority. Hughes predicted (in 1938) that such people would be likely to "express collective discontent with their position, as an ethnic group, in the new system"; and of course, they did. Hughes, then, is adopting the second model we have discussed: the view that opportunity influences one's cultural outlook and a changed opportunity changes one's outlook. As Hughes once said in conversation, "tradition is sacred only so long as it is useful."

Guy Rocher, however, explains the Quiet Revolution of the 1960s differently. Though Quebec had already become an industrialized society by the end of World War II, a large number of French Canadians "had maintained a preindustrial mentality" (see Rocher's paper included in this Section). Moreover, "they were living in democratric political structures without having the habits, the customs, and the ideas of a fully democratic society." After World War II, the cleavage between new opportunities and old ways of thinking became greater; culture lag produced strain in Quebec society.

Rocher sees the separatist terrorism of the 1960s and early 1970s as resulting from this strain. On the one hand, it results from the opening up of a moral vacuum once Francophones have rejected traditional values and have not found replacements. On the other hand, separatism also results from a gap in the rates of change between opportunity and expectation. Professor Rocher sees a strong connection between cultural values and opportunities, but he considers them equally important as causes of behaviour.

Hubert Guindon's analysis in the final excerpt below is different again. A key concept in his analysis is *secularization*: the declining institutional and political importance of clergy in Quebec society. For Guindon, Quebec begins to modernize most dramatically when lay Francophones begin to revamp traditional institutions, especially government, education, and the economy.

The process of Francophone self-assertion is political, and so is the Anglophone response. As Lord Durham said, these are "two nations warring in the bosom of the same state." For nearly two hundred years, neither culture has been able — despite war, politics and economic competition — to subjugate the other. According to Guindon, Francophone self-assertion in Quebec is not due to traditional (i.e., pre-industrial) cultural values or a temporary strain, but to unending cultural distinctiveness.

Will the two solitudes meet? Will the two cultures converge, and the two nations join together? From Lord Durham onward, no purposeful attempt to bring them together has succeeded. However, contact between the two societies is more frequent and open today than when Arthur Lower and Everett Hughes were writing nearly fifty years ago. Societies change very slowly. Only thirty years have passed since Quebec's Quiet Revolution began. We may have to wait another thirty years before seeing a clear indication of the likely outcome.

1

French-English Relations in Industry in Rural Quebec*

Everett C. Hughes

Quebec has always had industries which exploited the native resources of forest, sea, and lately, of the mines. In the present phase new major industries, which make little use of native materials except water and manpower, have invaded the province. Industries of this type are generally not on the frontiers of settlement, but in the very heart of the province. In the course of the last two decades, Quebec has become more urban than rural. It is now only slightly less industrial than Ontario.

Modern capitalistic industry grew up in a few centres, coincident with an enormous expansion of sources of raw materials and markets. Its spread has taken two forms: the first, still proceeding at a slackening rate, is the extension of its far-flung frontiers; the second is an inner expansion in which industry moves from its most intensely developed older centres to nearby less industrialized regions, where it finds a population accustomed to the main features of Western capitalistic civilization but not sophisticated with respect to its more extreme manifestations. Quebec and the southern United States are among the outstanding regions in which this inner expansion or "mopping up" is taking place.

Industrial development always engenders movements of population. But the pattern of movement in regions to which industry spreads is the reverse of that of the regions in which industry originally grew up. In the original centres the entrepreneurs and managers — few in number — were largely native: the labour force — large in number — was partly recruited by migration from a distance. Especially in the northeastern United States it has been the rule for management to be native and labour foreign and polyglot. In the regions to which industry spreads, the small but powerful managerial class comes from a distance and is culturally alien: the labour force is native and culturally homogeneous. The latter is the case in Quebec.

*Originally published as "Industry and the Rural System in Quebec," in *The Canadian Journal of Economics and Political Science*, IV, August, 1938, pp. 341-349. Reprinted by permission.

Hence the concern of the leaders of its traditional institutions with the repercussions of the new alien system upon the existing scheme of life. Underneath this concern lies unnoticed a functional relationship between the old system and the new.

However antithetical may be the spirit of the new industry to that of traditional Quebec, it is this very industry which allows the customary mode of life to persist. Based as it is on the indivisible family farm, the prevailing rural system presupposes a stable relation between population and tillable land. But the family occupying the indivisible farm is one of the largest in the Western world. How is this contradiction to be explained?[1]

First let us establish the fact of the stability of Quebec's rural population. If we arrange the 66 counties in a rank order starting from the county whose rural and village population of 1931 was furthest below that of 1871, and continuing toward that whose rural and village population of 1931 was highest above that of 1871, it is only after the forty-sixth county that the cumulative total of 1931 becomes equal to that of 1871.[2] These 46 counties form a block with the St. Lawrence and Ottawa rivers as an axis, extending from the Saguenay to the Ontario boundary. Their rural and village population was 705 578 in 1871; in 1931 it was 705 240. This unchanged total is, of course, a result of the manner in which these counties were selected. The significant thing is that they turn out to be a block of contiguous counties, the heart of Quebec.[3] This block contains the major urban centres of the province, it also is the seat of most of the settled, prosperous agriculture.

The rural population of these counties has long been either stationary or declining. Four of them actually decreased in total population between 1851 and 1861. In the same decade 21 of them grew by an amount less than their expected natural increase. In later decades more counties were added to those which lost all or part of their own natural increase. This is the more striking when one considers that most of the urban sections of these counties never ceased to grow. All the greater, then, was the sloughing-off of rural population. Now some of these counties are densely populated while others are not. Those of high density were the first to reach a maximum and then to lose. More recently even those of low density show a tendency to decline. (*Census of Canada*, 1931, vol. I, 109ff.) But, paradoxically, the downward trend of rural population has not been accompanied by a decline of agricultural production or of the number of people engaged in it. Indeed, it is the rule for the rural population to decline somewhat while agricultural production and the number employed in it are still growing (Lemieux et al., 1934).[4] But this decline, according to Lemieux and his associates, has been among the non-farm and part-farm rural population. Meanwhile two kinds of counties are still increasing somewhat in rural population: (1) those near urban centres, and (2) those in the early stages of colonization. But in the older sections of the latter, decline has already set in.

In sum, no further expansion of the rural population of these counties is likely to occur, except for a certain thickening about the cities. Farming is not declining, but the rural population is at a standstill. It is significant that this central block contains nearly all of the country in which the Quebec farmer does not supplement his income by other activities.

The remaining counties form two frontiers; one on the north, and the other on the southeast extending to the Gaspé peninsula. Their increase of rural and village population since 1871 is equal to that of the whole province. But that increase for the province was only 29 per cent; that of unincorporated districts, the strictly rural population, only 17 per cent. This is very small in relation to the rate of natural increase. These fringes have been of importance as symbols rather than as effective absorbers of population. Raoul Blanchard (1935, 1936, 1937a, 1938), the French geographer who has made a detailed study of the exploitation of land in Quebec, finds that the nominal farmers of these frontiers live to a large extent by other means. In the Gaspé peninsula, farming is usually practised in conjunction with fishing, lumbering, or work in the mills. Mr. Blanchard estimates that from one-half to three-quarters of the Gaspé men go to the woods in winter; some are at home only in fall and spring, between seasons of other work. He finds the same true, in varying degree, of the Saguenay — Lac St. Jean districts, of the southeastern counties abutting on Maine, and even of the inland parishes of the old counties of the lower St. Lawrence shore. The sparse population of the Laurentian mountain country notoriously depends more upon wood and tourists than upon agriculture. Life in these fringes does not, in short, generally conform to that pictured in the traditional conception of the self-dependent Quebec farmer. The Quebec frontier is chronic, quickened to real activity here and there by industries which make use of wood, minerals, and waterfalls, but offering little opportunity for expansion of a farming population independent of industry.

The depicted static condition of the Quebec farming population shows no new turn. In the last census decade the number of those gainfully employed in agriculture increased by only 3.8 per cent; the farm acreage by only 1.09 per cent. Although numerically static, the rural population is biologically very active. The compilers of the census estimate at 14 per cent the very least

natural increase in the population of Eastern Canada during any decade since 1871. It has been much higher in some decades (*Census of Canada*, 1931, vol. I, 109). Since the rate of increase is undoubtedly higher in rural Quebec than in other parts, 14 per cent is a good deal below the reality (Hurd, 1937a).[5] But using this figure, it appears that in no decade since 1871 has rural Quebec's loss by emigration been less than 50 per cent of its natural increase; in some decades, it has lost over 80 per cent.[6] It is obvious that Quebec's rural population is kept static by an emigration that is neither recent nor sporadic, but old and continued. Given the prevalent birth- and death-rates, the population can remain as it is only if the emigration continues at its accustomed level.

Underlying the stationary population is a definite system of farm life. The proprietor, with the help of his numerous children, exploits the inherited family farm and passes it on intact to one of his sons. This is both ideal and reality. The ideal is written deep in Quebec lore, literature, and sermons. The reality, so far as proprietorship is concerned, is seen in the fact that 93 per cent of Quebec farms are operated by their owners and 4 per cent by part-owners. It is a reality limited by the number of farms, which decreased slightly between 1921 and 1931 (*Census of Canada*, 1931, vol. I, 83).

The expectation that a Quebec farm will be cultivated by its owner is great. It does not follow, as is often assumed, that every Quebec farmer's son may expect to own and operate a farm.

The familial character of farming is symbolized by the persistence of household arts in Quebec long after their disappearance in other parts of North America. It is shown statistically by certain comparisons with Ontario farms. In Ontario 44.7 per cent of all farms reported some hired labour in 1931; in Quebec only 28.2 per cent. Apart from housekeepers, the Ontario farm has 1.5 unpaid adult family workers; the Quebec farm has 1.9. In Ontario 77 per cent of all adult male farm workers belong to the family; in Quebec 89 per cent (Haythorne, 1938).[7] Even the ownership of machinery attests the familial basis of agriculture. The Quebec farmer is much more likely to own a threshing machine than is the Ontario farmer.[8] Dr. Horace Miner, who recently studied in detail a parish in Kamouraska County, found that practically every farmer there had one, usually a small old machine operated by horse-power or a gasoline engine. Where grain is a large cash crop, threshing is a community or inter-familial activity. In Quebec, the family threshes as the grain is needed. The machinery is regarded as part of the inviolable heritage which keeps the family independent (Miner, 1939; Gérin, 1938). The contrast between this attitude toward farm equipment and that of a western wheat farmer needs no emphasis.

The third feature of the rural system is indivisibility of the farm. Dr. Horace Miner has described minutely how in each generation, the farm family works out a cycle which culminates in the turning over of the land to a son when the farmer is about 60 years of age. In this parish the chosen inheriting son would be one of 9.6 children of whom six have survived. The father is constantly preoccupied with the problem of providing for the five to whom he can give no land. In the last instance they must leave the land, whether he finds a place for them elsewhere or not. They are morally obliged to go.[9]

This system persists only as long as all children save one of each generation leave the paternal farm. Since there is no increase in the number of farms, this means that in each generation large numbers of children sever themselves forever from the land. The expelled members have found places for themselves in the less settled parts of the province, in New England and the West, and, in recent decades, chiefly in the towns and cities of Quebec itself. The first outlet absorbs very few; the gates of New England are practically closed; the absorptive power of urban Quebec will probably decline. With the outlets dammed, one would naturally expect a backing-up of the excess rural population upon the farm. And indeed, the median age of farm operators did increase by two years in the last census decade, and the median age of unpaid family workers by one year (Haythorne, 1938).[10]

A congestion of population in the rural districts would threaten the historic system, in its moral, as well as its economic aspects. For it is a moral system, involving mutual rights and duties for each member of the family. A function of industry in Quebec — though not the purpose of its founders — has been to allow the family system to continue. So long as industry and auxiliary urban activities grow rapidly enough, the farm population of Quebec can remain as it is — that is to say, not a simple resultant of birth- and death-rates, but of the number of farms and the size of the family living on each. For under the system one couple only produces children on each farm in each generation. Of course, industry as a way of life, threatens many of the features of the traditional order. But the rural system, not industry, creates a great landless population in Quebec in every generation.

The manner in which excess rural population is drawn into an industrial town may be illustrated by the following case. Drummondville was formerly a small town living off the trade of a surrounding farming district. It once had a number of industries which used local resources — sawmills, a tannery, smelting furnaces. By the 1890s the wood had petered out. The chief industries had disappeared and the town was in the doldrums. Its population was smaller in 1911 than in 1891.[11] The families associated with the early industrial development had disappeared entirely or had left behind only ageing *rentiers*. When finally a power dam brought new industries, the old families had no part in them. Between 1911 and 1933, the population multiplied by 5.44 and the number of industrial employees by 30.4.[12] This revolution was wrought by two large dams, which brought six textile industries and a number of smaller auxiliary plants. In the fall of 1937, over 19 000 people lived in the community, an increase of some 17 000 since 1911, and of 15 000 since 1921.

It is evident that the population is new to the town. But analysis shows that it is native to the vicinity, and of country and village birth. The birthplaces of easily 60 per cent of the recorded male heads of families lie within a radius of 30 miles from the town; 73.8 per cent of them were born in a group of ten nearby counties which I shall call the *region*. It is a parallelogram whose long sides are the St. Lawrence River and the foothills of the Appalachian Range. Its short ends, east and west, are the Yamaska and Chaudière rivers. The plain as it rises from the St. Lawrence decreases in fertility and in density of rural population. Every county in the region has contributed heavily to Drummondville's population; none outside has done so. The break is sharp in all directions. No other town approaching Drummondville in size and industrial importance is to be found within the limits of the region. The draw is heaviest from two fertile St. Lawrence shore counties which have exported population in this general direction for a hundred years (Blanchard, 1937b: 174). Conspicuously missing are families from the Montreal district, although that city is but 65 miles to the west.

The draw of population to Drummondville stops abruptly less than 20 miles west of the town toward Montreal. Likewise missing are families from the Sherbrooke and Three Rivers districts, both closer than Montreal. The Drummondville population is coming *to* town, not out from other cities.[13]

Early in this paper reference was made to communities in which labour is native and management foreign. That Drummondville is of this type may be shown by analysis of the class structure. Every industry of any size was founded at the instance of some company operating elsewhere. Managers and technical staff were sent to Drummondville to build and operate plants. These people are immigrants to the town; a majority of them are not Canadians. None of them is French Canadian. In addition, a number of English-speaking foremen, skilled operators, and clerical workers were imported. Such people, with their families, constitute about one-twentieth of the population — an alien and socially isolated element, mixing little with the native population and not at all with the native labouring population. The poorer of these alien people live among French people in the inner part of the town. The dominating managers and technicians are becoming somewhat segregated in the more desirable outlying sections. The segregation is not complete, for there are many local French people of the upper business and professional classes who live in the same districts.

The business and professional class is as completely French as the first class is English. It is probably even more local in origin than is the population as a whole for its nucleus is of old residents. Some French labour came from New England, but no important professional or businessmen did. Of the seven lawyers, five were born within a few miles of the town; the other two not 50 miles away. Seven of the 14 physicians were born within the region, and the others in the province, except for the one who is English. The upper business class is perhaps even more native to the town. The middle and lower business class is likewise completely French. Of the 486 business and service units in the town, 455 are owned or managed by French. While we do not know the birthplaces of these people, I know from my acquaintance with the town that most of them originated within the region.

Industrial workers, the most numerous class, are almost exclusively French. Some of the smaller industries have no more than half a dozen non-French workers. Before many years skilled work, in addition to unskilled, will probably be performed by French alone. While some of the French workers live in the same districts as English, they are the most segregated class of all. About the town have grown satellite villages inhabited by them alone, in which lives nearly half the entire population. In the typical industrial town in North America, the poorest sections — always the largest — are occupied by immigrants. In Drummondville such sections — also the largest — are occupied exclusively by natives. Insofar as they have come directly from the farm, they have never before lived in communities where there was any considerable class of people above them. In their new home, apart though they be, they experience for the first time the constant presence of a group far superior to them in both standard of living and authority. At the same time, though they suffer nostalgia for the independent farm life which they have left, most of them are aware that they are fatefully out of it. No great wonder that they attribute the trials of the new life not only to the industrial system but to the fact that it was introduced and is controlled by aliens. Their compatriots' monopoly of business and the professions may mitigate but does not re-

move this feeling. For the greater prizes in the new Drummondville are competed for in industry.

Less thorough but adequate information about other towns shows that this is a typical Quebec industrial centre. Some differ in that they were English towns prior to the coming of industry. In that case the business and professional classes contain both English and French. The frontier mining, wood-pulp, and smelting towns are characteristically company towns, without a previously established native business and professional class. Such towns draw their population from a greater distance and probably from a much wider territory, for they are men's towns while Drummondville and other textile centres are family towns. But in all the same general pattern prevails. The labour is largely native; the management is alien to the native culture. The source of the industrial population is to be found in the rural situation which we have described.

One must accept and honour the statement that French-Canadian survival is an heroic cultural miracle. That tribute should not obscure the hard ecological fact that Quebec's closed rural system — the basis of its culture — could neither have developed nor have survived without an open and absorbent North America. For the system must eject a large part of its human product in each generation. Perhaps the most crucial new feature of the situation is that those now being ejected live in the midst of their native region, rather than elsewhere. This is of social psychological portent. For it appears that the emigrant *déraciné* who lives far from home is likely to express his dissatisfaction in an individual effort to get ahead in his new surroundings; a mass of *déracinés* near home is more likely to express collective discontent with their position, as an ethnic group, in the new system.

Notes

1. For comparisons of birth-rates of the provinces and of the French and English see W. Burton Hurd, 1937, 40-57.

2. Rural and village population is that of country districts and of incorporated places of less than 1000 population in 1931. The general effect of this method of compilation would be to increase the rate of growth of rural and village population. The ordinary method would show an even smaller increase of rural and village population, thus accentuating the statement made here. The village population has multiplied by ten since 1871, but as it is only 130 000 now, it is not significant.

3. Enclosed in this block, but not counted because they had higher increases of rural population, are Sherbrooke, Drummond, Chambly, and Champlain. Examination proves that the apparent rural increase in these counties is really a growth of urban centres.

4. Of the 25 Quebec counties included in this study, 24 are in the block here discussed. The following pertinent points are made: Quebec farms were originally smaller than those in other provinces, and only now are catching up; there has been no decrease in the average size of the Quebec rural family, but the proportion of single persons over 15 years of age has increased while the proportion under 15 has declined. This indicates that the decrease in farm population is of persons too young to migrate.

5. Hurd's figures, corrected by him for differences of age distribution of women, show that in 1931 English rural women had only 63 per cent of the number of children under five years of age had by French rural women; French urban women had only 61 per cent.

6. Hurd finds that the net rural-urban movement in Quebec for the decade 1921-31 was 19.2 per cent of the rural population of 1921. This was probably about all of the natural increase of the decade.

7. Haythorne's compilations (1938) are based on the census of 1931. In Kamouraska County, Quebec, Dr. H. Miner found it said that a childless couple did not succeed at farming.

8. Haythorne reports that 28.9 per cent own threshing machines. In the lower St. Lawrence region the figure is 47 per cent; in the middle St. Lawrence region, 32 per cent; 25 per cent own gas engines.

9. Miner, Gérin, and the few agronomes with whom I have talked agree that if a farmer succeeds in acquiring a second farm, he nearly always gives it to a second son. He thus in effect establishes a second family. A part of the system has been the assumption by the inheriting son of full and exclusive responsibility for his parents in their declining years. A notary in Drummond County says that the system is endangered in his district by the rising cash cost of providing food, clothing, and medical care for the ageing parents.

10. Dr. Miner found in St. Denis a number of young men whose presence was thought anomalous because they had passed the age of expected emigration. In a sermon the curé urged them to leave the community to find work, as they were a burden upon their families.

11. As late as 1911, 1165 of the 1885 industrial workers in Drummond and Arthabaska counties were in the log products, lumber and furniture industries, and in creameries. The rest were engaged in a wide variety of small

industries which produced mainly for local markets (*Census of Canada*, 1931, vol. III, Table IX).

12. Compiled from the *Census of Canada*, 1911; *Census of Manufacturering Industries in the Province of Quebec*, 1934; and parish records.

13. This information was compiled from parish records kindly made available by the curés. The clergy takes an annual census of all families, both Catholic and Protestant. The birth-place of the male head was recorded for 1345 of the 3426 families listed in 1936. Omission of this item ran by streets and blocks, indicating that some census-takers were less punctilious than others. The least complete records were found in an outlying parish whose population is almost completely French and of the working class. A perfect recording would probably show an even larger percentage of people of local origin.

2

The Quiet Revolution in Quebec*

Guy Rocher

The Quiet Revolution: Why?

In an article that in other ways recalls the imperialistic role that the United States had played in the Third World, Lucian W. Pye (1964) opens the way to answering the question of why the Quiet Revolution took place in the sixties. "The relative immunity to insurgency of highly complex industrial societies, at the one extreme, and of homogeneously integrated traditional communities, at the other, points to the crucial reason why the problem of insurgency is so closely related at this time in history to the transitional and underdeveloped new nations of the world. The process of social and psychological disruption that accompanies the downfall of traditional societies opens the way to a host of sharp cleavages within such societies."

After World War II, Quebec was precisely no longer a "homogeneously integrated tra-

ditional community." During the previous decades, Quebec had become an urban and industrialized society, with a rapidly declining minority of French Canadians living on farms and in rural villages. On the other hand, Quebec was in the process of becoming a "complex industrial society," without still being an advanced and highly complex one. Although it was a more advanced industrial society than many of the new nations in Asia and Africa, it was still in the "transitional" stage of a society in the process of being industrialized. Economically speaking, in terms of industries and finance, Quebec has been, and still is, lagging behind the province of Ontario. It doesn't have the large diversity of industries that is to be found in Ontario, and it suffers from an unbalanced economic development because of the high concentration of its industries in the metropolitan area of Montreal at the expense of the rest of the province, which is not the case in Ontario. On the other hand, one can say that it is a more advanced industrial society than the Maritimes and some Prairie provinces.

But, more significantly, it is in sociological rather than economic terms that postwar

*Originally published as "The Quiet Revolution and Revolutionary Movements Among French Canadians," in Richard A. Preston (ed.) *Perspectives on Revolution and Evolution*, series number 46, Duke University Press, 1979. pp. 238–267. Reprinted by permission.

Quebec can be regarded as a transitional industrial society. Alexis de Tocqueville gives us an interesting lead as to what happened in Quebec in the fifties and the sixties. In his introduction to *De la démocratie en Amérique* (1968), Tocqueville compared the state of democracy in France and in the United States. He said that in France, the democratic revolution had taken place in what he called "le matériel de la société," which, in his language, meant the political structures of the French society. But he added that the democratic revolution had not reached the laws, ideas, habits, and customs of the French. The French democratic revolution was therefore incomplete, and it was hard to know in what direction French society would move in the future. Tocqueville said that he had discovered that the democratic revolution was much more advanced in the United States, in the sense that it had taken place not only at the political level, but it had also penetrated and permeated the daily life of the Americans, their spirit as well as their legislation. What Tocqueville called "le principe de la démocratie" ("the principle of democracy"), which was the egalitarian principle, had developed in the United States more than anywhere else in the world "et, marchant avec les moeurs, il a pu se développer paisiblement dans les lois." With his extraordinary lucidity, Tocqueville added that democracy was in his view not necessarily an absolute good because he thought there was no such thing as an absolutely good democracy. But he had finally reached the conviction that, in Europe, "nous arriverons, comme les Américains, à l'égalité presque complète des conditions." It was this irreversibility of the trend toward more and more democratic societies, a trend that could be observed over several centuries, according to Tocqueville,

that brought him to the conclusion that the consequences of the democratic revolution in the United States had to be well understood, in order to forecast and, if possible, modify the future of the European societies.

I think this observation by Tocqueville can help us understand the origins of the Quiet Revolution in Quebec. There are two ways in which this analogy applies. First, I have developed at length in *Le Québec en mutation* (Rocher, 1973) the idea that after World War II, Quebec had become a highly industrialized society, with the economic structure of an advanced industrial society. But the French Canadians, at least a large number of them, had maintained a preindustrial mentality, or at least the external visible elements of a traditional mentality. Their vision of the world, their attachment to the orthodox Roman Catholic beliefs, their strong family ties, their lack of capitalist ethics, their acceptance of the dominant role of the clergy, were among the main elements of the ethos of the French Canadians up to the 1950s. Because of those views — and I am sure that the causal relationship could be reversed and still be true — the French Canadians were not active elements of the development of industrial Quebec. They contributed the labour force, part of the technicians, and the professional bourgeoisie, but they did not provide the capital and the dynamic agents of the current changes.

Second, just like nineteenth-century French as described by Tocqueville, it could be said of Quebec French Canadians that they were living in democratic political structures without having the habits, the customs, and the ideas of a fully democratic society. For them, as for the French of the 19th century, the democratic revolution was not completed and they were still clinging to some values of the *ancien régime*.

After World War II, Quebec was still a "transitional" society because of the unbalanced development between its political and economic structures on the one side and the ethos and culture of the French Canadians on the other. Quebec was structurally urbanized, industrialized, and democratic, but culturally pre-industrial and still partly imbued with the spirit of the *ancien régime*. Quebec was surely one of the most interesting cases where the folk and traditional society survived in what was in other respects a modern industrialized society. The same situation still prevails even today in several areas of the United States and in other parts of Canada. But it was more striking in the case of the French Canadians because of their homogeneity in terms of ethnic origins, language, and religion.

After World War II, the cleavage between industrial and democratic structures on the one hand and a preindustrial mentality on the other became wider and wider. This is probably a case where Ogburn's theory of the "cultural lag" could be applied as one possible explanation of social change, or rather of cultural change. The notion of strain used by Parsons is also useful here. "*Strain* . . . refers to a condition in the *relation* between two or more structured units (i.e., subsystems of the system) that constitutes a tendency or pressure toward changing that relation to one incompatible with the equilibrium of the relevant part of the system. If the strain becomes great enough, the mechanisms of control will not be able to maintain the conformity to relevant normative expectations necessary to avoid the breakdown of the structure" (1961: 71). Such is, according to Parsons, the main "endogenous" source of change in the social system. If we use Parsons's paradigm of the four functional subsystems of the social system,

we can say that what we can call the structural changes that had taken place in Quebec were located in the economy-adaptation subsystem and in the policy-goal attainment subsystem, but that the latency-pattern maintenance and tension management subsystem lagged behind the two others, and that this was also partly true, although to a lesser extent, of the integration-societal community subsystem. In other words, the law was more advanced in the direction of the industrial and democratic society than the culture and mentality of the French Canadians.

The strain created by this "cultural gap" first appeared among some groups of intellectuals, probably at the end of the 1940s, but definitely in the first half of the 1950s. From those sources, which were then rather peripheral to the Quebec French-Canadian society, it spread progressively, but quite rapidly to some other groups, especially to the labour unions and to the Liberal party of Quebec. It is the latter that was finally to be the more visible, though not necessarily the more coherent, agent of the Quiet Revolution of the 1960s.

The Revolutionary Movements: Why?

It was precisely when the Quiet Revolution was at its height and in full swing in 1963 that the FLQ made its first appearance using violence, threats of violence, and a violent language. After having heard of violence elsewhere in the world and having read about it in the newspapers, the Quebeckers were suddenly confronted with terrorism as part of their daily life. Probably, as always occurs, their first reaction was one of incredulity accompanied by a profound feeling of malaise. It seemed unbelievable that people of our own ethnic group and nation would have recourse to violence for political purposes. Terrorism is good for others, for instance, Africans or Palestinians, but not for us! A subtle process of the denial of reality takes place at first. For instance, it was currently said and believed that the FLQ was probably made up of strangers, French leftist fanatics or "Pieds noirs" from North Africa, or at least that the FLQ was inspired by such strangers. Those perceptions were reinforced by the fact that the first FLQ member to be arrested was in fact a Belgian. But as time goes on, a community learns to live with terrorism and also with the idea that it is not the work of strangers but of its own people, maybe of one's relatives or of one's students or former students.

I think I am right in saying that terrorism first appeared to Quebeckers, French-speaking as well as English-speaking, as a "corps étranger." Whether the FLQ was made up of strangers or of Quebeckers was somewhat immaterial to the feeling that was widespread in Quebec that it was built on the model of revolutionary movements in some distant countries and that it was not and would never be a genuine Quebec institution. But then, as it maintained itself over time, one had to try to explain how it was that it actually existed and was largely constituted of French Canadians. Later, one had to try to understand why it was active for a period of seven years.

In my judgment, the most systematic attempt to deal with this problem in sociological terms is Raymond Breton's. According to him, the appearance of the FLQ was part of "widespread confrontations over the distribution of power and influence" that accompanied the Quiet Revolution, to the point that "there is hardly a single institutional sphere that has remained unaffected" (Breton, 1972). Breton lists what he calls the various "arenas" of conflict. These were the fields of education and of health and welfare, the federal-provincial network of relationships, work organization, an increased tension in the relations between the French Canadians and the other ethnic and linguistic groups in Canada, an increased tension within Quebec between various citizen groups and the governments and between students and the faculties and administrators of their institutions. He notes that those conflicts were not peculiar to Quebec but that they were more intense in Quebec than in the rest of Canada.

But how is it that in the context of this redistribution of power and influence some people came to use terrorism as a political weapon? Breton provides us with some explanations. The first one is what he calls the "dialogue de sourds" between the separatists and the federalists. As he points out, "a social political option such as the separatist one makes more difficult the use of the usual (legitimate) channels of conflict resolution. Given this kind of situation, we would expect a higher probability that some groups *on each side* of the issue will advocate the use of more extreme (non-legitimate) tactics to affect the course of events."

Second, Breton puts forward the hypothesis that the different separatist movements that existed at that time and that were not already unified, as they came to be by the end of the 1960s under the Parti Québécois, were unable to integrate and control their radicals. At first, as is pointed out by Breton, new associations and parties are not structured enough to cope with their more radical elements, who may then decide to create their own group, with a more radical ideology and using more violent means. Later on, the situation within associations and parties changes, but they then may become "too structured and rigidly controlled from the top," thus pushing the more extreme elements to break with the official party or association in order to go their own way. Finally, Breton reasons that after the first wave of terrorist action, the FLQ was engaged in what he calls "an escalation of violence" that was largely due to the failure of the previous phases to gain public support in the French-Canadian community and to inspire positive feelings in its favour.

Breton's explanations are quite valid, provided we take for granted that there were radicals among the French Canadians at the beginning of the sixties. It is true, as Breton points out, that there were "widespread confrontations over the distribution of power and influence" in Quebec in the sixties. But why did some separatists become radical and why did they decide to have recourse to terrorism, while many others did not? This is the question that Breton's hypotheses do not really answer. For this is a question for which there cannot be, at least for the time being, any clear and definite answer. We can only suggest plausible interpretations. Let me try some lines of explanation.

I think first that the cultural crisis that I have already mentioned provides us with some elements of explanation. The rapid change that took place in the cultural realm of the French-Canadian community brought with it the questioning of many traditional moral values. The acceptance of terrorism as a political weapon came to be symbolically associated, in the eyes of some youth, with the most complete rejection of the traditional ethics. Terrorism might therefore have been more profoundly related to a moral revolution than to a political one. For instance, for the extreme leftists of the journal *Parti Pris* — which was the main channel of ex-

pression of the young radicals of the 1960s — the Quebec of tomorrow was to be politically independent, economically socialist, and socially and culturally a nonsectarian society ("une société laique"). Of those three options, the last one was surely the most radical in terms of Quebec's long-standing religious traditions. This third option was the chief break with the traditional way of thinking in Quebec. It marked the most profound change of attitudes among the youth. The ideal of political independence had never been completely foreign to French Canadians; socialism was regarded as unacceptable, but not necessarily on ethical grounds. But when it came to complete religious neutrality in a society that had been under the aegis of the clergy and religion for over a century — this was the most important shift that was proposed. Recourse to terrorism was precisely in that line of thought, or better, it was seen as the logical end result of that line of thought. Therefore, we can hypothesize that for a certain number of youth in that period, when many moral values were being questioned, recourse to terrorism was the symbol of the most complete revolt against the past and the most radical break with the traditional values that had been associated with the economic subordination of Francophone Quebeckers and with many political frustrations.

One can see a confirmation of the value crisis that shook Quebec in the 1960s in the reformist movements among the Catholics that ran parallel to the radical movements. Whereas the latter were outside the Roman Catholic church and also against it, the former were taking place within the church and were part of it. They aimed at profound changes in the moral and dogmatic outlook of the church, as well as in the social doctrine and positions of the church in matters like capital-labour relationships, family planning and the use of contraceptives, the obligation of celibacy for the priests, the reform of the Roman Catholic liturgy. Laymen as well as priests, nuns, and brothers, adhered to those reformist movements, taking positions that were quite d'avant-garde compared to what was still regarded as acceptable in the Roman Catholic church in most countries at that time.

A second line of explanation has to do with the notion of "relative deprivation." Starting in the fall of 1959 with the Sauvé government, and then with the Liberal government of Jean Lesage, new aspirations were raised with regard to educational accessibility, occupational mobility, standards of living, and the relative autonomy of the Quebec government and of Quebeckers in North America as well as in Canada. But with the development of a separatist political option, the Lesage government, which was driven by the tide of the Quiet Revolution that had been prepared during the fifties, came to be regarded by some — especially among the youth — as being too moderate in its political aspirations and its economic as well as social reforms. What had now become possible, thanks to the educational and economic reforms of the Lesage government, appeared to some to be too little and too late when compared to all that had seemed to be possible. Therefore, the Lesage government, which at first appeared to be running too fast ahead of the population and which was in fact running ahead of at least a large proportion of the French-Canadian population, was suddenly bypassed by a minority that wanted more drastic reforms in order to meet higher aspirations for themselves and for the whole of Quebec.

Finally, it must be pointed out that, unlike what took place before the American Revolution in 1774 and 1775, the revolutionary ideology and the radical movements in Quebec were not born of repressive actions on the part of any of the governments. There were no "Intolerable Acts" passed by the Canadian and Quebec parliaments, and there was no harassment of the French Canadians. On the contrary, the FLQ made its first appearance not long after the backward and quite despotic Duplessis regime was over and when the more liberal and more progressive Lesage government was at its peak. Revolutionary movements may see the light in the trail of a liberal government as well as in a reaction against an oppressive one.

Failure of the Radical Ideology and Revolutionary Movements: Why?

We have already seen that the terrorist movements and the radical ideology died with the most violent wave of their existence, the kidnapping of James Cross and Pierre Laporte. How can we account for that unexpected end precisely when the FLQ seemed to be more active than before?

Can we say that it was an effect of the War Measures Act? Obviously, it could have been exactly the reverse. As has been illustrated many times in many circumstances, repression of violence usually provokes more violence and the vicious circle becomes tighter and tighter. Because almost 500 persons were arrested unnecessarily and held in jail incommunicado for days and weeks, and because the Canadian army was used in the streets of Montreal, a very hostile reaction to both the federal and the provincial governments for their brutal reaction was generated in some quarters. And this hostility was so acute and quite enough largely spread that it might have given birth to new revolutionary movements and to new waves of terrorism. And I can say that this was the expectation at that time. But contrary to those expectations, nothing of that sort happened and there has been no political violence in Quebec since 1970.

In the article previously quoted, Raymond Breton contributes one explanation of that fact when he says that the revolutionaries were led to an "escalation of violence" because of the successive failures of their actions. I don't think that Breton uses this as an explanation for the end of violence, because Breton didn't deal with this problem. But I think it casts an interesting light on what happened. It is quite true that there was such an escalation of violence, from the bombs in the mail boxes to the Armée de Libération du Québec (ALQ), finally to political kidnappings and murders. But the escalation of violence had a negative effect, not only on the general public opinion and population, but probably also on the members and sympathizers of the FLQ. That is why in the end the two small cells that kidnapped Cross and Laporte were desperately isolated, deprived of money and of effective support. When the kidnappings were done, and as long as Cross and Laporte were in the hands of the FLQ, one might have thought that the cells that were responsible for those actions were part of a vast network of members and sympathizers, or that they were carrying out a well-prepared plot. This was precisely the reasoning of the federal government when it proclaimed the War Measures Act and jailed some 500 people. But there was no plot of insurrection and there was no guerrilla support. As has been suggested above, the successive waves of violence had progressively exhausted the FLQ's and ALQ's small reserves of men, energy, and imagination.

A second reason for the failure of the radical ideology rests again in the moral sphere of the French-Canadian society. The traditionalist and religious mentality of the French Canadians was still too alive and also too spread out in the society to accept radical actions readily. The French Canadians in the sixties were willing to live with a certain number of changes in ethics and values, but the leap into radicalism was too great for them to make suddenly. For several decades, they had been fed with a conservative social doctrine of peace and order, of acceptance of all inequalities, of respect of any authority, and of the recognition of private property, especially of small private property. Lipset has been seeking the reasons that socialism has never taken root in North America (Lipset, 1950, 1967, 1970; Lipset and Laslett, 1974). Some of the reasons that serve to explain that fact in the United States and the rest of Canada also apply to Quebec, and there are others that I have already dealt with in other publications (Rocher, 1973). One of those obvious reasons is the influence of the Roman Catholic church and of its doctrine on the social thinking of the French Canadians. It is surely this lack of socialist as well as of radical tradition in French-Canadian culture that explains the almost universal negative reaction to the actions of the FLQ, their lack of real support in the population, and their escalation of violence when their successive failures to gain support finally generated. It would surely be interesting at this point to compare Quebec with Northern Ireland, where the IRA and the provisional IRA have had enough following among Irish Catholics to survive and maintain an active rate of intervention for several years.

A third reason for the failure of the radical ideology has to do with the economic structure of Quebec. In contrast with Ireland, Quebec is economically part of the northeastern part of North America, being economically and financially associated with

New England. The standard of living of the French Canadians, their ways of life, their aspirations are practically the same as the New Englanders, or just a little lower. In that respect, I think the young radicals of the 1960s made a false analysis of the revolutionary potential existing at that time among the French Canadians. They hypothesized that the Quiet Revolution was a sign that the French-Canadian working class was ripe for radical action, or at least for acceptance and support of radical intervention. But we know that such is not the case in North America, and maybe throughout the Western world. In a book that was on the whole badly received by the American social scientists and historians, both Marxists and non-Marxists (Wiener, 1975), Barrington Moore (1966) has effectively documented the fact that the only modern revolutions that have succeeded were revolutions by a peasant class against the coalition of landed lords and an urban bourgeoisie. Such was not the situation in Quebec, where the rural class has become numerically less and less important, although it has gained in organization and aggressiveness. But obviously the FLQ was not addressing the rural class, but the urban working class of the Montreal area.

It might also be that the radical ideologists of the 1960s made the mistake of taking French Canadians as a whole as "an ethnic class," to be analyzed on the model of the social class in the Marxist framework. This was a mistake that some of my best colleagues have also made (for example, Rioux, 1965), and I think that it led the FLQ to believe that, apart from a tiny French-Canadian bourgeoisie, the whole French-Canadian community was ripe for developing the equivalent of a class consciousness in the face of the Anglo-Saxon exploiters, and finally to act as a revolutionary social class. But this belief neglected the complex system of social stratification or social classes that exists among French Canadians.

One final reason that can be brought for the failure of radical ideologies and actions in Quebec is that they lacked support from the generations of active adults of that period. Radical ideology and the radical movements were developed and supported by young people in their twenties, most of them either students or former university students who had dropped out and also some young former high school teachers. But those youths found no support for their ideology and actions among the men and women of the preceding generation. The latter had suffered from the authoritarianism and backwardness of the Duplessis regime, and they had dreamed of changes that would bring Quebec back into modern society. In the 1960s, they were therefore engaged, some of them very actively, in shaping the Quiet Revolution that they had prepared and dreamed of. They were not ready to follow young people whose actions they saw as disturbances of, and threats to, the process of the Quiet Revolution.

Moreover, they had not been trained to terrorist methods and street manifestations. In the faculties of law or in the new faculties of social sciences, or in the schools of administration or public administration that they had attended, they had trained themselves to be agents of change either in labour unions or in governmental offices or commissions, but surely not as underground revolutionaries and street demonstrators. Therefore, they had little or no sympathy at all for the radical ideologies, which they regarded as too extremist and also too ideological to fit their more "scientific" training. Most of them were also opposed to the use of violence and terrorism, which they regarded as foolish and desperate political adventures, with no future at all in Quebec.

3

*Quebec and the Canadian Question**

Hubert Guindon

A century and a half ago, after the Rebellion of 1837, Lord Durham observed in his famous report that when he looked for the cause of the unrest, he found, to his astonishment, "two nations warring in the bosom of the same state." He proposed a simple remedy: "I believe that tranquility can only be restored by subjecting the province [of Quebec] to the vigorous rule of an English majority."

Where he to return today, Lord Durham would no doubt be astonished to learn that, despite the application of his proposed remedy, his initial observation holds true. Quebec and English Canada still seem to be "two nations warring in the bosom of the same state." Today the viability of Canada as a political entity remains in question. And for the Québécois it is *the* question, the distinctively *Canadian* question.

How are we to understand Quebec and its

place (or lack thereof) in Canada? For most English Canadians, the rise of the separatists in Quebec has been inexplicable. Quebec, that quiescent paragon of rural provincialism, has suddenly been transformed into a seat of rabid nationalists intent on the dismemberment of Canada.

If this change seems inexplicable, it is because it does not fit the political stereotypes and cultural myths that English Canadians long used to interpret Quebec as an archaic, traditional society. Ruled by an autocratic clergy fiercely possessive of its own powers and opposed to democracy, modernization, or social progress, Quebec, it was said, was a rural backwater of poverty, illiteracy, and political despotism.

This political/cultural vision of the French in Canada did not emanate from bigoted Orangemen. Strangely enough, it was the conceptual framework of the politically liberal Anglophone academics of the 1950s, and it was shared and disseminated by the "progressive" French-Canadian intellectuals in and around *Cité-Libre* magazine, who then lived in Montreal and went on in the 1960s and 1970s to work mainly in Ottawa. (That move may seem particularly surprising, but

*Excerpted from Michael Rosenberg *et al.* (eds.) *An Introduction to Sociology* 2nd edition, Toronto: Methuen, 1987. © 1988, Nelson Canada, A Division of International Thomson Limited. Reprinted by permission.

it was theoretically predictable. Minorities are often known to internalize the majority's view of themselves, and when people from a minority want to chart a career in the majority setting, it is a necessary precondition that they adopt the common mindset.)

I have argued elsewhere (Guindon, 1978) that the delegitimation of the Canadian state in the eyes of the Québécois is a consequence of the modernization of Quebec, which took off with the provincial government's massive intervention in the areas of health, education, and welfare. In this chapter I explore this issue at somewhat greater length and disentangle some of the separate threads in the modernization process. This necessitates distinguishing between secularization and political alienation.

The Secularization of Quebec Society

At the theoretical level, **secularization** is generally defined in terms of the shrinking importance of magic and religion, as a result of the expansion of science and the scientific method. The narrowing sphere of the sacred corresponds to the expansion of knowledge, at the expense of faith and myth. Yet to conceive of secularization as a fading of myths rather than an emergence of new ones is to miss the point. Moreover, this idealistic view of secularization fails to take account of how the process takes shape and how it unfolds historically.

If the theoretical perspective on secularization is often rooted in epistemology (theories of knowledge), the popular perspective is usually put more crudely in institutional terms of ignorance and education, as a byproduct of increased (mass) education. People erroneously assume that the world of knowledge and the world of meaning are the

same thing. In fact, education has or should have something to do with knowledge, while secularization has to do with the world of meaning, quite another matter indeed.

Secularization is a question of politics, not epistemology. Historically, secularization started with the separation of the Church from the state, with constitutional proclamations in France and the United States, not of a churchless society, but of a churchless state. In the case of France, this proclamation was made at the time of the Revolution to formalize the break with a feudal past. In the United States, the American Revolution needed to distance the state from an official religion (and therefore from all religions), in order to proclaim freedom of religion and accommodate the denominational pluralism of the citizens.

No such political imperatives ever existed in Britain or its dominion of Canada, where a break from feudalism never occurred (although the evolution of capitalism did) and where freedom of religion became politically tolerated and practised, not constitutionally proclaimed. Yet one can argue quite correctly that secularization took place in the 19th and 20th centuries in both Britain and English Canada. The process was the institutional consequence of the break from Roman Catholicism.

The term **institutional secularization** refers to the process by which institutions initiated, staffed, or managed by clerics came under lay control. In the 16th and 17th centuries, when the Protestant churches broke from Roman Catholicism, whole societies were deprived of the organizational structure of the religious orders whose missions were to aid the poor, to tend the sick, and to provide education (to the extent that it had been developed). Thus new institutions had to be organized on a community basis under the aegis of the Protestant churches, with increased lay participation through voluntary associations. For these structural reasons, the process of institutional secularization took place much earlier in Protestant countries than in Catholic countries. By the 19th century, voluntary associations were well established in Protestant countries and gradual secularization of institutions was taking place.

In contrast, the secularization of social institutions in most Catholic countries did not take place until after the middle of the 20th century.[1] In fact, both the number of religious orders and their membership increased dramatically during the 19th and early 20th centuries in Catholic countries; the Church became progressively more involved in social institutions during that period of transition when the poor, the sick, and the ignorant, as Everett C. Hughes once put it, no longer belonged to their kin and did not yet belong to the state.

This brief historical outline sets the stage for the analysis of the secularization of Quebec, which, it must be remembered, was — and still is — a Catholic society.

The Social Institutions

As the Quiet Revolution swept Quebec, the Church had neither the human nor the financial resources necessary to develop the educational and health-care institutions required to meet social needs as defined by the new middle classes. These needs were broadly defined indeed: nothing short of universal access to free education up to the university level, and heavy subsidies thereafter; free hospitalization for all citizens; and (later in the 1960s) free medical care. When the state accepted such a mandate, it sealed the fate of the Church in the whole area of social institutions. Such massive and rapid invest-

ment of public money required the development of a public bureaucracy to act on behalf of the public will (at least theoretically). Neither the Church as an institution nor the traditional community elites could be the agents of this institutional development. New elites — trained in everything from accounting to engineering, from personnel to industrial relations, from purchasing to architectural design — would swell the ranks of the new middle classes in the ever-growing public bureaucracies.

Although massive growth of public institutions took place during the 1960s, the traditional institutions had already felt great demands during the 1950s. Increasing enrolments had put pressure, for instance, on the traditional *collèges*, the institutions that had offered elite youths secondary and undergraduate education from a classical curriculum. (This *cours classique* was generally the only Francophone education available beyond the elementary level.) As the number of students rose, these institutions, once staffed almost exclusively by clerics, had to begin hiring lay teachers, who cost much more than clerics. Yet state subsidies amounted to very little — some $15 000 a year per institution. The same pattern was observable in health care. In brief, the demand for education and health care was outstripping the supply. The costs of expanding the existing facilities were essentially borne by their clients and, to a real but undocumented extent, by the Church — most of whose patrimony, one can assume, was spent in this transitional period of growth preceding the financial and administrative takeover by the state and its emerging professional bureaucrats.

Once the state decided to modernize and expand the educational system by the use of incentives, the secularization of the education system was greatly accelerated. This acceleration had nothing to do, as is commonly assumed, with a growing loss of religious belief or decrease in religiosity. Rather, it came from simple economic calculation at the community level. As long as the costs of education were borne locally, through taxes raised from local pockets, it made local economic sense to have clerical teachers, who cost much less than lay teachers because they lived communally and frugally and were low-level consumers. However, once the provincial government bore an overwhelming share of the costs of education, it quickly dawned on local business people (who made up most local school boards) that it made much more sense — if not to the total local community, at least to its merchants — to seek lay people with the highest possible qualifications. Not only were their salaries highly subsidized; they were big spenders with an assured income. In contrast to nuns and priests, lay teachers paid taxes and got married. Everyone — the hairdresser, the car dealer, the real-estate agent, and the insurance salesperson — could expect some share of the action. When principle and self-interest so neatly coincided, no wonder institutional change was both swift and harmonious.

While communities were securing immediate economic advantage, however, their control over local institutions was being sapped. Whether community elites were aware of this erosion or felt it was a fair tradeoff, the fact is that bureaucratic centralization soon eclipsed the importance of the community. Norms as well as subsidies started to come from outside. Since loyalty is most often a function of dependence, the loyalty of the teaching staff belonged no longer to the school board but to the professional association, which bargained with government for working conditions and salary.

In the process, school boards came to represent the government more than the community.

Similar analyses could be made in the realm of social welfare. The voluntary agencies that had traditionally been organized, staffed, and managed by the Church in local communities were now to be organized by lay professionals employed by state agencies.

The Exodus of Clergy

During the late 1960s and the early 1970s, Quebec, like English Canada, the United States, and some European countries, quite suddenly saw a new phenomenon: priests and nuns left their vocations in droves. Part of the process may be explained by ideological changes within the Catholic Church and part by the fact that the Vatican increasingly facilitated the release of individuals from their clerical vows. Equally facilitating these "defections" in Quebec was the fact that, contrary to the situation before the Quiet Revolution, priests or nuns who left orders could now quite easily find a place for themselves within the social structure. No longer were former clerics — especially priests — viewed as having committed spiritual treason by leaving the sacred calling; no longer could a defector cope only by either leaving the society or concealing his or her previous occupation. Suddenly, with the change in the social order, ex-priests could (and did) enter the growing ranks of the public and semi-public bureaucracies. The change was so thorough and so pervasive that priests who taught religion at the Université de Montréal, which holds a pontifical charter, were able, because of tenure, to keep their positions after quitting the ranks of the clergy and of celibates. Such a situation would have been inconceivable less than a decade earlier.

Paradoxically, the same reasons that had prompted men and women to enter the clergy in remarkable numbers in the none-too-distant past could also explain the sudden, massive exodus. Without doubting the selflessness and sincere motives of those who became priests, brothers, or nuns, one can argue that, in social terms, joining the clergy of Quebec had certainly not involved downward social mobility. For women, it had meant an assurance of comfortable, if austere, living quarters and an escape from the burden of large families and domestic chores, while gaining access to socially esteemed occupations in teaching and nursing. The lifestyle of nuns, although basically other-worldly, certainly matched and often surpassed the conditions under which most married women from the same social backgrounds could expect to live. The social distance that nuns maintained from the civil society was compensated by the deference given them by the laity. The majesty of their convents contrasted with the urban tenements their married sisters occupied. Deprived of the privileges of married life, they were equally spared its burdens; on balance, entering a convent was not — and was not perceived as — an irrational decision.

For men, joining the clergy, regular or secular,[2] meant entering a career that could lead to important institutional positions. In the secular clergy, the career paths mainly involved pastoral duties in the urban and rural parishes of a geographically circumscribed diocese. A young man began as a curate, receiving only a very low stipend beyond room and board, but could fully expect to become a parish pastor some day. Promotions, based primarily on seniority, would lead a parish priest from a small, possibly rural, parish to a large urban parish. As he moved from small to large parish, his income rose substantially because it was a function of both the wealth and the size of his parish. The "good income" years made a relatively secure retirement possible.

For the regular clergy, the career patterns varied according to the kinds of institutions run by the order — from novitiates for the training of future priests to colleges and sometimes universities, as well as shrines, publications, and social agencies involved with cooperatives or credit and trade unions. A man could aspire to positions of leadership, public recognition, and gratitude as his career reached its apex.

Quebec had long had a relatively high percentage of people who chose to follow these patterns. More or less simultaneously with the Quiet Revolution, decisions to enter the religious life suddenly shrank to a trickle, and defections increased dramatically, especially among younger nuns and priests — those who were beginning, not terminating, their careers. The shrinking role of the Church in the newly emerged social order was certainly a key factor. The Church, which had previously offered both full career patterns and social esteem, could now promise neither. One can also say that the Catholic hierarchy unwittingly helped to curtail the potential of clerical careers. Bureaucratic centralization of resources and decision-making, which became hallmarks of the new social organization, did not spare the Church itself. The career patterns of the secular clergy were drastically altered. Parish priests were suddenly transformed into functionaries on a fixed salary — and a low one at that. Any surplus resources were centralized by the bishop, who was, so the rationale went, in the best position to assess the needs of the various parishes and distribute the resources. Bureaucratically unimpeachable, this doctrine led to measures that sapped the morale of the secular clergy by suddenly eliminating the traditional pattern of rewards. Worse, parish priests and their curates realized that a priest who joined the ranks of the rapidly growing para-public institutions as a salaried professional made more than four times their income, was exempt from pastoral duties, could live in a private apartment, and, as a learned man of science, was more visible, better known, and socially esteemed in both the lay and the clerical worlds.

The Decrease in Religious Practice

"Tradition," Everett Hughes once pointed out in conversation, "is sacred only so long as it is useful." If tradition involves a mix of the sacred and the utilitarian, it follows that the first people to question its sacred character will be those for whom tradition is no longer useful. And indeed in mid-20th century Quebec, it was the intelligentsia and the new middle classes — whose careers and interests were no longer served by the traditional culture, institutions, or leadership — who first challenged the legitimacy of all three.

For traditional Quebec society, including the elites, visible religious practices were interwoven with almost every part of life. Many of these folkways all but disappeared over a very short time. For example, people had been accustomed to locate themselves by referring to the parish in which they resided; this custom rapidly disappeared as the majority of people no longer knew the names or the general locations of parish churches.

It would not be misleading to say that most of the population drifted into secularization through inattention. For the majority, estrangement from religious practice developed as a result of the Church's growing irrelevance in meeting their everyday needs. Schools were no longer linked to the Catholic parish; teachers were more apt to be lay than clerical; hospitals and clinics were professionally administered by specialists who lived far from where they worked, and neither knew nor cared to know about their clients in other than a professional capacity. The secularization of charity in the professionally operated agencies of the state left the Church not only with a shrinking role but also with half-empty buildings whose material upkeep became increasingly dependent on the continuing popularity of bingo.

The fall-off was evident both in the important decisions of life and in the minutiae of daily living. Stanley Ryerson has observed in conversation how deeply Quebec society has changed: nowadays, people no longer doff their hats or cross themselves when passing in front of a church. When what was commonplace has become bizarre, when automatic, unreflecting, customary behaviour becomes unusual over a very short time, one suspects that deep changes separate the present from the immediate past. In every respect except calendar time, centuries — not decades — separate the Quebec of the 1980s from the Quebec of the 1950s.

No longer visible, now basically silent, the Church, once a dominant institution in social and collective life, withdrew to service the spiritual and private needs of those still seeking its counsel. As its political clout faded, the voice of its critics became louder. The political liberals and conservatives maintain that the Church was, in large measure, responsible for the economic underdevelopment of Quebec, because it did not impart to its flock the "right" values, those that inspire entrepreneurial leadership and economic success. Under its leadership, they argue, Quebec's institutions failed to adapt to the requirements of a modern industrial society. The Marxists, on the other hand, take the Church to task for having collaborated with the Anglophone bourgeoisie in exploiting its flock, the working class. Both charges are ideologically inspired distortions. The Church, however, no longer answers its critics. Is this a dignified silence, or the sign of its collapse as an institution?

The Canadian Question

By the late 1970s, a modern and secular social order had indeed emerged in Quebec society. Quebec had put its internal house in order, in line with other developed societies. In spite of this — maybe because of this — Quebec remained politically restive. It was readying itself to challenge the legitimacy of another sacred institution: the Canadian state. The internal issue of Church and society having been resolved, the external issue of state and society rose to the top of the political agenda. For Quebec society that was *the* Canadian question.

A Lament for Two Nations

Seldom, if ever, do a conquered people give their consent to a conquering state. Conquered subjects' loyalty to the state is always suspect. This is so true that loyalty oaths are routinely administered to and taken by future civil servants. In times of crisis in national unity, these forgotten oaths become instruments of social control for those who fear for the state's security. The point is raised here not to underscore the vulnerability of those fragile freedoms known as civil liberties, but rather to call attention to the historically enduring price of political domination. Both those who created the state and those who are subject to it are forever condemned to wishful thinking: the first, to the dream of national unity, the latter, to the dream of national independence.

Those who dream of national unity are also forced to lament the absence of a commonly agreed-on history. In Canada in the 1960s, the Royal Commission on Bilingualism and Biculturalism went to great lengths and considerable expense to document this great gap. (On second thought, the commission might have realized it owed its very existence to that regrettable fact.)

Commonly agreed-on history presupposes a common celebration of either a glorious past or a common victory over an undesirable past. France can claim both; Britain can claim the first; the United States, the latter; and Canada neither. The cruelty of this observation is mitigated by the fact that political consensus can also be built on shared visions of the future. Such visions, however, must be based on the correction of history, not its denial. "Unhyphenated Canadianism" is a mirage based on the confusion of individual biography with group history. All immigrants have a biographical break with a past in which the country of origin somehow, to some degree, became undesirable — often because of denied opportunity or political persecution; the country of adoption, by the mere fact of receiving the immigrants, symbolizes a land of opportunity or a refuge from oppression, both of which are good reasons for thanksgiving. In contrast, the French and the English in Canada are burdened with historical continuity. In both cases, the breaking with the biographical past creates not a new citizen but a marginal one. And while marginal people may invest myths and create new visions, a new political order without group consent remains beyond reach.

A political order is a symbolically mediated structure. In other words, the state, to be legitimate, must rely on the substantial — not just formal — consent of the governed. Formal consent can be engineered by manipulation, trickery, propaganda, publicity, and deception, or it can be claimed on the basis of sufficient numbers alone. Shared consent, however, requires shared meanings, shared myths. The French and the English in Canada may have a common fate, but they share no political myths. The closest they have come was the belief that Canada was a partnership between the French and the English, an idea formalized in the **compact theory of Confederation**, which presents dualism as central to the nature of the state. John Porter (1965) spoke of "charter groups" — while admitting the junior status of one of them. Stanley Ryerson called Confederation an "unequal union." Lester Pearson, in striking the Royal Commission on Bilingualism and Biculturalism, spoke of the "two founding races." The commission, sensitive to the connotations that might be evoked by the word "race," preferred to speak of "two societies and two cultures." Pierre Trudeau watered the concept down still further, referring to two language communities (as though language without culture can be the basis of community) and many cultures. One need say no more to illustrate either the inability to define what Canada is or the incapacity of words to cover up an embarrassing social and political reality.

The last person to speak candidly about the social and political reality of Canada in unambiguous, well-established English words was Lord Durham, in his description of "two nations warring in the bosom of the same state." He recommended the subjugation of the French to the vigorous rule of the British, advice that was heeded but that did not succeed. Before Confederation, following this advice required thwarting democratic principles. With Confederation, those principles ensured political domination of the French nation.

Ever after, the word nation to describe the French fact in Canada was banned from the political vocabulary of Canadian academics and politicians. To make credible this semantic confusion, it became customary to refer not to the Canadian *state* but to the Canadian *nation* — creating unity not politically but semantically.

Such obfuscation obviously requires education. Denying reality rather than assuming it is characteristic of Canadian politicians, not of ordinary Canadian citizens. On leaving or entering Quebec, Québécois and non-Québécois alike quickly perceive the reality of cultural and social differences. Some people are dumbstruck by the differences. Others are paranoid about them. Both types of reaction testify to the reality of social and cultural boundaries. The fact that this dual reality cannot find a political expression in the Canadian political system constitutes its basic vulnerability.

The compact (or dualist) theory of Confederation, the myth that so many French Canadians clung to so that they could symbolically legitimate a dignified commitment to the Canadian state, suffered an ignominious death with the patriation of the Constitution in 1982; one partner, they discovered, could force patriation without the consent of the other. That the death blow was struck by a prime minister who was himself partly French-Canadian made it no less lethal; that it involved political trickery transformed the constitutional process from grand ritual into tragic farce, making the final demise of illusion seem unreal and senseless. Rumour has it that Prime Minister Trudeau's ruthlessness in patriating the Constitution was motivated by his frantic determination to secure a niche for himself in Canadian history. Secure a niche he did indeed; whether it will be an enviable one is quite another matter.

The destruction of dualism as a shared myth through the forcible patriation of the Constitution constitutes a proof by political action, rather than national argument, of a doctrine close to Trudeau's heart: that Quebec is a province *comme les autres*. In other words, Quebec is not the homeland of a people, it is merely a region of the country, one region among ten.

In legal fiction, Quebec has become a province *comme les autres*; in social reality it has not. It also is different economically; only in the province of Quebec is the economy controlled by a minority who differ socially, culturally, and ethnically from the inhabitants. This social and historical fact has arisen partly because of the Canadian state. Therein lies its tainted legitimacy. Therein, too, lies the reason it gave birth to the dream of national independence among its subjects in Quebec.

The Unreachable Dream

The dream of national independence in Quebec society took root when the "partnership" between French and English in the Canadian state was still a dominant theme in the political rhetoric. In effect, it was the suspicion that English Canadians did not in fact share this political myth that gave rise to the political alienation of the intelligentsia in Quebec society.

While the 1950s were ushered in by the strike in the asbestos mines, the 1960s were opened by the strike at Radio-Canada. Both events heralded basic changes in the socio-political order. The asbestos strike led to the Quiet Revolution a decade later. The Radio-Canada strike led, some 15 years later, to the election of the Parti Québécois. With the Quiet Revolution sprang up a modernized and secularized society, founded by the state and managed by bureaucratically employed professionals. With the independence movement was born an enduring, credible challenge to the legitimacy of an externally imposed political order.

As already stated, both strikes at first glance seem paradoxical. The asbestos strike involved a multinational corporation with English-Canadian management and French workers, but it led to a questioning of the Duplessis regime and the social power of the Church. The strike at Radio-Canada involved a conflict between producers and management within the exclusively French network of the CBC but ended by being defined in ethnic terms. Neither interpretation is really paradoxical. The contradiction between objective fact and social response would be real enough in normal times, but in times of social unrest and of heightened tension it is not unusual for an event to be invested with meanings that transcend what actually happens. The discrepancy signals the major redefinitions of historical situations that precede a challenge of a political order.

The strike at Radio-Canada, unlike many strikes, directly affected the intelligentsia and initiated their political alienation. Soon they scrutinized the federal government's institutions to ascertain the amount and level of participation of Francophones within them. They found this participation appallingly low, giving substance to the emerging conviction that the Canadian state is "theirs, not ours." Moreover, as the Royal Commission on Bilingualism and Biculturalism eventually substantiated, the few Francophones who did work in these institutions had to check their mother tongue at the door. At the Montreal Harbour Board, for example, bilingual civil servants received a routine memo from their Francophone boss: "Since everybody in the department is bilingual, from now on all memos must be written in English." It made perfect administrative sense internally. Externally, when leaked to the press, it made no political sense, except as an example of Lord Durham's "vigorous British rule."

The memo was quoted in the first of a series of editorials by André Laurendeau, the prestigious editor of *Le Devoir*. Some months later Prime Minister Lester Pearson struck the Royal Commission on Bilingualism and Biculturalism. Noble men filled with good intentions and alarmed by the strains threatening the state, the commissioners came forth with recommendations that perpetuated, rather than eliminated, those strains. By refusing to recommend a language regime based on territory, which would have ensured the Francophone majority in Quebec access in their own language to the large corporate sector of Montreal, they proclaimed Quebec the model for the treatment of "minorities" and urged the rest of Canada to follow suit toward their French minorities. In effect, they recommended leaving Quebec untouched, in terms of language policy, and adopting measures they thought would ensure the viability of French communities outside Quebec.

This viability could not be ensured, however, since postal services and radio and television programming in French were no replacement for a vanishing economic base. Furthermore, they could not convince the politically restive Québécois that Quebec was a model, since within that "model" they had to choose between a public-sector career in French or a private-sector career in English. If Quebec was to be a province *comme les autres*, as Trudeau insisted, it seemed elementary to correct that strange discrepancy. More skilled in provocation than in integration, Prime Minister Trudeau dismissed the terms of reference of the Royal Commission on Bilingualism and Biculturalism and proclaimed Canada to be bilingual and multicultural. While the proclamation pleased those citizens who were neither French nor English, it certainly did not guarantee any substance to ethnic cultures since they would not be celebrated in their own languages; what it did guarantee was state funds to enable colourful celebrations of official pluralism.

The official bilingualism adopted by the Canadian state was politically irrelevant for the modernizing Québécois majority and politically resented in most of English-speaking Canada. In Western Canada it smacked of privilege, since the few French Canadians living there were fully bilingual but now able to get federally funded French-language radio and television, not to mention bilingual labels on their cornflakes, while the overwhelming majority of neo-Canadians could not receive such services in their cultural languages. The reasons of state clashed with the logic of community, and the reasons of state prevailed, pitting the ethnic Canadians against the French Canadians. The very same result was achieved in Quebec by the failure of the senior government to act, leading, in 1974, the junior government under Robert Bourassa — no wild-eyed separatist but a tame Liberal — to introduce Bill 22, *la loi sur la langue officielle*. Replacing a 1969 act that had the same intent but was less comprehensive, Bill 22 announced that French was the language of the workplace and of government services. It also restricted Anglophone education to children who demonstrated a prior knowledge of the English language. Thus, although the new law was loudly denounced by the Anglophone media, one of its most immediate effects was to alienate from the Liberal party many of Quebec's new Canadians, who resented having to learn not one but two languages to qualify for effective citizenship.

The vocal opposition to Bill 22 in English-speaking Quebec was disseminated throughout the rest of Canada, leading the Canadian Air Traffic Controllers' Association (CATCA) to challenge, in 1976, the federal official language policy. Specifically, the air controllers, fearful of eventual bilingual requirements, struck to protest the use of French by Francophone pilots when talking to Francophone controllers; safety in the air was threatened, the union's public statements suggested, unless both parties had to use English at all times. Until now, implementation of the federal bilingual policy had been passively resisted, as the successive annual reports of the Commissioner of Official Languages ritually attested to. The CATCA strike was, however, an official challenge by a special-interest group. Trudeau responded by solemnly proclaiming in a television address that this challenge constituted a major threat to national unity, packed his bags, went off to Bermuda, and left the whole matter in the hands of Transport Minister Otto Lang — who promptly surrendered to the demands of CATCA.

Only months later, provincial elections brought to power, to the consternation of English Canadians, the Parti Québécois, whose announced goals included the peaceful attainment of independence for Quebec. One of its first actions was to complete the francization of Quebec that Bourassa had begun. It enacted Bill 101, *la charte de la langue française*, which makes French the normal language of work, education, and public life in Quebec. Basically, its authors considered Ontario the model for the treatment of the other official language. But what is normal in Ontario and elsewhere in Canada is considered by those regions to be outrageous in Quebec.

In response to the election of a "separatist" government in Quebec, Trudeau struck a Task Force on Canadian Unity, headed by Jean-Luc Pépin and John Robarts. Its report, however, did not take sufficient umbrage at Bill 101 and was not only ignored but swiftly denounced, on the very day of its release, by Don Johnston, MP for Westmount-St. Henri, then a Liberal backbencher but soon to be promoted to Trudeau's cabinet. Proud of his interview in the electronic media, Johnston eventually had the transcript translated into French and distributed in both languages to his constituents. In it, he solemnly proclaimed his and his constituents' rejection of the Pépin-Robarts Report. The grounds? First, history teaches us one thing: if you leave a minority at the mercy of a majority, its rights will not be protected. And that is what the Pépin-Robarts Report did. Second, our French-Canadian compatriots would be "condemned" to live all their lives only in French, a fate presumably worse than death. If Don Johnston was right about the fate of minorities at the hands of majorities, he made it the duty of every self-respecting Québécois to become an *indépendantiste*. By equating living one's life only in French to a sentence, he clearly shows that taking the role of the others is not an automatic consequence of living in their midst.

The Parti Québécois had won its electoral victory preaching **sovereignty-association** — political independence for Quebec within an economic union with Canada — but had promised to seek a specific mandate before attempting to negotiate the change with Ottawa. A referendum was announced for May 1980, and the federal Liberals combined with the provincial party to throw enormous amounts of money and advertising into the campaign. The referendum failed — a joyless victory of national unity. English Canadians stopped holding their breath, even when the PQ unexpectedly won another victory at the polls the next year. What the referendum had done was to make the dream of national independence unreachable.

Then Trudeau delivered on his promise of "renewed federalism"; in 1982 the Constitution was repatriated without Quebec's consent. The PQ resisted federal blandishments to sign, but in its eagerness to retain power, it loosened some requirements of Bill 101 (which even in its original form was felt by some Québécois to give insufficient protection to the French culture and language), and it announced a new, quasi-federalist platform that drove several well-known *indépendantistes* to leave its ranks. Those moves proved too much for the Quebec electorate. Although they had voted overwhelmingly against the Liberals in the federal election of 1984, sweeping the Conservatives to victory, a few months later they voted almost as decisively *for* the provincial Liberals — the party that, after all, had come to power in 1960 under the slogan *maîtres chez nous*.

The outcome of the referendum and the purge of the *indépendantistes* from the Parti Québécois spells not the end of Quebec's "national" movement, but the end of its embodiment by a specific political party. It also means that the strategy to achieve independence will not follow the route of party politics. A return to less institutionalized forms of political mobilization is not to be excluded.

Conclusion

This essay ends on a melancholy note of disillusionment with statesmanship and party politics in this country. It does not claim to be non-partisan or dispassionate. It is a plea, a public and desperate one, for the youth of this country to distance themselves from the political culture they are exposed to. It is especially a plea to young English Canadians not to accept either the new demonology on Quebec or the idea that all is returning to "normal" there, but to resolve to help to bring to birth eventually a state that will truly enjoy the consent of the governed.

Notes

1. The exception was France, where after the Revolution the state took over the direct organization of education, producing bitter internal conflict that lasted more than a century.

2. Catholic priests may be regular or secular clerics. The regular clerics are those who are members of a particular order, such as the Basilians, the Sulpicians, and the Jesuits, and live under its rule (hence "regular"); they take vows of celibacy, poverty, and obedience (to the hierarchy of the order). Although an order sometimes accepts the responsibility of running a parish, each views itself as having one or more special mandates, which in Quebec before the 1960s was most often education, health, or some form of social service for active orders. (Some orders are strictly contemplative.)

    In contrast, secular clerics take a vow of celibacy, but not of poverty or obedience. They work under the local bishop (whose assignment comes from Rome) and run most parishes, as well as other institutions under direct diocesan control.

    All nuns and religious brothers are regular clerics.

SECTION II

A British Fragment

Today, it would be difficult to find two more similar societies than the United States and Canada, especially English-speaking Canada. Nonetheless, over the years social science observers have reported intriguing differences between the societies. Many conclude that once we look beyond the marked similarities in ecology, urbanization, and political and economic conditions, we find differences in the ways Americans and Canadians behave and think, and in the ways their societies are organized. Specifically, English Canadian society is said to remain "British-like", unlike the United States. For example, English Canada is said to be more conservative than the United States. The explanation offered for this supposed difference is that English Canada was once **a British fragment**, and the British influence is conservative. Canada was settled by British immigrants who remained powerful over the years and maintained a close connection with British society as it once was. This imagery of the British fragment is the subject of this Section.

Like other major sociological images of Canada discussed here, this one has had many proponents. One prominent figure among them was the political historian, Louis Hartz (1955, 1964). In *The Founding of New Societies* (1964), Hartz joined with collaborators to compare several "fragment" societies, including Canada and the United States. According to Hartz, all societies of the New World had based their cultures on single ideologies taken from European societies which themselves possessed multiple ideologies. This narrowing to one ideology, he argued, occurs because only the most prominent political philosophy of founding immigrants catches on in a new society. In Hartz's words, "A part detaches itself from the whole, the whole fails to renew itself, and the part develops without inhibition" (Hartz, 1964: 9).

Hartz believed that, in Europe, conservatism, socialism, and liberalism each contributed to a varied political culture. Liberalism became a prevailing way of life only in English-speaking Canada and the United States, while conservatism and socialism were less important than in Europe. By a similar means, the colonization of New France (French Canada) had carried the conservative political principles of France's *ancien regime* across the sea to a new setting. Here they were safe-guarded from the attacks on feudalism that became ever more common in European politics. In the colonization of Anglo-America, liberal bourgeois culture migrated from Britain to a part of the world where the feudal mentality had never been known (Hartz, 1964; cf. Horowitz, 1966). In the colonization of French Canada, conservatism migrated and took root, however.

The historical processes just described do not give us reason to expect that English Canada and the United States will differ significantly. It takes an additional proposition — that there have been different formative events, with differing consequences for Canada and the United States — for us to expect differences between the Canadian and American societies today. This is the element that Kenneth McRae, a political scientist and one of Hartz's collaborators, added to our understanding. In McRae's view, the American Revolution provides an important key to explaining Canadian-American differences. Neither French Canada nor English Canada supported the American Revolution. This non-support reinforced loyalties toward the establishment in both parts of Canada, and set the stage for Canada and the United States to go in separate directions. As a result of the Revolution, English Canada moved closer to British society and culture, while the United States moved away from it.

According to McRae, there was also another formative event: the British Conquest of New France in 1759. This, perhaps surprisingly, led to the entrenchment in French Canada of the conservative French fragment, because the British takeover removed progressive economic entrepreneurs and top political leaders from French Canada. This left the conservative Catholic Church with primary influence over the French Canadian way of life. Thus, two European immigrant fragments meeting up with two formative events produced the two solitudes we described in Section I.

Early in the 1960s, S.M. Lipset, an American sociologist, shaped the theory of formative events in North America into a sweeping, yet detailed, socio-historical comparison of Canada and the United States (Lipset, 1963b, 1964, 1970). From a wide variety of data, Lipset concluded that Canadians have displayed a greater respect than Americans for tradition of all kinds: for tradition in social life (like permanent marriage), for traditional loyalties (like ethnic solidarity), and traditional relations of deference (to traditional elites and laws). Canadians seem to place law and order before freedom and equality, he argued. Canadians were also seen as less achievement-oriented, more collectivity-oriented, and more elitist. In all these senses, they were more British than Americans.

Lipset emphasized that Canada's major formative event turns out to be the flipside of America's. America's was the Revolution of 1776, Canada's the counterrevolution. He argued that the counterrevolutionary element in Canadian culture was provided, especially, by the movement of anti-revolutionary loyalists from the United States to Canada. In Lipset's words:

> once these events had formed the structure of the two nations, their institutional characters were set. Subsequent events tended to enforce "leftist" values in the south and "rightist" ones in the north. The success of the Revolutionary ideology, the defeat of the Tories, and the emigration of many of them north to Canada or across the ocean to Britain — all served to enhance the strength of the forces favouring egalitarian democratic principles in the new nation and to weaken conservative tendencies. On the other hand, the failure of Canada to have a revolution of its own, the immigration of conservative elements, and the emigration of radical ones — all contributed to making Canada a more conservative and more rigidly stratified society (1970: 60-61).

Lipset went on to argue that differences between the two countries were also reinforced by a continued British presence in Canada, in the form of monarchical institutions and the Anglican church. Also important were Canada's efforts, through its political elites, to set itself off from the revolutionary, anti-British, large and powerful neighbour to the south. In addition, Canada's orderly, governmentally planned and controlled expansion into the frontier reinforced conservatism, Lipset said. In the United States, western expansion was less orderly; great land speculation and entrepreneurship there reinforced values of achievement, self-orientation, and equalitarianism.

Lipset's theory, by now widely disseminated, has helped to form Canadian and American sociologists' definitions of Canada-United States differences. Yet Lipset's analyses have also been criticized, especially by sociologists in Canada. Lipset's claim of Canadian-American value differences is accepted as valid by most commentators only so long as it applies to historical, or pre-World War II, differences. But many authors have questioned the validity of Lipset's comparisons for recent periods (see, for example, the review by Brym, 1986). Critics believe Lipset's evidence of differences in recent times is inadequate and imprecise.

In making his case for recent differences, Lipset examined educational, legal, crime, and divorce statistics (1964: 174ff). Data from 1960 indicated that (1) proportionately fewer college-age (20-24) Canadians than Americans were enrolled in college and universities; (2) the ratio of police (and lawyers) to population was much greater in the United States than in Canada; (3) far fewer police officers were killed in action in Canada than in the United States, and crime rates for particular offences against person and property were substantially higher in the United States; and (4) Canada's divorce rate was significantly lower. The first finding was held to demonstrate greater elitism and lower achievement-orientation in Canada; the second and third findings, to demonstrate greater respect for public authority and the law in Canada and, thus, greater elitism and collectivity-orientation; and the fourth, to reflect Canada's greater traditionalism and collectivity-orientation.

Lipset also compared public attitudes towards authority, including political leaders, in the two countries. Americans believe more strongly than Canadians in the equality of all people and the dignity of the ordinary individual, he contended. For example, in the United States, all free men got the right to vote in 1845; this right was not attained in Canada until 1898. The number of voters was limited by property qualifications (i.e., unequal wealth) for half a century longer in Canada than in the United States (1964: 175ff; 1970: 44ff).

Symbols of the pioneer experience in the two countries also came under Lipset's scrutiny. He reported that the mythology of the American West was full of rugged individuals, for example, free-spirited, gun-slinging cowboys. Canadians do not imagine such wildness, he argued, when they think about the Canadian frontier. The Canadian West was dominated by red-coated enforcers of the law, the R.C.M.P., said Lipset, and this too is reflected in Canada's myths about its history. Indeed, Lipset observed that the purpose of the Canadian state, according to the British North America Act, was to secure the blessing of "Peace, Order, and Good Government", not liberty in the pursuit of happiness (1964: 183).

As we indicated, many Canadian scholars have doubted the applicability of Lipset's British fragment image to Canada today. In some cases, they believe the data support conclusions opposite to those Lipset has drawn. A few have attacked his way of explaining the observed value differences, arguing these differences can be explained by cultural lag if one assumes that Canada is similar to the United States, but falls culturally 20, 30, or 40 years behind it. By this reasoning, one should compare current Canadian data with American data from the 1940s or 1950s to measure the true depth of cultural similarity (see, for example, Horowitz, 1973; Clark, 1975).

Plausible alternative interpretations, not necessarily involving recent value differences, have been offered to explain the behaviour differences reported by Lipset. Among these is Horowitz's suggestion that higher United States crime rates result from the comparative absence in Canada of major racial strife (1973: 3). Others have attributed the difference to better policing and crime reporting in the United States. The divorce rate differences of earlier years may have resulted from different laws reflecting value differences that once held sway but do so no longer. The large increase in divorces immediately after liberalization of the Canadian divorce laws suggests that Canadians' shared values concerning divorce were not well-reflected in the earlier rates or in the laws prior to their being changed. Also, the educational participation differences may not have indicated Canada's greater elitism so much as proving that the country imported more of its trained personnel. Canada has historically relied on other, more developed educational systems, such as those of the United States and Great Britain, for its highly skilled workforce. This is discussed in the vertical mosaic in Section VII of this volume.

Some critics have asked Lipset to state more clearly which Canada he is analyzing in his comparisons. In some of his work, Lipset has ignored the Francophone solitude to focus on English Canadian-American comparisons. But in many of his analyses he has failed to maintain this distinction. Often Lipset's data measuring national rates of behaviour (the rates of crime or divorce, for example) consider English Canadians and French Canadians together without any distinction. Critics ask whether it is possible to make clear sense of such results, because of the great cultural and regional variations within Canada. Your readings in Sections I and V of this volume, on ethnic and regional variations, will suggest the magnitude of this problem with Lipset's approach.

Lipset (1985, 1986) has recently answered his critics with more data, extending his analyses into the 1980s. Our first selection in this Section summarizes Lipset's up-dating of his research. Drawing on an array of types of information — from attitude surveys, laws, crime, the arts, and various events — Lipset concludes that the pattern of between-country value differences, which he described earlier, still persists. According to him, distant formative events, from the Revolution onward, continue to affect people differently in English Canada and the United States. Lipset acknowledges, however, that if there is any change occurring it is toward greater similarity between the two countries. He also pays more attention to differences between French and English Canada, and concludes that Francophones have come to vary more from their English Canadian counterparts than from Americans. He emphasizes that the Québécois demonstrate greater liberalism in social attitudes, and more radicalism in politics, than Canadians in other provinces.

Lipset has always contended that the Loyalist exodus to English Canada (at the time of the American Revolution) provided Canada with conservative, Tory values, which reinforced the counterrevolutionary effect. David Bell and Lorne Tepperman take another look at this claim in the next article in this Section. Unlike Lipset, they conclude that the Loyalists differed little in political values and beliefs from colonists who remained in the United States. The only distinguishing difference between those who stayed and those who left, by Bell and Tepperman's reading, was that the Loyalists were "anti-American Yankees". They doubted the merit of pursuing independence for the colonies; they feared its consequences, economic and otherwise. In large part, this was because the Loyalists were more economically and politically dependent on ties with Britain than their fellow colonists who stayed behind.

This difference was enough, however, to set Canada on a divergent course from the United States. The Loyalists came to form a large part of the population of English Canada, occupying many of its key decision-making posts. Especially after the War of 1812 with the United States, which could hardly have decreased anti-Americanism, elites in British North America made sure to strengthen their ties with Britain, militarily, politically, economically and culturally. Immigrants from Britain were actively recruited. However, immigration from the United States was resisted; and some fairly unsuccessful attempts were made even to prevent Americans from owning property in Canada.

One of Lipset's claims has been that Americans may be more involved in voluntary associations than Canadians. He bases this hypothesis on his expectation that there will be greater collectivity-orientation among Canadians than Americans. This, he thinks, leads Canadians to believe that the state should address the community's problems, and that voluntary action is not necessary. Our next selection in this Section is a study by James Curtis and colleagues which tests the hypothesis of Canadian-American differences in voluntary association behaviour. The study draws data from two sets of national surveys conducted in the two countries in the

1980s. The findings show that there are few differences between English Canadians and Americans in voluntary association affiliation and involvement. The exception was for participation in church-related groups, in which Americans are much more involved. The authors attribute this latter difference to the greater competition for members among churches in the United States compared with those in Canada. Curtis *et al.* also conclude that voluntary association involvement rates are a poor measure of society members' collectivity-orientations because involvement can serve many purposes for individuals and their communities.

The final article in this Section, by Douglas Baer, Edward Grabb and William Johnston, illustrates the type of criticism that has been leveled at Lipset's claim that Canada continues to show evidence of strong British values. Indeed, their work provides the most thorough test of Lipset's views to date, among critiques using recent survey data.

The starting-point of the work by Baer and his colleagues is a belief that Lipset's analyses, however up-dated, do not directly measure the values of people living in the two countries. Baer *et al.* assume that only by asking people about their beliefs and attitudes can we really tap their values. They therefore compare the responses of adult English Canadians, Québécois and Americans to some sixteen pertinent questions asked in two recent nationwide surveys conducted in the two countries. The results of the Baer *et al.* study do not support Lipset's theory of contemporary English Canadian-American differences; there were no attitudinal differences in the direction predicted by Lipset's theory. The only consistent cross-societal difference was a slight tendency for the Canadians to answer questions moderately, rather than extremely. They seemed to prefer "agree somewhat" and "disagree somewhat" to "strongly agree" and "strongly disagree" in answer to the value statements presented for their assessment.

Baer and his colleagues wonder, in concluding, whether they have studied the kinds of beliefs and attitudes required for a proper measurement of the Canadian-American differences predicted by Lipset. However, they make a good case for using the particular data they examined. Their survey results should make us doubt the application of the British fragment image to contemporary Canada.

Lipset's image may capture a reality that is more historical than contemporary. Remember, however, that the data presented by Lipset are as much facts of Canadian and American society as the data studied by Baer and colleagues. Canadians are less likely to commit crimes, and they are less likely to divorce. And the countries do differ in laws and regulations, as

Lipset identifies. Lipset probably would argue that the differences in be-haviour rates, laws and such are as good (or better) indicators of the values in question as the data examined by Baer *et al.* In short, he might argue that in this case behaviour rates speak louder than words (i.e., survey responses). Baer *et al.* would not dispute that there are differences in behaviour rates between Canadians and Americans. Where they differ from Lipset is on what the proper interpretations of those differences are, and whether the case for particular Canadian-American value differences can be made with the evidence presented by Lipset.

Answers concerning contemporary Canadian-American value differences are not fully clear, then, even at a time when politicians and citizens are considering the possible cultural implications of free trade with the United States. There are also differences of opinion on the probable effects of free trade. Some see the Free Trade Agreement as simply an economic matter with little consequence for the culture of Canada. Others see it as leading to greater United States influence upon Canadian culture. The latter seems most likely to us. Free trade should further reduce Canada-United States cultural differences. This seems probable because free trade will tie Canada even more tightly into a North American economy, result-ing in more interaction between Canadians and Americans. This greater interaction should lead to greater similarity in outlook. Also, the American economy and cultural institutions are larger and stronger than their Can-adian counterparts. This should mean that Canadians are likely to undergo more change than the Americans, and that change will be in the direction of American culture. We shall soon know the answer, now that the free trade legislation has been passed in both countries. Meanwhile, what do you think? Is the case well made that Canada is currently more British-like than the United States?

4

The Cultures of Canada and the United States*

Seymour Martin Lipset

Theory and Approach

There is much to be gained, both in empirical and analytic terms, from a systematic comparative study of Canada and the United States. They have many of the same ecological and demographic conditions, approximately the same level of economic development, and similar rates of upward and downward social mobility. And alongside the obvious distinctiveness of Francophone Quebec, Anglophone Canadians and Americans have much in common in cultural terms as well. Yet, although overall these two people probably resemble each other more than any other two nations on earth, there are consistent patterns of difference between them. To discover and analyze the factors which create and perpetuate such differences among nations is one of the more intriguing and difficult tasks in comparative study.[1]

In this essay I shall focus on value differences between the two countries, that is, differences in that set of attitudes which tends to characterize and permeate both the public and private ethos in each country. The central argument of the paper is that Canada has been a more elitist, law-abiding, statist, collectivity-oriented, and particularistic (group-oriented) society than the United States,[2] and that these fundamental distinctions stem in large part from the defining event which gave birth to both countries, the American Revolution.

A brief characterization of the essential core, or organizing principles, of each society may help clarify the type of difference being referred to here. With respect to the United States, the emphases on individualism and achievement orientation by the American colonists were an important motivating force in the launching of the American Revolution,

*Excerpted from "Historical Tradition and National Characteristics: A Comparative Analysis of Canada and the United States," in *Canadian Journal of Sociology*, 11(2), 1987 (summer). Reprinted by permission.

and were embodied in the Declaration of Independence. The manifestation of such attitudes in this historic event and their crystallization in an historic document provided a basis for the reinforcement and encouragement of these orientations throughout subsequent American history. Thus, the United States remained through the nineteenth and early twentieth centuries the extreme example of classically liberal or Lockean society which rejected the assumptions of the alliance of throne and altar, of ascriptive elitism, of mercantilism, of *noblesse oblige*, of communitarianism. Friedrich Engels, among other foreign visitors, noted that as compared to Europe, the United States was "purely bourgeois, so entirely without a feudal past" (Engels, 1942: 467).

By contrast, both major Canadian linguistic groups sought to preserve their values and culture by reacting against liberal revolutions. English-speaking Canada exists because she opposed the Declaration of Independence; French-speaking Canada, largely under the leadership of Catholic clerics, also sought to isolate herself from the anti-clerical, democratic values of the French Revolution.[3] The leaders of both, after 1783 and 1789, consciously attempted to create a conservative, monarchical and ecclesiastical society in North America. Canadian elites of both linguistic groups saw the need to use the state to protect minority cultures, English Canadians against Yankees, French Canadians against Anglophones. In the United States, on the other hand, the Atlantic Ocean provided an effective barrier against the major locus of perceived threat — Britain — which helped sustain the American ideological commitment to a weak state that did not have to maintain extensive military forces. As with the United States, however, these initial

"organizing principles" in Canada served to structure subsequent developments north of the border. Although the content and extent of the differences between the two countries have changed over time, the contemporary variations still reflect the impact of the American Revolution.

Given all of the differences distinguishing the Canadian historical experience from the American, it is not surprising that the peoples of the two countries formulated their self-conceptions in sharply different ways. As an ideological nation whose left and right *both* take sustenance from the American Creed, the United States is quite different from Canada, which lacks any founding myth, and whose intellectuals frequently question whether the country has a national identity. Sacvan Bercovitch has well described America's impact on a Canadian during the conflict-ridden sixties.

> My first encounter with American consensus was in the late sixties, when I crossed the border into the United States and found myself inside the myth of America . . . of a country that despite its arbitrary frontiers, despite its bewildering mix of race and creed, could believe in something called the True America, and could invest that patent fiction with all the moral and emotional appeal of a religious symbol. . . . Here was the Jewish anarchist Paul Goodman berating the Midwest for abandoning the promise; here the descendant of American slaves, Martin Luther King, denouncing injustice as a violation of the American Way; here, an endless debate about national destiny, . . . conservatives scavenging for un-Americans. New Left historians recalling the country to its sacred mission. . . .
>
> Nothing in my Canadian background had prepared me for that spectacle. . . . To a Canadian skeptic . . . , it made for a breathtaking scene: a pluralistic pragmatic people openly living in a dream, bound together by an ideological consensus unmatched by any other modern society.

Let me repeat that mundane phrase: *ideological consensus*. . . . It was a hundred sects and factions, each apparently different from the others, yet all celebrating the same mission. . . . (Bercovitch, 1981: 5-6, emphasis in original)

Although interpreted in a variety of ways by different groups and individuals, the ideology of the American Revolution provides for each of them a *raison d'être* for the Republic — it explains why the United States came into being, and what it means to be American.

The contrast with Canada is a sharp one. Canada could not offer her citizens "the prospect of a fresh start, . . . because (as the Canadian poet Douglas Le Pan put it) Canada is 'a country without a mythology' " (Bercovitch, 1981: 24). To justify her separate existence, both linguistic cultures deprecated American values and institutions. As Frank Underhill once noted, Canadians are the world's oldest and most continuing anti-Americans (Underhill, 1960: 222; for an elaboration, see Kendall, 1974: 20-36). This stance was reflected in the writings of various Canadian observers in the 1920s who "discerned and condemned an excessive egalitarian quality derived from notions of independence and democracy that had been set free during the [American] Revolution" (Weaver, 1973: 80). Further evidence of such attitudes was gathered during the 1930s when the first efforts at a systematic sociological investigation of opinions in Canada concerning themselves and Americans were launched. One of the most important and prolific contributors to the research was S.D. Clark, then starting his scholarly career. He summarized the findings in the following terms:

Canadian national life can almost be said to take its rise in the negative will to resist absorption in the American Republic. It is largely about the United States as an object that the consciousness of Canadian national unity has grown up. . . .

Constantly in the course of this study we shall come across the idea that Canadian life is simpler, more honest, more moral and more religious than life in the United States, that it lies closer to the rural virtues and has achieved urbanization without giving the same scope to corrupting influences which has been afforded them in the United States. (Clark, 1939: 243, 245)[4]

As Clark suggests in this passage, Canadians have tended to define themselves, not in terms of their own national history and tradition, but rather by reference to what they are *not*: American.

These differences between Canada and the United States can be seen, not just in history or in the findings of social science research, but also in the novels, poems, and stories created by writers in each country. In fact, of all artifacts, the art and literature of a nation should most reflect, as well as establish, her basic myths and values. And many analysts of North American literature have emphasized the continuing effects of the "mythic and psychic consequences of founding a country on revolution or out of the rejection of revolution" (Brown, n.d.: 2).

Religion

The majority of Canadians adhere to the Roman Catholic or Anglican churches, both of which are hierarchically organized and continued until recently to have a strong relationship to the state. On the other hand, most Americans have belonged to the more individualist "nonconformist" Protestant sects.

Religion in both countries has become

more secularized in tandem with increased urbanization and education. For instance, Canadian Catholicism, particularly in Quebec, has modified the nature of its corporatist commitment from a link to agrarian and elitist anti-industrial values to a tie to leftist socialist beliefs. These variations, of course, parallel the changes in French Canadian nationalism. Public opinion research suggests that Francophone Catholics have given up much of their commitment to Jansenist puritanical values, particularly as they affect sexual behaviour and family size. This secularizing trend, although generally observable in both countries, has been less noticeable in the United States, particularly among evangelical Protestants. Americans, according to data from sample surveys presented below; are much more likely to attend church regularly than Canadians, and to adhere to fundamentalist and moralistic beliefs. And the continued strength of Protestant evangelical, sectarian and fundamentalist religion south of the border has meant that traditional values related to sex, family and morality in general are stronger there than in Canada.

A large body of public opinion data gathered in the two countries bear on these issues. Most findings are not precisely comparable because of variations in question wording. Fortunately, a research organization linked to the Catholic Church, CARA, has conducted a systematically comparative study of values in 22 countries, including Canada and the United States, where the data were collected by the Gallup Poll at the start of the eighties.[5] The two tables (4.1 and 4.2) which follow present some of the relevant CARA findings.

There is a consistent pattern in these data: Americans far outnumber Canadians generally in giving expression to Protestant fundamentalist beliefs, with Anglophones more likely to hold such views than Francophones. And, congruent with the variation in religious practice and belief, Americans appear to be more puritanical than Canadians, with Francophones the most tolerant with respect to sexual behaviour.

Table 4.1 Religious beliefs and values 1980–81, in per cent

	Americans	English Canadians	French Canadians
How important is God in your life? (1 = not at all; 10 = very important) Percentage choosing 9 or 10	59	44	47
Believe "there is a personal God"	65	49	56
Believe the Ten Commandments apply fully to themselves	83	76	67
Believe the Ten Commandments apply fully to others as well	36	28	23
Believe in "the Devil"	66	46	25
Believe in "Hell"	67	45	22
Believe in "Heaven"	84	73	58
Believe in life after death	71	61	63
Believe in a soul	88	80	80

Source: CARA, Center for Applied Research in the Apostolate, *Values Study of Canada* (code book) Washington, D.C.: May 1983.

Table 4.2 Family values 1980–81, in per cent

	Americans	English Canadians	French Canadians
Agree that "marriage is an outdated institution"	7	11	19
Believe that "individuals should have a chance to enjoy complete sexual freedom without being restricted"	18	18	24
Disapprove of idea of a woman wanting a child but not a stable relationship with one man	58	53	34
Agree that sexual activity must subscribe to certain moral rules	51	49	34

Source: CARA, Center for Applied Research in the Apostolate, *Values Study of Canada* (code book) Washington, D.C.: May 1983.

Law and Deviance

The difference in the role of law in the two countries is linked to the historical emphases on the rights and obligations of the community as compared to those of the individual. The explicit concern of Canada's founding fathers with "peace, order, and good government" implies control and protection. The American stress on "life, liberty, and the pursuit of happiness" suggests upholding the rights of the individual. This latter concern for rights, including those of people accused of crime and of political dissidents, is inherent in the "due process" model, involving various legal inhibitions on the power of the police and prosecutors, characteristic of the United States. The "crime control" model, more evident in Canada, as well as Europe, emphasizes the maintenance of law and order, and is less protective of the rights of the accused and of individuals generally.[6]

Property rights and civil liberties are also under less constitutional protection in Canada than in the United States. John Mercer and Michael Goldberg note:

In Canada . . . property rights are not vested with the individual but rather with the Crown, just the opposite of the U.S. where the Fifth and Fourteenth Amendments to the U.S. Constitution guarantee property rights. Interestingly, in the [recently enacted] Canadian Charter of Rights and Freedoms property rights (as distinct from human rights) were explicitly not protected. . . . Such a state of affairs would be unacceptable in the United States where individual rights and particularly those related to personal and real property are sacrosanct. (Mercer and Goldberg, 1982: 22)

The Canadian government has greater legal power to restrict freedom of speech and to invade personal privacy. Acting through an order-in-council, it may limit public discussion of particular issues and, as in 1970 during the Quebec crisis, impose a form of military control (see Callwood, 1981: 333-334, 341-342; Bell and Tepperman, 1979: 83-84; Smith, 1971). Comparing American and Canadian public reactions to violations of privacy by the government, Alan Westin writes:

[I]t is important to note that in Canada there have been some incidents which, had they happened in the United States, would probably have led to great *causes célèbres*. Most Canadians seem to have accepted Royal Canadian Mounted Police break-ins without warrants between 1970 and 1978, and also the RCMP's secret access to income tax information, and to personal health information from the Ontario Health Insurance Plan. If I read the Canadian scene correctly, those did not shock and outrage most Canadians. (Westin, 1983: 41)

That Canadians and Americans differ in the way they react to the law is demonstrated strikingly in the aggregate differences between the two with respect to crime rates for major offences. Americans are much more prone than Canadians to commit violent offences like murder, robbery, and rape and to be arrested for the use of serious illegal drugs such as opiates and cocaine. They are also much more likely to take part in protest demonstrations and riots. Although the United States population outnumbers the Canadian by about ten to one, the ratios for political protest activities have ranged from 20 to one to 40 to one.

Evidence from national opinion surveys in the two countries indicates that lower rates of crime and violence in Canada are accompanied by greater respect for police, public backing for stronger punishment of criminals, and a higher level of support for gun control legislation. For example, when asked by the Canadian Gallup poll in 1978 to rate the local, provincial, and Royal Canadian Mounted Police, a large majority (64 per cent, 64 per cent, and 61 per cent, respectively) said "excellent or good." The corresponding percentages reported by the Harris survey for local, state and federal law enforcement officials in 1981 were 62, 57, and 48.[7] In the early eighties, the CARA surveys conducted by Gallup found more Canadians (86 per cent) than Americans (76 per cent)

voicing a great deal or quite a lot of confidence in the police. There was no significant difference between the two Canadian linguistic groups on this item.

The lesser respect for the law, for the "rules of the game" in the United States, may be viewed as inherent in a system in which egalitarianism is strongly valued and in which diffuse elitism is lacking. Generalized deference is not accorded to those at the top; therefore, in the United States there is a greater propensity to redefine the rules or to ignore them. The decisions of the leadership are constantly being questioned. While Canadians incline toward the use of "lawful" and traditionally institutionalized means for altering regulations which they believe are unjust, Americans seem more disposed to employ informal and often extralegal means to correct what they perceive as wrong.

The greater lawlessness and corruption in the United States may be attributed in part to the greater strength of the achievement value in the more populous nation. As Robert Merton has pointed out, a strong emphasis on achievement means that "[t]he moral mandate to achieve success thus exerts pressure to succeed, by fair means if possible and by foul means if necessary" (Merton, 1957: 169). Merton accounts for the greater adherence to approved means of behaviour in much of Europe compared to the United States as derivative from variations in the emphasis on achievement for all. And the same logic implies that since Americans are more likely than their Canadian neighbours to be concerned with the achievement of ends — particularly pecuniary success — they will be less concerned with the use of the socially appropriate *means*; hence we should expect a higher incidence of deviations from conventional norms in politics and other aspects of life south of the 49th parallel.

Although the cross-national behavioural and attitudinal variations with respect to law and crime have continued down to the present, Canada has been involved since 1960 in a process of changing her fundamental rules in what has been described as American and due process directions. The adoption of a Bill of Rights in 1960, replaced by the more comprehensive Charter of Rights and Freedom in 1982, was designed to create a basis, absent from the British North America Act, for judicial intervention to protect individual rights and civil liberties.

While these changes are important, it is doubtful that they will come close to eliminating the differences in legal cultures. Canadian courts have been more respectful than American ones of the rest of the political system. As Kenneth McNaught concluded in 1975,

> our judges and lawyers, supported by the press and public opinion, reject any concept of the courts as positive instruments in the political process. . . . [P]olitical action outside the party-parliamentary structure tends automatically to be suspect — and not least because it smacks of Americanism. This deep-grained Canadian attitude of distinguishing amongst proper and improper methods of dealing with societal organization and problems reveal us as being, to some extent, what Walter Bagehot once called a "deferential society." (McNaught, 1975: 138; see also Whyte, 1976: 656-657; Swinton, 1979: 91-93)

Beyond these general distinctions there are specific provisions in the new Charter of Rights and Freedoms which set it apart from the American Bill of Rights. For example, to protect parliamentary supremacy, the Canadian constitution provides that Parliament or a provincial legislature may "opt out" of the constitutional restrictions by inserting into any law a clause that it shall operate regard-

less of any part of the Charter. In addition, the new rights do not include any assurance that an accused person shall have a lawyer, nor that he has the right to remain silent, nor that he need not answer questions which may tend to incriminate him in civil cases or in investigatory proceedings (Pye, 1982: 221-248; McWhinney, 1982: 55-57, 61; Westin, 1983: 27-44; see also McKercher, 1983).

The Economy: The Private Sector

The United States, born modern, without a feudal elitist corporatist tradition, could create, outside of the agrarian South, what Engels described as the purest example of a bourgeois society. Canada, as we have seen, was somewhat different, and that difference affected the way her citizens have done business.

According to Herschel Hardin, Canadian entrepreneurs have been less aggressive, less innovating, less risk-taking than Americans.[8] Hardin seeks to demonstrate that private enterprise in Canada "has been a monumental failure" in developing new technology and industry, to the extent that Canadian business has rarely been involved in creating industries to process many significant inventions by Canadians, who have had to go abroad to get their discoveries marketed (see also Brown, 1967; Bourgault, 1972; Hardin, 1974: 102-105).

This has been partly due to traditional management values and organizational processes (McMillan, 1978: 45).[9] Also important is the fact that, compared to Americans, Canadian investors and financial institutions are less disposed to provide venture capital. They "tend consistently to avoid offering encouragement to the entrepreneur with a new technology-based product . . . [or to] innovative industries" (Science Council of Canada, 1972: 123).

The thesis has been elaborated by economists. Jenny Podoluk found that "investment is a much more significant source of personal income in the United States than in Canada. . . . When Canadians have invested, the risky new Canadian enterprise has not been as attractive as the established American corporation."[10] Kenneth Glazier, in explaining the Canadian tendency to invest in the U.S. rather than in Canada, argues that

One reason is that Canadians traditionally have been conservative, exhibiting an inferiority complex about their own destiny as a nation and about the potential of their country. . . .

Thus, with Canadians investing in the "sure" companies of the United States, Canada has for generations suffered not only from labour drain and a braindrain to the United States, but also from a considerably larger capital drain. (Glazier, 1972: 61)

Data drawn from opinion polls reinforce the comparative generalizations about the greater economic prudence of Canadians. Studies of English and French speaking Canadians indicate that on most items, Anglophones fall between Americans and Francophones. When asked by the American and Canadian Gallup Polls in 1979 (U.S.) and 1980 (Canada) about usage of credit cards, 51 per cent of Canadians said they never used one, as compared to 35 per cent of Americans. The latter were more likely than Canadians to report "regular" usage, 32 per cent to 16 per cent. Francophones made less use of credit cards (64 per cent, never) than Anglophones (44 per cent, never). English speakers were also more likely to be regular users than French speakers.[11]

The Economy: The Public Sector

The proportion of the Canadian GNP in government hands as of the mid-seventies was 41 per cent, compared to 34 per cent in the United States; as of 1982 the ratio was 44 to 38 per cent (Nelles, 1980: 132, 143, n.28; United Nations, 1983: 22). Subtracting defence spending, roughly 2 per cent for Canada, and 5 to 6 per cent for the United States, widens the gap between the two countries considerably (see U.S. Arms Control and Disarmament Agency, 1982: 42, 71). Taxes as a share of total domestic product were 35 per cent in Canada as compared to 30 per cent in the United States in 1982 (*U.S. News and World Report*, 1984: 65).[12] Unlike "the United States, [Canada] has never experienced a period of pure unadulterated *laissez-faire* market capitalism" (McLeod, 1976; Aitken, 1959). The period since 1960 has witnessed a particularly rapid expansion in the number of crown corporations: fully 70 per cent of them were created in the past quarter of a century (Chandler, 1983: 187).

Research based on opinion poll interviews indicates that Canadians, at both elite and mass levels, are more supportive than Americans of state intervention. Summarizing surveys of high level civil servants and federal, state and provincial legislators, Robert Presthus reports:

[a] sharp difference between the two [national] elites on "economic liberalism," defined as a preference for "big government." . . . Only about 17 per cent of the American legislative elite ranks high on this disposition, compared with fully 40 per cent of their Canadian peers. . . . [T]he direction is the same among bureaucrats, only 17 per cent of whom rank high

among the American sample, compared with almost 30 per cent among Canadians. (Presthus, 1974: 463)

Differences related to party affiliation in both countries emphasize this cross-national variation. Canadian Liberal legislators score much higher than American Democrats on economic liberalism and Canadian Conservatives score much higher than Republicans. Conservatives and Republicans in each country are lower on economic liberalism than Liberals and Democrats, but *Canadian Conservatives are higher than American Democrats* (Presthus, 1977: 15).

Mass attitudinal data reinforce the thesis that Canadians are more collectivity oriented than Americans and therefore are more likely to support government intervention. In the 1968–70 studies of American and English Canadian attitudes discussed earlier, Stephen Arnold and Douglas Tigert found that, compared to Canadians, Americans are more opposed to big government and less likely to believe that government should guarantee everyone an income. They also reported that Americans are more likely than Canadians to take part in voluntary communitarian activities which, according to the authors, contradicts my assumption that Canadians are more collectivity oriented (Arnold and Tigert, 1974: 80-81). However, I would argue that the findings support this contention, since they demonstrate that Americans are more likely to take part in voluntary activity to achieve particular goals, while Canadians are more disposed to rely on the state. And in fact, a subsequent article by Stephen Arnold and James Barnes dealing with the same findings concluded: "Americans were found to be individualistic, whereas Canadians were more collectively oriented," more supportive of state provision of medical care or a guaranteed minimum income (Arnold and Barnes, 1979: 32).

The existence of an electorally viable social-democratic party, the New Democrats (NDP), in Canada, has been taken by various writers as an outgrowth of the greater influence of the tory-statist tradition and the stronger collectivity orientation north of the border. Conversely, the absence of a significant socialist movement to the south is explained in part by the vitality of the antistatist and individualist values in the United States. There is, of course, good reason to believe, as Louis Hartz, Gad Horowitz, and I, among others, have argued, that social democratic movements are the other side of statist conservatism, that Tories and socialists are likely to be found in the same polity, while a dominant Lockean liberal tradition inhibits the emergence of socialism, as a political force (see Hartz, 1955; 1964: 1-48; Horowitz, 1968: 3-57; Lipset, 1977: 79-83; 1983: 52-53).

However, there are other plausible explanations for the difference in the political party systems of Canada and the United States which suggest that the contrast in socialist strength should not be relied on as evidence of varying predispositions among the two populations. As I noted in an article on "Radicalism in North America," one of the main factors differentiating the United States from Canada and most other democratic countries has been its system of direct election of the President. In America, the nation is effectively one constituency and the electorate is led to see votes for anyone other than the two major candidates as effectively wasted. Seemingly, the American constitutional system serves to inhibit, if not to prevent, electorally viable third parties, and has produced a concealed multi-party or multi-factional system, operating within the two major parties, while the Canadian focus on constituency contests is more conducive to viable third, and even fourth, parties (Lipset, 1976: 36-52).[13] And many, such as Michael Harrington, former national chairman of the Socialist Party of the U.S., have argued that there is a social democratic faction in America that largely operates within the Democratic Party (Harrington, 1972: 250-269).[14]

Evidence, independent of the effect of diverse electoral systems, that the forces making for class consciousness and organization, linked to collectivity orientations, are more powerful in Canada than the United States may be found in trade union membership statistics. Canada not only has had much stronger socialist parties than America since the 1930s, but workers in the northern country are now much more heavily involved in unions than those in the south. By 1984, only 18 per cent of the non-agricultural labour force in the United States belonged to labour organizations compared to almost 40 per cent in Canada (Troy and Sheflin, 1985; Department of Labour, Canada, 1984: Table 1).[15] In the United States, the percentage organized in unions has fallen steadily from a high point of 32.5 in 1954, while in Canada the figure has moved up from 22.

Elitism and Equalitarianism

Elitism is presumed to be reflected in diffuse respect for authority, and in Canada contributes to the encouragement of a greater role for the state in economic and social affairs. Equalitarianism can be perceived as the polar contrast to elitism, in Tocquevillian terms as generalized respect for "all persons . . . because they are human beings" (Lipset, 1970: 38). Equalitarianism, however, has many meanings, not all of which are incompatible with elitism. Concep-

tualized as "equality of result," it enters into the political arena in efforts to reduce inequality on a group level. And, reiterating the arguments just presented, it may be said that Tory stimuli, elitist in origin, produce social democratic responses, efforts to protect and upgrade the position of less privileged strata.

Conceptualizing equalitarianism in this fashion leads to the expectation that nations which rank high with respect to the value of achievement, "equality of opportunity," will be less concerned with reducing inequality of condition. If the United States is more achievement oriented and less elitist than Canada, then she should place more emphasis on educational equality as the primary mechanism for moving into the higher socioeconomic positions. Canada, on the other hand, should be more favourable to re-distributive proposals, thus upgrading the lower strata, as, in fact, she is.

Robert Kudrle and Theodore Marmor note that "the ideological difference — slight by international standards — between Canada and the United States appears to have made a considerable difference in welfare state developments" (Kudrle and Marmor, 1981: 112). Canadian programs were adopted earlier, "exhibited a steadier development," are financed more progressively and/or are more income redistributive in the areas of old age security, unemployment insurance, and family allowances (non-existent in the United States), and medical care (Kudrle and Marmor, 1981: 91-111).

As of 1979, the percentage of Canadians aged 20-24 in higher education had risen to 36, but the comparable American figure had increased to 55.[16] The proportion of Canadians enrolled in tertiary education jumped by 125 per cent; that of Americans by 72 per cent. Americans, however, moved up more in absolute terms, 23 per cent to 20 per cent for Canadians.

Some analysts of recent changes in Canadian universities have referred to them as "Americanizations" (Bissell, 1979: 198). Canada not only sharply increased the number of universities and places for students, but her higher education institutions, following public policy, have changed. They have incorporated practical and vocationally relevant subjects, expanded the social sciences and graduate programs, and placed greater emphasis on faculty scholarship.

The changes in size and content of higher education in Canada should lead to a reduction in the proportion of persons without professional training who hold top jobs. Comparative data indicate that Canada has differed from America, and resembled Britain, in disproportionately recruiting her business and political administrative elites from those without a professional or technical education. As Charles McMillan reports, "Canadian managers tend to be less well educated than their counterparts in any other industrialized country with the possible exception of Britain" (McMillan, 1978: 45).[17]

This conclusion is documented by Wallace Clement's studies of business elites which reveal that the Canadians not only have less specialized education than the Americans, but also that the former are much more likely to have an elitist social background. As Clement reports, "entrance to the economic elite is easier for persons from outside the upper class in the United States than it is in Canada. . . . [T]he U.S. elite is more open, recruiting from a much broader class base than is the case in Canada" (Clement, 1977: 183, 209). Sixty-one per cent of the Canadian top executives are of upper class origin compared to 36 per cent of the Americans (Clement, 1977: 215-250, esp. 216; see also Safarian, 1969: 13).

Similar cross-national differences among top civil servants are reported by Robert Presthus and William Monopoli from studies done during the late sixties and early seventies (Presthus and Monopoli, 1977: 176-190). These revealed that a much higher proportion of Canadian than of American bureaucrats have been of upper class origin. Presthus explains the phenomena "both in industry and government" as reflecting

> strong traces of the "generalist", amateur approach to administration. The Canadian higher civil service is patterned rather closely after the British administrative class, which even today tends to symbolize traditional and charismatic bases of authority. Technical aspects of government programmes tend to be de-emphasized, while policy-making and the amateur-classicist syndrome are magnified. . . . (Presthus, 1973: 34, 98)

As with many other Canadian institutions, the civil service has been changing. A more recent survey of bureaucrats in central government agencies by Colin Campbell and George Szablowski finds that in "the past decade Canada has seen a remarkable influx of bureaucrats representing segments of the populace traditionally excluded from senior positions in the public service," and that many of those interviewed had "experienced rapid upward mobility" (Campbell and Szablowski, 1979: 105, 121). These developments may reflect the documented decrease in educational inheritance in Canada as the higher education system has grown (Manzer, 1974: 188-206).

Cross-national surveys conducted in recent years have explicitly sought to estimate support for meritocracy when contrasted with equality of result. Their findings point to strong differences between Americans and Canadians on these issues. In the fall of 1979, national samples in the two countries were asked by a Japanese research group to choose between the two in fairly direct fashion:

Here are two opinions about conditions existing in our country. Which do you happen to agree with?

A. There is too much emphasis upon the principle of equality. People should be given the opportunity to choose their own economic and social life according to their individual abilities.

B. Too much liberalism has been producing increasingly wide differences in peoples' economic and social life. People should live more equally.

Forty-one per cent of the Canadians chose the more egalitarian and collectivity-oriented option B. The proportion of Americans responding this way was 32 per cent. Clearly the pattern of responses suggests that Canadians value equality of result more than Americans, while the latter are more achievement oriented (Hastings and Hastings, 1982: 519, 520, 525).[18]

If greater commitment to equality of result leads Canadians to voice a higher preference for equality over freedom or liberty, as they do in the CARA study, the assumption that Canada is more elitist than the United States implies, as I noted in an earlier comparison of the two societies, that Canadians should be more tolerant toward deviants or dissidents than American, (Lipset, 1970: 46-48). I suggested that even without a due process system, the greater tolerance and civil liberties for unpopular groups in elitist democracies, such as Britain and Canada, as compared to populist ones reflected the ability of elites in the former to protect minority rights. Opinion studies from many democratic societies indicate that educated elites invariably are more tolerant than the less educated; hence the tyranny of the majority is less of a problem in a more elitist system. And the CARA data bear out the anticipation that Canadians would, therefore, be more tolerant than their southern neighbours.

Mosaic and Melting Pot: Centre and Periphery

In an earlier paper, I asserted that "Canada is more particularistic (group-attribute conscious) than the seemingly more universalistic United States" (Lipset, 1970: 55). These differences are reflected (a) in the Canadian concept of the "mosaic," applied to the right to cultural survival of ethnic groups, as compared to the American notion of the "melting pot"; (b) in the more frequent recurrence and survival of strong regionally based third parties in Canada than in the United States; and (c) in the greater strength of provinces within the Canadian union, compared to the relative weakness of the states.

The origin of these cross-national differences, as with those previously discussed, can be traced to the impact of the Revolution. American universalism, the desire to incorporate diverse groups into one culturally unified whole, is inherent in the founding ideology, the American Creed. Canadian particularism, the preservation of sub-national group loyalties, an outgrowth of the commitment to the maintenance of two linguistic sub-cultures, is derivative from the decision of the Francophone clerical elite to remain loyal to the British monarchy, as a protection against the threat posed by Puritanism and democratic populism from the revolutionary south. Given the importance of the French-speaking areas to British North America, the subsequent Canadian federal state incorporated protections for the linguistic minority, and the provinces assumed considerable power.

These differences could be expected to decline with modernization. Most analysts have assumed that industrialization, urbanization, and the spread of education would reduce ethnic and regional consciousness, that universalism would supplant particularism.

The validity of the assumption that structural modernization would sharply reduce ethnic and regional diversity and the power of federal sub-units has been challenged by developments both within and outside of Canada. From the sixties on, the world has witnessed an ethnic revival in many countries. In Canada, even prior to the revival, the values underlying the concept of the "mosaic" meant that various minorities, in addition to the Francophones, would be able to sustain a stronger group life than comparable ones in the United States. As Arthur Davis points out:

> [E]thnic and regional differences . . . have been more generally accepted, more legitimized [in Canada] than they have been in our southern neighbour. There has not been as much pressure in Canada for "assimilation" as there has been in the United States. . . . Hutterite communities unquestionably are granted more autonomy in Canada than in the United States. Likewise, the Indians of Canada, however rudely they were shunted onto reservations . . . were seldom treated with such overt coercion as were the American Indians (Davis, 1971: 27). . . .

The greater autonomy and coherence of ethnic groups north of the border is the result, not just of a different set of attitudes, but also of explicit government policies which reflect them. Ever since the publication in 1969 of the fourth volume of the *Report of the Royal Commission on Bilingualism and Biculturalism*, the country has been committed to helping all ethnic groups through a policy of promoting "multiculturalism" (*Report of the Royal Commission on Bilingualism and Biculturalism*, 1969). The extent of the government's willingness to support this policy was reflected in the 1973 establishment of a cabinet ministry with the exclusive responsibility for multiculturalism.

In addition, the government has provided funding to ethnic minorities for projects designed to celebrate and extend their cultures.

During the past two decades blacks have assumed a role within the American polity somewhat similar to that which the Québécois play in Canada. The call for "Black Power," in the context of demands for group, as distinct from individual, rights through affirmative action quotas and other forms of aid, has led the United States to explicitly accept particularistic standards for dealing with racial and ethnic groups. Much as Francophones have legitimated cultural autonomy for other non-Anglo-Saxon Canadians, the changing position of blacks has enabled other American ethnic groups and women to claim similar particularistic rights. In effect, the United States has moved toward replacing the ideal of the "melting pot" with that of the "mosaic."

Conclusion

Canadian provinces have become more disposed than American states to challenge the power of the federal government. Movements advocating secession have recurred in this century, not only in Quebec, but in part of the Maritimes, the Prairies, and British Columbia as well. The tensions between Ottawa and the provinces and regions are not simply conflicts among politicians over the distribution of power. Public sentiment in Canada remains much more territorial than in the United States, reflecting more distinct regional and provincial interests and values. In a comparative analysis of "voting between 1945 and 1970 in 17 western nations, Canada ranked among the least nationalized, while the United States was the most nationalized . . ." (Gibbins, 1982: 158).

Few Canadian scholars are ready to agree, as John Porter was, that the difference is derived from the continued influence in Canada of counterrevolutionary traditions and institutions, or that the variations represent a "choice of different sets of values, as the choice between a preference for the maintenance of group identities or for the diffusion of individual universalism" (Hueglin, 1984: 22).[19] Rather, they discuss a variety of relevant factors: "*societal* (economic, demographic, and international forces) and *institutional*)" (Esman, 1984; Smiley, 1984).

Two variables, both of which may be linked to the outcome of the American Revolution, appear to be most important. One is the role of the French Canadians discussed earlier. The other is the effect of the variation between the Presidential-Congressional divided-powers American system and the British parliamentary model. As Roger Gibbins emphasizes, "the Québécois . . . have used the Quebec provincial government as an instrument of cultural survival and, because the stakes are so high, provincial rights have been guarded with a vigour unknown in the United States" (Gibbins, 1982: 192).

I have paid more attention here than in my earlier writings to variations between the two Canadian linguistic cultures. The evidence indicates that Francophone Canadians vary more from their Anglophone co-nationals than the latter do from Americans. Quebec, once the most conservative part of Canada, has become the most liberal on social issues and had a quasi-socialist provincial government from 1976 to 1986. Clearly, as John Porter and others have emphasized, there are Canadian styles and values that differentiate both linguistic cultures from the American one.

The cultural and political differences between the two North American nations suggest why they occasionally have some difficulty understanding each other in the international arena. There are the obvious effects of variations in size, power, and awareness of the other. Canadians object to being taken for granted, and to being ignored by their neighbour. As citizens of a less populous power, they sympathize with other small or weak countries who are pressed by the United States. But beyond the consequences of variations in national power and interests, Canadians and Americans, as I have tried to spell out here, have a somewhat different *Weltanschauung*, world-view, ideology.

The United States and Canada remain two nations formed around sharply different organizing principles. As various novelists and literary critics have emphasized, their basic myths vary considerably, and national ethoses and structures too are determined in large part by such myths. However, the differences in themes in the two national literatures have declined in the past two decades. Ronald Sutherland and A.J.M. Smith, two Canadian literary critics, have both called attention to a new nationalism north of the border, one which has produced a more radical literature (Sutherland, 1977: 413; Smith, 1979: 236-237). But ironically, as Sutherland points out, these changes are making Canada and her fiction more American, involving a greater emphasis on values such as pride in country, self-reliance, individualism, independence and self-confidence.

It may be argued, however, that these changes, while reducing some traditional differences, have enhanced others. The new nationalism, often linked among intellectuals both to socialism and Toryism, seeks to resist takeover of Canada's economy and increased cultural and media influence by Americans, and its weapon in so doing is the remedy of state action. As Christian and Campbell have observed in this context: "Toryism, socialism, and nationalism all share a common collectivist orientation in various forms" (Christian and Campbell, 1983: 209).

Although some will disagree, there can be no argument. As Margaret Atwood has well put it: "Americans and Canadians are not the same, they are the products of two very different histories, two very different situations" (Atwood, 1984: 392).[20]

Notes

1. My initial treatment of this subject was presented in Lipset (1963a: ch. 7). The arguments presented there were elaborated in Lipset (1965a: 21-64). This article was subsequently updated and incorporated as a chapter in Lipset (1970: 37-75). The page references to the article here are to the 1970 edition, which has the widest circulation of the three. The current article is both an extension on the theoretical level and a condensation of the empirical content of a recent analysis (Lipset, 1985: 109-160).

2. For a review of propositions in the literature see Arnold and Barnes (1979: esp. 3-6). See also Vallee and Whyte (1971: 556-564) and Archibald (1978: 231-241).

3. Northrop Frye notes that English Canada should be "thought of . . . as a country that grew out of a Tory opposition to the Whig victory in the American Revolution. . . . [Quebec reacted against] the French Revolution with its strongly anti-clerical bias. The clergy remained the ideologically dominant group in Quebec down to a generation ago, and the clergy wanted no part of the French Revolution or anything it stood for" (Frye, 1982: 66). For a discussion of Canada's three founding nationalities, the English, the French and the Scots (those who settled in Nova Scotia were Jacobites) as defeated peoples, see MacLennan (1977: 30).

4. For a comparable report by a historian of the 1930s in Canada see Neatby (1972: 10-14).

5. See CARA (1983a). The percentages for the United States are based on 1729 respondents; for English-speaking Canadians, 913 respondents; and for French-speaking Canadians, 338 respondents.

6. These models are taken from the work of Packer (1964).

7. Data from the Roper Center, Storrs, Connecticut. A comparison of the attitudes of a sample of the public in Calgary in 1974 with those in Seattle in 1973 also indicate more positive attitudes towards police in Canada than in the United States (Klein, Webb, and DiSanto, 1978: 441-456).

8. As economist Peter Karl Kresl puts it: "Canadians have been described as a nation of 'sufficers.' By this it is meant that economic decision makers tend to be content with a pace of economic activity and a degree of efficiency that is not the maximum possible but is rather one that is 'adequate,' or that suffices. . . . Hand in hand with this is . . . the frequently observed lack of aggressiveness and competence on the part of much of Canadian industrial leadership" (Kresl, 1982: 240).

9. Canadian novelist Mordecai Richler has bemoaned Canada's lack of "an indigenous

buccaneering capitalist class," suggesting that Canadians have been "timorous . . . circumspect investors in insurance and trust companies" (Richler, 1975: 32; see also Friedenberg, 1980: 142).

10. As summarized in Hiller (1976: 144). John Crispo also notes the "propensity among Canadians to invest more abroad" (Crispo, 1979: 28; Kresl, 1982: 240-241).

11. Data computed at my request from Gallup studies in files at the Roper Center, Storrs, Connecticut.

12. The source is the Organization for Economic Cooperation and Development.

13. The argument that the difference in the voting strength of socialism is largely a function of the varying electoral systems has been challenged by Robert Kudrle and Theodore Marmor. They emphasize that the Canadian labour movement "is more socialist than is the U.S. labour movement and always has been" and conclude that "a real but unknown part" of the greater strength of the social democratic New Democratic Party, as compared to that received by American socialists, "may be reflecting a different underlying distribution of values from the United States" (Kudrle and Marmor, 1981: 112; see also Rosenstone, Behr, and Lazarus, 1984).

14. Norman Thomas, the six-time candidate of the Socialist Party for President, also came to believe that the electoral system negated efforts to create a third party, that socialists should work within the major parties (Harrington, 1972: 262).

15. In both countries, unions are much stronger in the public sector than in the private one. See also Rose and Chaison (1985: 97-111).

16. The data are from World Bank, 1983: 197; UNESCO, 1982: 111-143; *Statistical Abstract of the U.S.*, 1982-83: 159.

17. Writing in 1978, he suggested the gap still existed in spite of the growth in numbers of business students.

18. Further evidence that Americans emphasize achievement more than Canadians may be found in Geert Hofstede's (1984: 155-158, 186-188) multinational comparison of work-related employee attitudes.

19. This is Hueglin's characterization of the predominant perspective on this question, with which he disagrees.

20. For an excellent statement by a Canadian historian detailing the relationship between the diverse histories and contemporary North American societies in terms highly similar to those presented here, see McNaught (1984).

5

Founding Fragments and Formative Events*

David V.J. Bell and Lorne Tepperman

Kenneth McRae (1964) has pointed out that "Canada offers almost a classic instance of a two-fragment society." The older fragment broke off from France in the early 17th century, when Champlain first settled Quebec permanently in 1608. But, according to McRae, the sparsely populated colony did not take on its enduring character until nearly 60 years later, when it came under direct royal control. From 1663 onwards, French-style absolutism dominated the political development of the colony: "New France was a projection — a deliberate and official projection — into the New World of a dynamic, authoritarian society at the zenith of its power."

Geography kept the "absolutists" from completely realizing their plan. Lying on the other side of an ocean, the colony was months away from the royal officials in

France who tried to govern its affairs. The unsettled frontier offered a place of refuge to those *habitants* who found the European social order too limiting. Certain feudal customs failed to survive the transatlantic voyage without change; the social distance between *habitant* and *seigneur* in New France did not approach the immense gap in wealth and refinement that separated the French nobleman from the peasant (Diamond, 1972). Yet within these limitations the French fragment of Canada evolved according to the political culture of modified absolutism, adapting the social, political, and religious institutions of 17th century feudal France to its own needs.

On the other hand, colonial departures from the French model were neither accidental nor determined by the environment. In many cases colonial officials consciously sought to institute a different kind of feudalism in the New World, partly to avoid some of the abuses that troubled the Old. "Feudalism in France was an organic growth; in Canada it was a transplanted institution, and the French administration saw to it that in

*Abridged from *The Roots of Disunity: A Look at Canadian Political Culture*. (1979) Used by permission of the Canadian Publishers, McClelland and Stewart, Toronto.

the transplanting it was pruned of less desirable characteristics. The French monarchy had established itself in the teeth of feudal opposition and was in no mood now to offer the seigneurs sufficient independence and power so as to require the repetition of the experience" (Diamond, 1972). Thus the French crown deliberately denied the *seigneurs* important political, judicial, and military rights enjoyed by the French nobility (Clark, 1968). Likewise, steps were taken to protect the welfare of the peasants. Even their new name, *habitant*, indicated a better status than the Old World *paysan*.

In New France agriculture and settlement were the primary activities. Trade and missionary work disrupted them. A thriving fur trade challenged the feudal institutions, despite their modifications and improvements. Yet the fur trade was controlled from France, so it produced only a group of romantic outsiders — the *coureurs de bois* — and not a class of prosperous local merchants who might have fought the feudal ideology and its institutions.[1] The few capitalists who had gained a foothold in New France fell as the first victims of the British conquest in 1759.

Referred to by Francophones as *la cession* (a term that reveals their sense of betrayal), the end of French rule removed many nonfeudal elements and strengthened tradition at the expense of modernity. It "purified" the French fragment. The British took control of the fur trade, and local Francophone merchants and entrepreneurs returned to France. The new rulers disbanded the militia, which had provided a countervailing power for the *habitants*, from whose ranks the militia captain was always chosen. Many of the civil authorities dismissed by the British had also been aggressive businessmen. In the words of historian John Bosher: "There was an ambiguity in the royal financial administration of New France, indeed of the entire French kingdom. The system was almost as much a private enterprise as a public function" (Bosher, 1972: 116). Now the French merchants and officials were gone, and the impulse of bourgeois modernization deadened.

The only institutions surviving the conquest were the Catholic church (whose power expanded to fill the vacuum), the feudal landholders, and French language and civil law. Thus the dynamic forces for change were destroyed, while the traditional institutions were strengthened, with British colonial institutions superimposed on them.

At first no Assembly was elected; an Assembly was granted later when the newly arrived Anglophone colonists demanded it. But the Assembly became almost immediately the crucible of Anglo-French conflict. Ultimately French leaders used it to save rural tradition from the English impulse to change and modernize. In a now famous article Pierre Trudeau commented that the Francophones "had but one desire — to survive as a nation; and it became apparent that parliamentary government might turn out to be a useful tool for that purpose. [In 1837, the] Canadiens fought at Saint-Denis and Saint-Eustache as they would eventually rally for electoral battles or parliamentary debates whenever their ethnic survival seemed to be imperilled, as men in an army whose sole purpose is to drive the *Anglais* back" (Trudeau, 1968: 105).

No one can guess with any certainty the kind of society that might have evolved in Quebec if the British had not conquered New France. But it certainly would have been quite different. Quebec would probably have progressed and become cosmopolitan more quickly than it did. Perhaps it would have been clerical and feudal for a shorter time.

The conquest was survived by a group of traditional people sensitive to the threat posed by alien rulers and led by a clerical elite committed almost fanatically to guarding their people against the twin dangers of dispersal and absorption. "Therefore it was that the Church, profoundly convinced that to keep the race French was to keep it Catholic, came to look upon isolation as the chief safeguard for a racial individuality threatened on all sides by the advances of the New World" (Siegfried, 1966: 25).

The Canadian French proved remarkably ingrown. Efforts to attract emigrants from France had never enjoyed much success, despite offers of assistance that sometimes amounted to bribery. Almost the entire Francophone population of Quebec has therefore descended from about 10 000 original colonists who arrived between 1608 and 1760 (Henripin, 1968; Henripin and Peron, 1972). Even today relatively few surnames are to be found amongst the four and a half million Francophone Québécois.[2] The high rate of population growth this group achieved through natural increase alone averaged about $2^1/_4$ per cent a year for three centuries. This demographic feat, known as "the revenge of the cradle," has rarely been equalled in the world (Henry, 1961).

An almost total absence of Francophone immigrants after 1763 meant a very low level of "population turnover." Without "fresh blood," new ideas were few, and tradition was able to keep its grip on the population. No revolutions or upheavals broke the existing pattern. As the present century dawned André Siegfried observed that French Canada "never went through its 1789": "All the old beliefs have been preserved as it were in ice among the French of Canada, and it would seem that the great stream of modern thought has as yet failed, with them, to shake

the rock of Catholic belief" (1966: 22,25). Indeed, some church leaders thought the conquest was a godsend: it insulated New France from the sacrilegious turmoil of the French Revolution and allowed the church to propagate Catholicism of the unreformed variety in the New World.

In contrast, Canada's Anglophone society began as a more open, fluid fragment and has ever since been changed and enlivened by newcomers. These immigrants have come first from the United States, then from Britain, later from Europe, and most recently from Asia and the Caribbean. Anglophones and English-learning newcomers have dispersed into all regions. Yet from among the many groups that have come to settle in Canada, both Hartz's and Lipset's theories focus especially on the earliest settlers, the Loyalists. Unfortunately, scholars studying early English-Canadian history have disagreed more sharply over the Loyalists than over any other single issue or group.

Origins of Loyalism

One could say that the process that produced loyalism really began when the British acquired Quebec in 1763. During the negotiations leading up to the Treaty of Paris, which ended the Seven Years' War, Britain was sorely tempted to let France keep this area. Instead, Britain would have taken Guadeloupe, whose potential contribution to the English economy appeared more valuable than the "acres of snow" in continental North America. Finally, however, concerned about security and wishing to eliminate the French threat to the Thirteen Colonies, Britain passed up the chance to add the Sugar Island to its empire, and kept New France instead.

Defending this new territory meant spending more on weapons and supplies. The British decided that the American colonies ought to shoulder at least a part of the war debt and the added costs of policing the new lands. Removing the French threat to the Thirteen Colonies had, however, cut the bonds holding in check the colonists' ambitions for land. But for the moment Britain wished to keep American colonists from spreading into this wilderness that so invited settlement. Efforts to keep settlers out of this area, coupled with repeated attempts to tax the colonies to help pay for their own defence and administration, led almost unavoidably to the Declaration of Independence in 1776, and then to the American Revolutionary War.

In the years between 1763 and 1776, one thousand British military officers and merchants replaced the French fur traders and political officials in Quebec, settling mainly in Montreal and Quebec City. The elite of the Catholic church were allowed to keep their privileges. They even strengthened their hold over the Francophone population. With help from the clergy, a tiny British ruling class balanced itself at the apex of a Francophone society numbering about 80 000 persons. Under British military rule, Quebec lacked entirely those institutions of representative government found in all the English-speaking colonies of North America.

Nova Scotia was another recent British acquisition, also taken from France around the middle of the eighteenth century.[3] In 1755, many French-speaking Acadians were rounded up and exiled, the unlucky victims of a colonial policy of expelling or resettling inhabitants. Some Acadians managed to remain in Canada by disappearing into the back country of what is now New Brunswick and the Isle of St. Jean (Lower, 1977: 104).

The officially recognized population of Nova Scotia, however, consisted largely of transplanted New Englanders, later dubbed by J.E. Brebner (1969) "neutral Yankees."

These settlers were Yankees by birth and inclination, neutral by common sense and often reluctant choice. They probably would have preferred to join with their cousins in Massachusetts who had declared themselves independent from Britain. But for a variety of reasons Nova Scotia, the Fourteenth Colony, did not join the other 13. Nova Scotia's economy was not developed enough to support a drive to independence. Besides, the powerful naval garrison situated at Halifax made rebelling very risky. The relatively young colony also lacked a network of transportation and communication links that might have enabled nationalist anti-British feeling to spread and take hold. For all these reasons, Nova Scotia was destined to remain under British rule. During and after the American Revolution, about one-third of Nova Scotia's 14 000 inhabitants left to rejoin their relatives in New England; but most stayed behind (Bell, 1969).

To sum up, the major formative events of this period were three: the acquisition of Nova Scotia from France in the mid-18th century, the acquisition of New France in 1763, and the American Revolution. And of these three events, the last is the most important. Americans may recall it as the time the Thirteen Colonies threw off British rule. In fact, the American Revolution was a struggle to control all of North America.

For Canada it signifies, first of all, the *failure* of the revolutionaries to conquer Quebec and bring it under American rule. The failure to bring Nova Scotia into the Revolution was also important in a similar sense. Perhaps most important of all, the struggle brought to light the Loyalists of the American Revolution: colonists who opposed the Revolution and decided to leave for Canada rather than help build the American Republic.

The Loyalists were to play a major part in helping Canada to emerge as a separate nation on the northern half of this continent. In most important respects, the Loyalists founded English Canada. Depending on the sources one cites and how a Loyalist is defined, between 30 000 and 60 000 Loyalists emigrated to the Maritimes and to what are now Ontario and Quebec after the Revolution. At the time these regions comprised fewer than 15 000 Anglophones altogether. Thus English Canada came into being as a by-product of the American Revolution.

The Anglophone Fragment

Who were the Loyalists, a people who rejected — or, depending on one's point of view, were rejected by — the American Revolution? Our answer obviously depends on how we interpret the Revolution itself. Those who believe that the Revolution was a "social movement" tend to think that colonial American society was made up of two social classes, the privileged and the rest. The privileged favoured a social hierarchy, an established church, passive obedience to superiors, and government by an aristocracy. The underprivileged wanted universal equality (at least among white men), the separation of church and state, freedom from foreign domination, and representative government.

During the American Revolution, this interpretation argues, the underprivileged threw out their oppressors. The defeated Tory group then moved north to Canada, where it attempted to create another society based on hierarchy, the "establishment," and so on. W.S. MacNutt (1963: 92) has called this attempt the Loyalist dream of "Elysium." A.R.M. Lower puts it this way: "[The] loyalist movement withdrew a class concept of life from the south, moved up north and gave it a second chance . . ." (1977: 118). If this interpretation is correct, early English Canada might be characterized in Hartz's terms as a pure Tory conservative fragment. This interpretation is correct enough to prevent us from dismissing it out of hand. Yet, it obscures far more than it reveals, resting as it does upon three erroneous assumptions: assumptions about colonial American society, about the Revolution, and about the Loyalist migration.

Although interpretations of the American Revolution vary on this point (Ernst, 1976), one important school denies that an aristocracy of inherited wealth ever dominated colonial society. A leading proponent of this view is Harvard historian Bernard Bailyn (1959, 1968). Bailyn writes, "There were no 'classes' in colonial politics, in the sense of economic or occupational groups whose political interests were entirely stable, clear and consistent through substantial periods of time. More important, there was not sufficient stability in the economic groupings . . . to recreate in America the kind of stable interest politics that found in England so effective an expression in 'virtual' representation" (1968: 75).

Migrants from Europe to colonial America had been primarily members of the urban middle and lower-middle classes. These were spirited bourgeois activists, not a traditionally docile European peasantry. No wonder, then, the term "peasant" disappeared in favour of "farmer," suggesting the bourgeois character of American agriculture (Hansen, 1961).

If we take "aristocracy" to mean an inherited status based on land ownership, the term fails to apply in colonial America. But the word "elite" does apply, and distinguishing between elite and aristocracy is not trivial. It is a distinction we might make between the top group in contemporary American society, for example, and the top group in mediaeval England. An elite position is, to at least some extent, up for grabs; an aristocratic title generally is not.

As the Revolution progressed, the colonial society split apart, not "horizontally," along class lines, but rather "vertically," between those in each class who stood to gain and those who stood to lose by cutting ties with Britain. Nor did loyalty to Britain vary in any simple way with kinds of religious affiliation, degrees of political influence, or amounts of wealth. What is relevant is whether a person in question belonged to a religious group that dominated or was subordinate; whether he took part in the political or in the bureaucratic institutions of the colony (of which more will be said later); and whether his wealth came from trade inside or outside of the British mercantile system. These elements cannot be reduced to any single factor. As a result, the Loyalist elite cannot be distinguished from the Revolutionary elite working only with the usual categories of socio-economic or "class" analysis.

When contrasting the Loyalist and Revolutionary masses, the differences become even smaller.[4] In effect elite members were *pulled* into the Revolution by the various kinds of interest and dependency mentioned above. The masses, by contrast, were almost entirely *pushed* to participate, by force of group pressure and the example set by their leaders. On which side they ended up was largely a matter of chance. How the masses affiliated themselves depended chiefly on which political/military organization, Revolutionary or Loyalist, was stronger in the immediate area.

The Counter-revolution and Ideology

The counter-revolution did not, therefore, transfer north a pure, pre-modern Tory ideology, opposed to liberal values and full of yearning for the return to a feudal aristocracy.

Indeed most of the Tories were just as sympathetic to John Locke as their opponents. Besides, they found in Locke an entire arsenal of counter-revolutionary arguments to hurl against the supporters of Independence. Locke is well known for the passages, paraphrased in the Declaration of Independence, justifying revolution in the face of tyranny, "a long train of abuses and prevarications" that indicate the ruler's intention to enact a "system of slavery" against the people. The Tories were fully familiar with this side of Locke. Some of them even issued their own Declaration of Independence against the Revolutionary Congress, complete with a word-for-word preamble, naming George Washington the tyrant in place of George III and bitterly attacking his, rather than Congress', tyrannical acts.[5]

However, the Tories took much more comfort from the passages of Locke's *Second Treatise* that propose a counter-argument to the revolutionary doctrine. Locke distinguished between a tyranny that tried to impose a system of slavery on the people, and a government that was basically "just" but merely guilty of mistakes, even "Great Mistakes" resulting from "human frailty" rather than "evil design." Against tyranny violent revolution was amply justified. But anyone who attempts to use violence against a just government, said Locke, is himself "guilty of the greatest Crime, I think, a Man is capable of, being to answer for all those mischiefs of Blood, Rapine, and Desolation, which the breaking to pieces of Governments brings on a Country."

Any such "common pest of mankind" is for Locke the moral opposite of a "revolutionary"; he is instead a "rebel." He commits the crime of *re-bellare*, causing a return to the dreaded "state of war." Rebellion is quite different from the morally justified act of revolution, which literally means to "revolve back" to the time of good government that preceded tyranny (1965 [1690]).

Colonists were able, therefore, to subscribe to most of John Locke's principles and yet oppose the call to arms against Britain. Everything turned on deciding which George, George Washington or George III, was the *true* "tyrant."

Alike in subscribing to Locke's writings, the Whigs and Tories arrived at radically different conclusions. Contrary to Lipset's view,

the debate that raged before and during the Revolution did not pit democracy against aristocracy, equality against hierarchy, liberty against privilege, or new against old. The debaters disagreed about independence and national unification. The Whigs eventually argued that the colonies formed a nation; the Tories, that they did not, and that independence was impossible, even disastrous. The Tory counter-revolution was not based, therefore, in organic conservatism but in the timidity of colonial thinking, what some have called a "colonial mentality" (Bell, 1969).

Yet because the Loyalists had strong political and economic relationships to the mother country, their northward migration was bound to have "conservative" results. In attempting to recreate the pre-revolutionary Thirteen Colonies in Canada, the Loyalists would strengthen traditional ties with the mother country and their traditional role as go-between, or what we might now call a *comprador* elite (Clement, 1975). They would seek justification of their authority not from fellow colonists but from the mother country.

Notes

1. Historians have hotly debated the character of New France. Some have argued that prior to the conquest a thriving entrepreneurial spirit dominated the colony, but all was lost with the conquest. For a brief account of this debate see the articles reprinted in Bumsted (ed.) 1972.

2. Even this figure under-represents the number of descendants produced by this incredibly prolific society. Including Francophone progeny who left Quebec to move to other parts of Canada and the U.S., the total might approach ten million.

3. France had ceded Acadia (present-day New Brunswick) to Britain in 1713 but maintained a strong military presence in the area based in the garrison and naval fortress of Louisbourg, on what became Cape Breton Island. Louisbourg fell to the British in 1758 shortly after the Seven Years' War began. See Clark,

1959a, chaps. 1 and 2. For an assessment of historical differences in outlook between them see Wade, 1974, pp. 47-53.

4. It is often forgotten that nearly as many people fought for the British as fought against them. According to Wallace Brown, "Between 30 000 and 50 000 Loyalists fought in the regular army, at a time when Washington's army numbered only about 9000." *The King's Friends*, p. 249. These facts are borne out by the findings of Esther Wright (1955) and other students of the Loyalist colonial "masses."

5. The Loyalist Declaration of Independence is reprinted as Appendix A in Van Tyne (1959).

6

Do Canadians and Americans Differ in Their Joining Behaviour?[*]

James E. Curtis / Ronald D. Lambert / Steven D. Brown / Barry J. Kay

According to S.M. Lipset's hypothesis (1985; 1986), Canadians are less involved in voluntary associations than Americans. This is to be expected, he claims, because Canadians are more collectivity-oriented. Their greater collectivity-orientation makes "Canadians . . . more disposed to rely on the state" for solutions to the community's problems, while "Americans are more likely to take part in voluntary activity to achieve particular goals" (1986: 135; cf. 1985: 141 ff). Lipset emphasizes that the stronger tendency toward voluntarism in the United States is rooted in the greater sectarianism of American religion:

A large majority of Americans have adhered to Protestant sects, which had opposed the established state Church of England. These largely have a congregational structure, and foster the idea of an individual relationship with God.

Most Canadians have belonged to either the Roman Catholic or the Anglican churches, both of which had been hierarchically organized state religions in Britain and Europe. While efforts to sustain church establishment ultimately failed in Canada, state support of religious institutions, particularly schools, has continued into the present. Hence religious institutions have both reflected and contributed to anti-elitist and individualist orientations in the United States and countered them in Canada (Lipset, 1986: 119).

What is Lipset's evidence for the contemporary national differences in voluntary association activity? It turns out that the evidence, thus far, is not very compelling. The evidence for Lipset's argument comes from some of the data from two national adult surveys conducted by the Center for Applied Research in the Apostolate (CARA) in 1982 (Lipset, 1986: 135; 1985: 141).

Apart from the CARA studies, the only other relevant study is a comparison of national survey data on the extent of voluntary association affiliation in Canada, the United States, and four other democracies (Curtis,

[*]Abridged from "Affiliation with Voluntary Associations: Canadian-American Comparisons", *Canadian Journal of Sociology*, 14(2), 1989: 143–161.

1971). This study showed a different pattern of results from the CARA studies. Canadians and Americans had the highest, and similar, levels of associational affiliation: 64 per cent of Canadians and 57 per cent of Americans had one or more affiliations when unions were included (church affiliation was not included, but religion-related groups were). Thirty-six per cent and 32 per cent, respectively, had multiple affiliations. Comparisons excluding memberships with unions showed 51 per cent in Canada with memberships and 50 per cent in the United States; parallel findings for multiple memberships, with unions excluded, were 31 per cent and 29 per cent, respectively (Curtis, 1971: 874-75).

Given the inconsistency of his findings in comparison with those of Curtis (1971) and the difficulty of interpreting them, Lipset's intriguing thesis on voluntary association activity differences between Canadians and Americans requires more support before we can accept it with confidence. Our present purpose is, therefore, to explore other data for the contemporary period.

Comparison Procedures and Working Hypotheses

We begin with a closer look at the data from the CARA studies than Lipset provided. These studies are important because they were conducted using precisely the same procedure, in the same year (1982), in each country. Then we will make comparisons of data from similar national sample surveys of adults conducted in each country in 1984. We provide two types of comparisons: between Canadians as a whole and Americans as a whole, and between French and English Canadians, on the one hand, and Americans on the other.

Lipset's hypothesis led us to predict that both English Canadians and French Canadians would be lower on voluntary association affiliation (for membership *per se* and for multiple memberships) than Americans. Moreover, we expected that, regardless of other Canadian-American differences for specific types of memberships, Americans would be higher than both Canadian sub-groups on affiliation with those types of voluntary associations geared especially to providing care and service to fellow members of the community. Considering only the groups asked about in our data sources, Americans should be more involved than Canadians in charities, service clubs and organizations, and youth groups.

Comparing Canadians and Americans in 1982

The CARA surveys were conducted by the Gallup Poll organizations in each country, using the same questionnaire and research design (CARA, 1983a; Chagnon, 1986). Each of the North American samples was derived from random block sampling in urban areas, and quota sampling based on age and sex in rural and rural non-farm areas. In both countries these procedures result in samples representative of the adult population, aged 18 and over (for Canada, see Canadian Gallup Poll, n.d.). The sample size in Canada was 1254; there were 336 French Canadians and 918 English Canadians, defined by the language of the home. The American sample numbered 1729 English-speaking respondents. Each survey involved face-to-face interviews.

Two relevant questions on voluntary association affiliation were asked in these surveys: (1) "Which, if any, of the following do you belong to?"; (2) "And do you currently do any unpaid volunteer work for any of them?'' The respondents were handed a card displaying the following list of organizations and examples:

charities concerned with the welfare of people

churches and religious organizations

education or art groups

labour unions

political parties or groups

organizations concerned with human rights at home or abroad

conservation, environmentalist or animal welfare groups

youth groups (e.g., Scouts, Guides, youth clubs, etc.)

consumer groups

professional associations

none of these

Table 6.1 (the upper panel) shows the results of answers to the first question in each nation. It is clear from this table that Americans were more likely to report memberships in one or more organizations — 76 per cent of Americans versus 58 per cent of Canadians. Both English Canadians and French Canadians were lower on affiliations, with the English 10 per cent lower than Americans and the French at less than one-half the American rate. (The CARA results were not presented in such a way that multiple memberships could be computed.)

Table 6.1 Percentage with voluntary association memberships and by types of associations for French Canadians, English Canadians, all Canadians and all Americans: data from the CARA National Surveys, 1982

Memberships	French Canadians %	English Canadians %	Total Canadians %	Total Americans %
One or More Memberships				
Yes	38	66	58	76
No	62	34	42	24
Types of Memberships				
Charities	10	14	13	13
Churches or religious organizations	8	42	33	57
Education or arts groups	8	10	10	15
Labour unions	7	13	11	14
Political parties or groups	6	5	6	14
Human rights organizations	1	4	3	5
Conservation groups	3	5	5	6
Youth groups	7	11	10	12
Consumer groups	2	1	1	2
Professional associations	5	14	12	18
(N)	(336)	(918)	(1254)	(1729)

An inspection of the types of memberships held by Canadians and Americans (in the lower panel of Table 6.1) suggests that the higher level of affiliation on the part of Americans is largely a function of their greater membership in churches and church-related organizations. Twenty-two per cent more Americans than Canadians belonged to such organizations, and 15 per cent more Americans than English Canadians.

The CARA data do not allow us, however, to separate church membership from involvement in church-affiliated groups. Both are combined in the same question. This is a distinction of some moment. Many analysts exclude church membership from their conceptual and empirical definitions of voluntary associations on the grounds that some attendance at church services is virtually mandatory for many religions (for example, practising Catholics). Involvement beyond this in groups associated with the church is not required. It is presumably some of these associated groups which perform the voluntary services for the community that Lipset believes are more frequent among Americans.

The figure for French Canadian affiliations with churches and religious organizations is very surprising. Only eight per cent of French Canadians reported belonging to "churches and religious organizations". Surely French Canadians, who are overwhelmingly Catholic, belong to the Church and attend its services at a greater rate than this? Possibly the Francophone Catholics do not conceive of their church involvement as belonging to a voluntary organization; church affiliation and attendance are probably for many simply an expected part of their family and community involvement. Membership may be largely taken for granted. An interpretation along these lines was offered (personal communication, June 30, 1986) by Professor Maurice

Chagnon who conducted the Canadian study and provided us with the Canadian data. When we asked Professor Chagnon for his explanation of the lower rate of religious involvement for Francophones, he suggested that for many French Canadians one simply is Catholic; only for other organizations do they think about "joining" them. He believed that Francophone Canadians interpreted the question as referring to groups other than the Catholic Church, while Anglophone Canadians and Americans more often included churches in their answers. Whatever the explanation, this surprising result for Francophones suggests that we should approach cross-cultural comparisons of the CARA organizational membership data with caution. There is a need for further comparative data.

Table 6.1 also shows the involvement levels for the types of community service groups that we suggested would be crucial for tests of Lipset's thesis on the between-society differences in voluntarism in the interest of the community. Starting with "charities concerned with the welfare of people" we find exactly the same level of affiliation for Canadians and Americans, 13 per cent; the level for English Canadians was one per cent higher than this figure, and for French Canadians three per cent lower. Thus, there is little support for the Lipset hypothesis here. The same is true for affiliation with youth groups, which showed a one per cent difference between English Canadians and Americans (and two per cent difference between the total samples). The level for French Canadians was five per cent lower than for Americans, however. There were no specific questions relating to membership of service clubs and organizations in the CARA studies. (As we will see, they were included in the two 1984 studies.)

In which groups were Americans more frequent joiners than English Canadians, apart from the religious groups? The level for Americans was five per cent higher than that for Canadians in "education and arts groups", eight per cent higher in "political parties or groups", and six per cent higher in professional associations. Similar differences obtained for English Canadians versus Americans, and the differences were even more marked when French Canadians were compared with Americans. It is difficult to see, however, how higher involvement in these types of groups suggests that Americans are doing more volunteer work in the interest of the community. These groups do suggest an individual orientation, insofar as people may pursue their own interests

through them. But pursuit of one's interests will be common to nearly all types of voluntary associations, as we will emphasize below.

For the other types of groups asked about — labour unions, human rights organizations, conservation groups and consumer groups — the English Canadians and Americans were within one per cent of each other in membership levels, and French Canadians have lower rates of involvement for all except the consumer groups.

When we turn to Table 6.2, which reports on the frequency of current unpaid work in voluntary groups, we find even more results that contradict the hypothesis of Canada-United States differences. English Canadians

Table 6.2 Percentage currently doing voluntary work and by type of association for French Canadians, English Canadians, all Canadians, and all Americans: data from the CARA National Surveys, 1982

Memberships	French Canadians %	English Canadians %	Total Canadians %	Total Americans %
One or More Memberships				
Yes	23	37	33	34
No	77	63	67	66
Types of Memberships				
Charities	7	10	10	7
Churches or religious organizations	6	19	16	23
Education or arts groups	4	6	5	5
Labour unions	3	1	2	1
Political parties or groups	4	4	4	4
Human rights organizations	1	2	2	2
Conservation groups	2	2	2	2
Youth groups	6	9	8	8
Consumer groups	2	1	1	1
Professional associations	1	5	4	5
(N)	(336)	(918)	(1254)	(1729)

have slightly higher proportions than Americans in one or more of these "working" affiliations, at 37 versus 34 per cent, and the total national samples are at more or less the same level. French Canadians continue to report fewer affiliations (23 per cent). Nonetheless, French Canadians are about as involved as Americans in all types of groups, except religion-related and professional associations. English Canadians report slightly more working involvement in charities, and French Canadians show the same level of activity as Americans. Only in churches and related organizations do Americans exceed the involvement levels of English Canadians and of Canadians as a whole (there was a one per cent difference for professional associations).

Comparing Canadians and Americans in 1984

We turned next to the two national data sets gathered in the surveys conducted two years after the CARA studies. Each study employed face-to-face interviews. The Canadian National Election Study (CNES) involved a multi-stage, stratified cluster sample of people aged 18 and over, with systematic oversampling of the less populated provinces. After weighting to make the sample nationally representative, there was an N of 3380, with 2267 English Canadians and 822 French Canadians, as defined by the language spoken at home (Lambert, Brown, Curtis, Kay and Wilson, 1986). The National Opinion Research Center's General Social Survey (GSS) was conducted with a probability sample of the English-speaking population of the United States aged 18 and older, for an N of 1473 (NORC 1985).

Slightly different types of voluntary associations were asked about in each of the two surveys, but the lists were long in each case,

and longer than in the CARA studies. Fifteen specific types were asked about in the American survey, and there were 16 types in the Canadian survey. Also, each survey invited the respondent to report on types of groups not on the interviewer's list. Thus, in both cases, we get a thorough and quite similar probing of affiliations. Church affiliation (as opposed to church-affiliated groups) was not asked about in the voluntary association questions in these two studies.

The CNES survey asked the following question on voluntary associations, immediately after a similar question on union membership:

"Now I will ask you about some other kinds of clubs, organizations or groups that people may join. Please tell me whether or not you are now a member of each." (*The interviewer read the list.*)

NORC's American survey employed this question:

"Now we would like to know something about the groups and organizations to which individuals belong. Here is a list of various kinds of organizations. Could you tell me whether or not you are a member of each type?" (*Again, the interviewer read the list.*)

The types of groups asked about in each survey are listed in Table 6.3. To make comparable calculations of the total number of memberships for each national sample we adopted the conservative decision rule of including in the Canadian totals only those groups asked about in the American survey; groups asked about in Canada but not in the United States were excluded from the Canadian totals. These excluded groups, and their affiliation levels, are presented in brackets in the lower panel of Table 6.3. Thus, the Canadian measure of overall affiliation is based on involvement in fewer types of

Table 6.3 Percentage with voluntary association memberships and by types of associations for French Canadians, English Canadians, all Canadians and all Americans: data from the 1984 National Election Study in Canada and a 1984 NORC National Survey of Americans

Memberships	French Canadians %	English Canadians %	Total Canadians %	Total Americans %
Number of Memberships				
None	43	31	35	32
One	28	29	29	24
Two or more	29	40	36	44
Types of Memberships				
Fraternal	5	7	6	9
Service/Volunteer	8	12	11	10
Veterans	1	9	7	7
Political	9	10	9	4
Labour unions	23	18	18	14
Sports	19	27	24	21
Youth	4	7	6	9
School service	8	12	11	12
Hobby	5	9	8	9
Fraternity/Sorority				6
Nationality	2	3	4	3
Farm				4
Literary				9
Professional	12	17	15	15
Church affiliated	13	18	17	33
Others	1	1	1	9
Entertainment/Social	(12)	(14)	(13)	
Charitable	(11)	(14)	(13)	
Neighbourhood	(3)	(9)	(7)	
Public interest	(4)	(4)	(4)	
Credit union/co-ops	(19)	(26)	(23)	
Women's organizations	(<1)	(<1)	(<1)	
(N)	(822)	(2267)	(3380)	(1473)

groups (12 groups, plus the "others" category) than the American measure (based on affiliation with 15 different types plus "others").

Despite this imbalance in the number of types of groups considered in favour of the American sample, the results in Table 6.3 show much the same patterns as the previous two tables. Canadians are as involved as Americans in one or more associations: 65 per cent and 68 per cent respectively. Also, 69 per cent of English Canadians, but only 57 per cent of French Canadians, reported one or more affiliations. We observe, however, that Americans were more likely to report multiple memberships (two or more) than Canadians, although the spread between Americans and English Canadians was only four percentage points.

In the findings by types of memberships, again we see few differences except for church-associated groups. The latter are more frequent among American affiliations, replicating the findings from the CARA studies. Service groups showed similar levels of involvement on the part of both English Canadians and Americans, as did youth groups and school service groups. Also, surprisingly, there was not the same pattern of more Americans than Canadians in professional associations and political organizations, as in the CARA studies.

French Canadians once again showed lower levels of affiliation for several kinds of organizations — fraternal, veterans, sports, youth, school service, hobby, professional, religion-related, and other organizations. The level of religion-related group memberships for Francophone Canadians was 13 per cent, higher than the eight per cent figure for "churches and religious organizations" in the CARA study for the same language group. The 1984 figures for religion-related groups for English Canadians, Canadians, and all Americans were lower in the 1984 data than in the CARA studies, as we would expect given that the latter asked about churches and related groups combined, while the former asked only about the religious groups. These results, then, further suggest that we should be cautious in interpreting the CARA figure for the Francophones in the same way as the results for English Canadians and Americans.

The Canadian sample was asked the following additional question on church attendance:

"About how often do you go to church (temple, etc.)? At least once a week, two or three times a month, once a month, a few times a year or less, or never?"

The American sample was asked:

"How often do you attend religious services?" (The following categories were used as probes where necessary: "several times a week, every week, nearly every week, two or three times a month, about once a month, several times a year, about once or twice a year, less than once a year or never.")

The overall proportions of those who responded "never" in the two countries were somewhat higher for Canadians — 19 per cent for Canadians and 14 per cent for Americans. The percentages for English Canadians and French Canadians were 23 per cent and 13 per cent respectively. Moving to the highly active category, we were able to replicate the finding of a greater involvement level for Americans, at least compared with English Canadians. For attendance in church once per week or more, the figures were 35 per cent and 23 per cent, respectively. French Canadians resembled Americans at 36 per cent, and Canadians overall scored 29 per cent.

Conclusions

What the national comparisons for the 1980s show is similar levels of involvement overall and by type of association for Americans and English Canadians, with the exception of church involvement. For church affiliation, Americans exceed both categories of Canadians. Also, there are consistently lower levels of involvement for French Canadians overall and in several types of associations.

We find it impossible to conclude from these comparative results that Canadians in general are inclined to be less involved in voluntary associations than Americans. Indeed, in some cases, the differences for English Canadians and Americans run in the opposite direction from that predicted by Lipset's thesis. Lipset's theory leads us to predict Canada-U.S. differences in comparisons including both English Canadians and French Canadians. There seems to be no support for this theory when comparisons are made between Americans and English Canadians.

The comparatively high membership proportions reported for Canada probably result from basic structural and cultural similarities between Canada and the United States. For example, the two societies have similar high levels of economic development, and they are fairly similar with respect to the associated processes of urbanization, industrialization, the availability of formal education facilities, and the size of the middle-class strata. Although we cannot provide data here to support the point, we would suggest that the processes of urbanization and industrialization are highly correlated with social differentiation (see Booth, 1975). The result of these processes is many secondary groups and many opportunities for adult affiliation and participation in voluntary organizations in both the United States and Canada. English Canadians apparently avail themselves of these opportunities more or less as much as Americans. These major social change processes are probably more determinant of the contemporary extent of voluntary association affiliation in the two countries than events of political history that occurred some two hundred years ago.

Returning to Lipset's theory on between-society differences in collectivity-orientation, we should emphasize that a similarity of voluntary association affiliation levels in the two societies, by itself, does not invalidate the theory. We subscribe to the view that Canada is more collectivity-oriented than the United States, and for the socio-historical reasons described by Lipset in his several writings on the topic. The best evidence for this greater collectivity-orientation lies in other phenomena, however. It is manifest, for example, in different laws and formal procedures regulating the provision and funding of health, education and other social services in the two nations. It is also evident in differences in the levels of popular support for payment for such services through the public purse. Canadians clearly have taken more collective responsibility for seeing to the needs of the less advantaged through the state apparatus. More is left in the hands of voluntary and private profit-oriented organizations in the United States. Lipset has emphasized the latter, for example, in his description in previous analyses of the different experiences around medicare proposals and legislation in the two countries, (1963a,b; 1964; 1970). Also, in his recent papers, there is a very relevant discussion of the different proportions of the GNP held in governmental hands in the two societies (1985: 139ff; 1986: 133ff), with Canada being well ahead in this respect. In sum, Canadian society would appear to be both higher on collectivity-orientation than the United States and as high in voluntary association joining.

In retrospect, Lipset's extension of the

theory concerning Canada-United States differences in collectivity-orientation to predictions about national differences in affiliation
rates is probably faulty, because these rates
are poor indicators of the value orientation
in question. There are probably two problems with the extrapolation to associational
affiliations. First, voluntary groups and organizations are not exclusively arenas of voluntary action in the interest of the
community. The latter was, it will be remembered, Lipset's basic concern in raising the
issue of voluntary associations in the two
countries. Most voluntary associations surely
serve mixed purposes, whether for the society at large, for social sub-groups in the community, or for the members who join them.
For example, the same types of organization
have been shown to perform instrumental
and expressive outcomes for different members and for different segments of the wider
community (cf. Babchuk and Edwards, 1965;
Gordon and Babchuk, 1959; Warriner and
Parther, 1965; and Young and Larson, 1965).
It is presumably the largely instrumental purposes that best address the community's service needs (as we suggested when presenting
our working hypotheses) for charity, youth,
and service organizations. These groups
clearly have service to the wider community
as one of their mandates.

The second problem with using voluntary
associations as an indicator of differences in
individual versus collectivity-orientation has
to do with the differing reasons people join
groups. People with either individual or collectivity-orientations may join or start voluntary associations. Those moved by an
individual orientation might seek satisfaction
of their own interests in organizations,
whether this involves their expressive or instrumental needs. At the same time, those
moved by a collectivity-orientation might

pursue some of the same types of voluntary
association affiliations because they value
group activity, or because they wish to help
serve the community through these memberships. Moreover, people's individual and
collectivity-orientations may be acted upon
outside voluntary associations — for example, in the family and at work.

Even if voluntary association affiliations do
rather closely index individual versus collectivity-orientations, the comparative findings
suggest that for a case to be made for Lipset's
thesis we would have to show that the
churches and church groups reflect the orientations more prominently than do the
other voluntary associations in Canada and
the United States. After all, it is only here that
Americans truly exceed Canadians, or English Canadians, in involvement. We would
have to be able to show that the set of other
groups in Tables 6.1 to 6.3, which do not
show clear differentiation between English
Canadians and Americans, are less reliable
indicators of differences between individual
and collectivity-orientations. This is implau-
sible. Also, what we have said above about
voluntary associations' mixed purposes and
their members' mixed reasons for joining
would be no less true of the religious organizations. There is no sound theoretical reason for focusing on church affiliation
differences and ignoring the evidence of English Canadian-American similarity in associational involvement overall.

The differences in church affiliation and,
therefore, membership in religion-related
groups are clear and marked. How are these
best interpreted? It seems most reasonable
that the Canadian-American differences are
simply one of the consequences of the
greater sectarianism of the United States, described by Lipset. We need not attach a special meaning of individual and collectivity-

orientation differences to them in order to explain them. The greater sectarianism in the United States has led to a more differentiated structure of religious groups in American society than in Canadian society. According to one estimate, there were 223 distinct religious bodies in the United States compared to only 63 in Canada in the mid-1970s (Fallding, 1978: 145). An important consequence of this might be that there is more competition for members and, thus, more aggressive recruitment into the religious groups in the United States than in Canada. Bibby (1987) begins from the same historical events emphasized by Lipset but draws slightly different conclusions about their consequences for contemporary differences in religious behaviour. These historical differences have made for more of a marketplace of religion in the United States than in Canada. There are more numerous and more active sellers of religion in the United States. It is easy, then, to see how religious group memberships might be bought more frequently by Americans than by Canadians.

Given the evidence of between-nation similarities in affiliative behaviour presented above and the similar results in the earlier study by Curtis (1971), we would recommend a moratorium on assertions that English Canadians do not engage in voluntary organization activity as frequently as do Americans. This seems the wisest course of action until we have arrived at some significant evidence in support of differences in voluntary association activity beyond church involvement.

7

Reassessing Differences in Canadian and American Values

Douglas Baer / Edward Grabb / William Johnston

Introduction

One of the most interesting and provocative cross-national comparisons to appear in recent decades is Seymour Martin Lipset's thesis on the value patterns of the English-speaking democracies (Lipset, 1963a; 1963b; 1964; 1968a). Although his first work on this topic compared five countries, over the years he has focused almost exclusively on the more specific question of differences in the values and beliefs of Canadians and Americans. During this time, he has also altered certain aspects of his original interpretation to take into account some of the criticisms and unanswered questions raised by his argument (for example, Truman, 1971; Curtis, 1971; Horowitz, 1973; Crawford and Curtis, 1979). Nevertheless, Lipset's most recent writings have repeated his contention that important differences in Canadian and American values continue to exist (Lipset, 1985; 1986).

Lipset's thesis has been outlined in detail elsewhere and has been reviewed by several subsequent interpreters and critics (e.g.,

Truman, 1971; Bell and Tepperman, 1979; Grabb and Curtis, 1988; Baer *et al.*, 1990). In essence, Lipset has asserted that the Canadian and American nations were created out of distinct historical circumstances and institutional foundations, in spite of their early similarities as colonies of the British Empire. The United States, on the one hand, began with a liberal democratic revolution against British monarchical rule and the values of conservatism, elitism, and hierarchical control generally associated with that system. Canada, on the other hand, came into existence as a child of counterrevolution, affirming its loyalties to traditional English institutions, emerging as a distinct nation much later than the United States, and even now tied to Britain in tangible, if sometimes ambivalent, ways. As a result, although both nations are clearly identifiable as democratic states in the modern world, Canadians are seen by Lipset to have maintained a distinct British or "tory" flavour in their democratic values (cf. Horowitz, 1966). In particular, his view is that Canadians are less concerned about preserving equality, individualism, and freedom from control by government or others in power than are their southern neighbours.

Lipset's observations on the value patterns of Canada and the United States are intriguing to contemplate. Nevertheless, there are at least two kinds of difficulties in Lipset's thesis that become apparent on closer inspection. The first of these concerns numerous inconsistencies and contradictions in his argument. The second has to do with deficiencies in his evidence.

Problems in Lipset's Argument

Although Lipset's formulation is often inventive and imaginative, there are some important anomalies that have arisen in the argument over the course of its development (cf. Baer *et al.*, 1990). One apparent inconsistency in Lipset's thesis is his contention that Canadians are more strongly committed to values of "moral conservatism" than are Americans, but that Americans have a stronger sense of "evangelical Protestant moralism". Lipset perceives the latter orientation in the more restrictive attitudes that Americans have about marriage, the family, and sexual freedom (Lipset, 1968: 54-55; 1985: 125; 1986: 126-128). The problem with these two claims is that they make it unclear whether it is Canadians or Americans that Lipset believes are more conservative on moral issues.

A second problem arises in Lipset's discussion of the freedoms and rights of the individual. On the one hand, Lipset generally portrays the United States as the leading proponent of civil liberties for the individual citizen, yet elsewhere he readily acknowledges that Canadians show greater support than Americans for "freedom of political dissent and guaranteed civil liberties", especially in the case of minorities or groups outside the societal mainstream (Lipset, 1985: 129; 1968a: 39-40). This apparent contradiction is not really addressed by Lipset and once again makes his characterization of Canadian and American differences ambiguous.

A third difficulty in Lipset's formulation concerns his assessment of how equality is valued in the two countries. The original version of his argument explicitly identifies Canadians as more accepting of inequality than Americans, especially in such matters as the distribution of wealth or income to the population (Lipset, 1963b: 25, 89). However, more recently his view is clearly the opposite on this issue: Canadians are in fact more supportive of equal economic conditions for all citizens, while Americans are more strongly committed to equal economic opportunity, but not to equal conditions or distribution (Lipset, 1985: 144-145).

As a final illustration of inconsistencies in Lipset's argument, we can consider his treatment of the state and political power in the two countries. Canada is generally perceived by Lipset as a nation in which the state plays a dominant role, providing for most of the social needs of its citizens, intervening in private economic affairs, and if necessary overriding individual pursuits to protect and promote collective interests (Lipset, 1968a: 44, 49). In contrast, the United States is seen as more deeply imbued with "anti-statist and individualistic values", where each person's freedom to pursue his or her own interests is largely unencumbered by government control or concerns for collective goals (Lipset, 1985: 144). In this instance as well, however, Lipset makes what seem to be contradictory assertions, for he suggests that the United States is in fact "more centralized politically" than Canada, with a much stronger federal government. More-over, he also notes a greater dispersion of political power to regional and local governments in Canada compared with the United States (Lipset, 1985: 151, 157). These statements make it uncertain whether it is Canada or the United States that is more statist, in the sense of being more subservient to or dominated by the presence of big government.

Problems in Lipset's Evidence

We now have a sense of some of the conflicting and contradictory elements in Lipset's characterization of the value differences he perceives between the Canadian and American peoples. These problems are in turn related to the second set of difficulties in his work on this topic, which concern the evidence he uses to corroborate his claims for value differences. First of all, because his argument is often ambiguous or inconsistent concerning how the differences are manifested, the available evidence can be interpreted in whatever way best fits the argument. For example, if Canadians favour equal rights for minority groups more than do Americans, does this demonstrate that Canadians are more equalitarian or, as Lipset would have it, does this show that Canadians are more collectivist and particularist, putting the rights or needs of special groups (i.e., minorities) ahead of individual interests (Lipset, 1986: 144)? This pattern of placing the available evidence in the context most favourable to his argument is a common one in Lipset's writings.

Apart from this problem, a more obvious difficulty is that Lipset is unable to offer much direct evidence on the values, beliefs, or attitudes of Canadians and Americans. In-stead, indirect indicators such as crime rates, divorce rates, statistics on educational expenditures, and comments by journalists and other observers form the bulk of the support for Lipset's argument. When data on the orientations and perceptions of people themselves are offered, they come in most cases from unrepresentative samples. In order to test Lipset's argument adequately, it is essential that evidence from national-level, representative samples be employed, preferably on a range of issues that are pertinent to the differences he alleges.

The purpose of the present paper is to conduct just such an analysis. Using findings from recent representative national sample surveys in both countries, we are able to examine a series of issues that relate to Lipset's claims about Canadian and American differences. An additional feature of our analysis is that we have separated Québécois and English Canadian respondents when comparing the Canadian and American samples. As Lipset has recently acknowledged, there are reasons to expect important internal distinctions between French and English Canadians that would be blurred if the two groups were treated as a single entity (Lipset, 1985: 159). We proceed now to a description of the data and the items used in the analysis.

Data

Most of our findings are from the merged multi-national file of the "Class Structure and Class Consciousness" study obtained from the Inter-University Consortium for Political and Social Research at the University of Michigan (I.C.P.S.R.).[1] The Canadian data were collected in 1983, and the U.S. data in 1980.[2] In both countries, the universe consisted of adults, 18 years and older, who were working at the time of the interview. In Canada, 1785 labour force participants were interviewed; in the United States, 1498 labour force participants were interviewed.

From the full surveys, we chose a range of common items dealing with five general issue areas of relevance to Lipset's thesis: 1) perceptions of corporate power and profits; 2) attitudes about economic inequality and government social services spending; 3) feelings about labour unions and the rights of workers and management during strike situations; 4) beliefs about gender inequality; and 5) attitudes about family discipline and social control, especially in relation to crime (see Table 7.1).

To add to our list of issue areas, we also used data from two other surveys, both undertaken in 1984. These surveys are the Canadian National Election Study (N = 3277) and the American National Election Study (N = 2257), which contain two nearly identical items dealing with trust in government (see Table 7.2).[3]

Because of the inconsistencies and ambiguities in Lipset's formulation, it is not entirely clear what predictions Lipset would offer regarding each of these issue areas. However, based on what is implied in his more recent analyses, it is likely Lipset would expect that, when compared with Americans, English Canadians are less supportive of private business or corporate interests; more in favour of reducing economic inequalities and increasing social services; more supportive of labour over management; more supportive of legal punishments and family discipline to control crime; less in favour of equality regarding gender roles and women's opportunities outside the family setting; and more trusting of government. These predictions are consistent with Lipset's claims that English Canadians are more collectivist; more

egalitarian concerning economic conditions in society; more traditional on issues of restraint or social control; less influenced by a belief in equality of opportunity; and more deferential to state authority. As for the values of the Québécois, Lipset's current views suggest that they should be the most left-liberal or "quasi-socialist" of all (Lipset, 1985: 158); hence, if his assertions are accurate, Québécois respondents in our analysis should express the greatest opposition to corporations; the greatest support for both economic redistribution and the interests of labour; the least support for increased control and discipline; the most support for gender equality; and the greatest trust in state institutions.

Results

The responses to the survey items are shown in Table 7.1. The first set of questions considers attitudes about corporate power and profits. English Canadians agree more than Americans that "corporations benefit owners at the expense of workers and consumers." Among English Canadian respondents, 24 per cent agree strongly with this statement, and 42 per cent agree somewhat, for a total of 66 per cent. This can be contrasted with the 58 per cent of Americans who agree or agree strongly. Thus, on this item the results are consistent with Lipset's suggestion that English Canadians are less attached to a free enterprise oriented belief system. On this one issue, as well, we find as Lipset suggests that Québécois respondents are the least supportive of corporations. The next question, concerning whether big corporations have too much power, produces no consistent differences. For both English Canadians and Québécois, 83 per cent agree that "big

Table 7.1 Item wordings and distributions

		Agree strongly %	Agree %	Disagree %	Disagree strongly %
Corporate Power & Profits					
Corporations benefit owners	US:	19	39	25	17
at the expense of workers	Québ:	28	42	19	11
and consumers.[a,b]	Eng. Can.:	24	42	21	13
Big corporations have far	US:	54	27	12	7
too much power in [American]	Québ:	41	42	13	4
[Canadian] society today.[a,b,c]	Eng. Can.:	49	34	13	4
One of the main reasons for	US:	16	31	23	30
poverty is that the economy	Québ:	19	37	29	15
is based on private	Eng. Can.:	15	34	27	24
ownership and profits.[a,b,c]					
Inequality and Social Services Spending					
Many people in [the United	US:	33	37	21	9
States] [Canada] receive	Québ:	28	43	23	6
much less income than	Eng. Can.:	26	42	24	8
they deserve.[a,b]					

		Spend great deal more %	Spend somewhat more %	Spend present amount %	Spend somewhat less %	Spend great deal more %
Government social	US:	31	39	20	7	3
services spending	Québ:	25	34	32	7	2
(health, educ.)[a,b,c]	Eng. Can:	26	41	26	6	1

		Agree strongly %	Agree %	Disagree %	Disagree strongly %
Labour Unions					
During a strike, management	US:	32	16	22	30
should be prohibited by law	Québ:	46	24	15	15
from hiring workers to	Eng. Can:	37	18	21	24
take the place of strikers.[a,b,c]					
Striking workers are	US:	13	17	22	48
generally justified in	Québ:	8	13	24	55
physically preventing	Eng. Can.:	10	18	24	48
strikebreakers from					
entering the place of work.[a,b,c]					

continued. . .

		Workers win most important demands %	Workers win some demands, make some concessions %	Workers win a few demands, make major concessions %	Workers win nothing %
Imagine a strike.	US:	15	74	8	3
Which outcome would you	Québ:	12	72	14	2
like to see occur?[a,b]	Eng. Can:	11	72	13	4

		Agree strongly %	Agree %	Disagree %	Disagree strongly %
Gender Equality					
It is better for the family	US:	38	28	19	15
if the husband is the	Québ:	25	30	25	20
principal breadwinner	Eng. Can.:	32	30	22	16
outside the home and					
the wife has primary responsibility					
for the home and children.[a,b,c]					
If both husband and wife	US:	72	23	4	1
work, they should share	Québ:	66	31	2	1
equally in the housework	Eng. Can.:	71	25	3	1
and child care.[a]					
There are not enough women	US:	37	41	14	8
in responsible positions	Québ:	33	44	18	5
in government and private	Eng. Can.:	32	45	19	4
business.[a,b]					
Ideally, there should be	US:	26	32	26	16
as many women as men in	Québ:	38	39	17	6
important positions in	Eng. Can:	32	35	24	9
government and business.[a,b,c]					
Social Control and Crime					
In order to reduce crime,	US:	60	24	9	7
the courts should give	Québ:	43	28	19	10
criminals stiffer	Eng. Can.:	63	24	9	4
punishments.[a,b,c]					
If parents disciplined their	US:	53	27	13	7
children more firmly, there	Québ:	20	29	29	22
would be less crime.[a,b,c]	Eng. Can.:	40	33	18	9

Notes: a = Québecois and U.S. significantly different at p < .01
   b = English and U.S. significantly different at p < .01
   c = Québécois and English significantly different at p < .01
   All global Chi-square tests significant at p < .01

corporations have far too much power,'' but these figures are not substantively different from the U.S. proportion of 81 per cent.[4] One possible difference among the groups is the extent to which respondents indicate strong as opposed to moderate agreement: Americans are slightly more likely to ''agree strongly'' than English Canadians or Québécois. The third item in this set of questions asks whether poverty arises because of private ownership and profits. In this case, we once again find very little difference between English Canadians and Americans: 49 per cent of English Canadians and 47 per cent of Americans agree with this idea. Québécois respondents, however, show a higher level of agreement: 56 per cent of these individuals agree that poverty is attributable to private ownership and profits.

The second set of questions concerns attitudes toward inequality and social services spending. First, there is no substantive difference between the proportion of Americans and the proportion of English Canadians or Québécois agreeing with the view that many people receive less income than they deserve. For Americans, 70 per cent either agree or agree strongly with this statement, while for English Canadians and Québécois the proportions are 68 and 71 per cent, respectively. There is, however, a greater tendency for Americans to place themselves in the ''agree strongly'' as opposed to the ''agree'' response category. On the question of social services spending, there are significant differences among the three groups, with Americans indicating the most support for increases in spending, and Québécois respondents indicating the least support for such increases. This finding is exactly the opposite of that which would be predicted from Lipset's most recent formulations.

The next set of items relates to attitudes about labour unions. In Quebec, where hiring strikebreakers is illegal, it is perhaps not surprising to find that respondents are the most supportive of preventing management from employing strikebreakers. Among Québécois, 69 per cent agree or agree strongly with this prohibition, as opposed to 55 per cent of English Canadians and 48 per cent of Americans. On the other hand, English Canadians and Americans are more likely than Québécois respondents to condone the use of violence on the part of strikers to ''prevent strikebreakers from entering the place of work.'' Finally, Americans are somewhat more likely to prefer a strike outcome in which workers win most or some of their demands. Overall, evidence for Lipset's contention that Canadians are more supportive of labour cannot be found in these data.

On questions of gender equality, Americans are generally less supportive than the other two groups. Americans are significantly more likely to feel ''it is better for the family if the husband is the principal breadwinner'' and the wife stays home. There are no differences in the total proportions of individuals agreeing with the idea of equal sharing of housework, but Americans are slightly more likely to agree strongly, as opposed to giving merely an ''agree'' response, while Québécois respondents are slightly less likely to agree strongly. Very few respondents in any of the three groups disagreed with this item, as can be seen in the table. When asked if they agreed with the statement, ''There are not enough women in responsible positions in government and business,'' roughly the same percentage (77%) of individuals in each of the three groups responded affirmatively. Americans, however, were slightly more likely to give an extreme response (either agree strongly or disagree strongly) than Québécois or English Canadians.

On the issue of whether ''there should be

as many women as men in important positions", Americans are the least likely to agree or agree strongly (58%), Québécois are the most likely to do so (77%), and English Canadians fall roughly half-way between the other two groups (67%). This finding, along with the finding dealing with traditional roles (husband as breadwinner), is not consistent with Lipset's claim that Americans favour equality of opportunity more than English Canadians. However, the finding that Québécois respondents give more support to

gender equality than either Americans or English Canadians fits with his recent analysis of Quebec society.

The final set of items in Table 7.1 deals with issues of social control. Lipset's thesis suggests that Québécois will be less supportive of the state's use of tougher sentences for criminals and the family's use of greater discipline with children, and this notion is supported by the findings shown in Table 7.1. However, a consistent pattern of findings with respect to differences between

---

Table 7.2 Trust in government

No say:

Canada: "People like me don't have any say about what the government in Ottawa does."

	Agree strongly %	Agree somewhat %	Neither agree nor disagree %	Disagree somewhat %	Disagree strongly %
Québecois:	25	37	5	23	10
English Can.:	29	33	4	25	9

U.S.: "People like me don't have any say about what the government does."

Agree: 31%
Disagree: 67%
Don't know, no opinion: 2%

Don't care:

Canada: "I don't think the Federal Government cares much about what people like me think."

	Agree strongly %	Agree somewhat %	Neither agree nor disagree %	Disagree somewhat %	Disagree strongly %
Québecois:	35	32	4	17	12
English Can.:	34	28	2	21	15

U.S.: "I don't think public officials care much what people like me think."

Agree: 42%
Disagree: 56%
Don't know, no opinion: 2%

Americans and English Canadians cannot be found. Compared with Americans, English Canadians support stiffer punishments for criminals, but are less likely to call for more family discipline.

In total, then, the findings presented in Table 7.1 provide no consistent support for Lipset's thesis, and often are contrary to expectations based on his work. One possible difference of note is that Canadians, especially English Canadians, are less inclined towards "extreme" responses, but there is only weak evidence of this tendency.

Table 7.2 shows a final set of comparisons that address the problem of trust in government. Lipset's thesis implies that Canadians should be more inclined to accept government authority than Americans, and that Québécois will be even more likely to take this view, given their "left-liberal" belief system. In fact, however, it is Americans who have the greatest trust in government. The wording of the questions in the two surveys was virtually identical, although the U.S. National Election Study provided respondents with only two basic response options ("agree" or "disagree"), while strong agreement and disagreement were also possible responses in the Canadian study. Pooling the agree and disagree responses, we see that the differences between the two countries are quite substantial: 62 per cent of English Canadians, 62 per cent of Québécois, but only 31 per cent of Americans agree with the statement that "people like me don't have any say."[5] Likewise, 67 per cent of Québécois, 62 per cent of English Canadians, but only 42 per cent of Americans agree with the statement that public officials "don't care much what people like me think." These results are the opposite of what Lipset's thesis suggests.[6]

Discussion and Conclusions

Our purpose in this analysis has been to reassess Lipset's thesis on the values of Canadians and Americans. Both our review of his argument and our own findings cast considerable doubt on most of Lipset's claims about Canadian and American differences. With regard to English Canadian and American comparisons, in particular, we have found that the differences are largely insignificant or else work in the opposite direction to that suggested by Lipset's thesis. It is only in the case of the Québécois that Lipset's views receive much support. As his recent works argue, the Québécois are generally the most liberal on such issues as supporting organized labour, favouring gender equality, and questioning the need for more strict controls regarding crime and family life. The one difficulty in this case is that Lipset does not indicate how or why his thesis on value differences should lead to this prediction of greater liberalism among the Québécois. Rather, he simply asserts that "Quebec, once the most conservative part of Canada, has become the most liberal on social issues" (Lipset, 1985: 158).

Given the influential and longstanding nature of Lipset's thesis, the lack of support we have reported here is quite striking and may even be difficult to accept. Therefore, it is useful to end our discussion with some comments on what may account for the lack of support for Lipset's argument, as well as some speculations on directions that the analysis of Canadian and American values might take in the future.

One possible reason why we find little or no support for Lipset's argument may be that our evidence has somehow not considered the right questions. In other words, perhaps a different set of items would have yielded results more consistent with his thesis. Although this is possible, we think it unlikely because we have examined a rather wide range of issues in this analysis. Moreover, survey evidence from the 1960s and 1970s that deals with different topics from those addressed here has also revealed no clear support for his argument (Arnold and Tigert, 1974; Manzer, 1974; Grabb and Curtis, 1988).

A second possibility is that the process of attitude formation is a cyclical one and that Lipset's thesis may have received greater support during a different time. This prospect follows from the claim by some analysts that social and political climates, specifically in the United States, are subject to an "alternating process of conservatism and liberalism" (Schlesinger, 1964: 102). This could mean, for example, that our study in the 1980s happened to catch a tide of American conservatism, which would make Canadians appear relatively more liberal at this stage but not necessarily in a past or future time. Again, however, this possibility is unlikely. It assumes that Canada was not subject to the same type of liberal-conservative cycle in the 1980s, or else that Canada was moving in the opposite direction. Moreover, a similar assumption would have to be made about those earlier studies in the 1960s and 1970s that do not support Lipset. Such a series of coincidences seems highly improbable.

In our view, the reasons behind the lack of support for Lipset's thesis lie primarily with the argument itself. Apart from the inconsistencies we have already noted, another fundamental difficulty in Lipset's formulation is its undue reliance on a single historical event — the American Revolution — as the overriding cause of virtually all the subse-

quent differences that Lipset draws between the Canadian and American peoples (cf. Lipset, 1968a: 51). Of course, there is no doubt that the revolution was an important moment in American history and played a part in that country's eventual development. Even so, such subsequent occurrences as the American Civil War, the abolition of slavery, the mass immigration of European and other peoples, and the major wars of the twentieth century presumably had significant and complex influences on value patterns in the United States.

It should also be pointed out that Lipset's overall reading of the American Revolution and its significance for the United States has been seriously questioned (cf. Bell and Tepperman, 1979). Moreover, even if the revolution had the sustained impact on American society that Lipset suggests, it is by no means clear that the same could be said for its role in shaping Canadian values or institutions. Our own assessment is that the revolution's repercussions for Canada were far less serious than Lipset implies. We suggest it is expecting a great deal of one historical event, however momentous, that its influence on two different nations should both override all other influences and endure intact for more than two centuries.

To call Lipset's thesis into question, however, is not to contend that there are no differences between Canadians and Americans. In fact, our own evidence shows some significant divergences in attitudes and beliefs. It is Lipset's particular version of the differences that we believe is in doubt. For example, Lipset has pointed out that Canadians are more likely to save their money in banks and less likely to risk it in stocks than are Americans, and has seen these behaviours as a sign of greater Canadian conservatism (Lipset, 1985: 136-137). However, it seems to us that these activities could reflect something quite different, such as a tendency among Canadians toward caution or moderation. Moderation, rather than collectivism or particularism, might also be a better term for characterizing the more tolerant response to ethnic and political minorities that Lipset perceives in Canadian society. In this regard, we might note the slight tendency, which came to light during our own analysis, for Canadians to give more moderate or less extreme responses than Americans to some questions.

A similar conceptual issue can be raised concerning Lipset's treatment of the idea of individualism. For example, Lipset notes that Americans are more likely than Canadians to commit crimes and to divorce and concludes that these differences show Americans are more individualistic (Lipset, 1963b). However, to borrow a conceptual distinction from Durkheim, such behaviours could as easily demonstrate greater egoism, not individualism, in the American populace. Egoism for Durkheim entails an unbridled tendency to pursue personal desires or ends, regardless of the rights or needs of other people. According to Durkheim's view, the lower crime and divorce rates in Canada could actually demonstrate greater individualism among Canadians, since his concept of individualism always involved seeking personal goals while at the same time having regard for the laws of society and the rights of others (cf. Durkheim, [1893] 1964: 400-401).

These are just two illustrations of the need for greater conceptual precision and consistency in Lipset's attempt to characterize the value differences between our two nations. Greater attention to these and other theoretical or terminological weaknesses could help to eliminate some of the apparent contradictions in Lipset's evidence and general argument. Without some reconsideration of these and other problems, Lipset's conceptual framework will continue to be inadequate for helping us to understand fully the value differences of Canadians and Americans.

Notes

1. The data for the Class Structure and Class Consciousness Merged Multi-Nation file were originally collected by Erik Wright *et al.* Neither the original collectors nor the disseminating archive (I.C.P.S.R.) bears any responsibility for the analysis or interpretations presented here.

2. The Canadian data came from personal interviews as part of a study conducted by the Department of Sociology and Anthropology, Carleton University, and funded by the Social Sciences and Humanities Research Council of Canada (John Myles, principal investigator). The U.S. data were collected using telephone interviews.

3. Both of these surveys were administered as personal interviews, and sampled from a target population of adults of voting age in their respective countries. The data for the 1984 American National Election Study were originally collected by the Center for Political Studies of the Institute for Social Research, University of Michigan, under the overall direction of Warren Miller (Santa Traugott

directed studies in 1984). The data were made available by the Inter-University Consortium for Political and Social Research. Data from the 1984 Canadian National Election study were collected by R.D. Lambert, S.D. Brown, J.E. Curtis, B.J. Kay and J.M. Wilson, with funding from the Social Sciences and Humanities Research Council of Canada, and were made available by the study's principal investigators. In both cases, neither the original collectors of the data nor the disseminating archives bear any responsibility for the analyses or interpretations presented here.

4. The significant differences reported in Table 7.1 refer to differences among all categories, but when responses are pooled into "agree" and "disagree" categories, no significant differences exist.

5. The Canadian National Election study also contained questions referring to the *provincial* government instead of the federal government in Ottawa; these percentages, even in the case of Quebec, were almost identical: 67 per cent of Québécois, and 56 per cent of English Canadians, agreed with the "no say" statement in reference to the provincial government.

6. In analyses reported elsewhere, we find that the results shown here remain essentially unchanged when we take into account the possible confounding effects of additional variables, including income, education, age, gender, and class location (cf. Baer *et al.*, 1990).

A Closed Frontier

In Hollywood westerns, people settle cheap, open land. By taming a vast expanse of wild terrain, hostile Indians, and dangerous desperadoes, they prove that ordinary people really can create the kind of community they want to live in. This image of the American West that Hollywood has spread around the world — exciting, glamorous and even uplifting — has some basis in fact. Moreover, many American historians since Frederick Jackson Turner have argued that the frontier experience created a unique kind of society and culture in the United States. There, the coming of formal law and government often followed the building of frontier communities. Americans learned a lot about self-government by making and running such communities. The frontier was a training ground for personal and societal independence.

But whatever its merit as an explanation of American history, Turner's theory of the open frontier fails to describe Canada's settlement history. Canadian development is better described as the breaking open of a closed frontier, for Canadian settlers frequently came into an area after law and government had already arrived. Often, even representatives of the banks, churches and trading companies had arrived first.

The Canadian frontier was a closed frontier because it was a hard frontier. In S.D. Clark's words (1975):

> Canadian resources were generally hard to get at . . . What was called for in the opening up of this northern half of the continent were massive accumulations of capital, large-

scale forms of economic organization, long lines of communication and transportation, and extensive state support.

Settlers entered the frontier after bankers, engineers, railroad magnates and troops had staked a claim, so they came at the pleasure of those in control. Attempts at self-government and independence on the Canadian frontier had to challenge a powerful existing order, which would prove difficult and dangerous.

If Turner is the key theorist of the American open frontier, sociologist Rex Lucas can be considered the key theorist of the Canadian closed frontier. For Lucas, the typical Canadian frontier town is a single-industry "company town": a minetown, milltown or railtown its owner is using to exploit the raw resources nearby. (In this Canadian scenario, settlers are merely instruments of the owner.) Moreover, if American civilization is the "wild west" writ large, then Canadian civilization is a "company town" writ just as large.

People living in single-industry communities are practical, modest, deferential, willing to compromise. They could not survive in the company town any other way. But even Canadians who do not live in single-industry communities display similar traits. To learn the Canadian culture is to learn to tolerate adversity, not to oppose it. Sociologist S.M. Lipset has called this trait "conservatism" (see Section II of this book); novelist Margaret Atwood (1972) more accurately calls it a "victim mentality", and critic John Moss, (1974) the "mentality of exile". It grows out of the Canadian frontier experience.

But this line of thinking can be taken too far. Weak, uprooted and vulnerable Canadians may be; yet protest — social, political and religious — is a common, though largely forgotten, part of Canada's frontier history. In a paper included in this Section, S.D. Clark emphasizes the "importance of very similar forces in the political life" of Canada and the United States. Both nations shared the revolutionary or liberal inclinations that motivated the American War of Independence, he says. However,

> geography favoured the maintenance in this part of the continent of the controls of an Old World imperial, and later of a close federal, system(;) and . . . the effort to maintain these controls in face of the continuous threat of the expanding revolutionary community to the south led to the development of a form of government directly opposed to the principles of political organization growing out of the frontier experience of Canadian peoples.

Current political institutions and practices do not prove that earlier Canadians and Americans thought about democracy differently. It is simply that Canadians were more easily controlled than Americans, because of their harder frontier. Moreover, after the American Revolution, agents of the imperial government and newly arrived Loyalists controlled protest and reform in British North America even more strictly.

Thus, Clark and Lucas directly disagree about the frontier experience in Canada. Lucas believes that a harsh environment, foreign capital, and powerful vested interests have created a culture of accommodation and subservience in Canada. The closed frontier has closed up Canadian spirits. Clark denies this, claiming that differences between Canada and the United States arise out of differences in the opportunity to express progressive ideas, not out of a different preference for old ways.

This debate is like the one we examined briefly in the introduction to *Two Solitudes* (Section I): the debate over whether Francophones and Anglophones are culturally different in ways that will survive modernization, or merely different in ways that greater Francophone opportunity (due to urbanization and industrialization) will change.

Equally, one might ask whether Canadian-American differences are strong enough to survive urbanization, industrialization and, finally, free trade. Is Canada's closed frontier tradition a permanent part of our cultural identity or a way of thinking and acting that could easily disappear if Canadians freed themselves from economic dependency? An excerpt in this Section by Robert Brym helps us start to answer that question. Brym compares several regional (or what Clark would call "frontier") protest movements, to find the conditions under which they are strong or weak, left-wing or right-wing in politics. He concludes that certain conditions promote what he calls solidarity and proletarianization.

When both solidarity and proletarianization are lacking, no populist (or grass-roots) political movement will emerge. But when solidarity among farmers is great, a political movement will emerge. Its political outlook will be shaped by the extent of linkages with the local working class. For this reason, left-wing populism among Canadian farmers emerged in Saskatchewan — in the form of the Co-operative Commonwealth Federation (C.C.F) party — because links with the working class were strong and links with urban small business owners were weak. Right-wing populism, in the form of the Social Credit party, emerged in Alberta because the opposite conditions existed there.

Both Clark and Brym would agree that the Canadian culture, or state of mind, poses no obstacle to radical political protest. Political protest has always been possible in Canada and it has occurred in Canada. A better question, then, is why has protest occurred where and when it has, and why has it occurred less often than in some other societies. In answering this question, Professors Brym and Clark would part company. Clark would point to the closed, hard frontier as setting a limit on political mobilization and protest. But this limitation is the same for Alberta and Saskatchewan. The hard frontier theory does not help us to understand how political protest was possible in both provinces and took a different direction in each. Brym would answer that we cannot understand protest of any kind without knowing about the class linkages that underlie it.

In closing, then, the hard frontier image is important and attractive but, ultimately, incomplete. The notion that Canada's frontier is closed because it is hard marks a line of thinking that carries from Harold Innis (whose work is excerpted in the next Section), through Clark, to Rex Lucas. Lucas, in turn, takes the position, sometimes supported by Clark and always supported by Lipset (see the preceding Section), that differences in the frontier experience produce cultural differences between Canada and the United States.

Professor Clark sometimes implies that Canadians and Americans on the frontier are much more similar than we usually admit. Further, Professor Brym would argue that differences in their culture and history result from differences in class formation and conflict, not culture or environment *per se*. In Brym's eyes, ordinary Canadians are as active and successful in determining their own lives as Hollywood's ordinary Americans. By contrast, Clark and Lucas's Canadians look like losers; the winners are the powerful, vested interests and the hard frontier.

Brym's image of Canada is much more flattering to Canadians. It does not argue that the Canadian frontier is soft or open; but it does argue that frontier conditions are not the main factors influencing Canadian history. On this score, Brym would direct our attention to the class matters we discuss in Section VIII below.

Yet sectarian radical movements and third parties of the kind Brym discusses — Social Credit, CCF/NDP, Parti Québecois, and so on — have had only regional (even provincial) success. The Social Credit Party that exists today is very different from its original formulation, and indistinct from a farmer's version of Progressive Conservatism. The Parti Québecois has almost departed from Quebec's political scene, after a mere decade of dramatic importance. The NDP soldiers on with occasional provincial successes but no real chance of forming a federal government.

Perhaps the next stage of research is to ask, what are the differences between Canada and, say, England or Sweden or France, which have all supported exceptionally strong socialist (or labour) parties? Would answering that question force us to talk about Canada's closed, hard frontier and Canadians' historic dependence on the central government for peace, order, and enormous subsidies? We have certainly not heard the last word on this debate.

8

The Frontier and Social Organization*

S.D. Clark

Implicit in much of the writing on Canadian political history has been the assumption that an entirely different set of forces have shaped the development of democratic institutions in this country than in the United States. Whether because Canada learnt from the political experience of 19th rather than 18th century Britain, or because the tradition of the country has been more British, Canadians have been thought less inclined than their neighbours across the border to experiment with radical political solutions to their problems. Rather, they have sought through an orderly process to adapt their political institutions to changing circumstances. Thus the distinctive Canadian contribution to the development of democratic political organization has been considered the working out of the principles of responsible government within the framework of a system of imperial,

and later federal, control. The more radical principle of checks and balances, involving the separation of the executive and legislative functions of government, written into the Constitution of the United States, has been avoided as foreign to the spirit of Canadian political life.

That Canada has a political tradition more conservative than the United States would seem evident. This country remained within the British Empire, ultimately to secure separation by peaceful means; the people of the United States fought for and won their independence on the field of battle. The contrast today between the political institutions, and the informal processes of government, of the two countries reflects the different background of political development.

Concern to demonstrate the distinctiveness of Canada's political institutions, however, has led to a failure to recognize fully the importance of very similar forces in the political life of the two countries. The assumption that the Constitution of the United States grew out of the political experience of 18th century Europe, while the constitution

*Excerpted from "The Frontier and Democratic Theory," *Transactions of the Royal Society of Canada*, vol. XXXVIII, series III, June, 1954, Section Two. Reprinted by permission.

of Canada (that is, the unwritten part determining the form of parliamentary government) grew out of the political experience of 19th century Europe, overlooks as Turner emphasized a half-century ago the extent to which the principles of American government reflect very directly the political experience of American frontier peoples. What this paper seeks to demonstrate is that Canada shared in the revolutionary tradition of this continent which found its fullest expression in the American War of Independence and the principle of checks and balances written into the American Constitution, that, however, geography favoured the maintenance in this part of the continent of the controls of an Old World imperial, and later of a close federal, system, and that the effort to maintain these controls in face of the continuous threat of the expanding revolutionary community to the south led to the development of a form of government directly opposed to the principles of political organization growing out of the frontier experience of Canadian peoples. Thus what has been thought of in Canada as an orderly process of adapting political institutions to changing circumstances has actually represented an effort to hold in check the kind of democratic forces which were growing up from within the Canadian community. Responsible government developed in reaction rather than in response to the true democratic spirit of the Canadian people.

For the three centuries of its history the North American Continent has been a breeding ground of economic, political, social, and religious experiments of various sorts. Such was particularly the case during the latter half of the 18th and the first half of the 19th centuries. These 100 years witnessed not only the Revolutionary War of Independence but most of the great utopian experiments in economic, political, and religious reform. It was not an accident that it was on the North American Continent that the ideas of the English utopian, Robert Owen, and the French utopian, Charles Fourier, were tried out or that on the Euro-Asiatic Continent were tried out almost a century later the ideas of the German utopian, Karl Marx. Great land masses present problems of control. The ineptness of political administration where distances are great breeds political discontent and offers opportunities for the growth of revolutionary movements. On the North American Continent political authority was established only in face of almost continuous resistance on the part of the population in outlying areas. The American people fought not one but many wars of independence. Thrown onto their own resources, the populations of isolated areas or of areas of new economic growth organized their own systems of control and, when central authority sought to establish itself, movements of revolt quickly developed. The committee of safety, the territorial convention, the bill of rights, a locally issued currency, and encouragement of smuggling and tax evasion afforded means of politically organizing the frontier and of securing its autonomy in relation to outside government bodies.

It was this insistence upon local autonomy, this separatist spirit, which was the dominant characteristic of those revolutionary or reform movements which grew up in the interior parts of the continent. Such movements sought to build the new society not by making over the old, but by separating from it. The reason, of course, lay in the economic and political weakness of the frontier community. The 13 small, scattered, English colonies of 1775 could not hope to reform the British Empire but they could escape its exactions by separating from it.

There was something of this intense localism, an almost sectarian exclusiveness, in all American reform movements of the frontier. The dominant urge of frontier populations was to be left alone, to escape the exactions and restrictions of outside political authority. This was not because the frontier was poor but because it was rich. As politically virgin territory, it offered almost unlimited opportunities for office seekers from the outside; its virgin natural resources invited economic exploitation. It was in the struggle for the control of these two things of value on the frontier — office and land — that there developed much of the resistance to central government. Reform on the frontier was directed against such social evils of the outside world as political patronage, the payment of excessive salaries to governmental officials, economic monopoly, a stringent money supply, exorbitant interest charges, and burdensome taxation. Remedy for the ills of the frontier was sought in the effort to develop its own means of exploiting its economic and political resources.

It was no easy task for the central authorities to hold in check these separatist movements, to put down what amounted in effect to revolts against the state. Such movements had enormous advantages in geography and in the fanatical zeal of their leaders and followers growing out of strong feelings of righteousness. Where few qualifications for office were insisted on, an unlimited supply of people to fill positions of leadership and trust was available. Frontier conditions made for great mobility of agitators, self-appointed prophets, and organizers. On the other hand, the difficulties of policing, the ineptness of officials unfamiliar with local conditions, and the limitation in the supply of trained personnel handicapped severely governments seeking to impose their authority from the outside. When force was resorted to, a rebelling population, by delaying tactics, by hit-and-run raids, and by scattering when faced with a force more formidable than its own, could make the cost of defeating it so great as to discourage any determined effort directed to such an end.

Yet it would not be correct to say simply that the state was powerless to deal with frontier movements of revolt in America. The fact was that in that part of the continent which became the United States the authority of the central government was seldom employed with any resoluteness of purpose in putting down such movements. The American political society tended to be highly tolerant of the non-conforming elements of its population. The very weakness of the military forces of the country until recent years has been a reflection of such tolerance.

The constituted political authorities in the American society had no reason to be greatly concerned about movements of political separatism except when, as in 1776, they threatened to carry the population out of the British Empire or, as in 1860, they threatened the dismemberment of the Union. Rather, until recent years at any rate, such movements have constituted an important means of extending and strengthening American society. The major task of that society has been the conquering and occupation of a continent. In undertaking that task, it faced no organized political community on the continent as powerful as itself. There were, however, two serious claims to the continent which had to be destroyed if the Manifest Destiny of American peoples was to be realized.

The first, of course, was that of the North American Indian. Experience had demonstrated the costliness of trying to subdue the Indian by open warfare and the use of regular armies. The Indian enjoyed the advantages of all frontier people: great mobility, thorough knowledge of the terrain, and familiarity with the kind of weapons and tactics most suitable for frontier warfare. In challenging the claim of the Indian to the continent, accordingly, reliance was placed upon the resourcefulness (and unscrupulousness) of the white settlers. Treaties with the Indians solemnly entered into by the government were disregarded by these land-hungry settlers, and resistance on the part of the red man was used as an excuse for wars of extermination. The advance of American white society on the continent took place by means of this continuous pushing back and destruction of the native by people who took the law into their own hands. The same result would have been secured in the end, and at much less cost in human life, had the central government maintained a greater degree of order on the frontier, but only by delaying the advance of the white man's civilization. By tolerating the frontier settler's exercise of a large measure of independence, by granting in effect a large degree of autonomy to frontier communities, the American society was able that much more speedily to complete the occupation of the continent.

The second important claim to the North American Continent was that of the overseas empires. In the effort to destroy this claim, the interests of the British governing authorities before 1760, as of the central governing authorities of the united colonies or united states after 1776, were closely identified with the interests of the American frontier population. With no standing army on the continent sufficiently powerful to challenge the French Empire in America before 1760, and no navy sufficiently powerful to challenge the British Empire in America after 1776, the claims of the American political society to the continent were most successfully championed by the advancing frontiersmen fighting on ground on which the advantages were on their side and often through acts of warfare which were formally repudiated by the responsible governing authorities. Frontier armies or border raiding parties played an important part in the French-English wars, the War of Independence, and the War of 1812-14, while the two later invasions of Canadian territory, by the Patriots in 1838 and by the Fenians in the 1860's, were carried out entirely by armed forces of this sort. Spanish and French claims to the southern part of the continent were attacked by military forces of a similar character.

The invasion of territory outside the formal jurisdiction of the American political society was not simply an act of aggression of a land-hungry people. Frontier populations were land-hungry, but land hunger became closely identified with an interest in political reform. To wrest territory away from the control of France, Britain, or Spain was to "liberate" not only the territory but the inhabitants from the control of an Old World empire system. Here was to be found the significance of the revolutionary movement in the strengthening of the continental claims of the American political society. Wars with neighbouring communities assumed something of the character of wars of independence. In terms of the local scene, for instance, there was little essential difference between the border fighting in the Seven Years' War, the Revolutionary War, the War of 1812-14, and that which took place after the Canadian rebellions of 1837. In all these cases, the drive to liberate Canada came largely from what was then the American West, and in all of them, important support was obtained from within the Canadian community. Frontier populations on both sides of the border faced much the same problems and readily joined forces in protesting against the exactions and restrictions of outside political authorities. Within the continental situation, such movements of protest meant inevitably the weakening of the position of the overseas empires and the consequent strengthening of the position of the American political society.

Until at least the present century, thus, American expansionism and American reformism were closely linked to one another. The doctrine of Manifest Destiny found important support in the doctrine of revolutionary republicanism; or, to look at the matter from the other side, the isolationism of the American Republic was born out of the isolationism of the frontier and was a natural response to a situation where the nation felt no real threat to its position within the American continental system and craved no allies. What this meant was a form of government based upon the principle of a separation of powers and a limitation of centralized authority. Though in the writing of the Constitution of the American Republic powerful conservative interests, identified with sound finance and the promotion of overseas trade, did succeed in securing certain safeguards against the development of a system of political irresponsibility, the separatist-isolationist spirit of the American political community was too strong to be effectively checked by particular constitutional expedients such as the method of the election of the president or federal senators. American political theorists may have read Blackstone and Montesquieu, but the form of government they devised was one which reflected very directly the frontier political experience of American peoples.

In Canada there was not lacking among the people a frontier political experience similar to that of American peoples. Developing as the American frontier did through the spread of settlement into the interior of the continent, the Canadian frontier offered an almost equally fertile field for the growth of movements of a reform or revolutionary character. The insurrection of the *coureurs de bois* and the generally uncooperative attitude of the population during the period of the old régime, widespread disaffection in Nova Scotia and Quebec during the American Revolutionary War and in Upper Canada during the War of 1812-14, the rebellions of 1837, the Irish riots and the Clear Grit movement of the 1850's, the Red River and Northwest rebellions of 1870 and 1885, the development of militant miners' associations in the Klondike following the gold rush, the Winnipeg general strike in 1919, and the rise of the western agrarian political movement in the 1920's and of the Social Credit movement in the 1930's afford examples of efforts upon the part of Canadian people to create for themselves a better world in which to live. As across the border, these movements were essentially separatist and anti-authoritarian in character.

But whereas in the United States the development of separatist political movements meant freeing the expansive energies of the frontier and thus strengthening the political society as a whole, in Canada it meant exposing the frontier to forces of American expansion and threatening thereby the separate political existence of the Canadian community. The Canadian frontier lay alongside the line of advance of the American, and, while it could be reached only with great difficulty by armed forces moving out from the established centres of government, it could be swiftly invaded from across the border or from it Canadian rebellious forces could as readily withdraw to American territory. John

Allan, William Lyon Mackenzie, Joseph Papineau, and Louis Riel found refuge in the United States when rebellions they had led in Canada failed, and new rebellious uprisings were plotted on the other side of the line with the aid of American sympathizers. What this meant, therefore, was that any assertion of greater independence on the part of the Canadian frontier society drew it closer to the American and paved the way for its ultimate absorption.

Had the advantages of geography been all on one side, of course, no effort to maintain in the northern part of the continent a politically separate community would have been successful. But though American expansionism threatened Canadian lines of communication with the interior, no American liberation movement was sufficiently powerful to completely destroy in this part of the continent the claims of a rival political power. Canada maintained her separate political existence but only by resisting any movement on the part of her population which had the effect of weakening the controls of central political authority. The claims to the interior of the continent were staked not by advancing frontiersmen, acting on their own, but by advancing armies and police forces, large corporate economic enterprises and ecclesiastical organizations, supported by the state. The Canadian political temper, as a result, has run sharply counter to the American. Those creeds of American political life — individual rights, local autonomy, and limitation of executive power — which have contributed so much to the political strength of the American community have found less strong support within the Canadian political system. Canada sought political strength through alliance with the North American Indian and the support of ties which bound her people to the Old World and to a highly centralized federal system. In turn this meant a political system which emphasized the responsibility of governing authorities and tended to concentrate power in the hands of the executive. In this respect, it is easy to exaggerate the change which came with the establishment of responsible government in Canada. The two-party, cabinet system of government grew out of those conditions of rule in Canada which required the maintenance of a highly centralized political community and, as such, it stood sharply opposed to the separatist principles of political organization growing out of the frontier experience of the Canadian people. In the 1830's the Canadian frontier community found its true champions in Joseph Papineau and William Lyon Mackenzie. Responsible government came not as the climax but the anticlimax to the long struggle in Canada to secure the reform of colonial institutions. It represented an accommodative movement in the political organization of the Canadian community.

Enough perhaps has been said to indicate the nature of some of the forces which have determined the character of development of the political institutions of this country. It is not the purpose of this paper to examine in any detail recent political developments which have taken place in Canada or the United States. The fact, however, that the United States today appears to be more intolerant of radical political movements than Canada or her other immediate neighbour, Mexico, may seem strange in the light of what has been said above.

If this is so, the reason in part would seem to lie in the changed position of the United States in world affairs. To say this, however, is to risk exaggerating the difference between the political temper of the United States of today and of the United States of the past. The American people are perhaps no more intolerant of nonconformity within their midst than they ever were. What they are intolerant of, as they have always been, is any interference in their affairs from the outside. The attack of Joseph McCarthy upon Communist influences in the government of the United States was a clear and genuine expression of the American frontier, isolationist spirit. It was no accident that McCarthy came from the Middle West and represented an ethnic-religious minority population in the United States. His attack was directed not against poor, downtrodden people crying for a voice in the affairs of the state but against powerful political leaders, of unquestioned social respectability, largely of Anglo-Saxon background. Critics outside the country might well pause to consider not the intolerance which found expression in McCarthyism but the tolerance which made it possible for McCarthyism to develop. In Canada it would be hard to conceive of a state of political freedom great enough to permit the kind of attacks upon responsible leaders of the government which have been carried out in the United States. More careful examination of the American community in general, and perhaps of the academic community in particular, would probably reveal that, in spite of the witch hunts in that country, the people of the United States enjoy in fact a much greater degree of freedom than do the people of Canada. We could scarcely have a witch hunt when we have no witches!

Such considerations suggest the need for caution in the use of such terms as radical and reactionary. A student of Social Credit in Alberta is quickly made aware of the fact that here was a movement which from one point of view could be thought of as radical, from another point of view as reactionary. The same would seem to have been true of the McCarthy movement in the United States. It is not sufficient to say that these were movements which went "bad," because of their unfortunate leadership or for some other reason peculiar to themselves. What appears evident is that all those movements which grew out of the American — or Canadian — frontier were of this character, radical in the sense that they involved a break from established political practice, reactionary in the sense that their efforts were directed towards the creation of a more simple, primitive type of political world.

The farm movements of the western United States or of western Canada, for instance, sought the reform of political institutions not in a strengthening by more subtle means of the responsibility of the governors to the governed but by the development of simple, direct means of popular control over government. Thus the convention, referendum and recall, election of public officials, rotation of offices, and group representation were intended to weaken the executive branch of government and thereby strengthen the voice of the people in the affairs of the state. As instruments of political separatism, such forms of popular government were highly effective. They afforded a means of mobilizing the resistance of a population, often geographically remote and isolated, to a political authority which failed to give adequate expression to its interests.

We have been too much inclined perhaps to exaggerate the political intelligence of frontier populations. It comes hard to one brought up in Alberta to suggest that the people of that province who thought of themselves as in the vanguard of reform actually had only a limited appreciation of the complexities of modern government and no great understanding of the conditions necessary for the preservation of individual rights and a sense of community responsibility. In a cultural sense, the frontier was not a rich and progressive but a poor and retarded society. Its effort to break from the old political and social system of which it had been a part and to create a new system of its liking involved the disowning of a heritage which it had in large measure lost and the building anew of a political and social life with tools fashioned out of its rough and limited experience.

This fact becomes evident when it is recognized that the political reform movement was only one of many forms of frontier protest. Religious sectarianism, vigilantism, medical quackery, mob rioting, tax evasion, smuggling, and political apathy were other means of resistance by a frontier population to the interferences of an outside society in its affairs. What was apparent in all the various kinds of movements which came out of the frontier was an underlying attitude of irresponsibility with respect to the affairs of the larger community. The frontiersman was a difficult person to govern in that he was not prepared to accept the normal obligations of a member of society.

If what is said here is true, one is forced to the conclusion that the development in Canada of parliamentary institutions of government within the framework of the British imperial, and later the Canadian federal, system represented a more enlightened approach to the problem of government in the modern world than did the development of those forms of political organization which found expression in the constitution of the United States. Canada can assume a more responsible and thus more effective role in world affairs than can the United States not because its government is less responsive to the people but because its government's freedom of action is not continuously hampered by the behaviour of irresponsible parties and groups. In this sense, McCarthyism did represent a reactionary force in American political life.

In another sense, however, McCarthyism might be thought to represent a progressive force. By bringing about a break from established practice and forms of organization, the frontier separatist movement had the effect of weakening the hold of tradition upon men's thoughts and actions and thus in making possible a more rational approach to society's problems.

9

The One-industry Community*

Rex Lucas

The One-industry Community in Canada

The community of single industry is significant to Canadian society for several reasons. In the first place a considerable proportion of the population lives in this type of community, and half lives in communities of 30 000 or less. Second, because of the nature of Canadian geography and the distribution of natural resources, there is little chance that the total number of such communities will decrease. At least one writer has suggested that the number of single-industry communities will increase (Robinson, 1962). The third reason is that many Canadians have been brought up in this type of community. Perhaps the majority of the citizens of the larger, more diverse communities of the nation have had their attitudes, expectations, and behavioural patterns moulded within

the peculiar social structure of the single-industry community. Finally, this peculiar structure is common to both French and English Canada.

Isolation

The one-industry community exists to house the employees who exploit the area's natural resources; the location of the community, within a few miles, is predetermined by the location of the resource, the electric power necessary for the process, or the technical requirements imposed by the transportation system that moves the products. For this reason the communities are, almost without exception, found in the sparsely settled parts of the country. Indeed, if we trace them by province we find many communities of single industry in the rugged interior of Newfoundland, none in the farm-based communities of Prince Edward Island, a few in the more rugged parts of Nova Scotia, and far more in New Brunswick. There are a few south of the Saint Lawrence River and only one or two in Southern Ontario — that area lying south of

*Excerpted from Rex Lucas, *Minetown, Milltown, Railtown*, Toronto: ©University of Toronto Press 1971. Reprinted by permission of University of Toronto Press.

North Bay and Sudbury. The majority of these communities lie in northern Ontario and northern Quebec — the area characterized by the production of pulp and paper, gold, copper, nickel, and where the transcontinental railways pass through the preCambrian shield wilderness. Moving west, the communities of single industry hug the northern boundaries of the prairie provinces; the few to the south are located above the oil deposits and coal seams. A high proportion of the population centres of the Yukon and the Northwest Territories are communities of single industry and the remainder are found in the rugged terrain far from the fertile valleys of British Columbia.[1]

The peculiar location and isolation of these communities almost guarantees that they remain communities of single industry. The economic and technical factors that were instrumental in locating and developing communities of single industry are the same factors which rule out additional industry, diversification of the economic base, and expansion of population. In areas where the communities are close to a larger population and market they become diversified, expand, and so are no longer communities of single industry. One notable exception is the mining community where several competing companies work the same ore body; another is the community with an abundance of cheap electrical power fortuitously located where two basic resources such as minerals and forests can be exploited.

Communities of single enterprise are and remain isolated. Physical and geographical isolation, however, is a relative quality. At one end of the continuum there is the isolation of the community whose only contact with the outside is through infrequent air service; at the other end, is the community surrounded by 50 miles of scrub forests with

the closest community 60 miles away by road. People living in a Northern Ontario railway community on the main line of one of the transcontinental railways with dozens of passenger and freight trains daily pausing for servicing and change of crew, may feel, and in some senses are, isolated, and the same thing applies to individuals living in the community three hours' drive by first-class highway from a major city.

It is clear that these people are not talking about social isolation as it is usually defined in the social sciences. They are not talking about "failure of the individual through inability preference or whatever to establish or maintain communications with those about him (Lapiere, 1954: 330)." This isolation is not related to the interpersonal relationships *within* the community, but rather to the relationship between citizens of the community and others in outside communities. The preoccupation with this quality of life persists despite mass communication. McLuhan's global village is not meaningful to them in terms of interpersonal relationships or potential relationships with others. The isolation of the single-industry community seems to refer to the potential relationships of the individuals with other groups and communities outside their own. The phenomenon is probably quite close to the vicinal isolation, the physical separation which isolates and limits accessibility, as discussed by Becker; "nature presents man with his geographical location; culture provides his vicinal position (Becker, 1957: 164-5)."

That these definitions of isolation are subtle is supported by the preliminary findings reported by Matthiasson. Residents of an isolated community of single industry ranked services and facilities that should be available in a typical resource community; the first four were: entertainment and recreation, income in relation to cost of living, housing and accommodation, and good access to cities in the south. The services in their own community which needed improvement were, in order of frequency of choice, access to cities in the south, communications, medical facilities, and entertainment and recreation. Yet, when given a check list of terms descriptive of northern living, "isolated" was ranked fourth, after "friendly," "expensive," and "challenging" ("gossipy" was fifth). The responses could be interpreted in a number of ways, and the author carefully points out that the findings are still preliminary and incomplete (Matthiasson, 1970; Center for Settlement Studies, 1968).

In extreme isolation there seem to be geographical and measurable restrictions on the interrelationships possible with people of other communities. On the other hand, although there are few restrictions of this type imposed on an urban dweller, he seldom takes the opportunity of making contact with a neighbouring city or village. This suggests that isolation is a feeling, which, while based upon physical fact, has little relation to any absolute standard of geographical location.

The feeling of isolation discussed by respondents in communities of single industry is probably more closely related to their attitudes and opinions on the limitation of alternatives than it is to geography. In this sense, people feel isolated in Vancouver, Toronto, San Francisco, Boston, Halifax, New York, or London. This raises the question, isolated from what? The answer seems to be that the individual feels removed from the possibility of taking part in some desired activity. The feelings of isolation expressed by some respondents, although perhaps extreme in communities of single industry, are also found in diversified urban areas. On the other hand, there are people in both urban areas and communities of single industry who do not yearn for what is not there. This suggests that isolation, rather than being unique to the community of single industry is shared to some degree by many people in many types of communities, both urban and rural.

Single Industry

We now turn our attention to a second variable, that of single industry. If we leave the population and the degree of isolation constant what happens if we add a second industry to our community? If the second industry has the same resource base, such as two mining companies working on one ore body, there are a series of implications. To begin with, there are two sets of management personnel moving in and out of the community. Inevitably one of the two industries is defined as a better industry to work for and stratification is affected by the greater prestige attached to the Smith Company than the Jones Company. At the same time, however, because there are two work structures and two bases for stratification, there is a more complex set of formal and informal patterns of association. Further, the level of observability is reduced considerably; despite the fact that the size of the community has remained constant there are many activities in the Smith Company which would not necessarily come to the attention of all who work in the Jones Company.

The interaction between people and the role of the two corporations in the community depends largely on the early history of responsibility undertaken by the corporation in the development of the community — the degree of support for local organizations, the support and subsidization of recreation facilities and so on. Corporate competitiveness is introduced by the second industry. The two corporations are vulnerable to polite blackmail by the citizens, their associations, and organizations; almost inevitably the corporations are forced to vie for the goodwill of employees and their community associations. This at least opens the possibility for citizens to feel that their social and political action could affect their lot in life. The addition of a second industry then, provides a potential flexibility in social life.

All other variables held constant, the addition of a second industry does not affect the institutional and professional services available in the community. It does not increase the number of doctors and dentists or teachers or alternative streams in the school system; it does not affect the nature of the relationships with professional people; it does not affect the range of occupational choices open to the youth; it does not affect forced migration or the range of available marriage partners.

If, instead of two industries sharing the same resource base, an industry with a different base is introduced, more widespread ramifications are expected. If, for instance, a pulp and paper mill and a mine share the same community, the social differences are highly intensified. The two resource bases accentuate the differences in reputation of the two firms; the differences in the type of work have important ramifications for the prestige structure within the community. Because the two firms are unalike, different types of expectations are attached to their activities as well as an intensification of their competition. There is a wider variety of local jobs but the migration level from the community remains much the same. Further, the institutional and professional aspects of community life remain much the same regardless of the second industry.

Fishing, Farming and Commercial Communities

Social patterns and attitudes in a small industrial community are, however, quite different from those in a community built upon fishing and farming (and perhaps trapping), or in a centre based upon commercial and distribution services. The fishermen or farmers share occupations characterized by an indeterminacy and insecurity often classified as "acts of God." The return for work is ruled by changes in the weather, the season, and other variables not controlled by man. Men often cope with these unknowns by being fatalistic; if this is not a good year, next year may be, but in any event, there is nothing to be done about it. Although all are subject to these uncontrollable events, their social consequences are differently experienced because there are variations in the amount of capital that each man brings to his occupation — land acreage, fishing boats, stock in the store, and so on. His success depends upon the amount of work he does, the hours worked, and the scheduling of these hours, as well as the intuitive or "art" quality of his work — the right time to plant or harvest; where at this tide, in this season, with this moon, the fish are found; what loss leader brings customers to the store. The stratification of fishing, farming and commercial communities, then, depends upon a range of complex variables that are not incorporated in any industrial hierarchy. No individual earns a fixed income; his income is not guaranteed by skills, educational background, learning or age.

At the same time, the individual's position in the stratification structure is obscure because the symbols are far more varied and subtle than would appear from his pay cheque. The individual in a single-industrial hierarchy can spend his money in various ways, but everyone knows the amount he is paid; this knowledge, along with his occupation category, symbolizes his position in a stratification hierarchy. In a fishing, farming, or commercial community the returns are not clearly and definitely known in a monetary sense and the symbols of social status are indeterminate — in order to evaluate the status of a farmer, no one is sure whether to look at the barn, the house, the herd, the number of vacations, the number of paid employees, the clothes, the machinery, the type of car, or the amount of money borrowed. The symbols of position, then, can be highly specialized or very diverse; in this situation curiosity about the innuendo or the real story behind a particular set of symbols becomes tremendously important; it is under these conditions that a high level of speculation and gossip is devoted to the evaluation of the position of the individual.

In contrast with the industrial town, this type of community is made up of many independent but interrelated capitalists. Each man starts with some capital investment, and together with his talents, judgment, and labour, he carries out his work operating under a general level of luck. Although he can blame fate and impersonal forces, he has no industry to blame. He has no industry to use; he knows that recreational facilities, the school, his church and other institutional facilities are a product of his own participation and that he cannot call upon any local industry to assist him to build and maintain them. Similarly his position in the hierarchy and his relation to his fellows is not dependent upon a corporate structure. His relationship with store owners differs because the farmer, fisherman, and store-keeper are all entrepreneurs. In contrast, the institutional complement of professional services is much the same as in the community of single industry; the professional services rendered by doctors, dentists, teachers, and clergy are subject to many of the variables discussed previously. The level of role observability is much lower than in the community of single industry. This is partly because each man has his "own domain" as insulation and partly because status attributes are not achieved within the single structure. Observability is low and the level of curiosity and gossip is high.

The Community of Dominant Industry

Occasionally people refer to Oshawa, Hamilton, Sault Ste Marie, or even Ottawa as a one-industry town. This, of course, is a misnomer; they are not one-industry towns but rather communities with a dominant industry. Superficially, the community with a dominant industry has many characteristics of the one-industry town because the giant industry is seen as having an untoward effect upon the whole community. Executive decisions about how much, if anything, is to be contributed to a certain cause, changes in technology, when to lay off employees, raising employment qualifications — decisions in any area — have wide-spread implications for all citizens. The dominant industry, then, is seen as being responsible for the community and it is given a large share of the blame when things go wrong, and perhaps some credit when the community thrives.

It is clear, however, that the social stratification in a community of dominant industry is far more complex than that of a small community of single industry. Whether the dominant industry is surrounded by dependent and contributing industries or whether the other industries have independent bases, each industry tends to have different working conditions, pay scales, rates of promotion and so on. This, then, complicates the overall view of the general stratification of the individuals and families in the communities as illustrated by attempting to compare the ranking of the presidents of three companies — the large automobile manufacturing company, the firm that supplies it with safety glass, and the firm that manufactures bathing suits in the same community.

Community Size

Once the community has a large population, the role of industry is not so crucial in the non-work facets of community life; the institutions of the community are more varied and larger in number, the recreational services are more diversified with many added participation groups; the range of and competition among the stores is increased; alternative education streams are found; the quality and number of teachers is increased; the range of medical institutions, doctors, dentists and specialists in the medical and paramedical fields is enlarged. Medical aid is always available and the relationships between the patient and doctor are far less complex than in a small community; with any luck the patient may have a physician long enough that he is able to maintain a continuing medical history.

But although an increase in the size of the community seems to be crucial in changing the whole nature of the relationships between individuals, the assumptions held, the patterns of behaviour, and the distribution of responsibilities, this may be more apparent than real. If we consider, for instance, the metropolitan area, characterized by many industries, many stores, services, and a most complex institutional structure, we find that the round of life of most families is not very different from that of a one-industry community. Many families in the suburbs, in fact, go through the various stages of the development of their community, or their piece of community, as evidenced by the work of White (1956) and Clark (1966). Although the family shares a geographical base with a few hundred thousand other families, and potentially has at its service a thousand doctors and a thousand dentists and thousands of teachers and thousands of stores, schools, churches, and recreational outlets, life is restricted to a small segment of this potentiality. Many social relationships are confined to the immediate area. Despite the size of the community, friends and relatives form the bases of the most meaningful relationships (White, 1956).

Personal Relationships

One of the features of interpersonal relationships in the urban area that distinguishes it from the small town is neither the kinship relationships nor the primary relationships, but the lack of in-between civilities. The number of accumulating biographies and obligatory ritual exchanges is not as great. But, this is merely a matter of degree, for before long, the housewife finds out that the sister of the supermarket cashier is ill, and the cashier will enquire abut the housewife's little girl who is not accompanying her. The breadwinner knows that his secretary is having "man trouble," or that his fellow-welder's wife has cancer. One by one, repetitious meetings elicit greetings, until, over the years, in the most impersonal of areas, the individual accumulates a number of greeting and speaking acquaintances.

Within this area of kinship, neighbours, and friends there is a high level of role observability; but the urban family is able to carry on activities outside this web of relationships and so achieve a certain level of privacy. The breadwinner of the family characteristically moves several miles to his work and it is unlikely that neighbouring families have breadwinners working in the same industry. Thus men's successes and failures at work are not common knowledge within the neighbourhood. But as White and others have pointed out, because neighbours are never sure of the social status of the individuals in the neighbourhood, court or street, and as they are never sure which symbols should be accepted as indicative of what degree of success, the level of probing and curiosity is probably more extreme than it is in the community of single industry where the position of the individual at work, at home and in the community is well known to all.

Community Services

The city abounds with facilities and opportunities that are never utilized and for many, at least superficially, the life round of the suburban family is amazingly similar to that of the family in the single-industry community. The basic difference is that the urban resident has alternatives that are seldom used; the availability, whether used or not, affects social definitions which have a great importance to the individual and his attitudes. It is one thing to choose not to select certain alternatives and it is another not to be able to choose. Within our society it is not so important whether one goes dancing or bowling or whether one spends a dispropor-

tionate amount of money on food, a house, an automobile or whether one belongs to certain organizations, whether one goes to the ballet every night or goes to a concert twice a week, as it is to have a choice of not doing it. The absent services seem to make the heart grow fonder.

The Community of Single Industry and Canada

When people share a community, its problems and its limitations, consciously or unconsciously they work out ways of dealing with difficulties and conflicts. Ideas, norms, traditional practices, social expectations, and knowledge are transmitted, created, and shared over the years in the community and at work — these are the cultural facts. Behaviour is also related to the structural facts, such as the patterns of interaction among individuals and collectivities in the community and the division of labour and organization of work.[2] People share a way of life, and responses to problems are accepted because they have met with success. Those who are born and brought up in such a community unthinkingly take over many of these social habits and definitions.

People who share a community tend to share an outlook toward it and the world outside. These attitudes become important because, as W.I. Thomas stated, "if men define situations as real they are real in their consequences (Thomas and Znaniecki, 1958: 81; also Merton, 1968)." We have noted the preoccupation with isolation on the part of many respondents, but another commonly expressed attitude is that "small towns are a great place to live." These respondents list the advantages — "great hunting and fishing," and "wonderful outdoors life, right on your doorstep"; it is very rewarding to "know everyone in town" — city life is too impersonal, too many people. The extent to which these types of attitudes are transmitted to the young is impressive; when a questionnaire, on the advantages and disadvantages of remaining in their community of single industry (Railtown), was administered to high school students, 90 per cent talked of healthy outdoor life and friendliness.

Other attitudes and behaviour deal with persistent problems or intrinsic limitations and restrictions. Interviews disclosed at least two ways of handling these limitations. Despite the complaints, and sometimes the unhappiness expressed by respondents, many talked with a sense of inevitability. Whether the respondent was living in a community of single industry by choice or by default, temporarily or permanently, the comments suggested that there was nothing that could be done about the difficulties because they were inherent in the nature of the community. Further, these problems were minor compared with the fear that technological and economic change might bring about the disappearance of their whole way of life. Indignation is rarely associated with fatalism; people learn to live within limitations.

A second method of coping with limitations was the lowering of the level of expectations, particularly noticeable when interviews from the four stages of community development are compared. At the recruitment stage, respondents are indignant about their housing, medical, and shopping services. In the stage of maturity, young people who have been born and brought up in the community view it with affection for it is the only world they know; their parents have adjusted expectations and behaviour to adapt to an inevitable situation. The rebels who were unable to live within the strictures have

long since left.

When people have to share a community with neighbours, acquaintances, and workmates, they find it useful not to antagonize their associates. When they do not have absolute faith in their doctor, they remember that he is the only person who stands between them and illness. When conflict is considered futile and damaging, the working out of problems and difficulty is constrained, cautious, and conservative. Resignation to events is common.

A great number of people in both French and English Canada live within the strictures of communities of single industry. One-half of the population of the country lives in communities of under 30 000, in which size imposes restrictions only a little less severe. When the migration from these communities is taken into account, there is an additional large proportion of urban dwellers whose basic outlooks, expectations, and behaviour were formed within these small communities.

It is little wonder, then, that when describing Canada, Kaspar Naegele wrote, "Individually by contrast with the individual American the Canadian seems older, more self-contained, more cautious, less expressive (Naegele, 1964)." John Porter comments that Canadian literary plots "do not deal with the clash of social forces, social progress, social equality or the achieving of other social mobility. Rather, they tend to be, as R.L. McDougall has pointed out, concerned with personal values, personal relationships and private worlds — worlds of gloom and despair at that (Porter, 1967: 53)."

S.M. Lipset concludes that Canadians are "conservative, authoritarian, oriented to tradition, hierarchy and elitism in the sense of showing deference to those in high status (Porter, 1967: 55)." Whyte and Vallee talk of "a kind of pragmatic reasonableness which discourages open dispute (Vallee and Whyte, 1964: 849)." George Ferguson, comparing general trends in Canada and the USA talks of "the slightly slower tempo of life, the less volatile reaction to events, the more sober, more conservative attitudes of men, the higher degree of sabbatarianism, the greater gift for compromise and the middle way (1960: 5)." "If Canada is an 'unknown country' this is, in an important measure, a matter of choice. It is a consequence of a widespread wish to avoid ridicule, emotional display, public quarrels, obvious discrimination, and injustice, and to cultivate instead a certain shrewd and indirect managing of social reciprocities (Naegele, 1964: 512)."

This wide range of evaluative phrases has been used to describe Canadians. Taken in sum, then, Canadians are seen to be self-contained, cautious, less expressive than others, diffident, constrained, melancholy, and resigned to misery, in the belief that man is encompassed by forces beyond his control which strike out completely to destroy him. So they seek escape from their feelings of futility and denial in isolation and withdrawal, personal relationships and private worlds. They are conservative and authoritarian, oriented to tradition, hierarchy, and elitism, resigned to undemocratic and authoritarian practices. They prefer pragmatic reasonableness to open dispute, and so the conservative syndrome is fostered. Decision-making of elites is accepted and no wrong is seen in the fact that many of the latter virtually or actually inherit their positions. They place emphasis on the maintenance of order and predictability and the persistence of an ascriptive status. To them it seems right and proper for a given ethnic group to appropriate particular roles and designate other ethnic groups to less preferred ones. Canadians are envisaged as having a less volatile reaction to events, and more sober and conservative attitudes of mind together with a high degree of sabbatarianism. They are modest, with a sense of realism, and a gift for compromise and the middle way[3]

One would be hard put to find a more accurate evaluation of the residents of single-industry communities in Canada.

Notes

---

1. Many of these communities lie within the so-called mid-Canada corridor. See Rohmer, 1970.

2. This distinction between cultural and structural facts is analytical only in that it differentiates two distinct ways of looking at the same phenomenon. See Kroeber and Parsons, 1958, 582-3.

3. Many consider that the level of abstraction of "national character" is so great that the concept is meaningless; the abstraction obscures regional, linguistic, ethnic, institutional, and individual differences. Some feel that national character is a stereotype which "denotes beliefs about classes of individual or objects which are 'preconceived' . . . a belief which is not held as an hypothesis buttressed by evidence but is rather mistaken in whole or in part for an established fact." (Jahoda, 1964: 694). Stereotypes, of whatever kind, are important because they influence social action. Those who support the sociology of national character claim that it is legitimate: "Like an impressionist painting, national character appears when a body of

countrymen are viewed from an appropriate distance. If one observes the population from a great distance its members may be identifiable only as Western or Latin-American or Oriental. If one approaches individuals closely, they appear as social types . . . If one approaches closer still, all the blazing richness of the unique individual comes into focus blurring all else. However, assume an 'intermediate' distance from a group of countrymen and common features they display as nationals appear once more." (Martindale, 1967: 31.) Recently, in the course of research, the writer asked 144 senior high school students in Manitoba to complete the following sentence: "Canadians as a group are known for. . . . " Sixty-four per cent gave a flattering response, 25 per cent gave a neutral one, and 10 per cent an unflattering one; 76 per cent of 96 senior high school students from Ontario and Quebec gave positive responses, including such words as "peace loving," "democratic," "friendly," "responsible." This suggests that at least some of us like ourselves even if social analysts have described Canadians differently, as seen above. Clearly, these are different perspectives which may be useful depending on the frame of reference and purpose.

10

Canada's Regions and Agrarian Radicalism*

Robert Brym

The first half of this century witnessed the electoral successes of a left-wing populist party in Saskatchewan (the CCF) and a right-wing populist party in the neighbouring province of Alberta (the Social Credit).[1] Meanwhile, in the Atlantic provinces, there was little agrarian radicalism at all. Why this should have been the case is not immediately apparent. Nor has much attention been devoted to the problem.[2]

I shall seek to demonstrate that regional variations in Canadian populism may be explained in terms of variations in the type of social organization and class structure typical of different parts of the country. Specifically, I have been led to ask (*a*) how the structures of the wheat, ranching, and subsistence farming economies differ from province to province and within provinces; and (*b*) what

kinds of coalitions are formed between farmers and other segments of the population in different regions. I shall suggest that answers to these questions enhance our understanding of why certain ideologies took root in one place rather than another; and why in certain regions large parts of the farming population were successfully mobilized for protest while in other regions they were not.

In the middle of the 19th century, Montreal and Toronto based financiers and industrialists were faced with the uncomfortable prospect of a United States no longer prepared to engage in free trade, and the reality of an England convinced that the protected Imperial market was an anachronism. It was in large measure in response to these exigencies that a "national policy" was formulated: by uniting the colonies of British North America and settling the west with the surplus population of Europe it was hoped that an internal market capable of replacing the United States and Britain would be created. In execution, the settlement of south-

*Excerpted from "Canada's Regions and Agrarian Radicalism," in Himelfarb and Richardson, *Sociology for Canadians*, first edition, McGraw-Hill Ryerson, 1980. Reprinted with permission.

western Alberta provided beef for the domestic market. The settlement of Saskatchewan and eastern Alberta provided wheat for both domestic and foreign markets. And the settlement of the Prairies as a whole provided a market for the manufactured goods of the east.

C.B. Macpherson (1962 [1953]) has aptly referred to the Prairies as an "internal colony" of Canada. High tariff barriers on manufactured goods protected eastern industrialists but forced Prairie farmers to pay inflated prices for their implements. Freight rates were arranged so as to discriminate against the West. The entire marketing infrastructure was monopolized by eastern interests who could therefore to some degree set the prices paid for wheat and beef. Credit was controlled by eastern banking houses which charged seemingly exorbitant interest rates. It was largely in reaction to these facts of western life that populist political movements emerged.

It is significant that farmers were able to participate in these movements only because they had first been welded into a solidary group by a number of forces. Because the West produced only a few basic goods, farmers were affected more or less uniformly by fluctuations in the prices of these commodities. They also faced similar marketing and production problems. And they were all compelled to come into often acrimonious contact with eastern business interests and their local agents. Before the farmers had ever conceived of entering the realm of radical politics, their common class situation had in fact prompted them to form cooperative associations as a means of partially eliminating the profits of middlemen (Colquette, 1957; Wright, 1956). Marketing and consumer cooperatives not only functioned as schools for collective action, but led in turn to the blossoming of other voluntary associations. As late as 1950 the average Saskatchewan farmer belonged to four or five cooperatives (Lipset, 1968b [1950]: 54). And in a typical municipality there was more than one voluntary organization for every 21 persons (Willmott, ND [1964]: 5, 66).[3] Political protest was greatly facilitated by the pre-existing dense network of ties which bound western farmers together.

All this stands in sharp contrast to the history of agriculture in the province of New Brunswick, which is a history of social isolation. The reasons are several: political, economic, and geographical. The pattern was already set in the 18th century. Loyalists fleeing the American revolution were granted large tracts of land by the British regime in what is today eastern Canada — so large that, instead of living in communities, the settlers lived alone and apart in the bush. As the doyen of New Brunswick historians, the late W.S. MacNutt, wrote: "There was nothing to compel a man to live in proximity to and in emulation of his neighbours . . . . The isolated way of life bred a spirit of individualism" (1963: 88). Agriculture languished until the mid 19th century, partly because powerful lumber merchants and shippers profited from a scarcity of agricultural goods in the province and therefore sought to suppress its development (1963: 278), partly because the booming timber trade employed the vast majority of people (1963: 182). Only in the 1850s, when the industrial revolution in Britain prompted the construction of steamships and therefore hastened the decline of the market for New Brunswick square timber, were settlers driven to subsistence agriculture (Easterbrook and Aitken, 1956: 243). The farm population thus rose until the 1890s. But New Brunswick's agricultural sector did not become highly commercialized, in consequence of which few farmers ever got past the subsistence level and farm population decreased from the 1890s on.[4] By the 1940s farmers ceased to be the largest single group in the province's labour force (Priscepionka, 1963: 85). But even from the mid-19th to the mid-20th centuries, when agriculture in New Brunswick was at its height in terms of the number of persons it employed, the land was far from propitious. Sharply contoured terrain and generally low fertility soil allowed some farmers to prosper only in scattered areas in the river valleys and along the coastline (Brookes, 1972; Putnam, 1939).

These then appear to have been the principal factors which produced a farming economy largely of the subsistence type in New Brunswick. Table 10.1 provides several indices of the degree to which farming was divorced from the market. In 1941 some 67 per cent of farms in the province were marginal

(i.e., subsistence or part-time) operations, compared to only 18 per cent in both Alberta and Saskatchewan. Average cash income per farm was substantially less than on the Prairies; so was average capital investment per farm.

The preponderance of subsistence farming meant that there was no need in New Brunswick for the kinds of cooperative ventures which blossomed in the West, and therefore no social mechanism within which a collective spirit could be generated. Why form an organization to market crops when there are no crops to be sold on the market? For that matter, why come into contact with other farmers at all? Already in 1924 Louis Aubrey Wood noted that the "[cooperative] movements in the Maritime Provinces are now in a dormant state except in certain localities." He was certainly overly optimistic to add that they "undoubtedly will flourish again" (1975 [1924]: 304). Fifteen years

Table 10.1 Selected statistics on agriculture in New Brunswick, Saskatchewan, and Alberta, 1941

	New Brunswick	Saskatchewan	Alberta
Percentage of work force employed in agriculture	28 (n = 44 515)	58 (n = 197 009)	48 (n = 148 617)
Income from farm products/farm	$883	$1 431	$1 810
Investment/farm	$2 534	$6 460	$7 129
Mortgage debt/farm	$171	$1 127	$959
Owner-operators as percentage of total farm operators	92	53	63
Tenant- and part-tenant operators as percentage of total operators	7	47	37
Type of farm as percentage of total:			
grain and hay	2	65	47
livestock	2	3	13
subsistence and part-time	67	18	18
mixed, other	29	14	22

Source: Government of Canada (1941: Vol. 7, 296-320, Vol. 8, pt. 1, 306-61, pt. 2, 1268-1355, 1440-51)

later there were only 32 shareholders and members of farmers' cooperative business organizations per 1000 rural residents over the age of 14 in New Brunswick. The comparable figure for Alberta was 326, for Saskatchewan, 789[5].

All this is politically significant because, generally speaking, the more farmers produce for a market rather than their own subsistence, the more likely they are to join farm organizations (Jacobsen, 1969) and thus form part of a solidary group. And, as many studies have shown, the higher the level of a disadvantaged group's solidarity, the more politically active and radical its members tend to become (Oberschall, 1972; Tilly et al., 1975). Here then is one important factor that helps explain why Prairie farmers have tended to be more radical politically then their counterparts in Atlantic Canada. It must be emphasized that New Brunswick farmers were not only more atomized than farmers in the West, they were also less proletarianized. James McCrorie (1971), R.T. Naylor (1972a), and Peter Sinclair (1973) have recently emphasized that Prairie farmers were not, despite what they may have thought of themselves, workers (in Marx's sense of persons who are divorced from the means of production and therefore forced to sell their labour power on the market); rather, they were members of the *petite bourgeoisie* (persons who own and operate their means of production). The problem with this categorization is that it is unnecessarily rigid: it fails to take sufficient account of the fact that classes are historically developing sets of social relations; that a class may be in the process of decomposition and transformation (e.g., from *petitie bourgeoisie* to proletariat); and that, at any given time, some groups within a class may have advanced further along the path of transformation than others.

This more dynamic view of class is particularly helpful when it comes to analysing the structural roots of ideological divergence between Prairie and New Brunswick farmers. As Maurice Dobb (1963 [1947]) has shown for the European case, and as Max Hedly (1976) has more recently demonstrated for central Alberta, the process of proletarianization is often marked by the growing indebtedness of independent producers — a process which culminates in the loss of control over means of production. The data in Table 10.1 indicate that this process had in the 1940s hardly begun in New Brunswick but had advanced considerably in the West. Thus, the average mortgage debt per farm was much lower in New Brunswick than in the other two provinces. So was the percentage of tenant and part-tenant farm operators. New Brunswick farmers were not, then, reliant to any great extent on others for employment or credit, and were in this sense less proletarianized than farmers in the West.[6] Herein, I submit, lies a second source of political conservatism among New Brunswick farmers.

The major exceptions to this general pattern in New Brunswick — these help prove the rule — were the counties of Carleton and Victoria. (For other exceptions, see Brym, 1979). If, as I have argued above, the average money income of farmers is a good measure of the degree to which a farming region consists of economically self-contained units or, at the other extreme, of farms unified by market forces, then it is significant that Carleton and Victoria farmers had considerably higher average incomes than farmers in the rest of the province. And if indebtedness of independent producers is a good measure of proletarianization, then these same two counties again stand out as those containing by far the most proletarianized farming population (see Table 10.2).

Table 10.2 Selected statistics on New Brunswick Agriculture and UFNB vote

	Victoria and Carleton counties	13 other counties
Mortgage debt/farm, 1931	$524	$157
Income from sale of farm products/farm, 1921	$1 949	$1 250
Potato acreage, 1910	8 785	31 648
Potato acreage, 1921	21 584	41 185
Percentage UFNB vote, 1920 provincial election	61	14

Sources: Canadian Review Co. (1922:717); Chambers (1921:415-16); Chapman (1976:100); Government of Canada (1921: Vol. 5, 96-8, 176-82; 1931: Vol. 8, 154-5, 159-61); Government of New Brunswick (1962:39); Hyson (1972:201-4).

Notes: (a) Because of new information in Chapman (1976) regarding the third party vote in Northumberland county, the percentage UFNB vote outside Victoria and Carleton has been changed from 11, in the original version of this table, to 14 here. (b) Data on mortgage debt were not collected by the government in 1921. (c) The constituencies of Saint John City and Moncton City have been omitted since they are urban constituencies. (d) For four of the constituencies one can state only the probable affiliation of third party candidates, and in deciding these affiliations I have followed the judgement of Hyson (1972:203-4); all the King's, Queen's and Restigouche third party vote, and half that in Sunbury, have been categorized as UFNB.

In an often quoted passage in *The Eighteenth Brumaire of Louis Bonaparte,* Karl Marx (1971: 130) explained the conservatism of the mid-19th century French peasantry by likening the small isolated peasant holdings of that country to so many potatoes in a sack. Nothing really held the potatoes — or the French peasantry — together. Ironically, it was precisely the potato which bound farmers in Carleton and Victoria counties together and therefore distinguished them from most farmers in New Brunswick. According to one geographer, the "most extensive and easily cultivable soils of the entire Atlantic region" are to be found in these two counties (Brookes, 1972: 31) and, especially after the First World War, the export of upper St. John river valley potatoes to the United States and Cuban market became a major provincial industry and the biggest money earner of all agricultural sectors (Blanchard, 1938: 14, 50). Carleton and Victoria were

the two biggest potato-producing counties and two of the three fastest growing (see Table 10.2).

Did the greater solidarity and proletarianization of farmers in Carleton and Victoria produce greater radicalism among them than among farmers in other parts of the province? Very much so. The United Farmers of New Brunswick originated in Carleton county; the only federal third-party candidate ever elected in New Brunswick history — T.W. Caldwell, a Progressive candidate in 1921 — represented the constituency of Victoria-Carleton; five of the seven to nine successful UFNB candidates in the 1920 provincial election came from the "potato belt;"[7] and in 1920 an average of 61 per cent of the vote went to the UFNB in Carleton and Victoria counties, compared to an average of only 14 per cent in the rest of the province (see Table 10.2). This suggests that the more similar a subregion in New Brunswick was to the West in terms of the two structural variables discussed above — levels of solidarity and proletarianization of farmers — the more similar it was politically.

But Carleton and Victoria *were* exceptional, and for the province as a whole populism was therefore much less of a force to be reckoned with. It would in fact not be too much of an exaggeration to claim that agrarian radicalism in New Brunswick was stillborn. The UFNB had nearly 10 000 registered members in 1921 (Canadian Review Co., 1922: 731) but its strength soon failed. For reasons too complex to discuss here (see Brym, 1979), in the 1925 provincial election the party lost all the seats it had picked up five years earlier.

Let us now turn to this paper's second theme: the social basis of ideological divergence between Saskatchewan and Alberta farmers. By now it has become something of a sociological commonplace that the texture of political life is in some measure a product of the *inter-class coalitions* which predominate and compete within given settings (Moore, 1966; Tilly, 1976 [1964]). It is important that we pay careful attention to this fact in the present context, for farmers represent an intermediate social group with ideological views far less cohesive, homogeneous, and unambiguous than those of workers or entrepreneurs (Macpherson, 1962 [1953]: 221-30). Farmers are quite malleable ideologically, and therefore particularly susceptible to being swayed politically by other social groupings with which they may coalesce. Much like C.Wright Mills' "white collar" strata, they are "up for sale; whoever seems respectable enough, strong enough, can probably have them" (1951: 354). Neither the Social Credit nor the CCF parties were supported exclusively by farmers, and in order to understand why

some farmers backed one party rather than another it is necessary to examine which non-farming groups were aligned with farmers in the two provinces.

The Social Credit party in Alberta had been preceded in office for 14 years by a more left-wing populist party, the United Farmers of Alberta. Before the Depression the UFA had rigorously excluded from its ranks small town merchants and other middle-class townspeople, since it regarded them as the exploiters of the farmer. But the years following 1929 brought about a marked change in this antagonistic relationship. Jean Burnet notes in a report on field work conducted in the area around Hanna, Alberta, that during the Depression "farmers and merchants became more aware of their interdependence through the business failures which marked years of little rain and low prices," and agrees with one local businessman's observation that the drought "brought the farmers and townspeople closer . . . the store would give the farmer credit when the banks wouldn't give him a loan." Simultaneously, "the farmers began to lose confidence in their own strength and ability; it became increasingly apparent that neither as individuals nor in concert could they attain a secure social and economic position without the co-operation of townspeople" (Burnet, 1947: 403).

It is of more than passing interest that the meteoric rise of the Social Credit party paralleled — more accurately, was a manifestation of — this growing coalition between farmers, on the one hand, and small town merchants, teachers, professionals, and preachers, on the other: the "rise of Social Credit represented a new political bond between farmer and small town man" (Burnet, 1947; cf. Irving, 1959: 99, 232, 241 ff.) In fact the Social Credit party did not originate in rural Alberta but in the city of Calgary. It next spread by means of a massive organizational campaign to the small towns of southwestern Alberta, and only then penetrated the countryside. As the data in Table 10.3 on the social composition of the party leadership clearly demonstrate, Social Credit was first and foremost a party led from the town, not the farm.

Table 10.3 Occupational composition of elected representatives: CCF, Saskatchewan, 1944 and Social Credit, Alberta, 1935 (in percentages)

	CCF (N = 34)	Social Credit (N = 45)
Farmer	53.5	24.4
Worker	16.8	0.0
Businessman	5.3	20.0
Professional	0.0	23.3
Teacher	20.6	25.6
Clergyman	0.9	6.7
Housewife	2.9	0.0
Total	100.0	100.0

Source: Normandin (1936: 377-94; 1945: 628-42)

Notes: (a) If more than one occupation was listed for an individual, that person's score was divided proportionately among the appropriate categories. (b) The occupations of nine representatives in each of the parties were not given.

It was otherwise in Saskatchewan, where various labour parties had had a relatively harmonious relationship with agrarian radicals for at least 15 years prior to the CCF victory of 1944 (Lipset, 1968 [1950]: 99-117; Young, 1969a: 13-36).[9] The provincial election of that year saw urban and small town workers give overwhelming support for, and the urban and small town middle class register overwhelming opposition to, the CCF. This, too, was reflected to some extent at the leadership level (Lipset, 1968 [1950]: 197-243). One notes from Table 10.3 that the CCF leadership consisted of over 53 per cent farmers and about 17 per cent workers; this compares with just over 24 per cent farmers and no workers in the leadership ranks of the Social Credit party of Alberta in 1935.[10] Also, some 20 per cent of the Social Credit group consisted of small businessmen and over 55 per cent of persons from various white-collar strata; the comparable figures for the CCF group were just over 5 per cent and 21 per cent, respectively.

These data are especially significant if they are placed in the context of what is known about various groups' typical patterns of political behaviour in situations which generate large-scale social unrest. Members of most intermediate strata, such as farmers and independent professionals, have been known to fall either on the left or the right of the political spectrum. Small businessmen are prone to participate in right-wing extremist movements. And workers are inclined to become left-wing extremists.[11] This being the case, it may be suggested that what pushed farmers in Alberta to the political right was, at least in part, the small town *petit bourgeois* element with which they coalesced; while part of the reason for the Saskatchewan farmers' left-wing orientation was the fact that they coalesced with urban and small town workers.

But this is not the whole story. The Social Credit party's influence did not stop at the Alberta border; the party was also making very significant inroads among the Saskatchewan non-rural middle class by the time of the 1938 election in that province. Why then did the Alberta pattern not repeat itself? Or, stated otherwise, why did Social Credit in Alberta capture most of the farm vote while in Saskatchewan it failed to do so? Unfortunate timing probably had something to do with the party's lack of success in Saskatchewan. No political bond between farmer and small town businessman had been forged by the end of the Depression, and since the return of prosperity witnessed the resumption of antagonism between these two groups there was little chance for any such union to be effected (Lipset, 1968 [1950]: 199). Also significant was the fact that the Social Credit party in the late 1930s suffered from a "crisis of legitimation," having failed to implement many of the most important reforms it had promised on its way to power in Alberta (Sinclair, 1975: 13). But quite apart from these two factors, it may be tentatively suggested that there was a deeper structural reason for the Social Credit party's success in rural Alberta and its lack of success in rural Saskatchewan. This had to do with provincial differences in the social organization of agriculture.

In Saskatchewan 65 per cent of farms grew wheat for their principal source of revenue in 1941 and 3 per cent raised livestock. The corresponding figures for Alberta were 47 per cent and 13 per cent. The political significance of these differences can best be appreciated by referring to the ethnographic work of John Bennett (1969) on ranchers and farmers in a typical Prairie subregion.[12]

According to Bennett, ranching on the Prairies was characterized by relatively low overhead costs, high profitability, and small fluctuations in the price of beef — factors which contributed to the relative economic security of ranchers. Wheat farming, on the other hand, required greater capital investment, returned lower profits and was subject to relatively wide price fluctuations. Two important consequences followed. First, wheat farmers were less secure economically, a fact which contributed to the greater social in-

stability of that group. This was well demonstrated during the drought and depression of the 1930s, when ranchers were considered such good credit risks that bankers happily sustained them while "many farmers were foreclosed or simply went broke and departed" (Bennett, 1969: 180). Second, the relative lack of investment and the stability typical of ranching led to "continued individualistic operation, and a rejection of co-operative and collective organization" (Bennett, 1969: 181).[13] In contrast, the high overhead costs for land and equipment typical of wheat farming necessitated more co-operative ventures: by pooling resources investment costs of individual farming operations could be kept to a minimum. The contrast between rancher and farmer is well summarized by the following insightful remark of a Prairie farmer:

> There's quite a difference between the farmer and the rancher, or any stockman. I suppose it has something to do with the fact that the farmer trades with the world. He sells grain to the world, and he buys machinery and a great amount of supplies from all over the world. Now compare this to the rancher, who gets his lease land for practically nothing, and buys little more than a fistful, at least until recently. He needs little and can afford to be completely independent (quoted in Bennett, 1969: 212).

The divergent cultural and ideological consequences of these two forms of agricultural adaptation should be apparent. Ranchers tended to feel that they were "romantic, isolated entrepreneurs" and developed an "elitist" outlook on life. The pattern of culture associated with farming, on the other hand, emphasized "egalitarianism" and a "collective spirit" (Bennet, 1969: 185, 213). The fact that there were considerably more wheat farmers and fewer ranchers in Saskatchewan than in Alberta may help to explain why the CCF took root so easily in rural Saskatchewan and Social Credit met with such success in the Alberta countryside. The CCF, by emphasizing the necessity of redistributing wealth for the collective good, co-operatively organizing the marketing and consumption of goods, and collectively attending to the welfare of the population appealed to a set of values grounded in the very work situation of the farmer. Social Credit, by attacking what Thorstein Veblen called the "vested interests" and simultaneously defending the virtues of capitalism, and by favouring rule by "experts," appealed to the more independent, entrepreneurial, and elitist bent of the rancher. This argument is supported by John Irving's observation that the Social Credit party first spread from the city of Calgary to the surrounding area of southwestern Alberta — where ranching is a more important part of the agricultural economy than in any other part of the province — and only later found less enthusiastic support in other areas (Irving, 1959: 60-1).[14] Moreover, if we compare (a) the single census division in which livestock sales represented the highest proportion of agricultural revenue of all census divisions and (b) the single census division in which the sale of grain and hay represented the highest proportion of agricultural revenue of all census divisions,

we find that in 1935 the Social Credit vote in (a) exceeded the Social Credit vote in (b) by 8.3 per cent. If the five top census divisions of each type are compared, the Social Credit vote was 5.2 per cent higher in divisions of type (a) than in divisions of type (b). The relationship between Social Credit vote and relative predominance of ranching is not strong — largely, I would suggest, due to measurement problems[15] — but it does indicate that the ranchers, with lower levels of solidarity and proletarianization, had a greater propensity to vote Social Credit than the wheat farmers.

Essentially, my argument concerning the three provinces boils down to these propositions: (a) high levels of solidarity and proletarianization, combined with strong ties to the working class and weak ties to the urban *petite bourgeoisie,* facilitated the emergence of left-wing populism among Canadian farmers (as in Saskatchewan); (b) moderate levels of solidarity and proletarianization, combined with weak ties to the working class and strong ties to the urban *petite bourgeoisie,* facilitated the emergence of right-wing populism (as in Alberta); (c) low levels of solidarity and proletarianization hampered the emergence of populist movements (as in New Brunswick).

Notes

1. The distinction between left- and right-wing populism may be drawn partly in terms of economic principles (the left tends to favour the nationalization of at least large property holdings more than the right), partly in terms of political principles (the left tends to favour popular political sovereignty more than the right). For a general discussion of

this point, see Caute (1966). For details concerning the CCF and Social Credit on the Prairies, see Richards and Pratt (1979).

2. Two qualifications are in order. First, one does come across remarks in the literature which attribute regional variations in populist movements to different *cultural* orientations on the part of different population groups. Thus, the predominance in Saskatchewan of British and European immigrants who had been exposed in their countries of origin to socialist ideologies is sometimes said partly to account for the appeal of the left-wing CCF in that province; the predominance in Alberta of American settlers who had been exposed in the United States to the American populist tradition is said to have been causally related to the spread of Social Creditism there; and the predominance of conservative groups of Loyalist and Acadian stock in the Atlantic provinces is sometimes associated with the failure of populist movements to have met with much success in that region (Grant, 1937-8: 289; Morton, 1950: 83; Naylor, 1972: 253; Young, 1969a: 15-16; 1969b: 5). In an earlier version of this paper I sought to demonstrate through the use of census data and election returns that the posited differences between the national origins of Saskatchewan's and Alberta's populations were so slight that they cannot account for the relevant political differences; and that in some parts of Atlantic Canada with putatively conservative populations, populism was relatively successful. I have not discussed this point in any detail here because several readers of the earlier paper convinced me that I had transformed some passing remarks which may be found in the literature into a full-blown argument, and thereby erected something of a straw man.

Second, a convincing *political-historical* explanation for the divergent developments in Alberta and Saskatchewan has been proposed by Peter Sinclair (1975). But Sinclair, in common with Lipset, (1968 [1950] ixxii);

Young 1969b: vi), and others appears to have assumed the absence of major *social* differences between the two provinces. The present paper may thus be regarded as an attempt to explore some of the social foundations underlying these unique political histories.

3. Willmott's data are from the early 1960s, so one would assume, given the preceding waves of rural depopulation, that the ratio was considerably higher in earlier decades.

4. On the question of how different forms of capitalist underdevelopment have variously influenced the growth of social movements in Atlantic Canada and the Prairies, see Brym (1979); Brym and Neis (1978); Sacouman (1977); Sacouman 1979).

5. Calculated from data in Government of Canada (1941: Vol. 7, 296-320); Richards (1940: 38). While the population data are from the 1941 census, figures on cooperative memberships are for the year 1939. The latter do not include cooperative insurance companies, credit societies, telephone cooperatives, and farmers' institutes; if they did, one would expect the differences among the provinces to be even greater.

6. This does not mean that growing indebtedness *per se* is the same thing as proletarianization. It is only when growing indebtedness occurs in the context of alienation of productive resources from independent producers that it may be considered an index of this process. In Victoria and Carleton counties this was clearly happening. For example, in the area around Bath about 10% of farm families abandoned their farms between 1920 and 1925 because a cost/price squeeze drove them into unmanageable debt.

7. Reports concerning the number of successful UFNB candidates vary, probably because some of the Independent candidates who were farmers by occupation are considered by some writers to have been UFNB candidates. See Chambers (1921: 114, 403-5,

409, 413); Chapman (1976: 100); Hyson (1972: 45); Trueman (1975: 29); Woodward (1976: 48).

8. Interview with Professor Murray Young (6 December 1976, Fredericton), in the 1940s a CCF activist and candidate in New Brunswick.

9. The UFA also displayed a certain willingness to cooperate with workers, but not with workers' parties (Young, 1969a: 17-18, 33).

10. The Social Credit party in Alberta also had some working-class support in 1935, but mainly among unemployed and unorganized workers (Grayson and Grayson, 1974: 308-9; Irving, 1959: 244ff.).

11. The literature which could be cited to support these statements is voluminous. However, the reader's attention ought to be drawn to Nolan and Schneck (1969), a study of political attitudes among small businessmen and branch managers in Wetaskiwin, Alberta.

12. The need to recognize the social heterogeneity and consequent political diversity of North American farmers has recently been underscored by Michael Rogin (1967: 267-8 and *passim*). He masterfully criticizes those American social scientists who argue that right-wing McCarthyism and left-wing agrarian radicalism were both supported by farmers and were therefore similar ideologically (see Bell, 1963; cf. in the Canadian context, Naylor, 1972) by demonstrating that different types of farmers supported the two movements. Of particular interest in the present context is his discussion of wheat farmers (who manifested high levels of social solidarity and dependence and tended to support left-wing agrarian parties) and corn farmers (who were more independent, less solidary, and tended to support McCarthy).

For discussion of this point, see Rogin (1967: 97-9, 107-9, 140-2, 162-5).

13. To the best of my knowledge it was only in 1977 that the first beef marketing board was being seriously considered in Canada (in the province of Manitoba). According to the CBC national television news of 17 March 1977, small ranchers supported this development while large ranchers opposed it.

14. See also Richards and Pratt (1979: 152), where it is noted that "by the turn of the century the ranching-landowning-urban business bourgeoisie of Alberta was a significant, albeit regional fraction of Canada's capitalist class. By contrast Saskatchewan . . . offered fewer opportunities for regional capital accumulation" since it lacked a diversified economic base.

15. These percentages were calculated from data in Government of Canada (1931: vol. 8, 675-7): Normandin (1936: 395-400). Census divisions had to be matched with constituency boundaries through the use of maps — a hazardous task, but probably not a source of systematic error. The much more serious problem with the calculations (and probably the reason that the posited relationship between relative predominance of ranching and Social Credit vote did not show up more strongly) has to do with the size of census divisions in Alberta. On the average, each of Alberta's 17 census divisions is very roughly half the size of the entire province of New Brunswick. Within a given division one can therefore probably find both considerable ranching *and* wheat farming. My argument about the political consequences of ranching versus wheat farming cannot, in other words, be adequately tested until calculations are made using much smaller units of analysis.

SECTION IV

Metropolis and Hinterland

As we saw in the last Section, the image of Canada as a frontier has a long and fruitful history. Sociologists and historians have emphasized that the hard, closed Canadian frontier was more often acted-upon than actor in its own right. But if the frontier is merely acted-upon, understanding Canadian history means identifying the key actors who shaped the frontier and its settlers. It means contrasting the powerless frontier with its associated, powerful non-frontier. Out of such contrasts emerge sets of opposites, all quite similar: centre versus margin, core versus periphery, and metropolis versus hinterland. To understand the history of the frontier (the margin, periphery or hinterland) means understanding the goals that motivated people in places of wealth and power — that is, in the centre, core or metropolis.

Harold Innis, Donald Creighton, Arthur Lower and S.D. Clark led the historical analysis of Canada's frontiers. (For a discussion of each author's work, see Carl Berger (1976).) They found that Canadian society was, and is, a complex web of relationships between metropolises and hinterlands. This introduction will develop that insight into an image of Canada.

First, historians and sociologists found that development in each hinterland (by which we shall always mean *frontier*, *periphery* and *margin* as well) has typically been driven by decisions made in an associated metropolis (by which we shall always mean *core* and *centre* as well). That is, important decisions are rarely made in the hinterland itself. Neither are they made in a great many metropolises: only in one particular metropolis.

One hinterland-metropolis relationship is central to each important economic development in Canadian history — to the development of cod fisheries, the fur trade, the gold rush, the wheat industry, the petrochemical boom, and so on. Each relationship determines where development will occur and, often, where protest will erupt. So, for example, the fur trade was originally directed from Montreal. No other city played a major part in that industry or influenced the fur-collecting and trading hinterland. Equally, the wheat industry was originally centred in Winnipeg; Toronto, for example, had little to do with wheat marketing or speculation. On the other hand, Toronto has always had a lot to do with mining and still keeps up its metropolitan role in that industry.

Second, every large Canadian metropolis has been linked to a major non-Canadian metropolis. Historically, Quebec City was tied to Paris, Montreal and Kingston to London, Halifax to Boston and New York, Toronto to New York (and secondarily, to London through Montreal). Investment capital flows through these linkages. None of these linkages is static. In fact, Canadian cities are rapidly attaching themselves to foreign economic centres like Tokyo and Hong Kong. Smaller Canadian cities like Vancouver, Calgary and Edmonton are following Toronto and Montreal's lead in forming linkages outside Canada.

These facts are important for several reasons. Such outside links mean that Canadian development is largely under foreign control and it always has been. In the twentieth century the form of foreign control has simply shifted, from portfolio and bond investment to direct ownership and operational control (Hutcheson, 1978; Levitt, 1970). (Note, however, William Carroll's claim (1988; also, in this Section) that this pattern has recently changed.)

Sociologists Daniel Chirot (1977), Wallace Clement (1977) and others have argued that as direct foreign linkages into regional centres increase, Canada's economy will develop less evenly. Foreign investors with different goals are free from significant coordination or control and will be able to develop different regions of the country at different rates. Regional conflict within Canada will increase because of uncoordinated, unequal investment. (Free trade with the United States will give us the chance to find out if this prediction of greater regional inequality and conflict is valid.)

Third, research shows that Canadian metropolises typically control other Canadian metropolises. For example, Toronto was originally just a small financial centre and a hinterland of Montreal. Likewise, Winnipeg was once just a hinterland of Montreal, and Edmonton a hinterland of Toronto, though each (that is, Winnipeg and Edmonton) has, in turn, dominated a surrounding area. This fact holds true whether we are talking of secondary metropolises under a larger metropolis, or of such genuine frontiers as newly built mining or logging communities.

Finally, and ever more often, the largest Canadian metropolises dominate non-Canadian hinterlands. More and more Canadian capital is being invested outside the country. Some is even going to major cities of the United States, where Canadian real estate holdings have grown very large. But by far the largest bulk of Canadian investment is in third world countries. In this respect, Canada is becoming very similar to the United States, Britain, France, Italy, West Germany and Japan; nations that met at the economic summit in Toronto in June 1988. Each has huge investments in the third world and a strong wish to see poor debtor nations meet their financial obligations.

Canada's role as metropolis to a third world hinterland began early in this century. Canadian banks and trust companies were investing in Central and South American utilities — in electric power, railways and tram systems, telegraph and telephone facilities — before World War I. Indeed, they were doing this at the very time Canadian industrialists were having trouble raising capital in Canada for their own development. American industry was able to enter and dominate the Canadian economy because Canadian entrepreneurs could not raise the capital that would allow them to compete effectively. Thus, the American takeover of Canadian industry, resources and utilities was, in one sense, caused by the Canadian takeover of Central and South American economies.

Think of a chain of metropolises, each controlling or consuming the next weakest. In this image, Canada is just another link in an international chain of capital that reaches from the top economic centres of the capitalist world — New York, London and Tokyo chief among them — to the lowest reaches of the third world: down to Mexico City, then the Mexican countryside; to Lagos, then the minor Nigerian cities and towns; to New Delhi, then a hundred thousand Indian villages; and so on.

The readings in this Section illustrate many of these aspects of the metropolitan chain. Harold Innis's brief excerpt, from a book about the fur trade in Canada, points out that the producer and the consumer of staples — the hinterland and the metropolis — affect each other, even if unequally. Canada has helped shape the industrial growth of the United States, Innis says, by acting as the gateway for American goods into the British

Empire. Moreover, "as a producer of staples for the industrial centres of the United States", Canada has made "her own contribution to the industrial revolution of North America and Europe." Much has changed since Innis wrote those words in 1930. By 1970, many felt Canada's nationhood was threatened by American domination of the economy. Not surprisingly, Arthur Davis (see his excerpt below) and many other nationalists saw Canadian society primarily in relation to the "American Empire". Because the history of Canada "has been in large part a reaction to the activities of foreign empires"; and because "after the first World War, the Americans (had) quickly displaced Britain as the primary influence on Canadian society"; therefore, it was possible for Davis to argue that "the most important perspective for Canadians . . . to grasp is the present situation of American society."

This view showed Davis did not have a strong belief in Innis's earlier view that metropolis and hinterland influenced one another symbiotically. On the contrary, in Davis's view, Canada was an American puppet and, as such, needed to understand the puppeteer to understand its own history. Accordingly, "the chances for a successful confrontation with the United States may well be better in Mexico or elsewhere in Latin America than in Canada." Canada is too much a part of the American empire now, Davis believes. But if a revolutionary social transformer is to emerge in Canada, "he — or they — will come from, or be identified with, one or more of the underclass and regional hinterlands of North American society": in Canada, a French Canadian or a western farmer.

To simplify, Davis thinks we only need to know about the metropolis to understand the hinterland, and Innis thinks we need to know about the effects of metropolis and hinterland on each other. More recent work by Gordon Laxer returns our attention to the hinterland exclusively. Professor Laxer argues that the defeat of popular agrarian movements and the failure to develop military industry played a major part in allowing the United States (metropolis) to dominate Canada (the hinterland). Weaknesses in hinterland social organization — not strengths in the metropolis — ensured an eventual "branch plant economy", or economic dependency.

This view is similar to Robert Brym's, examined in the previous Section. Each thinks the frontier, or hinterland, can defend itself if appropriate actions are taken. Such actions would include political mobilization (in both cases, by farmers); a radical (that is, class-conscious) program of action; and cooperation across class, ethnocultural and linguistic lines. Thus, for Laxer, the relevant question is not, why did the American metropolis win? But rather, why did the Canadian hinterland lose? But for Laxer, as for Arthur Davis, the metropolis-hinterland relationship is not symbiotic; it is one of Canadian dependency and submission.

William Carroll makes the metropolis-hinterland image even more compelling. He does away with any simple notions of either symbiosis or dependency. Capitalism is a network of relationships within which nationality plays little part, and the largest, wealthiest power has most to say. By this reasoning, Canada would not necessarily be any better off if the United States disappeared into the sea tomorrow. The structure of capitalist relations — within which Canada is merely a middle-range imperialist power — would simply continue with a new metropolis at the helm.

Like any network or system model, this one of Carroll's implies dispersed (or hidden) control. Attention has shifted back to the relationship between metropolis and hinterland, or rather to the relationships between all countries within the system, many of which are both metropolis and hinterland. This image makes allocating blame or even explaining causation almost impossible. In a world system, no single country, no single class, no single group or person is — or could be — to blame. What is more, no simple action will change the situation.

In part, the changing portrayal of the metropolis-hinterland relationship in Canadian history and sociology reflects a maturing social science. Images of the world usually become more complex as we know more and understand more. In addition, changing images reflect trends in political ideology — in nationalist sentiment, for example — which often flare up and die down unpredictably. Davis's article might never have been written in the free trade atmosphere of the 1980s; and Carroll's piece might not have had a favourable reception in the nationalistic (Canada can do no wrong) early 1970s.

Most of all, however, these changing images of the hinterland-metropolis relationship reflect real changes in the relationship between Canada and the United States; and among regions within Canada. As various staples gain or lose value, the regions in which they are found gain or lose wealth and power. Today, metropolitan status is almost as changeable as frontier status. Power comes to a city or nation, then slips away again. It seems that nothing is constant but people's preference for metropolitan, rather than hinterland, status.

11

The Importance of Staple Products*

Harold Innis

Fundamentally the civilization of North America is the civilization of Europe and the interest of this volume is primarily in the effects of a vast new land area on European civilization. The opening of a new continent distant from Europe has been responsible for the stress placed by modern students on the dissimilar features of what has been regarded as two separate civilizations. On the other hand communication and transportation facilities have always persisted between the two continents since the settlement of North America by Europeans, and have been subject to constant improvement.

Peoples who have become accustomed to the cultural traits of their civilization — what Mr. Graham Wallas calls the social heritage — on which they subsist, find it difficult to work out new cultural traits suitable to a new environment. The high death rate of the population of the earliest European settlements is evidence to that effect. The survivors live through borrowing cultural traits of peoples who have already worked out a civilization suitable to the new environment as in the case of the Indians of North America, through adapting their own cultural traits to the new environment, and through heavy material borrowing from the peoples of the old land. The process of adaptation is extremely painful in any case but the maintenance of cultural traits to which they have been accustomed is of primary importance. A sudden change of cultural traits can be made only with great difficulty and with the disappearance of many of the peoples concerned. Depreciation of the social heritage is serious.

The methods by which the cultural traits of a civilization may persist with the least possible depreciation involve an appreciable dependence on the peoples of the homeland. The migrant is not in a position immediately to supply all his needs and to maintain the same standard of living as that to which he has been accustomed, even with the assistance of Indians, an extremely fertile imagination, and a benevolent Providence such as would serve Robinson Crusoe or the Swiss Family Robinson on a tropical island. If those needs are to be supplied he will be forced to rely on goods which are obtainable from the mother country.

*Originally published in *The Fur Trade in Canada: An Introduction to Canadian Economic History*. Revised edition 1956 ©University of Toronto Press, 1956. Reprinted by permission of University of Toronto Press.

These goods were obtained from the homeland by direct transportation as in the movement of settlers' effects and household goods, involving no direct transfer of ownership, or through gifts and missionary supplies, but the most important device was trade. Goods were produced as rapidly as possible to be sold at the most advantageous price in the home market in order to purchase other goods essential to the maintenance and improvement of the current standard of living. In other words these goods supplied by the home country enabled the migrant to maintain his standard of living and to make his adjustments to the new environment without serious loss.

The migrant was consequently in search of goods which could be carried over long distances by small and expensive sailboats and which were in such demand in the home country as to yield the largest profit. These goods were essentially those in demand for the manufacture of luxuries, or goods which were not produced, or produced to a slight extent, in the home country as in the case of gold and of furs and fish. The latter was in some sense a luxury under the primitive conditions of agriculture in Europe and the demands of Catholic peoples. The importance of metropolitan centres in which luxury goods were in most demand was crucial to the development of colonial North America. In these centres goods were manufactured for the consumption of colonials and in these centres goods produced in the colonies were sold at the highest price. The number of goods produced in a north temperate climate in an area dominated by Pre-Cambrian formations, to be obtained with little difficulty in sufficient quantity and disposed of satisfactorily in the home market under prevailing transport conditions, was limited.

The most promising source of early trade was found in the abundance of fish, especially cod, to be caught off the Grand Banks of Newfoundland and in the territory adjacent to the Gulf of St. Lawrence. The abundance of cod led the peoples concerned to direct all their available energy to the prosecution of the fishing industry which developed extensively. In the interior, trade with the Indians offered the largest returns in the commodity which was available on a large scale and which yielded substantial profits, namely furs and especially beaver. With the disappearance of beaver in more accessible territory, lumber became the product which brought the largest returns. In British Columbia gold became the product following the fur trade but eventually lumber and fish came into prominence. The lumber industry has been supplemented by the development of the pulp and paper industry with its chief reliance on spruce. Agricultural products — as in the case of wheat — and later minerals — gold, nickel, and other metals — have followed the inroads of machine industry.

The economic history of Canada has been dominated by the discrepancy between the centre and the margin of western civilization. Energy has been directed toward the exploitation of staple products and the tendency has been cumulative. The raw material supplied to the mother country stimulated manufactures of the finished product and also of the products which were in demand in the colony. Large-scale production of raw materials was encouraged by improvement of technique of production, of marketing, and of transport as well as by improvement in the manufacture of the finished product. As a consequence, energy in the colony was drawn into the production of the staple commodity both directly and indirectly. Population was involved directly in the production of the staple and indirectly in the production of facilities promoting production. Agriculture, industry, transportation, trade, finance, and governmental activities tend to become subordinate to the production of the staple for a more highly specialized manufacturing community. These general tendencies may be strengthened by governmental policy as in the mercantile system but the importance of these policies varies in particular industries. Canada remained British in spite of free trade and chiefly because she continued as an exporter of staples to a progressively industrialized mother country.

The general tendencies in the industrial areas of western civilization, especially in the United States and Great Britain, have had a pronounced effect on Canada's export of staples. In these areas machine industry spread with rapidity through the accessibility of the all-year-round ocean ports and the existence of ample supplies of coal and iron. In Great Britain the 19th century was characterized by increasing industrialization (Fay, 1928) with greater dependence on the staple products of new countries for raw material and on the population of these countries for a market. Lumber, wheat, cotton, wool, and meat may be cited as examples of staple imports. In the United States (Beard and Beard, 1927) the Civil War and railroad construction gave a direct stimulus to the iron and steel industry and hastened industrial and capitalistic growth. These two areas began to draw increasingly on outside areas for staples and even continental United States has found it necessary with the disappearance of free land, the decline of natural resources, and the demand for new industrial materials, notably rubber, to rely on outside areas as shown in her imperialistic policy of the 20th century. Canada has participated in the industrial growth of the United States, becoming the gateway of that country to the markets of the British Empire. She has continued, however, chiefly as a producer of staples for the industrial centres of the United States even more than of Great Britain making her own contribution to the industrial revolution of North America and Europe and being in turn tremendously influenced thereby.

12

Canada as Hinterland
Versus Metropolis*

Arthur K. Davis

Since the 17th century, Canadian history has been in large part a reaction to the activities of foreign empires. Until 1760, it was the French impact that was pre-eminent; then came the British impact for over a century and a half. After the first World War, the Americans quickly displaced Britain as the primary influence on Canadian society — a trend that was reinforced by the rapid decline of Britain itself to a satellite status within the American orbit. So far had the American fact developed in Canada by the 1960s that George Grant felt constrained to write his well-known essay on the demise of Canadian nationalism (1965). Yet the American influence on Canada began long before the 1920s. Its origins go back at least to the war of the American colonies of independ-

dence, 1776-83. And when we review the origins of the national policy during the third quarter of the 19th century, it is not too much to say that Canadian history and socio-economic development during the century of Confederation just ended have been a secondary reaction to the initiative of American events. It has indeed, been a pale reflection of American stratagems and American drift.

The stirrings toward nationalism and independence in Quebec today may, however, open the way to an alternative to "continentalism", which means the continued drift into an affluent but second-class status within the burgeoning American empire; for the price of affluent continentalism includes not only second-class status, but also "homogenization" — the eroding of particularistic communities like the French-speaking Canadians, the Indians of Canada, the Eskimos, and many other presently unique groups in Canada.

Meanwhile, the most important perspective for Canadians — both in and outside Quebec — to grasp is the present situation

*Excerpted from "Canadian Society and History as Hinterland Versus Metropolis" in Richard J. Ossenberg (ed.), *Canadian Society: Pluralism, Change and Conflict*, Scarborough, Ontario: Prentice-Hall Canada Inc., 1971. Reprinted by permission.

of American society. The prospect appears grim. Let us consider the surge and down-swing of oppositions within American society. In our view, this pattern is a key to contemporary Canadian alternatives.

Nearly a decade ago, the present writer argued that decisive structural change comes from oppositions, and that there had been no major oppositions in American society since approximately the time of World War I (Davis, 1960). It is too early to assess the opposition role of the American Black revolt: this may yet prove to be America's best hope. In the meantime, we may review the two major confrontations in the United States during the history of that Republic.

The first was that leading to the American Civil War, 1861-65. It consisted of the competitive clash between two increasingly divergent societies — North and South — both based on capitalistic economies which had to expand or perish. By mid-century, the outcome of the contest was no longer doubtful. The northern coalition of commercial and industrial interests, linked with the western farmers, steadily forged ahead in wealth and power. In 1860, with the election of Lincoln, the control of the national government passed to the new order. It only remained to win the Civil War and make the victory official. As usual, the old regime preferred to initiate a desperate counter-revolutionary war rather than to acquiesce in its own displacement. We quote from historians Charles and Mary Beard.

> Viewed under the light of universal history, the fighting was a fleeting incident; the social revolution was the essential portentous outcome . . . The capitalists, labourers and farmers of the North and West drove from power in the national government the planting aristocracy of the South . . . The physical combat merely hastened the inevitable. As we remarked at the time, the South was fighting against the census returns that told of accumulating industrial capital, multiplying captains of industry, expanding railway systems, widening acres tilled by free farmers. Once the planting and the commercial states, as the Fathers with faithful accuracy described them, had been evenly balanced; by 1860 the balance was gone . . . Viewed in the large, the supreme outcome of the civil strife was the destruction of the planting aristocracy which, with the aid of northern farmers and mechanics had practically ruled the United States for a generation (1927: 54, 99).

No other war in American history, before or since, ever made such an indelible impression on the minds, the memories, and the traditions of the American people and their descendants — both North and South.[1]

The second great opposition in recent American history began to take shape soon after the end of the Civil War. As the immense expansion of post-war American industrialism got under way, nurtured by the new protective tariff, by public subsidies to transcontinental railroads, and by the fabulous resources of the West, rumblings of discontent and revolt appeared among workers, miners, farmers, and various other colonials. Frustrated farmers, excluded from the feast for one reason or another, organized to raise hell instead of corn. Strikers fought pitched battles with police and militiamen across the country. Socialist splinter groups sprang up here and there, and numerous other strange counsels and cults alarmed the ruling burghers. By 1900, a fledgling indigenous Socialist movement led by Gene Debs was under way. In 1912, the various Socialist groups together received 6.3 per cent of the popular vote for the presidency. But since then, the combined Socialist percentage of the American presidential vote has steadily declined. It was seven-hundredths of 1 per cent in 1956.

What happened? Why did the emerging opposition collapse? Why did the opposition to capitalism, generated by capitalism as predicted by Karl Marx, collapse immanently in the United States — where the lack of non-capitalistic alternatives and the absence of anti-capitalistic traditions should theoretically have made for a classic case of socialist displacement of capitalism? The basic reason seems to have been the over-success of American capitalism.

The fantastic resources of the American heartland; the absence of any competing traditions of rival aristocracy; a vast domestic market protected by a high tariff; an endless supply of cheap immigrant labour; friendly politicians in control of the national government (which owned more than half of all land in the nation in 1860) who were eager to help and to share; these are the factors pointed out by the historians Charles and Mary Beard in their *Rise of American Civilization* as the key elements in the "triumph of business enterprise".

We explain American economic and social development, then, in terms of capitalism evolving under unique domestic, geographic, and international conditions — a perspective applicable to any other capitalist society with appropriate modifications in the components. This approach has not prevailed among the majority of American historians and intellectuals. The more common focus has been upon the development of the western frontier. In a famous essay in 1893, "The Significance of the Frontier in American History," F.J. Turner (1921) portrayed the westward movement as perennial rebirth, as a movement away from European influence and toward American uniqueness, and as the basis of democracy and prosperity. Despite its genuine insights, this viewpoint obscures at least as much as it reveals. It embodies a large element of nationalistic parochialism. Set in our larger and more realistic frame of reference, however, the Turner thesis helps

to bring out the central fact that throughout its course the American republic has resorted to expansion in order to escape its domestic contradictions and tensions. And when the western frontier was essentially closed in about 1890, expansionism had to continue abroad. If the historians missed this key point, the more perceptive business and political leaders of the United States from the earliest days of independence were in no doubt where their interests lay.

And when, much as Marx had predicted, capitalism began to generate the resisting forces of labour organizations and populist agrarian revolts toward the end of the 19th century, those thrusts in the case of the United States were turned aside by a combination of sharing the goodies at home and imperialistic expansion abroad. The crisis of the 1890s threatened by the closing of the frontier was resolved in part by extending the necessary economic expansion and investment frontier beyond the national boundaries. Indeed, as William A. Williams, another American historian, has shown, it was the rural colonials — farmers and small town processors in the American hinterland — who pressed most strongly for market expansion abroad. Some of the disappointed colonials moved to the Canadian prairies for a second try.

In other words, interest groups that feel deprived often strive first and foremost to improve their position in the going economic system. With a few adjustments, the system then carries on with some new faces at the head table. A parallel conclusion was reached by McCrorie in his recent study of the Saskatchewan farmers' movement in the 20th century.[2] The American farmers got markets; later they received subsidies. American labour turned to "business unionism." The real process was much more complex, naturally.

The foreign expansion of business was decisively and irreversibly reinforced by the effects of two relatively cheap world wars that brought still further American economic growth, and which wrecked the rival British, French, German, and Japanese capitalistic empires. But these same world wars, in destroying America's rivals, also cleared the way for the communist and nationalistic revolutions in Russia and China, thus closing off vast regions of the world to American business expansion, and forecasting an ultimate confrontation between the American empire and the rising new socialist world.

On another level, the domestic Keynesian and social security reforms have likewise bolstered the fairy tale American version of capitalism since the 1930s. In our own generation, the military and space budgets, which Thorstein Veblen would have called waste, have operated as additional investment frontiers. In truth, the limitless sky has become the limit. It all adds up to the most fantastic success story in human history. It staggers the imagination.

My central concern, however, is not the dynamics and contours of American history, but certain consequences that appear to follow from them, in the light of our dialectical premise. Since the first World War, there has been an absence of great oppositions in American society. Competition has been sharp, often nasty, sometimes violent. In our own day, assassination has become a standard political response; consider the cases of Malcolm X, Martin Luther King, the Kennedy brothers, and the hunting down of the Black Panthers. But no new philosophy, with organizational resources and potentially decisive mass support, has arisen to challenge seriously the prevailing pattern of corporate structures and middle class style of life. The hippies have opted out of their own encap-sulated thing; some student groups may drop out, turn on, or even sit in;[3] the Blacks — so far — simply riot; the old left is largely defunct; the new left — at least in the foreseeable future — has far less organizational and mass support than has George Wallace's reassertion of traditional White racism. Practically everyone that matters, power-wise, in the United States accepts the traditional American middle class way of life. The protests seem negative; none of them sounds positive — with the possible exception of certain stirrings among the Blacks.

At the moment, the best hope for a great change in American life seems to be in the emerging non-racist socialist humanism of such Black leaders as the late Malcolm X and Eldridge Cleaver. Whether these types can secure the necessary mass support among both Blacks and Whites is still a question mark. Surely no country in the world, for its own interest, has greater need for a social revolution that the United States. And the interest of the rest of the world in a new American revolution is equally compelling. In estimating the American future, therefore, we should reserve judgment on the potential of the Black revolt.

Meanwhile, the present absence of major internal oppositions acts as a block to the necessary structural changes that might adapt the United States to the modern world. The investment frontiers abroad are successively being closed out by the rising revolutionary tides of nationalism and communism. The Soviet Revolution of 1917, the Chinese upheaval of 1949 have slammed the door on American expansion in those vast and heavily populated heartland regions. Latin America could follow suit any day, any year. Yet, in this mounting crisis, there is as yet — apart from the aforementioned murmurings — no dialogue, no positive opposition in American society. On the contrary, there is rigidity and nativistic revivalism. In this perspective, the decline of American society may have set in two or three generations ago. It is interesting to note that Toynbee, in his study of civilizations, puts very early in his grand cycle the shift from a creative to a dominant (i.e. uncreative) minority, even though a long period of increasing national power and glory may follow.

The oppositions to American society and to the American ethos are today external rather than internal. This further impedes meaningful dialogue between Establishment and Opposition, by virtue of the emotional barriers of patriotism, nationalism, and racisim. Yet without such a dialogue, without massive and positive oppositions, the United States may well become increasingly obsolete, like the dinosaurs that in a long ago age failed to meet the challenge of their own time. Unfortunately, the United States still bestrides the world like a muscle-bound and inflexibly programmed colossus. It holds the fate of all of us in a finger tip poised above a nuclear push button.

The problem of the United States in 1970 is not primarily Vietnam. "Uncle Sam" could get out of Vietnam tomorrow without fundamentally altering his underlying dilemma. Indeed, the real problem of American society is not even the ghetto-encapsulated Blacks. The crisis, the failure of nerve, the Achilles heel of American civilizations surely lies in the colossal, almost indescribable failure — and need — to face up to itself.

The central issue of the mid-twentieth century is how to sustain democracy and prosperity without imperial expansion and the conflicts it engenders . . . The way to transcend tragedy is to reconcile the truths which define the tragedy . . . To transcend tragedy requires the nerve to fail . . . For the nerve to fail has nothing at all to do with blustering and self-righteous crusades up to or past the edge of violence . . . For Americans, the nerve to fail is in a real sense the nerve to say that we no longer need what Turner calls "the gate of escape" provided by the frontier . . . The traditional effort to sustain democracy by expansion will lead to the destruction of democracy.

So wrote William A. Williams in 1962 (307–9). Using different terminologies, a number of writers have come to similar verdicts — Veblen, Sorokin, Walter Lippman, Paul Sweezy — to name but a few.

"Over-success as failure" — this is the tragic verdict on the American republic, seen from afar by the present writer in 1970. In all the checkered course of human history, no other national rise has been more brilliant or more meteoric. No nation's fall could be more cataclysmic. It might well engulf not only Canada, but most of the world.

Once there was way to get back homeward,
Once there was a way to get back home . . .
(The Beatles, 1969)

Once upon a time it was not too late to retreat. But not any more.

The dreadful impasse in the United States, the mindless rigidity of American societal development during the last three of four generations — especially since World War I — this is what Canadian society has bought (or sold) into, and is now confronting. That the American Blacks in alliance with other underclass and dissident groups may break through the reigning conservative orthodoxy that pervades the American Establishment (including both major political parties) is not impossible. But it seems uncertain. Is the consequent drag upon Canadian society inevitably fatal?

Let us first consider the objective pessimism of George Grant, a perceptive Anglo thinker, a dissenting product of the Tory establishment of eastern Canada, and chairman of the McMaster University Department of Religion. He argues that in Vietnam the American empire is destroying an entire nation in order to preserve its domination, and that Canada is an integral and subordinate part of the United States order (1969: 63, 65).

In the light of our dialectical premise, we think there may be something more to be said. Regional and class oppositions have been more prominent in Canadian society during the half-century since the first World War than in the United States. And the half overt, half latent opposition between Canada and the United States still lives.

Today the prime confrontation within Canada, combining partly overlapping regional, ethnic, linguistic, and class oppositions, is that between Anglo Canada and French Quebec. It is wholly possible that Quebec may yet be the salvation of Canadian society, especially if Quebec opts for independence — as seems increasingly likely. And in our dialectical perspective, this domestic confrontation — particularly if Quebec moved decisively toward socialism (as she would almost certainly be compelled to do, in order to manage successfully her natural and human resources for national French-Canadian survival) — might awake unforseen reactions and resources in English Canada. To be sure, these reactions might produce either a collapse into the American camp or a spine-stiffening resolution to remain different.

There are only two basic alternatives for Canadian society in the foreseeable future. One is a continued drift toward continentalism which means further absorption into the American capitalist empire. This policy, which since World War II has been pursued largely without public debate by most elements of the Canadian elites — the policy makers in the private, public, and governmental corporations — anti-national and therefore anti-Canadian. The other alternative is a Canadian Castro. This means socialism: expropriation of selected foreign and domestic major corporations, closer control of certain other key industries, and the overall planning of the use of our major resources for national purposes and public services.

But there may also be intermediate possibilities, such as the watered-down socialism of René Lévesque. According to certain lines of contemporary economic thinking, it is apparently desirable to leave a fairly large private sector in the economy, perhaps along Scandinavian lines, particularly in "small business", but also in a few large scale industries. In principle, however, the choice lies between American imperialism and Canadian socialism.

Compensation for expropriation? In principle, yes But unforeseeable circumstances would doubtlessly control the amount. At one end of the range of possibilities is a minimal token compensation, based on the argument that past profits should be weighted off against present value. At the other end of the range is full compensation for present value. The pattern could vary for different industries. Here we may revert to a remarkable occurrence in Quebec. Some years back, the Province of Quebec nationalized an American owned corporation — Quebec Hydro — and borrowed the money from the Americans to pay for the take-over. We should all reflect at length upon this significant event. We might just possibly make it financially worthwhile for the Americans (who know a good business deal when they see one) to finance Canadian independence. And we could always hope to scale down the interest rate in due time. In any case, there are other sources in the world for borrowing capital for investment and for compensation. The Americans understand competition — or so they say. Let them compete with France, the Soviet Union, Japan, and so on for the financing of Canadian independence.

Still thinking in terms of metropolis-hinterland oppositions as a core concept in the history and the future of Canadian national development, we may suggest that the coming confrontation between Quebec and English Canada may be the best promise for both parties to that great dialogue. In Quebec's drift and thrust toward independence, it is secondary that a subjected and exploited nationality may some day soon recover its freedom. That would be no more than poetic justice for past wrongs. What really matters is what Quebec may do to stimulate the revival of independent nationalism in the rest of Canada. And even more important, perhaps, is what such socialist and nationalist development in the form of two independent nations north of the American border might do for the United States. That may be too optimistic, of course. Yet the fate of homo sapiens may well rest upon the issue: Can the United States recover — or more accurately, achieve — a national identity and national policy that is compatible with the emerging revolutionary mainstream of the rest of the world? Consider the words of W.A. Williams, American historian in the classic tradition of Charles Beard:

> For the rest of the world, be it presently industrial or merely beginning to industrialize, is very clearly moving toward some version of a society modeled on the ideal of a true human community based far more on social property than upon private property. That is what the editors of *The Wall Street Journal* meant in 1958 when they candidly admitted that the United States

was on "the wrong side of a social revolution." The socialist reassertion of the ancient ideal of a Christian commonwealth is a viable utopia. It was so when the Levellers asserted it in the middle of the 17th century, and it remains so in the middle of the 20th century. It holds very simply and clearly that the only meaningful frontier lies within individual men (and women) and in their relationships with each other. It agrees with Frederick Jackson Turner that the American frontier has been a "gate of escape" from those central responsibilities and opportunities. The socialist merely says that it is time to stop running away from life (Williams, 1961:487).[4]

All this may seem speculative, of course, but it is not entirely so, given the dialectical promise herein adopted. It is one task of the sociologist to clarify alternatives, regardless of how improbable they may appear in the light of current professional and political orthodoxies. Having said that, it may be well at this point to emphasize the importance of contingencies in social affairs. We may plan our futures, yet much depends on the larger trends of the times. For example, the National Policy that constituted and guided Canadian Confederation over most of the past century was "planned" only in a limited sense. Fowke has put the matter in this way:

> The National Policy was not by itself sufficient to make Western development possible on the scale eventually attained. The establishment of the prairie wheat economy, which may be regarded as its first major economic triumph, was accompanied by tremendous economic expansion throughout the entire Canadian economy, and was an integral part of a complex of dynamic forces which pervaded the western world. Professor Mackintosh has spoken of the "conjuncture of favourable circumstances" which marked the transition from the 19th to the 20th century and which gave to Canada three decades of unprecedented expansion. This conjuncture of world circumstances created the opportunity for

Canadian expansion, but a half-century of foundation work along the lines of national policy has prepared Canada for the opportunity (1957: 70).

R. Heilbroner points up the same argument in even stronger terms:

For the common attribute of contemporary events is not their responsiveness to our designs, but their indifference to them . . . . History less and less presents itself as something we find or make, and more and more as something we find made for us (1959).

Yet part of this deepening impasse may be due to the fact that the United States, like King Canute forbidding the tide, is attempting to stand against and to turn back the rising swell of anti-colonial and communist revolutions that are sweeping much of the world in the 20th century.

This brings us to our final issue. By contrast with the United States, Canadian society has been characterized as "pluralistic." This means that ethnic and regional differences for example have been more generally accepted, more legitimized than they have been in our southern neighbour. There has not been as much pressure in Canada for "assimilation" as there has been in the United States — though it is easy to exaggerate the importance of the American "melting pot" ideology (in the case of the Negro, and the southwestern Mexican-American, for instance) — just as one may readily over estimate Canadian tolerance for ethnic differences. Canadians seem to prefer Indians and Blacks to keep their distance. Yet the Hutterite communities unquestionably are granted more autonomy in Canada than in the United States. Likewise, the Indians of Canada, however rudely they were shunted onto reservations when the fur trade no longer needed their labour and the eastern

Anglo Establishment wanted their land for white settlement, were seldom treated with such overt coercion as were the American Indians. Above all, the English and the French, despite the conquest and subordination of the latter, had to arrive at a *modus vivendi* that involved mutual compromise and autonomy as well as exploitation.

Another way of describing and perhaps of partially explaining Canadian pluralism is to observe the fact that capitalism never developed to such extremes in Canada as it did in the United States. The American colonies broke their ties early with England, and the philosophy of laissez-faire Manchesterism could run wild until the rise of new internal oppositions late in the 19th century. Even then, as we have seen, the competitive challenges of the labour and the agrarian movements were blunted by taking the rebels into the feast and paying for this by means of foreign economic expansion. In England, on the other hand, elements of pre-industrial classes and values survived industrialization. The first reforms in the 19th century were sparked, not by the "new men of Manchester", but by Tories from the old landed classes motivated by feudal norms like *noblesse oblige*. Something of these restraining values seems to have carried over into English Canada. And French Canada has embodied still other and different traditions.

Now, however, all Canadian particularisms are threatened by what George Grant calls the "homogenizing and universalising power of technology" (1969: 69). What kinds of community do the various segments of Canadian society want? This is one of the key questions posed by the Alberta Indian leader, Harold Cardinal:

The new Indian policy promulgated by Prime Minister Pierre Elliot Trudeau's government . . . in June of 1969 is a thinly disguised programme which offers nothing better than cultural genocide . . . . Indians have aspirations, hopes and dreams, but becoming white men is not one of them (1969: 2, 3).

The Indians, according to Cardinal, want a respected place in Canadian society, but they also insist at least in some degree on remaining Indians.

A similar theme is voiced by René Lévesque, leader of the Quebec independence movement:

> We are Québécois. What this means first and foremost . . . is that we are attached to this one corner of the earth where we can be completely ourselves: this Quebec, the only place where we have the unmistakable feeling that "here we can be really at home." Being ourselves is essentially a matter of keeping and developing a personality that has survived for three and half centuries. At the core of this personality is the fact that we speak French . . . . We are heirs to the group obstinacy which has kept alive that portion of French America we call Quebec . . . . This is how we differ from other men and especially from other North Americans . . . (1968: 14-15).

In calling for an independent Quebec, Lévesque is striking out for the survival of a major Canadian particularism. He is arguing that only in their own sovereign state can French-speaking Canadians develop their own special style of life and shape their own institutions. Unlike the Indians of Canada, the independence movement in Quebec has such assets as numbers, concentration of population, organizations of all types, important natural resources, well developed economic enterprises, and so on. The Indians are scattered, divided into over 500 bands on more than 2200 reservations, further separated into 11 language groups, and for the most part poverty-ridden.

In affirming that the survival of various nationalisms in Canada requires (among other things) a shift to a socialist economy, we must refer to the thesis of André G. Frank concerning "underdevelopment". Although Frank based his analysis on Latin American studies, his conclusions seem equally applicable to Canada:

> Underdevelopment is not due to the survival of archaic institutions and the existence of capital shortage in regions that have remained isolated from the stream of world history. On the contrary, underdevelopment was and still is generated by the very same historical process which also generated economic development: the development of capitalism itself (1966: 23, 1967).

The history of the fur trade in Canada is a classic illustration of this thesis. The development of the fur trade tied the Indians to a world market as colonialized workers managed by others. When the fur industry declined, capital migrated to other sectors of the economy, and the Indians were left stranded and by-passed in a world they did not make. Now the Indians are beginning to knock on the door of the modern world. They no longer wish to be a poverty-ridden rural proletariat, they are not content to move into urban slum ghettos. Nor do they wish to be merely "brown white men". They want to be different it seems; they want to be Indian.

The Frank thesis can be applied also to Quebec. Modern economic development came relatively late to Quebec, compared to Ontario, and it came mainly for the benefit of Anglos. Now Quebec is catching up, but Quebeckers, too, wish both to retain their cultural differences and to have more of the economic goodies.

If this approach is valid, it greatly reinforces the argument that the salvaging of Canadian pluralisms requires a socialist economic base. The economic aspect of the issue is essential, but it is clearly not the only essence. There is also among many Indians, the Quebeckers, and perhaps among many other groups such as students and young people as well, a quest for community. Socialism by itself does not guarantee community. There is still the problem of large scale bureaucracy. Much experimentation in making bureaucratic organization more responsive to the control and needs of its members and clients is still needed. But a regime of social property rather than private property seems one obvious prerequisite of the next great phase of North American society. If that society has a future — a big "if" — the American empire must be de-colonialized. What Quebec and the Indians of Canada appear to be seeking to escape from is their dependent and colonial status. English Canada's branch-plant condition relative to the United States economic empire is objectively parallel in certain respects to the hinterland status of the Indians and French vis-à-vis the Anglos in Canada. But English Canadians have not yet awakened to their dependency and fate in the homogenizing and expanding American empire.

The coming confrontation between English and French Canada — if it does occur — may help to change all that. Lévesque's insight seems valid, in the light of our dialectical frame of reference.

> As for the other Canadian majority, it will also find our solution [independence for Quebec] to its advantage, for it will be set free at once from the constraints imposed on it by our presence; it will be at liberty in its own way to rebuild to its heart's desire the political institutions of English Canada and to prove to itself, whether or not it really wants to maintain and develop on this continent, an English-speaking society distinct from the United States (1968: 28).

Looking back and looking ahead, the Canadian Centennial of 1967 may well prove to be a watershed in Canadian history, an interlude between eras. This is the view suggested by our conception of Canadian history and society as a dynamic sequence of oppositions, irregularly and alternately latent and overt between overlapping hierarchies — regional, class, ethnic, urban-rural — of metropolis-hinterland relationships within North American society. Does this schema have any predictive value? If it does, then it could inform policy.

In the present writer's judgment this modified dialectical approach seems to "fit" the Canadian and North American past reasonably well. Whether it will continue to offer a realistic interpretation in the future, only time will tell. Life is full of surprises. Somewhere in his postscript to *War and Peace*, Tolstoy remarks that some interpretations of modern history are like "a deaf man answering questions which no one has asked".

The mythical scientific analyst must assume a completely deterministic premise. If he knew all the factors in a situation and their relative weights and vectors — currently an impossible "if" — he could predict the resultant outcome of that situation. The actor, however, cannot know all the factors in his action situation; therefore he has "choices". Hence we suggest no more than this: A dialectical approach illuminates the past and perhaps also clarifies the future alternatives of Canadian societal development. In other words, it fulfills what C. Wright Mills called the interpretive task of classical social analysis. All we are certain of, at this point, is that for such a purpose the dialectical frame of reference is superior to the orthodox structural-functionalism of academic sociology.

Is it unrealistic to take into account this dialectical perspective as one factor in making policy decisions in various interest-groups in Canadian society? For example, is it reasonable to suppose that Quebec or Canada can "confront" the American colossus and still survive? The answer seems obvious. Why not? We never know until we try. And if nothing is attempted, then the drift into the American empire will simply continue. What the fate and value of American society will be is presently indicated in the obscenities now proceeding in Vietnam. American policy in Vietnam — and potentially in Latin America — is like the Assyrian armies that flayed alive thousands of their opponents, only it is mechanized and on a vastly greater and more "efficient" scale. If the heart of American society is Main Street, its cutting edge is in Vietnam, and there is an organic link between the two aspects. This is barbarism, not civilization.

Many turning points of history appear to be a chancy process of "slipping successfully between the icebergs". The collection of puny American colonies was able to achieve its independence from the superior might of the British empire because Britain was preoccupied by a major war with France. The Bolshevik revolution in Russia succeeded because the hostile western powers, exhausted by a world war, could not muster sufficient force to smother it. Castro led a successful revolution in Cuba, right under the nose of the United States, partly because of American involvements in Asia and Europe and partly because the Americans assumed they could do business as usual with the new leader as they had always done with previous rebels in Cuba and Latin America. When the Americans finally woke up, it was too late.

Contrary to George Grant, therefore, we believe that nationalism in Quebec and in English Canada is not necessarily defeated. But it will require a socialist transformation to salvage and rebuild what remains and even that may not be enough.

The American empire is not merely a hemisphere but a global operation. It seems appropriate for students of Canadian society to take into account so far as possible key developments all over the world.

Looking at that larger picture, the chances for a successful confrontation with the United States may well be better in Mexico or elsewhere in Latin America than in Canada. A "successful confrontation" may be defined as one that leaves the people of the world both alive and fit to live. Mexico has vitality, great numbers, longer and deeper roots in distinctive Indian and Catholic cultures, a revolutionary tradition, and so on. On an even larger canvas, as Sorokin suggested during his last years, the best hope for a viable and humane stabilizing of the world may lie with Oriental societies — Japan, China, and India — especially the latter two. These societies have already made extensive progress in adapting such western patterns as science and technology to their own ancient cultural heritages, and in "kicking out the White man" (Sorokin, 1964: 64). Indeed, during most of world history the leadership of civilization has rested with the river-valley imperial societies of the near East, India and China. Perhaps the meteoric rise and evident decline of Western Europe during the last few centuries is but a passing episode.

This massive transition, however, could well be cut short by nuclear war, precipitated by the terminal convulsions of the American juggernaut in the face of rising domestic and external opposition. That would be the end of all of us. Meanwhile, we may offer one final thought. If a new Gene Debs appears to lead a revolutionary transformation in the United States, he may perchance be a Black. In Canada, he will probably be a French Canadian or a western farmer. He — or they — will come from, or be identified with, one or more of the underclass and regional hinterlands of North American society.

Notes

1. When the death of latter-day American hero-presidents like Franklin Roosevelt and John Kennedy were memorialized and publicly solemnized, the poem invariably recited was Walt Whitman's great elegy to President Lincoln: "When Lilacs last in the Dooryard Bloomed". The greatest American national crisis evoked the greatest national poem. Subsequent American crises, because they have been lesser, have merely echoed the greatness of that earlier day.

2. All that my friend Roy Atkinson, President of the Saskatchewan Farmers Union, is trying to do by organizing a National Farmers Union is to give farmers an effective trade association such as most other categories of capitalistic entrepreneurs have long enjoyed. A more conservative truly capitalistic goal could hardly be imagined.

3. The student strikes and the march on Washington in Spring 1970 provoked by the Kent College killings and Nixon's move into Cambodia may have been a step towards organization and mass support on campus however fleeting.

4. Copyright © 1961 by William Appleman Williams.

13

*The Branch Plant Economy**

Gordon Laxer

"The market is reserved for Canadian manufacturers. The way for our Yankee friends to obtain a percentage of the Canadian trade is to establish their works in Canada." (*Canadian Manufacturer*, Jan. 16, 1891: 44).

This was the way Canadian manufacturers set out the welcome mat a century ago for the economic takeover of Canadian industry. The question of why Canada incurred so much foreign ownership of its economy at so early a point in its history has generated three standard explanations: the tariff; proximity to the United States; and weak nationalism amongst Canadian capitalists. This paper outlines an alternative explanation, focusing on Canadian policies which entrenched a conservative banking system, squandered enormous amounts of capital on superfluous railways and failed to develop strong armed forces before 1914. Rather

than seek an explanation in the inability of Canadian industrialists to control the Canadian market, this paper explores the policy consequences of the weakness of agrarian-based, popular democratic movements (1867-1914), the latter resulting from the peculiar interaction between class and the binational character of Canada.[1]

When contrasted with the experience of other nations, it is striking that the power of big business in Canada remained relatively unchallenged in a new settler society with a broad electoral franchise. Canadian farmers (owner-operators) comprised the largest component of Canada's labour force (1870-1910) but did not have the dominant influence on government policies their counterparts did elsewhere in the same economic phase. Why then were popular democratic movements so feeble during the formative period in which the nation state was established and the industrial structure set in its branch plant, resource-exporting mould? Why was the Canadian state not strongly nationalist during this time when foreign own-

*Excerpted from "Class, Nationality and the Roots of the Branch Plant Economy," in *Studies in Political Economy*, 21, Autumn 1986. Reprinted with permission.

ership became entrenched?[2] To ask these questions is to move from George Grant's uninteresting problem of why Canadian businessmen put profits above country, to an analysis of the weakness of popular economic-nationalism in Canada during the age of autarchy.

Nationalist-continentalist categories first arose around the National Policy debates a hundred years ago, and still affect our thinking in unconscious ways. The traditional reasoning goes like this: the conservative-nationalism of Canada's National Policy was predicated on the power of elite elements, a whiggish political philosophy and the British tie, while continentalism was associated with American liberal and democratic influences amongst Canada's farmers (Careless, (1954: 8-14; Landon, 1967; Smith, 1971). I reject this dichotomy and argue that instead the feeble "nationalism of the National Policy" resulted from the inability of Canada's ordinary people — farmers mainly but also workers — to impress themselves on the political system.[3] Nineteenth century nationalism was born, after all, with the popular struggle for democracy (Hobsbawm, 1962).

The European System

Was the achievement of an independent industrial economy an unrealizable dream for Canada then? Not if we confine ourselves to the economy. After all, Canada was the eighth largest manufacturing country in the world in 1867, and seventh largest by 1913 (League of Nations, 1945; Clark, 1960; Maizels, 1963; Kuznets, 1969).[4] Starting from weaker economic positions, Sweden and Japan overcame their respective staples-exporting and colonial-economic handicaps, and developed independent industrial econ-

omies. But the answer is yes when we consider the political, social and ideational environments of post-Confederation Canada.

In a seminal article written two decades ago, Mel Watkins (1966) argued that Canada's National Policy of tariff protection for domestic industry, public subsidies for private railways to the west, and immigration for settlement was little more than emulation of the "American system" of the 1820s. After assessing the Canadian copy of the American system as inadequate because Canada developed later and in an elitist way, Watkins raised the question of a third possibility, the "European system" for Canada.

By the term "European system", Watkins meant the institutional changes Alexander Gerschenkron (1962) has shown were crucial for the independent industrial development of the "backward" countries of Europe. In the late 19th and early 20th centuries, backward European countries rejected the economic liberalism that was trumpeted as the new religion in the early industrial starters, especially in England.[5] Instead they adopted strong, state interventionist strategies for economic development.

To understand the importance of the European system for "late follower" countries — those passing through initial industrialization between 1870 and 1914 — we must examine the changed conditions for embarking on development in that era. Canada was among a handful of late follower countries which began to industrialize about a century after England, and about half a century after France, the USA, Switzerland and Belgium. The other later followers were Sweden, Italy, Russia and Japan.[6]

In the hundred years after economic transformation started in England, the cost of beginning industrialization had climbed considerably, especially with the invention of the railway and steel-making. To find the capital needed for development, late follower countries had two options: discover new sources of domestic capital, management and technology, and supplement this effort with foreign borrowings — the independent route; or, encourage foreign businesses to do the job by means of subsidiaries — the dependent route. The independent route was the European system.

The dependent or easy road to rapid development resulted from the failure to adopt the institutional changes of the European system (or its equivalent, as in Japan) during initial industrialization. It was purchased at the price of diminished political, economic and technological sovereignty. I have argued elsewhere that economic development was thereby retarded in the long-run (Laxer 1985a). Canada was the only late follower country that clearly took this route (Czarist Russia partly did) and the only one that did not achieve an independent and fully-developed manufacturing economy (Laxer 1985b).

Popular-Democratic Movements in Canada

Canadian farmers did not, for the most part, consciously seek to build an independent industrial Canada during initial industrialization. Far from it.[7] Most were trying to develop the family farm and prevent the incursions of industrial capitalism from sweeping over them and their communities. But that does not mean that the objective consequences of policies advocated by organized farming groups would not have led to a variant of the European system. We shall see that in fact, farmer-led movements, while generally seeking different goals altogether, supported policies along the lines of the European system.

After 1837, farmers' movements flickered, on occasion brightly, over the next 80 years of nation building and industrial transformation. Once, in 1894, the farmers' Patrons of Industry came close to winning office in Ontario. They had numbers on their side in this era. In 1881, the agricultural work force (mainly owner-operators) made up 48 per cent of the total labour force (Haythorne, 1941: 29). But as a group, farmers had little influence on state policy during this formative period.

It was only in 1919-1922, after initial industrialization was completed and farmers were reduced to one-third of the labour force, that agrarian political movements held centre stage again. Aided by significant numbers of Labour members, these movements took office in three provinces including Ontario, and showed strength even in such unlikely places as the Maritimes, British Columbia and Quebec.[8] In the federal election of 1921, the farmers' Progressive Party won a third of the seats, with preponderance from the prairies (Morton, 1978; Wood, 1975: 301–9; Forbes, 1983:15).[9]

Such a flowering of political strength was not seen amongst workers and their allies before, during, or after initial industrialization. Individual labour MP's here, a handful of Independent Labour Party members there, even briefly the (Marxist) Socialist Party of Canada as Official Opposition in British Columbia just before the First World War, did not constitute a serious bid for power by working class movements.[10] Nor was a syndicalist route to power possible.

During the transition period to industrial capitalism, it was no doubt easier for aristocratic landlords to rule in older societies than for independent farmers to hold or share elected power in new settler societies. Aristocrats, the ruling class in the pre-industrial order, generally could retain power by maintaining strict limits against the rising tide of democracy and popular nationalism. Farmer power in new settler societies, however, required an early and quick victory for a broad franchise and the power of elected government. This occurred at an early point in the new settler societies of the United Sates, Australia and New Zealand, in which popular-democratic movements quickly swept away parties advocating rule by large property holders (Laxer, 1985b). In some older societies such as Sweden, the transition to democracy did not spell the diminution of agrarian political power, at least for a while. As noble power began to decline in the 1870s and 1880s, the influence of independent farmers grew (Rustow, 1955: 9-47). As Canada did not share the tendency to agrarian political influence during initial industrialization, an important issue is left to be explained.

Agrarian Political Weakness in Canada

The forced union of English and French in Canada had disastrous effects for agrarian-based populism after the 1837 rebellions, creating a contrasting situation with liberal democracy's usual development in new settler societies. Liberalism rests on beliefs about private productive property and the market economy, but does not necessarily imply political democracy. In fact, democracy was added on to liberalism in every western society which later adopted liberal-democratic systems (Macpherson, 1977: 23). The transition from aristocracy to liberal democracy usually involved a period in which substantial property holdings began to replace inherited social position as the key to political rights. This was the period in which whiggery or plutocracy (rule by the rich) was the dominant ideology.

Whiggery usually found fertile soil in older societies with feudal pasts, where aristocratic and plutocratic bases for political rights could co-exist, if uneasily. In new settler societies in temperate climates where slavery or new types of serfdom could not be established easily, plutocratic ideologies usually withered quickly in the rising tide of 19th century democracy (Hartz 1955: 89). This was the case in Australia and New Zealand. Even in the United Sates, where an "aristocracy" of slave-owning planters arose in the southern states, the Federalist and Whig parties died by the 1840s. Canada was the exception. Even though feudalism never had deep roots here, plutocratic ideology — often referred to as the British conservatism of restraint — had a suprisingly long life (Harris, 1967: 7).

The unusual character of 19th century Canadian politics did not depend on a peculiar class structure and indeed Canada's social formation was typical of new settler societies transplanted from northwestern Europe. The usual stance of emerging capitalists in the age of revolutionary liberalism was typified by alliances which took place during the American revolution when the merchants joined forces with southern planters and free agrarians to demand independence from colonial rule and a broadening of democratic rights (Hofstadter, 1951: 3-17). In Canada, however, the emerging big bourgeoisie provided the strongest support for continued British colonialism and the arbitrary rule of appointed officials.

The bourgeoisie started off in the usual way. A small number of British-American merchants moved to Montreal between the

Conquest (1760) and the Constitution Act (1791), took over most of the fur trade from the French merchants, and began a political agitation typical of their class. They demanded representative government for the middle class, and an end to British military rule. But as soon as their campaign for a legislative assembly succeeded in the 1790s, they abruptly reversed themselves (Ouellet, 1980a; Creighton, 1937; Wade, 1968).

In what was to become a firm pattern in Canadian history, the ethno-national question intervened to divert politics away from division along class lines. By carving out a separate colony for Loyalist settlers in Upper Canada in 1791, Britain left the growing number of English-speaking merchants of Montreal surrounded by a sea of French Canadian habitants in Lower Canada. Even though the British were greatly overrepresented, French Canadians controlled the legislature in the Lower province. John Richardson, the leader of the Montreal merchants, complained of his frustrations as an elected representative in the new legislature: "Nothing can be so irksome as the situation of the English members — without numbers to do any good — doomed to the necessity of combating the absurdities of the majority, without hope of success (Wade, 1968:97)."

The attitude of French Canadian politicians disturbed Richardson and his friends. Instead of pushing for freedom of enterprise and capitalist progress as Montreal's big capitalists expected of a parliament, the Francophone majority used representative government to win recognition for their ethno-national collectivity, and championed the class interests of small-holding farmers who opposed many of the aims of commercial business (Trudeau, 1968: 104). The merchants' answer was to help curtail the colonial Legislature. Thus the big merchants turned against liberal democracy and supported a reactionary and colonial brand of whiggery.

Sectionalism and Popular Democratic Movements

In almost every decade from the 1850s until the First World War, significant popular-democratic movements challenged the power of commercial and industrial capitalists. Unfortunately, most of these movements fell into the trap of French-English division. In this context big business ruled with ease, and even allowed itself the luxury of public expressions of division amongst various factions, such as manufacturers versus bankers and railway magnates (Clark, 1959b: 10).

Agrarian movements in Canada from the 1850s to the 1930s were overwhelmingly petit bourgeois in character, representing the interests of owner-operators in the struggle to preserve the family farm. Other participants in agriculture (farm labourers, tenant farmers, seigneurs, forced labourers) that in other societies played important roles at times, were either absent or of little importance.

Farm labourers, comprising about one fifth of the male agricultural work force in 1891 and less than that earlier, were the only group of significant size outside of the agricultural small business class. They failed however to form cohesive communities and bring their weight to bear on the political system. The majority were irregular or seasonal workers who moved in and out of an agricultural working class, while another large portion were the sons (rarely the daughters) of farm proprietors. Only a small portion were permanent hired hands. Thus agrarian movements in Canada were of and by the small business class, usually comprising all family members (Haythorne, 1941: 213).

Labour shared many of the concerns of farmers, and attempts were made to forge a farmer-labour alliance to strengthen the "producing classes" against the "monopolists". In 1886 and again in 1893-4, serious efforts were made to unite the two groups. Although some cooperation occurred around Patron of Industry candidates in the 1894 Ontario election, an alliance was not to be (Smart, 1969:47; Hann, 1975:21; Kealey, 1982:387–91). Failure may have been due partly to the timing of the attempts. In 1886, labour was at its zenith and the farmers' movement was at a low ebb, while in 1893-4, it was the reverse. More important though, the attempted alliance foundered on divergences in class interests. As self-employed businessmen, farmers found labour's demand for an eight-hour day hilarious and, as sometime employers of casual labour, costly. The same applied to labour opposition to assisted immigration, a cheap source of agriculture labour (Wood, 1975: 103; Shortt, 1972: 225-9, Craven and Traves, 1979: 19-20).

The Patrons of Industry, despite its name, was a farmers' organization. At base there was resentment over the maldistribution of wealth. It seemed to the farmer that those who engaged in physical toil, the "producers", earned the least, while those employed in non-physical occupations did not create wealth yet earned the most (Hann, 1975: 12-20). The Patrons favoured low cost government, tariffs for revenue and not industrial protection, and an extension of democratic rights; they opposed railway control of prairie land (Wood, 1975: 114). Although these movements attracted wide support, they could not topple national governments. Sev-

eral decades later, even though farmers had become a minority of the population, agrarian parties scored considerable electoral success by championing these same issues. Why were farmers not politically powerful at the time when they comprised a plurality of Canadians?

Ethno-national division was in large part responsible. Sectional tensions ran high in the early 1890s when the Patrons emerged. The second Riel rebellion and the subsequent hanging of Riel set English against French, and at a temperature rarely seen in Canada.

Tempers flared again in 1888 when Honore Mercier settled the long standing Jesuit claim to estates seized in the Conquest by offering monetary compensation. Most English Canadians were incensed when the Quebec Premier requested that the Pope determine how the compensation should be divided between Jesuits and other Church bodies (Linteau *et al*, 1983: 251) Despite the offer of some compensation to Protestant education, Orange reaction to papal "interference" in Canadian affairs was swift. D'Alton McCarthy, head of the Imperial Federation League and a promising young Conservative, joined with the Grand Master of the Orange Lodge, forming the Equal Rights Association to battle against Catholic Church influence, to end French domination, and to abolish separate schools in Ontario and Manitoba. Despite concerted attempts by its leaders, the Patrons of Industry could not stay out of these conflicts (Watt, 1967).

The populist dream of forming a national party to fight for the rights of farmers was not realized at this time. The Patrons of Industry, like the Dominion Grange before them, did not develop into a pan-Canadian movement. They made little headway amongst French Canadian habitants who instead were joining Church or government-led agricultural associations during that era (Letourneau, 1952: 146-62; Linteau *et al.*, 1983: 421-6). Sectionalism was not conducive to farmers' politics. When ethno-national issues predominate, as they did in the late 19th century, it is difficult to appeal to class unity.[11]

Canadian politics had peculiar features during national unification and early industrialization which allowed anti-democratic ideas to live for an unusually long time in a new settler society, and the largest class, independent farmers, made little political impact during the period when their numbers and economic strength were at a peak. Now we turn to a third related element: the weakness of a popularly-based Canadian nationalism that contrasted for example, with the Australian experience (Younger, 1970: 403-429).

The truth was that Confederation aroused little enthusiasm amongst ordinary Canadians. Robert Haliburton (1869: 1), poet of the Canada First movement who created the myth of "Canada as a northern country inhabited by descendents of northern races", lamented the prosaic manner in which British North America was unified: "Confederation . . . created as little excitement among the masses as they would feel in the organization of a joint stock company." Young intellectuals in both English and French Canada wanted to change this.

Canada First was an Ontario-centred nationalist movement founded in 1868 by young followers of the assassinated D'Arcy McGee. Four years later, the Parti National emerged out of the anti-Confederation Rouges Party in Quebec and embraced the new, enlarged Canada.

Both movements espoused popular-dem-ocratic reforms such as the secret ballot, broadening the franchise, ending patronage and corruption, tariffs to foster industry, and greater independence in setting foreign policy (Berger, 1970: 68-77; Rumilly, 1975: 70-6). Another loose group of nationalists in English Canada, people like Phillips Thompson, A.W. Wright and E.E. Sheppard who were more progressive than Canada First, had connections with the emerging labour movement and, except for the latter, joined in the Patrons crusade (Hann, 1976). However, these nationalist movements did not form a pan-Canadian alliance or develop a popular-democratic version of the National Policy, even along the lines of the European system, basically because of the chasm in ethno-national relations in Canada. Before the Canada Firsters could get very far in creating myths that would provide "some cement more binding than . . . a mere community of profit," they became embroiled in the Metis question in Manitoba (Foster, 1968 [1871]: 29). Would the West become a settlement of "French half-breeds" or an extension of Ontario? Colonel Denison, a leading member of Canada First, advocated an "armed emigration" of Ontarians to the West to stamp a British character on the new region. Canada First rushed to the defence of the "Canadian Party" in the Red River and took up the cause of Thomas Scott, an Orangeman executed by Riel's provisional government. On the other side was the Parti National, which campaigned with some success on the maltreatment of Riel in the 1872 federal election.[12]

The nationalist movements had well-defined views of Canada's identity and could appeal strongly to popular, emotional attachments to their respective sections of the country. Yet these ethno-national and at times racist appeals led only to national conflict, not national unity. A popular, pan-Canadian nationalism based on sentiments and identities seemed impossible. The Canada-wide nationalism that did emerge during these years, John A. Macdonald's National Policy, confined its pitch to such prosaic symbols as the tariff and the promotion of home industry. The opening of the Canadian West was the only element that could excite the imagination. Pan-Canadian nationalism has ever since had this dull quality: an obsessive emphasis on geography or "mappism" (to use Abraham Rotstein's phrase) and economic prosperity.

Canadian Farmers and State Policies

It is commonly thought that Canadian farmers were laissez-faire liberals. If so, greater influence by farmers would have led to a diminished state role during initial industrialization. Since Alexander Gerschenkron showed that laissez-faire policies were inimical to the European system, then agrarian political dominance in Canada would have hurt, not helped, the development of independent, secondary manufacturing in Canada.

The idea of farmer hostility to government intervention is based on several misconceptions. Regarding the tariff, the most controversial issue, farmers often lined up on one side, and the Canadian Manufacturers Association on the other. Farmer support for Alexander Mackenzie's "laissez-faire" government (1873-1878), and opposition to government expenditures for canal and railway projects give the appearance of farmer opposition to state intervention. Reginald Whitaker argued that "toryism", the creed of the dominant capitalists, favoured intervention, whereas the popular liberal-democracy of the petit-bourgeoisie held to the unregulated freedom of enterprise (Whitaker, 1977: 32). The historical evidence does not support these arguments. Canadian farmers favoured intervention, but of a different kind to that supported by commercial and industrial capitalists.

Farmers were ambivalent about tariffs in the 1840 to 1914 period. They tended, as in other countries, to support duties on agricultural imports and oppose tariffs on manufactured goods.

On other forms of intervention, the farmers' position depended on class interest, not ideology. In the 1830s, the agrarian-based Reformers of Upper Canada fought for more competitive banking, while 50 years later the Grangers pushed for state-owned banks. These policies seem contradictory but in each case were attempts to break the commercial banking monopoly which provided inadequate farm credit. Farmers displayed the same flexibility towards intervention in transportation projects, supporting cheap government and opposing many of business' railway projects, yet demanding government-owned railways and more road building (Ouellet, 1980b: 153; Wood, 1975: 104). Farmers did not adhere to laissez-faire in principle. If state intervention was thought of benefit, farmers supported it; if not, they stood in opposition. The same was true of farmers in the USA and Australia in the 1800s (Broude, 1959; Butlin, 1959).

Farmers repeatedly tried to scale down Canada's grandiose railway schemes between the 1850s and the First World War, but without effect. With capitalists firmly in control, the state encouraged the squandering of enormous amounts of capital (Stevens, 1962: 155, 227). Backed by state finance, railway contractors usually adopted expensive British methods of construction rather than the much cheaper American or Swedish ones.[13] This had a different effect in Canada, with its long distances and sparse population, than it had in densely-occupied and capital-rich Britain. As well, railway duplication became endemic and Canada earned the dubious distinction of possessing the most miles of railway per capita in the world.[14]

In consequence, record amounts of British portfolio capital were borrowed, especially on the eve of the First World War. These capital imports fostered the establishment of American branch plants in Canada by rapidly boosting the size of the Canadian market. In a complicated triangular adjustment, Jacob Viner (1975: 288) showed that "the capital borrowed by Canada in Great Britain entered Canada largely in the form of American commodities." Hindered by Canadian tariffs and patent restrictions from exporting to Canada, many large US firms jumped over the border and set up branch plants in Canada (Wilkins, 1969: 78). Once established, American branch plants in Canada stimulated the further importation of manufactured goods from the United States (Viner, 1975: 288). Thus the failure of Canadian farmers to impose their views of cheap government on the state during initial industrialization contributed to Canada's heavy reliance on both foreign portfolio and foreign direct investment.

Finally there was the strategic factor that often leads an economy to find industrial maturity through technological innovation. In contrast to other countries, Canadian farmers were not especially military-minded, a fact explainable in terms of the way the nation state was created. Agrarian-based reform movements did not lead the struggle for Canadian independence. Rather, it was the commercial capitalists of central Canada who led reluctant peoples into Confederation in 1867.

Unpalatable as it may seem, the advent of mass democracy was related to the development of modern armies. Revolutionary France had the first armed people, when the *levée en masse* was raised to defeat the professional armies of emigré nobles who sought to restore the ancien regime. The relation between democracy, popular nationalism, and mass armies was not confined to old world societies however. The historian, William A. Williams, argued persuasively that the driving force behind American expansionsim during most of the 19th century, came from the farming majority who believed that freedom was connected to an expanding frontier (Williams, 1969). If Canadian Confederation had been an agrarian-democratic project, it is likely that Canada would have been more independent from Britain and would have developed larger and more independent forces before the First World War.

By volunteering to be a "Dependency of the Empire", Canada did not develop strong armed forces. The Empire, along with America's Monroe Doctrine, it was thought, would protect Canadian independence.[15] In consequence, Canada did not develop a domestically-owned and innovative engineering industry under the protective care of an independent military policy. Instead Canada relied almost exclusively on foreign technology, and this was a major factor in the emergence of the branch-plant structure.[16]

Conclusion

Despite a good industrial beginning, Canada failed to adopt the European system which led to independent development in other late follower countries (Laxer, 1985a). Instead of pointing a finger at Canadian capitalists for not protecting their own bailiwick, I have indicted the whole of the social formation. For capitalists everywhere, profits come first. What marked Canada off from other advanced countries was that other classes did not gain state power and guard the domestic ground for native capitalists. Foreign ownership and a truncated manufacturing sector were the result.

It has been argued that the Canadian state missed the opportunity of moving to independent industrialization because of the ways class and ethno-nationality intersected.

Inequalitites between the two nations, starting with the Conquest, led to a sectional politics that strengthened big capital and weakened popular-democratic forces. It was a peculiar situation for a new settler society in the democratic age. Popular forces, primarily agrarian, failed to take a leading role in creating the nation state and transforming the economy during the initial phase of the industrial revolution. The usual strategies of late follower countries were not pursued.

Notes

1. There are other explanations. Herbert Marshall *et al.*, *Canadian-American Industry: A Study in International Investment* (Toronto, 1976 [1936]), listed factors leading to the influx of US branch plants. The majority of reasons had to do with markets, but lower wages in Canada, the working clause of the Canadian patent law, and the availability of natural resources in Canada were also listed (pp. 198-217). They missed two major explanations: municipal bonusing of foreign subsidiaries, and export barriers erected to induce the processing of raw materials (Ontario's manufacturing condition). See R.T. Naylor, *The History of Canadian Business 1867-1914. Volumes I and II* (Toronto, 1975) and H.V. Nelles, *The Politics of Development, Forests, Mines and Hydro-electric Power in Ontario 1849-1941* (Toronto, 1974).

2. By 1913, there were 450 US branch plants in Canada, dominating the growth industries of the 20th century: the chemical, electrical, machinery, appliance and auto and related industries. US capital was also prominent in the resource sector with such companies as

INCO, Imperial Oil and International Paper. F.W. Field, *Capital Investments in Canada* (Montreal, 1914), pp. 39-52.

3. This term was first used by Craig Brown (1966).

4. Paul Bairoch (1982) disagrees. His estimates, which he noted in correspondence, are subject to error for the smaller industrial countries, place Canada 20th in 1860 and 13th in 1913 (p. 289). I use the earlier estimates because they coincide with other quantitative and qualitative information about the period. See Laxer, 1985a.

5. The state was interventionist in early American development, a role often overlooked by later ideologues of the laissez-faire persuasion. See W.A. Williams, *The Contours of American History* (Cleveland, 1961), p. 211.

6. "Late follower" countries began industrialization on a wide scale in the 1870s or 1880s and had more than 1.0% of world manufacturing by 1913. The timing of Germany's development fell between that of early follower France and the United States, and that of the

late followers. For a discussion of the timing of initial industrialization in each of the advanced countries, see Gordon Laxer, *The Social Origins of Canada's Branch Plant Economy, 1837 to 1914* (Doctoral dissertation, University of Toronto, 1981). Several countries were excluded from late follower designation. Czechoslovakia was not an independent country until 1918, and there is not adequate data on manufacturing in the Netherlands prior to 1914 to be certain of manufacturing levels. See Maizels, 1963. Although it had barely over 1.0% of world manufacturing in 1913, Australia was excluded because much of its industry entailed processing raw materials before exporting. See Laxer, 1985a.

7. Thomas Crerar, House Leader of the Progressives, urged Canada to develop "the natural resources of the country." Morton, *The Progressive Party in Canada* (Toronto, 1978) p. 116.

8. The Progressives ran 20 candidates in Quebec in the 1921 election, and received 18.5% of the vote in those constituencies. Chief Electoral Officer, *General Election 1921* (Public Archives of Canada, 1977), M-4212.

9. In Ontario, the United Farmers (UFO) won 43 seats to Labour's 12 seats, while in Manitoba the United Farmers (UFM won 28 seats to Labour's 6. Morton, 1978: 85, 228. See Sacouman, 1979, regarding the weakness of popular-democratic movements in the Maritimes then.

10. Literature on early labour and socialist parties is scattered. For a start, consult A. Ross McCormack, *Reformers, Rebels and Revolutionaries: The Western Canadian Radical Movement 1899-1919* (Toronto, 1977), pp. 53-97; Gregory S. Kealey, *Dreaming of What Might Be: The Knights of Labour in Ontario, 1880-1900* (London, 1982), pp. 204-247; and Martin Robin, *Radical Politics and Canadian Labour* (Kingston, 1968).

11. Kealey and Palmer (1982: 381) make a similar point in relation to working class unity in the 1890s.

12. The Parti National's leader, Louis Jette, personally defeated G.E. Cartier on the Riel issue.

13. British railway philosophy, born during a glut of capital, was to build solidly with high original cost and low upkeep in contrast to the American philosophy, born of capital shortage, to build cheaply and make improvements as revenue allowed (G.P. de T. Glazebrook, *A History of Transportation in Canada* Vol. 1 (Toronto, 1964), p. 66. The following railways were built according to the expensive British methods: The Grand Trunk and the Great Western in the 1850s (p. 166), the Intercolonial in the 1870s (Easterbrook and Aitken, *Canadian Economic History*, p. 412) and the National Transcontinental (Glazebrook, 1964, Vol. 2, p. 137). On the other hand, the CPR and Mackenzie and Mann's Great Northern were built according to the American standard (Glazebrook, 1964: 145): Harold Innis, *A History of the Canadian Pacific Railway* (Toronto, 1923), p. 102.

14. In 1914 Canada had 57 km of railway per 10,000 people, compared to 44 km in Australia and Argentina, 41 km in the US and 25 km in Sweden. See Kenneth Buckley, *Capital Formation in Canada* (Toronto, 1974), p. 52, regarding overbuilding Canadian railroads.

15. In 1902, Laurier suggested that the Monroe Doctrine protected Canada and obviated the need for an effective standing army (Stacey, 1940: 68).

16. For the connections amongst defence, foreign ownership and technological dependence see Laxer, (1985b).

14

Dependency, Imperialism and the Capitalist Class*

William K. Carroll

Toward Reconceptualism

Any theory of world economy need have two elements: (1) a model of accumulation, and (2) "a theory of the relevant division of the world for purposes of considering that accumulation as international" (Weeks, 1981: 118). The historical-materialist theory of modern imperialism incorporates a model of accumulation based on the extended reproduction of a capital-labour relation, whose motion is subject to certain objective tendencies. Capitalist accumulation occurs as both an exploitative and a competitive process which compels individual capitalists to concentrate and centralize their capital while they develop the productive forces of society. Capital also expands in a spatial sense, first in the form of trade but later as the export of money capital and productive capital. This formulation then

> converts its theory of accumulation into a theory of the world economy by locating it explicity in the context of *countries*. What makes a political territory a "country" is that the territory is controlled by a distinct ruling class, the vehicle for such rule being the state. Materialists identify their theory of the world economy as "the theory of imperialism," which can be defined as the theory of the accumulation of capital in the context of the struggle among ruling classes (Weeks, 1981: 121).

Apart from the capital-labour relation itself, the dominant focus here is not on bilateral relations between the "core" and "periphery" but on the internationalized process of accumulation and the relations it engenders (a) among capitalist ruling classes (inter-imperialist rivalry/cooperation), (b) between advanced capitalist ruling classes and ruling classes in backward countries (the articulation of modes of production), and (c) between ruling classes and oppressed peoples

*Originally published as "Dependency, Imperialism and the Capitalist Class in Canada," in Robert Brym (ed.), *The Structure of the Canadian Capitalist Class*, Garamond Press, Toronto, 1985. Reprinted with permission of Garamond Press and the author.

(national oppression/liberation; Weeks, 1981: 121-2; cf. Brewer, 1980: 80; Howe and Sica, 1980: 241).

Above all, modern imperialism is the historical culmination of the tendencies of capitalist concentration, centralization and internationalization identified by Marx. The phenomenon arose around the turn of the century as capital in the advanced countries became reorganized in the monopoly form of "finance capital" and exported to the most profitable outlets (Lenin, 1970; Bukharin, 1973; Hilferding, 1981).

Essentially, finance capital integrates the specific forms of capital — industrial, merchant, and loan — into articulated circuits of accumulation (Thompson, 1977; Clairmonte, 1982) controlled by "financial groups" of allied capitalists who own or manage giant firms (Aglietta, 1979: 252-3). Depending on particular historical circumstances, this *coalescence* of capitals is attained and sustained by means of a series of relationships, including the intertwining of share capital through investment banks, holding companies, etc., the institutionalization of long-term credit relations, the interlocking of corporate directorates, and familial ties (Menshikov, 1969: 158-84; Lenin, 1970: 706; Bukharin, 1973: 71-3 Overbeek, 1980: 102-3).

The formal circuit of finance capital also to some extent characterized the competitive capitalism of the 19th century, allowing Marx (1967, Vols. II and III) to dissect and analyze its constituent parts. Under advanced capitalism, however, it is important to note the following points:

(a) Much of the total social capital has been concentrated into a relatively few large units.

(b) Since large scale production requires enormous amounts of financing, the provision and control of financial capital (whether as bank loans, bond purchases or stockholding) take on great strategic importance.

(c) These developments imply that the few capitalists owning large blocks of corporate shares or controlling major financial institutions — typically organized into groups of associated capitalists — comprise the most powerful bourgeois fraction: an elite of finance capitalists.

(d) In the earlier era the process of internationalization occurred within circuits of commercial capital as the export of commodities. Under imperialism these circuits continue to internationalize as trade relations are extended and the world market broadened, but in addition, capital exports occur on a large scale, first as financial capital in the form of loans and stock (portfolio and direct investments), more recently as productive capital (the internationalization of the production process itself; Palloix, 1977; Cypher, 1979a; cf. Bukharin, 1973).

The reasons for this capital export encompass both the opportunities and the exigencies that emerge as capital becomes monopolized. On the one hand, as it develops, finance capital breaks down institutional barriers to international capital mobility. The corporate form of organization and close links between industrial and financial capital allow foreign subsidiaries to be established and financed without the capitalist having to migrate. On the other hand, tariffs erected by other capitalist states discourage the expansion of domestic production for export while encouraging establishment of branch plants behind tariff walls (Hilferding, 1981), a fact of recognized significance in the Canadian case (Naylor, 1975; Clement, 1977). Also, to a considerable extent, monopolized price structures in the domestic economy can only be maintained through reinvestment of profits in nonmonopolized sectors where there is no danger of eroding monopoly positions through overproduction in the home market (Szymanski, 1981: 38; Bukharin, 1973: 122-3). Thus, a portion of the surplus value produced within large domestic enterprises is capitalized elsewhere. The low wages and rent on land in less developed countries and colonies serve as a particularly strong magnet for investment as capital gains the capacity to become fully internationalized (Lenin, 1970: 716; Hilferding, 1981). All these constraints and opportunities give rise to an international network of dependence on and connections of finance capital'' (Lenin, 1970: 715) in which national monopoly fractions jostle for spheres of investments and shares of the world market while they export capitalist relations and forces of production to each other's home markets, and to the developing periphery.

Canadian Imperialism

The theory I have outlined can be used to good advantage on the issue of Canadian capitalism. Development of an indigenous fraction of Canadian finance capital around the turn of the century, and its subsequent expanded reproduction, are well-established historical facts. Leaving aside for the moment the issue of foreign investment in Canada, the period from 1870 to 1910 can be recognized as one of very rapid accumulation of financial and industrial capital, marked in 1881 by the coalescence of the country's largest financial institution — the Bank of Montreal — and its greatest industrial undertaking, the Canadian Pacific Railway (Niosi, 1978: 87). The close financial and directorate relations between these major monopolies were to form an axis for a financial group of corporations and capitalists that may still be fairly described as the bedrock of Canadian finance capital.[1] Following on the heels of this coalescence came a progressive centralization of manufacturing capital, first with the combination movements of the 1800s and 1890s and ultimately in the intense merger movements of 1908 through 1913 (Stapells, 1927; McLennan, 1929; Bliss, 1974). An indigenous financial-industrial elite composed of a few dozen highly interlocked capitalists in control of major banks, railways, steamship lines, manufacturing plants, mining firms, stock brokerages, and insurance companies consolidated in this period (De Grass, 1977: 115-23). Nor did the concrete manifestation of this finance capital remain confined to the Bank of Montreal — CPR interests. In Toronto, concentration of industry and finance gave rise to a financial group around George A. Cox's Canada Life Assurance Co. and the Canadian Bank of Commerce (Drummond, 1962: 211).

By the second decade of this century, an advanced form of indigenously-controlled capitalist production, circulation and finance was in place in Canada. At the apex of this finance capital stood the dominant fraction of the Canadian bourgeoisie, a small elite of monopoly capitalists whose interlocking investments and corporate positions effectively fused big industry with high finance. The subsequent reproduction of this dominant fraction has been abundantly documented in a host of corporate network analyses (e.g., Park and Park, 1973; Piedalue, 1976; Sweeny, 1980; Richardson, 1982; Carroll, 1982, 1984).

But the historical hallmarks of imperialism have been evident not simply in the internal structure of the Canadian bourgeoisie. As it attained monopoly form at the turn of the century, a portion of Canadian capital began to search for profitable outlets on an *international* basis. During the course of its developments international expansion of Canadian finance capital has taken a variety of forms, from the monopolization of banking and insurance in Cuba and of infrastructural industries in several Latin American countries (Park and Park, 1973: 126-8, 136-55; Naylor, 1975: Vol. II 252-64) to the multinational enterprises — and international in-banking consortia — of the post-war era (Neufeld, 1969; Moore and Wells, 1975; Litvak and Maule,1981; Rush, 1983: 282-4).

The theory of imperialism together with the fact of Canadian monopoly capital provide grounds for reconsideration of two issues that bear closely upon Canadian political economy. On the one hand, what dependency theorists mistook to be a universal process of "underdevelopment" in the Third World can be recognized as a *conjunctural* phenomenon in the broader history of imperialism; on the other hand, the *specificity* of Canadian capitalism can be distinguished from the more general features that Canada has actually shared with most other imperialist powers.

Let us consider each of these points in turn. It is generally held that the era of modern imperialism can be periodized into an *early* phase, in which financial capital exported to the periphery spurred the limited production of infrastructure and of raw materials for export to advanced capitalist economies; and a *late* phase which, in the wake of the long crisis of 1914-1945, has brought a broad range of industrial production and a predominance of capitalist production relations to an increasing number of [less developed countries] LDCs (Howe, 1981; cf.

Brewer, 1980; Szymanski, 1981).

In the former period capitalist development of the periphery occurred at a slow pace, due to a conjunction of conditions both internal to peripheral social formations and integral to the imperialist powers' regimes of accumulation.[2] The period since the Second World War,and especially from about 1960, may be characterized as one of unrelenting capitalist internationalization. Having attained political independence, many LDC's have successfully encouraged industrial development through state capitalism, subsidies, tariffs, and international cartels, as industrial capital has flowed from advanced capitalist countries to take advantage of cheaper labour and expanding Third World markets (Cypher, 1979a: 39; Szymanski, 1981). Transnational production, now made feasible by a new wave of technology such as air cargo, containerized shipping, and commercial satellites (Cypher, 1979b: 521) and generating in its turn a supranational banking system, has brought a qualitatively new level of international interdependence, a world economy characterized by global corporations and banks (Hawley, 1979: 80-1).

This post-war movement toward internationalized production carries several important implications for our understanding of Canadian capitalism and the Canadian bourgeoisie. If "underdevelopment" was not primarily a *cumulative* process organically rooted in the metropolis-satellite relation but a *conjunctural* phenomenon in an era of monopolization and capitalist internationalization, it follows that relations between countries cannot be adequately comprehended with the use of its theoretical complement, "dependency." To appreciate the position of Canadian capital within an increasingly *interdependent* imperialist system, we must begin not from an abstracted bilateral relation conceptualized by means of the metropolis-hinterland metaphor, nor even with a single agency, as in the multinational corporation, but from the totality of international capitalism and its dynamic tendencies.

Canada and the Internationalization of Capital

The Tendency Toward Capitalist Cross-Penetration

Initiated by the massive American expansion into Canada and Europe, the post-war internationalization of capital has engendered a multilateral cross-penetration: circuits of national finance capital quite often cross political boundaries, whether as merchant capital (foreign trade), financial capital (loans, interest, dividends) or industrial capital (transnational production). From 1960 to 1972 among member countries of the Organization for Economic Cooperation and Development (OECD), the average annual growth rate of total foreign direct investment was nearly 12% or one-and-a-half times the same countries' average growth in Gross Domestic Product (GDP). At present, about three-quarters of world foreign direct investment is concentrated in the advanced capitalist countries, compared with two-thirds in the 1960s (Portes and Walton, 1981: 142; Marcussen and Torp, 1982: 25).

The result of this interpenetration has been a general tendency toward increased foreign control in the *advanced* economies. In Britain, U.S. subsidiaries' sales alone accounted for 22% of the GDP in 1976, up from 13.5% nine years earlier. In France, more than 50% of sales in the petroleum, agricul-

tural equipment, electronics and chemical industries are presently attributable to foreign-controlled firms. In West Germany, foreign investment predominates over German capital in oil refining, glass, cement and brick production, food, electrical machinery and iron and metals. As in Canada, foreign investment in Europe tends to concentrate in large companies, reflecting its character as internationalized monopoly capital. For example, "among West Germany's 30 largest corporations are nine foreign subsidiaries, including Exxon, GM, Ford, IBM, Texaco, and Mobile Oil" (Syzmanski, 1981: 502). By way of comparison, a recent listing of the largest corporations in Canada also reveals the presence of nine foreign subsidiaries in the top 30, among them GM, Exxon, Ford, and Texaco (*Financial Post 500*, June 1983).

Although the overall levels of foreign, particularly American, investment in Canada are definitely higher than those in other imperialist countries, this example does put what is often depicted as a unique Canadian situation into a proper international perspective. Moreover, since most capital flows have occurred between monopoly capitalist countries it is doubtful that the *importation* of capital — abstracted from the totality of intercapitalist relations — can provide an unambiguous indication of any country's position in the world system. In this respect we can begin to understand the problems in Levitt's (1970: 25) depiction of Canada's post-war importation of U.S. capital as a "regression" to dependence and underdevelopment at the hands of the American transnational corporation.

Forms of Capitalist Internationalization

Analysis of the dynamics of foreign direct investment does not, however, tell the whole

story of post-Second World War accumulation. Studies of world capitalism tend to focus exclusively on transnationals, and this
results in an oversimplified analysis in which
large, international and apparently uncontrollable companies are identified as "the objective enemy of the people" (Barkin,
1981: 159). This motif of "domination by the
multinationals" is a central element in Canadian dependency studies (Panitch, 1981: 9).

However, transnational corporations represent only one form of internationalized finance capital (Nabudere, 1979: 50; Portes
and Walton, 1981: 140), and, depending on
the internal character of the host society,
need not necessarily be the most pernicious.
Levitt (1970) and others have constrasted the
beneficial developmental effects of portfolio
investment with the regressive ramifications
of foreign direct investment, destroying indigenous entrepreneurship, closing off opportunities for accumulation by the national
bourgeoisie, and culminating in the "appro-
priation in perpetuity of the economy's surplus" (Watkins, 1970: xii). To the contrary,
several recent analyses of international capitalism stress the similar effects of *both* these
forms of foreign investment in social formations where capitalist production relations
are, or are becoming, predominant. Direct
and portfolio investment both bring a local
accumulation of capital and return flow of
wealth to the capital-exporting country. Although direct investment implies a form of
multinational control and a flow of repatriated profit, if the investment is to be maintained, a share of the profit must be kept in
the country. In the final analysis, the rate of
reproduction of this capital "depends on
conditions of accumulation in the receiving
country relative to the returns on capital that
might be obtained by redeployment" (Friedman, 1978: 143). Warren has pursued the

larger implications of this rather basic fact of
modern capitalist accumulation:

> To the extent that political independence is real,
> private foreign investment must normally be re-
> garded not as a cause of dependence but rather
> as a means of fortification and diversification of
> the economies of the host countries. It thereby
> reduces "dependence" in the long run (Warren,
> 1981:176).

Warren's point is especially well taken *vis-
à-vis* the Canadian case, where the capacity
has existed not simply to *transpose* foreign
investment into indigenous circuits of accumulation, but more recently to *reclaim* much
of the foreign-controlled capital that contributed to Canada's economic growth during
the post-war boom. On one hand, the existence in Canada of an advanced capitalist
economy with an extensive and integrated
domestic market for both capital and consumer goods has allowed domestic industries to reap multiplier effects as foreign
investments cross the circuits of domestic
capital in associated economic sectors (cf.
Amin, 1974; Palloix, 1975: 76; Williams,
1983: 4). The excellent post-war growth record of the Canadian steel industry, for example, is related in part to the expansion and
emergence of such major steel consumers as
the automobile makers and pipeline companies, just as the full development of an oil
and gas sector has supplied industrial and
residential consumers with an abundant
source of fuel at relatively low prices. Similarly, increases in the size of the work force,
resulting from capital accumulation under
both foreign and domestic control, have increased demand for products such as automobiles and food and beverages (cf. Warren,
1981: 142).

However, as we have seen in recent years
(Niosi, 1981; Carroll, 1982: 106; Resnick,

1982), the advanced form of Canadian capitalism renders foreign direct investment less than permanent. In fact, between 1970 and 1981 foreign control of all capital employed in non-financial Canadian industries fell from 36 to 26 percent (Niosi, 1983: 132). Because they possess the independent financial power that accrues to an advanced economy, capitalists in Canada (as well as crown corporations) have been able to patriate foreign-controlled companies through share purchases, just as they have been able to expand their investments abroad.

It is instructive here to take note of the recent shift in imperialist investments on the periphery, from equity participation (portfolio and direct investment) to the use of loans and credits (Marcussen and Torp, 1982: 26-7). As the global economic crisis had deepened in the past decade, international banking capital, often through such institutions as the IMF, has shifted its emphasis from supplying multinational corporations with working capital to providing enormous amounts of long-term credit to LCDs with balance of payments deficits (Hawley, 1979: 86). Unlike portfolio and direct investment, such internationalized loan capital does not necessarily entail local investment, at least not at a rate adequate for repayment of the principle. Rather, as the historical example of British imperialism in Egypt shows (Luxemburg, 1951: 429-39), "the debt-service implied by massive loans can greatly outweigh the local accumulation of capital" (Friedman, 1978: 142), especially when growth is trade-related and when protectionism is on the rise in the advanced capitalist countries (as in presently the case; Hawley, 1979: 88).

The desperate need for lenders, in order to avoid the dire consequences of national bankruptcy in a growing number of countries has now led to the re-establishment of an extreme form of neocolonialism: institutions such as the International Monetary Fund require Third World governments to submit their economic policies to surveillance by international finance capital (Kolko, 1977: 14-15; Phillips, 1980: Szymanski, 1981: 250-2). The proud participation of Canadian bankers with other monopoly capitalist powers in these relations of imperialist domination is well known.

Inter-Imperialist Relations in the Post-Second World War Era

In sorting out the *specificity* of Canadian capitalism, we should bear in mind the crucial difference between the generally stimulative, relatively atomized, and increasingly cosmopolitan form of foreign investment that predominates in Canada and the wholly parasitic and highly centralized economic relation that has been imposed upon large sectors of the Third World.

To appreciate this difference it is necessary to examine the character of relations not simply between center and periphery, but *among imperialist powers themselves*. In particular, U.S.-Canada ties need to be viewed against the backdrop of American hegemony which provided essential direction in reconstituting world capitalism after the Second World War. In this period, inter-imperialist relations were not marked by the rivalry which had spawned both world wars, but by the hegemony of one power acting to enhance and preserve the unity of the entire capitalist system in the face of internal and external threats.[3]

After the Second World War, the potential for socialist revolutions in Western Europe and in South East Asia gave the United States — which enjoyed enormous financial and technological advantages over its competitors — a compelling interest in reconstructing European capitalism and converting Japan from a defeated nation to a junior partner in containing communism in the East (Nabudere, 1977: 156-8). These objectives were accomplished under the formal aegis of the Bretton Woods Agreement and Marshall Plan (Arrighi, 1978: 96) with the willing consent of the old pre-war bourgeoisies of Europe and Japan, who were for the most part restored to their positions as ruling classes (Dann, 1979: 70).

America's role as a state above states had appeal not merely by virtue of its contribution to the viability of world capitalism as a whole. With the reconstruction of Europe, U.S. capitalists secured an increasing demand for American goods, without which the U.S. economy probably would have stagnated (Marcussen and Torp, 1982: 18). At the same time, through its Open Door strategy, the U.S. effectively dismembered many of the colonial relations that had benefitted its rivals, replacing them by a system of open trade and investment more congenial to American interests. The new regime of post-Second World War imperialism would witness the eclipse of particular "spheres of influence," as formal colonial ties of classical imperialism were replaced by informal multilateral relations with "client states" (Nabudere, 1977: 145-6).

In this period of hegemony, most world capital exports emanated from the booming U.S. economy and were placed internationally on the basis of long-term comparative profits prospects. During the Korean War years, dominated by U.S. fears of a shortage of strategic raw materials, Canada received half of all U.S. foreign direct investment (Levitt, 1970: 163). U.S. capital remained skeptical of the economic and political viability of

European capitalism, and reluctant to expand across the Atlantic, despite the exhortations and incentives of the U.S. government (Tugendhat, 1973: 50). Confirmation of Europe's recovery as a reliable and lucrative locus for U.S. capital came with the creation of the Common Market in 1957. Thereafter, Europe attracted an enormous flow of U.S. direct investment (Nabudere, 1977: 156; Castells, 1980: 105-6).

The legacy of post-war American world hegemony gave rise in the 1970s to serious concern in other imperialist countries about the "American challenge." Ironically, this was coupled with an eroding basis for that concern, as the period of unrivalled American dominance was drawing to a close. Canadian expressions of consternation about "Americanization" (e.g., Levitt, 1970; Lumsden, 1970; Robert Laxer, 1973) need to be viewed, again, against the broader pattern of inter-imperialist relations. In Europe, U.S. direct investments, concentrated especially in basic industries, brought the same sorts of dominance relations in the areas of technology and marketing as have been observed in post-war Canada (Poulantzas, 1974: 162; Dann, 1979: 72; Marcussen and Torp, 1982: 21). The tremendous amount of U.S. direct investment flowing to Europe was perceived by some fractions of European national capital as a definite threat; however, "in the longer perspective this view was probably an exaggeration, and the importance today of U.S. investments is partly that of an external pressure contributing to a fast concentration and centralization process among the national capital groups in Western Europe" (Marcussen and Torp, 1982: 22) — an insight that was not lost on Canada's Royal Commission on Corporate Concentration (Canada, 1978: 408).

The international dominance relations

that grew up under the wing of American hegemony, however, were ultimately to erode the U.S. position in world capitalism by fostering revitalized national economies capable of competing directly with American capital (Camilleri, 1981: 141). The very high wage rates and strong dollar that characterized the American imperial state presented opportunities to the high-skill but low-wage economies of Western Europe and Japan, whose post-war expansion, like Canada's, was built on a massive outflow of exports (Barnet, 1980: 240). These same countries welcomed American direct investment as a means of expanding and strengthening domestic capitalist production (Warren, 1975: 139; cf. Frank, 1979: 121; Castells, 1980: 105-6). Because the European and Japanese economies had relatively little capital tied up in ageing and obsolete equipment, they were able to realize the "merits of borrowing" while the financially and technologically stronger U.S. paid the "penalty of taking the lead." U.S. companies often found it more costly to introduce technology, since they had to take into consideration the book value of existing fixed capital (Cypher, 1979b: 521). Moreover, as the leading economy, the U.S. bore much of the costs of *developing* new technology, which could then be incorporated into the productive structures of competing economies, allowing them to grow more rapidly (Szymanski, 1981: 517; cf. Warren, 1980: 180; Niosi, 1983: 132).

The ironic effects of international accumulation under the hegemony of American imperialism became visible in the 1970s, in two respects. First, parts of the formal structure of *Pax Americana* — such as the dollar standard — were jettisoned (Arrighi, 1978: 102-3) as the competitive position of American capital visibly deteriorated. The de-

cline of the United States from unrivalled dominance is evident across a range of indicators, from per capita wealth (Szymanski, 1981: 495) and the shrinking U.S. share of the world market in such industrial goods as steel and machine tools (Barnet, 1980: 273-5) to the decreasing number of the world's largest firms based in the U.S. (Frank, 1979, Szymanski, 1981: 496; Droucopoulos, 1981) and the declining U.S. Share in the world capital exports (Nabudere, 1977: 203; Szymanski, 1981: 504).

Secondly, as a regime of multilateral capitalist internationalization emerged, several of the socio-economic problems interpreted by dependency theory as consequences of foreign direct investment actually came to characterize the American metropole, only to spread to other advanced economies as the crisis of the 1970s and 1980s deepened. Massive capital exports from the U.S. led to a relative *stagnation* of internal production, as the foreign operations of U.S. based multinational corporations (MNC's) effectively competed with domestic American establishments (Baran and Sweezy, 1966: 23; Friedman, 1978: 134; 138-9; Castells, 1980: 109; Portes and Walton, 1981: 146). Developments such as deindustrialization in the American northeast have, ironically, been linked by Portes and Walton (1981: 154-61) in the American case to U.S. direct investment *abroad* (cf. Barnet, 1980: 275; Seidman and O'Keefe, 1980; Bluestone and Harrison, 1982). Similarly on the matter of foreign trade, Barnet and Muller (1974: 217) had described the "Latin-Americanization of the United States," as the American economy "becomes increasingly dependent on the export of agricultural products and timber to maintain its balance of payments and increasingly dependent on imports of finished goods to maintain its standard of living".

The story, of course, does not end with an American "regression to dependence," recalling Levitt's description of post-war Canada. With a devalued dollar, rising costs of production in Europe, and an ineffectual trade union movement at home, U.S. exports have recently become more competitive in world markets, and U.S. as well as foreign capital has been returning to the American economy (Barnet, 1980: 275; Portes and Walton 1981: 184) As a consequence of investment flow to the U.S., the pattern of unilateral American investments in Canada, Western Europe and Japan is in the process of being superseded by a tendency toward *cross-penetration* of capital. Again, the recent Canadian experience simply reflects this broader trend; whereas in 1970 there were $6.6 of U.S. foreign direct investment in Canada for $1 of Canadian direct investment in the U.S., by 1979 the ratio was 3.5 to 1 (Niosi, 1983: 133).

The International Formation of the Bourgeoisie

Capitalist internationalization has also had an impact on the formation of the bourgeoisie. With growth of an international capital market and cross-penetration of investments, and with development of supracapitalist institutions such as the World Bank, the IMF, and the Trilateral Commission, the "contours of an international capitalist class are emerging" (Portes and Walton, 1981: 174; Frieden, 1977: Goldfrank, 1977, Sklar, 1980), a fraction of internationalized finance capital conscious of the manner in which transnational capitalist production divides labour against itself while enabling the freest flow of capital (Hymer, 1972: 99-103; De Cormis, 1983).

This nascent class formation is evident in the international network of corporate interlocks studies by Fennema and De Jong (1978; summarized in Fennema and Schijf, 1979: 319-20). These researchers investigated interlocking directorates among 176 large corporations from twelve countries — including Canada — and found one large connected network of European and North American companies and a smaller network of Japanese corporations, detached from the first. The existence of an international network of the largest companies in Europe and North America puts into a broader perspective Clement's notions of a Canadian economic elite that is "distorted" by the presence of foreign-affiliated compradors (Clement, 1977: 117), and a "continental elite" that expresses the symbiotic but ultimately dependent ties of Canadian capitalists to the American metropole (Clement, 1977: 179-80). Canada's bourgeois formation certainly appears distorted in comparison with an autarkic ideal type in which "the economic elite would be contained within a national economy and controlled by citizens and residents of the nation" (Clement, 1977. 123). But relative to other capitalist classes that are being similarly restructured by the process of internationalization, the "comprador" elements within the bourgeoisie in Canada are not particularly exceptional, especially since they tend to occupy relatively peripheral positions in the structure of Canadian corporate power (Carroll, Fox and Ornstein, 1981, 1982; Carroll, 1982, 1984). By the same token, while there is no doubt that a "continental elite" of leading Canadian and American capitalists exists, it can perhaps be most fruitfully viewed as a segment of a larger, international network that has developed with capitalist cross-penetration in the post-Second World War era.

The Legacy of Capitalist Internationalization

Lastly, the internationalized capitalism that has matured in the period since the Second World War has brought important changes to the manner in which capital accumulates within national boundaries. The upshot of a transnational network of capitalists and their finance capital is that ". . . increasingly the dynamics of the world capitalist economy cannot be understood with reference to a single nation or group of nations. Productive decisions are now made on a global scale" (Barkin, 1981: 156).

With the development of internationalized monopoly capital an increasing disjuncture appears between the big bourgeoisie's accumulation base and the state's national boundaries, making it hazardous at best to assign "nationalities" to financial groups. According to Friedman, "it is just as serious an error to reduce international capital to its place of origin as to assume that all capital belongs to the place where it is employed" (Friedman, 1978: 141). As Rowthorn's (1975) discussion of post-war British capital illustrates, there is no simple relation between the strength of a "national fraction" of monopoly capital and the vitality of a national economy or the "independence" of a national state. Indeed, in Rowthorn's view it was the very international *strength* of British big capital in the post-Second World War era that led to a *weakening* of the domestic economy and state: ". . . as the British economy became more integrated into a global capitalism over which the British state had no control, it became increasingly vulnerable internationally and the potential benefits to big capital of a straightforwardly aggressive nationalism development have dwindled accordingly" (Rowthorn, 1975: 174-5).

Rowthorn's analysis of the "denationalization" of British monopoly capital and its contribution to that country's industrial decline, together with the example of diminishing American hegemony, provides an important lesson in the dynamics of capitalism and nation-states in the present era. Simply put, all transnational enterprises, irrespective of their "nationality", have the flexibility to play one set of workers off against another. On these grounds, given the strength of Canada's "own" multinationals, it is very misleading to attribute the problems that beset Canadian workers to the dominance of "foreign" capital. By reconceptualizing Canada as an imperialist power in an era of internationalized capitalism we can avoid the error, common in Canadian dependency analyses, of imputing to capitalists a voluntaristic capacity to do business on the basis of such patently noncapitalist considerations as patriotism. Ideological chimeras aside, the accumulation process is in fact highly constrained by competitive struggles around class-structured prospects for producing, appropriating and realizing surplus value at a given time and place (Walker, 1978: 30; Brewer, 1980: 276). Indeed, to the extent that imperialism has integrated the entire non-socialist world around capitalist relations of production and exchange, the logic of allocative decisions is now global even when transnational capital is not involved in a given activity (Barkin, 1981: 158).

The ultimate implication of capital's internationalization is a strong tendency for the law of value to operate more directly than ever on a world scale, producing in the present moment uneven patterns of economic fragmentation, truncation, and state-imposed "austerity" in imperialist countries such as Canada, the United States and Britain as well as in the Third World, as the international division of labour is violently restructured under the weight of global crisis (cf. Kolko, 1977: 20-1; Walker, 1978: 32, Portes and Walton, 1981: 16). In these circumstances, criticizing foreign firms for "disregarding the needs of the national economy," or blaming indigenous capitalists for "selling out the country" and "stultifying industrial development," "or lamenting the "relative dependence" of the state on foreign capital only obscure the structural bases of contemporary capitalism in Canada behind an exaggerated concern with the peculiarities of Canadian "dependency."

There is of course a pressing need to grasp the *specificity* of Canadian capitalism. The great contribution of the Canadian dependency school has been to direct critical attention to that specificity and, in the process, to create the space for a resurgence of radical scholarship that has had some success opposing the received ideology of liberal continentalism. But although the dependency approach has placed the issue of specificity on the agenda of Canadian scholarship it seems that the very problematic of dependency has tended to hamper understanding in at least two ways. There has been a certain "insularity of focus" (Panitch, 1981: 28) on imputed political and economic effects of Canada's particular relationship with the United States. This has obscured the fact that many "symptoms" of Canadian dependency are, as we have seen, consequences of the internationalization of capital in the post-Second World War period, evident in all or most advanced capitalist societies. Related to this first problem has been a tendency to impose *qualitative* distinctions between Canadian capitalism and other advanced capitalist economies, where differences are perhaps better viewed as matters of degree.

A concept that holds promise as a means of capturing the specificity of various capitalist societies, whilst avoiding the problems outlined above, is that of the *regime of accumulation*: the manner in which labour power and means of production have been concretely configured into a functioning social economy (cf. Aglietta, 1979; Therborn, 1983: 42). As I shall now seek to establish, the strong presence in Canada of U.S. monopoly capital, especially since the Second World War, furnishes a good example of how a feature of Canadian capitalism previously explained in terms of the peculiarly dependent logic of Canadian development can be fruitfully analyzed by considering Canada's specific regime of capitalist accumulation.

Canada's Regime of Accumulation and U.S. Direct Investment

The issue of U.S. direct investment in Canada ultimately turns on the way in which capital became monopolized and internationalized in the early phase of modern imperialism. It is crucial to note in this connection that the difference between Canada and Europe is essentially one of the *timing* of American capital exports to particular countries. As Schmidt (1981: 92) points out and we have seen above, Canada simply presents the first case of a more general phenomenon in the internationalization of capital. Nevertheless, in Canada the extent of U.S. control in sectors such as automobiles, petroleum, and electrical equipment has been especially great.

The question is: What class-structured conditions made these investments more attractive to American capitalists than possible investments elsewhere, while limiting the extent to which Canadian capitalists could directly compete in the same industries? These conditions can perhaps be best comprehended as a conjuncture of interrelated features, several of which have been recognized by Canadian dependency writers. In the early decades of the 20th century, for instance, surplus American capital was attracted both because of Canada's proximity — in light of the technical limits on intercontinental enterprise (cf. Clement, 1977: 6) — and because of the protected and expanding market that Canada provided as a high-growth capitalist economy in its own right *and* as a member of the British Commonwealth (cf. Drache, 1970; Clement, 1977; Williams, 1983). By the same token, for a number of reasons which Panitch (1981) has incisively analyzed, Canada's working class developed in the late 19th century as a relatively high-wage proletariat, placing constraints on the extent to which Canadian capitalists could compete with the large and technologically advanced U.S. firms that concentrated their Canadian investments in what were to become the growth industries of the second industrial revolution (McNally, 1981: 55; cf. Clement, 1977: 59; Hutcheson, 1978: 95).[4]

In conjunction with this first constraint on indigenous capitalists was the tying up of enormous amounts of finance capital in the construction and operation of a domestic transport industry. Again, the differences between Canada and other capitalist countries in this regard should not be overdrawn. In general, the development of railways has been a fundamental aspect of capitalist industrialization (Singelmann, 1978: 17), a fact well documented in the Canadian case by Pentland (1981: 145-8; cf. Palmer, 1983: 60-2). The importance of the transportation industry to modern regimes of accumulation has been explained by Richard Walker (1978: 31):

A general aim of capital is to lower its time of circulation, i.e., the speed of self-expansion of capital. Geographic movement of capital is one aspect of the circulation problem as a whole, the most specifically *geographic* problem for capital is in overcoming the barriers which (absolute) space presents, and the primary way capital overcomes this barrier is by what Marx called "the annihilation of space by time" — i.e., speeding up physical movement, especially through the development of transportation and communication systems.

In Canada the vast expanse of space to be annihilated, relative to the size of the home market, necessarily entailed a proportionately very large outlay of capital to the transportation sector, leaving a relative scarcity of indigenous finance capital for the rising industries in which American capital came to predominate. Thus, by 1923, 60% of the total assets of the 100 largest non-financial corporations — and nearly 40% of all industrial and merchant capital in Canada — was claimed by just two indigenous enterprises — the CPR and CNR (Canada, 1937: 21-2, 330). In the meantime, subsidiaries of U.S. corporations had become well entrenched in several expansive branches of Canadian manufacturing.[5]

In short, a regime of monopoly capitalism emerged in Canada at the turn of the century on the *dual* premises of (a) international concentration and centralization (U.S. direct investment) and (b) domestic monopolization (formation of indigenous financial groups such as the CPR — Bank of Montreal interests). The post-Second World War period of American economic and political hegemony in the capitalist world culminated in the late 1950s in the enlarged presence of U.S.-controlled monopoly capital in Canada, together with an intermingling of powerful U.S. financial groups with Canadian finance capital (Park and Park, 1973: 15).

These facts have been interpreted by Levitt and others as symptoms of a cumulative regression to dependence, but a more meaningful issue to explore in light of post-Second World War developments in the imperialist system is the *rate* at which the accumulation base of the Canadian bourgeoisie has been internationalizing, compared with the rate at which other imperialist class fractions have been expanding their circuits of accumulation within Canada. The three decades seem to divide evenly into two periods. Between 1946 and 1961 — the era of unrivalled American international hegemony — foreign direct investment grew at a rate faster than that of Canadian direct investment abroad. In the 1960s, and especially the 1970s, however, the opposite pattern came to prevail. From 1950 to 1965, U.S.-controlled capital in Canada accumulated more rapidly than Canadian-controlled capital in the U.S., but by the mid-1970s Canadian capitalists were augmenting their U.S. investments at a rate more than twice that of U.S. direct investment in Canada. Moreover, since 1966 there has been a clear tendency for Canadian capital to internationalize beyond the economies of the United States and the British Commonwealth.

On balance, Canada seems to present the example of a middle-range imperialist power in an era of thoroughly internationalized monopoly capitalism. The post-Second World War pattern of accumulation makes it clear that a focus on Canadian dependency ascribes increasing significance to a phenomenon that has been in decline. This decline is both *relative* to other advanced capitalist economies, as monopoly capital has further internationalized, and *absolute*, as the proportion of Canadian industrial capital under U.S. control has dropped while indigenous capital exports have continued to expand. The resilience and recent consolidation of Canadian finance capital is further underscored by findings from studies of corporate interlocking that the network of large Canadian companies is increasingly focused around predominantly indigenous interests (Carroll, Fox, and Ornstein, 1981; Carrol, 1982, 1984).

This is not to deny that Canadian finance capital, along with other imperialist fractions is beholden to the American military machine in order to protect its substantial investments in the Third World and keep the Soviet Union in check. These same capitalist fractions also yearn to share in the stimulative benefits of the current U.S. economic recovery, even as they resent the American attempt to recover lost economic space by projecting its political power (Petras and Morley, 1982: 6, 30-1). Canadian monopoly capital, while presently more *independent* of singularly American interests than it has been in several decades, is deeply involved in a complex structure of international politico-economic relations in which the largest imperialist power necessarily plays a focal role.

Notes

1. (cf. Ashley, 1957; Johnson, 1972; Chodos, 1973; Park and Park, 1973: 104-7). It is worth pointing out that this initial fusing of financial capital with industrial capital invested in means of transportation was by no means a phenomenon unique to Canada, but reflected the enormous financing requirements of railways everywhere. See, for example, David Kotz's (1978) account of the similar course followed by finance capital in the United States.

2. Discussion of these conditions is well beyond the scope of this paper, but can be found in Kay (1975). Brenner (1977), Phillips (1977), Cypher (1979a) and Szymanski (1981).

3. Camilleri, 1981: 141; cf. Arrighi, 1978: 96-103; Cardoso and Faletto, 1979: 182; Castells, 1980: 104-9; Szymanski, 1981: 492.

4. Panitch's account has recently been challenged by Drache (1983), who notes that from 1870 through 1930 American wage rates were consistently higher than Canadian wage rates. This observation, however, has no relevance to Panitch's central claim that the Canadian working class developed as a high wage proletariat "not only relative to the Third World but relative to the capitalisms of Europe" (1981: 16). More fundamentally, Drache grievously misrepresents the thrust of Panitch's argument, which is not that "the relatively high wage levels of the Canadian working class at the end of the 19th century retarded the rate of capital accumulation" (Drache, 1983: 27), but that "industrial production in Canada had to expand on the basis of *relative* surplus value, the application of extensive fixed capital to the production process to expand labour productivity" (Panitch, 1981: 19) — an undertaking for which large American corporations were favoured.

5. We ought not to push this account beyond its limited purpose in explaining the relatively large share of U.S. Direct investment in certain Canadian industries. One legacy of the very extensive involvement of Canadian capitalists in the manufacturing sector from Canada's industrial revolution on (Phillips, 1979: 11) is the list of Canadian MNCs engaged principally in manufacturing: Seagrams, Northern Telecom, Massey-Ferguson, Moore Corporation, Bata Shoe Company, Canada Packers, etc. (Moore and Wells, 1975: 79-90; Litvak and Maule, 1981).

SECTION V

A Fragile Federation

Sociologists Lorna Marsden and Edward Harvey (1979: xiii) begin their book on social change in Canada, *Fragile Federation*, with a quotation from Mordecai Richler:

> Canada is a fragile, loosely knit confederation comprised of the Yukon, the Northwest Territories, and ten squabbling provinces, their interests and loyalties, largely regional, conflicting more often than not.

This image of Canada as **a fragile federation** reminds us how strong and important regional, provincial and local communities are in Canada. Just as Richler suggests, many (most?) Canadians are more influenced by, and feel more attachment to, the regions in which they live, than to the nation as a whole. For this reason, the Canadian nation is always at risk of flying apart into separate, independent and inward-looking sub-societies.

What is the reason for this fragility, and what are the roots of Canada's disunity? Scholars have put forward many explanations, some of which are discussed in other sections. There is, first, the problem of two solitudes. Colonial competition, war, and Lord Durham's compromise solution gave rise to the British North America Act, which wrote biculturalism and bilingualism into law. All our major institutions are built on this major bicultural fault line. Other fracturing results directly therefrom, chiefly the ideology of multiculturalism and the vertical mosaic.

Canada's geography and terrain have also made the nation more fragile. Until very recently, travel and communication across Canada have been difficult and costly. Population is sparse, distances great. Ecosystems and ecological concerns differ greatly across regions; so do climates, flora and fauna, and ways of making a living. To bridge so many different kinds of land and living arrangements, and to travel and communicate across this sparse, often unforgiving terrain, have required enormous planning and capital. The number of dollars needed *per capita* has made state intervention, hence state control, inevitable. For this reason, Canada — unlike the United States — has had to develop from the centre, under central control. A highly centralized system is more rigid than a decentralized one, other things being equal. Such rigidity also means greater fragility.

A foreign demand for staples has historically driven Canada's economy. This kind of economy is highly vulnerable to fluctuations that Canadians are unable to control. Today other nations may want Canadian furs (or fish, or wheat, or gold, or oil), tomorrow they may not. As the demand for a staple soars, employment levels and wage levels rise. Everyone is better off. New communities are built; immigrants arrive to do new jobs. But as the demand falls, often suddenly and without warning, wages fall, people are laid off, immigration is reduced to a trickle, and communities shut down. Canada's economic system is tremendously fragile.

This image or metaphor portrays Canada as characterized by (1) a weak central government and strong regional governments; (2) a somewhat passive citizenry; and (3) elites who tie the nation together at the top. According to this image, regionalism is strong because nationalism is weak; economic development is regional, not national; and geography conspires against national unity. In this context, elite individuals play an extremely important role. In particular, they channel communication and organize compromise among the society's competing fragments. They must play this role because ordinary people cannot and do not. Ordinary people lack the knowledge and power to run Canadian society. Some observers believe the explanation is psychological or cultural. According to Margaret Atwood (1972), Canadians see (and portray) themselves as the victims of impersonal forces; they have a victim mentality. Or, they are too ready to defer to authority, too traditional and elitist to challenge the ruling elites for control (see the excerpt by S.M. Lipset in Section II; also, Friedenberg, 1980).

This functionalist image of Canada (see, for example, Durkheim, 1964 [1985]; Giddens, 1978) sees people as objects or commodities, pushed around by natural and human laws. Behaviours are mere social facts. This outlook fails to see people as conscious and aware, acting effectively in their own interest. Or, at best, it sees them as easily duped by a need to conform to social expectations. Equally, it sees elites as acting in the social interest, not in their own self-interest. What would result if we were to stand this functionalist model on its head? What if Canada were not fragile, or the fragility had a completely different origin?

By such a reverse reasoning, elites are seen as the cause of Canada's fragility, not its cure (Bodemann, 1984). Coming chiefly from upper class origins, Canadian elites have historically taken advantage of economic opportunities to further their own interests. They have prevented economic development from benefiting more Canadians; and they have obstructed better planning and more democratic decision-making. Ordinary Canadians have struggled, usually in vain, to get the information and power they need to control their own lives. But links with British and American upper classes have helped the Canadian elite keep power in their own hands (Clement, 1977).

Not all protest against the ruling class has been in vain, however. Protestors' actions have won important rights and freedoms. Thus, protest is not proof of Canadian society's fragility, much less the cause of such fragility. On the contrary, conflict and protest show the strength of Canada's social fabric. In the face of great odds — geographic, economic, and political — ordinary Canadians again and again claim their right to exercise control.

Depending on where you stand, Canada's federation is fragile and elites hold it together; or it is strong, but a self-interested upper class injures it time and again. According to the first image, regionalism is Canada's chief social, economic and cultural fact of life. According to the reverse image, a semi-feudal competition between local elites produces this thing we call regionalism. Regional loyalty and inter-regional conflict exist because elites want them to.

Michael Bodemann (1986) sees the first image emerging clearly in the writings of S.D. Clark, whose work we have examined in earlier sections. Clark's line of thinking continues in the excerpt by Lorna Marsden in this section. Professor Marsden ends her analysis by denying that class conflict brings about social change in Canada. Instead she argues that a theory of social change must focus on "leaders of Canadian society (who) make their decisions to bring about or oppose change mainly in terms of regional, economic or cultural interests." These national leaders tie Canada, on the one hand, to the core countries that influence us most economically, politically and culturally; and on the other hand, to regional elites who represent narrow economic, cultural (ethnic and language) and political interests. National elites, then, try to make up for the fragility that narrow or selfish regional interests bring into being.

Patricia Marchak gives the alternative point of view in her article in this Section. Unlike Marsden, she does not see Canada as fragile simply because geographic, linguistic and ethnic isolation produce wide regional variations. Neither do economic relations that favour one part of the country (central Canada) over the rest necessarily cause fragility. Nor, finally, does Marchak see elites as the do-gooders in Canadian history. Despite the divisive role that Canada's economic elites have played, and the enormous effect of foreign-owned multinational organizations, Marchak is interested to note the growth of nationalist sentiment. Where, she asks, has this sentiment come from; what has produced it? Marchak answers that ordinary skilled and white collar Canadian workers have become more nationalistic as they have found out that Canadian control over large organizations, whether public or private, best serves their interests.

Ralph Matthews takes the middle ground, seeing regionalism both as cause and effect. Like Clark, Matthews can see regionalism arising out of concrete historical, geographic, economic and political circumstances. As such, regionalism proves something about Canadian society: at the very least, that Canada is far from homogeneous. Social differences and inequalities lead to competition, struggle, protest: in a word, fragility. But like Bodemann and Marchak, Matthews can also see individual Canadians as effective actors in a play they have written. Thus, regionalism is also a state of mind, a source of values, meaning, and motivation. Better this regionalism, this differentiation and competition, than faceless, detached uniformity, he would say.

The subjective assessment of regional differences may be far different from the objective assessment by outsiders. People learn, add to and cherish the regional culture simply living their ordinary lives in a particular time and place. Elites are quite unimportant from this standpoint. The Canadian nation is no more or less than the flexible federation of many strong identities. Such flexibility may even provide a strong basis for Canadian nationhood, and prove not to be fragile at all.

What evidence would help us decide which image — the fragile federation image or its reverse — better explains Canadian society past, present or future? This question is hard to answer because agreeing on the terms of reference is difficult. Even if we can agree that the survival of Canada as an independent nation-state is our goal, people will disagree about the role of central elites, and whether they have played a beneficial (functional) role or a harmful one. This is the very disagreement we see between Marsden and Marchak.

We might take as our criterion Canada's survival as an autonomous culture. But if so, Matthews would probably say that no such culture has ever existed: Canada is a federation of regional cultures, and a strong one, but not a unified, single culture. Where cultural unity is concerned, central elites have done as much harm as good. Elites are not the key factor, for a culture persists at the grass-roots or not at all.

The question is vague and the evidence is complex, so it is hard to draw a final conclusion about which way the evidence points. Canada seems much less fragile today than it did in the 1970s when the economy was slumping, Quebec nationalists threatened to take the province out of confederation, and foreign multinationals controlled much more of the Canadian economy than they do today. At the same time, Canadians may also have become more at home with Canada's fragility, or persuaded of Canada's real strength. The latter view is the burden of Richard Gwyn's book, *The 49th Paradox* (1984). Gwyn argues Canadians need not fear for their society and culture; both are strong enough that nothing — not even free trade with the United States — can destroy them.

Different positions on the fragility issue imply different social and political policies. If we think Canada really is a fragile federation, the Meech Lake Accord and free trade with the United States make no sense whatever: they will destroy what little is left of Canada's unity and autonomy. We all have the rare opportunity to see a sociological theory tested within our lifetimes.

15

Social Change and Canada's Regional Federation

Lorna Marsden

Economic and Population Parameters

Any type of social change — from a planned change such as the building of a new airport outside Toronto to the formation of an entirely new set of social and economic relationships between one province and the rest of the federation — is the product of decisions taken by some that mobilize resources and arouse countervailing actions in others. The ways in which this happens are patterned or institutionalized. How can that pattern be identified? First, in order to understand why a situation becomes ripe for change, the forms of economic development need to be understood. H.A. Innis made a most powerful contribution to the study of Canada when he talked of "cyclonic development" to describe the movement into an area of powerful technologies, often backed by foreign capital, to exploit a primary resource. These technologies bring workers, goods and a demand for services, and a partnership between the interests backing the

development and those controlling the society, thus achieving a meeting of political and economic leaders in a set of common interests (Marsden and Harvey, 1979). This pattern of economic development has had certain long-term effects on Canadian society and the way in which our social institutions work. In brief, these long-lasting effects are: a bias in favour of large-scale production of primary commodities that is capital intensive, rather than labour-intensive, and geared to the demands of mass production technology; the centralization of power and authority at the federal level as the political and economic elites move to protect the investments and stability of the developing communities; and the pattern of the use of foreign capital and technology to develop resources on a large scale, with a concomitant reliance on foreign markets and the tax benefits accruing to governments from resource development.

The historical economic development of Canadian society is one of the parameters which must be considered in studying social change because it leads to an understanding of the various economic and political interests that are at work in our society. But another rather different parameter which is often overlooked must also be considered and that is the study of the growth, relative size and characteristics of the Canadian population. In using any theory of social change to explain change in Canada, one must consider the relative size of any sector of the population in proportion to that of other societies. To illustrate this, one might consider the relative size of the scientific community in Canada, not only to look at problems of scale of markets. scale of investments and the numbers of available workers, but also at their distribution. The foreign dominance of industry might be the explanation for Canadian research and development's being conducted outside the country, but would it be possible to do that research and development within Canada? We find, for example, that a higher proportion of Americans than Canadians have post-secondary education, and, more specifically, the United States has a higher proportion of engineers than Canada (Marsden and Harvey, 1979: 121-122). It would be a long jump indeed to conclude from this that certain types of changes would or would not occur in Canada. The point is simply that, in the face of some popular assumptions about similarities between the two countries, it is important to look at the characteristics of the population, or the work force, as in this case, and the relative dis-tribution of people in the societies being compared.

A second aspect of the population issue to be considered when studying social change is ethnic pluralism. As a result of the demand for labour in Canada, it has been a political necessity (made into a political virtue and ideology) to ensure that ethnic rights will be respected — the ethnic mosaic as opposed to the American melting pot approach. It is not asserted here that there is a mosaic or a melting pot, but rather that in explaining the processes of social change the ideological necessity to encourage structural but not behavioural assimilation has certain pressures attached to it.

Finally, one must look at the distribution of people not only between urban and rural areas but across the country. For example, in trying to analyse the resurgence of nationalism in Quebec, it is instructive to look at the dramatic drop in the birth rate in Quebec since 1958, the intensive urbanization within that province, and the assertion of control over immigration by the government of Quebec.

Canada in Relation to The U.S.A.

One might argue, and with cause, that every society has an economic history and a population history and that these, therefore, cannot be new or useful ideas. They are, however, necessary ingredients in any attempt to explain our society. What makes Canada significantly different from other societies examined by modernization theorists or neo-Marxists is the extent of the foreign domination of its economy, or its relative situation in the world system.

We have drawn heavily upon the work of Daniel Chirot (1977) in discussing this feature of the study of social change in Canada, because Chirot stresses the importance not only of patterns of investment and the penetration of ruling elites in societies like ours, but also the importance of the importation of values and ideas in institutionalized forms from core societies. Chirot's thesis is that while the twentieth century began with several dominant economies (those of Britain, the United States, Germany and France), as the century went on the United States became the dominant economy in the capitalist world system. A rival system of communist development also grew and was dominated by the USSR. We will not explore his evidence here but concentrate on the place of Canadian society in this world system. His argument is that core societies are both economically and culturally dominant; that is, that capital investment and control of technology lead to the export of economic goods and ideas and of social ideas. He argues that "world science and technology, as well as methods and theories of social, political and economic organization, have been dominated by the core societies. This is in keeping with their expected role, for, by definition, a core society causes other societies to change (whether by force or example). Core cultures are dynamic, and they originate ideas that others adopt or try to adapt to their local conditions" (Chirot, 1977: 40).

As the century has progressed, Canada has been increasingly dominated both culturally and economically by the United States. Chirot argues that the stratification system of a society is affected by its relationship to the core society. In a totally peripheral society, for example, an international elite may run the modern sector while the majority of the population carries on in relatively traditional and insular ways. In a semi-peripheral society like Canada, however, the relationship is both more widespread and more subtle.

Everyone in our society is aware of Canada's relationship to the United States. As a consequence, the political and economic elites must operate to maintain the good will and investment of the core economy and to satisfy the demands of their own clientele.

How do entrepreneurs in Canada maintain a position of power in Canada? — by introducing innovations, maintaining profits and creating stability in their businesses, and that means in their labour forces. This is also true of the political elites on the national level. So, being a member of the elite in a semi-peripheral society requires a good working relationship with similar elites in the core economy. Elites in Canada articulate the model of development of their core society for their own constituency of Canadians. They also articulate, in a negative critique, the rival models of development. All this is part of their attempt to maintain their own elite position with Canadians and their relative position of power in the Canadian elite hierarchy (Campbell and Szablowski, 1979). But Chirot's thesis goes beyond this linkage of the core. He argues that it is in the interests of the core economies to keep semi-peripheral societies open to their influence both in terms of economic interests and cultural interests. As part of this, the elite in core economies may engender regional or cultural rivalries within semi-peripheral societies in order to protect their domination. He says, ". . . the cultural diversity in many new semi-peripheral societies means that substantial portions of the population still do not accept the legitimacy of the state. This not only opens states to meddling in their affairs from the outside, it makes their very survival problematic" (Chirot, 1977: 223).

Having examined Chirot's thesis on the basis of the available Canadian evidence, we argue that Canada remains semi-peripheral and it is this that accounts in part for the contemporary struggle within Canada over provincial rights and interests. This struggle is a major force of social change in economic relations, in political institutions and in social relationships.

What makes social change happen? Social changes occur when people take decisions which result in the restructuring of social relationships, such as when a new factory is built or a community is zoned differently; when groups of workers decide to move to jobs outside their own economic region; when a network of people decide that a proposed change in social legislation or in community planning is against their interests and form together to oppose it. Social changes can occur suddenly as in a revolution, or slowly as in the cumulated patterns of family life that have resulted in the legitimation of divorce, two-job families and child-care centres. While there are many varieties of patterns of social change, what we are attempting to delineate are the major influences on the ways in which people make decisions to take action. Most of the people who take action for or against change are leaders in the community, region or economic sector. The majority of us accept decisions for change from those in positions of authority. Always, however, there are ordinary citizens who join together to press for changes or to oppose them. Our approach is not to examine the precipitating factors to action, nor the way in which people explain their own decisions, but to look for what we call dynamic forces or major interests which appear to mobilize Canadians in the direction of change.

Actors in Social Change

As for the actors in this process of change, the people through whom the major sets of interests or dynamic forces operate, it can be argued that two types predominate. First, the elites and the upper class of Canadians are responsible for most planned change. While we argue for the existence of an upper class ("those who work for the state in both political and bureaucratic wings, as well as in the capitalist class" (Marsden and Harvey, 1979: 135)), elites take precedence in the study of social change. Porter, describing elites and their internal dynamics, says "It is elites who have the capacity to introduce change, but changes bring about shifts in the relations between elites" (Porter, 1965: 27). Elites in any sector are the decision-makers whose actions lead to economic and social change and who respond to other sources of social change. It is in the immediate interest of elites to be conscious of countervailing forces, not only internally among elites as Porter describes it, but also in social movements which operate most often against the interests of the elites.

Social movements are the second type of change agents. They are found only in modern societies because they are a product of a legitimization of change. A social movement can be defined as "a spontaneous development of norms and organization which . . . contradict or reinterpret the norms and organizations of the society" (Marsden and Harvey, 1979). Social movements are not simply collective actions. They are not mobs, or masses, or spatial movements. They have group conciousness and show coordinated actions.

Social movements can be divided into three types. The first consists of collectivities that band together to make changes in their own lives and to maintain an existence separate from that of the larger society. These social movements, which Banks (1972) calls "self-help" movements, may become institutionalized at some later time or may continue to exist as pockets of resistance to the institutions of the society, renewing themselves periodically. An example of these is the union movement which in some of its earlier forms was a self-help movement but which has become one of the major elite institutions in the society. In contemporary Canada, there is a continuous stream of social movements designed to protect a set of ideas or ideals from the ravages of the establishment — communes, religious sects, and the particular urban variants of communities bound to restricted diets, forms of exercise and self-defence (groups which form a way of life for their membership). The objective of such groups is not the conversion of the society but resistance to the incursions of planned or elite-based social changes.

The second type of social movement is what Banks calls "cause movements". This type of social movement has an issue or cause which it wishes governments, churches, unions or other institutional powers to adopt. The groups form to resist change, especially planned change, and to try to influence the wider community. Protest movements of various kinds, from farmers' protests to the women's movement, have abounded in Canadian social history. This type of social movement is more socially significant than the self-help movement. Certain features of the dynamics of such social movements are characteristically Canadian. Very often they are regionally based, but if they are not, maintaining a national organization and identity usually either hardens the group into part of the established powers (and thereby shifts it into the other type of change agent) or leads to real instability within the group. For example, in the early women's movement in Canada, formed around the issue of suffrage, the national organization fell apart as a consequence of regional loyalties once the vote for women was won (Marsden and Harvey, 1979).

In addition to being inclined to a strong regional base, cause movements are quite often culturally specific. They may recruit on that basis or have within their bounds different factions or groups based on cultural loyalties and relationships.

In certain instances, one might argue that class interests are paramount. The "People or Planes" cause movement was based upon the defence of property so that, even though there were substantial differences in the economic circumstances of those involved, it was a property-based movement — literally.

Finally, the third type of social movement is the revolutionary movement. The most notable example of this in Canada was the *Front de Libération du Québec* (FLQ) which was active in Quebec in 1970.

The Dynamic Forces for Change

To what do elite and class groups respond? Why do social movements and their leaders pursue particular causes? In *The Fragile Federation* (Marsden and Harvey, 1979), it was argued that the "movers" in Canada press for or against changes on the basis of three types of social forces that dominate their decision-making and planning. We described those forces as sets of interests — regional, cultural (meaning ethnic and language interests mainly) and social class. These interests constitute the dynamic forces that lie behind the impetus to social change, whatever precise form the change may take and whoever proposes and carries out (or resists) the change. Thus, in examining the relative contributions of change of government or economic planning, voting behaviour, capital investment, farmers' movements, or revolutionary cells, one should search first for the regional, cultural and class interests underlying the change. While class interests are fundamental generators of social action and change, these interests are not highly visible in Canadian social behaviour because they are fractured by the rival and overwhelming importance of language, ethnicity, or religion, or by regional identities. We assert that there is an economic basis to cultural and regional interests but not necessarily a class basis.

The argument presented here goes somewhat further than that and suggests that the first stage of the analysis of social change in Canada should involve an examination of regional interests, because only among the very small national elites will regional interests not be paramount. Indeed, even there, power is maintained — as the formation of governments, councils and commissions shows — by the mobilization of support in the regional base. In the majority of decisions, the impact of regional interests and loyalties must be considered the most powerful force to be examined.

Regions have been identified by a number of criteria but it seems preferable to think of them as synonymous with provinces. It is the provincial governments that have the major jurisdiction in those areas of social life which deeply affect the vast majority of the citizens within a geographical area — social and welfare policy, urban and municipal policy, and education.

The second most powerful force to be analyzed in examining social change in Canada is that of culture. Included in culture are the combination of language, religious and ethnic groups and behaviour by which people identify themselves. The bilingual nature of this country is too well understood to require discussion here, but, as some social scientists have demonstrated, language is never enough to explain social behaviour. An entire cultural and social framework accompanies a language and is the underlying basis of nationhood. Nationalism, which is based upon subjective feelings, is a powerful motivating force. Canada has two official languages and exists as two nations culturally, but places explicit ideological emphasis upon the existence of an ethnic mosaic. This structural, but not behavioural, assimilation is officially encouraged. It is reinforced by informal association. It modifies individuals' perceptions of their economic position and class interests. The intimate and primary nature of cultural loyalties and relationships has two important consequences that affect our understanding of social change. If there is a choice to be made, those who identify with a nation or ethnic subculture will consider these interests before economic interests. Those who have no strong cultural identification are lacking in an important aspect of their social identity and consequently may not have a reason for choosing one path rather than another.

Ethnic relations must be taken into account in pressing for social change. In Canadian social planning the interests of the Francophone, of Quebec as a province, and of the government's need to balance the interests of Quebec and those of English Canada, will be factors in most decision-making on social programmes. Further, it can be argued that few ethnic or language loyalties transcend regional ones. The structure of most cultural organizations is federalist, that is, provincial and local branches culminate in a small national organization.

The dominant theories of social change, suggest that class interests, when they become conscious interests, are the most powerful dynamic force of change. That may be true elsewhere but there is little evidence that this is the case in Canada.

Chirot (1977) puts forward two propositions about the nature of stratification and division within semi-peripheral societies that relate to the forces which we assert are most powerful in Canada: (1) It is not correct to say that development ends ethnic division, not as long as there exists a culturally based division of labour in which certain culturally defined groups continue to occupy only certain economic positions; and (2) Development does not end regionally based hostilities if it perpetuates regional inequalities in power and wealth.

Our attempt to develop a theory of social change, then, depends upon our abilities to show empirically that (1) regional differences in wealth and power are linked to the class structure and the role of economic elites as the leaders of social change in Canada, and that (2) cultural (ethnic and language) differences are expressed in regional terms.

Canadians with economic and political power in the central core of the country and in the federal government, relate most closely to the core countries for both historical and constitutional reasons. There is a long standing and powerful tension between the federal and provincial economic and political elites. The regional or provincial leaders relate both to the central or national elites and directly to the core countries, while the majority of people in Canada tend to find their sources of identity and group consciousness in regional and cultural allegiances. These strains diffuse the creation of a national culture or loyalty, and as a consequence, constrained by the need for constant innovation and change in order to maintain economic development and social stability, the leaders of Canadian society make their decisions to bring about or oppose change mainly in terms of regional, economic or cultural interests.

16

*Regions and Nationalism**

M. Patricia Marchak

This essay advances three arguments: (1) that prior to the full-scale development of multinational enterprises in the postwar period nationalism within Canada was impeded by the alliance of interests involving the Canadian financial elite and foreign industrialists; (2) that this alliance has led to concentration of manufacturing industries in the central region of Canada but has failed to generate secondary industry elsewhere, with the result that regional loyalties have tended to override national ones; and (3) that postwar growth of the multinational corporations has undermined the position of the indigenous financial class, has created mobility frustrations for the upper middle class, and contributed to the emergence of a very large number of public service employees, all of whom derive declining benefits from continentalist policies. This is the basis of an increase in Canadian concern with national development, culture, communications and sovereignty.

One of the most significant characteristics of the Canadian financial elite throughout its history has been its failure to promote indigenous industrial development. The original terms for banking activity, the imperial preference trading arrangements, the terms of reciprocity agreements with the United States, and the other economic interests of the financiers have all made it more profitable for Canadian financiers to invest in mercantile activities and utilities at home while lending abroad for industrial enterprise based elsewhere (Hammond, 1967; Acheson, 1969; Myers, 1972; Tulchinksy, 1972). This has resulted in the slow and incomplete industrialization of Canada, a persistent dependency on export staples trade, and dependence on first London, and then the North-Eastern United States for economic leadership. It has also led to the development of strong communications links between Canada and the United States which have certainly rivalled if not surpassed the efficacy of links within Canada.

*Excerpted from "Nationalism and Regionalism in Canada," *Canadian Review of Studies in Nationalism*, Vol. VII, No. 1 (Spring), 1980, pp. 15-30. Reprinted by permission.

While encouraging foreign investment in industry and the establishment of subsidiaries in the resource and manufacturing sectors, the Canadian bankers did retain control over finance and the utilities. Indeed, it was their interest in the railroads which paved the way to Confederation. In Underhill's judgment:

> What Macdonald did was to attach to the national government the interests of the ambitious, dynamic, speculative or entrepreneurial business groups, who aimed to make money out of the new national community or to install themselves in strategic positions of power within it — railway promoters, banks, manufacturers, land companies, contractors and such people. They provided the drive behind his so-called National Policy, and they stood to reap the greatest benefits from it. They also required lavish expenditure of taxpayers' money in public capital investment if their ambitions were to be realised (1964: 24-25).

With respect to the railways, it might be argued that East-West communication was well developed by the indigenous elite. However, railways alone do not create a nation, and other media of communication — both the more obvious such as transportation into hinterland regions, the press, cultural institutions, a national school curriculum, and the less obvious, such as higher rates of internal migration rather than emigration to other countries, or the emergence of common interpretations of national history — were slow to develop. Further, where cultural media did develop, either through public intervention as in the creation of the Canadian Broadcasting Corporation and the National Film Board, or through natural growth as in the establishment of a Canadian comic books industry during the Second World War, they were obliged to compete with foreign media or South-North links on

disadvantageous terms. Part of the disadvantage was the relative size of the market for commodities and cultural influences. But another part consisted of the underfinancing of indigenous enterprise and the increasing dependence on American imports and American subsidiaries for manufactured goods.

The underfinancing was not, as is sometimes asserted, a function of a lack of funds in Canada. By 1880 the Bank of Montreal was one of the leading lenders on the New York Stock Exchange (Hammond, 1967: 167). Canadian funds during that critical period were directed to the industrial corporations in Britain and the United States, where shorter term financing and lower risks were attractive incentives compared to the requirements for new industries in Canada.

By the 1920s the ultimate "centre" for a large part of economic activity in Canada was the United States, and specifically in those regions containing the greatest number of head offices for parent corporations. Toronto and Montréal, the regional bases for the Canadian financial institutions and elite, were mini-metropoles in a continental economy. They were, however, necessary links in that economy. Canadian wealth was important to the growth of American corporations, and continued to be important through the Second World War. The integration of the two economies was consolidated with the military agreements of the immediate postwar period, especially the Defence Production Sharing Agreements. By the end of the 1950s, Canada's economy was contained to a larger degree than that of any other industrial country within another nation's economy. By the mid-1960s, foreign-owned firms accounted for 58 per cent of the Canadian manufacturing sector as a whole, between 50 and 100 per cent of the high value-producing industries such as machinery, transport equipment, chemicals, and petroleum, and 63 per cent of the mining industry (Government of Canada, 1972: 20-22).

This has had consequences throughout the society. Political sovereignty is limited where economic decisions are made outside the nation's borders and in terms of essentially non-national interests. All economic decisions are subject to agreement by those who actually have economic power: balance of payments, the development of alternative export markets, Canadian foreign policy, Canadian financial legislation, Canadian tax laws, and Canadian legislation designed to protect or encourage Canadian culture are all subject to non-national controls.[1]

The effects have not been contained within the economy. Scientific endeavour has been severely restricted where industrial research is carried on primarily in the head offices of dominant corporations and those offices are not within the nation. Canada's underdevelopment in this respect has increased in direct proportion to degrees of foreign investment (Bachynski, 1973; Britton and Gilmour, 1978). This is but one area in which workers have been obliged to seek jobs outside Canada, with the result that emigration rates have always been very high and have been particulary so amongst well-educated and skilled Canadians. Brain Drain

Foreign subsidiaries became dominant in cultural areas as well as manufacturing. Books and periodical publishing, film distribution and theatre chains were among these. Children of the 1950s and 1960s received their school instruction from American textbooks, and as television became a major cultural medium another generation became conversant with American styles, commodities, language, politics, and interpretations of the larger international community. The effects tended to be self-reinforcing. As Ca-

nadians became ever more dependent on foreign products, foreign employment, foreign science, and foreign culture, they became less confident about their own abilities, judgments, and culture. The British definition of "excellence" which informed much of early Canadian culture was displaced by an American definition. There was little room for the development of a distinctive Canadian culture.

The lack of a national culture, however, did not prevent the growth of regional cultures. These developed in spite of the American influence and in consequence of the extremely uneven industrialization of Canada.

The original centres of commerce for the fur trade, the banks, and the railways continued to be the financial and manufacturing centres of Canada after Confederation. Manufacturing was increasingly under foreign ownership, but it provided the Montréal-lower-Ontario heartland nonetheless with an industrial economy. The Atlantic, rural Québec, Prairie, West Coast, and Northern regions, however, remained dependent on agriculture or the export of resources. These differing economies both attracted different populations to their regions and encouraged the growth of different kinds of skills and viewpoints amongst them.

The distinctive features of metropolitan regions are their high regional wealth relative to hinterland areas, their high employment in manufacturing and managerial trades, their high ratio of urban residents, and their relatively large number of cultural institutions. Ontario has the highest average income in Canada, the highest proportion of income earners in high income brackets and the lowest proportion of families in low income brackets. Québec, divided between Montréal and an extractive base, is somewhat poorer overall, poorer than British Columbia, for example, but much wealthier than the Prairies and the Atlantic regions.[2] Ontario is the most urbanized region of Canada, with 82 per cent of its population residing in the southern urban centres.[3] A third of the total labour force in the Ontario-Québec heartland is employed in manufacturing industries. They are skilled workers in assembly lines, clerical and professional workers in bureaucracies, and branch-plant managers for the multi-national subsidiaries. Another 20 per cent of the labour force is employed in finance, real estate, and trade (Dominion Bureau of Statistics, 1969; Census of Canada 1971, 94-717). The metropolitan characteristics to which this heartland conforms are functions of the concentration of industry and finance in these regions, a concentration which is in turn dependent on the successful exploitation of resources from the hinterland regions.

That such concentration in the central Canadian region has always been a feature of Canadian society is now well documented (Clement, 1975). From their origins, four of the five major banks have had their head offices in Montréal or Toronto. At the present time, these banks control some 93 per cent of the banking industry, and 96 financial corporations altogether, the vast majority located in the same region, control 67 per cent of all financial assets (Neufeld, 1972; Statistics Canada 1970a: 194-215). Of all manufacturing establishments, 72 per cent were located in Québec or Ontario in 1920 and 67 per cent are located there today (Statistics Canada, 1970b). According to the 1972 CALURA reports, less than half of one per cent of all corporations in Canada controlled 63 per cent of the total assets, 41 per cent of the total sales, and 57 per cent of the total profits: the head offices in Canada were pre-

dominantly in Ontario and Québec (Statistics Canada, 1972a: 19).

The line of authority, however, does not typically end in Ontario or Québec, except for the financial and utilities industries. The larger corporations are American, the average American corporation is three to four times the size of its Canadian counterpart (Statistics Canada, 1972a: 20). Nearly three-quarters of the taxable income reported by American-controlled corporations in 1972 was generated in the Ontario-Québec area (Statistics Canada, 1972a: 23). What these financial statistics indicate is that there is a concentration of wealth and control in the Ontario-Québec region relative to the rest of Canada, but that this is itself linked to a larger concentration in the United States.

Only a fraction of the population becomes wealthy as investors and financiers in a situation such as that found in the heartland of Canada. Nonetheless, the population which gains employment in the manufacturing, trade, and finance industries improves its material position. Thus the objectives of the financiers are in the short-term the objectives of the rest of the population. The mini-metropolis flourishes through the manipulation of capital: it gains cultural centres, universities, hospitals, roads, and welfare services. Its role as broker for the real metropolitan interests is a lucrative one, and the trickle-down effect to the rest of the population in that area is a beneficial one.

However, the edifice rests on the continued export of raw materials from other regions, the continued dominance of the transportation facilities for conveying the raw materials, and the continued control of finances at the Centre. Two sources of threat to this arrangement have always been potential: the American interests could move directly into other regions, thus bypassing the financiers and transportation magnates of central Canada; or the other regions could develop alternative arrangements and rival metropoles. A history of communications and economy in Canada is in part a history of manoeuvres by central Canadian interests to avoid either of these developments, and of attempts by populations in hinterland regions to limit the control of the central Canadian bankers.

The most virulent source of discontent with the bankers — known locally as "the East" — had traditionally been the Prairie farmers. Many of the first generation came as peasants, with strong ethnic identities. They were settled as ethnic groups not accidentally but as explicit government policy. Their task was to clear the farmland, rear large families, and keep to themselves. The nostalgic picture now presented of their past is of extended families celebrating Bruegel weddings, but this version is invariably interrupted by memories of the Depression. Depression memories are the core of the culture, and are still quickly evoked in debates on the relative prerogatives of Albertans and Canadians, for example, over oil royalties and taxes. The reason for this is that the Depression, from the perspective of Prairie dwellers, was in large part a consequence of the greed of the Canadian Pacific Railway, Federal Government, the bankers, and the manufacturers of "the East."[4]

The cultural and economic gulf between the Prairies and Central Canada was most apparent during the Depression. Economically it took the form of bank foreclosures on farmlands, high rail costs for grain exports, high interest rates on loans, all sharp reminders to prairie dwellers that they were not part of the "establishment" and had no control over their livelihoods. Culturally and politically it was expressed in rejection of the established churches and political parties. Fundamentalist sects and social movements became characteristic features of population organization: both the Social Credit Party and the Cooperative Commonwealth Federation were born on the Prairies during the Depression. They promoted both community control and private enterprise. The control was aimed at the oligopolistic capitalists of central Canada; the private enterprise at the family farms.

There was no parallel development in central Canada. Politics had long been a series of choices between two virtually indistinguishable parties, both dedicated to maintaining a system by which the rest of the country provided the staples, the elite of the area controlled the money, the larger part of the population was employed and earning relatively high incomes even during the Depression, and internal trade within the manufacturing multi-national corporations appeared to create a favourable balance for Canada — meaning lower Ontario and Montréal. The inability of this population to comprehend the continuing radicalism of the West was a measure of their divergent experiences of Canada.

The bucolic prairie society began to disintegrate with the end of the war and the development of the oil fields. The family farms and ethnic communities did not disappear, but around them the oil industry built an empire. The industry was American-owned, and for the local residents it represented a major break with the "Eastern establishment." The ground rules changed, and the culture changed with it. Suicide, rape, crime, mental illness, and divorce rates increased almost in direct relationship to the influx of foreign money, managers, and materials. The income gap widened. Nearly a quarter of the population by 1972 earned under $5000. A disproportionate number of them lived in the rural areas where they could no longer avoid the money economy. At the same time, the proportion whose earning exceeded $25 000 topped British Columbia's rate, even though the two provincial incomes clearly favoured the coast (Statistics Canada, 1972b). The disparities extended to the various prairie regions. Saskatchewan became increasingly impoverished on its agricultural base, and its youth migrated to Alberta, British Columbia, and Ontario. Manitoba fared slightly better. Alberta swelled with new-found riches.

British Columbia, by contrast with Ontario, is still a frontier society. Its turn of the century company towns have not disappeared. They were two-class towns then, isolated and violent, and they spawned the socialist parties and militant unions which fought viciously with the traditional and conservative craft unions of Ontario throughout the first several decades of the 1900s. They have not changed greatly, though they have added schools and paved streets and company housing. What has changed in the meantime is that Vancouver has grown rich on the resources, and its wealth has turned British Columbia into Canada's second wealthiest province.

The wealth in British Columbia is distributed much more evenly than in Ontario: there are few owners and financiers by comparison (Statistics Canada, 1972b; Marchak, 1975). Its labour force is also different: there are larger proportions of unionized workers in primary industries, fewer managers, professionals, and clerical workers, and more of the managers and white-collar workers are employed in the public service (1971 Census, 94-717).

American control is considerably lower in British Columbia than in any other region, and although Canadian Pacific owns much, the forestry industry is not a typical branch-plant operation. Head offices are in Vancouver, and manufacturing subsidiaries — planing, saw, pulp and kraft mills — are located through the lower mainland and elsewhere in the United States and Canada while controlled in British Columbia.

In addition, the government (both in the form of a right-wing Social Credit movement and in that of a leftish NDP) has steadily moved in on the cash-flow. It owns a major hydro-electric corporation and its several subsidiaries, continues to struggle for ownership of its new provincial bank, has bought into the forest industry, and purchased enough shares of other corporations to obtain a voice at the directors' meetings. It has produced some limited legislation aimed at returning some of the corporation profits to government coffers and restricting their real estate ventures.

A phenomenally high rate of immigration has always been a feature of British Columbia society. The fur trade, the gold rush, the mining towns, the forestry camps, and finally the attractive sea-bounded city of Vancouver with its promise of wealth lured solid prairie-folk as well as others to the coast. At the 1971 census, a third of the total population had been born elsewhere in Canada, and the westward flow continues (Kubat and Thornton, 1974). The result is an unsettled population, a basic demographic factor which increases the already unsettling effects of a frontier resource-based economy. This no doubt underlies the statistical profile: the highest suicide rates, the highest rate of criminal convictions, the highest proportion of labelled mental cases, one of the highest rates for rape, an enormous rate of cannabis convictions, an astronomical rate of divorce. British Columbia also has the highest number of intermarriages involving Jews and Gentiles, Catholics and Protestants, and the largest number of people admitting to having no religion.[5]

British Columbia is clearly a different kind of society than Ontario. It lacks the historical roots: no significant proportion of its population can trace an ancestry in the area, and there is no well established elite. Elsewhere in Canada there is the occasional warning that if British Columbia fails to cooperate with Ontario, it will become a fifty-first state. This is unlikely: the eastern interests own more of British Columbia than do the American corporations and are themselves the most closely integrated into the American economy. The Coast still sells its forestry products to the United States on a fairly straightforward trading arrangement, and has a more diversified market outside the United States for its minerals as well as its pulp and paper than have the Eastern manufacturing industries. Moreover, British Columbia, by virtue of retaining it simple class structure and its resource-based economy, is not in fact like its nearest southern neighbours either in industrial structure or in attitudes and politics. A Socialist party was the official opposition in 1903, and under various names social democratic parties have held steady electoral support ever since.

The Maritimes, rural Québec, and the northern regions are yet further cultures and economies, each with its peculiar history and social structure. All suffer much poverty as hinterlands, having either no resources valuable to the metropolitan regions, or no control over the markets and values of the products they have. Their economies are controlled elsewhere, an elsewhere that receives a large proportion of the talented young whose futures cannot be secured in their homelands.

One seldom thinks of peasantries in connection with Canada except in terms of those farming populations imported from Europe to keep the Americans off the prairie wheatlands. Yet there are some of the attributes of peasantries among the fishing population of Newfoundland: individual farmers of the sea related in a kind of client-patron relationship to market-brokers who in turn are integrated into a system of large packing houses.[6] The Indians of the fur-trade suffered similar relationships.

Close communal ties are characteristic of regions which are largely rural, geographically or linguistically separated from the metropolitan and manufacturing areas, and poor. The Maritimers are geographically isolated, their economy having been left in limbo when Confederation consolidated the interests of central Canada. Their isolation allowed them to cultivate their peculiarities — the dialects, the humour, the dancing, the fishing ballads — none of which has parallels in Central Canada. Isolation in the north and Québec is even more evident because the local populations are ethnically and linguistically different from the outsiders. Half the population of the Northwest Territories is Indian or Eskimo; 80 per cent of the population of Québec is French (1971 Census, 92-731).

This combination of geographic and ethnic isolation provides the base for preserving indigenous cultures, especially where it is apparent — as it is in both regions — that the indigenous population forms a single economic class in contrast to the English-speaking southerners who manage the economy. In the Northwest Territories wages in 1971 provided a median income of under $4000. A quarter of the registered labour force was unemployed. A total of 115 individuals in the Northwest Territories and Yukon combined earned over $25 000 that year (1971 Census, 94-709). This income distribution is obvious; the classes appear as unofficial castes: southern managers and technicians who return to suburbia at the end of their tour of duty, and the local labourers — Indian, French, and permanent.

The fact is that much of Canada has been neither industrialized nor urbanized throughout the past century. Company towns, strung-out farming settlements, ranch-lands, marginal tourist resorts, fishing villages, frontier townsites — outside of the heartland Canada has been made up of these. They have manufactured little besides a folklore which is rich with rage and humour, and though they have sported the coca-cola signs in the same way as do the Mayan towns in the Yucatan, they have not become replicas of American life. They could not because they have lacked the urban core, the ideology of successful imperialism, and the history and economic base of the American empire.

While an authoritative study of regional cultures in Canada has yet to be published, a superficial examination of regional literature suggests some of the historical differences in perspectives across the country. Baird's *Waste Heritage*, Graham's *Earth and High Heaven*, and Ross's *As For Me and My House* are entirely regional in setting, problematic, characterization, and solution.

Some common conditions have characterized the various regions of Canada. The railroads, subsequent transportation routes, the CBC, the NFB, and the widespread exposure to American media and consumer goods all provided shared experiences, values, and perceptions. In addition, the frequent and continual migrations from the rural and poorer hinterlands to the urban and industrial regions have produced populations with experience of larger areas of the country. Finally, both the experience of the two wars and the necessary propaganda in support of Canadian participation and for conscription enlarged the share of the population which might consider itself Canadian and imbue the term with significance. Nonetheless, regional diversity and the massive inflow of American culture, together with the economic ties to the United States, inhibited a distinctly Canadian "sense of community" common to all. By the mid-1960s, George Grant (1965) could write a lament for the Canada that never emerged and meet widespread agreement with his thesis.

Yet in the late 1960s and early 1970s, there appeared to be some consensus that a new sense of national identity was emerging, although only indirect support exists for this belief. At the federal government level, several small moves have tended toward repatriating Canadian industry, screening proposed take-overs with a view to "protecting the public interest," and restricting the non-Canadian content of some media. Canadian independence movements have grown in both numbers and general popularity. They are found on both the right and the left of the political spectrum, and they have members in all regions of the country. They have affected academic associations, trade unions, and political parties.

This flowering of nationalistic sentiments a century after Confederation requires some explanation. In part it rests on the gradual erosion of regional loyalties as ethnic identities in the West decline and urbanization increases. But it is linked as well to a less obvious process. The benefits to be derived from a policy of continentalism by Canada's financial class are threatened, and the benefits to be derived from a greater degree of national sovereignty are increasing for middle classes throughout the country. These classes are the main carriers of the new nationalism.

The Canadian financial community played a vital role in the early development of American branch-plants and, continuing through the 1960s, it provided a larger share of new investment funds for American corporations than its American counterparts. However, corporations are increasingly able to finance their own expansion — a fact demonstrated in the increasing shares of funds derived from reinvested profits.[7] Take-overs of Canadian companies are no longer a typical means of American expansion.[8] Vertical integration can occur without external financing, and in spite of laws restricting new investments.[9] In short, the power to make decisions about the Canadian economy has increasingly become a power held not by Canadian financiers, still less by Canadian parliaments, but by American-controlled multinational corporations. Their decisions — regarding location of plants, investment, expansion, employment, costs, supplies, prices, technological developments, and much else — are not subject to the will of parliament, to majority vote, or even to public perusal. They are made in the interests of the parent corporation, the location of which is not in Canada.

Politicians who have over the past century viewed the Canadian national interest as coincident with the expansion of these corporations are faced with a double-bind situation: their party finances derive primarily from the large corporations (Paltiel, 1970), but the cost of such support results in the depletion of power held by their own class in Canada. Originally created to represent

that class's interest in parliament, the two major parties are no longer able to defend such interests and simultaneously to maintain their own financial base.

The multi-nationals, moreover, import their own managerial elite. The larger the corporation, the greater the frequency with which the presidents, executive officers, and members of directing boards are American citizens. For firms with non-resident ownership exceeding 50 per cent, presidents were not Canadian citizens in 55 per cent of the cases studied by the Gray Task Force (Government of Canada, 1972). Similar proportions pertained on boards of directors.

It might be expected that the large corporations, being dominant employers of Canadians, would gain the loyalty or at least the tacit support of the population, especially from that sector whose mobility into white-collar and managerial jobs is tied to corporate growth. However, the employment of this class is geographically restricted. Where head or regional head offices and major manufacturing plants are located, white-collar and skilled workers have employment. In areas dependent on resource extraction and consumer sales, the corporate demand for these workers declines. In British Columbia, for example, the top 50 corporations in terms of assets directly employ only 12 per cent of the total labour force. A quarter of these are being employed by the forestry industry with head offices in the region. Compared to Ontario, the managerial/professional and clerical groups are small in British Columbia. Even with large allowances for indirect employment, the corporations employ a smaller proportion of the British Columbian labour force than various government agencies. Similar proportions may be found in other hinterland areas: thus there is no large body of multi-national support by virtue of employment in resource regions, and no strong middle class associated with the corporations.

In the metropolitan regions support is tied to employment, but two factors undermine this. First, mobility is closed at the top by American supervisors, managers, executives, and by the need to change countries for mobility within the technical and scientific research areas. Secondly, technological advances diminish the needs for labour of all kinds, including now skilled and white-collar labour. This is, of course, equally true of Canadian companies, but as the expansion of the North American economy decelerates and even contracts, it becomes apparent that job priorities will be retained for the nationals of the corporation. In the event of employment cutbacks, whether because of technological developments or because of a recession, Canadian workers have less to gain now from American corporations and unions than at any time in the past.

Associated with the relatively low employment in private corporations in the hinterland regions is the high employment in government agencies. Schools, universities, hospitals, legal institutions, welfare agencies, transportation and communication spheres, hydro and other public utilities have all become major employers in these regions. This is partly in response to the demands from industry itself. Corporations have relied on governments to build transportation and communication systems necessary to their operation, for legal and fiscal policies useful to their expansion, for the purchase of products, especially in the heavy manufacturing industries, and to provide education and social services for their labour force. In addition, governments have had to expand employment where technological advance and cut-backs in the economy would otherwise create large pockets of unemployment, and government services by their nature tend to be labour rather than capital-intensive.

Hubert Guindon (1964), Charles Taylor (1965), and others have noted that Québec separatism is most virulent in these public service agencies (see also Bourque and Laurin-Frenette, 1972). The situation for Anglophones in the other provinces is not identical with that of the Québécois, but they do suffer similar frustrations from blocked mobility (as in the universities dominated by American academics) and similar identifications with regional and national governments in contrast to foreign corporations. These workers have no vested interest in the growth of foreign-controlled multi-national corporations but do have much to gain from an intensified nationalism.

In summary, then, the evolution of Canadian nationalism has depended on the loss of benefits for an indigenous elite in the continentalist system. As foreign multi-national corporations have become more independent of Canadian sources of finance, this elite has lost its central and vital role in the continental system. At the same time, the managerial class and some groups within the skilled and white-collar class have developed reasons for supporting a more nationalistic position. Among these reasons are blocked mobility within the foreign corporations and employment tied to the strength of regional and national governments.

Notes

1. The limitations are discussed at length and with specific examples in Government of Canada (1972).

2. Median income in Ontario for 1972 was $11 425, compared to the national median of $10 367. Incomes in British Columbia, Québec, the Prairies, and the Atlantic Provinces followed in descending order. The distribution for British Columbia is less dispersed than that for Ontario, but both of these provinces have considerably smaller proportions of income below the $5000 level than other regions. A quarter of the Atlantic Provinces population earned less than $5000. Statistics Canada, *Income Distribution by Size, 1972* (Ottawa, 1972), Table 3, "Percentage Distribution of Families by Income Groups and Regions, 1972."

3. Kubat and Thornton, (1974), Table P-1, based on census data.

4. The depression on the Prairies has received some attention from writers, including James H. Gray, *The Winter Years* (Toronto, 1966); Michael Horn, *The Dirty Thirties: Canadians in the Great Depression* (Toronto, 1972), and more recently Barry Broadfoot, *Ten Lost Years, 1929-1939* (Toronto, 1973). The suspicion held by farmers that they bore the brunt of it has gained supporters. The experience for the heartland was a loss of affluence, but for the West it was a loss of livelihood and faith. The rise of the Social Credit Movement as one response is described in John A. Irving, *The Social Credit Movement in Alberta* (Toronto, 1959); of the CCF as another in Leo Zakuta, *A Protest Movement Becalmed* (Toronto, 1964).

5. These statistics, based on Statistics Canada, have been grouped together and analyzed by Werner Cohn in "Jewish Outmarriage and Anomie: A Study in The Canadian Syndrome of Polarities," *The Canadian Review of Sociology and Anthropology*, 13, No. 1 (February, 1976), 90-105. Also, *1971, Census of Canada, Religious Denominations by Age Groups* (cat. no. 92-732).

6. For descriptions along these lines, see T. Philbrook, *Fisherman, Logger, Merchant, Miner: Social Change and Industrialization in Three Newfoundland Communities*, Study No. 1. Newfoundland Institute for Social and Economic Research (St. John's 1966), and other studies published by the Newfoundland Institute.

7. Government of Canada (1972) Tables 9 and 10, pp 24-26, and further discussions throughout the text. In the period 1960-1967, retained earnings provided 38 per cent of all expansion funds; Canadian capital, 21 per cent.

8. Rates increased up to 1970 and appear to have been declining since then. Figures are shown in Government of Canada (1972), Table 11, p. 64.

9. This fact has prompted the Task Force to point out that restrictions on new takeovers or purchases would no longer curb foreign ownership. Expansion could now advance without hindrance through re-investment of profits made in Canada (Government of Canada, 1972).

17

Regionalism as Effect and Cause*

Ralph Matthews

"Orthodox" Economic Interpretations of Regional Development and Regional Disparities

In 1977, the Economic Council of Canada published a major study of regional disparities in Canada. Surprisingly, only eight pages of this work are devoted to theoretical and conceptual perspectives on the nature of regional disparities. In these eight pages, five economic theories of regional disparities are identified: the Staples Approach, the Development Approach, the Neo-Classical Approach, the Keynesian Approach, and the Regional Science Approach.

*Excerpted from "Understanding Regionalism as Effect and Cause," In Dennis Forcese and Stephen Richer (eds.), *Social Issues*, 2nd edition, Scarborough, Ont.: Prentice-Hall Canada Inc., 1988. Reprinted by permission.

The Staples Approach

According to the Economic Council of Canada, the Staples Approach explains the differences between regions in terms of "the varying availability and marketability of natural resources." (1977: 29) In this, the economists who espouse this framework are little different from many ordinary Canadians who generally see economic prosperity as the result of our abundant natural resources, and who conversely tend to regard societies which are not economically well off as lacking such plentiful resources. However, those who argue in this manner may be misled by the uniqueness of the Canadian economy where so much of our wealth is derived solely from the extraction and sale of resources. A cursory look at other societies will quickly show that some of the world's most advanced economies are not based on resource extraction (e.g., Japan), while countries with enormous resource potential still have been unable to benefit fully from it (e.g., Brazil, Mexico). Much the same is true of the differences between the regions of Canada. The relative wealth of southern Ontario is certainly not attributable to any strong resource base as there are few resources within several hundred miles. Conversely, the Atlantic provinces have always had abundant iron ore, coal, gold, forests, fish and hydroelectric power, but have remained poor throughout most of this century. To be sure, one might argue that the situation is different for Western Canada which derives much of its wealth from oil, potash and timber. However, as the recent economic crisis in the Western Canadian oil industry attests, it is not simply the presence or absence of a resource which determines whether large-scale economic benefits accrue to the region. The other critical factor is the activity of other countries in limiting or expanding their supply of oil to the West. The Economic Council of Canada itself makes much the same point when it concludes that "resources are only one of many factors determining the productivity of a region or nation. . . ." (1977: 24)

The problem is that while recognizing the external limitations on resource development, the Economic Council's treatment of the Staples Approach to resource development has grossly over-simplified the way in which that perspective incorporates other social conditions. In particular, recent works using this perspective have focused on *who benefits* from the development (or non-development) of available resources (cf., Watkins, 1973, 1975, 1977: Matthews, 1980, 1983; 193-215). Such a perspective has a number of significant advantages. First, it focuses attention on the power and class structure in a society, and how those who dominate this structure influence and benefit from resource exploitation. Second, it permits analysis of the ways in which the class structure of different regions in a country may be competing for benefit from a single

resource. In this way, the Staples Approach has been transformed from a purely economic theory of resource development to a framework which takes into consideration the social structural conditions which affect how and where resource development takes place.

The Development Approach

Staple resources are not the only factors which have been singled out by both economists and sociologists as instrumental in the development or underdevelopment of a country or region. As the ECC study notes:

> . . . Attention has also been directed to many other factors including capital accumulation, infrastructure, education and human capital, the level of technology, agricultural modernization, social structure, and attitudes . . . . (1977: 25)

The report uses the label "Development Approach" to encompass any and all such explanations of the causes of regional differences and disparities. As a general rule or principle, it can be stated that all such approaches attribute regional differences and/or disparities to a supposed *lack* of some social, economic, political or cultural condition in one region, and to its supposed presence in another.

While the report does not single it out for special attention, one factor frequently cited as explaining regional disparities is the supposed differences among Canadian regions in the quality of their *entrepreneurship* and in the social and cultural conditions which favour the development of entrepreneurship. For example, the conclusion of Roy George's comparison of business enterprise in Ontario and Nova Scotia, published under the title *A Leader and a Laggard* (1970), finds no "economic" factor clearly responsible for such differences, and that such differences must therefore be attributable to the different quality of entrepreneurship in the two provinces.

George's work is closely allied to David McClelland's more general analysis of economic underdevelopment (1961, 1969, 1971). McClelland explains underdevelopment as a consequence of a lack of "achievement motivation" on the part of the economic leaders of economically depressed areas. He argues that most successful entrepreneurs have, within their inner psyche, a "need for achievement" (1971: 110), and are not simply motivated by economic greed. For McClelland, underdevelopment at either a national or regional level is, therefore, a consequence of poor socialization in need of achievement by a society.

One advantage of works such as those of George and McClelland over some of the other interpretations of the causes of regional underdevelopment is that they avoid the tendency of explaining all development in terms of purely economic considerations, and accept that men can have more than just economic motivations. However, such explanations also have their shortcomings. For example, they frequently fall prey to a basic logical error which is apparent in George's work. George never really examines whether there are differences in entrepreneurship between Ontario and Quebec. In fact, he studies almost everything but entrepreneurship. His evidence for differences in entrepreneurship rests only on the fact that the other factors he examines don't appear to make any difference. However, a study of entrepreneurship (and cultural factors affecting entrepreneurship) also might not reveal any differences.

But the biggest objection to what may be described as "psycho-economic" interpretations of regional differences is that such analyses frequently combine a stereotypical understanding of the residents of a region with a form of analysis that essentially "blames the victim" for his or her own misfortune. Thus, there is little or no evidence to suggest that there is really any difference in basic entrepreneurial motivation among the regions of Canada. Given the opportunity, it is likely that certain residents of each region would demonstrate large amounts of entrepreneurial drive.

The Neo-Classical Approach

From a neo-classical economic perspective, "the immediate cause of regional problems is commonly diagnosed as market failure." (Economic Council of Canada, 1977: 26) This is because the fundamental premise of the neo-classical perspective is the classical economic belief in the necessity of a freely fluctuating market economy; free, that is, from virtually all forms of policy involvement by government that might hamper the ability of any business to do exactly what it wants to do.

Ironically, neo-classical economists usually identify as interference those government policies which are designed to increase the economic and social well-being of underdeveloped regions. In Canada, they have singled out for particular attention government policies with respect to minimum wages and transferring capital from developed to underdeveloped regions with the intent of narrowing the differences in material well-being among the regions (cf., Courchene, 1976, 1978).

According to the neo-classicists, the high levels of unemployment found in the poorer regions of Canada are a direct consequence of government minimum-wage legislation which keeps wages artificially high and makes the region unattractive to industrialists who would establish themselves there only if the wage rates were lower. Transfer payments to poor provinces are seen to have similarly negative effects. First, they are blamed for introducing into the region money which was not rightfully earned there. Thus, it is claimed that they shore up high wage rates which otherwise could not be maintained. Second, they allow people in the region to live better than would "naturally" be the case. Though this may be desirable on humanitarian and social grounds, it is seen by the neo-classicists as undesirable on economic grounds. They contend that transfer payments artificially improve living conditions in poor regions and permit people who otherwise would migrate elsewhere to live there. This includes the unemployed and seasonally employed who find little incentive to move when government assistance keeps their incomes high, and it also includes some of those who are employed but who might leave for higher-paying jobs elsewhere if their incomes were not buoyed by artificially high wage rates and transfer payments (Courchene, 1970, 1974a, 1974b).

In sum, the neo-classical position is one of paradoxes. Regional unemployment is believed to be caused by minimum wage rates and the resultant high wages. Regional underdevelopment is seen to be caused by too much government assistance aimed at reducing it. It would appear that, from a neo-classical perspective, no government program of regional assistance can ever be successful as it will only deal with the symptoms rather than with the causes of regional economic differences. From a neo-classical perspective, Canada's regional economic disparities will only be eliminated when the federal government gives up trying to help Canada's underdeveloped regions and cuts off aid to them, and when provincial governments are forced to eliminate minimum-wage legislation.

It should be apparent that the neo-classical position has major social implications despite its claim to deal only in matters of supply and demand (cf., Matthews, 1976, 1981, 1983). First, many of the government policies it opposes have been developed for essentially humanitarian reasons. For example, minimum-wage legislation was designed to protect the least-skilled workers in a society from unscrupulous employers who would try to pay them less than a living wage. Similarly, many of the transfer payments to the underdeveloped regions take the form of social welfare assistance paid out to those who are in most need. The elimination of such assistance would produce considerable hardship among the poorest segment of the population in Canada's underdeveloped regions.

If, in the long run, the region began to prosper, it might be argued that the end justified the means. However, it does not necessarily follow that prosperity will occur if the proposals of the neo-classicists are put into practice. For example, among the industries attracted by low wage rates are those which must pay lower wages in order to survive. An influx of such industries into the poorer regions of Canada will not eliminate regional economic disparity, it will only institutionalize it. Canada will then always have regions in which people must work for less than what is deemed acceptable in other regions. Furthermore, any attempt by the workers of the poor regions to unionize so as to raise wages will have to be opposed by the companies which employ them, as any increase in wages will likely put the companies out of business. Any government attempt to raise wage rates will likely be met by threats from such companies that they will close down if they are not compensated by government aid in the form of tax breaks or outright subsidies. Under such circumstances, all that will have happened is that government grants to people in need will now have been replaced by grants to companies in need.

The neo-classicists argue that anyone who isn't better off than he/she could be elsewhere can always leave, and that such people will likely do so, thus opening up jobs for those who are unemployed. However, such a position simply misunderstands the role of migration out of Canada's poorest provinces. The neo-classic position thus assumes that, when times are bad, people will leave poor regions. However, this author's own (unpublished) study of the relationship between unemployment rates and out-migration rates for each of the four Atlantic provinces indicates that these two factors are inversely rather than directly correlated. Contrary to what might be expected, the lowest levels of out-migration occur when the unemployment rates are highest. The reason for this would seem to be that unemployment and migration in Atlantic Canada are a function of factors in other regions, and not the result of local conditions. When times are bad in Atlantic Canada (i.e., unemployment is high), unemployment is high in the more prosperous regions as well. Thus, there is nowhere for the excess labour force (i.e., the reserve army of the unemployed) to go. Their only opportunity for out-migration occurs when times are good in other regions, but these are also the very times when times are good in the Atlantic region as well. In short, the neo-classical position incorrectly assumes that conditions in poor regions *push* people

out. The evidence suggests that it is the *pull* of other regions which is the fundamental incentive to migrate.

The Keynesian Approach

Keynesian economics is based on the realization that the market alone will not guarantee full employment, and that the capitalist system has a tendency to fluctuate between growth and depression over time (Economic Council of Canada, 1977: 27-28). Keynes argued that government could take positive action to level out the pattern of boom or bust inherent in capitalism. This approach obviously stands in marked contrast to the neo-classical position.

The Keynesian framework can be used to explain the nature of regional economic disparities. These are also seen as fluctuations in the capitalist system which can be evened out through state action. As the Economic Council of Canada's study of regional disparity notes, modern-day Keynesians frequently argue that business will not risk locating in an area in which there has been a pattern of economic failure (1977: 28). In this sense, regional economic disparity takes on the characteristics of a self-fulfilling prophecy, and Keynesians argue that government action is needed to overcome this resistance.

Together with the growth centre strategy, Keynesian theory has provided justification for much of Canada's regional development policy aimed at industrial and urban development. Much effort has gone into attempting to lure manufacturing interests into unattractive regions by offering them large economic incentives. These incentives include outright grants of money, tax concessions and cheap access to available resources.

One cannot help wondering about the

wisdom of trying to eliminate regional poverty by giving money to powerful industries based in rich areas (either inside or outside Canada) if they agree to establish a branch operation in one of Canada's poorer regions. Furthermore, it would appear that this approach to dealing with regional economic disparity at no time gives any consideration to the possibility that business itself may be the ultimate cause of regional disparity because it is in the interest of capitalist enterprises to maintain areas of the country where unemployment is high and where resources can be obtained cheaply.

Marxist Analyses of Regional Disparities

From a Marxist perspective, regional disparity is a natural and endemic characteristic of capitalism, and is directly related to the goal of capitalism itself. Capitalism is designed to amass wealth, not to distribute it evenly, either in class terms or in regional terms. If capital is to be accumulated, it must be accumulated somewhere in the country and, by extension, other regions of the country must therefore suffer from a comparative lack of wealth. From a Marxist perspective, regional economic disparity is thus seen as an inevitable consequence of the capitalist system (cf., Mandel, 1973: 2).

Furthermore, regional disparity is seen by the Marxist as "functional" to the capitalist system. The "absolute general law of capitalist accumulation" is that "[c]apitalism overworks part of the labouring population and keeps the other part as a reserve army, half or entirely pauperized (Karl Marx, as quoted in Anderson, 1974: 12). Marxists argue that this is a necessary consequence of

capitalism because capitalism, by its nature, needs labour force flexibility. It needs a large "surplus army of the unemployed" (cf., Holland, 1976: 41-43) which it can draw on and lay off at will as market conditions fluctuate through the boom and bust cycles that both Marx and Keynes identified as endemic to capitalism. Regional disparity gives it this flexibility as the poorer regions contain large numbers of unemployed and marginally employed workers who flood to the industrialized areas when times are good, and who simply return home again when times get bad. Such workers have the added advantage that they do not constitute a direct drain on the central industrial economy, but on the economy of the poorer regions to which they return. Thus, central industry never has to pay the full cost of supporting its labour force. According to the Marxists, the principal role of the underdeveloped regions is to furnish labour reserves.

Marxists argue that the second major role of underdeveloped regions within a capitalist economy is as a major source of resources and capital. Capital and resources constantly drain out of the underdeveloped regions into the developed ones. This is done in a number of ways. One of the most obvious is the extraction of raw materials from the underdeveloped regions for processing in the more developed ones. However, capital is also drained out in other ways such as taxes, national banking policies and procedures, and public and private expenditures. One of the "aims" of industrial capital, as seen from a Marxist perspective, is to convince people everywhere that they need its manufactured products. Thus, the potential capital savings of each person is drained out of the underdeveloped regions to buy goods that are produced elsewhere. Likewise, regional governments are convinced that they must buy the latest equipment for their people, including medical and educational facilities, planes and modern factories with labour-saving equipment. All of these drain the underdeveloped region of its capital which it might otherwise have used for its own economic development, and this process thus ensures the continued underdevelopment and dependency of that region. Conversely, much of the industrial activity of the developed regions is financed with capital drained out of the poorer ones.

The third function of underdeveloped regions, according to Marxists, has already been alluded to. Not only do such regions provide surplus labour and capital for the developed regions, they also provide an additional market for the products of those developed regions. Most Marxists contend that capitalism contains a weakness within its organization. Because the capitalists take some of the surplus value out of the system, there is simply not enough available to purchase all the goods made. Thus, if the system is to continue, new markets must also be available. Underdeveloped regions serve this function admirably.

In assessing the legitimacy of this Marxist perspective, it seems fair to state that it has one major advantage over the more "orthodox" interpretations of regional differences. Whereas most orthodox economic explanations essentially treat the economy as a distinctive and independent system operating separately from the general social system, the Marxist framework thoroughly integrates economic considerations with social ones. Indeed, if there is a fundamental strength to Marx's analysis, it is that he took the accumulation of wealth (i.e., capital), which is seemingly the most purely economic aspect

of capitalism, and involved it as part of a largely *social* process involving a distinctive pattern of social relationships between ownership and labour. Whereas capitalist "orthodox" economists usually view the economic realm in simply instrumental terms, Marxist economists emphasize the social system that shapes it.

The Marxists' fundamental concern with class is undoubtedly the most obvious indicator of their concern with the impact of general social relations on economic activity. For Marxists, all economic activity is essentially class activity, and the forces of production cannot be adequately explained without reference to the class relations which grow out of them.

This concern with social class is an integral part of the Marxist explanation of regional differences. Regional disparity is seen as essentially the regional manifestation of the general pattern of class exploitation in capitalist society. The dominant class interests are those of the capitalist class within the developed regions. It is their interests which are most served by the process of regional exploitation of resources, capital and labour. In short, from a Marxist perspective, regional divisions and disparities in society are virtually inseparable from the more general social class divisions within the society, and are explainable in class terms.

Finally, it should also be noted that the Marxist explanation of regional differences and disparities differs from more orthodox economic interpretations in another way. Whereas most of the other frameworks we examined see the "cause" of regional disparity as lying in the underdeveloped region, this is not true of the Marxist framework. From a Marxist framework, regional disparity is not caused by some lack or failure of the underdeveloped region, but results directly from the influence and power of the developed region within the capitalist society. The key concept here is power. Regional disparity is the result of the power of a developed region to enforce its will on a poorer one. It is a result of the power of a dominant class, based primarily in the developed region, to manipulate the situation in the underdeveloped region for its own gains. Thus, from a Marxist perspective, regional differences and regional disparities are the product of social processes as much as of economic processes.

Recent Sociological Approaches to Regional Dependency in Canada

In addition to the general Marxist interpretation of the nature and causes of regional differences outlined previously, recent approaches to regional underdevelopment have been influenced by two "new" schools of Marxist theory known respectively as "dependency theory" and "mode of production" analysis. Dependency theory was developed by Latin American sociologists to explain the continued economic underdevelopment of their countries. Underdevelopment is seen as the consequence of the historic *dependence* of their countries on the economically advanced and industrialized ones. The most widely known exponent of dependency theory is André Gunder Frank who describes the world as a series of interlocking metropolis-hinterland relationships in which underdeveloped countries are the exploited economic hinterlands of the more developed countries (1969: 146-147). Most of Frank's work has focused on the relation-

ship between nation-states. However, a far greater body of dependency analysis has attempted to investigate and analyze the internal operations of Latin American countries. These studies have paid considerable attention to the relationship between the industrialized "developed" areas and the exploited or "underdeveloped" areas of the same countries. In particular, there has been a focus on the interrelationship between the traditional class structure based on preindustrial modes of production and the more modernized class structure centred around new industrial and urban developments (cf., Laclau, 1971; Palma, 1978). Though dependency theorists rarely use the term "regionalism," their work constitutes a form of regional analysis.

Even though some dependency theorists do deal with regional modes of production, the regional class structures which grow out of them, and the relationship between the class structures of different regions and countries, they have tended to come under heavy criticism by those who engage in "modes of production" analysis and who seem to equate dependency theory with the earlier (and rather unrefined) work of Frank. The essential thrust of the modes of production perspective is that, instead of focusing on the dependency relationship, a more accurate understanding of the social and economic structure of a society can be obtained through a focus on the different modes of production involved in any society. Such a focus, it is argued, will highlight the different class structures which have evolved out of the intersection of different modes of production within the same society (cf., Taylor, 1979; Wolpe, 1980: Chilcote and Johnson, 1983). Thus, it is possible to examine in detail the different "contradictory class locations" (Wright, 1978) that exist in a society as it "evolves" from one mode of production to another.

In the Canadian context, several recent sociological works employ varying dimensions of Marxist, dependency and mode of production analysis. Thus, Clement's analysis of the "Political Economy of Regionalism in Canada" (1978) was an attempt to directly apply to Canadian society some of the dependency theory insights concerning the relationship between social class and regionalism. Clement argued that it is not Ontario that dominates the underdeveloped regions of Canada; rather, the domination of these regions is directed by the dominant capitalist class in Canada whose primary place of residence is in Ontario, Montreal and Vancouver. Clement also borrowed from the work of the Marxist theorist Johan Galtung (1971) when he argued that this dominant class is assisted in exploiting underdeveloped regions by the economic elite of those regions who have been coopted by outside interests.

Matthews (1983) has also based much of his analysis on the dependency and modes of production perspectives. His work attempts to show, conceptually and through example, the way in which the dependency of the underdeveloped regions of Canada is "created." However, unlike most others who employ dependency theory, he argues for the incorporation of a more "voluntarist" perspective to offset the tendency of dependency theory to produce rather structural and teleological analysis. Such a perspective, he argues, would focus on the way in which the actions of specific individuals contribute to the structural dependency of a region. It would also focus on how individual residents of dependent regions perceive the external processes which tend to make them dependent, and also on how they attempt to "operate" within the context of that structural dependency.

The Identification of Regional Differences

There is no doubt that there are "real" or "objective" regional differences in Canada. As Tables 17.1 to 17.3 clearly show, such differences can be easily documented. Most studies use such facts not just to demonstrate that regional differences exist, but that there are real disparities among them. Put somewhat differently, the presentation of lists of *objective* indicators is of little relevance, and what is more important is the transformation of the objective indicators into *subjective* indicators designed to support a particular perspective or argument.

One of the most important efforts in this regard is the major study of regional disparities in Canada by the Economic Council of Canada, published under the title *Living Together: A Study of Regional Disparities* (1977). Beginning first with "Demographic Differences," the study documents clearly that there are significant regional differences in rate of population growth, natural increase, migration, urbanization, rate of urban growth, family size, fertility rate, and youth and dependency rates (1977: 32-54). This is followed by a similar documentation on regional differences in material well-being with respect to per capita income, unemployment and labour force participation rates (1977: 40-56).

However, the most interesting feature of this study is that it does not simply stop with the presentation of demographic and economic indicators of supposed "disparity," but follows with an analysis of what it terms

Table 17.1 Urban population distribution of Canadians by provinces, 1971 and 1981

Province	% Urban 1971	% Urban 1981	Number of cities over 50 000 people 1971		Number of metropolitan areas 1971	
			1971	1981	1971	1981
Newfoundland	57.2	58.6	1	1	1	1
Prince Edward Island	38.3	36.3	0	0	0	0
Nova Scotia	56.7	55.1	2	2	1	1
New Brunswick	56.9	50.6	1	2	1	1
Quebec	80.6	77.6	13	20	3	4
Ontario	82.4	81.7	20	27	9	10
Manitoba	69.5	71.2	2	1	1	1
Saskatchewan	53.0	58.1	2	2	2	2
Alberta	73.5	77.2	2	3	2	2
British Columbia	75.7	78.0	2	5	2	2
Total			45	63	22	24

Source: Compiled by the author from data contained in Statistics Canada, *Canada Year Book, 1974*, and *Canada Year Book, 1985*.

"Social Indicators and Other Social Measures" (1977: 56-59). Presumably, these are included to show that regional disparity is as much a social problem as an economic one. This list includes indicators of housing, education and wealth. *Housing* is measured in terms of crowding index based on the number of persons per room in the houses of each region, and on the availability of household telephones throughout each region. *Health* is measured primarily in terms of the per capita expenditure on medical services and number of physicians per person in each region. *Education* is identified using indicators of school attendance, per capita expenditure on education by region and level of educational achievement.

However, there are two problems with such indicators, both relating to the issue of the subjective interpretation or "meaning" of indicators. First, it is hard to see what is particularly "social" about some of these indicators since they relate to the cultural, behavioural, organizational or psychological character of society only in the most superficial way. It is difficult to determine just what the social dynamics involved are. Second, it is questionable whether these indicators really tap the *meaningful dimensions of regional disparity as far as the residents of such regions are concerned*.

To illustrate this latter point, it is helpful to examine the indicators chosen by the Economic Council a little more closely. Looking first at the Council's indicators of housing, the data clearly show that the provinces of Atlantic Canada have a higher ratio of persons per room per house than does Ontario. This seems to provide clear grounds for the claim that the Atlantic region suffers from regional disparity. However, had the Economic Council decided to use home ownership as an indicator, a very different pattern might have emerged. In many of the rural com-

Table 17.2 Employment by occupation and province, Canada and the provinces, 1983

Occupational Category	Canada	Nfld.	P.E.I.	N.S.	N.B.	Que.	Ont.	Man.	Sask.	Alta.	B.C.
					Total — Both Sexes						
	%	%	%	%	%	%	%	%	%	%	%
Managerial/ Professional	24.3	19.9	21.8	21.6	20.6	24.6	25.3	23.0	19.1	25.5	24.0
Clerical	17.1	13.7	14.5	16.5	15.3	18.0	17.3	16.3	13.4	17.0	16.9
Sales	10.3	8.5	9.1	10.6	10.0	9.6	10.5	10.5	9.4	11.0	11.6
Service	14.5	13.2	18.2	16.2	16.0	14.8	13.8	14.0	14.2	14.2	15.8
Primary	7.0	10.9	18.2	8.0	8.5	5.2	5.0	10.5	22.8	9.6	6.7
Processing	13.5	17.1	7.3	11.7	12.5	15.0	15.4	12.6	7.9	8.4	11.1
Construction	6.0	8.2	7.3	8.0	8.2	5.2	5.5	5.7	6.6	7.7	6.1
Transportation	3.5	4.7	1.8	4.0	4.6	3.7	3.0	4.0	3.6	4.0	4.1
Crafts and Materials Handling	3.8	3.8	1.8	3.4	4.3	3.9	4.2	3.4	3.0	2.6	3.7
Total	100.0	100.0	100.0	100.0	100.0	100.0	100.0	100.0	100.0	100.0	100.0

Source: Percentages calculated by the author from Statistics Canada, *The Labour Force*, July 1983.

Table 17.3 Average earnings as a per cent of national average income, Canada and the provinces, 1946-1981

Province	1946	1951	1956	1961	1966	1971	1981
Newfoundland	—	93.0	81.4	85.7	77.5	79.5	74.9
Prince Edward Island	90.0	78.9	77.8	75.9	69.0	66.7	70.6
Nova Scotia	91.2	85.0	84.3	84.3	81.3	83.4	89.8
New Brunswick	88.9	83.1	82.5	79.4	79.5	78.5	77.7
Quebec	96.7	97.8	97.2	97.1	99.0	97.4	93.7
Ontario	104.4	104.8	106.2	106.1	105.7	107.6	102.9
Manitoba	93.0	93.9	91.3	93.7	98.7	89.1	93.6
Saskatchewan	103.1	92.5	85.7	88.7	90.4	79.6	101.3
Alberta	92.5	97.9	96.0	97.2	96.0	96.8	112.6
British Columbia	99.8	105.5	108.5	105.5	107.7	106.5	107.6
Canada	100.0	100.0	100.0	100.0	100.0	100.0	100.0

Source: Calculated by the author from data on earned income for the specified years contained in Revenue Canada, *Taxation Statistics*.

munities and small towns of Eastern Canada, a large majority of residents live in homes built by themselves or their forefathers. These homes are not financed by bank mortgages, but are owned "outright" by their inhabitants. Indeed, the rate of actual home ownership is higher there than in the more urbanized provinces where a large proportion of the residents are either paying off mortgages or renting. Yet for the working class and marginally employed, outright home ownership is critically important for, should they become unemployed (a likely condition for most of Canada's poor and unskilled), no one can take the roof from over your head (cf., Iverson and Matthews, 1968). For the residents of such poor provinces, there can be little doubt that home ownership is a far more important factor than the slightly higher ratio of persons per room. Yet by this criterion, it is Ontario and Quebec that have the highest level of "regional disparity" in the country.

With regard to "health," it seems relevant to ask whether it is more important to have more physicians per capita than anyone else, or to live longer. If the latter is the case, then it is Central Canada that again seems to suffer from disparity when compared with Atlantic Canada. Per capita longevity is certainly greater in each of the four Atlantic provinces than in the central provinces. Even the choice of number of physicians per capita can be questioned as illegitimate on the grounds that it ignores the vital role provided by other health care professionals. If one takes that into account, it is interesting to note that Prince Edward Island has the highest per capita number of nurses in the country. As long as there is access to a physician, this surfeit of nurses may actually mean a higher level of personal health care than elsewhere.

One can even question the legitimacy of some of the educational indicators used by the Economic Council, again on the grounds that they do not capture the meaningful dimensions of life in the so-called regions of regional disparity. For example, the ultimate goal for many of the residents of Atlantic Canada is to find a way of making a living that will permit them to remain in their home communities and not have to move to another province. Given this, having a higher education may actually be a disadvantage rather than an advantage. To train for highly skilled jobs that are not available in the region may, in fact, be "disfunctional" to a person's underlying life goals. Such training may mean that they can only get work in Ontario, a region considered by many as an undesirable place to live because of its high level of urbanization and industrialization.

Though the preceding discussion of indicators may seem overdrawn to some, the underlying issue that it is intended to demonstrate remains valid. The issue is that a full understanding of the dimensions of regional differences must involve an understanding of the subjective dimensions of *regionalism*. We have already discussed one aspect of this, namely the way in which economic and social indicators become subjectively interpreted to demonstrate supposed regional disparities. However, there is a second subjective dimension which requires consideration — the social psychological dimension which argues that the residents of a particular region are likely to develop certain social psychological orientations, simply by virtue of having spent all or a significant part of their life in a particular region.

Some writers use the term "regionalism" in a general way to refer to any aspect of regional study. In such usage, regionalism becomes the study of regions. However, it seems analytically useful to limit the use of the term to refer to the subjectively meaningful social psychological dimensions of regional living, and that is the way the term will be used throughout the remainder of this paper. Three such dimensions seem to be of particular importance. One dimension is the "identification" of a region as unique or distinctive by those who live there, and perhaps also by those who live outside it. This phenomenon analytically precedes, but is closely related to, the second social psychological dimension of regionalism which is "identification with" a particular region. This involves the belief that those people who inhabit the same general area are, in some sense, identifiably different in outlook and values, and perhaps even in behaviour, from those who live elsewhere. The third social psychological dimension of regionalism is the "commitment to" a particular region by those who live there. This commitment is both a social psychological and behavioural dimension which, for example, accounts for residents of an underdeveloped region preferring to remain there in spite of the supposed economic and social disparities which characterize its way of life.

Taken together, these three phenomena comprise the dimensions of "extragroup closure" whereby the members of a particular group identify themselves as distinctive from the larger society surrounding them (cf., Martindale, 1960: 377-380). Though this phenomenon has, in the past, been used largely to help explain the formation of distinctive ethnic "communities" within a society, it can be just as fruitfully employed to explain the formation of what are, in the minds of their residents, distinctive regional communities and ways of life.

In sum, it has been argued here that the "Identification of Regional Differences"

involves both the objective delineation of regional differences and the subjective assessment of these differences. Furthermore, it is argued that the analysis of regionalism involves more than just the listing of differences in economic and social organization. Such structural regional differences also have their social psychological counterpart in the way in which the residents of a region identify their region, identify with their region and demonstrate commitment to their region through their actions.

Regionalism as Explanation

One of the earliest and most sweeping condemnations of the use of region as an explanatory variable is found in the work of political scientist Richard Simeon. In his words:

> We must first recognize that in no sense is it [regionalism] an explanatory variable: by itself it doesn't explain anything. If we find differences of any sort among regions, it remains for us to find out *why* they exist; regionalism is not the answer. In this sense, regions are simply containers whose contents may or may not differ. (1979: 293)

While it is not clear exactly why Simeon makes this claim, his reference to regions as "containers" would seem to suggest that he is trying to emphasize that "space" or "area," in and of itself, is not a determinant of social and political behaviour. However, his generalization seems as unnecessarily sweeping as the position he is trying to oppose. To be sure, space or area may not *determine* behaviour in the sense that very different types of social behaviour are possible in the same or similar areas. To argue otherwise would be to make the same error as those early sociologists who saw climate as *determining* individual behaviour. On the other hand, as geographers can demonstrate, the geographic features of a particular area or region can certainly have an influence on the types of social organization and social behaviour that develop there.

Even more importantly, at least in the context of our analysis in the previous section, Simeon does not distinguish the difference between *region* as territory and *regionalism* as a social psychological measure of one's sense of identification with and commitment to a particular region as a place in which to live. While region simply as territory may indeed explain little, people do come to identify with their region of residence and with those who live there with them. As a result, over time they may actually come to think differently and have different attitudes and values about certain matters than people in other regions. The result of these different attitudes and values is that, in response to certain problems and issues, the people of one region may, by and large, actually *behave* differently from people who live elsewhere. In short, while region as territory may explain little, the fact that people live there over time and develop a sense of regionalism may actually explain a lot. The problem then becomes something of a methodological conundrum. Regionalism, using "region of residence" as a dependent variable, may actually explain quite a lot in a whole variety of independent variables.

However, Simeon's condemnation of "region" as an explanatory variable is only one of many different ways in which the explanatory power of "region" and "regionalism" have recently been challenged. Another approach is to be found in the work of Gibbins (1980) on Western Canadian regionalism. His argument is essentially a "cultural ho-

mogenization thesis." He suggests that, in the past, Western Canada was unique in its ethnic and religious diversity from the rest of Canada and, as a result, had its own distinctive pattern of politics, political parties and other aspects of social life. However, he contends that recent changes have "eroded the distinctiveness of the prairies" (1980: 66) with the result that it now has a way of life that is much like that of the rest of Canada (1980: 92).

To understand Gibbins' arguments and some of the problems with them, it is useful to compare them to the relatively well-known sociological approach to social and economic development known as "convergence theory." Championed by such sociologists as Kerr (1960) and Moore (1965, 1979), this position contends that, as societies modernize, they pass through similar stages and become more alike — indeed, it was assumed that they would become more and more like the United States of America which was accepted as the ideal society by such ethnocentric writers. Time has shown that most underdeveloped societies and regions do not become willing copies of the more developed ones.

Much the same response can be raised against Gibbins' work. He is too willing to emphasize the general ways in which the regions of Canada have become alike, and too unwilling to explore the extent to which real differences in attitudes, values and behaviour remain. Indeed, the methodology on which Gibbins' work is based is such that he measures virtually everything except regionalism. We would emphasize again that a growing similarity among regions in terms of rural-urban balance, ethnic diversity, occupational structure, political affiliation and any number of other such characteristics does not necessarily mean that the extent of identification which the residents of each region have with the place they live is breaking down. Nor does it mean that their sense of regional commitment has lessened. Only if one could establish that such dimensions of "regionalism" are in decline would one be in the position to argue that regionalism is no longer a meaningful feature of Canadian society. Moreover, even that is not enough to suggest that regionalism is not an explanatory variable in Canada. To do this, one would have to determine that region of residence and/or regionalism was no longer a significant explanatory variable with regard to some other set of attitudes, values, or behaviours.

One study which does attempt to establish the extent to which there are significant regional differences in attitudes and values in Canada was carried out by Blishen and Atkinson (1981). Using the data from the 1977 Quality of Life Study, they conclude that "no major regional cleavages in personal values exist in this society, although there are some regional differences in the degree to which certain values are emphasized." (1981: 18-19) They note that in only one of the 11 values they studied does region account for more than 2 per cent of the variance in values, and that this was probably attributable to value differences held by French Canadians and British Columbians (1981: 10).

At first consideration, Blishen and Atkinson's findings would appear to provide the proof of similarity in regional values that is missing from the claims of Simeon and Gibbins. However, once again it is necessary to question the qualities being measured. Blishen and Atkinson base their analysis on the replies of respondents who were asked to rank the relative importance of 11 "values" such as love, security and prosperity. However, the relationship between these values and regional concerns is not obvious, nor is it stated by the authors. That residents of all regions place similar weighting on love, security and prosperity again should not be taken as evidence of any lack of regionalism, regional identification or regional commitment. In short, there does not seem to be any necessary relationship between regionalism and the values analyzed by Blishen and Atkinson.

In addition to the various works just discussed, there is another body of recent work that explicitly criticizes those who argue that region of residence and regionalism have explanatory power. These are the works written from a Marxist perspective which generally contend that any "effect" previously attributed to regional differences or to regionalism is not the product of distinctive regional differences as much as it is a consequence of the considerable social class differences among the various regions of Canada. The major work from this perspective is that by Ornstein *et al.* (1980). The significance of this work lies in the fact that the authors avoid the trap of claiming that "region of residence" has no significance, and that all differences among regions are totally due to class factors. Rather, they suggest that there is something of a balance between region and class, with region being more significant with regard to local level issues and class being more significant at the more general level and at the level of overall ideology. The strength of their work also comes from the fact that they attempt to support their hypotheses with sophistical empirical/statistical analysis. Finally, their work also benefits from the fact that they employ both Marxist (i.e., relationship to the means of production) and non-Marxist (i.e., socioeconomic status of occupations) measures of the social class of their respondents.

Ornstein *et al.* also use the data from the 1977 Quality of Life Study in their analysis. Their focus is on the "layers" of political attitudes in Canada. These range from specific attitudes toward particular parties and governmental institutions through attitudes toward general systems of government to the most general level of attitudes toward political ideology and the distribution and use of power (1980: 233-234). They hypothesize that region of residence is only important at the level of the most local specific attitudes, and that as one moves up the hierarchy of increasing generality, the layers become increasingly explainable only in class terms. Based on their analysis, they conclude that the explanatory power of region versus class is much as they predicted (1980: 267-268). Moreover, they contend that they have demonstrated this using *both* Marxist and non-Marxist methods of operationalizing the class origin of respondents.

While Ornstein *et al.* have done far more than anyone else in determining the comparative explanatory power of region of residence versus social class, it should be noted that their work also has some limitations. For example, it contains no evidence of the extent to which regionalism as a social psychological orientation as described above remains a significant feature of Canadian life. Nor does it in any way examine the extent to which regionalism, so defined, is an explanatory variable. If, as has been argued previously, region of residence leads to an increased sense of regionalism (as previously defined), then there is nothing in this work which directly examines that relationship. Moreover, it is possible that "regionalism" as an intervening variable is a stronger predictor of differences in other attitudes than is region of residence *per se*.

Moreover, Ornstein *et al.* are also limited by their specific concern with certain political values. We have no way of knowing from this study whether region of residence or regionalism is significant in influencing attitudes and values in areas other than politics. Indeed, certain aspects of their analysis suggest that regional differences are weak only when the issues involved are primarily class related, such as support for labour unions. Region of residence appears to remain a strong predictor of attitudes with regard to broader social concerns such as support for social welfare (1980: 257-258).

Two papers by Matthews and Davis (1986a, 1986b) have attempted to examine (a) the extent to which regionalism can still be shown to be a significant feature of Canadian society, (b) the extent to which regionalism, as here defined, can be shown to have explanatory power, and (c) the strength of this explanatory power *vis-à-vis* such other variables as social class, status (SES) and ethnicity.

The data for these works are again taken from the 1977 Quality of Life Study. As that survey was designed for another purpose, it is not always possible to find questions in it which directly probe the dimension of regionalism of most interest. However, several of the key dimensions are at least touched upon. It should also be noted that, given the way in which the data were coded, the only indicator of region that could be used was province of residence. As it is likely that some regions overlap more than one province while not comprising all of any single province, this must be regarded as a crude indicator that is likely to underrepresent the extent of regional differences in Canada.

There are three questions which relate to the extent of regionalism. These include questions concerning whether each respondent considered himself/herself "Canadian first" or "a provincial resident first," the preferred province of residence of each respondent and the level of satisfaction of each respondent with his/her province of residence. If the first of these questions measures the level of "identification" with province of residence, then identification is very low indeed. The majority in each province saw themselves as Canadians first or equally Canadian and provincial residents (Matthews and Davis, 1986a). However, it may be that the comparative character of this question tends to underrepresent the still strong level of identification that most Canadians have with their home province. This is certainly supported by the answers to the other two questions where it is clear that the overwhelming majority of residents in each province prefer to remain where they are, and are generally very satisfied with the quality of life they enjoy there (Matthews and Davis, 1986a). Certainly, there is no doubt from the answers to these questions that regional "commitment" remains extremely high in Canada.

The explanatory power of region of residence was examined in several ways in these two papers. First attempts were made to determine the extent to which the replies to the three questions described above were related to other factors. Responses to the identification and provincial satisfaction questions were shown to be statistically related to several "regional concerns" as well as general satisfaction with life in Canada (Matthews and Davis, 1986b). In contrast, socio-economic status was not statistically related to any of the provincial concerns or satisfaction with life in Canada (Matthews and Davis, 1986b).

The evidence discussed above supported the notion that measures of regionalism were related to attitudes and values concerning some other aspects of Canadian life, while a measure of social class appeared to have no such relationship. Given this, a more complex statistical analysis was undertaken to determine the comparative influence of province of residence, identification with province of residence, preferred province of residence, satisfaction with province of residence, class, socio-economic status and ethnicity on a whole variety of other attitudes and values related to federal-provincial relations. The analysis of covariance measured the impact of all of the dependent variables simultaneously while controlling for their interaction effects. The analysis generally demonstrated that province of residence was consistently able to explain more variance in the various attitudes and values than were status, class or ethnicity. However, the measures of identification, satisfaction and commitment to province of residence by themselves tended to explain less variance than did class or ethnicity (Matthews and Davis, 1986a).

The findings of these two papers can certainly not be taken as conclusive. The dimensions considered and the measures of both region and regionalism employed were little more than approximations which likely underestimated the significance of region of residence and regionalism in Canada. A study aimed directly at measuring the nature and extent of regionalism is clearly needed. However, the one conclusion that can be derived from these studies is that region of residence and, to a lesser degree, regionalism still remain significant explanatory variables.

SECTION VI

Accommodating Elites

Who rules Canada? Who makes the decisions that most shape the country's history? Who decides on major issues before the country now, and influences its future? These questions have been central to Canadian sociology at least since John Porter posed them and offered tentative answers in *The Vertical Mosaic* (1965). His view that Canada was run by a set of competing but **accommodating elites** provides the starting point of this Section.

The debate between followers of Porter and their opponents is often complex, so we will begin with a very simple version of the debate, then progressively sketch in details. First, imagine two kinds of powerful groups in Canadian society: elites who hold top positions in the society's most important organizations; and the upper class who have typically inherited wealth (and everything that goes with it — influence, social standing, respectability) from their parents. Note that the key feature of elite positions is that they are tied to organizational control; the key feature of upper class positions is their inheritance, or passage within a single family from one generation to the next.

The first question at issue is, what is the connection between elite position and upper class inheritance? Are upper class people more likely to become elites than other people, and if so, why? Further, does it matter how elite positions are filled, that is, do elite position-holders from different class backgrounds behave differently?

Elite positions are to be found in economic organizations (for example, bank president or executive officer of a manufacturing company), in government (elected prime minister or appointed deputy minister), and in a variety of other organizations, such as labour unions, the Red Cross, the CBC, universities, and so on. Often these organizations are in conflict or, at least, fail to share the same goals and interests. We should therefore expect their elites to be in conflict or, at least, to promote opposing goals and interests. But is that what happens? Do elites openly conflict? Or do they accommodate, that is, cooperate with one another, and if so, how and why? Moreover, if elites do accommodate to prevent or minimize conflict, is it because cooperation is in the best interest of their respective organizations? Or because elites, coming mainly from the same (upper) social class background, share similar values and goals, whatever organization they may work for? Or, finally, is it because some parts of society — especially the economy — are able to dominate others (for example, universities, labour unions, government), forcing compliance and apparent cooperation?

At the very least, we can imagine two extreme images of Canadian society. Call one the accommodating elite image, the other the capitalist class control image. According to the first, elites in different sectors of society fight hard to promote the goals of their own organizations. Each sector, each organization has some power in this conflict. However, more often than not elites cooperate with other elites because this will, in the long term, further their organization's interests; because elites have a fundamental commitment to avoid upsetting the social order; and because many of the people with whom they are interacting (in conflict) are acquaintances, friends, members of the same social class (with the same background experiences), and perhaps even kin.

By this line of thinking, a complex society with many legitimate competing interests requires both conflict and accommodation of this kind. Each sector, each organization, each elite person will have a fair share of wins and losses, successes and failures in such a pluralistic system. Within this framework, class of origin is relatively unimportant. Elites are fighting to further their organization's interests, and not their own, much less those of their social class.

The capitalist class control image is almost entirely the opposite of this first accommodating elites image. It assumes that competition and conflict between sectors, organizations and elites is less common than collusion and domination. Those in control of the economic sector, and within that sector, the largest, wealthiest organizations (in Canada, the banks and other financials) will control all other sectors of the economy, all other organizations, and thereby all other elites. They do this, in part, by controlling the state, that is, by controlling both elected and appointed officials; and in part, by controlling access to capital, the ultimate source of all power. In turn, this dominant economic elite is filled by people from the hereditary upper class and by a very few new capitalists. Thus, the elite structure of society simply duplicates the capitalist class structure. What appears to be elite accommodation is simply cooperation among capitalists and their agents.

The following questions have been raised in the debates around Porter's image of power: (1) *How many elite groups* are seriously involved in controlling Canada, that is, how plural are the elites, and are there one, two, or even more powerful groups? (2) How *closed or open* is the recruitment of outsiders into the elite and where do elite members come from when there is turnover? (3) *How accommodating are the power-holders?* Are the elites cohesive, with shared outlooks, or do decisions come only after deep and bitter conflict? Are elites members of the capitalist class or at least the tools of it, or do they serve a more varied set of class interests?

The selections in this Section address these three questions. Before turning to the selections, however, let us outline Porter's image of accommodating elites a little more fully because of its great influence upon the literature that followed. Porter saw Canada as ruled by five elite groups. These were people in the top positions in each of five broad areas of social organization in Canada: in major economic corporations, political organizations, bureaucratic (i.e., government bureaucracies), labour organizations, and ideological (i.e., church, educational, and media) organizations. Strong corporate, bureaucratic, political, labour, and ideological elites each had enormous power. The distribution of power among elites was due to the placement of the elites at the tops of large organizations, each with its own wealth, power and mandate provided by long-standing values and norms, to perform different services for Canadians.

Porter did conclude, however, that the economic or corporate elite had been most successful, most powerful, in seeing that its interests had been served over the years. Holding second place, by the same criterion, was the bureaucratic elite. This elite was made up of high ranking civil servants, the mandarins of government. The most powerful of these were in the federal bureaucracy, but this elite was said also to include high ranking personnel of provincial bureaucracies. Thus, in Porter's judgment, the elites said to provide cement to the society in the fragile federation image

— the regional bureaucratic elites — were not among the most powerful. But these regional elites were not to be ignored for the reasons cited under the fragile federation imagery. Moreover, the other national elites — political leaders, labour leaders, and ideological leaders — were said to be even weaker.

Porter gave several reasons for the paramount strength of the corporate and (federal) bureaucratic elites, not the least of which were the enormous economic resources each could command, and the fact that these sectors employed huge proportions of the Canadian working population. Moreover, according to Porter, these sectors provide better paying and more stable careers than are enjoyed by politicians and labour leaders. For the latter reasons, the corporate and bureaucratic sectors are able to recruit the most talented workers for their bureaucracies.

Porter saw two trends in the distribution of power, each resulting from the greater bureaucratization of the elites' supporting social organization. First, power was being concentrated in fewer and fewer hands in each elite sector. Second, corporate and bureaucratic elites were growing progressively dominant over the other elites. So, in answer to the first question raised above, Porter saw a plural set of elites, with two more powerful than the others, and saw this dual system becoming more strongly established with the passage of time. Political scientist Robert Presthus's (1973) image of duality and accommodation ran along the same lines as Porter's but with the strong implication that political and bureaucratic elites were most determinant in key decision-making. Compared to Porter, Presthus minimized the role of the corporate elite.

Porter addressed the second question of how closed the elite groups were by studying the social backgrounds of their members around 1951. His procedure was to look at the characteristics (including social class backgrounds, ethnicity, religion and gender) of elite members and compare them with the characteristics of the general adult population. In this way Porter was able to estimate roughly how over- and under-represented in the elite were certain types of Canadian. (He found the appropriate data on elites in biographies, directories and census data.) He showed that, of all elites, the economic elite was least representative on all of the counts just mentioned; but each of the elite groups had some form of exclusivity. The economic elite was defined by Porter "as the 985 Canadian residents holding directorship in the 170 dominant corporations, the banks, insurance companies, and numerous other corporations" (1965: 274). Within this group, a high proportion had fathers in the economic elite before them; most had inherited their positions; and only a few had worked their way into the elite by establishing their own firms or by taking over existing firms. In addition, over fifty per cent of the economic elite had upper class origins, while only about one per cent of the general population did. Thirty-two per cent of the elite had middle class backgrounds; and only eighteen per cent had working class backgrounds, even though over eighty-five per cent of the general population had such origins. In terms of ethnicity and religion, the vast majority of the economic elite were English-speaking Protestants, even though more than thirty per cent of all Canadians were French-speaking Catholics. Less than one per cent of the elite were Jews, who made up one and one-half per cent of the general population. "Economic power belonged almost exclusively to those of British origin," Porter concluded (1965: 286). Most dramatically, perhaps, there were no women in the corporate (economic) elite, despite their (roughly) fifty per cent representation in the population.

The exclusivity of the other elite groups was less marked on most counts, but exclusion was always a factor. People of middle class and French Canadian backgrounds were found more frequently in the bureaucratic, political, and ideological elites, but people with middle class and upper class backgrounds and people of British origin were still over-represented, and people of non-English and non-French backgrounds were seldom to be found. Only the labour elite came close to representing average Canadians on class and ethnicity. But even here, women were seriously under-represented.

Despite much conflict and much accommodation between elites, Porter concluded that accommodation eventually held sway. He drew this conclusion by studying economic, political, and social issues that had faced the country, and seeing how decisions about these issues affected each elite's interests.

> Elites both compete and cooperate with one another: they compete to share in the making of decisions of major importance for the society, and they cooperate because together they keep the society working as a going concern. Elites govern institutions which have, in the complex world, functional tasks. The economy must produce, governmental bureaucracies must administer, governments must govern, the military must maintain the defences, and the churches, or some counterpart in the epoch of the mass media, must continue to provide a view of the world in which the whole process is legitimate and good and in conformity with dominant social values. It is elites who have the capacity to introduce change, but changes bring about shifts in the relations between elites. Because they all have power as their institutional right they can check each other's power, and, therefore, cooperation and accommodation, as well as conflict, characterize their relations (1965: 27).

The elites compromise to get on with their respective businesses, and also because each has an independent power base of its own. Further, Porter argued, no elite could fully dominate because the others would object collectively:

> The argument is then that power tends towards an equilibrium of competing elites. The checks and balances which are everywhere considered desirable do not come from control by the masses or from the membership of the corporate bodies which elites represent. Rather they come from the tradition of independence built up by elite groups within a system of juridical norms. Elites guard jealously their spheres of activity and the previously appropriated options which they claim to be theirs. Big business is always beating off the bureaucratic octopus, whether governmental departments or regulatory agencies; politicians can enhance their power by arousing public sentiment when large corporations exploit too much.
>
> In this respect the "rights" about which we have spoken and which appear to limit the exercise of power are really the rights of institutional elites to organize and carry out their activities. If one elite threatens these rights it will be challenged by other elites whose positions are threatened (1965: 214).

The accommodations of the elites are facilitated, too, by a pronounced sharing of values and interests, Ported contended. Each of the elites, he felt, had many members who subscribed heavily to the idea that corporate capitalism was "for the common good"; and they shared in the "Western" values of democracy, nationalism and Christianity. They came to these common views, Porter believed, through the similarities of their social backgrounds, their similar training in upper class schools, and their repeated interaction on boards of directors and through memberships in the same clubs. These were not unlike "a web of kinship and lineage which provides cohesion to primitive life" (1965: 304).

In his answer to the question of the role of class in power distribution, Porter stopped well short of concluding that there was a dominant capitalist class. He considered this possibility, and rejected it. As he said, he found the Marxist theory of the state, according to which "the economic . . . system is the master" (1965: 206), too simplistic. He drew this conclusion despite the evidence, which he accepted, of the greater strength of the corporate elite, and despite his belief that the corporate elite's interests were entrenched in values shared by the other elites. He was impressed by the "counteracting power" (1965: 522-23) of the other elites. We have to wonder, however, whether this power was more an unrealized potential than an exercised force. Of course, Porter would have replied that it was both.

It is on the role of social class, especially, that Porter's work has been most seriously criticized. Many insist that the capitalist class exercises enormous control through the corporate elite and the state (generally including Porter's bureaucratic and political elites, and the judiciary). The other elites in this alternate theory are forced to accommodate or simply to lose power. This is just the view that Libbie and Frank Park put forward in their study, *Anatomy of Big Business* (1973 [1962]). As their Marxist perspective would require, the Parks began by asking "Who owns Canada?". Their view was that "control is ownership and without ownership control vanishes" (1973: 11). They studied a class of persons "that owns and controls the mines and mills and factories of Canada" (1973: 10) and those at the centre of the "financial and industrial corporate structure", including "the chartered banks, the members of whose boards of directors make up the 'Who's Who' of the dominant financial groups" (1973: 71). They reported on the frequent interaction and shared backgrounds of members of these groups, much as Porter did. But they went beyond Porter's work by emphasizing that the financial elite had presided over the selling off of Canadian natural resources and industry to foreign-based interests. They described an increasingly powerful external economic elite, a phenomenon that Porter discussed only briefly (1965: 214-45, 1966-73). Unlike Porter, the Parks did not go much beyond the economy and the economic elite to study other sectors and elites.

The relationship between foreign ownership of the Canadian economy and the country's national power structure was the focus, too, of Wallace Clements's, *The Canadian Corporate Elite* (1975, see also 1977). Clement showed that the corporate elite, around 1971, was often tightly tied into the corporate elite of other countries, especially that of the United States. He found it necessary, therefore, to distinguish between "comprador elites" and "indigenous elites" within the Canadian corporate elite. The comprador elites were people working for foreign-owned operations in Canada. They administered these organizations as branch plants, with most major policies likely to originate in the foreign-based parent organization. The indigenous elites were people who controlled firms that were Canadian-owned.

Clement worked from a Marxist perspective and was guided by the following principle:

> No matter what institution is the most powerful, a society reproduces itself through the production of means of living (food, clothes, shelter), and, therefore, the economy is always a fundamental activity, whether organized by religious, political, military, or business leaders. Those who control the economy are a powerful elite within any modern society (1985: 562).

Consistent with this view, Clement reported that Canada was characterized by capitalist class control, much of it exercised from outside Canadian borders, but operating through a Canadian-based corporate elite. He saw only limited accommodation occurring at the elite level, between the corporate elite and the state elite. Clement saw a type of parallel development occurring for the comprador and indigenous (corporate) elites, with little foreign-Canadian conflict, and reported that "the process of compradorization has been sector specific" (1977: 293). The indigenous elite of an "overdeveloped financial and transportation/utilities system in Canada" (1977: 291) was not under threat of displacement by the influx of foreign capital. However, "the effect on weak capitalists in production was, of course, to bring about their downfall" (1977: 293).

Clement also assessed the social backgrounds of the Canadian corporate elite using data twenty years more recent than Porter's. Comparisons between Clement's results and Porter's must be made cautiously, however, because Clement used a slightly different definition of corporate elite. Clement's results suggest that the corporate elite became more exclusive (i.e., less representative of the general public) between 1951 and 1971. By 1971, 61 per cent of the elite had upper class backgrounds, compared with 50 per cent at the time of Porter's study, and 23 per cent came from the middle class, with six per cent from the working class. Eight per cent were French Canadians versus 29 per cent in the general population, and by 1971, Jewish Canadians were fully four per cent of the elite, although still only about one per cent of the general population. Yet only about one per cent of the elite in 1971 were women; this exclusion had gone unchanged. Clement also compared his list of dominant economic organizations with Porter's and concluded that there had been "an increased centralization and concentration of capital into fewer and larger firms" (1975: 168).

Clement conducted a parallel study of the media elite, defined as people who were at the apex of privately owned media organizations (the CBC and other public agencies were excluded). Here, too, Clement found a class and ethnic bias in the social background of the elite. But more important, he found a great deal of overlap in personnel between his corporate elite and the media elite, and much inter-linkage between the two elites by virtue of their members' sitting beside each other on the same boards of directors. Clement argued that this showed that the two elites were not as separate or independent as Porter had suggested.

Our excerpts in this Section begin with Porter's observations on Clement's work in *The Canadian Corporate Elite*, which were originally published as the "Foreword" in Clement's book. Porter is obviously pleased with those aspects of Clement's analyses that replicate and extend his own analyses, but shows no sympathy for Clement's conclusion about corporate-media inter-connections, via boards of directors. Porter delineates what Clement would have to show in order to prove that corporate and media elites are effectively the same.

In the next selection Clement summarizes some of his findings from the *Canadian Corporate Elite* project and reminds us that the corporate (especially, financial) elite is not weak simply because it acts as mediator in the sphere of circulation, rather than as an extractor of surplus through production, it is just different from a lot of national bourgeoisies around the world. Clement then goes on to argue why he believes plural-elite versus accommodation images of power are misleading. Here he emphasizes how, and why, accommodations between the state elite and the corporate elite tend to reinforce arrangements that are in the interest of the capitalist class.

Next we present one of Michael Ornstein's studies that compare the beliefs and values of members of different elites. Until such studies as this, people often argued that we could not determine whether elites shared a common outlook because their members are not inclined to respond to interviews. Sociologists assumed they were too busy and private; yet Ornstein found that it was not difficult to interview the elite. He studied the responses of a national sample of members of different elites in respect to questions on social welfare policy, rights of workers, foreign investment, and taxation. This allowed Ornstein to compare executives of the largest Canadian corporations, executives of medium-sized firms, top-level federal, provincial and municipal politicians, top-level federal and provincial civil servants, and trade union leaders. As might be expected, the trade union leaders were comparatively left-leaning in their beliefs, while economic leaders gave responses considerably to the right of politicians and the bureaucratic elite.

At this level of policy beliefs, some differences between the elites do appear. There is not the level of elite consensus that Porter and Clement might have expected. However, the different portions of the economic elite showed only very small differences in beliefs, suggesting that economic forces tend to unite the capitalist class in its outlook.

In the final selection, S.D. Berkowitz criticizes Porter and Clement for providing too little information on the structure of elite relations. Berkowitz questions their data and conclusions on three key issues: intercorporate control, foreign domination, and social backgrounds of the corporate elite.

We have not seen the last word of research and theory on images of the Canadian elite structure.

18

A Single Elite or Multiple Elites?*

John Porter

Radicalism has retreated in our universities, as elsewhere in North America, at a rate which has surprised, and no doubt relieved, those who viewed it with panic and as a permanent feature of academic life. While university administrators are not likely to ask in harmony where all the student radicals have gone, the fact remains that the social criticism expressed by our young people a few years ago seems to have become dulled.

Some of these student radicals have graduated to become faculty members. Still radical, they are now more at home in the library and with the pen than in the lists with their loud-hailers. As scholars their attitude to *The Vertical Mosaic* has changed. Some charge that its errors are egregious, that its author has sinned, to paraphrase at least one meaning of that expression, by missing his Marx.

I have never been dogmatic about the theories and frameworks by which we seek to give order to the facts that emerge from our research. As far as inequality is concerned, the facts often speak for themselves regardless of the framework within which they are presented. I doubt that the picture of inequality which I drew would have been much different or any more demanding of attention if I had had a prime concern for theoretical or definitional purity to the point at which I might have become bogged in a scholastic morass, my data sinking with me.

If my younger critical colleagues speaking with the conviction of evangelists, a happy state of mind denied to me throughout, feel that they have an exclusive hold on truth, I am not likely to challenge them. Rather I would say, "Fine! Go Ahead! Do it your way, but at least do it!" For there is much to be done to demonstrate the pervasiveness and endurance of inequality in Canada. Unless there is some slogging after the facts, theoretical debates are abstract and hollow whether the schoolmen who engage in them are medieval or contemporary. Hence from the point of view of human betterment I view much of the radical criticism as carping rather than constructive.

*Originally published as "Foreword" in Wallace Clement, *The Canadian Corporate Elite: An Analysis of Economic Power*, Carleton Library No. 89, Toronto: McClelland and Stewart, 1975, pp. ix-xv. Reprinted with permission of Carleton University Press.

Wallace Clement is not wholly in the company of the carpers. He is radical in that, like many of us, he does not see the key to human welfare as lying within the institutions of modern capitalism, but he has the good sense to realize that social change depends on the accumulation of evidence that leads us ineluctably to conclude that we must bring it about. He points out what he considers to be the shortcomings of *The Vertical Mosaic*, and goes on from there to present us with an impressive assemblage of information that we cannot ignore if we are concerned about the inequalities that stem from the present concentration of economic power as it is found within Canada, and as it has been created by the investing metropolises of the world.

Mr. Clement's contribution is important in several respects. To me perhaps the most interesting is his meticulous following, within the limits imposed by new forms of data collection, of the same procedures I used twenty years earlier to measure economic concentration and the social origins of the economic elite. I have often been asked if the structure of power and mobility into the elite in Canada has changed since I studied it, the questionner often implying that things must surely have changed because the image of the open society in which he believed he lived, he earnestly wished to retain. Now Mr. Clement has answered that question, as far as the economic and what he calls the media elites are concerned, with evidence that some will find startling but with which few can find reason to be pleased. The economic elite of 1972 is more exclusive in social origins, more upper class and more closely knit by family ties than in 1952. Nor has there been any sizable entry into the board rooms of our major corporations of Canadians who are not British in their ethnic origin. So social structures are slow to change.

By employing the same methods to investigate the concentration of economic power and to identify dominant corporations and trace their interlocking directorships to establish the 1972 economic elite, the author has been able to show a trend and provide the beginning of a time series or a social indicator to tell us something of the direction of social change in the formation of Canada's economic elite. This is a significant advance over the so-called cross-sectional study when only one point in time is considered. It is to be hoped that Mr. Clement will continue and others will follow his example in this important development in Canadian sociology.

Another significant difference which the present study was able to exploit, and which I think is worth noting, is the greatly increased availability of data. The Corporations and Labour Unions Returns Act, requiring both corporations and trade unions to file, if they are federally chartered, as most important ones are, a great deal of information previously held confidential, has meant a great cutting down in time and work required to marshal the facts of economic concentration. Also, some provincial legislation has forced more disclosure through such things as insider trading reports. Gradually Canadians may be becoming aware of the importance of information, collected by governments and other research agencies, for social planning and improving the directing capabilities of our social system. Such information is not important for policy-making and monitoring only, but also in making judgements about the quality of our society.

Another important contribution of this present work is the attempt the author makes to provide historical depth to his analysis. Such a time perspective is essential for thorough class analysis for it is continuity over generations of established families that gives an upper class its tenacity and endurance and accumulated wealth. He adumbrates from Canadian history a pattern of relationships between those who direct economic activity and those who control the major sources of investment, at first in France, then England and finally the United States. Canada's position as a recipient of investment in its staple products and natural resources has given Canadian businessmen an *entrepôt* or go-between role which has in the twentieth century given those Canadians, whom Mr. Clement calls the indigenous elite, a continuing control over finance, commerce, transportation and utilities. As a consequence there has been a neglect of entrepreneurial talent, a gap in managerial skill for manufacturing which, as the Herb Gray Report reminds us, persists until today. In all this Mr. Clement is eclectic in drawing upon a growing body of entrepreneurial and elite history both of which represent a new resource for the Canadian social scientist.

In his discussion of what has become the most salient feature of Canadian economic structure, foreign control, Mr. Clement distinguishes between what he calls the indigenous Canadian elite, much confined to its historic go-between role, and the "comprador" elite (a term as delightful for the image it evokes as it is suitable for the relationship it describes), which serves as the agent of foreign, particularly American owners. As decision-makers the compradors are the servants of outsiders who are labelled the "parasitic elite" living off the avails of their investments short of the point where we as hosts are so enfeebled that we can no longer nurture our guests who, for whatever else they produce for us, produce also a national enigma. Contemporary Europe is acquiring a proletariat euphemistically referred to as "guest workers". Canada has acquired a bourgeoisie of guest owners. But as Mr.

Clement points out, the surviving indigenous elite is also capitalist and many of the comprador elite are capitalists lured by the lucrative take-over bid to transfer their capital to the custody of the foreigner. He provides us with a fascinating account of his three elite types and leaves us with the anticipation that there is more to come when he turns his attention to the "parasites" and the intricate web of multinational enterprises that make us so much periphery to their centre, hinterland to their metropolis.

Less striking than the evidence that the economic elite has become more closed, which I take to be the significant contribution of this study, is the part of the book that deals with the mass media. Perhaps that is because it is such a short time since the Senate committee report, which is drawn upon heavily, brought the picture of concentration in the mass media up to date. The story is much the same as with major economic institutions. A higher proportion than formerly of newspaper circulation, radio listening and television viewing is controlled by the major chains in the hands of upper class families. That this has taken place in Quebec as well as in English-speaking Canada is the most important change noted. Very little is said about public broadcasting or about, for example the role of Radio Canada in Quebec in the formation of national sentiments in that Province or the emergence of educational television, or the political struggle for the control of television and cable systems. Nor can we judge from the analysis the effectiveness of the public control of broadcasting, or whether the public interest is better served by public regulation as with the broadcast media than it is with the printed media which has so far escaped public surveillance with those dubious press councils devoted to self-regulation.

Since the author's purpose in this examination of the mass media is to show that those who own big business also own the mass media and therefore must use their power to subvert the public interest, it is surprising that he does not deal with the phenomenon of the Senate committee itself. He shows the Senate is closely associated with economic power through the number of corporate directorships held by Senators. Why then did they agree to this exposé? Surely not to satisfy the ego or enhance the career of Senator Davey.

I suppose I find the mass media chapters less than satisfactory because, beyond the intrinsic interest of the Senate committee findings, the author argues in them a questionable theoretical point not unrelated to my earlier references to those radical critics with whom I am reluctant to engage in duals of sophistry about analysing power.

In *The Vertical Mosaic* I adopted what might be called a plural elite model which, very simply, stated that the power of economic, political, bureaucratic, military and other institutions tend to be separated because they perform different tasks for a society and, in so doing, become specialized, and hence there is always a tendency for power also to be separated. At the same time the overall coordinating and guidance needs of the society require interaction between the various elite groups. It therefore becomes a matter of empirical investigation to discover the extent to which these coordinating and guidance needs lead to an aggrandizement of power, to the creation of what might be called a power elite or a ruling centre such as exists, for example, in communist systems where party membership provides the linking mechanism.

In the final chapter, Mr. Clement argues that the links he has shown between the owners of the major mass media complexes and the corporate world and the upper class refute any theory of plural elites because they provide examples of two functionally separated tasks, that is the creation of ideology on the one hand, and sheer economic or money making on the other, which are under the control of the same elite, the corporate. From this position he throws doubt on the separateness of other elites, political, bureaucratic, church, intellectual and so forth, and seems much inclined, in order to conform to a radical orthodoxy, to take as writ that all institutions serve the evils of capitalism. Thus he moves away from his role as a justifiably angered, but reasonably objective investigator.

As to the particular point on which he tries to build his case, the ownership and control of the mass media, the matter is very marginal once the question is asked whether capitalists own the mass media primarily for economic gain or to produce ideology to legitimate their other exploitative behaviour. I suppose the test case would be where capitalists continued to operate newspapers and broadcasting stations at a loss, subsidized from their other activities, to serve their ideological interest. I would think such a case difficult to find. To quote one of his own sources, "Bassett could make more out of a dead *Tely* than a live one."

Other elites, politicians, senior government officials, clergy, intellectuals, generals are not directly linked to profit making enterprises. The degree to which their functional separateness and institutional specialization becomes mitigated because of the over-all coordination and planning of a complex society should, I think, remain a problem to investigate rather than be subject to premature theoretical closure, a point which Mr. Clement curiously makes from time to time. If all elites have similar social and educational backgrounds, if they are intermarried or join the same exclusive clubs, all that becomes important evidence to be weighed in making a judgement of how narrowly recruited our elites are, and from which we might infer their broadly similar interests in the survival of a corporate capitalist economy.

We should always remember that to others the evidence might not be so convincing. Thus it seems to me to argue which theory is right, that of plural elites or that of a power elite or that of a ruling class, is futile. Each may have its own particular attraction as a guiding framework for research, but they remain hypotheses to be tested by evidence. Unfortunately, in the study of power, unlike some other fields of inquiry, the evidence is not sufficiently conclusive or generally agreed upon that an hypothesis can be universally accepted or rejected. We might well wish it could be, but our desire for certainty should not overwhelm our critical capacities.

19

Public and Private Power*

Wallace Clement

Canada in the Continental Context

There are a number of indicators that Canada is actually part of the North American economy rather than self-contained within the Canadian nation-state. In other words, Canada's economic and political boundaries do not always coincide.

The process of structural compradorization has been proceeding steadily over the last 20 years. Indeed, it was found that 29.2 per cent of the dominant positions in the Canadian economy are either within U.S. controlled subsidiaries or held by persons born in the U.S. The evidence from the present study illustrates that the Canadian indigenous elite have had an active role in U.S. controlled companies operating in Canada. While 29.2 per cent of the dominant positions are U.S. comprador, only 15.8 per cent of the Canadian born elite are. Conversely, three quarters of the Canadian born elite are indigenous with autonomous Canadian controlled bases of power. In other words, the Canadian indigenous elite is also recruited to sit on U.S. controlled branch plants. A good deal of evidence was provided which illustrated that this indigenous elite remains viable. For instance, the proportion with their main careers in family firms has increased over the past 20 years, the youngest group of elites are more likely to be indigenous than the middle age group, and almost 20 per cent fewer of the comprador elite are of upper class origin with half the comprador elite coming from the middle class while almost two thirds of the indigenous elite are upper class, with this rising to almost three quarters for the multiple directorship holders.

The Canadian economic elite is, however, a specialized elite. As was documented, the traditional elite has chosen to centre itself in transportation, utilities, finance and the mass media. In so doing, it has stifled the development of indigenous social forces in most manufacturing and resource activities — the

*Excerpted from *The Canadian Corporate Elite: An Analysis of Economic Power*, Carleton Library No. 89, Toronto: McClelland and Stewart, 1975. Reprinted with permission of the author and Carleton University Press.

sectors which are actually engaged in the creation of surplus in a capitalist society. In the process it has become allied with foreign capitalists in these surplus-creating sectors. The scope of the traditional indigenous elite's power within the continental context remains to be examined but it should not be surprising to find that they have an important place in this larger context. Their viability within the Canadian context, as an expression of the upper class, has been illustrated but if they do not have a powerful position within the continental context they are vulnerable to U.S. industrial capitalists. This rather unique development of elite configurations makes the Canadian corporate elite atypical compared to other industrialized liberal-democracies. Panitch and Whitaker have summarized some recent work on Canada's development saying: " . . . from the start it was a resource hinterland within a mercantile-imperialist framework. The kind of bourgeoisie which emerges from this political economy is a conservative mercantile and financial type which inevitably is dependent upon the dynamic, creative, *productive* industrial bourgeoisies of the metropolis, first British, then American. Canadian capitalists are typically bankers who today make their profits by channeling Canadian surpluses into American takeovers. In other words, finance *capital* has led to industrial *capital*, but financial *capitalists* have not become industrial *capitalists*; instead they have provided Canadian funds for American industrial capitalists. Thus Canada lacks a *national* bourgeoisie in the sense that the U.S.A., Britain, Germany, France, and Japan have national bourgeoisies" (1974: 52). But to say Canada "lacks a national bourgeoisie" like other liberal-democracies is not the same as saying it does not have a national bourgeoisie. The difference is that the Canadian bourgeoisie is primarily a commercial one,

engaged in circulation rather than production while in other nations the bourgeoisie is typically both industrial and financial. The fragmentation which has resulted does not mean the total bourgeoisie is not powerful — indeed, it may be more powerful because of the continental context. It does mean, however, that the Canadian component must commit itself to the continental context to remain strong. In the meantime, indigenous industrial forces are restrained, their mobility limited, and the independence of the Canadian nation-state by-passed. The power of the indigenous commercial elite and the foreign industrial elite reinforce one another in the continental context. The following passage provides some insight into the way a representative of this indigenous elite perceives Canada's place in international capitalism:

> Canada should rely on its comparative economic advantages in determining which economic sectors to develop and how to pace that development, W. Earl McLaughlin, president and chairman of the Royal Bank of Canada, said yesterday. "Let our comparative economic advantages speak for themselves, and let us avoid any artificial diversion of our economic structure into costly and inefficient forms", Mr. McLaughlin told the Canadian Club . . . The Royal Bank chief executive added: "Let us try to avoid the misjudgment — or personal vanity — which proclaim one form of activity to be intrinsically superior to another, whether that be resource development, high technology manufacturing, or service industries" (*The Ottawa Journal*, April 18, 1974: 9).

In other words, just because the Canadian corporate elite has chosen to extract its surplus as mediators in the sphere of circulation, this should not be judged as being somehow "inferior" to extracting surplus through production. This ideology of the traditional financial elite certainly fits well with its historical and contemporary role in the Canadian economy. It certainly fits well with W. Earl McLaughlin's position: he has the best of both worlds, his ancestors having sold out to General Motors of the U.S. in the early 1900s, he now has six dominant directorships plus a directorship on General Motors Corp. (Detroit).

By developing a powerful national base in the circulation sectors, the indigenous Canadian elite has been able to operate internationally among the most powerful world capitalists. By servicing U.S. control of most of the resource sector and much of the manufacturing, the indigenous elite has reinforced its position within Canada and in the international capitalist system. They have accepted an international "division of labour" and their role in it as mediators. To say that Canada's bourgeoisie is not like most other liberal-democracies is certainly correct; to say there is no national bourgeoisie fails to acknowledge the powerful position Canadian financial capitalists have had and continue to enjoy.

The question of "dependency" on the U.S. is much more complex when the important place of Canadian financial capitalists is introduced. For instance, is the bourgeoisie "dependent" on the workers because they create surplus? Are the Canadian commercial capitalists "dependent" on U.S. industrial capitalists because they control the creation of surplus? Of course, the parallels are not synonymous because U.S. industrial capitalists obviously have a better organized base of power than do Canadian workers, but it does serve to illustrate that the notion of "dependency" is, at least, paradoxical. If the indigenous Canadian elite were to suffer severe losses to its "turf" in finance, transportation, utilities and the media, then it could be said it was being drawn into a "dependency" relationship but as long as it maintains control over these key institutions, then it has an independent base of power with which it can enter into an alliance with foreign capitalists. This subservience has not yet arrived and, in the face of threats, it has been successful in using its political power to ensure protection. Again, to say the traditional elite has entered into a "partnership" with U.S. industrial capitalists is probably correct; to say this is a "junior partnership" is to underestimate the power this elite wields nationally and internationally.

The existence of a powerful Canadian commercial elite controlled by the upper class and of a predominantly foreign elite in production, means that Canada remains a "low mobility" society. Concentration and centralization in commercial sectors has been the result of indigenous forces while these same processes in the productive sections have been imposed from outside. The result is an economy which is highly structured with few mobility avenues for those outside the upper class. A few middle class Canadians have experienced individual mobility with compradorization but even this avenue has had many of its uppermost positions filled by the indigenous elite. In light of the earlier findings that few from outside the upper class are able to make the shift from insider positions to the executive or outsider positions, it is probable that this middle class comprador elite is trapped in the branch plants of U.S. subsidiaries but a conclusive answer to this must await an analysis of the continental economy.

Canada as a Liberal-Democracy

To use C.B. Macpherson's words, the "democracy" of a liberal-democracy is not a "kind of society" but simply a "system of government". As has been evident throughout this book, neither the economic nor mass media domains in Canadian society are in any sense democratic. The "freedom" of liberal-democracy is limited since it must be placed within the framework of gross inequalities pervasive throughout society which confine that freedom. The structured inequality evident in the corporate world becomes reflected in the inequality of access to decision making positions. Mediating between structure and opportunity in capitalist society is ownership of property. Laski indicates, in part, how the selection and screening process under corporate capitalism operates when he says: "Once the right of employment is dependent upon the will of the owner of property, it is in his power to make occupation a function of orthodoxy" (1935: 208). It can be expected that acts of firing or, more subtly, "freezing-out" the undesirable by promoting those seemed suitable, will lead to the perpetuation of similar social types and privileged status for those similar to the power holders. This should be viewed as a consequence, rather than a cause, which follows from the way a society is organized. That it exists, should cue the analyst to examine stable patterns of relations which encourage and permit its development.

It is important to understand that social classes transcend the individual in at least two crucial ways. First, since classes are the product of relationships between structures, they continue as long as the structures continue. Consequently, classes have a continuity which lasts over generations because the structures and relationships which create them have continuity. Second, class positions are typically transferred intergenerationally and here, for instance, Poulantzas would agree: "It is true that in the capitalist mode

of production and a capitalist social formation, social classes are not castes, that agents are not tied by their origin to determinate places . . . . But it is also true that the effects of distribution show themselves in the fact that . . . the vast majority of bourgeois (and their children after them) remain bourgeois and the vast majority of proletarians (and their children after them) remain proletarians" (1973: 54). Poulantzas is arguing that education is not itself social class but does, in fact, serve to transfer class positions intergenerationally within families, but the cause of social class is "the positions themselves" within capitalist production. An alternative way used earlier to express these two dimensions of social class is through the concepts of condition and opportunity where condition refers to the structure of society based on relations of production and opportunity to the intergenerational transfer of positions within the structure of relationships. Within liberal-democracies there is not attempt to achieve equality of condition. As a result, their stated goal of equality of opportunity is severely limited. Even if Canadian society is highly structured and if there is unequal opportunity, some would still argue that everyone is "protected" by the variety of interest groups operating in the great "pluralist arena" — balancing each others' particularistic interests against the general good. This argument will now be examined.

The Pluralist Arena?

It has been argued by some observers of liberal-democracies that a great variety of "interest groups" operate to ensure that everyone gets a "fair" voice in the management and direction of society. Connolly identified two "types" of pluralism, one which "views the government as the *arena* where major group conflicts are debated and resolved" and another which "sees major social associations, especially organized labour and the corporation, involved in a balancing process which operates largely outside the government; the government acts more as *umpire* than as participant, setting rules for conflict resolution and moving in to redress the imbalance when one group goes too far" (1969: 8). Pluralists generally focus on "consensus" and the idea of a "balance" of social forces. It ignores the systematic biases evident in class based societies and the reflection these have on relations between the state and corporate worlds. The pluralist model assumes "free willed" individuals who will come together when they detect injustice and voice their concerns through the many "access points" in the state. What this ignores is the fact that individuals are not "free willed" but subject to dominant ideological systems; what it fails to acknowledge is the unequal allocations of resources necessary to mobilize and realize concerns.

Pluralists assume that the state will be an unbiased mediator of interests but fail to recognize the possibility, as Miliband argues, "that the state might be a rather special institution, whose main purpose is to defend the predominance in society of a particular class" (1969: 3). Schattschneider has summarized the critique quite poetically when he writes: "The flaw in the pluralist heaven is that the heavenly chorus sings with a strong upper class accent" (1960: 35). There is little reason to assume that the existence of several institutional bases of power (such as corporations, the state or mass media) necessarily lead to a "countervailing" or even competitive system. It needs to be demonstrated that various segments of society are organized into roughly equally powerful

agencies and further that these are indeed competitive with one another. Neither of these positions has been empirically verified and evidence presented earlier indicate that some segments of society, such as the dominant Anglo upper class, have much more pervasive power than any other segment. Indeed, as Paul Sweezy has wittily remarked: "Some of the alleged countervailing powers may veil more power than they counter" (1959: 71). Common ideologies, class backgrounds and relationships serve to solidify power holders, not bring them into opposition. Structured interlocks, combined with social ties, serve to create a system of mutual benefit and dependence between leaders of dominant corporations and other institutions. By failing to conceptualize dominant organizations as part of, and intimately involved in, the larger social system, pluralists fail to understand that these dominant organizations are not simply passive conductors of values; rather, they shape values and activate the values of those in control. Values are not "free-floating" variables but a part of life that changes and is changed by social situations. Large organizations represent values in themselves and further act to shape and develop other select values.

Interest group theorists, a version of pluralists, have a long theoretical and empirical history in social studies but one of their greatest difficulties is the tendency to identify organized pressure groups as a sign of strength rather than weakness. As Nettle has argued, many are simply "shells" engaged in a form of "shadow-boxing" (1969: 291-302). The powerful have direct access to state leaders and do not have to be organized into "interest groups" which provide a façade of importance but lack the substance of direct access. One such study by Robert Presthus of interest groups in Canada is subject to such a critique. He says: "Although our sample includes a cross-section of virtually all types of interest groups, one common characteristic is that none of them are 'profit making'. Many, of course, are creatures of activities which are themselves profit-making" (1973: 73). Only those groups which hang out their shingles and call themselves "interest groups" are defined as important for the power process of Canadian society. He eliminates, by definition, those sectors of corporate power which deal directly with the state and defines in the very groups Nettle argued are engaged in "shadow-boxing". It would be wrong to conclude that Presthus is not capturing an important aspect of the power process in Canada. What is important, however, is to recognize that he is only including one aspect — the formal interest group level — while ignoring direct interaction by corporations and their elite with members of the state elite. Moreover, it is not correct to place on the same level the Canadian Manufacturers' Association and other interest groups such as the Lions' Club, the Loyal Orange Lodge, or Association Cyclists Canadienne. The consequences of these latter groups "getting their own way" is on a totally different level, as is the weight they carry in the political domain.

In spite of limitations outlined, Presthus was able to detect "the tendency of governmental elites to reinforce the going distributive system" in Canada such that "the consequences include a virtual monopoly of access by established groups which tend to enjoy major shares of political resources". This, Presthus argues, is because of "the vital issue of practical politics which, all else being equal, compels governmental elites to defer to those who command the most powerful institutional structures in finance, industry and the mass media" (1973: 350, 352).

Inequality inherent in a class-based society, particularly in one which has concentrated power in a few dominant institutional orders, becomes reflected in the political domain whereby those with the most in turn are able to command the most advantageous arrangements with the state.

Presthus' position is that "elite accommodation" acts to "ensure some rough equilibrium among the contending group interests . . . . elite accommodation may be regarded as a structural requisite of any democratic society in which policy decisions are the result of negotiation and consultation among the elites concerned . . . . Elite accommodation is inherent in the process of democratic government" (4). Moreover, he claims this reflects "an underlying pluralism" which offers "the hope of finding some way to overcome pervasive modern schisms between labour and capital, social classes, and indeed, between government and the governed" (24-25). These may be the aspirations of "elite accommodation" but the consequences have been of quite a different nature. Indeed, Presthus' own findings show that the "consequence of the going system of elite accommodation is a reinforcement of the *status quo* in terms of the existing pattern of distribution of public largesse and political power. Functional ties and established clientele relationships tend to crystallize existing power relationships. As we have seen, it is understandably difficult for new or substantively weak interests to penetrate the decision-making process. . . . The perhaps inevitable inequalities in political resources among interest groups mean that government, to some extent, is pushed into the anomalous position of defending the strong against the weak" (349). It is difficult to understand how Presthus can characterize such a system as "ensuring some rough equilibrium"; rough indeed! To argue as Presthus does, that this structure is "inherent" and inevitable" does not justify his calling it "democratic" without twisting the use of that word so badly as to leave it without meaning. It is one thing to identify a structure and its consequences; it is yet another to advocate and celebrate the inequalities of liberal-democracies.

The Nexus of Public and Private Power

Collegiality as a principle of decision making by elites was considered earlier as it was elaborated by Weber (1947: 392ff). Following this, Porter has identified two main aspects of collegiality: "First, it greatly increases the range of knowledge which can be brought to the making of major decisions and policies .... Secondly, collegiality helps to reduce power by requiring that it be shared among colleagues who represent the various and often conflicting interests of the larger group". The importance of these groups is stressed by Porter when he says that "within institutional systems and between them, control crystallizes within the ambit of these relatively small collegial groups" (1965: 218-220).

The way collegial groups are formed and particularly the relative power of their components should be placed within the context of Laski's notion of how dominant interests respond to emerging social forces: "a class which controls the power of the state will not surrender it if surrender involves the abdication of its privileges. It will reform when it must if reform does not mean the destruction of what it regards as essential. But it will only reform when it believes that concessions can be made without essential sacrifice.

On any other terms, a ruling class will fight" (1935: 316). Within this framework, it can be anticipated that collegial groups formed in the post-war era between the state and corporate interests will attempt to operate on the level of reforms which do not involve "essential sacrifice" to the prevailing order. The rudimentary principle which is left unchallenged is that of private power as expressed in captial — the same principle which confines equality of opportunity and condition in liberal-democracies.

The state is a major candidate as a location for collegial activity because it has two advantages. First, it has the power to tax the population thus providing such surplus as may be necessary to undertake its policies, although the capacity of the corporate world in this respect should not be understated, and second, the state is also backed by what Weber and Laski both called "coercive authority". While it is correct to argue that dominant elements in society are forced to respond to underlying social forces and movements, it is also important to remember Laski's point that it is the dominant elements which usually choose how to respond and their response is conditioned by some basic issues for which they will be willing to fight.

How is it that collegial decisions are worked out and what are the consequences for the populace? In a period of optimism, W.L. MacKenzie King, later to become Prime Minister of Canada, argued: "It is altogether probable that Collectivist ideals, and in particular what they represent of the community idea and improvement in the status of Labour, will vastly expand their influence in the years to come. This is but continuing a natural evolution which experience has wholly justified. A belief in the wisdom and justice of a measure of State interference succeeded the older conception of *laissez faire*, which looked to unrestricted competition as the ideal in matters of industrial organization. Regulation, especially as respects a minimum of social well-being, is more and more the accepted order of to-day" (1918: 230). King's optimism has not been totally borne out in Canada, although the collectivist structure he envisioned does bear some resemblance. The essential harmony of interests between the state, labour and industry is a model more resembling the top of society than its base. Michels' prediction seems much more accurate: "Sooner or later the competition between various cliques of the dominant classes ends in a reconciliation which is effected with the instinctive aim of retaining domination over the masses by sharing it among themselves" (1962: 343).

Structurally, both King's and Michels' frameworks resemble one another but the anticipated consequences are radically different. King's image is of harmony among all people while Michels' is of a basic division between ruler and ruled with harmony limited to the rulers. Even today the debate is a relevant one with the critics arguing that the elite accommodation or collectivist models really mean a coalition of the powerful dominating others while its defenders say this "balanced" coalition is the wave of the future and of benefit to all. Both agree that it means concentration of power in the hands of a few.

What then are the roles of public and private power in a liberal-democracy like Canada? Louis St-Laurent, as Prime Minister of Canada, represented the way he saw the role of the state in these terms: "I don't think that free enterprise requires that governments do nothing about economic conditions. Government can — and I believe governments should — pursue fiscal and commercial policies which will encourage and stimulate enterprise and wise government policies can do

a lot to maintain the right kind of economic climate" (quoted by Lamontage, 1969: 69-70). O'Connor has offered an explanation which goes a long way in explaining why the state "should", in St-Laurent's terms, "encourage and stimulate enterprise". O'Connor says that the state has succeeded in socializing a number of aspects of production in liberal-democracies, particularly risk, but what it has not socialized are private profits or control over private decision making. His argument is that the fiscal policies of the state in liberal-democracies are tied to the tax base of corporate activity such that "state expenditures remain integral to the process of private accumulation. In the event that state spending is not tied to the needs of private capital, there will occur a reduction in the rate of economic growth, and, hence, the tax base and the possibility of financing future expenditures" (1970: 79). The fiscal policy of the state is tied to the prosperity of private capital since it is growth which generates taxation revenues, a basic ingredient of policy implementation. However, the long-term productivity of the corporate sector "requires the expansion of the state sector" O'Connor maintains, thus making them interdependent in their relationship (1972: 25). The political economy of the state is such that it requires higher levels of involvement in order to meet demands made on it. To do so continues to require higher levels of revenue. The critical point appears when its revenues can no longer support escalating demands.

But who benefits? As long as production expands, at least that component of labour tied to big unions and large corporations gains in real income terms but it is not so clear that the rest of labour gains. Given the biased way state subsidies are offered to corporations, big corporations gain while smaller ones are allowed to pass by the way. But it is not enough to say big corporations gain; it is actually those at the top of these corporations who gain through higher salaries and through dividends from profits. Without explaining that there are people involved in these processes, there is a failure to understand how the major instruments of income and wealth distribution in capitalist societies operate. The distributive mechanism of the prevailing system serves to reinforce and perpetuate existing inequalities. To the extent that the state encourages and supports these mechanisms, public capital is used to promote private gains.

To argue that liberal-democracies are characterized by a "mixed economy" of public and private capital is to miss the point of how they are "mixed" and in what proportions. When public capital is used to support private capital the mixture is not "balanced" but has the effect of reinforcing and maintaining inequalities. The gains to be made are still private gains and the power is still private power.

The pressure by dominant interests within the state and corporate worlds has been toward increasing the stability of society through planning but given the existing inequalities, it is evident that this means further consolidation of already concentrated power centres and the reduction of boundaries between public and private power. To argue that the state has become more involved in economic activities without specifying the character and purpose of these activities fails to see the complementarity of these actions with those of private capital. State expenditures have been directed toward stabilizing relationships within the population and as a means of funneling surplus to dominant economic interests. In other words, what has frequently been understood as encroachments by public power on private power turns out in practice to reinforce and strengthen private interests. The future of the state and private capital have become identified as complementary and each has become mutually dependent upon the other. In order to coordinate these coincidental interests, there have evolved a series of forums and associations, created by and for the state and corporate elites. The majority of benefits from these types of arrangements accrue to those most capable of demanding them — the already powerful.

20

*The Political Ideology of Canadian Elites**

Michael Ornstein

Our analysis of capitalist class ideology is based on interviews with executives of the largest Canadian corporations and a comparison sample of medium-sized corporations. These interviews are set in the context of the opinions of top-level federal, provincial, and municipal civil servants and elected officials, and trade union leaders, all gathered as part of the same survey. For many of the items, the responses of a representative sample of Canadians were also available for comparison. The analysis of ideology is divided into four sections which deal with social welfare policy, labour relations, foreign investment, and the powers and taxation of different sectors of business.

Methodology

Measures of the political ideology of the capitalist class and of state officials, trade union leaders, and the general public were obtained in surveys conducted in late 1977 and early 1978. Although researchers in the tradition of elite theory (Barton, 1974, 1980; Higley, et al., 1979; Eldersveld, et al., 1975) have used survey data, surveys have seldom been used to address questions such as those dealt with here. In Canada, Fournier (1976) and McKie (n.d.) have surveyed business executives, but most studies have relied on documentary sources (Bliss, 1974; Mellos, 1978). One important advantage of sample surveys is that they permit the investigation of issues about which there is little public debate, on which business has not played a public role, or on which executives' public statements are likely to be rhetorical. Of course, surveys are much less suitable for detailed analysis of policy development. Implicit in this paper's approach, and consistent

*Excerpted from 'The Political Ideology of the Canadian Capitalist Class' in *The Canadian Review of Sociology and Anthropology*', Vol. 23: 2, 1986.

with a structuralist approach, is the assumption that the study of ideology cannot be reduced to the study of political action.

Measuring Ideology

As Larrain (1979) notes, widespread theoretical debate and little consensus exist concerning the definition of ideology (see also Hänninen and Paldán, 1983). This paper views ideology in what Larrain (1979: 14) describes as a "positive" sense, as "the expression of the world view of a class . . . the opinions, theories, and attitudes, formed within a class in order to defend and promote its interests." The term "ideology" is used in this paper instead of "attitudes" in order to draw attention to its substantive focus — on class relations and the role of the state — and to its methodological focus — on interpreting the responses to individual items in terms of more general ideological perspectives.

In each of the five policy areas our analysis focused on important current issues at the time of the survey. Our discussion of the results is informed by two cautions. First, as Merleman (1968) and Offé (1974) persuasively argue, the study of issues that have become the subject of public date conceals the unexamined assumptions that prevent many issues from entering policital debate — systematically excluding issues that might lead to fundamentally alter the structure of power. There is also a danger of overinterpreting the responses to individual questions because of unintentional biases in item wording, and the context provided by earlier items in the questionnaire and carelessness on the part of the interviewer and respondent may combine to undermine validity. In part, these difficulties are addressed by analyzing the business executives' responses in the context of the state and labour respondents.

Sample and Variables

The 142 big business respondents were chief executives (or other top executives designated as their substitutes) of a random sample of corporations chosen from the 1976 *Financial Post* ranking of the largest firms. The comparison sample of 43 chief executives of medium-sized business was selected from lists of firms supplied by the Boards of Trade in the 12 largest Canadian cities (with the number of selections proportional to their populations), which makes it difficult to advance strong claims about its representativeness. None of the medium-sized firms had more than 200 employees; the mean was 50 and the median, 59 employees. While much smaller than the large corporations, the medium-sized businesses are also not small retail stores or workshops.

The sample of civil servants includes approximately equal numbers of federal deputy and assistant deputy ministers, provincial deputy ministers, and department heads from the 12 largest Canadian cities, while the sample of politicians includes approximately equal numbers of Members of Parliament, provincial cabinet ministers in each province, and mayors and city councillors from the 12 largest cities. The sample trade of union leaders includes the presidents of the 50 largest trade unions in Canada and top officials of the major trade union centrals.

The "neo-staple industry variable" divides corporations between the spheres of production and circulation, as defined by Clement and Naylor, and according to whether they are Canadian and or foreign controlled. For the large corporations only (no measure is available for the medium-sized firms) capital intensity is measured by the ratio of corporation sales to assets, a convenient but somewhat flawed indicator. Core-periphery differences are examined by comparing the large and medium-sized corporations and (for large, industrial corporations) by the sales-to-assets ratio.

The measure of class background refers to the work done by the respondent's father when the respondent was 16 years of age, in particular his occupation, whether he owned a business, and, if he did, the size of the business, and (for non-owners) whether he supervised other workers. Regrouping Wright's (1976) categories, three class categories for family background were formed: the "bourgeoisie" includes the owners and top managers of business with 50 or more employees, the "medium and petty bourgeoisie" includes the owners of all business with less than 50 employees; and the "working class" includes all non-owners, including semi-autonomous employees and supervisors.[1]

Results

In each table the top panel compares the corporate executives as a whole to the samples of civil servants, politicians, and trade union leaders and, when possible, to the general public. The second panel of each table addresses the arguments about core-periphery differences by comparing the executives of large and medium-sized businesses. The third to sixth panels, which refer only to the executives of large corporations, examine the effects of industry, nation of control, "neo-staple industry," and class background.

Social Welfare Measures

The first three items in Table 20.1 measure how much effort, compared to levels of effort at the time of the interview, that respondents believed the government should put into health and medical care, providing assistance to the unemployed and helping the poor. Effort was defined as "the proportion of our total resources which is spent in each area." The fourth, fifth, and sixth items measure responses to the statements: "there is too much of a difference between rich and poor in this country;" "unemployment is high these days because it is too easy to get welfare assistance;" and "people with high incomes should pay a greater share of the total taxes than they do now."[2]

For all six items, capitalists are most conservative, trade unionists on the left, and civil servants, politicians, and the general public somewhere in between, just where depending on the particular issue. The business executives were more conservative concerning redistribution than general welfare measures. Only 13 per cent of the executives believed the rich should carry more of the tax burden, compared to 34 per cent of the civil servants, 54 per cent of politicians, 84 per cent of the trade unionists, and 59 per cent of the general public. By comparison, about 40 per cent of the business executives supported greater efforts to assist the poor. The two items bearing on the unemployed also find the capitalists far to the right of the other groups.

Contrary to monopoly capitalist theory, there are no systematic differences in the positions of the executives of large and medium-sized corporations. Not only are five of the six comparisons below statistical significance, but the directions of the differences are inconsistent.

While there were no consistent differences among executives from corporations in the five major industry categories, the executives of foreign-controlled corporations were somewhat more liberal than their Canadian counterparts. The largest difference involved the statement that welfare payments increase unemployment, a statement with which 56 per cent of the executives of foreign corporations and 68 per cent of the executives of Canadian corporations agreed. Because there were no industry differences this effect could not result from the concentration of foreign capital in certain industries. An examination of the "neo-staple industry" typology supports our prediction that the most conservative element of the capitalist class is the Canadian "mercantile" fraction — although the differences among the four categories are not large. In the sphere of production, the executives of foreign-controlled corporations were generally more conservative than their Canadian counterparts.

Although family background has a significant effect on the responses of four of the six items in Table 20.1, not all the differences are in the expected direction. Among executives with "bourgeois" backgrounds, 85 per cent agreed that welfare payments raise unemployment, compared to 72 per cent of executives with petit bourgeois and small employer backgrounds and 55 per cent of executives with working-class backgrounds. On support for the poor the effect of class background is in the opposite direction: about one half the executives from bourgeois and small employer backgrounds supported greater assistance to the poor, as compared to only one quarter of the executives from the working class.

Only one of the six items is related to the sales-to-assets ratio. That item is the measure of support for the unemployed which is strongly, positively related to the sales-to-assets ratio. Thus executives of labour intensive firms were *more* likely to support the unemployed, suggesting that they were not especially fearful that social welfare measures would decrease the labour supply.

The results of the bivariate analysis discussed so far are qualified by their basis on single-item measures and the small numbers of respondents in some of the categories. To address these shortcomings, a multiple classification analysis (not shown in any table) of two multi-item indices measuring opinions on social welfare efforts and on redistribution of income was undertaken. This additional analysis shows that, when family background is held constant, the effect of nation of control disappears. Executives from petit bourgeois and small employer backgrounds were more liberal than executives from the bourgeoisie and the working class.

Rights of Workers

On labour relations issues, the business executives were again to the right of the other groups. The capitalists were most isolated in responding to the statement "employees should be represented on the boards of the companies for which they work," with which only 17 per cent of the executives agreed or strongly agreed, compared to 50 per cent of civil servants, 57 per cent of the politicians, 42 per cent of the trade union leaders, and 69 per cent of the general public. For the other items in Table 20.2, and particularly for the evaluation of the power of trade unions, the executives proved only slightly more conservative than politicians and civil servants. Executives overwhelmingly favoured the existing level of workers' compensation, opposing the increase of payments to injured workers after their injuries.

Table 20.1 Support for social welfare measures by group, type of firm, and social origin (% distribution)

Independent Variable	Amount of government effort for health and medical care			Amount of government effort to assist the unemployed			Amount of government effort to help the poor			There is too much difference between rich and poor			Unemployment high because welfare too easy to get			People with high incomes should pay more taxes			No. of cases
	Less	Same	More	Less	Same	More	Less	Same	More	Disagree	Neither	Agree	Disagree	Neither	Agree	Disagree	Neither	Agree	
Group																			
Capitalists	26	68	6	47	37	16	10	50	40	64	14	22	22	13	65	85	2	13	(185)
Civil Servants	14	72	14	33	40	27	4	56	40	38	13	49	47	13	40	54	12	34	(129)
Politicians	12	71	17	22	43	35	6	45	49	44	12	44	54	8	38	45	9	46	(147)
Labour	0	28	72	4	32	64	2	13	85	6	6	88	86	2	12	8	8	84	(53)
General Public	3	50	47	26	46	38	4	55	41	18	18	64	22	10	68	26	15	59	(3289)
Size of Firm																			
Medium	21	67	12	58	23	19	12	49	39	71	22	7	20	24	56	78	5	17	(43)
Large	28	68	4	44	40	16	10	50	40	62	11	27	22	10	68	87	1	12	(142)
Industry																			
Industrial	24	72	4	40	39	15	8	54	38	63	13	24	24	7	69	88	1	11	(72)
Resources	19	71	10	43	43	14	10	28	62	65	10	25	40	20	40	90	0	10	(21)
Transport, utility	31	61	8	41	42	17	8	54	38	64	0	36	18	9	73	90	0	10	(13)
Merchandising	40	60	0	40	33	27	13	47	40	50	17	33	9	0	91	83	0	17	(15)
Financial	38	57	5	43	48	9	15	57	28	61	11	28	6	17	77	83	6	11	(21)
Nation of Control																			
Canada	34	62	4	49	36	15	12	52	36	55	11	34	12	8	80	85	1	14	(73)
Foreign	20	74	6	38	46	16	7	48	45	69	12	19	32	12	56	89	2	9	(69)
Neo-Staple Theory Industry																			
Canadian-'Mercantile'	41	54	5	49	36	15	16	51	33	58	12	30	9	13	78	84	3	13	(39)
Foreign-Productive	20	73	7	42	43	15	8	46	46	70	14	16	35	14	51	89	2	9	(59)
Canadian-Productive	26	71	3	50	35	15	9	53	38	53	9	38	15	3	82	85	0	15	(34)
Foreign-'Mercantile'	20	80	0	11	67	22	0	60	40	63	0	37	13	0	87	87	0	13	(10)
Class of Father																			
Bourgeois	31	61	8	50	42	8	12	47	41	66	17	17	9	6	85	86	3	11	(34)
Petit bourgeois	24	74	2	39	44	17	2	46	52	54	16	30	19	12	30	80	0	20	(45)
Working Class	29	66	5	46	36	18	16	57	27	4	65	31	34	12	54	94	0	6	(54)

Note: *N* is in parentheses.

Table 20.2 Labour relations issues by group, type of firm, and social origin (%)

Independent Variable	Amount of government effort for workman's compensation			Raise workman's comp. to pay level before injury			Prohibit employers from hiring strikebreakers			Put employee representatives on company boards			Power of trade unions			
	Less	Same	More	Disagree	Neither	Agree	Disagree	Neither	Agree	Disagree	Neither	Agree	Too little	About right	Too much	Much too much
Group																
Capitalists	19	72	9	67	17	16	78	8	14	70	13	17	0	11	55	34
Civil Servants	13	75	12	50	19	31	57	12	31	26	24	50	2	21	57	20
Politicians	4	75	21	49	16	35	57	13	30	33	10	57	3	22	58	17
Labour	0	37	63	24	4	70	4	4	92	29	29	42	57	34	9	0
General Public	4	51	45	—	—	—	29	16	55	15	16	69	8	31	48	23
Size of Firm																
Medium	23	72	5	57	29	14	82	9	9	51	16	33	0	9	40	51
Large	17	72	11	70	14	16	76	8	16	76	12	12	0	11	60	29
Industry																
Industrial	17	73	10	66	17	17	79	8	13	73	14	13	0	13	51	36
Resources	10	76	14	78	5	17	65	20	15	75	20	5	0	9	62	29
Transport, utility	15	77	8	70	15	15	61	8	31	83	0	17	0	0	69	31
Merchandising	14	79	7	77	8	15	92	0	8	72	14	14	0	20	73	7
Financial	25	60	15	74	10	16	79	0	21	84	0	16	0	10	75	15
Nation of Control																
Canada	18	69	13	73	9	18	75	6	19	75	12	13	0	10	67	23
Foreign	16	75	9	67	18	15	78	10	12	76	12	12	0	13	54	33
Neo-Staple Theory Industry																
'Canadian—Mercantile'	18	69	13	75	11	14	77	3	20	86	3	11	0	8	76	16
Foreign—Productive	15	75	10	67	19	14	78	12	10	79	12	9	0	12	52	36
Canadian—Productive	18	70	12	72	6	22	73	9	18	62	22	16	0	12	56	32
Foreign—'Mercantile'	22	78	0	67	11	22	78	0	22	60	10	30	0	20	60	20
Class of Father																
Bourgeois	20	69	11	78	11	11	82	6	12	89	11	0	0	6	64	30
Petit bourgeois	12	77	11	66	16	18	75	7	18	67	13	20	0	9	63	28
Working Class	21	68	11	70	12	18	76	9	15	77	10	13	0	16	57	27

Similarly, three quarters of the capitalists opposed prohibitions on the hiring of strikebreakers, compared to the majority of the public that supported this measure.

As predicted by segmentation theory, executives of medium-sized companies were more opposed to trade unions than their counterparts in large corporations. On the other hand, executives of medium-sized companies proved somewhat *less* likely to oppose increases in workman's compensation and the placing of employees on company boards. Although the individual items differed significantly, capitalists' positions on labour relations issues are not consistently related to nation of control, industry, or family background. Multivariate analysis of scale measuring attitudes towards labour revealed only one significant effect: as predicted by monopoly capital theory, executives of capital-intensive corporations were more sympathetic to labour. Although none of the groups within the capitalist class deviated from the generally conservative line on labour relations issues, very large differences existed between the business executives and state officials, trade union leaders, and the general public.

Foreign Investment

Business executives were much more favourable to foreign investment than state officials, labour leaders, and the general public. Sixty-five per cent of the executives said that foreign investment had at least "mostly good" effects on the Canadian economy; only one in six believed that integration of the Canadian and American economies was too great (compared to at least one third of state officials, labour leaders, and the general public); one half believed that foreign investment should not be subject to any

screening. For each of four areas of the economy — manufacturing, petroleum, banking, and merchandising — executives were the most likely to want to "encourage" or "strongly encourage" new investment. However, attitudes differed considerably towards investment in the four areas: 81 per cent of the executives wanted to encourage foreign investment in manufacturing, compared to 77 per cent for petroleum investments, 51 per cent for merchandising, but only 25 per cent for banking. At the opposite extreme were the labour leaders, at least one quarter of whom would "discourage" or "strongly discourage" new investments in each area. The pattern of politicians' and civil servants' support for foreign investment in the four areas was similar to that observed for executives, but the state officials were somewhat less likely to encourage investment. Outright continentalism gained little support from any group. Even among executives, only one in six supported closer economic integration with the U.S.

In the context of their overwhelmingly positive view of foreign investment, there were some differences within the business community. Executives of medium-sized companies were somewhat less enthusiastic about foreign investment than big business executives. Comparing industries, executives in the financial and merchandising sectors most strongly supported foreign investment, while transportation and utility executives were the least supportive. Surprisingly, there were no differences between the executives of Canadian and foreign-controlled corporations or among the categories of the related "neo-staple" industry categorization. Consistent with previous findings, the executives from small business backgrounds were the least supportive and executives from big business backgrounds the most supportive of foreign investment; executives from working-class families had opinions somewhere in between.

There is a very high degree of consensus in the business community over foreign investment, not only with regard to more general questions, but also concerning investment in four different sectors of the economy. The strongest opposition to foreign investment was found among the executives of medium-sized firms and among executives from small business backgrounds. However, these differences within the capitalist class exist in the context of generally strong pro-investment attitudes.

The Power and Taxation of Business

Not surprisingly, corporate executives are unlikely to say they possess too much power or have paid too little in taxes. And, once again, the trade unionists differed most sharply from the executives. For example, 10 per cent of the executives said that large industrial corporations carried too small a part of the total tax burden, compared to 39 per cent of the civil servants, 34 per cent of politicians, and 94 per cent of trade union leaders. Only the items dealing with the power of and taxes paid by small business produced a consensus among the different groups of respondents. For the other items, the differences among the business, state, and labour groups were much larger than the differences within the capitalist class.

Responses to the questions about the power of large corporations demonstrated sharp differences among the four groups: only one quarter of the executives said the corporations had too much power, compared to 63 per cent of the politicians, 74 per cent of the civil servants, 91 per cent of trade union leaders, and 74 per cent of the general public. Civil servants were more likely than politicians to believe that business was too powerful and corporations too lightly taxed.

There were large differences between the executives of medium-sized companies, four in five of whom believed that large corporations had too little power, and the executives of large corporations, about half of whom took that position. A similar difference appeared in evaluations of taxes paid by small business. Over one third of the executives of medium-sized companies believed that large corporations had too *little* power in Canadian society, compared to one quarter of the executives of large corporations.

The responses to the questions about taxation reflect rivalries among industries, since the executives of each branch of industry described their own taxes as too high and the taxes of other branches as too light. For example, only 5 per cent of the executives of the financial corporations said that banks were too lightly taxed, as compared to 30 per cent of industrial executives; 84 per cent of transportation and utility executives said resource firms were too lightly taxed, as compared to 58 per cent of industrial executives.

Executives of foreign-controlled corporations were less likely than those of Canadian-controlled corporations to believe that they were too highly taxed. In spite of the high level of foreign investment in the resource industry, 71 per cent of the executives of Canadian-controlled corporations, compared to 58 per cent of the executives of foreign-controlled corporations, described the resource sector as too highly taxed. The belief that industrial firms are too heavily taxed was strongest among Canadian firms in the sphere of production; strongest among foreign-controlled corporations in the sphere of circulation.

Table 20.3 Attitudes on the power and taxation of business by group, type of firm, and social origin

Independent Variable	Power of large corporations—too much	Power of financial sector—too much	Power of small business—too little	Tax burden of small business			Tax burden of large industrials			Tax burden of banking, financial			Tax burden of resource firms		
	Percentage			Too light	About right	Too heavy	Too light	About right	Too heavy	Too light	About right	Too heavy	Too light	About right	Too heavy
				Percentage distribution											
Group															
Capitalists	27	28	61	1	59	40	10	56	34	24	58	17	13	24	63
Civil Servants	74	56	73	4	50	46	39	51	10	65	33	2	43	41	16
Politicians	63	43	73	2	38	60	35	47	18	50	43	7	28	38	35
Labour	91	81	62	4	68	28	94	6	0	90	10	0	82	18	0
General Public	74	–	67	–	–	–	–	–	–	–	–	–	–	–	–
Size of Firm															
Medium	37	26	81	2	41	57	23	47	30	39	46	15	16	29	55
Large	24	28	55	1	65	34	6	59	35	20	63	17	13	22	65
Industry															
Industrial	21	29	58	0	65	35	7	61	32	30	58	12	15	27	58
Resources	32	33	45	5	65	30	9	48	43	5	70	25	5	24	71
Transport, utility	31	23	62	0	33	67	8	54	38	18	55	27	8	8	84
Merchandising	27	33	53	0	64	36	0	43	57	23	46	31	29	7	64
Financial	20	20	50	0	89	11	5	79	16	5	84	11	5	26	69
Nation of Control															
Canada	21	24	45	0	66	34	8	51	41	18	59	23	11	18	71
Foreign	26	33	66	2	65	33	5	67	28	24	67	9	15	27	58
Neo-Staple Theory Industry															
Canadian—'Mercantile'	24	21	47	0	71	29	5	65	30	14	67	19	11	16	73
Foreign—Productive	26	32	62	2	68	30	5	71	24	25	69	6	13	30	57
Canadian—Productive	18	27	41	0	59	41	12	35	53	22	50	28	12	21	67
Foreign—'Mercantile'	30	40	80	0	44	56	0	44	56	1	57	29	22	11	67
Class of Father															
Bourgeois	14	22	42	0	77	23	8	53	39	19	65	16	9	17	74
Petit bourgeois	26	22	65	2	67	31	11	60	29	22	63	15	21	26	53
Working Class	24	33	55	0	58	42	0	63	37	19	60	21	8	25	67

Within big business, executives of more la-bour-intensive corporations tended to give stronger support to small business on both the taxation and power issues. This probably reflects the fact that, among large corporations, the labour intensive firms are the most similar to smaller businesses and are likely to operate in industries with considerable numbers of small and medium-sized firms. Class background had little effect on responses to these issues.

Summary and Conclusions

The major elements of the ideology of the capitalist class include 1) strong opposition to redistribution of income and support for cuts in assistance to the unemployed, combined with a traditional, paternalistic support for greater aid to the poor; 2) the belief that trade unions are too powerful and strong opposition to legal changes favouring the labour movement; 3) opposition to most forms of government investment; 4) strong support for foreign investment, outside of banking; and 5) support for small business. Whatever its past role in the enactment of social reforms, these data show plainly that the Canadian business community opposes virtually all efforts at further social reform and given the power would roll back many present programs.

The survey revealed very large ideological differences between business executives and the state officials. Not only are these differences substantively meaningful, but they are much larger than the differences between major fractions of the capitalist class. At least at the time of the survey, policy making involved substantial conflicts between capital and the state with different strategies for managing a capitalist economy and society.

While these findings run counter to the instrumentalist stress on the influence of business on the state, the survey results do not permit us to choose among alternative explanations of the ideological conflict between capital and state, including pressure from subordinate classes, the state's legitimation role, and fiscal imperatives.

There were some ideological distinctions between the monopoly and competitive sectors; executives of medium-sized companies took more liberal positions on income redistribution and the appointment of employee representatives to company boards, but they were also more fearful of the power of trade unions. While the last of these findings is in keeping with the general argument that larger corporations can better accommodate the higher wages and higher taxes produced by more liberal state policies, our data suggest that corporations in the competitive sector are generally more and not less supportive of state intervention — precisely the opposite of what monopoly capitalist approaches would predict. This suggests that, increasingly, small business executives have come to recognize that state intervention is required to protect them from the power of large corporations. However suggestive these results, the magnitude of these core-periphery differences should not be exaggerated. On many issues ideological differences cannot be discerned between the executives of large and medium-sized corporations, and, for the issues on which differences occur, the magnitudes are smaller than the differences between the business, state officials, and labour leaders.

Similarly, there are some ideological differences between executives of corporations in different industries and between the executives of Canadian and foreign-controlled corporations. As suggested by Clement's finding that they have experienced more occupational mobility than their counterparts in Canadian-controlled corporations, the executives of foreign-controlled corporations proved somewhat more liberal. This difference disappeared when a statistical control for family background was introduced. However, these effects of family background and nation of control were largely confined to items dealing with social welfare programs and with taxes, and did not extend to labour relations issues and foreign investment. The industrial differences also did not extend across the different aspects of ideology.

The relative weakness of ideological differences between major sectors of the capitalist class testifies to the power of the economic and social mechanisms uniting the capitalist class. Those mechanisms include the capital mobility between sectors, interlocking directorates, and business executive participation in various educational, charitable, and social institutions. Whatever its internal divisions, the Canadian capitalist class shares a common ideology that can serve as the basis for its political mobilization.

One political implication of these findings is that efforts to incorporate weaker fractions of the capitalist class into populist political alliances will not likely succeed. The competitive fraction of the capitalist class is distinguished by its strongly anti-union ideology, and on other issues it is only slightly more liberal than big capital.

Notes

1. Among the executives of large corporations, 34 were from bourgeois backgrounds, 45 from petit bourgeois and small employer backgrounds, and 54 from working-class backgrounds. It is difficult to imagine how methodological differences could account for the very large difference between this distribution and Clement's and Porter's findings about the social backgrounds of what they describe as the corporate elite. Therefore there must be a large difference between the class origins of the top *executives*, who served as respondents in this study, and Clement's "corporate suggests elite," which includes the *directors* of dominant corporations, many of whom inherited their wealth and directorships.

2. The responses to all the items were trichotomized: "depends" answers were placed in the medium category and "strongly (dis)agree" and "(dis)agree" responses were collapsed, as were "much more (less) effort" and "more (less) effort" responses. The eta values given in the bottom of the tables were computed using the full range of responses, scored linearly.

21

Corporate Structure and Elites[*]

S.D. Berkowitz

Intercorporate Control

The question of "intercorporate control" has probably been one of the most hotly debated in Canada in recent years. When Porter wrote *The Vertical Mosaic*, the question of foreign control of Canadian industry was not the burning issue it was to become only a few years later. For a variety of technical reasons, it was also not possible to appreciate the full impact of foreign control/ownership on the economy.[1] Indeed, throughout the book, Porter gives the effects of foreign ownership relatively short shrift except where they can be seen to have a measurable impact on corporate concentration[2] or on the defensive strategies adopted by firms in avoiding foreign takeovers.

The publication of the Watkins Report (The Task Force on the Structure of Canadian Industry) in 1968 engendered greater awareness of the question, but, once again, the data it was based upon were incomplete.[3] Within a few years, however, with the greater availaibility of information, both the issue of foreign ownership and the larger question of centralization of economic power in Canada were fully joined.

Foreign Domination

Clement's *The Canadian Corporate Elite* takes the issue of foreign impacts on the Canadian economy far more seriously than Porter. In fact, in an important sense, it is the point upon which his entire analysis turns. His stratification of elites into "indigenous," "comprador," and "parasite" sub groups (1975: 36), for instance, is based on a variant of the "core-periphery" or "metropolis-hinterland" model in which different nation-states take up roles within an international capitalist economy. The role played by a country within this global system then determines its internal system of stratification — including divisions within its elite:

[*]Excerpted from "Corporate Structure, Corporate Control and Canadian Elites," pp. 233-259 in S.D. Berkowitz (ed.) *Models and Myths in Canadian Sociology*. Butterworths, 1984. Reprinted by permission.

Although it will be emphatically argued in subsequent chapters that Canada's economic system is not separate or detached from a wider capitalist system, it is none the less [sic] valuable to examine Canada's place within the wider system and analyze the implications of this for Canadians. For now it is sufficient to note that the issue of whether Canada is "dominated" by U.S. capitalists or in a "junior partnership" with them is at least as problematic and much more complex than these simple assertions suggest. While this [?] is probably correct for what will later be called the comprador elite, it does not accurately describe the traditional indigenous elite. The indigenous elite is better understood as being in an alliance with foreign capital as a full partner resulting from an historical division of labour. (Clement, 1975: 33)

Note here that Clement extends what is essentially a geographic or spatial metaphor to social groups, i.e., he generalizes from core and peripheral areas to core-tied ("comprador") and periphery-tied ("indigenous") elites. According to the model he adopts, "internal contradictions" among "dominant class factions" result from the process of the "uneven development of capitalism" in "dependent" regions (R.H. Frank, 1967).

There are several reasons why it is particularly interesting that Clement applies this model to the Canadian case. First, by treating Canada as an "imperialized" country, Clement ties his analysis of foreign domination back into the work of the Toronto School — especially Innis's — and, simultaneously, links it to a more theoretically explicit model of development. This is useful because the Toronto School avoided truly general theory construction. At the same time, modern core-periphery theorists have characteristically paid little attention to the concrete economic and social mechanisms through which "dependency" is developed and sustained. By explicitly relating these two bodies of work

to his problem Clement has built an important bridge between Toronto School enthusiasts — such as R. Laxer (1973), J. Laxer (1970; 1973), Watkins (1973), and Hutcheson (1973), — and the work of a more self-conscious international theory group.

Second, while Clement encompasses work by a number of writers with intellectually modest goals who dealt with the issue of Canadian-American economic relations immediately before *The Canadian Corporate Elite* was written — such as Levitt (1970), and Naylor (1972b), — it extends their arguments by placing them in the larger context of a complex set of international economic ties. This is, in one sense, quite interesting: the "debate" over foreign ownership was cycling back and forth over the same ground at the time — with fewer insights added as it "progressed." But Clement does not follow up on the consequences of this notion of a "global" capitalist system. At best, his injunction that we study Canada in the context of the world economy is a kind of academic pietism: when it comes down to concrete cases, Clement either resorts to a tried-and-true focus on bilateral exchanges between Canada and the U.S. or dredges up Toronto School platitudes about Canada exchanging British Colonialism for American neo-Colonialism. He makes no attempt to use the notion of multi-lateral economic ties analytically.

Finally, Clement recognizes that Canada does not fit easily into either the unconventional ("core-periphery") or the conventional ("modernization") model:

It is often argued that multinationals bring extensive investment into capital poor areas, either geographically defined or developmentally defined, but the example of Canada suggests otherwise. Between 1960 and 1967, new capital inflow from the U.S. amounted to $4.1 billion but counter to this, outflows in the form of remittances to U.S. parents amounted to $5.9 billion, a net outflow of capital from Canada to the U.S. of $1.8 billion. . . . The argument that U.S. investment comes to Canada because capital is scarce . . . runs counter to the evidence . . . [it] indicates that mostly Canadian capital, or capital generated from retained earnings by Canadian operations of foreign firms, finances large amounts of foreign investment. (1975: 109)

Rather than reject his assumption that Canada is a classic "dependent" or "modernizing" country, Clement assumes that the models are flawed. This, once again, is unfortunately typical of much of the work by sociologists on Canadian economic development: they seem bound and determined to "fit" Canada into one of the prevailing models on the basis of a cursory reading of the data and, at the same time, to ignore important results obtained by those using these same models. Thus, the "fits" involved are quite often superficial. For instance, the same argument about the indigenous generation of investment capital that Clement puts forward can, in general terms, be made with regard to "developed-dependent" countries in Latin America (Fuentes, 1963). Both the "developmentally defined" (modernization) and "geographically defined" (core-periphery) models recognize that there is a pattern associated with investment which will generate a different balance of flows at different stages in the process. The differences between the two schools have to do with how one interprets the observed use of retained earnings or indigenous capital for reinvestment and the net outflow of payments in the "mature" phase: modernization theorists — and here Rostow (1971) is probably the best example — see it as a prelude to "takeoff." Core-periphery theorists see this pattern as evidence of continuing dependency.

The historical evidence on the subject is mixed. Some "developed-dependent" countries have broken out of this status. The United States itself, for instance, was a net capital debtor until after World War I. Others, like Chile or Argentina, have not. In retrospect, whether or not countries have been able to break out has depended, in large measure, on the magnitude and sectoral sources of capital outflows. The Canadian literature has dealt with these questions only superficially.

What is most striking here is that, whether they follow one school or another, the overwhelming majority of Canadian researchers concerned with the impact of foreign corporate control on the Canadian economy have done no serious analytic work with data on capital flows. Like Clement, they simply present their data, intone platitudes, and think that this is sufficient. It is not. In most cases, the interactions and effects of foreign investment within an economy — in particular, a "mature" one — are varied and complex. Usually they are so complex that we need elaborate and detailed models to separate them out. They cannot simply be determined by "eyeballing" raw numbers.

For instance, J. Laxer argues that the principal effect of American foreign investment has been to retard and reduce Canada's manufacturing capacity, relegating it to the status of a service economy:

As Canada has moved more completely into the American economic orbit, the nature of the American impact on the manufacturing sector has altered. Since World War II Canada's manufacturing industries can increasingly be characterized as warehouse assembly operations which rely on imports of technology, machinery and parts and components. Moreover, as U.S. investment in Canada has more and more derived from the reinvestment of profits made in Canada and from loans on the Canadian money market, the net flow of dividends out of Canada has surpassed the inflow of new foreign investment. . . .

A striking feature of Canadian manufacturing is the relatively small percentage of the country's work force it employs. In 1965 only 24.5 per cent of the paid non-agricultural work force in Canada was employed in manufacturing. By 1971, the percentage had dropped to 21.3 per cent.

Among Western countries, only Greece and Ireland have a lower percentage of their work force employed in manufacturing. For the United States the comparable figures are these: in 1965, 29.7 per cent of the paid non-agricultural work force was employed in manufacturing; in 1971 the figure was 26.3 per cent. (Laxer, 1973: 129)

With these and similar statistics as a base, Laxer goes on to argue that Canada is being "de-industrialized" and that this "de-industrialization grows out of the nature of Canadian capitalism and its relation to American capitalism (1973: 146)."

What is most striking here is the rather one-dimensional way Laxer looks at the problem — almost as if he had the "answers" before he compiled the data. There are, in any case, a variety of factors which might explain them. First, multinational companies act so as to minimize taxation (Caves, 1982; Adams and Whalley, 1977; Aharoni, 1966; Brooke and Remers, 1970). Since they are in a good position to shift profits from one country to another by varying the transfer prices associated with non-traded goods (a fender for a GM automobile, for instance), they can affect a series of book transfers which result in higher rates of dividends and other income, i.e., they can borrow money in Canada rather than reinvesting income, that parent corporations claim back in the form of dividends and other income. Since Canadian corporate tax rates are, for certain industries, consistently higher than in the

United States, there is an incentive to do this.

Second, technology transfers — a machine tool sent to Canada by a U.S. parent, for instance — are usually reckoned at some relatively arbitrary book value. If, during the period in question, an increasing proportion of U.S.-to-Canada transfers were in the form of capital goods — and Laxer himself suggests that they might have been — and, at the same time, there were incentives towards minimizing these stated values, then the *apparent* rate of external investment would decline. Since Laxer locates the greatest shift in flows in the high technology area, this is a real possibility.

Finally, changes in patterns of capital investment must be viewed over a long time period. Capital recovery may occur in some industries in as little as three to five years. In most cases, it takes much longer. Thus, in considering aggregate data which lump all investments together, we must look for cyclic patterns before resting our case on data drawn from one specific time period. There are standard statistical techniques — similar to those used in calculating seasonally adjusted unemployment — which can be used to do this where long time series data are available (Hamburg, 1970).

In any event, Laxer presents no convincing evidence for the belief that changes in the pattern of American capital investment in Canada are part of some larger strategy for shifting production back to the United States. First, note that the apparent proportionate decline in paid non-agricultural workers is higher (3.4 per cent) in the United States than in Canada (3.2 per cent). The apparent relative decline (decline as a proportion of the total) is two per cent higher in Canada during the period in question — nothing with which to go running to the newspapers. Second, the period Laxer has chosen was one in which there was a marked increase in the proportion of women in the labour force in both countries. Since proportionately fewer women are employed in manufacturing, this, in itself, would tend to reduce the proportion of the total labour force in manufacturing — despite an enormous increase in employment, generally.

Third, the reason women were able to enter the labour force in such numbers was that there had been a secular trend towards the growth of the service and government sectors of both economies. Part of this, at least, built on itself: as women entered the labour force they generated a demand for services to replace part of their household labour, e.g., laundry services, fast food franchises. This, in turn, led to further growth of service sector employment — in some cases for women — and so on.

Finally, in recent years there has been a multilateral — not simply a bilateral — shift towards a pattern in which workers in various countries sub-assemble components at different stages in the production process. This long-term trend is the result of (a) an increasing international division of labour and (b) variations in labour costs.[4] This is a fact of life which *all* western industrialized countries, not simply Canada, must face. In many cases, these shifts are the result of contractual arrangements rather than, as Laxer might suspect, decisions by multinationals to "relocate" production.

My point, of course, is not that Laxer's conclusions are wrong — some may well be right — but that we have no way of assessing them given the limited nature of his analysis.

Centralization of Power

The ultimate goal of any study of corporate power, of course, is to locate the centres of that power and to circumscribe the group(s) that wield it. *The Vertical Mosaic* and *The Canadian Corporate Elite* both find the source of economic power in Canada in a set of large private business corporations. The men occupying the upper reaches of these corporate hierarchies are the ones best situated to wield this power. Porter:

> The economic elite of Canada has been defined. . . as the 985 Canadian residents holding directorships in the 170 dominant corporations, the banks, insurance companies, and numerous other corporations not classed [sic] as dominant. (1965: 274)

Clement:

> The corporate elite is. . . . that set of positions known as senior management and directors within dominant corporations . . . [Since] the elite is defined as the [role occupants of the] uppermost positions only within dominant corporations, not all corporations . . . the corporate elite may then be said to correspond to the "big bourgeoisie." (1975: 5-6)

Both Porter and Clement stress that, in order to function as an elite, it is necessary for this group to be bound together by common backgrounds, social ties, and life experiences.[5] Common patterns of birth and residence facilitate this. Both Porter and Clement observe that their elites are overwhelmingly located in Central Canada — particularly in Montreal and Toronto — although at least some elites may be found in other regions. Clement systematically explores the birthplace of members of this elite, discovering that Central Canada is overrepresented relative to the population as a whole.[6] These distributions mirror those for Canadian business enterprises and corporate wealth.

The Canadian "economic elite" or "corporate elite," according to both authors, is overwhelmingly Anglophone, of British origin and Protestant religion (Porter, 1965: 285-90; Clement, 1975: 231-40). It is disproportionately drawn, both Porter and

Clement maintain, from the upper-middle and upper classes (Porter, 1965: 291; Clement, 1975: 224-30). Private school education and private club membership are common among members of the group (Porter, 1965: 283-85, 304-305; Clement, 1975: 240-49). They are disproportionately university educated for people in their age-cohorts (Porter, 1965: 279-85; Clement, 1975: 240-43) and tend to have been trained in technical specialties or in law, commerce and finance (Porter, 1965: 274-79; Clement 1975: 240-42). Their children tend to intermarry, they grace one another's tables, and they interact in a variety of other informal ways. Thus they form, both authors agree, a coherent social group. This group tends to exclude — to varying degrees — French speakers, Jews, and other ethnics.

Moreover, in recent years, the economic base for the power of this group has grown through mergers, acquisitions and other consolidations of capital. According to Clement, major consolidations of Canadian capital occurred during and after the First World War and in the 1950s (Clement, 1975: 80-102). In the 1960s, the expansion of the activities of foreign-owned multinationals led to a corresponding increase in the power of "comprador" elites connected with them (Clement, 1975: 109-12). This also led, however, to a weakening of the social boundaries around the corporate elite because access to positions in Canadian subsidiaries of multinationals was controlled by non-Canadian parent firms (Clement, 1975: 112-6).

On balance, then, the Porter-Clement analysis of economic power in Canada circumscribes a group which closely resembles that identified in various Canadian regionalisms: what the Saskatchewan populist calls "those snotty bastards down East," the Newfoundlander "those rich Mainlanders," and the Québécois nationalist "les Anglais." This is one reason why both books are so popular: they play into and lend academic legitimacy to "what we already know." Both are, in this sense, good journalism but bad sociology because, as a scientist, it is a sociologist's job not simply to present interesting distributions, but to show *why* they occur: to tease out the essential underlying features of social structure which lead to the construction of the world as we observe it. Both books fail to do this in a number of ways.

First, only the most deliberately naive would expect that those persons occupying key positions in the Canadian economic structure would be randomly drawn from the population. Even without strong institutional constraints, the general structure of societies, skill requirements, times of immigration, and so on would yield a non-random distribution of certain group traits — in the absence of specific elite-generated pressures and mechanisms. The faculty of the department of sociology at the University of Toronto in 1972 — the same year for which Clement gathered his elite data[7] and hardly what one would call a branch of the economic elite — was 56.6 per cent WASP, 3.8 per cent French, 26.4 per cent Jewish, and 13.2 per cent other ethnic. Thus, in a year in which Clement reports that the general population was 44.7 per cent WASP, the proportion among sociologists was 11.9 per cent more. Whereas 28.6 per cent of the general population was French, the percentage among sociologists was 24.8 per cent less. Jews were only 1.4 per cent of the total population, but 26.4 per cent of sociologists. Other ethnics were 25.3 per cent of the Canadian population, but 13.2 per cent of the sociology faculty. In the same year, the economic elite, according to Clement, was 86.2 per cent WASP, 8.4 per cent French, 4.1 per cent Jewish and 1.3 per cent other ethnic (Clement, 1975: 232, 237).

What are we to make of these data? Toronto sociologists decidedly over-represented certain groups and underrepresented others. But why? Are they subject to the same familial and economic pressures which Clement claims forged the economic elite into an exclusive club over a period of 200 years? By contrast with the economic elite, the Toronto sociology department had expanded rapidly in the 1960s. It was much younger: over two-thirds of its members were under 50, while 70 per cent of the corporate elite were over that age (Clement, 1975: 218). Many sociologists had recently migrated to Canada. Thus, we would expect the department to disproportionately represent non-Charter groups.

We can begin to appreciate this if we reduce the *number* of Jews proportionate to their percentage in the general population, and increase the number of other ethnics in the same fashion; holding the number of WASPS and French constant. In this fashion, we generate an artificial faculty of size 46 in which 65.2 per cent are WASP, 4.3 per cent French, 2.2 per cent Jewish and 28.3 per cent other ethnic. The results of this procedure are shown in Table 21.1.

This begins to look more like the distribution of Clement's corporate elite. If we then rescale the age distribution among sociologists to fit that of the corporate elite, and recalculate an ethnic distribution on this basis, we generate an artificial group of size 35 which is 85.7 per cent WASP, 6.7 per cent French, 4.7 per cent Jewish, and 2.9 per cent other ethnic. In this distribution, French-speakers are under-represented relative to the corporate elite and other ethnics over-represented. This is to be expected since Clement's data includes elites in Montreal as well as Toronto.

This procedure reveals that, by "fitting" constraints, we can generate a distribution for another group which closely mirrors the ethnic background of Clement's corporate elite — but without any of the specific assumptions he makes about the forces determining the composition of that group. Since the factors at play in our experiment had an impact on the composition of *both* groups, they cannot be intrinsic to the corporate elite but must have been related to general changes going on in Canadian social structure, i.e., changes in patterns of immigration, age structure within institutions, etc.

Second, Porter and Clement have an obligation as scientists to doubt the conclusions of their own research, i.e., not simply to "make a case," but to weigh and assess alternative explanations. There is no evidence of even a slight sensitivity to this question in

Table 21.1 Distributions of ethnicity within various groups

Econ. elite		Sociologists		Gen pop.	Sim. 1	Sim. 2
WASP	86.2%	56.6%	(30)	44.7%	65.2%	85.7%
French	8.4	3.8	(2)	28.6	4.3	6.7
Jews	4.1	26.4	(14)	1.4	2.2	4.7
Other	1.3	13.2	(7)	25.3	28.3	2.9

their examinations of the mechanisms leading to the creation and centralization of power within the WASP-dominated, Eastern establishment group they identify. Clement's treatment of the role played by Jews in the corporate elite is, perhaps, the most obvious example in *The Canadian Corporate Elite* of how advocacy can get in the way of scientific objectivity.

Clement assumes that, as in Porter's assessment, Jews are marginal to any system of socio-economic power in Canada. Thus, in describing the corporate elite, he begins by telling us that there are *"only* 32 Jewish-Canadians" included in his corporate elite (1975: 237). Later he cites a 1939 study by Rosenberg to justify the assertion that "[Jews'] participation [in the corporate system] is, for the most part, peripheral to the economic elite and located in the high risk sectors of trade and real estate (1975: 238)." Clement, however, has a problem: in the case of every other ethnic group — especially WASPs — he has rested his case on the fact that a given group is either "over-represented" or "under-represented" in the corporate elite relative to the general population. As Clement himself tells us, Jews constitute only 1.4 per cent of the general population, but 4.1 per cent of the elite group. Put another way, the Canadian corporate elite contains just under three times the number of Jews we would expect at random — or we can view them as 200 per cent over-represented.

This fact is hard to ignore, but Clement tries:

A closer examination of the firms with which they are associated explains why they are 4.1 per cent of the elite and only 1.4 per cent of the population. Of the 32 Jews, 28 are associated with one of the five long established corporations in the beverage industry, three in trade and one primarily in real estate. These are tightly-held family firms with only six families accounting for 25 of the 32 Jewish members of the elite. Outside these family firms, Jews have much less economic power in dominant financial corporations, holding only five of the dominant bank directorships (2.4 per cent) and two dominant insurance company directorships (1.2 per cent). In other words, their representation in financial corporations is well below their proportion of the entire economic elite (1975: 237-38).

What is most disturbing here is that, when Clement speaks about other large family holdings — such as the Irving's or Sifton's — he does not treat them as "only" family capital: when WASPs control whole industries in some region, it is taken as evidence of enormous personal power. When Jews do, it is seen as a *prima facie* case of marginal status.

If there is a single inviolate rule of science it is the notion that one should let the data have their say. Clement is breaking this rule with impunity. The "long established corporation in the beverage industry" Clement refers to above is, of course, Distillers-Corporation Seagrams Ltd. The family involved is the Bronfmans. We know from data published by Statistics Canada (Statistics Canada, 1978) that the Bronfmans control literally dozens of corporations in a wide range of financial and industrial areas. Yet, they are only noted episodically in Clement's account. Other highly significant Jewish families are not even mentioned — including one which is now gradually buying lower Manhattan from the natives. When Clement talks about Jews outside of these "family firms,"[8] he notes that they "only" hold "five of the dominant bank directorships" for "2.4 per cent" of the total. Once again, this is 170 per cent of what we would expect them to hold at random.

This goes beyond stubbornness: it takes a real commitment to one's model of WASP exclusiveness to persist in the face of this kind of evidence that families like the Bronfmans wield enormous financial power on both sides of the border. The costs are also clear: Clement has failed to detect one of the most important interfaces between Canadian and American capitalism.

Finally, both Porter and Clement have failed to provide readers with a realistic context within which to view the trends towards centralization of power which they observe. We know, for instance, very little about the demography of their corporate elites (Tepperman, 1977). Thus, when they talk about inter-marriages, we have little idea how likely they are. We have anecdotal accounts of club membership, but, once again, little sense of the opportunity structure surrounding them. Clement, in particular, seems to be extremely concerned with the "place" of Canadian capitalism within a worldwide scheme. Yet, is this an issue with any practical referents: is the American real estate developer who is dealing with the Bronfmans, for instance, really concerned about whether, in the abstract, Canadian capitalists are "junior partners" or acting out a rule in an historic division of labour? The practical questions surrounding foreign ownership or centralization of power have to do with what economists refer to as "welfare effects": who derives what benefits from what sets of arrangements and who bears the costs. The costs and benefits of centralizing production within a few firms are, for example, not self-evident. They require some considerable study since they vary a great deal from industry to industry and from market to market within the economy. Similarly, the tradeoffs between concentration and dispersal of economic decision-making within a vast country such as Canada are not matters for speculation, but ought to be treated in a theoretically and empirically consistent way.

Conclusion: Toward A Structural Theory of Canadian Corporate Elites

It is ironic that what has been hailed as "the most Canadian of books," *The Vertical Mosaic*, should be so closely wedded to its American counterparts. Its basic analytic framework is not much different from that in C. Wright Mills' classic study of American society, *The Power Elite* (1956), which was published some nine years earlier. As such, it owes much to Weber's notions of power and social organization, to Mosca and Pareto's treatments of elites, and to a kind of domestic North American populism in which one sees the "big guys" — usually in the "East" — as the major source of domestic woes and foreign entanglements (Berkowitz, 1976).

This is also true of *The Canadian Corporate Elite*. While Clement tends to borrow the rhetoric of neo-Marxist writers — such as Frank or Domhoff — his basic overall analytic schema is not much different from Porter's: "elites" are still defined as functional groups thrown up by institutional hierarchies and closely identified with dynamics in each of several relatively autonomous social and cultural spheres. The basic thrust of argument in both books is to show that certain social groups disproportionately monopolize access to key positions within these institutions and important channels of communication between them.

What is missing from all of this is a sense of social structure. Access to favoured goods in a society — such as wealth, prestige and power — is governed by a series of structures at different levels of the system (Berkowitz, 1982). These vary from society to society: there is no particular reason why the barriers which impede access to certain favoured goods in one should act in the same way in another. In fact, given that societies may have widely varying institutional histories, it is extremely unlikely that any two will structure inequality in precisely the same way.

In Britan and France, for instance, accents act as a sorting mechanism to discriminate classes and regions from one another. As in George Bernard Shaw's famous tale, persons without "appropriate" accents are barred from certain circles. This is, to some extent, true in the United States as well (Kavaler, 1960; Wechter, 1937). But no one has shown that accents are used in this way in Canada, and it is unlikely that they would be given the newness of most upper class social circles. However, there are undoubtedly other signals that perform the same function. No doubt, for instance, French Canadians without pronounced French overtones in their speech or Jews without "Jewish" inflections find it easier to function in the *haute monde* than those with these traits.

By borrowing heavily from their American counterparts, both Porter and Clement — perhaps inadvertently — have fallen into assuming that certain features of social structure in Canada operate in substantially the same way as they do in the United States. The American educational system, for instance, is large and varied. Some colleges and universities function as national institutions: they draw their student body from across the country and around the world. They clearly see their role as training "the next generation of leaders," within each locale, for the tasks involved in running the system. Competition for places in these institutions is

fierce, since each applicant knows that only a few will be chosen from a given city or state. Other American educational institutions clearly exist to serve some regional or local clientele. These schools are easier to get into and the branches of government which often support them are usually successful in pressuring administrators into accepting a large number of local sons and daughters. Thus, while their student bodies may include a sprinkling of out-of-state or foreign students, the primary base for the student population is within a limited, local geographic locale. Still other institutions — usually state colleges — are not only geographically limited in focus but really specialize in some few forms of highly specialized training geared to the needs of a local area. Some institutions are private, some public, some closely affiliated with religious denominations, some are closely tied to particular industries or companies. Thus, precisely where one goes within this panoply of possibilities is quite important and will have strong implications for his or her future careers and life chances.

The college and university system is structured quite differently in Canada. Most students prefer — and provincial legislatures have agreed — to attend university in their home cities. As we noted in the first chapter, until very recently this has meant that a single institution, the University of Toronto, had all but monopolized the lion's share of teaching in English Canada. Within Québec, McGill had functioned the same way for Anglophones. Both institutions, as a result, have been huge and entrance requirements, in American terms, comparatively low.[9] Student bodies, as a result, are quite heterogeneous with respect to both abilities and class background.

When the members of Porter's and Clement's elites were growing up, these institutions were probably more elite than they are today. At the same time, students had fewer options. Thus, when Porter says that "Of the 118 [men] born and educated in Canada, 42 graduated from McGill science and engineering faculties, 35 from Toronto, and 4 from Queen's", (1965: 277) he implies a great deal more than he ought to: "This common educational background can make for homogeneity of social type (1965: 277)." While this may be true for the 1929 graduates of, say, MIT or Caltech, it is at least unproven that it is as meaningful here. Even a cursory examination of the subsequent careers of the graduates of Toronto and McGill in these years would reveal a far wider scatter of paths than those of elite American scientific institutions.

Clement commits the same error. When he talks about the lawyers in his corporate elite, he says:

> All the lawyers are trained in Canada with half attending Osgoode Hall and about one fifth going to each of the University of Toronto and McGill; Dalhousie, University of Manitoba, Laval and University of Montreal are also important.

There are 113 law schools in the United States. They are elaborately stratified and rated. Students, moreover, are aware of this and of the career implications of attending one or the other. During the period when the American counterparts of the Canadian economic elite were the appropriate age, there were between 90 and 100 such schools. At the time that most of Porter or Clement's elite were attending law school, there were only two in the province of Ontario. McGill was the only wholly Anglophone law school in Québec. Since Canadian law schools have tended to be quite oriented to their own provincial bodies of law — i.e.,

they see their task as training lawyers rather than educating jurists — it makes sense to attend a school within one's own province. Thus, Clement is not saying very much in this paragraph that we did know know by definition: the distribution of elites among law schools is undoubtedly very close to a random one for all English-speaking law students at the time. All lawyers of the appropriate age — those practising on Bay Street and those in storefronts on Roncesvalles — would have had similar educational backgrounds in a way that American lawyers of the era would not (Smigel, 1969).

The point, then, is that, however Canadian elites are filtered out, these kinds of institutions do not do it and it is a false inference to assume that they do. Porter and Clement are probably on firmer ground when they view private school education as an elite-shaping experience,[10] but, once again, the term covers a myriad of different things in Canada and we have no precise way of sorting this out as one does in the United States.

If educational careers are not the mechanism through which elites are socialized and shaped in Canada, what is? Probably the family system. While both Porter and Clement deal, in a passing way, with the influence of particular families on the careers of their members, neither deals with family systems *qua* systems.

What is obviously needed is a study of the "structuration" of class in Canada comparable to those done by Berkowitz (1976) and Bertaux (1977) — for the United States and France, respectively — in which capital formation and family structure are explicitly related to one another. Given the history of "family compacts" in Canada, this approach is likely to yield even richer insights into the process in Canada than it did in other cases.

Notes

1. Brecher and Reisman, 1957, began exploring this issue. At the time — and until Statistics Canada began publishing these data in detail *Inter-Corporate Ownership* — it was often not possible to determine the exact proportion of a Canadian subsidiary's assets held by its foreign parent(s). Moreoever, until the late 1960s it was often all but impossible to disentangle the operating statistics of subsidiaries from those of their parents.

2. "Where there is no Canadian participation in a productive instrument called a corporation there is little difference between that situation and one where ownership is completely in the hands of one person or a group within the country. In these terms there is no difference between T. Eaton Company and General Motors of Canada. Nor does it seem to matter much from the point of view of the operation of the economic system whether these large pieces of private property are in the hands of Canadians or people of other nations." Porter, 1965: 246.

3. Indeed, until the publication of the 1975 edition of *Inter-Corporate Ownership* (1978) a method was used for determining proportion of foreign ownership which tended to *understate* foreign control. Statistics Canada now provides two statistics to reflect these different aspects of the problem. See Berkowitz *et al.,* 1976, for a detailed discussion of the issue.

4. A friend of mine in Canada recently wrote a book for a British publisher which was typeset in India.

5. Porter, 1965: 231; Clement, 1975: 5. "To demonstrate that a particular elite is also a social group requires that its structure be specified, that members of the group interact and are related to one another sufficiently to say they exhibit solidarity, cohesiveness, coordination, and consciousness of kind."

6. Sixty-eight per cent of Clement's elite was born in central Canada. See Clement, 1975: 224-25.

7. My source here was the 1973-74 academic calendar since it was compiled during 1972.

8. When Clement uses the term in this context, it sounds like it refers to a mom and pop grocery.

9. At the time I taught there, the mininum entrance requirements for the University of Toronto were high school graduation and a 65 grade point average from an Ontario high school. This is the equivalent of a "D" average in the United States, and would qualify a student for entrance into only the very lowest rungs of the system.

10. Porter, 1965: 283-85, 292, 295, 342, 528; Clement, 1975: 4, 6-7, 73, 91, 96, 176, 178, 180-81, 185, 188, 190, 192-95, 277, 240-47, 251, 267, 269, 272, 307ff, 308.

SECTION VII

A Vertical Mosaic

This Section presents material on what may be sociology's best known contribution to popular images of Canadian society: Canada as a **vertical mosaic**. This image refers to the fact that, historically, race/ethnicity and social advantage (in occupational attainment, income and power) have gone hand in hand. To some extent this remains true, although evidence suggests that Canada has changed appreciably in the direction of greater equality.

This image was made popular by John Porter's celebrated book of the same title. Porter, in describing how he arrived at this title, explained the meaning of the vertical mosaic as follows:

> In a society which is made up of many cultural groups there is usually some relationship between a person's memberships in these groups and his class position and, consequently, his chances of reaching positions of power. Because the Canadian people are often referred to as a mosaic composed of different ethnic groups, the title, *The Vertical Mosaic*, was originally given to the chapter which examines the relationship between ethnicity and social class. As the study proceeded, however, the hierarchical relationship between Canada's many cultural groups became a recurring theme in class and power. For example, it became clear that the Canadians of British origin have retained, within the elite structure of the society, the charter group status with which they started out, and that in some institutional settings the French have been admitted as a co-charter group whereas in others they have not. The title, "The Vertical Mosaic," therefore seemed . . . appropriate (1965: xii-xiii).

Porter's idea that social inequalities varied markedly by cultural background was new to the Canadian literature. So was his idea that these inequalities were supported by the wishes of a more powerful Anglo charter group, who wanted to remain advantaged in income, occupations and power. As Porter put it:

> Even at times in what purports to be serious social analysis, middle class intellectuals project the image of their own class onto the social classes above and below them. . . . The idea of class differences has scarcely entered into the stream of Canadian academic writing (1965: 6).

Sociologists before Porter had carefully described Canada's racial and ethnic inequalities, but none was heard as well as Porter. Most notable among predecessors with the same vision of Canadian society was Leonard Marsh. His analyses, in *Canadians In and Out of Work* (1940), covered much the same ground as Porter's, and in similar style, but they came 25 years earlier. Marsh's 500-page volume detailed the extent of inequalities of income and occupations in Canada, drawing heavily on 1931 census data. Among Marsh's conclusions were the following:

> Many Canadians are reluctant to admit that their country has a class structure. So far as social classes cannot be demarcated by a hard and fast line . . . this reluctance is understandable. But this does not dismiss the other evidence of the class division of the population which exists in terms of inequalities of wealth, opportunity, and social recognition. The barriers are not the horizontal ones of geographic regions or distinctive ethnic cultures but the vertical ones of a large socio-economic hierarchy. . . . Communities and classes intersect; perhaps in few places more than in Canada, which has regional and ethnic variety . . . of formidable magnitude. But these complications merely obscure, they do not eliminate the fundamental problems which class inequalities engender (1940: 403-404).*

Marsh's book enjoyed little of the popularity of Porter's book neither among academics nor the public at large (*The Vertical Mosaic* was even a best seller, for a time). The reasons for this difference are not fully clear, but the outbreak of World War II must have had something to do with it. The war undoubtedly occupied the attention of the general public and academics, leaving little room for concern with ethnic and racial inequality in Canada. By contrast, Porter's book was published just after Canadian Before the 1960s few universities had sociology departments at all and there were few sociological researchers in the universities or outside. *The*

Leonard C. Marsh, *Canadians In and Out of Work: A Survey of Economic Classes and Their Relations to the Labour Market*. (Toronto: Oxford University Press, 1940) pp. 403-404. Reproduced with permission.

Vertical Mosaic was, then, "in the right spot to be acknowledged as the centrepiece of a newly-legitimated and rapidly-expanding academic discipline. In that sense, . . . *The Vertical Mosaic* rode as many waves as it created" (Helmes-Hayes, 1986: 30). Porter's own guesses at why the book was so well received included the following:

> Canada was approaching a centennial and occasionally, in the range of celebration, questions were being asked about the kind of society that had been established. More importantly, perhaps, Canada was being torn by ethnic conflict which no amount of celebration could conceal (1975: ix).

Both Marsh and Porter described a Canadian society where racial and ethnic minorities tended to occupy lower occupational positions for which they had been imported from other countries, sometimes generations earlier. There was limited occupational mobility out of these entrance statuses; ethnic minorities tended to continue holding down the worst positions, getting too little education, and having too little power in the society. The vertical structure of income and occupational inequality contained a mosaic of types of people: it was made up of brightly distinct pieces at different levels in the structure, and these colours did not change locations over time.

Our first selection in this Section presents some of Porter's interpretations of data from the 1931 to 1961 Canadian censuses bearing on patterns of ethnic inequality in occupation and income. This section of Porter's book was titled "The Vertical Mosaic" before the whole book was given that title. As Porter's findings show, of all minority groups the visible racial and ethnic minorities have been the most disadvantaged and most burdened by the weight of the vertical mosaic. But Porter feared that many minority groups were being assimilated into mainstream society far too slowly for their own good, and for Canada's good. Faster assimilation required, he felt, more educational opportunity for the minority group members, and more freedom from influence by the ethnic community.

The next excerpt in this Section, Raymond Breton's classic study of ethnic communities, picks up on the second point. It shows just how significantly immigrants' ties with ethnic communities influence their integration into the community and the wider society. Breton coined the term "institutional completeness" to summarize the extent to which the ethnic group has its own churches, schools, mass media and recreational clubs, each often operating in the community's own language. Breton demonstrates considerable variation among ethnic communities in institutional completeness, then asks: what causes institutional completeness to vary in this way? Does it matter how institutionally complete or incomplete an ethnic group may be? How much, for example, does institutional completeness affect the willingness and ability of an immigrant to assimilate into the larger, non-ethnic society?

Breton finds that the degree of institutional completeness determines the proportion of individuals who have most of their personal relations within the ethnic group. Ethnic organizations discourage group members from going outside the community, providing instead a context within which community members can meet and socialize with other community members. The leadership of these organizations continues to raise the salience of ethnic membership. Organization leaders also pursue group interests and act to maintain or increase participation in the ethnic organizations. Thus, the internal politics of ethnic communities is enormously important in shaping the communal organizations and, through them, the rate at which immigrants and their children assimilate. In most cases, the more institutionally complete a community, the slower the assimilation of members into the wider society.

While they are not immigrant groups, Canada's Native peoples also provide excellent examples of institutionally complete ethnic communities that have been slow to assimilate into the wider society. Of course, here it is not just that organizations in the Native communities have discouraged their people from involvement outside the communities. The wider society has wanted it that way! The Canadian law has defined and legitimated a segregated status on reserves for Native peoples. The laws have dictated that minimal levels of ethnic institutional completeness must be developed by Natives in separated areas.

Bienvenue (1985) has emphasized that the approach that has been taken to Native peoples in Canada is consistent with the treatment of colonized peoples in various other parts of the world. First, Native peoples were killed and robbed of their valuable land. Later, they met with neglect and segregation on reserves. No group in Canada has suffered such extreme racism as the Native peoples. The problem of the Native peoples continues today. For example, Weinfeld's study in this Section will show (see Table 26.1) that Native Indians are the most disadvantaged in income of all major ethnic and racial groups, even after such factors as education, occupation and number of weeks worked are taken into account.

There are a few hopeful signs for the plight of the Native peoples, however. First, tougher anti-dissemination laws are making it harder for Canadians to practise racism openly. Second, the Native peoples are organizing to pursue more effectively their treaty land rights and claims for special status. Third, Native issues are getting a somewhat more sympathetic reception than in the past. Rick Ponting has documented the views of the general Canadian population on Native rights through a series of interview surveys. In an article in this Section he reports on some of the major findings from his most recent survey. He emphasizes that, because of a high level of sympathy, Canadian public opinion may be said to be permissive with regard to reform relating to Native rights and support for "self-government". But he also finds that knowledge of Native issues and the priority assigned to them are low, and that there is considerable opposition to Native claims for special status.

In the next selection, Frances Henry and Effie Ginzberg provide dramatic evidence of racial discrimination in employment. They conducted a field experiment on a sample of jobs advertised in Toronto newspapers. Two people made in-person applications to test whether employers preferred to hire White or Black applicants. Other experiments tested the reaction of employers to an "audible" minority, by telephoning employers who had advertised jobs. Combining the results of the two studies, Henry and Ginzberg estimate a discrimination ratio (for Toronto) of 3:1 in favour of Whites over members of visible minorities. Henry and Ginzberg's data clearly suggest that the vertical mosaic persists, at least for visible minorities.

Morton Weinfeld next reviews contemporary evidence of the level of ethnic and racial inequality. In doing so, he explores studies of ethnic and racial differences in socio-economic opportunities, studies of racial discrimination and prejudice, immigration policies and patterns, and human rights legislation. Weinfeld shows that "effective discrimination", in the sense of occupational and economic inequalities by ethnicity, has apparently disappeared now for all European immigrant groups. However, Weinfeld (like Henry and Ginzberg) finds less to cheer about in available data on the occupational and economic experiences of racial minorities. Some groups, like the Japanese, are doing comparatively well, but others, like Blacks and Chinese, are substantially disadvantaged. The disadvantages these groups experience are especially evident in statistics on the rate of return in income for higher education.

Weinfeld also reviews evidence of greater ethnic penetration into elite positions outside the economic elite — in government, the civil service, and the cultural sectors. Here, too, the visible minorities lag behind. Examining a variety of studies, Weinfeld concludes that measurable levels of racial prejudice continue, despite evidence that discrimination and prejudice are decreasing over time. Human rights legislation and immigration policies also show some positive changes, Weinfeld argues.

Thus, Porter's image of a society which locks certain ethnic and racial minorities into entrance statuses at the bottom of the occupational world seems to apply less to Canadian society today than it did a generation or two ago. The vertical mosaic imagery successfully captured what was occurring in a widespread way in Canada during the first half of the century and before; but there have been some profound changes in a more equalitarian direction since then (see also Darroch, 1979; Lautard and Loree, 1984). Those of us who advocate greater equality of opportunity will welcome the news that the vertical mosaic is disappearing. In the near future, "the vertical mosaic" may be only a memory: an historic image of Canada. First, however, the persistent racial inequalities described by Ponting, Henry and Ginzberg, and Weinfeld must disappear, and ethnic and racial barriers to elite entry be eliminated. There is quite a way to go yet.

22

*Ethnicity and Social Class**

John Porter

Ethnic Affiliation and Occupational Class

Immigration and ethnic affiliation (or membership in a cultural group) have been important factors in the formation of social classes in Canada. In particular, ethnic differences have been important in building up the bottom layer of the stratification system in both agricultural and industrial settings. If non-agricultural occupations are considered alone, there are ethnic differences in the primary and secondary levels of manufacturing and in service occupations. Depending on the immigration period, some groups have assumed a definite entrance status. It is interesting to discover what happens to these various groups over time: whether they move out of their entrance status and show by their subsequent occupational distribution that ethnic origin was not a factor impeding

their social mobility. If it was not, they will have achieved an equality of status with the charter group. On the other hand, where cultural groups tend to be occupationally specific, with successive generations taking on the same occupations as earlier generations, we can say that ethnic affiliation is at least a correlative factor in the assignment of occupational roles and thus in social class.

There are two ways of measuring the movement upwards from entrance status towards equality of status, that is, structural assimilation. One would be to observe the ethnic distribution of occupations where the latter are arranged in some rank order. A second would be to examine the roles at the top of our institutional hierarchies, the roles of power and command, to see what representation the non-French and non-British have at this level. This second method would tell us the extent to which the charter groups had accepted other cultural groups as equals, and which groups had achieved positions of power and which had not. The first of these methods we shall attempt now.

There are some difficulties with the first method because social processes are the result of a variety of factors operating together.

*Excerpted from *The Vertical Mosaic*, Toronto: © University of Toronto Press, 1965. Reprinted by permission of University of Toronto Press.

If we attempt to treat ethnicity as a single independent variable we are immediately confounded by many related variables that are impossible, because of lack of specific data, to hold constant. Religion has already been mentioned as an outstanding example. A large proportion of the earlier Irish and later European immigration was Catholic, and the general educational level of Catholics in Canada has been lower than that of the main Protestant groups. Thus Catholic religious affiliation may be as important a determinant of the stratification system as ethnic origin. The higher occupational levels of the non-Irish British immigrants or those of non-Irish British descent may be due as much to their Protestant orientations as to their affiliation to the charter ethnic group. Age and marital status distributions will also distort the occupational distribution of ethnic groups, particularly in earlier periods before family migration became more the rule. A further factor is the over-all change in the occupational structure — the general higher level of skill which has been mentioned earlier. It would be expected that all ethnic groups would share in some measure in this process. It is therefore difficult to separate mobility attributed to this factor from mobility attributed to moving out of entrance status. Finally, too, there are some difficulties attaching to the lack of uniformity in both occupational and ethnic origin statistics at different periods of time. In part, the problems of origin statistics arise because of changes in European national boundaries.[1]

It is necessary to remember the changing importance of agriculture in the economy. Some groups have become relatively more urban over time, and others have been predominantly urban from their period of first immigration. In the latter category are the Jews, who were 99 per cent urban in 1951 and 1961, and the Italians, who were 88 per cent urban in 1951 and 96 per cent in 1961. In degree of urbanization in 1951 and 1961 they were followed by the British (66 and 71 per cent) and the Polish (63 and 75 per cent). These four groups were the only ones that were more urban than the total population in both 1951 and 1961 (Census of Canada, 1951, Vol. X: 145-146; 1961, Vol. I: 2-5, Table 36). If the movement from farms to cities can be viewed as a process of downward social mobility, or at least a movement of unskilled labour, then groups which were predominantly in agriculture before the cityward movement began will be at a disadvantage compared to those groups predominantly urban throughout.

In the following analysis we unfortunately cannot use occupational rank categories that are wholly satisfactory. Some of them, such as "professional" and "unskilled labour" can be considered class categories. Clerical occupations can be considered "white collar" and therefore ranked above unskilled, personal service occupations, such as domestic service, cooks, janitors, waiters, and launderers, can be ranked between clerical and unskilled. "Commercial" is a general business classification which includes small traders as well as large ones, and therefore cannot be brought into a rank order. Financial occupations can be given a higher white collar rank. Agriculture is also too broad a category to be brought into a rank order because it includes wealthy as well as poor farmers.

An attempt will now be made to establish the proportions of each ethnic group in those occupational categories which can reasonably be taken as occupational rank or social class categories, and to compare these proportions with the proportions of the total labour force in these occupational categories. A group will be considered over-represented if it had a higher proportion at a particular level than did the total labour force, under-represented if its proportion was less than that of the total labour force. Compared to the British and French most of the ethnic groups to be discussed, taken separately, constituted only a very small proportion of the total population in both 1931 and 1951. The regional distribution is important, because the relationship between ethnicity and class will vary according to regional concentrations of all ethnic groups. We shall be concerned with changes over time, that is from 1921 to 1961.

For the 1931 census we shall look first at the immigrant portion of ethnic groups, and later at the "origins" of the total ethnic group, that is, immigrants and native-born combined. At both the 1921 and 1931 censuses British immigrants were more urban than rural, and engaged more in industrial and clerical opportunities than in agriculture. Less than 25 per cent of the British-Isles born were in agricultural occupations, compared to 50 per cent of the United-States-born, 40 per cent of the European-born, and more than 34 per cent of the Canadian-born. About 25 per cent of British-born males at the 1931 census were in manufacturing and construction occupations, compared to 15 per cent of the United-States-born, 15 per cent of the European-born, and 16 per cent of the Canadian-born. British-born immigrants were also over-represented and in slightly greater proportion than the Canadian-born in transport, trade, service, and clerical occupations. Although the Asian-born were more than 80 per cent urban very few of them were in the "British-dominated" occupations. Most Asian-born males were either in personal service (over 40 per cent) or in labouring occupations in secondary industry. About 20 per cent of European-born

males were labourers, compared to 12 per cent Canadian-born and 11 per cent British-Isles-born.[2] Although all female immigration up to this time went predominantly into service occupations, 17 per cent British-born females went into clerical occupations compared to 4 per cent European and 7 per cent Asian-born females.

Almost 25 per cent of the Central European and 40 per cent of the Eastern European immigrants were engaged in agriculture in 1931. A little more than 20 per cent of the Central European and 25 per cent of the Eastern European immigrants were in unskilled occupations in secondary industry. Within the Eastern European group 33 per cent of the Polish immigrants were secondary labourers. The high proportion of labourers in both Central and Eastern European groups shows the trend to increasing urban immigration when entrance status involved urban unskilled occupations. The onset of the depression of course was partly responsible for this increase in 1931. The same no doubt applies to Italian immigrants, 90 per cent of whom were urban, and almost 20 per cent of whom were labourers.

In the non-agricultural occupations, Italians were over-represented in mining (10 per cent compared to 3 per cent of the total immigrant work force), and Scandinavians in logging (5 per cent compared to one per cent of the total). Of Jewish immigrants in 1931, 99 per cent were in non-agricultural occupations; over 40 per cent were in commercial and almost 33 per cent in manufacturing occupations, compared to 8 per cent of all male immigrants in commercial and 12 per cent in manufacturing occupations. Of the small number of French immigrants (only 3 per cent of all immigrants) more than 33 per cent were in agricultural occupations, and the remainder were distributed about equally with all other immigrants in the occupational structure.

All immigrant groups shared in the trend of urbanization between 1921 and 1931. Some British moved from farms into manufacturing, personal service, and clerical occupations. In the Central European group relatively more were found as labourers in secondary industries (an increase from 14 to 21 per cent between 1921 and 1931), in part because of the arrival in the late 1920s of a number of Czechs and Slovaks. During the decade the Eastern Europeans also showed a drop in the proportion in agriculture and an increase in the proportion classified as urban labourers.

These tendencies associating ethnic affiliation and immigration with occupational status are accentuated when urban immigrants of the 1931 census are separated from rural, agricultural immigrants. Over 50 per cent of the urban Eastern European group and over 40 per cent of the Central Europeans and Italians were labourers in secondary industries. British, French, and Dutch immigrants were under-represented in the labouring group. The British had the highest proportion in clerical occupations. As Reynolds (1935) has shown in his study of the British immigrant in Canada the British provided a large proportion of the skilled and clerical workers in the decade both before and after World War I. There was in 1931 a greater proportion of British-born than Canadian-born in manufacturing, and in the more skilled metal trades there were twice as many.

So far, the occupational levels of immigrants alone have been considered, but in 1931 immigrants made up only 33 per cent of the labour force. The remainder, who were Canadian-born, all had a non-Canadian origin (as every ten years the census keeps insisting), so the ethnic composition and the occupational distribution of the Canadian-born must also be taken into account. The proportions of the Canadian-born of all origins in some of these occupational levels have already been indicated, but the association between ethnic affiliation and occupational level is more clearly demonstrated when immigrant and native-born are taken together.

If three broad occupational groupings — agriculture, professional and financial, and primary and unskilled labour — are taken from the 1931 census the status differences of that time become clear. Agriculture is included because the distribution of the various origins in agriculture indicates the proportions that were left for the other occupations. Professional and financial have been grouped together as high occupational levels, and primary (logging, fishing, and mining) and unskilled labour as low occupational levels. Class differences can be shown if ethnic groups are over- or under-represented at these levels: that is, whether they appear in greater or less proportion than does the total labour force at these levels. Males only are considered.

In 1931, 34 per cent of the labour force was in agriculture. The German, Scandinavian, Dutch, Eastern European, Irish, and French were all over-represented in that order in agriculture. The Scottish, native Indian, 'Other Central European' (mainly Balkan), English, Asian, Italian, and Jewish were all under-represented in that order in agriculture. The Germans, the most over-represented, had 55 per cent in agriculture, and the Jews, the most under-represented had 1.6 per cent.

In the professional and financial occupations (4.8 per cent of the labour force) Jewish, Scottish, English, and Irish were all over-represented. Jewish and Scottish were tied (7 per cent each), followed by the English

(6.4 per cent) and the Irish (5.8 per cent). All other origins were under-represented.

For the low level, primary and unskilled occupations (17.7 per cent of the labour force) the proportions were reversed. Jews were the most under-represented group (3.2 per cent), followed by German (12.4), Dutch (12.5), Irish (12.8), Scottish (12.9), and English (13.3). All other groups were over-represented. In the clerical occupations (3.8 per cent of the male labour force in 1931) which can be taken as intermediate between the high and low levels being considered, the three British origins and Jews were over-represented and all the other origins were under-represented.

There are three female occupations worth noting because they tend to reinforce the occupational class differences for males of the various origins. For females, the professional (17.7 per cent of the female labour force), clerical (17.6 per cent), and personal service occupations (33 per cent) together made up 68 per cent of the female labour force. With the exception of Jews all ethnic groups had more females in personal service than in clerical or professional occupations. The three British origins were under-represented in personal service occupations: English 29.2 per cent, Scottish 29.3 per cent, and Irish 27.1 per cent, compared to 33 per cent for the entire labour force. Also under-represented were Jews (7.4 per cent) and Italians (24.4 per cent). (Italian females were more in manufacturing occupations, particularly textiles.) In the clerical occupations Jewish (31 per cent), Irish (23.8), English (23.5), and Scottish (23) were over-represented compared to 17.6 per cent of the total female labour force. In the female professional occupations the Scottish, Irish, and French were over-represented. This is the only high occupational category for males or females

in which the French were over-represented, no doubt because of the teaching and nursing positions held by nuns. In this category of female professionals, the English and Dutch ranked close together. Both were slightly under-represented.

Some caution is necessary in interpreting this distribution of female occupations because unlike adult males, almost all of whom work or seek work, the participation of women in the work world outside the home probably varies by origin. As well the differences between the origins in the proportions married are important. However, there are some class differences, notably the high representation of some groups in the personal service occupations.

From this distribution of occupations, both male and female, a rank order of ethnic groups in the economic system of 1931 can be determined. There is little difference among the three British groups, and they and the Jews rank high. French, German, and Dutch would probably be ranked next, followed by Scandinavian, Eastern European, Italian, Japanese, "Other Central European," Chinese, and native Indian. This rank order of occupational status is, of course, rough, and it does not consider the intermediate occupations between the professional and financial at the top and the primary and unskilled jobs at the bottom. However, almost two-thirds of the 1931 labour force have been taken into account. It is by comparing the higher and lower levels that class differences stand out most sharply.

Two further observations might be made about this vertical arrangement of Canada's mosaic. One concerns the almost equal status of the three British origins, but in particular the equality of the Irish with the other two and their over-representation in agriculture in 1931. Canada must have lost a good proportion of the Irish Catholics, who, as we have seen earlier, did not become farmers, but rather provided a cheap labour market for the construction of the last century. In 1931 only one-third of Canada's Irish were Catholic (Hurd, 1937b: 214). No doubt Protestant immigration from Ireland exceeded Catholic in later periods, but it is also likely that large proportions of Irish Catholics emigrated from Canada. The second observation is about the relationship between occupational levels and period of arrival in Canada. The German and Dutch have relatively high status. Members of this group have been in Canada for a very long time, many of them having come at various times from the United States. These two groups were the most highly represented in agriculture. The low status of Italian and "Other Central European" groups reflects their later arrival and hence their entrance status at the time of the 1931 census.

The distribution of cultural or ethnic groups in the occupational system is a reflection of that process already referred to as structural assimilation. There is also the contradictory process of segregation. These have been measured by indices based on residential propinquity, intermarriage, and the adoption for Protestants of a Canadian religious affiliation such as membership in the United Church (Hurd, 1937b: 215 and Ch. VI).[3] It would seem that movement generally of a group through the class system is the result of a set of interrelated factors. Religion clearly plays an important role, for it reinforces language and cultural differences, reducing the possibilities for intermarriage, encouraging segregation, and helping to create differences in educational opportunity. Similarly, the emphasis placed on ethnic loyalties enhances both segregation and religious control, and the perpetuation of ethnic differences in class structures.[4]

The question now is whether the occupational levels of the various groups changed between the 1931 and 1951 censuses. Did the low level groups of 1931 move out of entrance status by decreasing their proportion in the unskilled and primary occupations? Was the general rank order of the various groups maintained in the interval? Were certain groups leaving agriculture more rapidly or more slowly than the decline of the total labour force?

All groups had a smaller proportion of their members in agriculture as the proportion of the total labour force in agriculture declined from 34 to under 20 per cent between 1931 and 1951. Within this general decline in agriculture the English became more under-represented and the principal agricultural groups, German, Dutch, Scandinavian, and Eastern European, became more over-represented. The movement out of agriculture affected proportionately more of the English than the other groups. The proportion of Irish, French, and Scottish declined in about the same ratio as the total labour force, and Jews and Italians were as much under-represented in 1951 as in 1931. These changes suggest that the European groups, more than the British, were remaining in agriculture. For the British in agriculture a greater proportion were farm owners, rather than farm labourers, than was the case with the European groups, although for all groups there was a decline in the ratio of labourers to owners.

In the non-agricultural part of the labour force the most significant change in the relationship between ethnic groups and occupational class level during the 20 years was the lower level of the French. In 1951 the French were almost as much over-represented in the primary and unskilled occupations as they had been in 1931, and were even more over-represented than the East Europeans (16.3 per cent of French compared to 15.6 per cent of East Europeans). Moreover, the gap between the French over-representation at this level and that of Italians and "Other Europeans" narrowed. In the primary and unskilled class which made up 13.3 per cent of the labour force in 1951, the Italians (22.9) changed places with "Other Europeans" (19.0) as the most over-represented, next to the Indians and Eskimos (60.3). The Scandinavians (13.8) remained slightly over-represented in this class. The groups under-represented in the primary and unskilled class were: Jews (1.8), German (9.6), Scottish (10.1), Irish (11.1), Asian (11.4), English (11.6), and Dutch (11.6). The Asians appear to have improved their position, but in 1951 more than 25 per cent of them were still in personal service occupations, compared to 3.4 per cent of the labour force.

In the professional and financial class Jewish and all British origins continued to be over-represented, and all other origins remained under-represented. Compared to 5.9 per cent of the labour force, 10.2 per cent of Jews, 8.4 per cent of Scottish, 7.5 per cent of English, and 6.8 per cent of Irish were in this class.

Some further important evidence on the relationship between ethnic affiliation and class level can be seen in Blishen's study (1958). Although his scale is based on the 1951 census and therefore cannot be applied to either the 1931 or the 1961 occupational distributions, it does provide important confirmation of the relationship between class and ethnic origin for 1951.

Blishen groups the ethnic origins in a slightly different way and combines male and female occupations. In class 1, the highest class, which contained .9 per cent of the labour force, only Jewish (2.9 per cent) and British origins (1.3) were over-represented. If classes 1 and 2 are combined to make the top occupational level they constituted 11.6 per cent of the labour force. Once again those of British (13.1) and Jewish origin (38.6) were over-represented; Asians (11.5), Russians (10.7), and Scandinavians (10.2) ranked higher than the French (10.1), but all were under-represented.

A similar pattern of rank can be seen if Blishen's bottom two classes are combined. Classes 6 and 7 together made up 40.9 per cent of the labour force. The groups under-represented in these lower classes were Jewish (23.8), British (33.9), and Scandinavian (40.0).

By 1961 the relative positions of the various groups had changed very little. The British have improved their representation in the professional and financial class while in all the rest of the classes they have slowly tended towards the total labour force distribution. The French, however, have become more under-represented in the professional and financial class, dropping from − .8 in 1931 to − 1.9 in 1961. In all the other classes they have been moving slowly over the 30 years towards the normal distribution, with their over-representation in the primary and unskilled class dropping from +3.3 in 1931 to +2.8 in 1961. Two other ethnic groups have become more under-represented at the professional and financial level. These are the Italians who dropped from − 3.3 in 1931 to − 5.2 in 1961, and the Indians who dropped from − 4.5 in 1931 to − 7.5 in 1961. All the other groups have improved their position at this level since 1931, the most outstanding being the Asian and the Jewish. The former has increased its over-representation from − 4.3 in 1931 to + 1.7

in 1961, and the latter from $+2.2$ to $+7.4$.

There are two possible reasons for the changes in relative status. One is the differences between ethnic groups in the occupational level of their immigrants. A large number of Italian labourers entered Canada between 1951 and 1961. Most of the Asian immigrants, on the other hand, had to be professionals in order to enter Canada. In fact over one-third of the increment to Asian professionals between 1951 and 1961 was due to immigration. Most of these were engineers or scientists. However, we cannot attribute either the rise of the Jewish or the decline of the French to immigration.

A second possible reason for the status changes of the 1950s is the differences between groups in the amount of schooling. For males, 5 to 24 years old, at school, in 1951 the Asian and Jewish groups were greatly over-represented and the French, Italian, and Indian were definitely under-represented in the male school population. Jewish and Asian groups were still very over-represented in 1961 although the Asians had dropped from $+18.0$ to $+5.3$. Although the relative ranking of ethnic origins by school attendance was roughly the same in 1961 as in 1951 the British became more over-represented while the French became more under-represented. The French appear to be falling behind in the general rise in school attendance, so it appears more than likely that the decline of the French in the professional and financial class was due to lack of schooling.

If the French and English live within the same class system, and there is no reason to say that they do not because they enter into economic relations with each other, the French have gained the least from the transition to industrialization. This proposition is in accord with many of the impressionistic statements which are made about French Canada. An analysis such as the one presented here simply puts in quantitative terms a process about which many have been aware. As we shall see, the relative status of the two groups for the country as a whole is intensified within Quebec where more than three-quarters of the French live.

The high occupational level of Jews is striking also, but again this fact is not particularly new for the more sophisticated observer. Jews are the most highly educated group in the country, and they are more heavily represented in the professions than any other group. They made up only 1.3 per cent of the labour force, but they made up 4.4 per cent of Blishen's class 1 in 1951. Their high representation in the higher occupational levels should not be confused with power, as it sometimes is, for Jews are scarcely represented at the higher levels of Canada's corporate institutions.

Notes

1. There is also a degree of unreliability about census origin statistics. See N.B. Ryder, 1955.

2. The data for the analysis in this section came from the following sources: *Census of Canada, 1931*, vol. VII, Table 49: *Census of Canada, 1951*, vol. IV, Table 12; Hurd, *Racial Origins*, chap. XII and Tables 65-69; and A.H. LeNeveu, 'The Evolution and Present-Day Significance of the Canadian Occupational Struc-

ture,' 1931 census monograph (unpublished), chap. III.

3. Recent studies in the United States indicate that intermarriage takes place between ethnic groups but within religious faiths. Protestants, Catholics, and Jews represent pools from which marriage partners can be drawn.

4. Political behaviour is one social activity which has changed with length of residence in Canada. The longer the residence the less likely are members of an ethnic group to support an "ethnic" candidate, and the more likely are they to support a party of their own choice. See Vallee *et al.*, 1957.

23

*The Effects of Institutions in Ethnic Communities**

Raymond Breton

Introduction

Many researchers, in attempting to explain the integration of immigrants, have stressed the factors pertaining to the social background, the motivation, and the primary group affiliations of the immigrant (Mills *et al.*, 1950; Warner *et al.*, 1945; Eisenstadt, 1954, 1955; Reynolds, 1935). In the present study the view was adopted that some of the most crucial factors bearing on the absorption of immigrants would be found in the social organization of the communities which the immigrant contacts in the receiving country. There are three communities which are relevant: the community of his ethnicity, the native (i.e., receiving) community, and the other ethnic communities.

It was also felt that the integration of the immigrant should not be seen from a purely assimilationist point of view in which integration is said to have taken place when the immigrant is absorbed in the receiving society. Integration was rather conceived of as taking place in any one of the communities mentioned above or in two or three directions at the same time. That is, an immigrant can establish a network of social affiliations extending beyond the boundaries of any one community. Finally, it is also possible for the immigrant to be unintegrated.

In the present paper the influence of the institutional completeness of the immigrant's own ethnic community on the direction of his social integration is examined. In other words, I will examine the extent to which the institutional completeness of the ethnic community is related to its capacity to attract the immigrant within its social boundaries.

*Excerpted from 'Institutional Completeness of Ethnic Communities and the Personal Relations of Immigrants,' *American Journal of Sociology*, LXX, No. 2 (September 1964), pp. 193-205. Copyright 1964 by the University of Chicago. Reprinted by permission.

Institutional Completeness of the Ethnic Group

Ethnic communities can vary enormously in their social organization. At one extreme, there is the community which consists essentially in a network of interpersonal relations: members of a certain ethnic group seek each other's companionship; friendship groups and cliques are formed. But beyond this informal network, no formal organization may exist. The immigrant who is a member of such a group will establish all his institutional affiliations in the native community since his ethnic group has little or no organization of its own.

Most ethnic groups probably were at one time — and some still are — of this informal type. Many, however, have developed a more formal structure and contain organizations of various sorts: religious, educational, political, recreational, national, and even professional. Some have organized welfare and mutual aid societies. Some operate their own radio station or publish their own newspapers and periodicals. The community may also sustain a number of commercial and service organizations. Finally, it may have its own churches and sometimes its own schools. Between the two extremes much variation can be observed in the amount and complexity of community organizations; the degree of institutional completeness in fact shows variations from one ethnic group to another.

Direction of Personal Affiliations

When the immigrant is transplanted from one country to another, he has to reconstruct his interpersonal "field". He will rebuild in a new community a network of personal affiliations (Eisenstadt, 1952). Such a reconstruction is accomplished through his activities to satisfy his immediate needs: making a living, learning the new language, participating in social life, going to church. To satisfy these needs he will use a certain institutional set-up; he will introduce himself into a social group. Which one? The native community? His own ethnic community? Another immigrant community of an ethnicity different from his own? Will he integrate himself primarily in one of these communities, or will he split his affiliations among them?

In the present paper two questions will be discussed: (1) Does the interpersonal integration of the immigrant in fact take place in different directions? In other words, to what extent are immigrants integrated in the native, their own, or another immigrant community? (2) To what extent does the institutional completeness of the ethnic community determine the direction of the interpersonal integration of the immigrant?

Data and Methods

The analysis of the effect of the community characteristics on the direction of integration was carried out through a comparison of the personal relations of immigrants from 30 different ethnic groups. The findings are based on data from interviews with 230 male immigrants in Montreal, Canada, 163 of whom were reinterviewed 14 months later.[1] In drawing the sample, no restriction was put either on the length of residence in Canada or on the ethnicity of the immigrant.

The sample was drawn in two stages. The first stage was an area sample in which 13 census tracts were randomly selected. The census tracts in which the number of immigrants was extremely small had first been eliminated. Of the 18 415 households in the 13 census tracts, 75 per cent were visited in order to enumerate their foreign-born population. From this enumeration a list was drawn of 1689 male immigrants 18 years of age or older who had been at least 15 years of age when they came to Canada. In the second stage, a sample of 350 was drawn at random from the list. Questionnaires were then administered in personal interviews.

The measure used to rate the ethnic communities according to their degree of institutional completeness is constructed from information on the number of churches, welfare organizations, newspapers, and periodicals in each ethnic community.[2]

The direction of the affiliations of the immigrant was determined by the ethnic character of the persons with whom he was in contact. The respondent was first asked whether during the week preceding the interview he had visited any people in their homes or had received any visitor himself. He was also asked whether he went to the movies, theatre, night clubs, dance halls, taverns, bowling alleys, or other similar places; whether he attended concerts, sporting events, or other entertainments of some sort; and if he did, whether he went alone or with other people. Finally, he was asked if he met socially some of his co-workers, if he had any. Information was obtained on the national origin and birthplace of each person met (identified by first name or some other symbol). Then the respondents were classified, according to the proportion of the people met who were from each group, as having a *majority* or a *minority* of their personal relations in their own ethnic group, among other immigrants, or among members of the receiving community.[3]

Attachments to Native and to Ethnic Communities

Most immigrants become absorbed into the new social system in the sense that they establish some personal attachment to it. But in which direction? Table 23.1 presents data bearing on the extent to which immigrants are interpersonally integrated inside or outside their own ethnic community.

The relations of the immigrants with their ethnic group seem quite strong as far as social ties are concerned. Indeed, nearly 60 per cent have a majority of their personal ties with members of that group, and comparatively few — approximately 20 per cent — have most of their relations with members of the native community.

If we examine the changes that take place as the immigrant spends more time in his new society, we find that the idea of the immigrant segregated from the native community, fits more closely, although far from perfectly, the situation of the recent immigration. But this situation changes more and more as the number of years spent in the receiving society increases. It is partly true that at one time the immigrant is drawn into the ethnic subsystem, but it does not take too long before he begins to break these ties and to form new attachments outside his ethnic community. Indeed, it is after six years in the host country that the ties with the native community show a substantial increase.

Institutional Completeness of the Ethnic Community

The presence of formal organizations in the ethnic community sets out forces that have

Table 23.1 Ethnic composition of interpersonal relations for total sample and by length of residence in receiving country

	Years of residence			
Interpersonal relations	*Total (N = 173)*[a]	*0-6 (N = 73)*	*7-12 (N = 57)*	*13+ (N = 43)*
Proportion with majority of their personal relations:				
In own ethnic group	0.59	0.70	0.58	0.42
In another ethnic group	.14	.15	.07	.21
With members of native group	.19	.10	.25	.28
In none of the above groups	0.08	0.05	0.10	0.09

[a] Respondents with no personal relations and those who did not give the necessary information are excluded.

Table 23.2 Institutional completeness and in-group relations

	Degree of institutional completeness of ethnic group		
	Low	*Medium*	*High*
A. Proportion of *individuals* with majority of relations within ethnic group	0.21	0.54	0.89
Number of individuals	(62)	(28)	(83)
B. No. of *ethnic groups* with majority of all relations within group	5 out of 21	4 out of 5	4 out of 4

the effect of keeping the social relations of the immigrants within its boundaries. It tends to minimize out-group contacts. This is what Table 23.2 shows. The communities showing the highest degree of institutional completeness have a much greater proportion of their members with most of their personal relations within the ethnic group: 89 per cent of the members of highly institu-tionalized communities, as compared with 21 per cent of those from ethnic groups with few or no formal organizations. The relationship between institutional completeness and in-group relations is about the same when the groups themselves, rather than the individual immigrants, are classified on these dimensions (Part B of Table 23.2).[4]

Social Organization
or Individual Participation?

Do the institutions of an ethnic community affect the social relations only of those who use them, or do they generate a social life that extends beyond the realm of the participants. Table 23.3 shows that the presence of churches in a community is related to more in-group relations even among those who do not attend the ethnic church.

The number of ethnic publications also affects the composition of interpersonal networks, but only among non-readers. The non-readers are much more likely to associate within their ethnic group if the latter has several publications rather than a single one, but the difference in the case of readers is not only much weaker, but in the opposite direction. This is perhaps due to the difference in the distribution of the members of each category of ethnic groups in terms of education, language read, or other relevant attributes. The size of the sample, however, does not allow a more detailed analysis.

If the immigrant is a member of a community with many publications, it does not seem to make much difference whether he reads them himself or not. If, on the other hand, there is only one publication, then it seems important that he be directly exposed to its influence if it is to affect the composition of his personal relations. We may note also that the respondents from communities with no publications at all are the most likely to associate outside their ethnic group.

Through what process does the institutional completeness of the community affect the composition of the interpersonal networks of the members of an ethnic group? There are at least four such processes that we can speculate about.

Substitution. The ethnic group succeeds in holding its members' allegiance by preventing their contact with the native community.

Table 23.3 In-group relations, by number of churches in ethnic community and church attendance[a]

	None	One or two		Three or more	
		No. of churches in community			
	None	*One or two*		*Three or more*	
		Non-national attendance	*National attendance*	*Non-national attendance*	*National attendance*
Proportion of respondents with majority of relations within ethnic group	0.12	0.62	0.85	0.82	0.98
N[b]	—	—	—	—	—

[a] *a* (effect of number of churches) = 0.16, $P(a \leqslant 0) < 0.05$; *b* (effect of attendance at a national church) = 0.19, $P(b \leqslant 0) < 0.02$.

[b] Respondents from communities without churches are not considered in the calculation of the index.

This measure of the effect of an independent attribute X on a dichotomized dependent attribute Y is the mean of the percentage difference in each pair of comparisons when controlling for other independent attributes. The sampling variance of this statistic is obtained by summing the variances of each percentage difference and dividing by the square of the number of paired comparisons through which these differences were obtained. This estimate of the variance and a table of the standardized cumulative normal distribution are used to find the level of significance. For the basis of this statistic see James S. Coleman, *Introduction to Mathematical Sociology* (New York: Free Press of Glencoe, 1964).

This is achieved by a process of substitution whereby ethnic institutions rather than those of the native community take hold in the immigrant's social life. Immigrants have to find jobs; if they belong to a religion, they will want to go to church; being members of an occupational group, they may wish to join a work association; like other members of a modern society, they will read newspapers, listen to the radio, and watch television; they will send their children to school, etc. The immigrant and his family establish a wide range of institutional attachments, inevitably, or nearly so, through the performance of their work. If these attachments are established within the native community, they will constitute channels for the formation of personal relationships with the members of that community.

If, however, the ethnic group develops its own institutions and forms its own associations, it will in this way control to a large extent the interpersonal integration of at least those of its members who become participants in the ethnic instead of the native organization.

Indeed, the findings presented in Table 23.3 show that, to the extent that there is actual substitution, that is to say, to the extent that individual immigrants do attend ethnic religious institutions instead of others, the expected effect on the composition of interpersonal ties is observed. But this effect through the process of substitution is fairly weak. If there is at least one church in the community, a large proportion of the immigrant's personal relations are contained within the social boundaries of the community. The increment in that proportion stemming from the individual's actual attendance at the ethnic church is not very large.

Extension within the community of the personal networks of the participants in institutions. The immigrants who belong to ethnic organizations value highly their nationality and, as we have seen, form associations within it. The organizations sustain and perhaps increase this group of "attached" individuals, who in turn nourish the national sentiments of non-participants and include them among their associates.

Organizations and associations in a community also raise new issues or activate old ones for public debate. The arousal of public interest in the life of the group probably results in greater cohesiveness of the group. For instance, the group may become united in some action against outside elements, such as over an immigration bill which would be detrimental to this particular group, or the expropriation of houses which would force a large number of families of that ethnic group to move away, or again the attempts of a non-national parish to have the national church closed down in order to increase its own membership.

Of course, issues which divide sub-groups within the ethnic community will also have the effect of keeping the personal relations within the ethnic boundaries. The attachments of the members of each sub-group will be strengthened. To the extent that they become polarized on the issues facing their group, association with individuals who are not members of the ethnic group will be less appealing, unless they could become allies in the conflict. An important controversy among Italians, for example, will make Italians associate among themselves in cliques fighting each other (Simmel, 1955: 13ff).

Leaders of organizations actively attempt to maintain or enlarge the clientele. This is particularly true if the rate of immigration is decreasing, and because of this the survival of some of the organizations comes to be in danger.

Type and Number of Institutions

Effect of Different Types of Institutions

Of the three types of institutions included in the index of institutional completeness — churches, welfare organizations, and newspapers and periodicals — religious institutions have the greatest effect in keeping the immigrant's personal associations within the boundaries of the ethnic community. This is shown in Table 23.4 where the effect of the other types of institutions is controlled. In both cases, the presence and number of religious institutions explain about the same proportion of the variation in the dependent phenomenon (40 per cent and 45 per cent).[5]

The weight of the religious institutions can be attributed to the dominant role they hold in the community. Churches are very frequently the centre of a number of activities; associations are formed and collective activities are organized under their influence and support. Also, the national sentiments of

the immigrant find support in having experiences in church very similar to those in the country of origin — the language is the same; the images used in preaching are the same; the saints worshipped are also those the immigrant has known from early childhood. Moreover, religious leaders frequently become advocates and preachers of a national ideology, providing a *raison d'être* for the ethnic community and a motivation for identification with it.

Publications have the second most important effect on the immigrant's interpersonal network. The presence of publications in the ethnic community explains 35 per cent of the variation in the proportion of in-group relations.[6]

Newspapers have a role in promoting the national ideology and keeping alive the national symbols and values, national heroes, and their historical achievements. Moreover, they interpret many of the events occurring in the country of adoption in terms of the survival or interests of the ethnic community. It is the very business of the national peri-

Table 23.4 Churches, welfare organizations, publications, and extent of in-group relations

	No. of churches in community							
	Two or less	Three or more		Two or less		Three or more		
	Welfare organizations				Publications			
	None	Some	None	Some	None	Some	None	Some
Proportion of individuals with majority of relations within ethnic group	0.26	0.54	0.75	0.95	0.23	0.67	0.73	0.98
N	(61)	(48)	(4)	(60)	(70)	(39)	(11)	(53)

a (effect of welfare organizations on in-group relations) = 0.24, $P(a \leq 0) \approx 0.05$; b^1 (effect of churches holding welfare organizations constant) = 0.45, $P(b_1 \leq 0)$; < 0.01; b^2 (effect of churches holding publications constant) = 0.40, $P(b_2 \leq 0)$ < 0.01; c (effect of publications) = 0.35, $P(c \leq 0)$ < 0.01.

odical or newspaper to be concerned with the events and personalities of the ethnic group.

Finally, the effect of the presence of welfare organizations is the least. It explains only 24 per cent of the variation. This, we presume, is due to the fact that these organizations are not concerned with the national interests of the community. They deal with people in need of food, shelter, clothing, or medical attention. They have to support "human" feelings rather than "national" feelings; nevertheless, the existence of such organizations points to the presence of an active elite in the community which perhaps has its influence on the community's cohesiveness through channels other than the welfare organizations themselves. Also, their existence has a negative effect on contact with the host community: immigrants in need who address themselves to ethnic organizations miss a chance of contact with the "native" community.

Variation with Increasing Number of Formal Organizations

What most differentiates one community from another in its capacity to control the social integration of its members is not so much its having many formal organizations as having some as opposed to none at all.

The first organization makes the greatest difference. Second, third, or further additions have an effect on the extent of in-group relations, but much smaller than the effect of the first organization, or in the opposite direction. A drastic expansion occurs in the ethnic interpersonal network when the ethnic community ceases to be an informal system and acquires some first elements of a formal structure. This expansion continues as the formal structure develops but in increments smaller than the initial one.

Change in Composition of Interpersonal Networks

If the ethnic community to which he belongs determines to a certain degree the composition of an immigrant's interpersonal network, it should also show some effect on the rate at which the immigrant changes his personal associates as well as on the kind of people he includes among, and abandons from, his personal relations.

Changes took place in both directions: some immigrants associated more within their ethnic group, some less. Of those who were not members of an ethnic interpersonal network at the time of the first interview, 22 per cent were included in one a year after; on the other hand, 17 per cent of those associated mostly in their ethnic group had become interpersonally integrated in the native group.[7]

The changes in the composition of the immigrants' personal relations were then approximately as likely to be in the direction of the ethnic community as in that of the native community. This fact is of crucial importance for this study indeed; it serves to validate the scheme used in the analysis. It supports the idea that the integration of immigrants cannot really be studied without taking into account the fact that it can be achieved in at least two directions, that is, within the native or within the ethnic community, and that the integration can take place as frequently in one as in the other direction. Integration within the ethnic community cannot be ignored under the assumption that it is relatively unimportant or that it occurs relatively infrequently.[8]

The degree of institutional completeness of an immigrant's ethnic community is one of the main factors determining the direction of the change in the composition of his personal relations. As Table 23.5 shows, the immigrant who is a member of an institutionalized ethnic community is more likely to have shifted to a high proportion of in-group relations than the one who belongs to a less institutionalized one (29 per cent as compared to 18 per cent).

Also, Table 23.5 shows that the immigrants who had no personal relations at the time of the first interview and acquired some between the interviews acquired different kinds of associates depending on the degree of institutional completeness of their ethnic group. If the immigrant is a member of a group with organizations of its own, he is three times more likely to have acquired associates within his own group than if he is a part of a group with a more informal social organization (62 per cent as against 20 per cent).

The degree of institutional completeness and the magnitude of the ethnic interpersonal network are interdependent phenomena. It can be argued that the existence of an informal structure in an ethnic community is a prerequisite for the appearance of formal organizations. But it is also true that once

a formal structure has developed it has the effect of reinforcing the cohesiveness of already existing networks and of expanding these networks. This expansion is achieved mostly by attracting within the ethnic community the new immigrants. A community with a high degree of institutional completeness has a greater absorbing capacity than those with a more informal social organization. The present findings on the changes in the composition of personal relations show the difference between the two types of ethnic communities in their ability to exert influence on the direction of the interpersonal integration of the immigrant.

On the other hand, the ethnic community does not seem to have much effect in preventing some of its members from establishing relations outside its boundaries. The proportion who had most of their relations within their own ethnic group and who now have most of them outside of it is the same for members of communities with either formal or informal social organization. The proportions, however, are based on a very small number of cases.

Table 23.5 Institutional completeness and change in ethnic composition of personal relations

Proportion of relations within ethnic group	High degree of institutional completeness			Low degree of institutional completeness		
	Wave II			*Wave II*		
	Minority	*Majority*	*N*	*Minority*	*Majority*	*N*
Wave I:						
Minority	0.71	0.29	17	0.82	0.18	34
Majority	.15	.85	60	.14	.86	7
No personal relations	.038	0.62[a]	13	0.80	0.20	10

[a] $d(0.62 = 0.20) = 0.42$ is significant at the .03 level.

Conclusion

Having found that the institutional completeness of the ethnic community is an important factor in the direction of the social integration of immigrants, it is interesting to speculate about the determinants of this property of an ethnic community. There seem to be at least three sets of factors related to the formation of a public for ethnic organizations.

First, the ethnic group may possess some differentiating social or cultural attribute which can set it apart from the native community. Language, colour, and religion are prominent among these features, but other traits and customs of a group can bring about the same result. The more different the people of a certain ethnicity are from the members of the native community, the easier it will be for them to develop their own institutions to satisfy their needs.

In the present study, it was found that a difference in language was associated with a high degree of institutional completeness. It was also found among ethnic groups with a different language that the higher the proportion in the ethnic group who are ignorant of the native languages (French and English), the higher the degree of institutional completeness of the group.[9]

The differentiating characteristics of an ethnic group constitute the basis for the formation of a clientele or a public for ethnic organizations. The mobility potential of the immigrant is reduced by such factors; he is more confined to his ethnic group. This is particularly true — or perhaps only true — when the differentiating features are negatively evaluated by the native community.

The second set of factors related to the degree of institutional completeness has to do with the level of resources among the members of the ethnic group. If a large proportion of the members of an ethnic group have few resources of their own, as indicated for instance in rural origin and lack of occupational skills, then there is in this ethnic group an important "clientele" to support welfare and mutual benefit organizations. Such a situation is likely to incite a "social entrepreneur" within the ethnic group to try to organize something for the new immigrants in need, seeing there an interesting opportunity for himself. His rewards would be either monetary profit, prestige in the community, more members for his church, or more buyers for his newspaper. In the present study, a strong positive relationship was in fact found between the proportion of manual workers in an ethnic group and the degree of institutional completeness of that group.[10]

A third set of factors relates to the pattern of migration. The number of immigrants of a given ethnicity and the rate at which they arrive are relevant factors in the formation of an ethnic public. Perhaps a more important factor is whether the migration is an individual or a group phenomenon. Immigration during certain periods of time or for a given ethnic group can be the result of discrete decisions by individuals experiencing similar conditions in their country of origin; but it can also be a more or less organized group response, ranging from the migration of a group (such as a sect) under a leader to the pattern in which a migratory chain is established over a few years within a kinship network or a village and funds are collected in the new country to pay the passage of others from the native village or city (Petersen, 1958; Price, 1959). Such factors provide very different sets of conditions for the development of ethnic institutions.

Ethnic communities are formed, grow,

and disappear; they go through a life cycle.[11] They probably begin either as simple aggregates of individuals, as amorphous informal groups, or as fairly well-structured informal groups. This group can constitute a public for ethnic organizations, a set of opportunities for social entrepreneurs. The organizations established by these entrepreneurs will maintain themselves as long as a public exists to use their services, or as long as the ethnic identity of the organization is important for the members of the ethnic group. The very existence of such organizations, as the findings of this paper show, act to strengthen this identity. But other mechanisms also operate,

such as the fact that the leaders of the organizations have a vested interest in these organizations and will attempt in various ways to strengthen the ethnic identity so as to keep their public as large as possible.

If the rate of migration is low or nil, the ethnic public will progressively decrease, because even a high degree of institutional completeness will not prevent some integration into the native community. With time — and it may be quite long — the ethnic organizations will themselves disappear or lose their ethnic identity, completing the life-cycle of the community.

Notes

1. The first wave was done during April, May, and June, 1958; the second during July, August, and September, 1959.

2. In referring to degree of institutional completeness, what is meant is the *relative degree*, not the absolute degree. First of all, not all the organizations are included. The schools, for example, are left out and — what is even more important — so are voluntary associations, which are not only numerous but also very significant in the social life of any ethnic community. However, it seems reasonable to assume that the distribution of these associations among the various groups would be about the same as the distribution of the organizations presented above. Second, there are probably minor errors in the above list. Some ethnic groups may have a welfare organization, for example, which was not listed in the sources used.

3. No attention is given here to the difference between those with affiliations in two or

three communities and those whose affiliations are concentrated in a single one. Consideration of such differences would be revealing as regards both patterns of change over time and the social and psychological impact of the ethnic homogeneity or heterogeneity of affiliations on the immigrant personality and behaviour.

4. In order to test the relationship between institutional completeness and the composition of personal relations, several factors were held constant: the size of the group, its residential concentration, the proportion of professionals in the group, the similarity and the difference of the language of the group with those of the natives (English and French), the proportion in the group who are ignorant of the native languages, years of residence in Canada, and occupational status. The relationship held under all these controls. The strength of the relationship was reduced by as much as one-third in only one case: when the proportion ignorant of the native languages was held constant.

5. The number of cases in certain cross-classifications did not allow an identical break for each type of organization. It was done as a check, and the results were in the same direction.

6. The estimate of the effect of the presence of publications remains the same when it is computed while holding constant the presence of welfare organizations.

7. If there had been no panel dropouts, the proportions changing in each direction would probably not have been different. Indeed, if we compare those who changed address with those who did not, under the assumption that the dropouts were mostly movers, we find that the movers were more likely to change the composition of their personal ties than the non-movers during the period between the two panel waves, but in both directions: among those who had mostly in-group relationships at the time of the first panel wave, 13 per cent more of movers than of non-movers had changed to a majority of out-group contacts by the time of the second wave; among those with a majority of out-group contacts, 11 per cent more of movers than of non-movers changed to a majority of in-group relationships.

8. There are two other possibilities: the immigrant may become interpersonally integrated in another immigrant group of an ethnicity different from his own, or he may remain an isolate.

9. Institutional completeness is high in one group out of eight whose language is also spoken by the native community and in 12 out of 22 whose language is different. Also, it is high in six of the 13 groups with less than 20 per cent ignorant of the native languages and in six of the seven groups with 20 per cent or more not knowing these languages. (No data were available for two of the ethnic groups with a language other than French or English.)

10. Of 13 ethnic groups with less than 50 per cent of their workers in manual occupations, two are high on institutional completeness. Of the 14 with 50 per cent or more of their workers in manual occupations, seven have a high degree of institutional completeness. (No occupational information was available for three of the ethnic groups.)

11. The community life-cycle approach to the study of the integration and acculturation of immigrants is well represented by Thomas and Znaniecki, 1920; and Galitzi, 1929.

24

Canadians' Responses
To Native Peoples*

J. Rick Ponting

Introduction

Following the federal government's policy paper on Indian affairs in 1969 and the 1973 Supreme Court of Canada decision on the Nishga land claim, Indian and Native issues acquired much greater significance for Canadian policy makers. With the constitutional entrenchment of aboriginal rights and of a series of First Ministers' Conferences (FMCs) to define and elaborate those constitutional rights, aboriginal affairs achieved a prominent position on government agendas in the 1980s. However, since the 1987 FMC's failure to reach an agreement on aboriginal self-government, Native leaders have struggled to maintain that position. Hopeful of increasing the political incentives for governments to act on Natives' demands, Native leaders have shown greater interest in moulding non-Native public opinion in favour of those demands. Even before public opinion polls were cited by one Premier as justification for not entrenching an explicit right to self-government in the constitution, some Native strategists had concluded that they have no choice but to improve non-Native public opinion toward Natives. Aboriginal organizations have therefore published full page advertisements in prominent newspapers, commissioned their own polls, and shown considerable interest in academic surveys on Native issues.

Given this political context, it is interesting to examine non-Native public opinion and to ascertain how it has changed since the mid-1970s. That was precisely the thrust of a national survey conducted by the author in fall 1986; its findings are the focus of this paper. The 1986 sample was large, random,

*Revised version of a paper presented to the Ninth Biennial Conference of the Canadian Ethnic Studies Association, Halifax, N.S., October 14-17, 1987. The research reported herein was conducted with the aid of a Sabbatical Leave Fellowship from the Social Sciences and Humanities Research Council of Canada (SSHRCC) and with funding from SSHRCC (Research Grants Division), the Multiculturalism Directorate of the federal Department of the Secretary of State (Canadian Ethnic Studies Research Programme), the University of Calgary, and the sale of reports issuing from the study. Data for the 1976 study mentioned herein were collected under a generous grant from the Donner Canadian Foundation. The author expresses his sincere appreciation to these supporters of the projects and to the respondents, research assistants, and other support staff members without whose assistance the projects would not have been possible. Data collection in 1986 was done under contract by Decima Research Ltd.

and included only non-aboriginal persons residing in the ten provinces. The 1834 interviews were conducted face-to-face in the respondents' homes. Unless otherwise specified, all remarks below pertain to this 1986 data set.[1]

Main Findings

Little Knowledge, Low Priority

Canadians know very little about aboriginal affairs, pay little attention to most aboriginal matters in the mass media, and attach a low priority to aboriginal issues. The evidence to this effect is overwhelming. Almost one third of the sample does not know the meaning of the term "aboriginal people." When explicitly asked, only a bare majority would include the Métis as aboriginal people. The majority has never heard of the Indian Act (56 per cent) and is unaware of the existence of aboriginal rights in the constitution (52 per cent). Over 55 per cent are unaware of any difference between status Indian and non-status Indian. Sixty-one per cent classify themselves as "not at all familiar" with the Lyell Island controversy in the Queen Charlotte Islands, while 60 per cent are not at all familiar with the main status Indian lobby group, the Assembly of First Nations. Almost 40 per cent said they are "not at all familiar" with "a constitutional conference involving the Prime Minister, provincial premiers, and Native leaders."[2] Over one third of the sample would not even hazard a guess when asked approximately what per cent of the Canadian population is Native, while over 40 per cent (including a majority in each of the three most westerly provinces) estimated that Natives constitute more than 8 per cent of the national population. (The correct answer is around 3 per cent.) By means of a complicated analysis, it was concluded that around 15 per cent of Canadians are almost totally oblivious to aboriginal matters in this country.

The opening question of the survey asked respondents to rank, in order of importance to the respondent, five "problems facing Canada today," one of which was "improving the social and economic situation of Canada's Native people." If this can be taken as representative of Native issues in general, we can say that Canadians attach low priority to Native issues, for less than a quarter chose this as their first or second priority in the list of five problems. The five problems and the percentage of the sample choosing each as its first or second priority are: "protecting the natural environment," 67 per cent; "reducing the national debt," 65 per cent; "improving the rights of women in Canada," 24 per cent; "improving the social and economic situation of Canada's Native people," 23 per cent; and "reaching a free trade agreement with the U.S.A.," 20 per cent.

Opposition to Special Status

With the exception of a select few situations, Canadians manifest a pronounced tendency to reject what they view as "special status" for Natives. This is shown in the curve in Figure 24.1, which plots the distribution of the sample on two indexes, one of which is the index of support for special status for Natives. A respondent's score on this index is his or her average score on four items dealing with special institutional arrangements for Natives. As with most of the indexes in the study, this one comprises statements with which respondents are asked to indicate their degree of agreement or disagreement, on a five-point scale ranging from "strongly agree" to "strongly disagree". The statements in the index of support for special status for Natives are shown below, and are followed by the per cent of the sample agreeing (strongly or moderately) and then the per cent disagreeing (strongly or moderately) with each one:

> If Parliament and the elected leaders of the Native people agreed that some Canadian laws would not apply in Native communities, it would be all right with me (38 per cent vs 44 per cent);
>
> Native schools should not have to follow provincial guidelines on what is taught (22 per cent vs 67 per cent);
>
> Native governments should have powers equivalent to those of provincial governments (31 per cent vs 51 per cent); and
>
> Native governments should be responsible to elected Native politicians, rather than to Parliament, for the federal government money they receive (28 per cent vs 44 per cent).

In Figure 24.1 we observe that most respondents fall at the unsupportive end of the scale measuring support for special status for Natives. Even stronger opposition to special status is found in most questions which explicitly use the word "special." For instance, when given two statements — one of which described special institutional arrangements for Natives and one of which did not — and asked to choose the one that comes closer to their views, it was repeatedly found that almost two-thirds of respondents opted for the statement that denied special status to Natives. One concrete example of this is Q.57, where the two statements were: "For crimes committed by Indians *on Indian reserves*, there should be special courts with Indian judges"; and "Crimes committed by Indians on Indian reserves should be handled in the same way as crimes committed elsewhere." Sixty-five per cent chose the latter, while only 27 per cent favoured the former.

This opposition to "special status" is probably rooted both in the longstanding opposition of many English Canadians to spe-

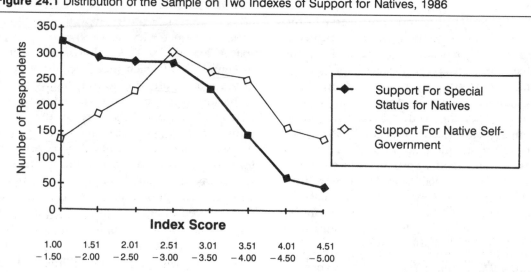

Figure 24.1 Distribution of the Sample on Two Indexes of Support for Natives, 1986

cial status in Confederation for Quebec, and in a norm of equality which is widely held among Canadians.

The only exception to this opposition to special status for Natives is issue areas which tap Canadians' sensitivity to Natives' special relationship with the land.

Support for Self-Government and Native Rights

To the author's surprise, the aforementioned antagonism toward special status coexists with a support for Native self-government. For many Canadians self-government is less a manifestation of special status than a basic democratic right of self-determination. This interpretation is suggested by the fact that in Figure 24.1 the curve representing the distribution of the sample of an index of support for Native self-government exhibits a markedly different shape than the curve for the index of support for special status for Natives. The curve depicting support for Native self-government is akin to the famous bell-shaped curve and the average score is slightly to the supportive side of the mid-point of the scale.

The index of support for Native self-government is made up of four items. A respondent's index score is his or her average score across the four items. The items are listed below, and are followed by the percentage of the sample agreeing (strongly or moderately) and then the percentage of the sample disagreeing (strongly or moderately):

It is important to the future well-being of Canadian society that the aspirations of Native people for self-government be met (42 per cent vs 33 per cent);

Those provincial premiers who oppose putting the right to Native self-government in the Constitution are harming Native people (38 per cent vs 34 per cent);

Most Native leaders who call for self-government for Native people are more interested in promoting their own personal career than in helping Native people (30 per cent vs 41 per cent); and

The constitution of Canada should specifically recognize the right of *Indians* to self-government (41 per cent vs 40 per cent).

Similarly, in answering the question of how much effort government should put into protecting the rights of Native people (given that putting more effort into this area would require a shift of money from other areas), a largely plurality (45 per cent) favoured more effort, while only a small minority (14 per cent) favoured less effort. (Thirty-two per cent felt that the present amount of effort devoted to this is about right.) Further evidence of support for such rights as the right to self-government can be found in the fact that when asked which of three things (on a list provided) is needed most by Canadian Indians, a similarly large plurality (44 per cent) chose "more rights in the constitution" over "less control by government" (33 per cent) and "more money from government" (7 per cent).

General Sympathy

To some extent, the above support for Native self-government and Native rights is a reflection of a more general positive orientation toward, or attitudinal support for, Natives. This might be called "sympathy", if that word can be stripped of connotations of condescension. Overall, the Canadian population tends to be more sympathetic than antagonistic toward Natives. This observation is based on respondents' scores on two composite indexes — the index of sympathy for Natives and the index of sympathy for Indians. On both indexes the average score for the sample fell well above the mid-point of the scale. Further evidence comes from other questions not included in any of the above four indexes. For instance, a majority (57 per cent) disagreed with the statement, "Indians are a bunch of complainers" (only 23 per cent agreed), and a large majority (71 per cent) disagreed with the statement, "The more I hear and see about Indians in the news media, the less respect I have for them" (only 13 per cent agreed). A large plurality agreed (48 per cent vs 29 per cent disagreeing) with the following item in the index of Indian sympathy, "Indians deserve to be a lot better off economically than they are now." This suggests that there is a moral component to the aforementioned general orientation of support for Indians and other Natives.

Sensitivity to Natives' Special Relationship to the Land

Respondents exhibited a surprisingly high degree of supportive opinion for Natives on matters related to land and land-use conflicts. This is captured in the most straightforward manner by responses to the following statement, "Where Natives' use of land conflicts with natural resource development, Native use should be given priority." A slight majority agreed with this view, while only one third disagreed.

Another question, inspired by the situation of the Lubicon Indians in northern Alberta, brings into bold relief this sensitivity to Natives' special relationship to the land. Respondents were asked which of the following three statements comes closest to their own view:

Native land claims should *not* be allowed to delay natural resource projects at all;

Natural resource development companies should not be allowed to even set foot on land claimed by Natives until those Native land claims have been settled; or

I haven't given any thought to the matter of land claims and natural resource development.

The pro-Natives statement was chosen over the pro-development statement by a margin of 2:1 (42 per cent to 19 per cent). Thirty per cent chose the third statement, and another 11 per cent said "none of the above" or expressed no opinion.

Similarly, on yet another question a large plurality (48 per cent vs 37 per cent) disagreed that giving Native people special hunting rights "just isn't fair." In the 1988 follow-up study, when the question was reworded to deal with special fishing rights, rather than special hunting rights, the results were virtually identical.

Regional Variation

Although all of the foregoing is applicable to Canada as a whole, such generalizations obscure important variations from one region of the country to another. Those regional variations take on considerable practical significance when one remembers that many of the reforms sought by Natives require the approval of provincial governments.

In some provinces, notably Saskatchewan, British Columbia, and Alberta, support for Natives is clearly rather low, while in Quebec and Ontario support is high, regardless of which of the four aforementioned scales we use to assess that support. Table 24.1 shows provincial/regional average scores for each of the four indexes mentioned above. Scores on each index could range from 1.0 to 5.0, and considerable variation from province to province can be found on each of these scales. The most extreme interprovincial variation, however, is found on the index of support of special status for Natives, where the difference between the most supportive province (Quebec) and the least supportive province (Alberta) is 0.82 scale points.

Table 24.1 Provincial average scores on four indexes of attitudinal support for Natives, 1986

	Scale			
	Sympathy for Indians	Sympathy for Natives	Support for special status	Support for self-government
Total Canada	3.29	3.22	2.56	3.11
Atlantic Region	3.09 (4)	3.12 (5)	2.49 (4)	2.92 (4)
Quebec	3.44 (1)	3.24 (2)	3.04 (1)	3.33 (1)
Ontario	3.40 (2)	3.35 (1)	2.51 (3)	3.15 (2)
Manitoba	3.39 (3)	3.13 (3.5)	2.54 (2)	3.10 (3)
Saskatchewan	2.91 (7)	2.96 (7)	2.28 (5)	2.81 (7)
Alberta	3.08 (5)	3.13 (3.5)	2.22 (7)	2.91 (5)
British Columbia	3.04 (6)	3.03 (6)	2.23 (6)	2.89 (6)

Range of each scale = 1.00 to 5.00. Numbers in parentheses are rank order within each column.

Regional variation is also pronounced on other measures not shown in Table 24.1. For instance, the proportion of the public which is oblivious to Native issues is much larger in Quebec than in the other provinces. In addition, familiarity with Native matters tends to be regionally-specific, as illustrated by the fact that over three-quarters of British Columbians classified themselves as "very familiar" with the Lyell Island controversy in the Queen Charlotte Islands, while only 15 per cent of Maritimers and five per cent of Quebeckers put themselves in this category. Even on issues that are clearly of national applicability, such as aboriginal rights in the constitution or amendments to the Indian Act to remove sex discrimination, regional variation is found in respondents' degree of familiarity.

support for aboriginal people, on the one hand, and knowledge or familiarity with aboriginal issues on the other hand. Quebec, for instance, is the most supportive province, but the least knowledgeable. Yet, even if we consider Quebec to be a special case and remove Quebeckers from the analysis, the relationship between knowledge or familiarity and attitudinal support for Native people remains negligible. However, in interpreting these findings, we must bear in mind that the measures of knowledge used in this study were crude and did not cover a very broad base of Native conditions.

It is also interesting to note that the data failed to support the hypothesis that persons over-estimating the size of the Native population in their province would be most likely to be antagonistic toward Natives.

Tenuous Relationship Between Sympathy and Knowledge

At best, there is only a very weak and inconsistent relationship between attitudinal

Importance of Two Perceptual Variables

Although the type of knowledge measured in this study proved inconsequential in influencing opinions on Native issues, that does not mean all knowledge or perception is unimportant. Indeed, two variables emerged as strongly related to attitudinal support for Natives on all four scales discussed above. These variables are the perception of the adequacy of government financial assistance to Natives, and perceived capability of aboriginal governments. The questions were phrased as follows:

> In your opinion, is the financial assistance which government gives to *Native people* far too much, a bit too much, about right, a bit too little, or far too little? and

> In general, if Native governments were adequately funded, how would they perform in meeting the needs of Native people — would they be more capable than the federal government is in meeting Natives' needs, less capable than the federal government at this, or would they be about equally as capable as the federal government?

The more capable a respondent perceived Native governments to be (in relation to the federal government) and the more inadequate (rather than excessive) he or she perceived government financial assistance to Natives to be, the more supportive were the respondent's scores on the indexes of support for self-government, support for special status for Natives, sympathy for Natives, and sympathy for Indians. However, whether the perceptions shaped the attitudes, or vice versa, is difficult to ascertain.

Canadian Public Opinion Permissive of Reform

At the national level, the Canadian adult population is not set to launch a bitter backlash against politicians who bring about reform to increase aboriginal Canadians' level of self-determination. Rather, public opinion is permissive of a wide range of such governmental actions. This conclusion is based on several observations. First, a large minority of the Canadian electorate is oblivious to

what happens in the realm of Native affairs and shows little or no sign of becoming politically activated in response to controversial issues, for their obliviousness extends even to those controversial issues. Secondly, Canadian public opinion is not polarized into two hostile camps of so-called "red neck racists" and "bleeding heart liberals". These extremists of the left and right are a very small proportion of the adult Canadian population. Thirdly, persons who are consistently supportive of aboriginal people outnumber those who are consistently antagonistic by a margin of about two to one. Among the adult Canadian population as a whole, the distribution of opinion is generally more favourable than antagonistic, except where certain forms of special status or special privilege are perceived.

Given that a large plurality of the Canadian population is unstable, but more positive than negative, in its views toward aboriginal people, that opinion could probably be made more positive through strong opinion leadership, such as that demonstrated by the Pope during his 1987 visit to a Northwest Territories Native community. However, persistence in that leadership is necessary. Furthermore, its effectiveness will be undermined if no effort is made to bolster perceptions of the competence of Native governments and perceptions of the magnitude of Natives' needs for financial assistance in comparision with what is being provided.

Decline in Support for Natives?

Several of the questions posed in a 1976 national survey co-directed by the author, were reproduced in identical or substantially the same form on the 1986 survey. Among these were six from the 1976 Indian sympathy index. Figure 24.2 portrays the distribution of

Figure 24.2 Distribution of the Sample on Index of Sympathy for Natives, 1976 & 1986

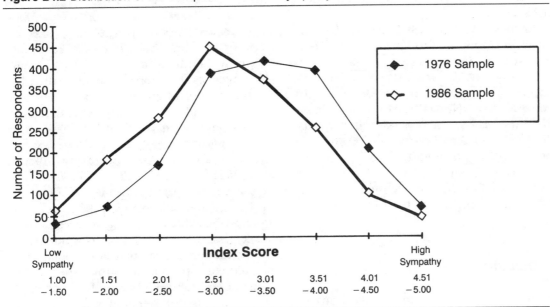

the 1976 and 1986 samples on the six-item composite index, which we might call the index of comparative sympathy. It *appears*[3] that, as measured by these scale items, support for Natives has declined significantly over the last ten years. Although not shown here, it was found that the apparent decline occurred in every province and region.

However, a few words about this apparent decline in support are warranted. First, it takes on practical significance only if the items included in the index are judged to cover a sufficiently wide range of the subfields about which we could conceivably have asked. Secondly, in light of the events of the last decade, it might be that the main significance of this finding is that the decline in support has not been greater. (Remember that the average scores of respondents on three of the four indexes were above the neutral point on the scale.)

Writing about public opinion in the U.S.A., Anthony Downes (1972) observes: "American public attention rarely remains sharply focused upon any one domestic issue for very long – even if it involves a continuing problem of crucial importance to society." He goes on to identify five stages in the "issue attention cycle," as follows: (i) the pre-problem stage; (ii) alarmed discovery and euphoric enthusiasm; (iii) realizing the cost of significant progress; (iv) gradual decline of intense public interest; and (v) the post-problem stage. In light of the dynamics of the issue attention cycle, whereby publics tend to become bored with issues after their repeated mass media exposure, we might well have expected a less supportive level of opinion than we found in 1986. It is possible that the apparent decline in attitudinal support for aboriginal people over the ten-year period is merely a slower than normal manifestation of the normal evolution of public opinion on social issues in advanced industrial societies.

Downes (1972) notes that not all major social problems go through the issue-attention cycle. Social issues that are likely to go through the cycle share the following characteristics: (i) only a minority of the population is suffering (ii) a majority or a powerful minority in the population is benefiting significantly; and (iii) the issue has no intrinsically exciting qualities (or no longer has such qualities). All three of these conditions could be said to characterize the situation of aboriginal people in Canada today.

Conclusion

In closing, we turn to the implications of the findings for academic and applied endeavours.

One of the most salient findings from an academic perspective is the structure of the public, particularly the substantial portion of the population which is oblivious to Native issues and the near-majority which is somewhat unstable in its opinions on Native issues. Awareness of these features of the structure of the public should serve as a warning beacon to remind academics to guard against reifying the public, for that sector of the population which expresses views on Native issues to an interviewer is not at all coterminus with that sector of the population which is interested in Native issues and involved in discussing Native issues and registering opinions with decision-makers.

This reinforces Blumer's (1948) critique of public opinion studies like the present one which focus on the mass public and assign equal weight to all respondents regardless of their connection with social networks, their degree of influence over others, and their propensity to register their opinion through

political action. Clearly, on Native issues the attitudes and opinions of the different sectors (the "oblivious", the "consistent", and the "inconsistent") of the public are of rather different political significance and probably of rather different causal origin. This suggests that global or abstract theories of the causes of prejudiced attitudes will have little explanatory utility in the Canadian context, and what is needed instead is the specification of highly particularized social settings where one or the other causal theory is applicable. That is, we need to identify the regional, ideological, social psychological, and social characteristics of different situations under which different theories of prejudice are valid. Thus, just as students of ethnic identity realize that ethnic identity is situationally specific, we should regard the causes of prejudiced (or even favourable) attitudes as different depending upon the sector of the public to which individuals belong and the other characteristics of their social situation. This therefore calls for a more micro-level analysis of the mass public. It also calls for research at the elite level in an attempt to discover how political leaders and decision-makers interpret and evaluate Native issues.

The practical significance of the findings is multifaceted. Because this is the focus of other papers (Ponting, 1987 a-d, 1988 a,b), it will not be developed in depth here. Rather, a few brief points will be listed with little or no elaboration. First, it is apparent from Canadians' low levels of knowledge and familiarity with Native affairs that Native leaders who wish to have the backing of favourable public opinion need to engage in imaginative, innovative, and attention-grabbing tactics which will help to educate nonnatives not only to the needs and aspirations of Natives, but also to such basics as who aboriginal people in Canada are. (The need for Francophone spokespersons is particularly acute.)

Secondly, public opinion would permit significant reform in the relationship between Natives and the non-Native society and its government. This is particularly true if care is taken in public pronouncements to justify that reform in terms of equality, multiculturalism, conservatism, and participation, and if the issue of "special status" is addressed directly so as to alleviate concerns that special arrangements for Natives are a form of special privilege.

Thirdly, there is an underlying predispositional compatibility between support for Natives and aspects of the aforementioned ideologies (for example, the desire by both Indians and conservatives to reduce the interference of government in the daily life of individuals). However, the opinion leadership to date has been insufficient to bring this compatibility to the fore so that it will influence the opinions of individuals on Native issues. To apply the insight of Philip Converse (1964) from a different realm of public opinion, we can say that the *constraint* imposed upon peoples' opinions in the Native affairs realm by their views in other realms (for example, multiculturalism, government in general) is very weak. That is, despite the logical coherence of these views on different aspects of contemporary life, they do not form a tightly knit ideology or system of belief and opinion. Hence, one task of Native leaders who seek to reverse any possible erosion of supportive public opinion is to provide to the mass public the cues that make those linkages explicit.

Fourthly, once those linkages are made explicit, Native issues will be less on the periphery of public consciousness and public opinion; they might even be in a position to "ride the coat-tails" of some other cognate issues (e.g., environmental protection, multicultural protection, national self-determination). If this is not done, it will be exceedingly difficult to fight the issue-attention cycle to keep Native issues on the agenda of the federal and provincial governments of Canada, unless Canadian Natives are prepared to rely more heavily upon the controversial (even within the aboriginal population) strategy of embarrassing Canada internationally. Yet, even the strategy of international embarrassment is not particularly effective with provincial governments, for they are much more insulated from international political pressures than is the federal government. Thus, the challenges facing Native leaders are formidable.

Notes

1. The confidence limits for the 1986 data are as follows: in 19 out of every 20 national samples of the same size drawn in Canada, the results would fall within about plus or minus 2.3 percentage points of the results found in the present study.

2. In a follow-up survey of 1200 randomly selected Canadians interviewed by telephone in September 1988, this figure remained high (37 per cent), despite the intensive media coverage of the March 1987 constitutional conference on aboriginal issues.

3. Results from the 1988 follow-up survey strongly suggest that a proof-reading error on one question in the 1986 survey introduced a slight distortion into the 1986 data. That is, the decline in sympathy from 1976 to 1986 was probably slightly *less* than was indicated by the 1986 data. The refinement permitted by 1988 data merely reinforces the conclusion that support for aboriginal peoples is remarkably persistent.

25

Racial Discrimination in Employment*

Frances Henry and Effie Ginzberg

Until the publication of our report *Who Gets the Work?* (1985) efforts to demonstrate that there is racial discrimination in the Canadian employment arena have been limited to census data analysis, personal reports of victims of discrimination, and attitude studies. Each of these three types of research is limited in its capacity to prove that discrimination based on race is actually the cause of discrepancies in income and access to employment. Critics, sceptics, and racists have easily been able to doubt the presence of racial discrimination in view of weaknesses inherent in these indirect measures of discrimination. *Who Gets the Work?* sought to test directly for the presence or absence or discrimination in the Toronto labour market through the process of field testing — a quasi-experimental research technique.

For the first time in Canada, a study tested racial discrimination in employment by actually sending individuals, White and Black to apply for advertised positions in order to find out if employers discriminate by preferring White to non-White employees. We believe we were successful in proving definitively that racial discrimination in Canada affects the employment opportunities of non-White Canadians. Whites have greater access to jobs than do equally qualified non-Whites.

Our study was guided by two questions. One, is there a difference in the number of job offers that White and Black applicants of similar experience and qualifications receive when they apply to the same jobs? And two, are there differences in the ways in which White and Black job applicants are treated when they apply for work? Both questions were tested by two procedures: *person testing* and *telephone testing*.

*Originally published in James Curtis *et al.* (eds.), *Social Inequality in Canada*, Scarborough, Ontario: Prentice-Hall Canada Inc., 1988. Reprinted by permission.

Defining Discrimination

Discrimination can take place at any point in the employment process. It may exist in such areas as recruitment, screening, selection, promotion, and termination. At the level of employee selection, for example, discrimination against non-Whites can take place when job applicants are called to the initial interview. To the extent that the employer's staff or the other employees themselves practise discrimination, either as a result of racial attitudes of the interviewer or because of instructions to screen out non-Whites as a matter of company policy, non-Whites will not get beyond the initial screening of job applicants. Similarly, in terms of promotion policies, non-Whites may be hired at lower levels, but their promotion to the upper ranks is effectively stopped by discriminatory barriers to mobility. For example, the employer may believe that the other employees will not accept a non-White as their supervisor.

Discrimination in employment can be intentional as well as inadvertent. Employers may not realize that their practices and policies have the effect of excluding non-Whites. The use of standard tests of personality or intelligence to select employees places certain minority groups at a disadvantage since they come from cultures other than the one for which the tests were designed. Recruiting through in-house word-of-mouth techniques often excludes minority applicants since they do not hear about available positions. Requiring Canadian experience and education can effectively eliminate non-Whites, many of whom are immigrants, from job opportunities even though such experience is not necessary to successful job performance.

Thus, there are numerous types of discrimination and numerous ways in which discrimination can be carried out. Our study concentrated essentially on the entry point and/or the selection procedure. In this study, the dynamics of discrimination are studied as discriminatory practices occur, that is, when a job seeker either makes an inquiry on the phone or comes in person to be interviewed. It is at this point that the applicant can run into a prejudiced employer or "gatekeeper" who either presumes that non-Whites are not desired or merely acts according to company policy. The telephone inquiry is particularly crucial at this stage since it is often the first approach made by the job applicant. An individual can be screened out, that is, told quickly and efficiently either that the job has already been filled or that the applicant's qualifications are not suitable. In all likelihood, the applicant will not know that he or she has been the victim of discrimination.

For the purposes of this study, we defined discrimination in employment as those practices or attitudes, willful or unintentional, that have the effect of limiting an individual's or a group's right to economic opportunities on the basis of irrelevant traits such as skin colour rather than an evaluation of true abilities or potential.

In-Person Testing

In the in-person testing, two job applicants, matched with respect to age, sex, education, experience, physical appearance (dress), and personality, were sent to apply for the same advertised job. The only major difference between our applicants was their race — *one was White and other, Black*. We created four such teams: one junior male, one junior female, one senior male, and one senior female. The younger teams applied for semiskilled and unskilled jobs such as gas station attendant, bus boy, waitress, and clerk and sales help in youth-oriented stores. The senior teams applied for positions in retail management, sales positions in prestigious stores, and waiting and hosting positions in expensive restaurants. The senior team members were, in fact, professional actors. Applying for middle-class type jobs meant that they would be required not only to present a sophisticated image but also to participate in a fairly demanding job interview. Professional actors, we believed, would be more convincing in playing the many roles required for this project. The résumés of the team members were carefully constructed to be as alike as possible. In order to further control possible biases, the staff of testers was changed several times so that no individual personality could account for the results.

The younger teams were composed of high-school and university students who would normally be applying for the same types of job that they applied for in the testing situation. Since we were not testing for sex discrimination and did not want this type of discrimination to account for any of our results, the male teams were sent to traditionally male jobs and the women went to jobs traditionally associated with women's work. In some types of jobs, for example waiter/waitress, both men and women were acceptable. Men and women were sent to such jobs but never to the same job. Each tester had a different résumé for the various types of positions that he or she was applying for, so each member of the senior female team, for example, carried several résumés, one for a secretary, another for a retail sales assistant, a third for a dental technician, etc. Each résumé contained the names of references supplied by business people and friends who had agreed to support our re-search. Our applicants could thus be checked out by a potential employer who could obtain a reference for the applicant. In actuality, only two employers ever called for references.

Research Procedure

Each evening, a listing of jobs would be selected for the next day from among the classified advertisements. Some types of jobs were excluded such as those involving driving, where licences could be checked. Jobs which required highly technical skills were also excluded.

The testers were instructed either to go to a certain address or to phone for an appointment. They used standard Canadian accents when phoning since we did not want them to be screened out over the phone. The testers would arrive within approximately one half-hour of each other so that there was little chance that a job had been legitimately filled. In most cases the Black applicant went first. After their interviews the testers completed a summary data sheet especially designed for this project in which they wrote down the details of their treatment and the kinds of information they had been given. Their résumés listed telephone numbers which were in actuality lines connected to the research office. Call-backs for second interviews or with offers of employment were received and recorded by the researchers. On-the-spot offers to the field testers were accepted by them. In the case of call-backs and on-the-spot offers, employers were phoned back, usually within an hour and informed that another position had been accepted, in order to make sure that employer could fill the vacancy as soon as possible.

Research Results: The In-Person Test

In three-and-one-half months of field testing, the testers were able to apply for 201 jobs for a total of 402 individual applications.

For our purposes, racial discrimination in employment was tested in two ways. First, was an offer of employment made to one of the applicants, both applicants, or neither applicant? Second, during the interview, were there any differences in the treatment of the two applicants? The following tables present the numerical results.

Blacks received fewer job offers than Whites. Of a total of 37 valid job offers, 27 went to Whites, 9 to Blacks, and in one case both were offered the job (Table 25.1). There were an additional 10 cases where both were offered jobs, but these were for commission sales which involved no cost to the employer. Our overall results therefore show that *offers to Whites outweigh offers to Blacks by a ratio of 3 to 1*.

We had thought that the nature of the job might influence whether Blacks or Whites would be hired. Only Whites received offers for managerial positions or jobs as waiters and waitresses or hosts and hostesses in the restaurant trade. A Black was offered a job in the kitchen when he had applied for a waiter's job!

As noted above, the second measure of discrimination was whether differential treatment had occurred during the interview. Table 25.2 presents the results.

Blacks and Whites were treated differently 36 times and in all cases but one the White applicant was preferred to the Black. The ways in which differential treatment took place provide a great deal of insight into the

Table 25.1 Offer of a job versus no offer.

	Number	%
Both offered job	10	5.0
White offered job; Black not	27	13.4
Black offered job; White not	9	4.5
No offer to either	155	77.1
Totals	201	100

Table 25.2 Treatment of applicants.

	Number of cases
Treated the same	165
Treated differently	36

nature of discrimination and its subtleties. Differences in treatment were sometimes very blatant, as the following examples show.

1. Mary, the young Black tester, applied for a sales position in a retail clothing store and was told that the job had already been taken. Sylvia, our White tester, arrived a half-hour later and was given an application form to fill in and told that she would be contacted if they were interested in her.

2. In a coffee shop Mary was told that the job of cashier was taken. Sylvia walked in five minutes later and was offered the job on the spot.

This pattern occurred five times. Another form of differential treatment was as follows: the Black was treated rudely or with hostility, whereas the White was treated politely. This occurred 15 times.

3. Paul, our White tester, applied for a job as a waiter. He was given an application form to fill out and an interview. He was told that he might be contacted in a week or so. Larry, the Black tester, was also given an application form and an interview. But as the Manager looked over Larry's résumé, he asked Larry if he "wouldn't rather work in the kitchen."

4. Applying for a gas station job, the White tester was told that there were no jobs at present but that he could leave a résumé. The Black tester was told that there were no jobs, but when he asked if he could leave a résumé, he was sworn at: "Shit, I said no didn't I?"

Another form of differential treatment occurred when the wage offers to Blacks and Whites were different. There were two occasions where the Black tester was offered less money than the White tester for the same job. On a few occasions, derogatory comments were made about Blacks in the presence of our White testers. The Blacks being referred to were our own testers!

These results indicate that Black job seekers face not only discrimination in the sense of receiving fewer job offers than Whites but also a considerable amount of negative and abusive treatment while job hunting. The psychological effects of such experiences became evident in the feelings expressed by the research staff. The Black staff felt rejected and some doubted their own ability: "I was beginning to wonder what was wrong with me and why Jean [the White tester] was so much better than me."

In sum, the findings of the in-person test reveal that in 48 job contacts, or 23.8 per cent of the cases, some form of discrimination against Blacks took place. These findings indicate that Blacks and Whites do not have the same access to employment. *Racial discrimination in employment, either in the form of clearly favouring a White over a Black, even though their résumés were equivalent, or in the form of treating a White applicant better than a Black, took place in almost one-quarter of all job contacts tested in this study.* When we examine the results of telephone testing, we will see that this pattern of discrimination occurs again and, if anything, more clearly and strongly.

Research Results: The Telephone Test

We have all had the experience of calling for a job and being told that the job has been filled. We experienced a twinge of disappointment but we rarely felt the need to ask ourselves seriously if we have been told the truth. Members of minority groups have good reason to question whether they have indeed been told the truth. Our study tested this by having callers phone numbers listed in the classified employment section of the newspaper to present themselves as job applicants.

In total, 237 job numbers were phoned. Each job was called four times, once by someone with no discernible accent (apparently a White-majority Canadian), once by someone who had a Slavic or Italian accent, once by a Jamaican-accented caller and finally by a person with a Pakistani accent. Many different jobs were called ranging from unskilled labour, secretarial, and service, to skilled trade, to managerial. To exclude sex discrimination, callers did not cross traditional sex-role categories. Men were of the same age, education, number of years of job experience, and so on for each type of job. Callers were "older" for jobs requiring more experience and maturity. A profile was provided for each of the callers for each type of job so that they had a secretarial profile, a managerial one, one for waitressing and so on. Jobs to be called were selected from among those that had not appeared in the newspaper the previous day; they were all new jobs. Callers within each sex were given identical lists of jobs to call on the next day and were instructed to begin their calls from the top of the list and proceed in order down the list. All callers were to begin the calling at the same time so that the time span between callers would be minimized. All callers were instructed to use standard English, full sentences, and correct grammar so that the lack of language would not be a discriminating factor against them.

In the telephone testing, discrimination was said to occur when one caller was told that the job had been filled while another caller was told that the job was still available. Discrimination was also said to take place when one caller-applicant with a certain set of qualifications was screened out and told that he or she did not qualify although other callers with the same qualifications were told that they did qualify and were invited to apply. Another form of discrimination was identified as occurring when callers were treated differently from one another in that some and not others were screened to see if they had the experience the employer sought. It has been argued that screening some applicants and not others is not necessarily discriminatory. However, if there is not systematic discrimination present, then we would expect all racial or immigrant groups to be subject to the same proportion of screening.

Results of this procedure were that in 52 per cent of all jobs called there was some form of discrimination present. Either one of our testers was told that the job was filled when another tester was told that the job was open, or one of our testers was treated differently in that he or she was screened while another was not.

There were nine instances where our accented callers were told that they did not qualify for the job even though they presented the same experience and qualifications as the White-majority callers. Needless to say, the White callers were told by these same nine employers that they qualified and were invited to apply. In addition, the employers did not perceive the need to screen all of the four minority-accented callers to the same degree. Employers who treated callers differently, that is, the 123 employers who discriminated in some way, never screened non-accented callers. Italian- or Slavic-accented callers were screened 5 percent of the time and the two non-White minority callers received three times as much screening as the Whites, on between 15 per cent and 20 per cent of all their calls.

Minority-accented callers did not receive the same information about the status of the job as did Whites. Forty-eight per cent of the jobs were closed to Blacks and 62 per cent were closed to Pakistanis in that the employers told them that the job was filled when the non-accented caller was told that the job was available. Statistical analysis revealed that there were significant differences in the treatment and the type of information that Whites and non-Whites received about work. The Toronto employers discriminated against immigrants in general but to a significantly greater degree against non-White immigrants.

The results of our telephone testing demonstrate that to secure 10 potential job interviews a White Canadian has to make about 11 or 12 calls. White immigrants have to make about 13 calls. Racial minorities must work harder and longer since they must make 18 calls to get 10 potential job interviews. Clearly there are differences in what Whites and non-Whites are being told over the phone about the availability of work in Toronto. And, as noted in the in-person testing, discrimination does not end when a job interview has been obtained.

A Ratio of Discrimination

An Index of Discrimination was developed by combining the results of the in-person test and the telephone testing to demonstrate the degree of discrimination experienced by equally qualified persons prior to actual employment. On the phone, Blacks were told that the job was closed to them 20 per cent of the time, whereas the job was closed to

Whites only 5.5 per cent of the time. In the in-person test, Blacks experienced discrimination in some form in 18.3 per cent of their job contacts. If these figures are translated into the actual chances of having success in the job search, the figures become even more revealing. Blacks have a 64 per cent chance of getting through a telephone screening, which means that they can secure 13 interviews out of 20 calls. But their chances of actually getting a job *after* an interview are only about 1 in 20. White applicants, on the other hand, are able to pass through screening very successfully, 87 per cent of the time. They can achieve an interview in 17 out of 20 calls. Out of these 17 interviews they manage to receive three offers of employment. *The overall Index of Discrimination is therefore 3 to 1*. Whites have three job prospects to every one that Blacks have.

Conclusion

The results of this study clearly indicate that there is very substantial racial discrimination affecting the ability of members of racial minorities to find employment even when they are well qualified and eager to find work. This study examined discrimination only at the very early stages, or entry level, of the employment process. Once an applicant is employed, discrimination can still affect opportunities for advancement, job retention, and level of earnings, to say nothing of the quality of work and the relationships with co-workers.

The findings also support the results of other types of studies done in Canada. We know that indirect measures of discrimination, such as those which reveal income disparities between Whites and non-Whites, all come to similar conclusions: non-Whites in this country are discriminated against. Our studies suggest that discrimination is more widespread than has been thought. Employment discrimination appears not to be the result of a few bigoted employers; there is a system-wide bias against hiring non-Whites. The systemic nature of the discrimination implies that attempting to change the behaviour or the attitudes of individual discriminators will not address the problem. What is required is redress at the system level in order to remove the barriers to the employment of non-Whites so that all Canadians, regardless of colour, can achieve their full potential.

26

*Trends in Ethnic and Racial Inequality**

Morton Weinfeld

Immigration

At Confederation, Canada's population was almost exclusively of French or English origin. Over the years, the immigrant groups have increased their proportion in the Canadian population.

In 1871, the British and French comprised almost 92 per cent of the Canadian population. Following the mass migrations of the late 1800s and early 1900s, the balance began shifting. By 1911, their proportion was down to 84 per cent, and by 1931, to 80 per cent. Immigration was curtailed in the 1930s and the through World War II, only to pick up again in the 1940s. The proportions for 1951 through 1981 were 79 per cent, 74 per cent, 73 per cent, and 72 per cent (the latter figure computed only for single origin claimants).

*Excerpted from ''Ethnic and Race Relations,'' in James Curtis and Lorne Tepperman (eds.) *Understanding Canadian Society*. Copyright © McGraw-Hill Ryerson Limited, 1988. Reprinted by permission.

There has also been a continuing diversification of the sources of immigrants. Great Britain remains the major country of origin for Canadian immigrants, though some of these British immigrants may belong to other ethnic or racial groupings. But the sources of immigration have moved from Great Britain and Northern and Eastern Europe to Southern Europe (Italy, Greece, Spain, Portugal) in the post-war period, and to countries in the developing world.

Public perception of these changes in Canada's ethnic composition may be heightened because of the tendency of the more recent immigrant groups, both Southern European and visible minority groups, to congregate in the major Canadian cities under the glare of media and political attention.

Analysts of immigration in Canada monitor the degree of ethnic or racial exclusivity which has characterized Canadian immigration policy. Canada, like most countries, has set its immigration policy in terms of quantity and origin of immigrants to meet perceived economic needs and national self-interest. Toward the end of the 19th century, large numbers of European immigrants were recruited to fill the open private expanses, to create a population presence sufficient to prevent any American expansion northward, and to help unite the new Canadian state from coast to coast. Ever since, Canada has adjusted immigration to meet various manpower needs, seeking out alternatively unskilled and highly skilled manpower, the latter to meet Canada's historic lack of highly trained human capital. Even today, immigrants continue to meet economic needs, some arriving through the points system as highly qualified professionals. Others, often refugees, work at low level jobs many Canadians would not accept.

Throughout the 20th century, Canada preferred European immigrants. Until 1962, geographic quotas that discriminated against non-Europeans were in effect. Beginning in the 1960s, and culminating in the 1967 Immigration Act, a new points system was introduced which was supposedly racially and ethnically neutral. Independent immigrants would receive points for universal attributes, such as knowledge of English or French, educational and occupational skills, etc. The points system, combined with provisions for family re-unification, has changed the composition of Canadian immigrants. But critics say that the system may be biased against non-White immigrants. For example, there were too few Canadian immigration offices in some Third World countries relative to the demand. Awarding points to prospective immigrants for job offers in hand might also favour Europeans, who could better make such arrangements. The immigration officer may award up to ten points at his/her discretion, an area where latent racism might surface. Even emphasizing education may penalize Third World immigrants, who may not be as likely as Europeans to have higher education, or whose educational credentials might be discounted. Ironically, by admitting highly skilled immigrants from developing nations, Canada stands accused of promoting a "brain drain" and hindering their economic development.

Canada in the 1980s has declared itself decisively committed to a two-pronged policy regarding Canada's ethnic and racial minorities. First, is the achievement of a true equality of opportunity by eliminating invidious discrimination, creating a climate of intergroup harmony. Where needed, government will act affirmatively to increase opportunities for minority groups, primarily visible minorities, often through the role of human rights commissions. Second, is the commitment to encourage minority groups to retain their cultures and promote their communal survival by guaranteeing their freedom of association and, where needed, by supporting their efforts at communal and cultural development. These two orientations define cultural pluralism in Canada today. Multicultural policies and ministries aim primarily to achieve this second objective.

Equal Opportunity and Multiculturalism

The first major step taken to protect human rights in Canada was the Canadian Bill of Rights, passed as an Act of Parliament in 1961. The bill addressed equality in only one clause, which maintained: "the right of the individual to equality before the law without discrimination by reason of race, national origin, colour or sex." The Bill of Rights proved ineffective as a defence of minority rights. Several provincial statutes limiting discrimination were likewise not authoritive.

Another step to protect minorities was the

introduction of hate literature amendments to Canada's criminal code in 1966. These amendments prohibited the advocacy or promotion of genocide, and provided that a person "who, by communicating statements, other than in private conversation, willfully promotes hatred against any identifiable group," was guilty of offence. This provision against group defamation knows no parallel in American legislation, where it might be construed an abridgement of free speech. For close to two decades, the hate literature amendments remained largely dormant. They were used only once, in a 1981 case involving promotions of hatred against French Canadians in Essex County, Ontario; a lower court conviction was overturned on appeal (Berger, 1981: 271). At any rate, in 1985, there were two convictions under these sections of the criminal code. The first conviction involved James Keegstra, an Alberta social studies highschool teacher who had been charged with promoting anti-Semitism in his classroom over a ten-year period. Keegstra argued that an international Jewish conspiracy lurked behind all the events of recent world history (Bercuson and Wertheimer, 1985). The second case was the Ontario conviction of Donald Andrews and Robert Smith, charged with promoting hatred against non-Whites in their white supremacist publication, *Nationalist Report*. They argued that non-Whites should be segregated from Aryans and repatriated.

These convictions and that of philo-Nazi publisher Ernst Zundel under a different section of the criminal code, raised painful questions. During the trials, courts were used as forums for the propagation of hatred. Some Canadians felt that the extensive media coverage of the trials could lead to an increase in anti-Semitic or racist sentiments, quite apart from offending the sensitivities of mi-

norities by the factual reporting of racist messages. One study, however, found that the opposite took place: Canadians who followed media reports of the Zundel trial became more sympathetic to Jews, not less (Weimann and Winn, 1986.) These trials brought into focus value conflicts between two important Canadian societal principles: opposition to racism and bigotry, and freedom of speech and expression. The Canadian courts have confirmed that the willful promotion of hatred against minority groups lies outside the protection of free speech.

The next legislative initiative on behalf of minority protection, and civil rights generally, was the passage of the Canadian Human Rights Act in 1977, and corresponding measures passed around the same time in all Canadian provinces. This Act, while also lacking constitutional entrenchment, went much further than the 1961 Bill of Rights Act, and established the Canadian Human Rights Commission as a watchdog and champion for victims of discrimination.

While these efforts to protect minorities were occurring, parallel steps were taken to enact a multicultural policy, and to assist Canadian ethnic groups in enhancing their own cultures. The idea of multiculturalism emerged from volume IV of the Report of the Commission on Bilingualism and Biculturalism in the 1960s. That volume dealt with the contribution of the "other ethnic groups" to Canada. The dualistic English and French focus of the Commission tended to make the other ethnic groups insecure, feeling they somehow would be relegated to second class status. In 1971, a multicultural policy was enunciated, which committed the Canadian government to the support of ethnic groups and their activities, and led to the setting up of a bureaucratic machinery, The Secretary of State for Multiculturalism to channel financial support to various minority groups. In promulgating the policy, the Canadian government also endorsed the "multicultural assumption" that a positive sense of one's own ethnic identity would lead to tolerance and respect for other groups. Thus, multiculturalism, it was felt, would promote harmony. Research in Canada and elsewhere has generally not found strong support for this view. Rather, evidence suggest a kind of ethnocentric effect, so that greater preoccupation with one's own group makes one more distant from and antipathetic to others (LeVine and Campbell, 1972, Berry et al., 1977). Both the prohibition against discrimination and the commitment to multiculturalism have found their way into the new Canadian constitution and, specifically, the Canadian Charter of Rights and Freedoms.

Section 15 prohibits discrimination on certain grounds, and explicitly permits affirmative action programs based on preferences for disadvantaged groups:

15.1 Every individual is equal before and under the law and has the right to the equal protection and equal benefit of the law without discrimination and in particular, without discrimination based on race, national or ethnic origin, colour, religion, sex, age, or mental or physical disability.
15.2 Subsection (1) does not preclude any law, program or activity that has as its object the amelioration of conditions of disadvantaged individuals or groups including those that are disadvantaged because of race, national or ethnic origin, colour, religion, sex, age or mental or physical diability.

The Charter of Rights and Freedoms does not nullify the Human Rights Act of 1977, with its more detailed protections against discrimination in employment in federal agencies or Crown corporations. It is not yet clear how far these protections of section 15

will extend. This section only came into effect in 1985, as provinces were given three years from passage in 1982 to bring their provincial statutes in line with the Charter. Historically, Canadian courts have not been as vigorous as American courts in interpreting or extending statutes to maximize the rights of citizens. Indeed, it is still unclear whether the protections of section 15 extend to all areas of public life or simply those under explicit federal jurisdiction.

One nagging problem is that the provinces may opt out of the requirements of section 15 by passing legislation under section 33, the "notwithstanding clause." In other words, a province could invoke section 33 and then, for a five-year period, pass and enforce a law discriminating against non-Whites, redheads, or any group. Section 1 of the Charter also provides an escape from the requirements of non-discrimination, due to "reasonable limits prescribed by law as can be demonstrably justified in a free and democratic society." These "reasonable limits" would be defined by courts on a case by case basis if challenged.

Section 15.2 also highlights a fundamental difference in human rights in Canada and the United States, regarding affirmative action. In the United States, neither the Civil Rights Act of 1964 nor the fourteenth amendment of the constitution contain wording legitimating affirmative action. In fact, they require states to guarantee to every person equal protection of the laws, and prohibit any discrimination (along the lines of Canada's section 15.1). The impetus for affirmative action in the United States has come from executive orders, namely, directives from the White House, which have been periodically sustained by court decisions (Benokraitis and Feagin, 1978). Thus, the constitutional basis for affirmative action is much less explicit in the United States than in Canada.

Two other sections of the Charter are important for ethnic groups. The first is sections 2 (c,d), which grant to "everyone" (not only to citizens, as for democratic rights) freedom of peaceful assembly and of association. These freedoms facilitate the creation and growth of ethnic voluntary organizations. Section 27 is a vague section whose aim is probably rhetorical; in fact, constitutional experts do not know what the clause may mean practically, or how courts might eventually interpret it (Hogg, 1982; Tarnopolsky, 1982: 345-442).

"The Charter shall be interpreted in a manner consistent with the preservation and enhancement of the multicultural heritage of Canadians." For example, if a person's multicultural heritage involves regular use of marijuana, or beating one's spouse (offences under the Criminal Code), Canadian courts would not likely accept a defence under section 27.

The broad Canadian constitutional and legal context tries to maximize individual rights and freedoms, while recognizing the role of group rights. The concern with group rights, with collectivities, such as ethnic or language groups or Native peoples, reflects a heritage of continental European political thought and experience, where history was shaped largely by intergroup clashes and emerging nationalisms. It has certainly been a dominant preoccupation of the French minority in Canada. The concern with individual rights and freedoms reflects the legacy of the British philosophy and historical experience. The liberal tradition, from John Locke to John Stuart Mill, was concerned with the relations between the individual citizen and the state; the idea of the social contract linked individuals with their ruler.

We should note that Canada's constitution remains unfinished. If amendments like those agreed to in the spring of 1987 come into effect, power may flow from the federal government to the provinces. Yet, when it comes to the issue of the protection of minority rights, some might argue that it is the federal government that has a better track record than the provinces. Changes in the federal-provincial balance of power may well have repercussions for Canada's ethnic and racial minorities.

The Canadian government faces a difficult task. In promoting equal opportunity and prohibiting discrimination on the basis of ascribed characteristics, such as ethnicity or race (section 15), Canada is positing the irrelevance of ethnic and racial origin to participation in Canadian society. The sentiment is that people should be judged as human beings, with intrinsic worth, and not prejudged by membership in a given group.

On the other hand, by enshrining in the Charter recognition of either group rights or the importance of ascriptive characteristics such as ethnic origin, and by promoting ethnic cultures and organizations through multicultural policies, Canada is stressing differences among people. From this perspective, ethnic origins and cultures are important.

Classical sociological theory suggests that it will be hard to achieve both objectives at the same time. Social theorists have suggested that as societies become more urban, modern, and industrialized, people in these societies will shed ties to the past and adopt more contemporary identities, becoming a universal "citoyen" or "tovarich." Ethnic and racial origins, like religious ties, would become less important. This suggests that when Canadian immigrant groups or group members become more fully acculturated as Canadians, they will become less, not more, committed to retaining their ancestral identities and cultures. How are immigrant groups faring in Canada today on these broad dimensions?

Equal Opportunity for Ethnic and Racial Minorities

There are several ways to measure the extent to which minority group members enjoy equal opportunity in general, and equal economic opportunity in particular. One could examine a group's education, occupation, and income level compared to the societal average. A second approach, popular in Canadian ethnic studies, focuses on ethnic representation in elite sectors of the society. In both approaches, we might conclude that underrepresentation is caused by prejudice and discrimination.

A third approach focuses on prejudicial attitudes held by the majority group or acts of discrimination reported by minority group members. The legal framework described earlier deals only with acts of discrimination; no governmental mechanism regulates prejudicial or stereotypic attitudes held privately by Canadians, or patterns or private, intimate behaviour.

The Mosaic: Still Vertical?

Most recent evidence suggests that the immigrant groups are more and more resembling the dominant British group in levels of socioeconomic status, as measured by education, occupation, and income. For all European immigrant groups, effective discrimination and resulting inequality have all but disappeared. This can be seen from Table 26.1, and from the more sophisticated analysis in Table 26.2. In the latter table, we can see the income gaps which remain for

average minority group incomes, as deviations from the national average, controlling for sex, nativity, occupation, age, number of weeks worked, and education — all of which influence incomes. As both tables show, European ethnic groups do as well as or better than the national average. For example, consider Italian Canadians, a group which ranked poorly in Porter's original analysis in *The Vertical Mosaic*. In 1981, Italian Canadians earned just slightly below the male and female average incomes. However, as seen from Table 26.2, the deficit of slightly over $500 from the national average was fully explainable by the other demographic characteristics of Italian Canadians, specifically a large immigrant component and below average levels of educational attainment. Indeed, Italian incomes are even higher than we might expect, by about $150.

Comparisons between 1971 and 1981 show a reduction in the proportional disparities for various minority groups from the national mean income. This can be seen by comparing the percentage differences for 1971 with those for 1981 in Table 26.2.

There is convergence going on. This has been found by Darroch (1979) in his study on indices of occupational dissimilarities, which have been narrowing since 1931. Other studies of generational mobility and stratification also point to the decreasing role of ethnic origin per se as a determinant of status attainment (Ornstein, 1981, Tepperman, 1975).

Yet if we focus on visible minority groups we see a mixed picture (Table 26.1). Some groups, like the Japanese, are doing very well. Those grouped as Indo-Pakistani likewise earn incomes above the Canadian average, due largely to an educational and occupational profile, which is well above average. This grouping may even be earning

Table 26.1 Demographic characteristics of selected ethnic groups[a] in Canada, 1981

	Black[b]	Chinese	Czech & Slovak	Dutch	Filipino	German	Greek	Italian	Japanese	Jewish	Polish	Portuguese	Scandinavian	Indo-Pakistani[f]	Indo-Chinese[g]	Ukrainian	Yugoslavian	All Canada
Size in 000's	241	300	86	408[f]	76	1100[f]	164	872	46	294	254[f]	195	283[f]	222	56	746	128	24 200
% born in Canada	20	27	58	66	21	—	43	54	75	66	41	26	83	24	10	89	41	84
Age Structure																		
% 0–14	24	24	20	20	31	15	29	24	22	20	12	29	14	—	30	23	24	23
15–24	18	19	17	21	11	20	16	20	16	14	15	19	16	—	25	19	16	19
25–44	42	35	31	30	42	30	32	20	31	30	30	31	32	—	35	28	32	29
45–64	13	16	22	21	13	25	18	20	23	18	22	17	24	14	—	20	21	19
65+	3	7	11	7	3	10	4	6	8	15	7	3	16	3	—	10	6	10
% with Ethnic[c] Mother Tongue	—	73	49	40	46	34	75	60	46	13[h]	50	81	19	53	75	37	—	13
% with Ethnic[c] (F.B.)	—	—	22[e]	7[e]	40[e]	10[e]	57	41	23	4	21	65	2	43	72	12	—	7
Home Languages (N.B.)		31																
% able to speak[d]																		
English	91	81	98	95	98	95	89	80	95	99	90	75	95	86	68	99	—	82
French	18	4	10	6	3	5	17	22	5	30	9	16	4	7	28	5	—	32
Neither	—	19	—	1	1	1	6	—	—	1	1	20	1	—	18	—	—	1
% living in																		
Toronto	51	31	17	8	39	7	41	37	29	40	20	47	13	36	17	—	33	12
Montreal	20	6	6	1	6	2	31	19	3	32	7	12	3	7	22	—	5	12
Vancouver	3	29	8	7	14	6	4	5	27	5	5	4	20	17	7	20	8	5
All 3	74	66	31	16	59	15	76	61	59	77	32	63	36	60	46	20	46	29

% unemployed																	
Male	7.2	4.2	3.6	—	3.5	3.4	6.5[g]	4.5	3.1	4.7	—	5.3[g]	3.9	4.8	8.4	—	4.8[g] 6.1	6.5 7.4[g]
Female	8.5	5.4	6.4	—	4.0	5.5	7.1	6.9	5.0	6.9	—		6.0	9.8	12.2			8.7
Occupation																	
% Mgr. & Admin.	n.a.	8	10	9	—	9	7	6	10	19	4	—	8	5	9	6	9
% Technical/ Scientific	6	11	12	—	7	—	—	—	12	13	—	—	9	9	6	6	7
% Medicine/Health	11	5	5	—	21	—	—	—	—	7	—	—	5	5	—	3	10
Education																	
% < grade 9	11	21	18	31	9	40	31	36	11	12	25	20	15	20	22	23	20
% some university	18	28	30	55	60	20	14	12	29	41	33	50	35	29	17	18	16
average male income	14.9	15.1	19.2	—	15.1	—	14.6	16.2	18.7	26.4	—	14.9	—	17.6	10.5	17.1	16.9
average female income (in 000's)	9.2	9.0	9.5	—	11.6	—	7.6	8.0	9.4	12.0	—	7.7	—	8.6	7.0	8.6 13.7[g]	8.4 12.7[g]

[a] Unless specifically indicated, data are for Canadians who indicated whole or partial ethnic identity for the specific group.
[b] Includes Caribbean. (May include some Whites and Asians as well.)
[c] "Ethnic" languages refer to languages other than English or French.
[d] Bilinguals (English-French) are included, leading to double counting and percentages greater than 100.
[e] Single figure denotes home language for both foreign-born and native (Canadian)-born combined.
[f] For those reporting single ethnic origin.
[g] Single figure denotes rate for males and females combined.
[h] Yiddish and Hebrew.
[i] Includes persons who reported an origin from the Indian subcontinent such as Indian, Pakistani, Bengali, Gujarati, Punjabi, Tamil, Sinhalese, Sri Lankan, or Bangladeshi.
[j] Includes persons reporting Thai, Vietnamese, Kampuchean/Cambodian, Laotian, Malay, or Burmese origin (over 70% of the immigrants from these groups in Canada in 1981 had come within the previous three years).

Source: *Socio-Economic Profiles of Selected Ethnic/Visible Minority Groups.* Multiculturalism Canada, March 1986.

incomes lower than their credentials warrant. On the other hand, with 75 per cent of the group foreign-born, problems of immigrant adjustment and integration may play a role. Indo-Chinese Canadians earn well below the Canadian average, despite high levels of educational attainment. This may reflect discrimination and the undervaluing of their educational credentials, as well as the fact that most of those responding were recent refugees from Southeast Asia.

Blacks and Chinese, as seen in Tables

Table 26.2 Effect of racial and ethnic origin on the mean income of ethnic/racial groups in the employed labour force in Canada, 15 years and over, 1971 and 1981

	1971[a]			1981[b]		
Ethnic groups	Gross effect as deviation from grand mean	Deviation from grand mean %	Ethnic groups	Gross effect as deviation from grand mean	Deviation from grand mean %	Net effect[c]
1. Jewish	+3544	59.0	Jewish	+6262	44.6	+2936
2. Japanese	+ 938	15.6	Czech & Slovak	+2137	15.2	+ 63
3. Austrian	+ 744	12.4	Hungarian	+1902	13.5	+ 20
4. Russian	+ 348	5.8	Scandinavian	+1860	13.2	+1035
5. Brit. Isles	+ 294	4.9	Ukrainian	+ 795	5.7	+ 213
6. Czech	+ 105	1.7	Polish	+ 721	5.1	− 223
7. Slovak	+ 84	1.4	German	+ 652	4.6	+ 275
8. Hungarian	+ 56	.9	Croat. & Serb.	+ 459	3.2	+ 378
9. Polish	− 92	− 1.5	British	+ 356	2.5	+ 104
10. Italian	− 164	− 2.7	Dutch	+ 77	2.2	+ 77
11. Scandinavian	− 195	− 3.2	French	− 501	− 3.6	− 204
12. German	− 233	− 3.7	Italian	− 509	− 3.6	+ 149
13. Finnish	− 235	− 3.9	Other	−1113	− 7.9	− 278
14. Other	− 325	− 5.4	Chinese	−1295	− 9.2	− 931
15. Netherlands	− 384	− 6.4	Black	−1588	− 11.3	−1680
16. French	− 424	− 7.1	Greek	−1894	− 13.5	− 796
17. Ukrainian	− 642	− 10.7	Portuguese	−2002	− 14.3	+ 627
18. Negro	− 919	− 15.3				
19. Chinese	−1026	− 17.1				
20. West Indian	−1536	− 25.6				
21. Nat. Indian	−1868	− 31.1				
x̄ = Canada	6004		Canada	14045		

[a] 1971 raw data from Li (1980).
[b] 1981 raw data from Li (1986).
[c] Net effect of racial and ethnic origin controlling for sex, nativity, occupation, age, number of weeks worked, and education (Li (1986)).

26.1 and 26.2, remain substantially victimized. They earn well below what might be expected, given other background characteristics, particularly educational attainment, which is above the Canadian average for both groups. The only solace here is that Li's data for 1971 and 1981 (Table 26.2) show the disparities seem to have decreased. In 1971, Chinese incomes and Black incomes were 17 per cent and roughly 20 per cent (Negro — 15 per cent, West Indian, 26 per cent) below the Canadian average; by 1981 these gaps were reduced to 9 per cent and 11 per cent, respectively.

Some indication of the persisting problems of minority groups can be seen from Table 26.3, which describes mean incomes

of university graduates for a selection of ethnic and racial groups, for both native-born and foreign-born Canadians. With a few exceptions (Korean, Japanese, and Portuguese, for the Canadian-born, and Portuguese for the foreign-born), the European minorities earn more than do the visible minority college graduates. Part of this variation could be explained by differences in the types and extent of university education, as well as by discrimination.

Thus, in moving up the stratification system, equal opportunity exists for Canada's White immigrant groups. Visible minorities still have far to go, but there is variation in the rates of progress or achievement of differing minority groups that cannot simply be

Table 26.3 Rates of return for higher education for selected ethnic or racial groups, Canada, 1981

Canadian-born			Foreign-Born		
Group	Incomes rank	Mean incomes, university graduates	Group	Incomes rank	Mean incomes, university graduates
Jewish	1	32 235	Czechoslovak	1	32 214
Russian	2	30 073	Jewish	2	31 106
Korean	3	28 210	Finnish	3	26 788
Japanese	4	28 202	Yugoslavic	4	25 837
Finnish	5	27 350	Russian	5	25 297
Yugoslavic	6	26 366	Ukrainian	6	24 936
Czechoslovak	7	26 074	Greek	7	24 492
Greek	8	25 670	Chinese	8	24 015
Ukrainian	9	24 936	Black	9	22 191
Indochinese	10	24 783	Indo-Pakistani	10	22 108
Chinese	11	24 370	Japanese	11	22 094
Black	12	24 085	Korean	12	20 576
Portuguese	13	22 244	Indochinese	13	20 062
Filipino	14	20 749	Portuguese	14	19 762
Indo-Pakistani	15	13 186	Filipino	15	19 332

Source: Winn (1985, p. 691). Data from 1981 Census of Canada.

attributed to racism. For example, differences in Japanese and Chinese achievements in Canada can be explained by differences in immigrant proportion, amount and type of educational attainment, etc. (Li, 1980).

There has been a transformation of political life for immigrant groups. Through the post-war period, federal and provincial Cabinets have included increasing numbers of immigrant groups. Jews have served as premiers of provinces, as a Supreme Court Justice of Canada, and — in "Tory blue" Ontario — as a leader of the provincial Progressive Conservative party. A Black has been appointed Lieutenant-Governor of Ontario. Ed Schreyer's acceptance address for the governor-generaliship was in five languages: English, French, German, Polish, and Ukrainian. These advances and appointments are not tokenism — they have real symbolic value.

In the senior Canadian civil service, long a bastion of Anglo dominance reinforced through old boy networks dating back to MacKenzie King, similar penetration has occurred. One study found non-charter representation in the state elite increased from 3 per cent to 11 per cent between 1953 and 1973 (Olsen, 1980). Another study of 92 senior bureaucrats found 20 per cent of non-charter origin (Campbell and Szablowski, 1979).

Finally, Canadian culture, whether highbrow, as measured by appointments to the Royal Society of Canada or representation as senior professors or university administrators, or popular, as measured by representation in the various media as performers, directors, or producers, has also been transformed mightily in the post-war period. The children and grandchildren of immigrants, equipped with university or other training and the requisite freedom of expressions, have exploded onto the cultural scene. Another indicator of this openness is the proliferation on campuses of chairs, programs, or courses in ethnic studies.

To be sure, the visible minorities lag far behind (Owaisi and Bangash, 1978). These groups include large numbers of recent immigrants who have not yet developed the contacts that help them "make it" in Canadian cultural or elite sectors. The corporate elite will likely be most resistant to integration by visible minorities. But within the next two or three decades, these groups will likely increase their presence in political, social, and cultural elite sectors.

Racism: Discrimination and Prejudice

Social scientists study two broad types of discrimination. Overt discrimination refers to specific acts of discrimination directed against specific victims by specific perpetrators. It is illegal in Canada, and its presence can be established using rules of evidence in courts of law.

More complex is discrimination called structural, institutional or, most recently, systemic. Here there are no overtly identifiable perpetrators caught in a specific act of discrimination. Rather, minorities are penalized because of the historic, cumulative effect of past discrimination. In addition, minorities may be excluded from old-boy networks, and face unreasonable educational or job requirements, which may screen out competent employees from possible jobs or promotions. Lower educational performances can reflect cultural biases in testing, rather than cognitive deficiencies. These barriers will not be eliminated, in the view of some analysts, by simply legislating equal opportunity. They must be attacked directly, using affirmative action programs.

Thus, in Canada as in the United States, the fight to overcome discrimination has shifted from a concern with equality of opportunity to one with equality of result. Discrimination is no longer defined by the intent or motivation of the discriminator, but by the consequences of actions, rules, or procedures on minority groups. Statistical under-representation of minority groups is presumed to indicate discrimination (Weinfeld, 1981).

On the other hand, simply because a group has a high level of achievement, or individual group members are well represented in elite sectors, does *not* mean that racist sentiments — prejudice — as well as discrimination do not exist. The Bronfman family's money and power did not get patriarch Sam Bronfman into the Canadian senate. Some of the achievements of minority group members — one thinks of Jews and Japanese — may have been made despite historic and persisting racism, or even, surprisingly, because of it (Light, 1972). Even successful members of minority groups may suffer psychological distress because of persisting, if ineffectual, prejudice.

One way to measure racism is to poll majority Canadians about their attitudes or beliefs regarding immigrants. People can be queried about their personal relations with various groups, or asked to rank groups in terms of prestige.

If we look at Gallup poll data in Canada in the post-war period, we see a decline in explicitly racist attitudes, for example, on questions about approval of mixed marriages. Yet polls on immigration during this period have revealed decreasing support for higher immigration levels, as well as increasing preferences for quotas on countries of origin.

Other studies have found Canadians perceive a prestige ranking for ethnic groups (Pineo, 1977). Not surprisingly, the English and French are ranked highest, with visible minority groups ranked well below. These rankings correspond to social distances of Canadians from minority groups. Another study found Canadians were least "aware" of visible minority groups, compared to European groups. Studies that discovered rank orders of groups, as well as existing stereotypes, did not conclude that lower ranked groups were actively disliked. "The absolute rating of all groups were quite favourable" (Berry et al., 1977: 107).

One Toronto study estimated that about one-sixth of the respondents could be classified as "very racist." One-quarter of the respondents judged West Indians, Pakistanis, and Indians as inferior (Henry, 1978). This study, done in Toronto where minorities are concentrated and friction may be greater, may be more relevant that national Gallup polls.

One indirect measure of racism is interethnic and interracial marriage. Rates of interethnic marriage in Canada are high and increasing, primarily for the European ethnic groups. Yet out-marriage seems to be increasing even for interracial unions, and rates are higher among the native-born (Kalbach, 1970). Moreover, when minority groups intermarry, they select partners from the British (higher status) group in proportion to their weight in the population. Of course, such intermarriages can be interpreted both as acceptance by the dominant group and as loss of ethnic identity by the minority group.

Still another way to measure racism is through opinion surveys in which minority group members report their perceptions of their own conditions, or on the frequency with which they encounter discrimination.

(Evidence shows some minority group members perceive more victimization for their ethnic group in general than they have themselves experienced (Weinfeld, 1980: 5-15). One study of Blacks in Toronto claimed 59 per cent were victimized by discrimination (Head, 1975). An unpublished survey of West Indians in Montreal found 25 per cent claiming there is "very strong" prejudice, and 67 per cent "some prejudice" against West Indians in Quebec. (The same survey revealed 25 per cent had experienced no personal discrimination.)

A final way to gauge racism is by enumerating objectively verifiable incidents. Field studies in Toronto have found that employers clearly discriminate against non-White job applicants (Henry and Ginzberg, 1985). Another example of this approach is to tabulate the numbers of accepted complaints of discrimination of Human Rights Commissions in Canada. For example, from 1979 to 1983, the Commission investigated 531 complaints of discrimination based on national, ethnic, or racial grounds. (Investigation does not mean a finding of guilt.) The actual numbers of such complaints were 109, 94, 122, 113, and 93, certainly not a pattern of increase. Provincial Human Rights Commissions also hear complaints on these grounds.

Official statistic are notorious in underestimating the prevalence of discrimination, since most acts go unreported. But in any case, how can we interpret such numbers; do they indicate a serious problem? Are they a tip of an iceberg, depicting a society seething with deep rooted racial animosity, or are they relatively trivial? The same questions must be asked for the attitudinal survey data. What does it mean for the life of the country if 2 per cent – or 20 per cent – of Canadians are "racist?" But even a lowly 2 per cent denotes hundreds of thousands of adult Canadian racists – more than enough to poi-

son race relations if they were mobilized.

Racism and the fear of racism are part of the cultural climate separate from statistical trends. Consider the case of Jews in Canada. As indicated previously, Jews have done well economically and are well represented in elite sectors of Canadian society.

Yet periodically, and routinely, Jewish cemeteries, synagogues, or homes are defaced with swastikas, and Jewish defence agencies, such as the League for Human Rights of B'nai B'rith, tally such anti-Semitic incidents on a yearly basis. Perhaps, more important, racist and anti-Semitic organizations like the Western Guard publish and disseminate hate-filled material. Yet episodes such as the trials of Jim Keegstra and Ernst Zundel, and their coverage, affected members of the Jewish community, who found vile anti-Semitic cards reported daily in the media. One well-publicized act of bigotry may be more salient than a stack of poll data. The fact that diehard racist and anti-Semitic movements remain relegated to fringes of political life in Canada may be cold comfort to minorities whose dignity is brutalized and degraded.

What can we conclude? Many observers emphasize the continuing inequalities facing visible minorities and the need for further affirmative action. This was the thrust of Judge Rosalie Abella's landmark Royal Commission Report, *Equality in Employment* (1984). The federal government accepts that affirmative action is required to overcome "systemic" discrimination, which may lead to minority underrepresentation. The Report called upon Canadian businesses and, in particular, government agencies and firms dealing with government to implement "employment equity."

Employment equity is a term which the Report proposes to replace affirmative action. It is a set of procedures aimed at improving, where necessary, "the participation of women, Native peoples, disabled persons, and specified ethnic and racial groups in the workplace." While quotas are not acceptable, it is proposed that firms will have to devise timetables for increasing minority hiring, preferably on a voluntary rather than mandatory basis. Moreover, as long as there is no legislation requiring federally and provincially regulated employers to implement employment equity, the federal government is encouraged to adopt "contract compliance" as a means to pressure firms to conform. In this approach, firms hired by the government would be required to have employment equity programs.

Ethnic communities are becoming more active in attempting to pursue their collective interests by lobbying and petitioning governments. These interests may be domestic (fighting discrimination) or international (support for the homeland).

In earlier times, such preoccupations of citizens in a Western democratic polity led to charges of dual loyalty or of ethnic groups creating a "state within a state." The strength of multicultural ideology, and its consequences of energized ethnic polities, makes such charges unlikely. Ethnic Canadians are free to petition the government through their associations, as do Canadians active in other lobbying groups, such as environmentalists, manufacturers, farmers, women, etc. Canadian politicians are slowly becoming more sensitive to the "ethnic vote," i.e., making sure that party platforms and campaigns appeal to ethnic voters in ridings where such groups are concentrated. In this sense, Canada has lagged behind the United States in recognizing the role of ethnic issues and interests in political life (Litt, 1970).

SECTION VIII

A Class Society

John Porter begins his classic book *The Vertical Mosaic* (1965) with the statement "One of the most persistent images Canadians have of their society is that it has no classes." This belief, he feels, arises from the Canadian frontier experience which Porter characterizes as being much like the American one in that it promoted independence and equality. However, while Canadians today are willing to admit that modern urban society is unlike the frontier a century ago, they are likely to claim that most people today still belong to the same class, namely, the relatively affluent middle class. Moreover, they would argue, even people who do not belong to the affluent middle class have every opportunity of doing so. Opportunities for upward social mobility — for parents or, at the very least, for their children — are great and readily available. If inequality and class difference do exist, at least it does not matter. Class inequality matters less in Canada today than in any society that ever existed, they might argue.

However others, Porter included, have a different image of Canadian society. They see it as a society in which large class inequalities do exist and in which class matters for the lives of people and their offspring. We share that view with virtually all sociologists. But disagreement remains about the forms, causes and consequences of such inequality and about the possibilities of changing them. This section is, then, concerned with showing how Canada is **a class society**.

The term "social class" has been applied to persistent social inequalities in ownership of a variety of scarce goods: the means of production, wealth, income, prestige, and power. Sociology has been concerned with the sources and consequences of these inequalities ever since the origin of the discipline in European social thought in the nineteenth century. The problem of social inequality has been so central to sociology that Robert Brym (1988: 4) has emphasized that we must see it as one of the field's three "classic questions" (along with "the relationship of the individual and society" and "whether the determinants of social behaviour are more economic than cultural"). Some sociologists go even further, seeing class inequality as "*the* problem in sociology" (Giddens, 1980: 19). Little wonder, then, that we find the idea of a class society is one of the key images of Canadian sociology.

Alfred Hunter, who titled his book *Class Tells* (1986: 2), says that the interest in social class

> lies in the fact that it seeps into and shapes so many aspects of our experience, even if we are not always (or even often) aware of its presence and effects. It is not something which affects only some people or touches only some isolated corner of our lives. Whenever something is both scarce and valued, individuals and groups will compete for it, and some will possess more of it than others. And inequality is the usual state of our relationships with others and of the relations among groups, and equality the rare and limiting case. A phenomenon as pervasive as this is almost synonymous with social life itself, and any thorough-going theory of inequality, then, will necessarily represent a considerable feat of mental labour, tying together the full gamut of our life's activities from home to work to play. *

Two distinct types of social inequality have been identified by researchers working from two different sociological theories. One theory is derived from the work of Karl Marx (e.g., [1848] 1967), the other from writings by Max Weber (e.g., 1947). The Weberian approach became popular in Canadian and American sociology in the 1940s to 1960s (Hughes' and Porter's approaches in this volume are good illustrations) but currently the Marxian approach is ascendant (Clement's works in this volume provide an example).

In the Marxian approach, social classes, which are defined by ownership of the *means of production* and *labour power*, exist in all capitalist societies. The means of production include the machines, buildings, land and materials used in the production of goods and services. Labour power, the physical and mental capacity of people to work, is bought and sold

---

Alfred A. Hunter, *Class Tells: On Social Inequality in Canada*, 2nd edition (Toronto: Butterworths, 1986), page 2. Reproduced with permission.

for wages (or salary) by the owners of the means of production, or by their agents. Marxists identify three main classes: the *petite bourgeoisie*, who own their means of production, work for themselves, and do not employ others; the *proletariat* or working class, who do not own the means of production and sell their labour power for wages; and the *bourgeoisie* or capitalist class, owners of the means of production, who purchase labour power, acquire a living and accumulate wealth from surplus value provided through workers' labour.

The Marxian social class distinctions do not refer to types of occupation or levels of income. For example, a plumber could be a member of the working class (because he sells labour power and does not own a business); or he could be a small capitalist who owns a company and purchases the labour of several plumbers; or he could be a member of the petite bourgeoisie. Also, members of different classes may have similar incomes. An owner of a small engineering firm with a few employees may, in one year, earn less than a worker does, if that worker is a successful engineer employed by a large firm. However, capitalists generally have more power than workers to determine the distribution of wealth, because capitalists own and control the means of production and because the working class is not fully organized (for example, in unions or political organizations) to oppose them. Marxists believe that a conflict of interests (for example, wage disputes, and opposition by capitalists to the formation of unions) between capitalists and the working class is an inherent feature of capitalism. On the one side, capitalists try to keep wages low and productivity high to maximize their wealth; on the other, workers attempt to increase their share of the wealth through higher wages and to improve their working conditions.

The non-Marxists claim that social classes can also be defined through inequalities in income, educational attainment, power and occupational prestige, and they often study these forms of social inequality to the neglect of social class in the Marxian sense. They identify different kinds of social classes or statuses depending on which of the other dimensions of social inequality has been selected for study. People are categorized and ranked according to their income, occupational prestige, power or education. The same people may fall into different ranks according to different dimensions of social class. For example, the very rich, the middle class and the poor can be easily distinguished from one another by using standards of income and wealth; but people in the middle-income category (e.g., white-collar and blue-collar workers) will receive quite different degrees of prestige for their different jobs. By the same token, white-collar jobs usually carry more prestige and income, but this is not always the case. The same is true of differences in educational levels. People with secondary-school diplomas more often have white-collar jobs and higher incomes than people with less education; but some skilled blue-collar workers, such as electricians, earn comparatively high wages without secondary school diplomas. Finally, the respective amounts of power attached to different jobs, incomes and educational credentials are difficult to discern.

Weberians emphasize the distribution patterns of scarce rewards, for example, the numbers and social backgrounds of the people who acquire university educations or high prestige jobs; while Marxists emphasize the social activities and interactions of the classes, for example, who purchases labour power from whom and what is the rate of exploitation of one class by another. The Weberians are more likely to be concerned with explaining patterns of social inequality, while the Marxists study the way class conflicts produce social change.

Few sociologists would disagree that for a clear understanding of Canadian society we must know about all the social inequalities discussed above. Indeed, most images of Canada are concerned with one or another kind of inequality. Section I of this book deals with economic and power differentials between the two charter groups, Francophones and Anglophones; Section II covers struggles between Canada and its neighbour to the south; Sections III, IV and V address economic inequalities by region and relations between the regions; Section VI assesses the distribution of elite power and its relationship to class as ownership; Section VII covers racial and ethnic inequalities; and Section IX explores gender relations and inequalities. It is easy to demonstrate that social inequality is central to key sociological images of Canadian society. The differences in views in the literature will revolve around which form(s) of inequality, class ownership or another, is (are) most important in describing Canadian society and explaining its history.

A case can be made that social inequality is *the* substance of Canadian society. If anything, social class dynamics are the most basic to explaining Canadian history. This is the point that Clement argues in the first excerpt in this Section.

Perhaps the most dramatic way of portraying the effects of social class upon individuals is to show that it affects how long people live. Rich people are known to live longer, healthier lives than poorer people. For example, a study by Wigle and Mao (1980) has found, from data on 21 metropolitan areas in Canada, that the life expectancy at birth of men living in the most affluent areas of the cities was 6.2 years longer than for males from the least affluent areas. (The comparable figure for females showed less difference, at 2.9 years.) What accounts for the income-life expectancy association is still a matter of debate. The answer probably includes differential opportunities for good nutrition, medical care, housing and rest; differential risks of injury on the job; and differential lifestyle risks including the likelihood of smoking or excess drinking, suffering too much stress, and not getting enough fresh air and exercise.

In his selection Clement elaborates upon the differences between the Weberian and Marxist approaches to class, and commits himself to the Marxist approach because it gives greater emphasis to the role of class relations. This approach leads us, he emphasizes, to attend to class contradictions and tensions. The direction of Canadian history can be best understood by attending to class relations, according to Clement. He also emphasizes how classes and other social groupings — nation, region, gender and ethnicity — are bound together in numerous ways. In so doing, he provides reasons why we should have multiple sociological images:

> Class relations are everywhere but they never exist in pure form; that is, they always combine with other social relations. . . . These other social relations include gender, ethnicity . . . and region. These combined social relations have significant effects on one another. Class-blind analysts, like gender-blind ones, fail to grasp essential facts of social life.

The next article in this Section, by R. Jack Richardson, has close kinship with the Marxist research tradition. Richardson uses data from the 1970s and 1980s to describe significant recent changes in corporate concentration in Canada. Economic power has become concentrated in fewer and fewer hands within the capitalist class, he argues. This has occurred through the growth of huge conglomerates and the integration within them of financial and non-financial firms. Richardson shows that these conglomerates have gained control of the trust industry to achieve this integration. He also emphasizes that as part of these changes there has been a resurgence of family-controlled enterprises. It is these enterprises, and not management-controlled firms, that have become the risk-takers and the most innovative in this part of the economy. Richardson also shows that one consequence of recent trends in corporate concentration is that economic control has become much more concentrated in Canada than in the United States. The top 100 enterprises in Canada control a far greater proportion of all non-financial assets and profits than do the top 100 enterprises in the United States.

The next selection by John Goyder and Jim Curtis is more in the Weberian research tradition because it focuses on opportunities for intergenerational occupation mobility in Canada. It asks: "Over how many generations does a male's social origins affect his chances of getting ahead in occupation?'' The answer, from national survey data for adult males, is, perhaps astoundingly, three generations! What a man's grandfather did for a living will influence what he (the grandson) will do for a living, and, of course, the father's job has an even stronger influence. Happily, there appears to be no significant pattern of four generation effects; that is, great-grandfathers do not seem to influence great-grandsons. (We have no comparable data for women and their ancestors, unfortunately.)

In the final article in this Section, Dennis Forcese asks whether there is a reasonable prospect that working-class/capitalist-class conflict will lead to revolutionary change in Canada: a change toward greater equality of condition and opportunity as predicted by Marx. Forcese bases his predictions on the history of class conflict in Canada, a technique some may wish to quarrel with. He concludes from this that the likelihood of radical change is slight. The struggle between regions and ethnic groups over the distribution of scarce resources deflects the working class's efforts to organize for the pursuit of common interests, regardless of their region and social background. The ruling corporate and bureaucratic elites are inherently opposed to radical change, and very capable of defusing class conflict through such means as welfare policies. In addition, as Richardson shows us, the corporate sector has acquired an increasing capacity to control labour through concentration of ownership and control.

There seems little doubt that for the forseeable future the class society image will continue to be applicable to sociological analyses in Canada. This image will likely continue to require each of the elements emphasized by the authors in this Section. Social class and socio-economic status will matter in people's quality of life; class relations will be central to social change (and its hindrance); entry into the economic elite, or the most powerful segment of the capitalist class, by persons from other classes will continue to be minimal; inter-generational social mobility in the occupational structure will remain somewhat limited; and there will continue to be a heavy concentration of economic control and power within the capitalist class.

27

*Does Class Matter?**

Wallace Clement

Before addressing the question "Does Class Matter?" more systematically, it is worth briefly recalling two principal traditions of class analysis as inspired by Weber and Marx. For Max Weber, classes are sets of people who experience the same status positions vis-à-vis a series of markets. Classes are specified in terms of control (or its absence) over goods and services; individuals are the unit of analysis. Both objective and subjective aspects are involved, but Weber argued that there tend to be overall constellations of positions, such as the relation to property ownership, the ability to acquire goods and services, marketable capacities and social status, which may collectivize and act together. The amount of unity exhibited by any such collectivity was considered variable. Weber (1947: 425-429) divided everyone (that is, distributively) into "positively" and "negatively" privileged property classes and the "middle class." The criterion that seems to run consistently between each of these three major classes is the ability to acquire sufficient revenue to command a certain style or quality of life (which Weber terms "class situations").

The Weberian tradition of class inspired what are known as gradational class schemes. These are descriptions of different characteristics, such as occupation, educational attainment or social status, which can be used as evaluative tools measuring inequalities such as income distribution.

Contrasted to the Weberian tradition has been the Marxist one, which has stressed *relational* classes. Karl Marx was not attempting a scheme of ranks, but a theory of social change. As Z. A. Jordan has pointed out, Marx concentrated on the differentiation of social classes and ignored the stratification based on income, education or occupation. . . . He used the term "class" in the collective sense, that is, he spoke either of the class as a whole or of a certain class property which only a class as a whole, and not each and every member of this class, may have. For instance, when Marx described the proletariat as a revolutionary class, he did not wish to say that each and every

* Originally published in *The Challenge of Class Analysis*. Ottawa: Carleton University Press, 1988. Reprinted by permission of the author and Carleton University Press.

proletarian was a revolutionary, but that the proletariat as a whole had this characteristic (1971: 23).

Whereas distributive properties of individuals can be ranked for all members of society, such is not the case for Marx's collective notion of class, which includes not only social roles, but social action and people with varying awareness of themselves as class actors.

It has been argued within the Marxist tradition that specific "economic interests" are a "necessary" but not a "sufficient" condition for defining social classes (Ossowski, 1963: 71). Marx would seem to have confirmed this interpretation with his famous "sack of potatoes" remark in *The 18th Brumaire of Louis Bonaparte* when he said:

> In so far as millions of families live under economic conditions of existence that separate their mode of life, their interests and their culture from those of the other classes, and put them in hostile opposition to the latter, they form a class. In so far as there is merely a local interconnection among these small-holding peasants, and the identity of their interests begets no community, no national bond and no political organization among them, they do not form a class (1963 [1852]: 124).

For the purposes of this discussion, I will adopt the convention of defining classes in terms of property rights to the means of production and control over the labour power of others. The key in the following definition is that the classes are not merely categories, but relationships that are undergoing processes of change. The capitalist class controls property rights and commands the labour power of others. The working class is excluded from control over property and is obliged to sell its labour power. Estrangement from the *means* of labour and the *rights* of property are the key criteria for identifying the working class. This distinguishes them from the traditional petite bourgeoisie who control their own property (that is, access to the ability to labour). The modern petite bourgeoisie (or new middle class) performs the tasks of capital (which include surveillance and discipline along with co-ordination and direction) and the tasks of labour, thus exercising both the rights of property and the obligations of labour, even though, like the working class, it must sell its labour power (Clement, 1983).

The fundamental direct *contradiction* in this formulation is between the capitalist class and the working class, yet there are key *tensions* involving especially the trajectories of the new middle class and the traditional petite bourgeoisie. Relationally defined classes are always in tension: they are only in contradiction at particular historical moments. Tensions can promote social changes, whereas contradictions can transform entire epochs. Both are antagonisms, but of a different order.

The tradition of class studies in Canada has been influenced by both the Weberian and Marxist formulations (Clement, 1983). Currently class analysis is at a crossroads. It is under attack for being too limited and narrow, particularly with respect to gender, ethnicity and region, and overly rigid with respect to economic determination. I wish to make an argument for coaxing class analysis along a more nuanced, powerful path.

The academic exercise is not to *simplify*, but to *clarify* — to provide conceptual tools for richer understanding. Class, I contend, is one such clarifying concept, but one which has suffered greatly from simplification. I undertake to resurrect class from its contemporary abuse as a simplifying concept and attempt to raise it again to a clarifying one.

Part of the complexity of class is the fact

that its analysis proceeds at several levels of abstraction. Mino Carchedi, for example, has identified four such levels: the "pure capitalist economic structure," which primarily involves the logic of surplus value production; the "capitalist socio-economic system," which includes political and ideological dimensions along with the economic; the "concrete society," which is composed of several co-existing modes of production; and the "conjunctural level," which is a specific junction of a concrete society and the level at which political action occurs (1977: 18-23). A similar, yet less complex, set of levels has been identified by Ira Katznelson in his insightful book *City Trenches*. Most abstract is the level of capital accumulation and the mode of production. This is followed by the level of the labour market and workplace patterns. Finally, there is class as "a happening" rather than "a thing" whereby classes act as an historical collective (1981: 202-5). Analysis can proceed at any of these levels of abstraction and should be able, at least theoretically, to move between levels while retaining its integrity.

Increasingly there have been demands, particularly led by social historians, that class be understood and analyzed at the most concrete level of class action. In part this is a response to the limitations of abstractions that tend to be economistic, thus failing to capture the political, cultural and ideological richness of the totality of class not only as a structure but as an experience. Moreover, the dimensions of class as economic/reproductive, political/legal and cultural/ideological are, at the most, moments of one another. Class cannot be only any one of these; class can only exist in their combination. To quote Michael Burawoy's most recent formulation of this issue in *The Politics of Production*, "Any work context involves an economic dimension (production of things), a political dimension (production of social relations), and an ideological dimension (production of an experience of those relations) (1985: 39). (See also Przeworski, 1977). Class in this sense is the combined "effect" of all these dimensions. At the conjunctural level of analysis, class is manifest through each of these dimensions, as my recent research on the emergence of resistance among Canadian fishers attests (Clement, 1986). Such "effects" are transparent among unionized fishers who sell to capitalist enterprises or even the state, but it is also the case for the more translucent co-operatives. Co-ops are class-based institutions. During their formative periods of struggle they were typically directed against large capital, yet as they began to operate, their principal struggle became against labour. Anti-capitalist ideologies and practices were transformed into anti-labour ideologies and practices, both of which were comprehensible given the material conditions of co-op members and the market situation of co-ops as institutions. The Prince Rupert Fishermen's Co-operative, for example, has had its most bitterly fought struggles with unionized labour on the West Coast, including both the shore workers who process the fish and the crew on co-op member boats catching the fish. Labour has been the Achilles heel of the co-op movement and has dramatically affected the ideology and politics of class experience within that movement.

As I will argue in some detail, class relations are everywhere, but they never exist in "pure" form; that is, they always combine with other social relations (except at the very highest level of abstraction). These other social relations include gender, ethnicity, age and region. These combined social relations have significant effects on one another. Class-blind analysts, like gender-blind ones, fail to grasp essential facts of social life. A social scientist without a refined class tool is one ill-prepared to comprehend social relations. But class is more than an analytical tool. It is also an ideology and a practice. It involves not simply categories, but dynamic relationships.

Classes, I contend, never enter the political arena in "pure" economic form; that is, the political expression of class is always in combination with other forces whether they be over issues of nation, ethnicity, gender, region or even political party. Parties are not classes. Even in Sweden, where class has its clearest political expression, the Social Democratic Party is not identical with labour centrals, nor are either identical with the working class. Political parties, by their very nature, combine popular forces with class forces. To put the point even more forcefully, class forces can never exist alone in pure form at the concrete level; they must express themselves in other than strictly economic forms.

The primary contention of this discussion is that if one wishes to gain an understanding of Canadian society, class in isolation is not sufficient. Analysis requires gender, region, ethnicity, etc. Having said that, however, in order to grasp the essence of Canadian society, class is essential. Most enriching is the "chemistry" of class and other factors. The processes of class formation may be universal, but worthy of note are the specific configurations. While class "conditions" non-class cleavages (gender, region, ethnicity, etc.), it is also conditioned by them. I am not arguing that class is an independent variable and all others are dependent variables. Instead, these factors are relational and interactive, not determined but dialectic.

The most significant challenge to traditional class analysis in recent times has come from the women's movement. Transformations in the household and the labour force, broadly speaking the social division of labour, were the material bases for the women's movement. That movement, it has often been observed, has an internal class character in a similar sense that class is also "gendered." The challenge is to bridge the gap between the workplace, home and community. This connection has ben brought to the fore by women's greater labour force participation and the ensuing demands that have been articulated by the women's movement. Analytically these include issues of domestic labour and its impact on both paid labour and gender relations; politically it has involved struggles for day care, community services and family law reforms. Class issues have been affected in significant ways.

Ironically, the domestic labour debate has been overly economistic (Fox, 1980) focusing upon the production of value and productive/unproductive labour, exchange in the context of the reproduction of labourers, and labour power — all of which are class issues, but at the highest level of abstraction. Patriarchy, for example, is a concept germane to gender relations, yet it does not operate at that purely abstract level. Patriarchy is a power relationship between genders wherein men dominate women; men expand their freedom at the expense of women, including the economic, political and ideological manifestations of that domination. What I find most important is the "chemistry" of class and patriarchy. Patriarchy is *not* confined to the family or domestic labour, but is practised in the "public" work world as well; that is, there are gendered patterns of labour force segmentation and patterns of workplace domination (Armstrong 1984). There are no separate public and private worlds since each strongly shapes the other; each affects what is possible in the other through wages brought into the family or the availability for wage labour, depending upon the domestic situation. These issues are ignored at our peril, as Jane Barker and Hazel Downing's study of gender and the office illustrates. They call for "a recognition that where, when and under what conditions women's work is governed by the mechanisms of the family and patriarchy . . . patriarchal relations [are] increasingly firmly rooted in, and defined by the relations and needs of capital" (Barker and Downing, 1980: 65).

A further challenge has come from race and ethnicity. Some of the most exciting recent work in this field has placed class at the centre of such discussions. An excellent example is Ron Bourgeault's work on class and native people, particularly noteworthy since gender is so integral to his analysis (Bourgeault, 1983a, 1983b).

Calling upon my own research in the fisheries, the Native Brotherhood of British Columbia is a solid example of the intersection of class and race. Historically racial conflicts in the B.C. fishery included Japanese, native and white fishers in bitter rivalries where class was the terrain of struggle. The Native Brotherhood incorporates within itself class relations that bring it at times in alliance with the United Fishermen and Allied Workers Union and at times in conflict. Within the Native Brotherhood there are both seine captains who employ crew and the crew members themselves, whereas the union excludes seine captains who own their boats. This rivalry is also gendered since Native women tend to work in the fish processing plants, where the union is strongest, whereas the

Native Brotherhood represents Native men on the fishing vessels. It is impossible to comprehend adequately the West Coast fisheries without a firm grasp of gender, race *and* class.

A further feature too seldom examined with respect to class is age. Particularly noteworthy is the high unemployment among young people, but also the nature of the work they do experience. Increasingly they are being marginalized into part-time, non-union, low-skilled jobs. These jobs are expanding rapidly with the increasing use of franchises in areas of fast-food, retail stores, gas stations, etc. The responsibility of franchise holders is to supervise labour and direct operations according to the specified (and contractual) rules set by large-scale capital. This reduces large-scale capital's risk and its need to spend on the supervision and recruitment of labour. The class experience of young people who are the bulk of the labour force in franchise operations is being moulded. These jobs are uniform in every sense: clothing, procedures and practices. There is no room for innovation or initiative, and it is dead-end work. They do not even have to add — only be able to identify a "Big Mac."

This type of work is not developing talents, initiative or solid class traditions. In today's labour market, many young people find that when they are out of school this type of work is all that is available, often stringing together several part-time jobs to make ends meet. Recently Ester Reiter published her study of "Life in a Fast-Food Factory" (1986). She shows that Canadians now spend a third of their food dollar outside the home and much of that in franchise establishments that maximize the use of minimum-wage, part-time labour. She identifies "the emerging market importance of the young worker" as fast-food franchises reach industrial proportions wherein "young workers become ideal commodities; they are cheap, energetic, and in plentiful supply." It is worth quoting her findings:

> Making up about 75 per cent of the Burger King workforce, the youngsters who worked after school, on weekends, and on holidays were called "part-timers". . . . The daytime workers — the remaining 25 per cent of the workforce — were primarily married women of mixed economic backgrounds. . . .
>
> The women and teenagers at Burger King are under the sway of a labour process that eliminates almost completely the possibility of forming a workplace culture independent of, and in opposition to, management — there are indications that the teenagers and women who work in this type of job represent not an anomalous but an increasingly typical kind of work, in the one area of the economy that continues to grow — the service sector (Reiter, 1986: 321, 324).

The character of the working class is being transformed by such developments and is impacting disproportionately on young people and women who are structured out of the traditional industrial working class, which is unionized and male (not to mention central Canadian). Marginalization is not confined to franchises. Increasingly the central firms and employers (such as municipalities) are using subcontracting of non-union firms for cleaners, garbage collection and a multitude of services (airlines, for example, contract out as much work as possible). Alongside these practices is the increasing use of part-time workers in clerical and sales jobs. Again these disproportionately affect women and young people.

The drawing upon reserve labour pools is an issue that involves women and young people, but in Canada it is also a regional issue.

Region itself is a relationship; that is, regions can only be a region in relation to something else. Regions are not simply areas of unequal power. They are areas in relation to one another and connected in such a way that one is enhanced at the expense of the other. I would argue that regionalism is a consequence (rather than cause) of uneven economic development. Uneven development is historical, spacial and, most crucially, relational; that is, it represents the unfolding of unequal power relations with regional manifestations. The basis of these unequal power relations is class. Class in this case is manifest both at the level of control over capital accumulation and making pools of surplus labour available.

Class and region are bound together in numerous ways. A rather bold example is the so-called resettlement program in Newfoundland. It involved the transformation of the outport household as both a production and consumption unit. Families were relocated from outports to "centres" such as Arnold's Cove. Once moved, there was a commodification of their consumption patterns, involving food preparation, child care, clothing and shelter, which forced families to seek greater wage income. The Arnold's Cove resettlement was tied, not coincidentally, to the Come by Chance oil refinery project. Its failure left the people detached from their new jobs and from their previous means of realizing their labour power. Eventually they readopted fishing in Placentia Bay (although many had moved on to Ontario in search of jobs). To practise fishing, the men must return to their old berths in the abandoned outports during the week while the women work for wages in the new National Sea fish plant. The plant is supplied by two collector boats that make daily rounds to the fish camps. An available labour force was created by detaching people from their subsistence and means of realizing their labour power and drawing them into a situation where wages were required. These workers are "free" to remain unemployed should the fish plant follow the path of Come by Chance. Once again, it is evident that the class relations of this situation are not only regional, but gendered: men become *dependent* commodity producers and women industrial workers, both detached from earlier domestic commodity production which they shared. The major actors in this drama are the large-scale capitalists who control the oil refineries and the fish plants.

Not all social relations are class relations, but class affects all social relations; that is, gender, region, ethnicity, and so on are all *relational* concepts that are affected by class (although class does not *determine* these relations). This does not mean that gender, regional or ethnic groups are "classes." A key corollary of this argument is that classes *never* exist in isolation — "pure" classes only exist in abstraction. Conversely, classes are *always* conditioned by other social relations.

What needs to be stressed are relations and processes. At its highest level of abstraction, class struggle hinges on the contradiction between the development of the forces of production in capitalism and the limitations imposed by the relations of production inherent in that system. It is this contradiction that provides class with its dynamic, its motor force. At the socio-economic level the politics of class struggle include a history, culture and ideology that give life to basic economic situations. As Marx noted in the *Grundrisse* (1973 [1939]), "Society does not consist of individuals, but expresses the sum of interrelations, the relations within which those individuals stand." Classes are not "things." They are relations and processes.

Since these relations and processes are experienced through people, they never manifest themselves in "pure" form, but take on and are affected by the characteristics of people — that is, their gender, race, region, etc., all of which are themselves social characteristics. Similarly, objective positions in the labour process are not *identical* with class, nor is class reducible to such positions; yet these positions have social, political and ideological effects that contribute to the experience of class.

Having discussed some factors that interact with and impact on class, I will now briefly turn to some of the processes under way within class relations in order to reflect upon current changes.

A key process in the transformation of class relations is that of proletarianization. People enter the labour market because they are separated from the means to realize their labour power and must provide for their basic needs. The means of production are also their means of realizing their labour; that is, these are opposite sides of the same process whereby capital accumulates. Just as it is necessary for capital to accumulate or die, so is it equally necessary for labour to seek a place to utilize its labour power or perish. In the terms introduced earlier, when the traditional petite bourgeoisie experiences the effects of proletarianization, they increasingly come to resemble the working class or, if the process is completed, actually become members of the working class. There is also another side to the proletarianization process, which involves the differentiation of aspects of capitalist rights into the new middle class. As that new middle class declines in performance of the rights of capital and increases in performing the obligations of labour, it too experiences proletarianization (Clement 1983). Proletarianization is a *pro-*

cess; to be proletarian is a condition. They are part of a relationship between the rights of capital and the obligations of labour, on one side expressed in processes involving the traditional petite bourgeoisie and labour, while on the other side, the relation between capital and labour.

The new middle class arises out of the division of capitalist rights concerning surveillance and discipline, but also out of productive activities necessary for the working class which involve co-ordination and direction of the labour process. Surveillance and discipline involve the realization of surplus value (unproductive labour), while co-ordination and direction involve creation of surplus value (productive labour), to use a language appropriate to the highest level of abstraction (Poulantzas, 1977: 118). Whereas the traditional middle class was "independent" in the sense of not employing the labour power of others (aside from its family where patriarchy acts as a key relationship), the new middle class truly stands between capital and labour exercising both co-ordination and surveillance aspects of the labour process.

A central feature of the new middle class is its supervisory activity. I will take one piece of evidence from the International Class Structure Project concerning supervisors and work through some implications for types of control structures. In Sweden 8 per cent of the men and 6 per cent of the women are supervisors, while in Finland 5 per cent of each are supervisors. In the United States these proportions rise to 15 per cent for men and 12 per cent for women, while in Canada a similar 11 per cent of men and 9 per cent of women are supervisors (Finnish Class Project, 1985: 62). Don Black and John Myles have done some detailed analysis of similar patterns. Notable are the significant differences in the proportions of supervisors, but also in their types of activities. They report that "virtually all Canadian and American supervisors have sanctioning authority," which I have been calling surveillance and discipline, while "only a majority of the Swedish supervisors, have such authority. For the most part, Swedish supervisors merely co-ordinate the labour of others." This is what I have been calling co-ordination and direction (Black and Myles, 1985: 20). Black and Myles make an interesting observation: "What is most remarkable is the enormous amount of "administrative overhead" that goes into the work of control and surveillance in Canada and the United States. In the United States, almost 29 per cent of all employees are engaged in disciplining other employees as compared to less than 12 per cent in Sweden. For Canada as a whole the figure is 23 per cent but rises to 28 per cent in the extractive/transformative industries (Black and Myles, 1985: 22). The Swedes and Finns have much lower expenditure on supervision and adhere much more to administrative or bureaucratic forms of control. They also have a fearless approach to technology (which is made possible by labour market policies that ensure employment at decent minimum standards).

The introduction of technology is often a key point of struggle in relations between capital and labour in North America. Labour often resists because of the way technology is implemented (that is, to maximize capital accumulation rather than to improve the quality of work life), which in turn is determined by the industrial relations context of its implementation. Although both operate within capitalist economies, it is evident the Scandinavians have created a much more productive and less conflict-ridden system of industrial relations than in North America, where unproductive supervision flourishes. The Scandinavians have a system that provides much more autonomy for workers and has less need to spend on coercive control structures.

Bureaucratic control structures that operate in place of direct supervision are not without their problems. It is through bureaucratic structures that unions are often drawn into management's system of control. In order to protect the interests of present members, unions have often neglected part-time workers, who are often excluded from the advantages of concessions gained through bureaucratic arrangements such as grievance procedures, bidding for jobs, pensions, etc. Such arrangements often operate to the disadvantage of women and young people, as does the way technology is introduced into the office through automation (Morgall and Vedel, 1985: 93).

Automation is not uniform in its impact on the working class because the working class itself is not homogeneous by skill, industrial sector or gender, as will be argued in the following chapter. The point is that class and automation are not simple processes. They are uneven within the working class and have different effects on various fractions of the working class which correspond to variously skilled and gendered jobs. Assessing the impact of automation requires a textured understanding of class and class fractions.

Another aspect of class demanding careful attention is its so-called "subjective" side. This means more than "class consciousness" as traditionally understood by that term. It means class *experiences* and class *struggle*, which are actual manifestations of class. More important than "consciousness" per se is ideology, which provides an account or explanation for people's practices. The leading voice in this tradition has been E.P. Thompson who, in his classic *The Making of the English Working Class*, tells us that "class experience is largely determined by the productive relations into which men [and we should add women] are born — or enter involuntarily. Class-consciousness is the way in which these experiences are handled in cultural terms; embodied in traditions, value systems, ideas, and institutional forms. If the experience appears as determined, class-consciousness does not (Thompson, 1963: 9-10).

I have tried to apply some of these principles in two case studies of class formation and experience. In *Hardrock Mining* I focused on managerial strategies and workers' resistance as manifestations of class struggle. In the fisheries study, *The Struggle to Organize*, the focus was on differences in the politics and organization of capitalist, petty bourgeois and proletarian "characters" of unions, co-operatives and associations. The purpose was not only to distinguish organizational types, but to explain the behaviour of each. I used class analysis, for example, to explain differences in the ideology and behaviour between the two largest unions, the United Fishermen and Allied Workers Union, which excludes skippers who regularly employ three or more crew, and the Newfoundland Fishermen, Food and Allied Workers Union, which includes skippers. The class content within these unions explains their tendencies and concrete practices (Clement, 1981; 1986).

To this point attention has been focused on the working and middle classes, but some brief comments on the upper class are appropriate. Using my earlier studies on corporate power as a baseline, the theme here is continuity rather than change.

The actions of the ruling class make a difference for the lives of ordinary people.

The St. Lawrence, Newfoundland, fluorspar mines, formerly operated by the Aluminium Company of Canada, were reopened recently under the control of Minworth Limited, a British company. The Peckford government induced the company with exclusive rights to the rich fluorspar deposits and a forgivable grant for $6.8 million plus equity financing of $1.5 million. Transport Canada kicked in another $1.5 million to repair the docks. Why such concessions? Only 15 per cent of the town's labour force is currently employed, a situation that has persisted since Alcan withdrew in 1978. The town's council is so desperate for work that they struck a three-year agreement with Minworth that sets the following conditions: (1) wages will be set at $9 to $10 per hour (nearly half the rate for hardrock miners elsewhere in Canada); (2) employees will not join a national or international union, but may form a local association; and (3) no strikes. These are demeaning conditions, but the people are desperate and all three levels of the Canadian state are scurrying to satisfy the wishes of capital with all too little protection for the workers. Yet these are precisely the workers most in need of the ability to protect themselves: St. Lawrence has a lung cancer death rate twenty-nine times the Newfoundland average; radioactivity in the mines has been from two and a half to ten times maximum standards (in some sections 193 times recommended levels). A provincial Royal Commission in 1969 identified 150 miners who had already died from these conditions, with another 100 permanently disabled. It took five years after the first medical studies before miners were finally told of the medical dangers (*Toronto Star*, 19 October 1985; A1, A10). Should capital really be trusted again with the lives of St. Lawrence's workers?

It would be difficult to exaggerate the disparities of power between the ruling class and working class. The Canadian state is most accommodating to capital and both are highly integrated. The implications of this highly concentrated power are enormous for Canadians as consumers and as employees. The actions of the ruling class have consequences for everyone.

Why should one care about class theories? Theories are intended to lend insight into building explanations, which in turn guide the way individuals think about and act toward their society. It is the contention of this discussion that class can and should be an integral part of such an understanding. Class, however, cannot be narrowly understood if it is to fulfil its analytical promise. Class does matter, but not isolated from gender, region, politics, ideology, culture and classes in relation to one another. Indeed, without these various social relations class is a static, economistic category. With them it is a dynamic explanatory concept central to the social sciences and fundamental to everyday life.

28

*Economic Concentration and Social Power in Contemporary Canada**

R. Jack Richardson

Introduction

In the past decade or so, there has been a remarkable transformation of the Canadian economy. The degree of foreign control has begun a modest decline. Canadian multinationals have grown to such a point that Canada now ranks as the sixth largest home country for multinational enterprise (Niosi, 1985). The deregulation of the financial and transportation industries is producing short-term chaos among stockbrokers, truckers, airline passengers, and others.

The most significant elements of this transformation are three closely related developments: the resurgence of family con-

trolled enterprises; the growth of huge conglomerates; and the integration within these conglomerates of financial and nonfinancial firms. This paper presents an analysis of these revolutionary changes in the concentration of economic power between 1978 and 1985. But economic power, if it exists, extends beyond the economy to the political and social realms (Hilferding, 1970 [1910]; Panitch, 1977; Brym, 1985), consequently, the paper concludes with an exploration of the social implications of these changes in the structure of our economy.

Perspectives on Corporate Control and Economic Power

Market Power

Conglomerates are groups of firms under common control. They gained prominence during periods of rapid concentration of North American industry in the late nineteenth and early twentieth centuries. Because they are created by takeovers which

*Although they cannot be held responsible for any errors in judgement this paper may contain, I gratefully acknowledge the influence that Robert Brym, Alfred Hunter, Ralph Matthews, Jorge Niosi, Michael Ornstein, John Scott and Lorne Tepperman have had on the development of my approach to the sociology of economic institutions. I thank Robert Brym and Alfred Hunter for their critical comments on an earlier draft of this paper.

concentrate economic power, conglomerates have been the subject of extensive and critical investigation (for example, United States Department of the Interior, 1939). There has been a massive wave of corporate concentration and conglomeration in both the United States and Canada since the late 1970s. This has placed the control of our economic institutions into fewer and fewer hands, which in turn has inevitably increased the degree of market power they can wield.

Market power arises from the concentration and control of economic resources, combined with the ability to withhold those resources from the market (Weber, 1968). Capital can wield market power by delaying investment and closing down operations, thus creating job losses; labour by forming unions and calling strikes. Dominant enterprises can wield market power over their competitive suppliers and customers.

The Management versus Ownership Control Debate

Corporations may be controlled by an individual, a family or a small group of owners whenever they hold a block of shares larger than that which contending owners can mobilize to thwart them. When, in the absence of a control block, shares are widely dispersed, corporations are usually considered to be controlled by top management and their allies on the board of directors. Berle and Means, (1967 [1932]) concluded that this dispersal of shareholdings results from corporate growth. Hence, the larger the corporation, the more likely it will be controlled by management.

However, the locus of control has sociological significance only if it has social consequences. Some propose that the rise of management has opened social mobility and broken down old class barriers (for example, Parsons and Smelser, 1957; Aron, 1967). However, in a recent study of the Canadian trust industry (Richardson, 1988), the author discovered that the management which had controlled these firms largely formed an entrenched, hereditary group. It was the new owners who acquired the trust companies that displayed outstanding social mobility. It was largely these "nouveaux riches" new owners who transformed the moribund trust industry into the dynamic institution it is today.

The Theory of Finance Capital

The concept of finance capital refers to two parallel processes: one is the growth and concentration of financial and nonfinancial corporations; the other is the development of non-market ties, such as shareholdings and directorship interlocks (Hilferding, 1970). This integration results in the concentration of economic power in the hands of the few owners and chief executives who hold key positions in both the financial and the industrial realms of the economy (Niosi, 1978). This conceptualization of those who dominate a capitalist economy provides a rough synthesis of the Marxist and elite theorist approaches, because it views finance capitalists as the dominant fraction of the capitalist class (Fennema, 1982).

Hilferding's (1970) analysis of turn-of-the-century Germany found that the big banks became directly interested in the profitability of the industrial sector. They participated in building barriers to entry in order to permit large-scale industry to obtain monopoly profits. This coordinated activity by the dominant banks and industrials was cemented by an

integration of capital and directorship interlocks. Subsequent analyses of contemporary
patterns of directorship interlocks have supported the fusion of financial and industrial
capital in Europe, the United States and Canada (Fennema, 1982; Scott, 1985; Ornstein,
1984).

In Canada, the Bank Act largely prohibits
crucial ownership ties between banks and industrials. However, in the past decade the
trust industry has grown so rapidly that its
assets now amount to more than 80 per cent
of the Canadian assets of the banks (Richardson, 1988). Furthermore, this highly concentrated industry has also been integrated into
financial-industrial conglomerates. This has
provided the previously missing ownership
ties which reinforce the dominance of Canadian finance capital.

Harvey (1982) proposes that the modern
state rests on the foundation of finance capital and is dominated economically by a few
huge financial-industrial complexes. These
tend to set the pace of economic growth of
a society. Thus, it is to the advantage of the
state to act in the best interests of finance
capital in order to reap the many political
benefits of economic growth (Helferding,
1970; Harvey, 1982).

In turn, the interlocked spheres of interest
of finance capitalists provide the social cement which unites this "inner circle" and
permits it to establish not only economic hegemony but also political leadership (Useem,
1984; Ornstein, 1984; Carroll, 1986). Indeed, Useem (1984) shows that the inner
circle of finance capitalists has been very
effective in transcending narrow corporate
interests and in pressing the interests of finance capital on governments.

The following section presents data which
can test many of these propositions concerning the application of the theory of finance
capital to the contemporary Canadian case.

Corporate Concentration and Control

The assets of corporations in the financial
sector consist, primarily, of money in its various forms. Assets of nonfinancial corporations largely consist of less liquid assets, such
as physical plant and equipment and inven-
tories. Because of these differences, it is not
appropriate to consider financial and nonfinancial assets as equivalent, consequently,
this study will focus on nonfinancial assets.

The top 25 Canadian enterprises account
for 34 per cent of the total nonfinancial assets and nearly 33 per cent of the total profits
of the 391 212 Canadian industrial enterprises (Table 28.1). The top 100 enterprises
account for roughly 55 per cent of total Canadian nonfinancial assets and profits. Thus,
the remaining 391 112 enterprises (99.97
per cent) account for less than half the assets
and profits of the Canadian nonfinancial
sector. In contrast, the largest 100 American
enterprises account for only one-third of
nonfinancial assets and profits in the United
States (Francis, 1986). Clearly there is an extraordinary degree of corporate concentration in Canadian industry.[1] In concordance
with finance capital theory, it seems reasonable to conclude that a few huge enterprises
can wield market power over the nearly
400 000 smaller firms which fight for survival
in the competitive marketplace.

However, these data are but a snapshot of
1983. Comparable data over a reasonable
time period are not available from this
source, so *The Financial Post*'s data for the
397 largest nonfinancial corporations for the

Table 28.1 Nonfinancial enterprises in Canada, 1983

| Enterprise characteristics | Size ranking of enterprise | | | |
	Top 25	Next 75	Remainder	Total
Number of enterprises				
Foreign controlled	9	35	3 355	3 399
Government	4	5	39	48
Canadian private	12	35	387 718	387 765
Total	25	75	391 112	391 212
Financial Data				
		(mean, in $ millions)		
Assets	8 216.2	1 459.0	0.7	1.5
Profits	431.2	87.3	0.04	0.08
		(per cent of total)		
Assets	34.0	19.7	46.3	100.0
Profits	32.6	22.8	44.6	100.0

Source: Adapted from Supply and Services Canada (1984).

years 1978 and 1985 were analyzed to discover the process of corporate concentration.[2] We find that during this period the proportion of foreign-controlled assets of the largest corporations declined from 29 per cent to 26 per cent. This was largely offset by a two per cent increase in the government sector (Table 28.2).[3] Co-operatives maintain a constant one per cent share of nonfinancial assets.

Canadian corporate assets accounted for 43 per cent and 44 per cent of the large corporate nonfinancial sector in 1978 and 1985, respectively. Most notable, however, is the rise of ownership control, from 42 per cent to 60 per cent of Canadian corporate assets in a mere seven years (Table 28.2). Clearly, this trend in the control of large Canadian economic institutions contests the managerialists' claim that, as owners' original

shareholdings become diluted, large corporations ultimately become controlled by management.

However, these data were compiled on the basis of individual corporations, analysis of corporate concentration and control is more appropriately conducted when the unit of analysis is the enterprise (which comprises corporations under common control). Consequently, the Canadian corporate sector in *The Financial Post*'s listings were collapsed into enterprises. In 1985, there were 17 enterprises (comprising 46 of *The Financial Post*'s 397 corporations) with assets over $2.5 billion. This seemed to be a reasonable number (and size) of enterprises that could collectively dominate the Canadian corporate economy.

Table 28.3 compares the 17 largest nonfinancial enterprises in 1985 with the top 17

Table 28.2 *Financial Post's* largest nonfinancial corporations

| Corporation type | 1978 | | | 1985 | | |
	(n)	Assets $ millions	%	(n)	Assets $ millions	%
Total	(397)	214 658	100	(397)	462 067	100
Foreign controlled	(199)	62 712	29	(175)	119 819	26
Government controlled	(25)	57 213	27	(36)	133 709	29
Co-operatives	(10)	1 755	1	(16)	3 326	1
Canadian corporate*	(163)	92 978	43	(170)	205 213	44
*of which, control is by:						
–management	(48)	53 232	57	(44)	80 777	39
–family owners	(109)	39 207	42	(118)	123 354	60
–unclear	(6)	539	1	(8)	1 082	1

in 1978. Here, we find that the recent rise of family control reported in Table 28.2 is concentrated most strongly among the few dominant enterprises of the economy. In 1978, nearly two-thirds of the largest enterprises were management-controlled. This was a higher proportion of management control than was found among the larger population of 397 corporations. It provides some support to the proposition to the management control perspective that the larger the enterprise, the greater is the likelihood of management control. However, by 1985 we find a dramatic shift among the dominant enterprises from management to owner control. The number of dominant enterprises that are management-controlled dropped from 10 in 1978 to just six in 1985. The proportion of the total assets of this dominant group of enterprises declined from 65.8 per cent to just 41.8 per cent in this seven year period. What we are witnessing is the dramatic rise to economic dominance of a small group of Canadian capitalist families (listed in Table 28.4).

Table 28.3 also depicts a remarkable rise in corporate concentration in the period under analysis. In 1978, the 17 largest enterprises controlled 63.6 per cent of the assets of *The Financial Post's* largest Canadian corporations. By 1985, 76.2 per cent of the assets of the 170 largest Canadian nonfinancial corporations were controlled by just 17 dominant enterprises. To put it another way, while the assets of large Canadian nonfinancials roughly doubled in the seven year period study, the assets of the dominant 17 enterprises nearly tripled. More detailed analysis indicates that much of this increase among the dominant corporations resulted from acquisitions. In fact, 10 of the 30 largest enterprises in 1978 disappeared as they were taken over by four giant conglomerates.

From these data we can conclude that corporate concentration, a fundamental prerequisite for the exercise of market power and the functioning of finance capital, is clearly present in the Canadian economy. Furthermore, it is increasing at a remarkable rate.

Table 28.3 Seventeen largest Canadian nonfinancial corporate enterprises

Control	1978			1985		
	(n)	Nonfinancial assets *$ millions*	%	*(n)*	Nonfinancial assets *$ millions*	%
Management	10	38 906	65.8	6	65 335	41.8
Family owners	7	20 189	34.2	11	91 071	58.2
Total	17	59 095	100.0	17	156 406	100.0
(mean)		(3 476)			(9 200)	
Memo: Per cent of *Financial Post's* largest nonfinancial Canadian corporations			63.6			76.2

Table 28.4 Seventeen largest Canadian nonfinancial enterprises (by assets)

Enterprise	Nonfinancial assets (1985) *$ billions*	Locus of control
Bell Canada	28.2	Management
Edper/Brascan	27.4	Bronfman family (Toronto)
Canadian Pacific	21.4	Management
Olympia-York, etc.	17.3	Reichman family
CEMP, Seagram, etc.	13.2	Bronfman family (Montreal)
Thomson Group	8.3	Thomson family
Irving Group	6.5 (est.)	K.C. Irving
Nova Corp.	6.4	Management
Eaton's	4.1 (est.)	Eaton family
Trans Alta Utilities	3.7	Management
Genstar	3.4	R. Turner & A. McNaughton
Atco Ltd.	3.0	Southern family
Stelco	2.9	Management
Unicorp Canada	2.8	George Mann
Dofasco	2.7	Management
Weston Group	2.6	Weston family
Power Corp.	2.6	Paul Desmarais

We can also conclude that family-controlled enterprises have largely accounted for the dramatic growth of the dominant conglomerates. Subsidiary analysis reveals that it is largely the non-British, upwardly mobile families that have blasted their way into the command posts of the economy. The classical analyses of the Canadian corporate elite showed it to have been predominantly of upper class British origin (Porter, 1965; Clement, 1975). Therefore, this is an important new phenomenon in Canadian society: it signals potential changes in social mobility and ethnic stratification that are worthy of further study.

Finance Capital in Contemporary Canada

Recall that the concept of finance capital rests on more than just corporate concentration and market power; its second foundation stone is the merging of financial and nonfinancial capital. The concentration of Canadian financial capital in the five big banks is an oft-repeated social fact. Park and Park (1962) even propose that these banks control Canadian industry. But they are prohibited by law from owning or controlling anything more than a tiny fraction of the shares of industrial corporations and vice versa. At first glance, it would appear that the economic dominance of finance capital has not developed here in Canada.

However, the concept of finance capital focuses on people as wielders of institutional power, not just on capital. The integration of financial and nonfinancial spheres of capital can be achieved to some significant degree by the key executives who act as directors of both financial and nonfinancial corporations. These interlocking directors become links in a dense network that provides the social cement uniting both the dominant segment of the capitalist class and the dominant sector of the economy. Carroll, Fox and Ornstein (1982) conducted one of the most intensive studies of directorship interlocks ever undertaken. They concluded that the Canadian banks were the most densely connected of all of the 200 large corporations that were linked in a national network of interlocks. For this and many other reasons they determined that this intercorporate network was a manifestation of Canadian finance capital. (For a comprehensive analysis of the development of Canadian finance capital see Carroll, 1986).

The recent explosion in the growth of conglomerates has had a more direct effect on the development of finance capital. Apart from concentrating economic power, many of these conglomerates have begun to join both financial and nonfinancial corporations under common control. The three largest Canadian merchant banks have now come under the control of huge nonfinancial conglomerates. Most of the Canadian-controlled insurance industry (excluding mutual companies, which are owned by their policy holders) have recently been acquired by these same conglomerates.

The most significant integration of financial and nonfinancial capital, however, has resulted from the transformation of the Canadian trust industry. This industry has had a phenomenal growth over the past 20 years. The total assets it controls and administers have grown from $7 billion in 1965 to $181 billion in 1984. Now, trust company assets amount to more than 80 per cent of the Canadian assets of the chartered banks. They have emerged as a new force to rival the banks' influence on the Canadian financial scene (Richardson, 1988). Furthermore, while this industry appears to have acted as a passive investor in the past, its rapidly increasing corporate holdings now provide a base for it to exercise influence over the non-financial sector (Niosi, 1978).

As significant as all these recent trends in the trust industry may be, they pale in comparison with the importance of the latest development. Within the last decade every one of the ten largest Canadian trust companies (which collectively control over 90 per cent of the trust company assets) have been acquired by nine rapidly growing nonfinancial conglomerates — most of which are among the 17 largest conglomerates summarized in Table 28.3. Since that table represents only nonfinancial assets, it significantly underestimates the economic clout of these huge enterprises. This integration of concentrated pools of financial and nonfinancial capital is the latest and most significant step in the development of Canadian finance capital.

The concept of finance capital was originally developed to explain the dynamic rise of industrial Germany since the turn of the century. More recently, it has been used to explain the basic structure of contemporary economies in Western Europe and the United States (Fennema, 1982; Scott, 1985; 1987). Its application to the Canadian situation has been debatable. Indeed, the lack of development of finance capital has been used to explain the foreign control of the Canadian economy (Clement, 1975; Laxer, 1985b). Now, however, with the seminal work of Carroll, Fox and Ornstein (1982) and Carroll, (1986), and the evidence of the concentration and integration of financial and non-financial capital presented here, there can be little doubt that the concept of finance capital aptly serves as the organizing principle of the contemporary Canadian economy.

In addition to the retarded development of finance capital, the Canadian case may be unique in one other respect. Scott (1985; 1987) persuasively proposes that finance capital operates in Europe and the United States through "impersonal possession" of managerially-owned enterprises. In contrast, here in Canada control has become highly personalized. The majority of the dominant Canadian enterprises are now controlled by individual and family owners, and every one of the enterprises that gobbled up the trust industry is owner-controlled.

Conclusions: The Social Significance of Economic Structure

Canada has endured a comparatively high degree of corporate concentration. Indeed, there is ample evidence that the state has encouraged this kind of economic structure (for example, Innis, 1971). Even though their recent growth has been remarkable, conglomerates as a genus are nothing new. But the current species, which fuses the financial and nonfinancial realms, is a mutation of momentous import.

Now the conglomerated industrial, resource, real estate, communication, and marketing enterprises have gained access to the huge financial resources of the trust industry and other types of financial institutions. This small group of about 17 enterprises controls over three-quarters of the assets of large Canadian nonfinancial corporations. Thus, it forms the heart of Canadian finance capital. It has achieved the ability to perpetuate its own growth by its new-found access to the financial marketplace and to the savings of countless Canadians. This quantum leap in corporate concentration and the integration of financial and nonfinancial capital now provides a much stronger power base from which financial capital can exert its influence on the political process. Power is a relationship (Weber, 1968): this implies that the owners and executives who control a small number of huge financial and nonfinancial corporations (i.e. the finance capitalists) now dominate the smaller capitalists who control the remaining 391 000 corporations in the economy.

Furthermore, political power is related to the control of resources, concentration and organization (Brym, 1985; 1989). Thus, it seems sensible to propose that this small group of Canadian finance capitalists can increasingly wield political influence at the expense of the countervailing influence of other elite structures. In fact, Brym (1989) provides international evidence showing that the autonomy of the state is inversely related to the cohesion of the dominant class.

The Business Council on National Issues is recognized as the voice of finance capital in Canada. Its chairman, Thomas D'Aquino, clearly voiced its conception of the power of finance capital vis-à-vis other institutions: "No one tells us what to do, no one. We do what we want when we want to do it." (*Toronto Star*, November 17, 1988).

Space precludes a listing of illustrations of the influence of finance capital on the Canadian political process (see, for example, Richardson, 1988). However, the Canada-U.S.A. free trade agreement and the 1988 federal election is a good example. The large conglomerates which form the heart of Canadian finance capital are now growing so quickly and have such major sources of capital at their disposal that their major challenge is to find opportunities for further expansion (Francis, 1986). Opportunities are becoming limited in Canada because they already control over three-quarters of the assets that are worth acquiring, therefore, expansion into the United States is the logical next step. Indeed, several of these dominant conglomerates have already made some very large acquisitions of American financial and nonfinancial assets. Secure access to American markets and corporate assets is thus of the utmost importance to the well-being of these burgeoning giants. Consequently, they strongly support the objectives of the free trade initiative.

Although Brian Mulroney denounced free trade when he campaigned for the leadership of the Progressive Conservative (PC) party in 1983, he reversed his position and initiated the negotiations that produced a free trade agreement a few years later. This initiative was strongly supported by the Canadian Alliance for Trade and Job Opportunities — a one-issue lobby group attached to the Business Council on National Issues. In fact, this lobby group spent $3 million advertising the virtues of free trade just before the 1988 election. Still, however, more Canadians opposed the agreement than supported it. When the implementing legislation was blocked in the Senate, an election was called to "let the people decide." During the election, this lobby group spent $4.2 million on political advertising. Never before has the Canadian electorate been exposed to such a pervasive campaign. In fact, the funds this group pumped into the campaign greatly exceeded the combined total spending of the two opposition parties (*Toronto Star*, Nov. 22, 1988; *Time*, Dec. 5, 1988).

Although free trade was certainly not the only issue in the election, it was the dominant one. The Progressive Conservatives were the only party supporting the agreement. Thus, there can be little doubt that the overt massive support of finance capital was a significant factor leading to a PC victory with a parliamentary majority.

The ensuing speedy passage of the free trade agreement has economic, political and social consequences. In the economic realm, it secures Canadian finance capital's expansion opportunities. Blocked by diminishing opportunities at home, it can continue to expand by acquiring American corporations. In the political realm, the agreement severely restricts the Canadian government from intervening in the economy. This, of course, reduces the power of the political elite and correspondingly increases the power of finance capital. Surely it is illogical to conceive that any elite group would voluntarily relinquish power. So we can only conclude that the consolidation of finance capital has provided it with the political and social power that the theory of finance capital predicts.

Notes

1. In comparison with the United States and many other economies. However, there is probably an even greater degree of corporate concentration in some European economies, such as Sweden and Belgium (Fennema, 1982).

2. These data were derived from *The Financial Post* (1979; 1986). Both issues reported the 500 largest nonfinancial corporations. However, their method of compilation changed during this period. To achieve consistency, some of the smaller firms in a few industries were eliminated for the year 1978. The largest 397 firms survived and are compared with the 397 largest firms reported for 1985.

3. It is possible that these trends will be reversed with the implementation of the free trade agreement and the government's privatization program.

29

*The Jobs of Fathers, Sons and Grandsons**

John C. Goyder and James Curtis

Cumulative Effects in Family Ascription[1]

In analyses of mobility over two generations, the socio-economic characteristics of the father are usually taken as indicators of ascribed family status even though these may not capture the full implications of family background. Extensions of mobility models beyond these basic status variables have sometimes used attitudinal predictors (e.g. Duncan, Featherman, and Duncan, 1972), but seldom have they involved variables pertaining to other family members. However, the status of grandparents and great-grandparents might be expected to have some independent effect upon the status of respondents. If such effects were of any magnitude the impact of family status could be said to be cumulative over generations and the conventional .40 father-son correlation found in previous two-generational studies would understate the full degree of "family ascription" in the process of occupational attainment.[2] Thus, one way in which the addition of information on the statuses of grandfathers and great-grandfathers might lend perspective to interpretations of ascription is by clarifying the contemporary ascriptive importance of past generations.

The most direct manner in which grandparents may influence their grandchildren's occupational attainment is probably by direct adoption or guardianship. More subtle forms of influence might take the form of trust accounts and inheritances that bypass the father's generation. Along with the transmission of such resources, grandparents may have some role in socializing grandchildren if contact between them is frequent. Even lacking contact, the influence might persist posthumously as in the case where a grandfather is venerated and held up as a role model to the new generation.[3] The possible

*Excerpted from "Occupational Mobility over Four Generations," *Canadian Review of Sociology and Anthropology* 14 (3), 1977, pp. 221-233. Reprinted by permission.

influence of great-grandparents, which could not be supposed to be of any great strength, would seem likely to be exerted almost entirely through the form of reputation and role model. No doubt, individual cases can readily be found where grandparents or even great-grandparents could be seen to be influences affecting the socio-economic attainment of their progeny. This is certainly a theme which occurs in literature. Whether the transmission of resources, values, and role models over non-adjacent generations is of sufficient frequency and importance to be detectable in a general population is a question that only a survey analysis is likely to answer.

Data Source

Our data come from a set of mobility questions included in a political opinion survey conducted following the 1974 federal election. The survey used a national sample of Canadian voters (for fieldwork details, see LeDuc et al., 1974). The mobility questions were asked of males only (N = 1191, 1143 when weighted). Several previous three generational mobility studies (cf. NORC, 1953; Davidson and Anderson, 1937; Svalastoga, 1959; Zelan et al., 1968) have asked respondents to report the occupations of their fathers and paternal grandfathers, as well as their own. An alternative method of linking three generations, used in the Glass study (1954), is to ask respondent's father's and respondent's son's occupations. Judging from two recent reports on re-analyses of the Glass and NORC data sets (Ridge, 1973; Hodge, 1966, respectively) the two methods of constructing a comparison of mobility over three generations yield somewhat different results. Findings from the two re-

ports are difficult to compare because of the different analytical tools (and societies) involved in each, but Ridge (1973) appears to have found stronger direct grandfather effects than Hodge (1966) did. In the election study the two approaches were combined. Respondents were asked to report the "main" occupation of their paternal grandfathers, fathers, and eldest sons, as well as their own current occupation.[4] Responses were coded into 1971 Blishen scores (Blishen and McRoberts, 1976) and into a scale suitable for matrix analysis (Pineo and Porter, 1967: 61).

Findings

Correlational Results

The intercorrelations among the statuses of grandfathers (G), fathers (F), respondents (R), and eldest sons (S) are shown in Table 29.1. Farmers are a difficult group to code into an occupational SES scale because of their great heterogeneity; since they constitute a large proportion of occupations in Canada, the correlations are given first with farmers included (above the diagonal in Table 29.1) and then excluding farmers in each generation (below the diagonal). Including farmers, the correlation of respondent's and father's occupation, with a value of r = .38, follows closely the "western European model" (r of about .40) found in a number of such countries and in the U.S. (Svalastoga, 1965).[5] With farmers excluded, this figure drops to r = .33. Among grandfathers and fathers the effect of excluding farmers is to raise the intercorrelation of their occupations by .01 points.

Of principal interest for our purposes is the relationship grandfather's occupation has

Table 29.1 Intercorrelations of occupational status scores among grandfathers, fathers, respondents, and sons

Generation	G	F	R	S
Grandfather (G)	1.00[a]	.49	.22	.05
Father (F)	.50	1.00	.38	.13
Respondent (R)	.27	.33	1.00	.26
Sons (S)	.03[b]	.09[b]	.22	1.00

[a] Figures above the diagonal are for the total sample; those below the diagonal are for farmers excluded in each generation.
[b] $p. > .05$

with those of the succeeding generations. Over the generations the intuitively obvious pattern holds; the strength of association between grandfather's occupation and those of the following generations steadily declines. The results reported in Table 29.2 show that grandfather's occupational status retains a moderately large zero-order association with the occupational status of the third generation (respondents). A less obvious finding is that by the fourth generation (sons of respondents) family ascription due to the status of grandfathers, disappears almost entirely. The correlation of grandfather's with respondent's son's occupational scores ($r = .05$ with farmers, .03 without) fails the test for statistical significance and is so small that any possibility of cumulative ascription extending to the fourth generation is ruled out. The correlations involving eldest sons fluctuate somewhat according to whether all working sons are used or only those aged 25 or over. The coefficients reported in Table 29.2 include all sons. It may be more reasonable to analyse data only for older sons because they are relatively settled in their careers, but this dissipates the case base. Restricting the calculations to sons aged 25 or over, the association between grandfather's and respondent's son's occupation scores

declines to $r = .02$ with farmers included. This figure actually takes a negative value ($r = -.07$) with farmers excluded.

We have seen that there is some first order association between respondent's and grandfather's occupation. This, however, does not necessarily demonstrate that family status ascription is cumulative. Some degree of correlation between the occupations in these two generations is inevitable because both share a strong association with the intervening generation (Table 29.1). In fact, when the combined contribution made by grandfather's father's occupations in explaining variance in respondent's occupation is examined, the resulting multiple correlation is found to be little larger than the conventional two generation (father-respondent) correlation. Indeed, the correlation of $r = .38$ seen in Table 29.1 for fathers and respondents is raised only in the third decimal place. In the non-farm population the cumulative effect is larger but still not important (the zero-order $r = .33$ becomes a multiple $R = .35$). In sum, correlational analysis reveals an extremely low association between occupations over four generations, and over three generations a moderate association is found to possess only a minor cumulative component.

Table 29.2 Simple frequencies: Respondent's occupation by father's occupation by grandfather's occupation

Grandfather's occupation	Respondent's occupation	Father's occupation		
		White col.	*Blue col.*	*Farm*
White collar	White collar	67	19	3
White collar	Blue collar	11	19	2
White collar	Farm	0	1	6
Blue collar	White collar	45	55	5
Blue collar	Blue collar	18	80	8
Blue collar	Farm	1	2	1
Farm	White collar	37	56	54
Farm	Blue collar	18	47	89
Farm	Farm	3	4	46

Matrix Results

Both the correlational and matrix methods yield the conclusion that mobility between grandfathers and respondents' sons is high. A simple cross-tabulation of the two occupations, without resorting to controls for structural causes of mobility, exhibits no statistically significant association (p = .80). In this matrix, occupation was coded into seven broad groupings, and there are large proportions of great-grandsons in the blue-collar categories whose great-grandfathers were professionals or business owners. And, of course, there is a great deal of upward mobility by great-grandsons of manual workers. Only 20 per cent of great-grandsons of unskilled manual workers are also unskilled, while the rest are scattered throughout the other categories; 24 per cent are in the professional category. So, this analysis corroborates what the correlational analysis suggested, that occupational status ascription all but disappears after an interval of four generations down the male side of a family.

Table 29.2 shows the simple frequencies of respondents classified simultaneously according to their own occupation group and those of their grandfathers and fathers. To prevent having too large a number of cells, occupations were recoded here into the traditional white-collar, blue-collar, and farm scale. This grouping is only a crude categorization and for contemporary generations may over-simplify because of the overlap in incomes between lower white- and upper blue-collar occupations. However, it may also capture more reality for occupations in past generations, from a time when the blue-collar/white-collar boundary was more distinct. In examining the frequencies in Table 29.2, no separation is made between structural mobility (that attributed to changes in occupation distributions in each generation) and the underlying patterns often referred to as "net mobility." However, the over-all incidence of different status combinations seems to us to have intrinsic importance. It allows an understanding of what the occupational backgrounds of Canadians have typically been over the past three generations.

The single most frequent status combination observed in Table 29.2 is that of the blue-collar respondent whose grandfather and father were both farmers (N = 89). Indeed, as one would expect, over half of all respondents in the sample have farming backgrounds either in the father's or paternal grandfather's generation. The opposite pattern, that of migration back to farming by respondents having grandfathers in the industrial sector is, of course, infrequent. For example, only one respondent had a white-collar grandfather, a blue-collar father, and was himself a farmer. It can be observed that the incidence of consistency in occupational groups over three generations is, in terms of simple frequency, rather large. Sixty-seven respondents reported white-collar occupations in 1974 and said that their fathers and grandfathers also did white-collar work as their main occupations. The combination of blue-collar occupations over three generations is even more frequent (N = 80). And, the inheritance of farms over generations (N = 46) is by far the most common means by which respondents entered into farming. These consistent patterns, particularly those for the industrial sector, are of theoretical interest because they reflect cases in which the social structure has been impermeable. There are two other patterns of mobility over three generations that hold particular theoretical interest. One of these is the progression from blue-collar grandfather to white-collar father and back to blue-collar respondent. The other is the opposite; white-collar grandfather, blue-collar father, and white-collar respondent. These patterns are odd because, if all respondents fitted into them, father's occupation would correlate − 1 with both the grandfather's and respondent's occupations, while respondent's and grandfather's occupations would hold a perfect positive correlation. The pattern of blue-collar

grandfather, white-collar father, and blue-collar respondent is expressed in folklore by the saying "clogs to clogs is only three generation" (Apperson, 1929: 102).[6] This proverb seems to imply that mobility is likely to be sustained only over two generations and that somehow the class structure will reassert itself by the third generation. If this was true, then the opposite pattern, which we would term "reverse clogs," might also hold. Some incidence of these two patterns is to be expected merely by chance and according to the principle of regression towards the mean over generations (Allingham, 1967; Blau and Duncan, 1967: 199). That is, if occupational status was determined randomly, having no connection with the levels held in previous generations, sons of both high and low status fathers would generally be found to have occupations closer to the mean level than would their fathers. In fact, the frequency of the "clogs to clogs" and "reverse clogs" patterns does seem small (N = 18 and 19 respectively). Both are minor patterns in the over-all table and we will give below an assessment of whether they occur any more frequently than simple chance would predict.

A summary statistic representing the over-all direct association between grandfather's and respondent's occupation, net of father's occupation, can be generated with the matrix approach by making use of Goodman's (1972) "log-linear modelling."

The odds of a person being in white-collar work are stronger if both his grandfather and father were also in white-collar work than for any other combination of background statuses. The corresponding consistency effect for blue-collar respondents does not appear. Blue-collar background in the father's and grandfather's generation produces a mild probability that the respondent will be in farming and almost identical probabilities that he will be blue collar vs white collar. Clogs to clogs predicts a tendency for respondents having blue-collar grandfathers and white-collar fathers to be downwardly mobile to the blue-collar sector themselves. The rank order of probabilities for the occupational destination of such respondents is first farming, secondly white collar, and last blue collar. Thus, if anything, the "clogs to clogs" pattern occurs slightly less frequently than one would expect from the additive effects of the two previous generations. Similarly, the "reverse clogs" pattern finds no support; those with white-collar grandfathers and blue-collar fathers are most likely to remain blue collar themselves. We would not want to over-emphasize these findings. It should be remembered that in total these three-way effects are too weak to meet the conventional .05 level of significance.

Conclusion

The three-generation data bear on the interpretation of the degree of ascription in Canadian society by revealing the amount of mobility taking place between non-adjacent generations and by allowing tests of whether the degree of family ascription represented by the effects of father's occupation should be adjusted upward to take account of cumulative ascription effects over another generation. To recapitulate the main findings: (1) mobility between grandfather's and grandson's occupation is, not unexpectedly, a good deal greater than that over the two generations represented by fathers and sons; (2) when a fourth generation is included in the analysis, the mobility between great-grandfathers and great-grandsons is so great that there is no statistically significant asso-

ciation between the two sets of scores; and (3) cumulative effects in family ascription over three generations do exist, but they are not large in terms of increased variance explained.

A substantial upward revision in the interpretation of ascription in Canadian society does not seem in order in light of the results. In addition, the high level of mobility between non-adjacent generations seems a consideration which should enter into assessments of the degree of ascription in the Canadian social structure. To us, the patterns of findings suggest the "achievement" interpretation of Canadian social structure, although it is achievement in a limited sense. If the correlation between father's and son's occupations is .4 it is, of course, not diminished by our finding of a low correlation among more distant generations. In addition, it is probably small consolation to those dissatisfied with their occupational status to know that, if previous trends continue, their great-grandsons or grandsons are likely to end up at any occupational level. Nevertheless, from the point of view of describing social structure, the impermanence of family status over non-adjacent generations does suggest an achievement society rather than an ascriptive one.[7]

For the general public, the long-term perpetuation of family status seems to be much less than that found at the very upper end of Canadian society by writers such as Clement (1975: 72-269) or at the very bottom of the social order by studies of poverty (Gonick, 1970: Puxley, 1971: cf. Croll, 1971). Our findings do not contradict those from these other studies, of course. The two types of processes may well occur together: high over-all three-generation mobility in the general population along with low three-generation mobility in poverty and elite groups.

One of our colleagues asked, concerning

our analyses: "Why do powerful families fall and, conversely, how do lowly families rise?" Our main impression from the three and four generation findings is that over several generations the randomizing process is very pervasive in the general population. What we called the "clogs to clogs" and "reverse clogs" hypotheses, our main attempts at a theory of upward and downward mobility over three generations, were not substantiated. We would conceptualize the problem the other way around, arguing that the fundamental principle is that status regresses towards the mean over generations in the general population, and that efforts in theory construction should be directed to accounting for the exceptions to this rule. Some leads towards understanding how status is perpetuated over generations are suggested by the results described herein. For instance, the white-collar sector was found the group most likely to perpetuate status over at least three generations.

Notes

1. In this paper we understand "ascription of social status" to refer to the linkage between a person's status and different components of his family background statuses. We acknowledge that there are alternative definitions in the literature. The term "mobility" is a well-known but somewhat vague label and we employ it here because it conveys more to many readers than more technically precise but awkward phrases such as "achievement-oriented." Mobility encompasses two components: 1) the degree to which parental status is found to be unrelated to son's status and: 2) the distance moved by sons, upwards or downwards, from father's status. Our own conception of a highly mobile society is one having comparatively high levels on both characteristics. In the following analysis the issue of achievement vs. ascription is principally addressed in the correlational analysis, while the distances moved are seen more in the matrix analysis.

2. International comparisons have shown that the correlation of father's and son's occupation seems to cluster around r = .40 among the western European countries and the U.S. (Svalastoga, 1965: 176). Some interesting variations in mobility rates across a broader range of countries have been reported, but their importance has also been given rival interpretations (e.g., see Jones, 1969).

3. A form of mediated influence of grandfathers or grandsons would be where the grandfather trains the father to believe that high (or low) values ought to be placed on occupational success, high educational attainment, having authority and power, etc., and these values are then passed on to the grandson by the father.

4. The occupation questions were: Q76a "What is your occupation?" (Probe, "What exactly do you do?"); Q80a "Is your father living?"; Q80b "What is (was) his main occupation?" (Probe, "What kind of work does [did] he actually do? In what industry is [was] that?"); Q81a — same sequence for paternal grandfathers; Q82d — same for eldest son. The research design would have been enriched had questions been asked of female respondents as well as of males and for female family lines. We were offered the opportunity to ask mobility questions of a half-sample of males and females or of all males in the sample. We se-

lected the latter because a half-sample would have given us too small a number of respondents of each gender (especially working females) for proper analysis. Our findings here, and some reported elsewhere (e.g. Cuneo and Curtis, 1975, on the effects of mother's education), suggest that further work including information on the mother's side should give a very modest increase in variance explained.

5. The relationship between respondent's education and his occupation (r = .61) also follows closely the American figure (r = .60, reported in Blau and Duncan, 1967: 169).

6. Lipset and Bendix (1966: 74) note that the American version of this saying is: "Three generations from shirt-sleeves to shirt-sleeves."

7. If there is a sense in which some of the findings might be taken as lending additional serious support to the ascription interpretation of Canadian society it would be where one was, above all, impressed with the social distance (e.g. limited contacts) and temporal separation between grandfather's and grandson's statuses. One could argue that any statistical association, however weak, between the two statuses is theoretically important because with such great social distances between variables it is remarkable if the background status has any opportunity at all to affect the dependent variable. We are still left, though, with the fact of high levels of mobility from grandfather's to grandson's occupation.

30

Class Conflict and Prospects for Change*

Dennis Forcese

Class and Change

In the 19th century, Karl Marx and Friedrich Engels argued that the interests of capitalists and the interests of workers were inherently contradictory. Inevitably, class conflict would become overt, and the revolutionary victory of the workers would come to pass. For Marx and Engels, the concept of class was not just a description of the structure of economic control, but, more important, it was the key to a theory of social change. The working class, as a collectivity conscious of its relations to the property ownership of the capitalists, was to be the vehicle of societal progress, ultimately realizing full equality of condition in a communist society.

Although Marx offered no time frame

within which the revolution would occur, many observers have delighted in noting the apparent failure of Marxist predictions. Instead of becoming more impoverished, workers in developed societies have shared in industrial prosperity to an extent Marx failed to anticipate, while the *lumpenproletariat* have been extended considerable welfare privileges. In the place of class polarization, a "new class" of white-collar employees and professionals has developed, and serves to insulate the working class from the upper class. Rather than fewer and fewer capitalists controlling the means of production, ownership has been dispersed in corporate structures and amongst their shareholders and managers.

These features of modern capitalist societies are factual enough; it is their interpretation that is open to debate. The possibility of class action persists insofar as there persists a basic opposition of interest between owners and workers. The working class may share in industrial benefits to some degree, but, especially according to the concept of

*Excerpted from *The Canadian Class Structure*, third edition. Toronto: McGraw-Hill Ryerson, 1986. Reprinted by permission.

relative deprivation, they do not share to the point of satisfaction, let alone equity. The unemployed may be supported by the state, using funds collected from wage-earners, but they are not, thereby, somehow rendered full and equal participants in society. The middle class may have acquired some measure of job security and consumer capability, but they have not gained any greater control over the economy. Formal ownership may have largely passed from individuals to corporations, but ownership is not any less concentrated. On the contrary, it is more concentrated, given the size of modern corporations whose effective ownership is vested in one or a few individuals possessing blocks of shares. Changes in class affluence have not altered the fundamental relations of production and control in western societies like Canada. Nor have such changes prevented a steady and gradual shift in the direction of employment-dependence. That is, every year fewer and fewer Canadians are self-employed; they have become wage workers. The class of owners is becoming progressively smaller, and the class of workers progressively larger. At the same time, industries are becoming less labour-intensive and more dependent upon capital-intensive technology. Employment for workers is all the more precarious, as a result.

It is not a matter of rescuing Marxist theory, but of recognizing the continued salience of Marx's descriptions, however much he may have failed to anticipate the massive potential of industrial societies to produce and distribute wealth and to defer and control class opposition. Whether the opposition of interests of which Marx spoke and which does obtain in altered form in Canada will result in overt conflict and significant change is far more open to question.

The Working Class and Conflict in Canada

Controlled Conflict

Class conflict persists in the present state of labour relations, of course, and is manifest in strike action. Especially in the 1960s, the number of strikes, including many illegal and violent strikes, was conspicuous. And, in 1972, a brief but effective general strike took place in Quebec (Rinehart, 1975.)

If the number of strikes, and their duration, are taken as indicators, Canada is now experiencing aggressive labour-union activity. Consistently, Canada loses more time on the job through strike action than all but two of the industrial nations of the world. In large part, increased labour demands are a response to inflation and relate to a pursuit of immediate or short-term economic advantage, rather than any drive for basic change in social organization. In such two-party economic bargaining, unions are relatively successful in terms of gaining wage concessions. But when they have shown interest in influencing government policies, they have not been effective. Presthus has reported that, although many elected representatives in Canada believe unions to be effective pressure groups, and analysis of actual government decisions shows that, in fact, it is professional and business interests that are dominantly effective in this respect. (Presthus, 1974: 207.) Union influence seems to carry weight only at the point of specific bargaining confrontation. Unlike previous instances of conflict in Canada, labour actions have become conventionalized or institutionalized in a time of relative public affluence and general acceptance and legitimation of collective bargaining. Class conflict has not disappeared but, rather than becoming extreme, it has become and likely will continue to be increasingly oriented to wages rather than to significant structural change.

Organized economic bargaining has increasingly extended to white-collar workers and professionals. Teachers' unions, professors' unions on most Canadian campuses, and the large Public Service Alliance of Canada are examples of such unionization and, perhaps, despite their affluence, the mobilization of the hitherto placid middle-class. What is absent in such action, however, is an ideological component or sentiment that differs from hitherto prevailing "centre" attitudes of middle-class Canadians. Insofar as people are becoming increasingly engaged in confrontation with employers, it is purely out of local, short-term interest, and not an interest in the fundamental improvement of a class economic situation of any ideological conviction of an egalitarian sort.

The extent to which such pedestrian activities become radicalized will depend, in part, on the response of the government and employers, and on whether or not a major economic crisis occurs. Given economic disruption, middle-class persons have educational and organizational skills that are translatable into effective opposition politics. But that opposition is as apt to be conservative, as in the Saskatchewan doctors' strike, as it is to be change-oriented. A crucial variable will be perceived, relative, deprivation: economic jeopardy could bring about the class polarization Marxists anticipated so long ago. Hypothetically, massive inflation could precipitate a middle-class "revolution" — again, not necessarily or probably a left-wing revolution — involving skilled workers and professionals. Ominously, the conditions of the pre-war German Weimar Republic resembled such a hypothetical situation. But the likelihood for Canada is improbable.

Strikes, especially violent strikes characterized by vandalism, picket-line fighting, and police intervention, are bitter labour actions. However, the bitterness and anger do not render them challenges to the basic legitimacy of the society, with its established system of stratification and corporate and political authorities ranged in opposition to a union. Strikes are almost invariably wage-related, and not political challenges. The strikes are job-specific, and do not constitute a fundamental rejection of or attempt to alter the existing political and corporate systems. Moreover, striking unions in Canada are characteristically isolated. Not only is there rarely union solidarity with other unions, but often a striking union is pitted against a non-striking union, as in the case of striking inside postal workers pitted against mail carriers. In 1978, the Canadian Union of Postal Workers was, in fact, repudiated by other representatives of organized labour.

Massive strike action like the Winnipeg General Strike of 1919 may not have been initiated as a clearly articulated political action. But it became such a challenge, characterized by labour solidarity and a refusal to conform to government directive. In contrast, the labour union movement today is simply not cohesive. Rather, it consists of numerous non-coordinated organizations, diffused loyalties, and a quest for respectability.

In this context of limited labour action, there are, nonetheless, numerous illegal strikes and strike violence. Where such incidents produce police intervention, there is some exacerbation of class opposition, but it is usually fleeting and isolated. The Fleck strike, for example, where the Ontario Provincial Police intervened, had such a consequence, but it was not enduring. Similarly, when the CUPW refused federal government back-to-work legislation in October of 1978, that was an explicit challenge to government authority. But the challenge was, in turn, repudiated by the rest of organized labour, and CUPW capitulated, with some public humiliation.

Rejection of government authority is a more fundamental union and class action than are mere strikes over wage and other job-related issues. Yet it must be observed that its occurrences are few and far between, and seem to stem from government as much as from union initiative. For example, there is reason to suggest that the CUPW confrontation with the Trudeau government was not entirely unwished for by the government, who were seeking to re-establish a lost public popularity by "being tough" with a relatively isolated, unpopular, and militant union. Thereby, in sum, government legitmacy was enhanced, not eroded, and the union's standing suffered.

To exert serious pressure on government, and to make any inroads on class differentiation, inter-union co-operation is crucial in actions discrediting the government status quo. Failing this, as Rinehart remarks, "What collective bargaining does is institutionalize the conflict by subsuming it under a web of rules which is made explicit in a union contract." (Rinehart, 1975: 154.) Currently, we have a situation in which unions tend to be chiefly interested in wages and to display the passive respectability that repudiates more militant labour groups, as when, in 1978, the Canadian Labour Congress failed to support the striking inside postal workers. Conforming to the norms of bargaining effectively reinforces the system, and blunts the effects of class conflict.

Since World War II, labour relations have been characterized by ritualization. Labour unions now largely confine their activities to questions of wages and working conditions, while the state has provided a statutory legitimacy that has institutionalized collective bargaining and neutered periodic withdrawals of labour. Progression to a strike situation proceeds through extended periods of negotiation, conciliation, mediation, and arbitration. This paced ritualization allows the employer and the state a measure of predictability and protection that effectively reduces the value and power of the strike. In fact, the strike may now be planned for, costed out, and even timed, to allow an employer the opportunity to reduce a surplus inventory and/or effect wage savings that translate into a profit for the corporate or public operation.

Unions and the Labour Market

Ironically, insofar as labour unions and labour leaders themselves enforce compliance with the laws and conventions of Canada's collective bargaining system, they deter the power of labour, and sustain employers. Rather than challenge the industrial system, as in change-oriented political action or in national labour solidarity, Canada's unions win short-run economic benefits in exchange for collaborating in stabilizing the socio-economic system. The scenario of the political power of the strike, above all the "general strike," has scant bearing in modern Canada. The economism of Canadian unions is expressed as a tacit concession that welfare capitalism, controlled labour supply, underemployment, and unemployment are to be accepted, and no fundamental redistribution of resources is to be sought.

The dilemma of trade unionism is that

worker solidarity, cooperation, and class consciousness are unlikely, if not impossible, without trade union organization. Yet, with trade unionism, a structure of controlled adversarial game playing is institutionalized, effectively controlling and curtailing labour power and reinforcing the authority of employers and the state. Unions win concessions, they frustrate and deter authority and unbridled management, but they also sustain the fundamental relations of labour, capital, and the state. Thus one finds many experienced unionists and observers of unionism remarking upon unions as "policemen for the bosses" (Pfeffer, 1979: 317-326; Garson, 1975) with labour locked into contracts, bounded by laws, and monitored by both management and labour leaders. One writer, an academic who spent seven months as a factory worker in order to experience a workplace quite unlike the academic environment, remarks upon unions contributing to "the pacification, demoralization, and disorganization of [their] members as workers with a class interest." (Pfeffer, 1979: 137.) This consequence was not anticipated by Marx. In a letter to Engels, in 1875, Marx described a union as "the real class organization of the proletariat, in which it carries on its daily struggle with capitalism." (Marx and Engels, 1968: 338.) Yet, as he also noted, the "guerilla war" waged by unions dealt rather more with the effects rather than the bases of capitalism (Marx and Engels, 1968: 229), and, in consequence, allowed labour's accommodation to a capitalist class society rather than that society's destruction or change.

A modern comment is offered by Stanley Aronowitz (1973), by no means an academic merely passing through the working-class world. He spent almost 15 years as an industrial worker and a labour organizer, finally withdrawing, having concluded that American unionism was consolidating and reinforcing capitalism. More specifically, he argues that unions, and stratification or differentiation among grades of workers, sustain the myths of nationhood, mobility, and opportunity previously nurtured by school, church, and mass media. Moreover, the unions reinforce and concede the natural order of the labour market, with labour as just another commodity. (Aronowitz, 1973: 10.) In this way, labour unions become one of the institutional pillars of modern society and its class structure.

Ultimately, the role of organized labour in modern Canadian society is best summed up by an appreciation of its having conceded the essential acceptability of the labour market. As Marx, Weber, and so many others have agreed, capitalism is, above all, characterized by its ability to treat labour as a commodity for sale and a source of profit. Unions organize labourers, and thereby secure for workers some material benefits, security and protection. But they also stabilize and channel the labour supply, and, in effect, auction off their commodity, labour power. Whatever conscious motives one may attribute to labour leaders, the consequence of their activity is a symbiotic relation between unions and employers, with both of them intent upon economic regulation and stability. (Stewart, 1977: 14.)

Labour organizations formed to meet working-class objectives and enhance labour power have nevertheless maintained class society and insulated the state from conflict. Insofar as unions organize, systematize, and control the labour supply for employers, they are, as Mills wrote of union leaders, (1948: 6) "jobbers of labour power," with the task of selling workers "to the highest bidder on the best terms available." Unions also channel and resolve disputes and problems by vetting grievances, effectively sharing in the management of an operation. Similar generalizations are to be found throughout the sociological literature, whatever the theoretical school, whether functionalists or Marxists, with impressive agreement despite ideological differences. Although trade unions are a means to more effective worker opposition to capitalism, they tend to be "too much aloof from general social and political movements," just as Marx feared. They respond to "effects" rather than resorting to basic political action. (Marx and Engels, 1968: 229.)

Strikes

While routinization is achieved, privileged class interests also enjoy the benefits of union scapegoating. Strikes are perceived by most Canadians as costly and damaging, and the majority of Canadians who might otherwise support unions willingly would accept limitation upon the right to strike.

Yet strikes are actually the tolerable and controlled manifestations of routinized class conflict, a means of regulating and defusing class antagonisms. Although statistically Canada has one of the worst records of working time lost to strike action, in effect the consequences are far less dramatic than presumed. As previously remarked, such legal withdrawals of labour frequently play into the hands of the employer, at great cost to the striking worker. Often there is no real loss in production, in that, as predictable events, strikes may be preceded by production speed-up (Forrest, 1978: 8), or, during the course of a strike, by supervisory production. Meanwhile, an employer enjoys massive wage-savings often more than sufficient to pay for increased benefits in any new contract. The worker, on the other hand, forfeits income, often never compensated for by any nominal gain in wage rate.

Moreover, in a labour-market system of union- and employer-controlled adversarial relations and economism, and in a society characterized by other divisive allegiances such as ethnicity or region, strikes may work to the advantage of capitalists and the state by generating a widespread public hostility. Canadians, most of whom, objectively, are themselves workers or wage-earners, tend to sympathize with management, in so far as modern strikes are frequently perceived to be to their own cost as much or more than to the employers'. In fact, the perception is partially valid, for the public is more often harmed by the strike action, while employers are protected. Increasingly, strikes alienate a public of fellow class members by withdrawing a service or products enjoyed by the mass public and otherwise unobtainable, whereas the affluent employer will have access to alternate supply. Strikes of private and especially of public workers tend not to damage an employer or members of a dominant class so much as other workers; rather than challenging corporate or state authorities, modern strikes create support for state intervention and "labour-busting." Thereby strikes may offer the employer not only economic advantages, but also clear ideological advantages, deterring class solidarity and class consciousness. The striking workers will sometimes experience a measure of increased cohesion and of more pronounced hostility to an employer. But such increments are transitory, however great the emotion, for the fundamental relation of accepting economic dependency is not altered, and the employer is often economically regenerated and the union fiscally drained. At times, too, rather than keep its solidarity, a union will split, as members divide over the suitability and duration of a strike.

Strikes are a manifestation of class conflict, and represent labour's most powerful tactic. However, the power is squandered if withdrawals of service become routinized, ill-timed, and misdirected. Increasingly, they sustain industrial capitalism, in that they occur as segmented or local events, oriented around short-term benefits, and targetted ineffectively against employers and the state. Ironically, collective bargaining and legal strikes become a means of institutionalizing and diminishing class conflict, rather than focusing such conflict. Insofar as such institutionalized conflict is characteristic of Canada and other modern industrialist capitalist societies (Giddens, 1973: 287), class conflict is limited, and any potential for radical or revolutionary action is obviated.

Further, the conflict is often diluted and directed back to fellow class members. Not only are other unionists often the direct victims, as in public service strikes, but employers are more thoroughly protected from the consequences of a strike than are members of the public. In addition, there is conflict among unions, between better- and less well-educated workers, between rank-and-file members and union executives and hired experts (Westley and Westley, 1971: 37), between workers in one region and those of another, or between workers of one language group and those of another.

In sum, Canadian welfare capitalism and the inequalities vested in Canadian society persist because they meet no wide-ranging challenges or disruptions. Periodic disturbances are more apt to be directly experienced and suffered by wage-earning Canadians than by owners who are insulated by considerable wealth and resources. The disadvantaged are divided by contending al-

legiances, and by a "false consciousness" that is repeatedly reinforced in the daily experiences of first-hand contacts and media socialization. The working class is fractionalized and controlled to such a degree that drastic change is all but inconceivable, and effectively unrealizable. Piecemeal reformism or welfarism, a concession to the endurance of the industrial class system, is the empirical reality. Classes and expressions of class conflict exist, but the potential for producing action and change is slight, especially as Canadian unions avoid or prove incapable of sustained political partisanship or action.

For the securely employed blue- or white-collar worker, there is as yet no fundamental dissatisfaction with the existing system of economic distribution. For the marginally employed or the unemployed, shunned as much by organized labour as by corporate and government interests, protest organization and action is even more rare.

The Impoverished and the Welfare State

Unemployment is a basic indication of social inequity. The extent to which a society will tolerate the existence of a reserve labour army, dependent upon state payments for sustenance, is an indication of social morality. In Canada, unemployment is massive, the highest among comparable western industrial nations including the United States, the United Kingdom, and Australia. Moreover, unemployment is far higher than official employment rates indicate. Underemployment and marginal work, accounts, in some estimates, for 30 per cent of the labour force. (Gonick, 1978: 22-23; Braverman, 1974: 439-40.) Unemployment rates are diminished by periodic work. In addition, among the "hidden unemployed" are those on welfare assistance and not seeking work, those who have not registered, often in despair, as well as a massive student population, many of whom are students involuntarily in school by law and not for education. Witness the substantial enrolment increases experienced by Canadian universities in the 1980s, no doubt in part a response to diminished employment opportunities. One economist accounts for this in estimating the real Canadian unemployment rate as at least 20 per cent. (Gonick, 1978: 22.)

The unemployed and marginally employed are not a significant force for change, cut off as they are from organization and sustained in their subordination by welfare programs. The welfare state effectively pacifies deprived individuals, unless their ranks are drastically enlarged by persons previously enjoying superior economic advantage. Piven and Cloward (1971) have proposed that the history of welfare policy in the United States is one of response to successive economic crises. We might consider Canadian government welfare response to the Depression of the 1930s and currently to inflation and unemployment, as such. They are not policies that alter the distribution of resources or the structure of class, but stabilize them. As one not-so-radical group (the Senate Committee on Poverty) put it, the welfare system "has treated the symptoms of poverty and left the disease itself untouched." (Canada, 1971: xv.) But the programs were not designed to do otherwise. Moreover, stabilization is secured using revenues in large part obtained from wage and salary earners, rather than from business, in no way challenging the economic dominance of the ruling class. In a period of inflation and rising welfare costs, corporations in Canada, especially the banks, report record profits.

Welfare programs, or, in the current euphemism favoured by the Economic Council of Canada, "transfer payments to individuals," amount to taking from the not-so-poor and not-so-rich and giving to the utterly deprived. But only giving a little to the deprived; most of it comes back to the middle class. Remarkable biases exist in programs ostensibly designed to provide equitable systems of security. For example, a 1978 analysis of the Canada Pension Plan demonstrates the advantage to higher-income groups. In effect, allowing for savings from tax deductions, a person with an income of $6000 would make a net Canada Pension Plan contribution of $90.00. Moreover, the $6000 income earner is entitled ultimately to a mere 58 per cent of the full pension entitlement. In contrast, the person earning $50 000 is entitled to 100 per cent. Proportionately, the wealthier income earner pays much less for much more than the lower income earner. (see Table 30.1.)

The taxes that support "transfer payments" are paid by workers. In 1970, over 80 per cent of total income taxes in Canada were collected from persons earning under $20 000 per year. More startling, 41.6 per cent of total taxes were paid by persons earning between $5000 and $10 000. (Tarasoff, 1973: 1.) Taxes fail to redistribute income significantly, because the income share after taxes of widely disparate income groups is virtually unaltered. A slight income gain of one per cent may be measured for each of the two lowest income groups, and a mere two per cent income drop for the highest income group.

The very privileged tend to pay proportionately much less than wage workers. The Progressive Conservative budget of 1985, for example, merely exaggerated the advantage of the prosperous, especially in its capital

Table 30.1 Net contributions to the Canada Pension Plan for 1978

Earned income	Required CPP contribution	Tax saving from deduction	Net CPP contribution	Pension entitlement
$ 6 000	$ 90.00	$ 0	$ 90.00	58%
8 000	126.00	0	126.00	77
10 000	162.00	41.99	120.01	96
12 000	169.20	46.29	122.91	100
15 000	169.20	51.17	118.03	100
20 000	169.20	60.91	108.29	100
25 000	169.20	68.22	100.98	100
50 000	169.20	87.71	81.49	100

Source: National Council of Welfare, (March 1978).

gains provisions. The income tax system is notoriously regressive, making deductions to the advantage of persons with higher income. Rather than being a redistributive mechanism, the tax system consolidates privilege. (Gillespie, 1978.) When indirect taxes are also considered, such as those on clothing and all consumer items, we have all the more clearly regressive rather than progressive tax systems, insofar as the taxes paid by low-income earners constitute a far greater proportion of their income than do the taxes paid by higher-income earners, particularly those enjoying business profits rather than wages or salaries.

Most of these tax revenues, then, benefit the middle class, and are a further indication of the essential stability or maintenance of the system. In 1973-74, projected federal spending of tax revenues only apportioned 28 cents of the tax dollar for "health and welfare," and an additional 13 cents of the tax dollar for "economic development and support." (Tarasoff, 1973.) And much of this goes to middle- and upper-class persons, not only insofar as they receive profits from

economic development schemes, but also in that "health and welfare" spending includes medicare payments and hospital insurance payments to the provinces, family allowances, and veterans' allowances. A similar pattern of "redistribution" operates at the provincial level. The aged — especially women — suffer most from meagre levels of state-mediated support. (See Table 30.2.)

Generally, therefore, present government systems act to reinforce the class structure. Wage earners are taxed, whereas corporate profits remain relatively unscathed. Taxes, then, are returned as benefits to the relatively privileged. Extremes of wealth and poverty are not seriously affected, except for some necessary support of the impoverished, which, however humane, also serves to deepen the dependent state of its recipients and gloss over the persistence of disparities. There is no significant redistribution of wealth, but only a circular distribution.

Rather than offer genuine redistributive and security benefits for all Canadians, present state intervention only subsidizes employee-derived benefits for the middle class.

Table 30.2 Average income from public pension plans and private sources, poor and non-poor aged couples and unattached individuals, 1981

Income Source	Aged Couples[a]		Aged unattached individuals	
	Poor	Non-Poor	Poor	Non-Poor
C/QPP	$1 824	$ 2 263	$1 276	$1 973
Private pensions	1 075	4 885	1 679	4 787
Investments	748	7 161	1 176	7 107
Employment	913	10 984	1 206	7 731

[a]Couples in which both spouses were 65 or older in 1981.
Source: National Council of Welfare.

Of particular concern in Canada, where we have an aging population, is that few pension plans are comparable to the indexed pensions available to state employees. Moreover, increasingly, accumulated pension funds have been used by corporations and the state as a source of capital, with the funds "borrowed" at nominal interest charges. (Myles, 1979: 11-23.) Wages "banked" by workers are, in effect, reappropriated by the state or industry for their own investment and regulatory purposes. As a result, the Canadian welfare state, like other capitalist states, has not ultimately been the impartial arbiter of class interests, as it expanded so vastly throughout this century. Whatever the measure of relative bureaucratic or state autonomy and the extension of citizen rights to fundamental economic subsistence (defined relative to national standards of wealth) the state has nonetheless acted to legitimate and stabilize class society. The ruthlessness and indignity of pre-welfare class societies have been muted, but the class structure has been reinforced.

A relatively new economic device for the state is the promotion of lotteries. So lucrative as a source of revenue have public lotteries proven to be in Canada that the provinces and the federal government contested control of them — ultimately ceded to the provinces. Despite their wide acceptability as voluntary purchases, lotteries are a cruel form of taxation, disproportionately drawing monies from the disadvantaged with the lure of quick riches. In a sense, lotteries are welfare capitalism's Horatio Alger equivalent, insofar as they are a seductive promise of the possibility of better things. Yet the monies are applied by the state to finance its operations, often directly applied to recreational benefits for the middle and upper class rather than the working class. Ironically, the early success story in Canadian lotteries was Manitoba's — introduced by the New Democratic Party government of Edward Schreyer before lotteries were common elsewhere in Canada.

Social Change and Politics

A token lament is heard in the legislatures, the media, and the social science literature of the industrial democracies, to the effect that public participation in politics is slight. Voter turnout may be appraised as too low, party affiliation as too infrequent, and, generally, rates of participation in political campaigns and events too skimpy and apathetic. (Swartz, 1977.) Yet this level of political activity is precisely consistent with the persistence of "democratic" class societies, as Lipset (1965b) approvingly acknowledged in his functionalist analysis of social stability. Lipset's reasoning is offensive, premised as it is upon notions of working-class authoritarianism, irrational extremism, and ideological gullibility. But the conclusion is apt: stable class societies depend upon economism and limited and ritualized political action. Lipset (1960) observed that stable politics obtained when the degree of participation was modest, and when it was confined to electoral politics. Extremist political movements of the right or of the left, oriented to drastic change, are apt to achieve political success when they coincide with an extraordinarily high rate of political participation, including voting. For Lipset, this also means that extremist groups won power when they elicited the participatory support of the sectors of society normally inactive, specifically the working class. Insofar as unions are apolitical, and discouraging of class-oriented politics, they therefore may be seen as securing stable electoral systems.

In contrast to the fragmented and unpredictable politics of the 1930s, normal democratic politics are premised upon generalist centre parties that combine a variety of public interests. Above all, the Liberal Party in Canada has achieved such centre blandness, offering if not delivering something for everyone. Stable politics depend upon the dominant participation of the politically orthodox middle class, and their support of the centre parties. In Canada, for example, placid politics or normal politics are those in which the centre Liberal Party is hegemonic, as it has been through most of Canadian history, having elicited the support of the middle class — the social class to which the majority of voters belong. In 1985, the Progressive Conservatives under Brian Mulroney successfully, if perhaps only temporarily, displaced centre Liberal appeal, and, as the Liberal Party had done, achieved their electoral strength by appealing to the middle class. Middle-class political hegemony is not only tolerated but generally supported by organized labour. The Liberal Party and not the New Democrats have received the majority of working-class votes (Alford, 1963), an historic consistency that has encouraged the futile shift of the New Democrats to an indistinguishable and undistinguished centre position.

There have been several attempts in Canada to translate labour interests into a political party, most explicitly in support for the CCF/NDP. Yet one finds cleavage, tension, and conflict within the party (Westley and Westley, 1971: 38), as well as a general inability to demonstrate its utility to the working class, and so to win anything but a small minority of the working-class vote. In the main, the NDP party is perceived as the plaything of the "eggheads," of the middle-class intelligentsia who thus far have failed to live up to the traditionally-anticipated potential of providing effective and convincing leadership for the working class. Although, on the one hand, one can point to a Canadian "intelligentsia" having been crucial to the CCF/NDP and to Canadian "socialism" as founding influences (Avakumovic, 1978), the feeling is prevalent that the party does not really reach the working class.

The national NDP's commitment to cautious evolutionary politics, intended gradually to displace one of the older parties, has had the consequence of an increasingly bland and undistinguished "socialist" alternative — far from forming an official opposition, let alone a government in Ottawa. The glory of its early policy initiatives in the West has dissipated, and the party seems to have chosen the role of permanent critic or devil's advocate, responding in an *ad hoc* manner to circumstances, rather than generating and systematically promoting its own policy initiatives. In consequence, the party seems long since to have reached its saturation point where public support is concerned, with approximately 17 per cent of the popular vote in the last 15 years. The centre character of the NDP has featured middle-class political candidates and leaders, especially teachers and university instructors (Forcese and de Vries, 1977), and reactive political positions devoted to social criticism rather than policy positions. The de-radicalization of the NDP has won it some formal labour support, in endorsement and financial support from the Canadian Labour Congress (CLC). However, CLC contributions, amounting to $1.2 million in 1979 when the Liberals were defeated by Joe Clark's Progressive Conservatives, did not translate into votes and NDP seats; in fact, the NDP lost a seat in Ontario in 1979, (*The Gazette*, May 24, 1979.) Similarly, the NDP survived, but did not break out, in the Mulroney landslide victory that came after.

The significance of stable politics has to do fundamentally with the maintenance of a system of economic distribution. Insofar as legitimate politics are defined as consisting essentially of electoral politics, and especially the act of voting, the potential of politics for opposition and change is inhibited. All Western democracies depend upon routinized and narrowly defined politics (Giddens, 1973), wherein extended periods of public inattention give way to periodic, ritualized,

media events known as elections. Governments find routinized lobbies acceptable between elections, and a measure of conventional criticism. But group actions that challenge the operation of the state are threatening and intolerable for the dominant class interests in Canada.

Notably, politicized labour union action is intolerable. In North America, labour unions have allowed themselves to be defined as utterly apolitical. The economism of unions in Canada, as in the United States, has been institutionalized so thoroughly as to render political action by unions a form of deviance. Such, for example, is manifest in the attitude of the Canadian Labour Congress with respect to the militant activities of the Canadian Union of Postal Workers. Labour unions exist, in the view of union leaders as well as that of business and government, in order to enhance the market value of their commodity, labour. Moreover, that limited objective is further restricted to the routinized behaviours associated with the collective bargaining process. The stressful features of the process, such as strikes, are directed explicitly to short-term economic benefit, or some comparable improvement in working conditions, and tend to affect the immediate employer and public consumers rather than the real employers, such as the head office of a multinational corporation or the government. Additionally, such actions are themselves routinized and orderly.

Short-run objectives are, of course, not without significance to the lives of employees. But they are inherently limited objectives that offer no prospect of a fundamental or far-reaching change in the system of economic distribution. Nor does such institutionalized unionism tolerate job actions that constitute a challenge to the character and composition of the state. In 1976, with the imposition of wage and price controls, organized labour leaders began briefly to talk of political strikes. Joe Morris of the CLC speculated publicly that traditional opposition to political strikes might have to be abandoned. (*The Globe and Mail*, February 14, 1976). Yet this union sabre-rattling was a passing thing and never developed into a course to be seriously pursued. Traditionally in Canada, except in the West before the 1930s, strikes as political weapons have been considered abhorrent. Unions as political actors are abhorrent.

In Canadian unions, anyone calling for politicization is labelled an "ultra left" radical or communist. For example, when the Canadian Labour Congress was condemned for its failure to support striking postal workers, and a motion of censure was put by CUPE members at a CLC convention, the president of the CLC, Dennis McDermott, called for a purge of the "ultra left" in the labour movement. When such statements exemplify union executives and policies, organized labour is limited to seeking economic benefits within the parameters of the dominant class system, and deterred from seeking more thoroughgoing redistribution. The working class is co-opted, and fails to ever seriously threaten the basic inequities of class society. Manipulation by corporate interests and the state is not only tolerated, but ends in collaboration. Organized labour, therefore, is not a threat to the welfare capitalist society of North America, as at times it is represented to be. Rather, it is a legitimate participant in the process of maintaining the basic nature or profile of class society. This "adversarial" fashion of North American industrial relations is as much a process of "co-determination" in the sense of co-maintenance as are European systems of so-called "industrial democracy" or corporatism.

Even in more class-conscious societies than Canada, one finds that the activities of organized labour are preoccupied with immediate advantage. The frequency of strikes, or the willingness to resort to strike or other job action, does not usually translate into political action. In the United Kindgom, for example, the militant character of labour has not been expressed as an "effective political radicalism; and it has rarely been revolutionary." (Westergaard and Reisler, 1975: 7.) Although, in contrast to Canada, the British working class is politicized, by affiliation with the Labour Party, this is itself a routinization, an activity within the rules of the game, and the rules are those of the dominant interests in society. The situation of British unions, unable to alter the character of British class society, merely points up more sharply the far more thoroughly apolitical unionism of the United States and Canada, tied to the continental economic grid. Especially as unions also become a fashionable organizational device of the Canadian middle class, the labour movement in this country ceases to press for profound change.

Barring a major economic catastrophe, or some external intervention, there is little prospect of drastic action being taken within the Canadian class structure. The ruling class is not apt to undertake the erosion of its advantages, the middle- and working-classes are entwined in a feedback system of affluent, short-term economic competition, and the destitute are restrained in a web of welfare dependency. A proletarian consciousness consisting of an organized and effective opposition to the ruling stratum is improbable under existing conditions of competitive economic gamesmanship. In his optimism, Mills offered the remark that, "Because men are not 'class conscious' at all times and in all places does not mean that 'there are no classes' or that 'in America everybody is middle class.' " (Mills, 1951: 294.) But neither is it true that because people are class conscious sometimes, and because classes are real, that class contestation of a magnitude sufficient to realize structural change is likely.

Wage and salary workers hold the potential for political action, but it is not a potential apt to crystallize without a major catalyst. Economic breakdown on the scale of the 1930s, which economists confidently assure us is impossible, would be such a crisis. Conceivably, nationalist movements in Canada could also serve politicizing class actions. However, there is certainly no assurance that it would be action to the "left," and in aid of a more egalitarian society.

Johnson has argued that Canada has experienced a decline in the size and influence of the petite bourgeoisie — that is, small businessmen and farmers. In the past, he argues, such people have been in opposition to the working class, a statement not altogether correct in light of periodic working-class-farm alliance in Saskatchewan. But in the deterioration of their positions he suggests that perhaps there has been a polarization of class interests. (Johnson, 1972.) Similarly, Clement has argued that there has been a crystallization of class interests insofar as the capitalist élite in Canada has become more exclusive and difficult of entry. (Clement, 1975.) The validity of the arguments rests on a number of assumptions, not the least of which relates to the character of labour and white-collar action. Labour organized in international unions has always been very moderate in ideology and action, and salaried workers have always been conservative. (Mills, 1951.) The middle class mediates now between the owners and the working class. Should it become radicalized

in its union relations with its employers, then the polarization of which Johnson speaks may be realized. But it seems a tenuous hope, especially in light of the increasing entry of women into the labour force, constituting a new group to be "educated" to class consciousness while contributing to two-income family affluence.

In all probability, class-related hostility will continue to be most viably expressed as a reaction to regional differences. The regions in Canada have distinct interests and identities. Particularly as peripheral regions move effectively to develop in competition with central Canada, class conflict will manifest itself in regional conflict. But such regional/class conflict is itself subsumed within legitmated federal constitutional politics. The so-called rise of the middle class in Quebec (Guindon, 1964), a feature of industrial development and urbanization in the province, led to a vigorous separatist movement launched by the middle class, with the support of organized labour, who viewed their interests in opposition to Anglophone Canada. But, in the 1980s, separatism in the western provinces, exploiting the capital generated by sales of oil and natural gas, evolved as nothing more than a move to industrialize and compete with eastern Canada in secondary production.

Political exchanges between federal and provincial governments will produce some regional redistribution. But the radical tradition of the West and its well-established NDP socialist power base and, similarly, the language-based interests of Quebec at best produce intermittent regional separatist efforts that to some extent achieve redistribution of economic resources in amelioration of class distinctions. Fundamentally, however, Ontario and the Maritimes remain relatively unaltered in social structure and benefits. As the theory of relative deprivation would suggest, those regions that are experiencing developmental changes and social instability are those wherein deprivation will be perceived as salient and prompt social action. To put it crudely, central Ontario is on top, the Atlantic on the bottom, and the West and Quebec are the middle class who are apt to incite the Canadian middle-class revolution and perhaps along the way seriously alter the basic structure of inequality in Canada. But to count on the influence of such separatist movements, and to further expect that they would necessarily make for autonomous or semi-autonomous political entities that are more egalitarian than the present Canadian federal system, is to engage in naïve speculation. At best we could predict some redistribution of wealth in the nation's regions, but among the privileged classes.

Only some issue or event that will override present, conventional, welfare-related, political opportunities is apt to challenge the existing system of stratification. Hence our reference to regional separatism, and perhaps also nationalist opposition to foreign economic control, that might serve as foci of radical action, even though these issues are themselves readily distorted or conventionalized. But in the meantime, the privileged enjoy their advantage, and the underprivileged suffer the "structural violence" inherent in Canada's system of institutionalized inequalities.

The Double Ghetto

A *ghetto* is a city area populated by a minority group. The most famous historical ghettos are those the Jews occupied and the name derives from 16th century Venice where an area was set aside for Jewish settlement and became a large, thriving community. Institutionally complete, this community took care of its own and also provided goods and services for the outside gentile community. But despite its size, vigour, and importance to the city-republic of which it was a part, the Jewish community was considered alien and captive. Each night the gates of the ghetto were shut and locked: no one — neither Jew nor gentile — could enter or leave before daybreak.

We do well to remember this original meaning of ghetto when we consider the current image of Canada as a **double ghetto**, a term coined by Pat and Hugh Armstrong (1984) in a book of the same name. Their book, which is excerpted in this Section, is not about Jews (or other ethnic groups) in cities (or other geographic locales), but about Canadian women at work. The book's title conveys the sense that women are treated like an alien and captive population in Canadian society.

But what is the gate that is locked against women? Where is this imaginary ghetto and what does it look like? We can travel to Venice and see the physical remains of the Jewish ghetto. But where would we go to see the ghetto in, say, Toronto that locks in working women, or treats them like captive aliens? The Armstrongs might suggest that we start our sight-seeing tour with a bank, insurance office, or department store. At any of these, we will find large numbers of women working in jobs that pay poorly, command little respect or authority and hold little prospect of career advancement. Indeed, sales and service occupations are the ghetto in which we will find Canadian women.

Several facts about this ghetto are particularly ominous. First, there is every sign that it is getting larger. With the development of what Daniel Bell (1973) has called the "post-industrial society", more and more work in our society is of the "sales and service" variety, which tends to employ women disproportionately. As more women are entering the labour force, more work of the kind typically done by women is becoming available.

Second, efforts to improve the status of working women — to make them less alien and captive — have seen little and slow success. Unionizing the employees of banks, offices and stores has proved very difficult, for a variety of reasons. As a result, women's employment continues to be insecure and poorly paid, with little prospect of improvement. Upgrading the status of part-time work, which women do much more commonly (and by preference) than men, has also been slow. Moreover, affordable, good quality care facilities for the children of working mothers are few and increasing only slowly.

Finally, new technology poses a problem. Not only is new technology eliminating jobs in agriculture and manufacturing, traditionally male-dominated work, it is also eliminating jobs that women have traditionally done. New computer technology for information storage significantly reduces the need for large numbers of (female) clerical workers. Word-processing capability significantly reduces the need for large numbers of (female) secretaries and stenographers. New communications technology may largely reshape sales and service occupations, eliminating many (female) workers. An example of this is the introduction of the automated banking machine that has resulted in a considerable reduction in the hiring of (female) cashiers.

That is not to say that nothing is improving. There is clear evidence, for example, that women are starting to break out of their ghettos and into traditionally male-dominated professions (on this topic, see the article by Katherine Marshall in this Section). Key here is the growing enrolment of female students in traditionally male-dominated courses of study: engineering, architecture, medicine, and law, among others. Moreover, unionization has made some progress, and even male-dominated unions are taking more interest in what have until recently been considered "women's issues": day care, maternity leave, sexual harassment, pay discrimination against women, and so on. Affirmative action and pay equity legislation are becoming more common. Such legislation seeks to increase the proportions of women in positions from which they have traditionally been excluded or under-represented; to see that women are preferred — or at least given an even chance — for promotion; and to ensure that payment is equal for "work of equal value", whether that work is typically done by men or women.

So we have reason for optimism that the female ghetto will be broken open in due course: change is slow but progressing. Currently, however, the female ghetto is located in a sector of the economy which some have called the "secondary labour market." As we have noted, this market is unprotected by unions or professional associations, pays poorly, frequently hires and lays off people, gives (and requires) little job-training, and is highly vulnerable to technological unemployment. What are the gates that lock women into this ghetto?

This question requires a lengthier answer than can be given here. Sociologists know about the factors that lock women into the ghetto: discrimination against women, disadvantage by domestic duties, inappropriate educational preparation, and cultural incapacitation. These are all discussed at greater length elsewhere (Tepperman, 1989), but a few words will be said about each here.

For whatever reason, patriarchy — the domination of men — is part of our cultural heritage (Fox, 1988). It has a very long history, and some part of the male domination that persists today is simply a vestige from an earlier, agricultural period when a sexual division of labour may have been more necessary and was, in any event, more easily imposed. If we search beyond this cultural lag, or culture holdover, explanation, we realize that discrimination against women may be economically beneficial to men today. Pay discrimination allows male employers to pay female workers less than they would have to pay male workers; and discrimination in hiring and promotion reduces by half the number of people with whom male workers have to compete.

However, this explanation is ever less compelling, for those women suffering discrimination are consumers as well as producers, wives and daughters as well as competitors. Men may want to discriminate against women as producers and competitors, but not as consumers and kin. So it may be that, as more women enter the labour market, this contradiction will itself help to contribute to the elimination of gender discrimination.

Disadvantage by domestic duties is a very serious impediment to women's economic progress. As the excerpt by Meg Luxton shows, married women who work for pay customarily work a "double day": one day's work for their employer and another day's work for their family. A great deal of evidence from across Canada and elsewhere shows that when married women go out to work for pay, their husbands do not significantly increase the time they spend on domestic duties, even if there are young children in the household. Moreover, this inequality is apparently not lessening.

There are only so many solutions to this problem. Wives can try to compel their spouses and children to cooperate more; but so far such attempts have met with little success. Wives can simply work harder and risk their mental and physical health. They can opt for part-time rather than full-time paid work, especially while their children are very young, and there is evidence that many women are doing this. They can rely increasingly on paid domestic and child-care services (day-care, fast food, house cleaners, and so on). Or they can set their aspirations and expectations very low, that is, think of their employment as a job, not a career.

Evidence suggests that in traditionally male-dominated careers, where women would have the greatest difficulty lowering their aspirations and expectations, women's domestic lives are at the greatest risk. Marshall's excerpt below shows that, compared with women in traditionally female careers or mere jobs, women in traditionally male careers are less likely to marry; if married, less likely to remain married; or, if remaining married, less likely to bear children. It is virtually impossible to have a serious career and a serious marriage if you are a woman, since you are expected to carry your full weight in both activities. Men, by contrast, are culturally forgiven their lack of domestic involvement.

Part of the problem, again, is cultural and long-standing. It has to do with the way we value time. By assigning women a double day, we are saying several things about time and about women. Mainly, we are saying that housework is worth little in comparison with other kinds of work. Women are worth little, since they earn less than men at paid work, therefore, they should do the housework. That is to say, women's time is worth less than men's time. As Margaret Eichler writes in the article excerpted here, "when we cease to define people as dependents, or when the power position of a group of people changes, the value of their time will change."

If women accept the heavy domestic responsibility currently foisted upon them, they will find it hard to compete effectively with men at work. Moreover, if employers believe that women consider their domestic responsibility to be primary, they will see females as less valuable employees, since they are less available. Continued gender inequality at home will almost certainly ensure continued gender inequality in the workplace.

These factors aside, there is evidence that many women are continuing to train for occupations with limited potential for employment, promotion or pay. This self-limitation through educational streaming occurs well before post-secondary education begins. It begins at least by the time a student enters high school and selects her courses of study. Girls are less likely than boys to select academic, university programs of study. If they aim for post-secondary education, it is more likely to be for community colleges. And if they aim for university, it is more likely to be for a university program that is traditionally female dominated — arts, nursing, social work — and therefore that leads to careers that are less well paid than do the male dominated programs.

Finally, cultural incapacitation plays a part. Women are taught by our culture that they are incapable of many kinds of activity: that they are sexual objects and delicate pets, not thinkers, decision-makers, political actors. They are made to feel dependent, which justifies their subordination. While ever fewer women are accepting their second class citizenship, many still feel guilty about straying outside their prescribed ladylike roles.

These then are the gates that lock women into the gender-based job ghetto. But why a "double ghetto"? The answer comes from the excerpt on women's consciousness by the Armstrongs. Not only do men and women lead different work lives, for reasons already discussed, they also lead different married lives. As sociologist Jessie Bernard (1973) put it, every marriage is actually two marriages, his marriage and her marriage. His marriage is full of provided support, nurturance, physical caring. Her marriage consists of providing support, nurturance and physical caring, and of seeing to the children, the shopping, the house-cleaning, and so on.

Thus, just as there is a world of work that includes a female ghetto, so there is a world of marriage that includes a female ghetto: the ghetto of wives. Wives experience marriage differently from husbands, they experience parenthood differently from husbands, and they experience paid work differently from husbands. Because their daily experience (in every important particular) is different, their consciousness — or perception of the world — is different. They live in a different world, one that is subordinate, alien and captive: they live in a ghetto.

As noted in the introduction to this book, the images of Canada presented here are not unique to Canada. We do not claim that only Canadian women live in a double ghetto. On the contrary, evidence suggests that most women in industrial nations live in such a ghetto. However, there is some variation among nations in the degree of inequality women experience as workers and wives; some variation in the degree of captivity. This is an important fact. Canada is far from the worst place in the world to be a woman, but it is also far from the best. (It is also very far from what it should be, under an equality principle.) For this reason, the double ghetto is a compelling image describing contemporary Canadian life.

31

*Women and the Double Ghetto**

Pat Armstrong and Hugh Armstrong

Women's Work in the Home and Women's Consciousness

Clinicians are more likely to suggest that healthy women differ from healthy men by being more submissive, less independent, less adventurous, more easily influenced, less aggressive, less competitive, more excitable in minor crises, having their feelings more easily hurt, being more emotional, more conceited about their appearance, less objective, and disliking mathematics and science. (Boverman *et al.*, 1970: 4)

Without either subscribing to the view attributed to clinicians of what is "healthy"[1] or denying the clinicians' bias, it can be argued that many women fit this description. The issue is why they do so. If, as argued here, work is primary, it follows that this work has a profound effect on women's view of themselves and on their personalities, and that it should be the starting point for an explanation of women's consciousness.

Work in the home is unpaid, invisible. The long hours and inflexible requirements are not regulated by a contract limiting the demands of others. Little training is required — in fact, any woman can perform the work — and selection is based, not on skill, but on personal traits. Consequently, prestige is low. The work itself is dull, repetitious, boring, fragmented, and isolated. It is a service job, a job that consists of service to others. What does it mean to women's self-concept to work continuously at jobs that must be done but quickly disappear; to know that millions of others can also perform these tasks equally well; to know that even if they become more highly skilled, there will be little relationship between their work and their financial rewards; and to know that to quit would drastically change their lives without significantly improving job alternatives elsewhere?

Housework is useful, necessary work but because it is not paid a wage, because it is not exchanged directly in the market, it is unproductive. As Mitchell (1972: 27) explains:

Their socially useful work in the home is without value in capitalist terms, for they produce nothing that they can exchange for anything of equiv-

*Excerpted from *The Double Ghetto* by Pat Armstrong and Hugh Armstrong, (1978). Used by permission of the Canadian Publishers, McClelland and Stewart, Toronto.

alent value. The housewife has thus neither her labour power nor the products of it to sell. It is given in so-called "free exchange" for capricious maintenance by a husband. That such maintenance is capricious can be tested not only by the fact that there is no "standard" of maintenance that her work commands — the wife of a poor man goes poorly fed and poorly clad — but also by the fact that on the occasion of death or desertion the State is obliged to continue adequate maintenance only if the male provider has been a State employee.

It is not just that women are not paid a wage for housework. The lack of a wage represents a different relationship to the market. Unpaid labour is, by market standards, not highly valued. But it is also not subject to the discipline of the market. There is no relationship between hours, skills, performance, and financial reward. Consequently, it is difficult to establish comparable standards, to measure success. There is no opportunity for earned recognition. Since housework skills, hours, and performance are not related to pay or promotion, they are not evaluated in objective terms. Housework is not only unpaid and therefore devalued in the market terms that "count" in our society, but criteria applied to it are based on personal responses and needs rather than universal standards. Women are judged by themselves and others not according to their job performance but according to their response to personal needs. It is not surprising that women may often appear less objective, given that the job is both unrelated to economic rewards and based on individualistic criteria.

The significance attached to wage labour is reflected in the study of employed mothers conducted by Weiss and Samuelson (1958: 364). The majority indicated that some aspect of their work in the marketplace made them feel important more often than any aspect of their work at home. Since the work available to women outside the home tends to be poorly paid and not intrinsically rewarding, these findings suggest that any work for pay is more highly valued than work in the home. However, it cannot be assumed that pay alone is responsible for the greater worth associated with labour force participation. Work outside the home is visible: work in the home is invisible. Even if women receive low wages for their work outside the home, others are aware of their labour, and the social contacts that are usually part of this work make the tasks appear more meaningful both to the women themselves and to those working with them. As one of the women we interviewed recently put it:

> I could never see me sitting at home. Initially, I was home most of my married life, the first time, in fact. And I found it just totally boring. There's only so much housework you can do. There's only so much coffeeing you can do with the neighbours. And it just wasn't challenging. Your mind just seems to shrivel up. You just don't have to think. (Armstrong and Armstrong, 1983: 209)

When wives have a wage their power within the family often increases. The higher the income of the husband, the less likely the wife is to work. And according to Gillespie's (1972: 133) American study, the higher the income of the husband, the greater his power in the household. However, Hoffman (1960) found no power difference between working and non-working American women. This evidence, which appears contradictory, may merely reflect differences in the kind of jobs and wages available to women outside the home. Crysdale (1968: 278) found that in Canada's Riverdale, "when the wife's education and work role were comparable with those of her husband, a radical revision of the traditional roles of husband and wife in household duties and in sociability followed."

An important recent Australian study summarizes much of what we know about domestic financial decisions. One of its conclusions is that "Women who earned their own incomes were likely to have more say in the spending of total family income than were women who did not earn," but it goes on to observe that "It is difficult for women to share equally with men in the control of finances inside the home or more generally in economic power outside the home, when they have no income they can call their own, and so long as the labour market disadvantages them" (Edwards, 1981: 132, 133-34). Luxton (1983: 35) is among those to note that the wife's power in the household seldom approaches that of her husband unless their wages and work are roughly equal. The segregation of the labour force makes this situation less than common.

Housewives act more dependent on men when they are more dependent on men. Eichler (1973: 47) characterizes people who rely on others for financial support as "personal dependants." Because they are dependent on the support of others, they will be "very submissive, will attempt to please and control the master indirectly by manipulating him emotionally, whenever possible" (Eichler, 1973: 49). Men have greater access to concrete resources. Women, especially those who are full-time housewives, primarily have access to personal resources such as love, affection, and approval. Furthermore, women's work in the home requires concern with personal relations and thus they are more likely to use referent power to gain their ends.

Housewives have even less access to other sources of power. Their expertise is usually limited to household tasks like cleaning, washing, and cooking. Small wonder they often want to protect these areas of expertise both by continuing to perform these tasks and by elaborating them. The power gained from being the only person who knows how to run the washing machine or sort the wash may be small but it is important if this is your only area of expertise. Women are also seldom in a position of authority except in the case of children, and this authority is transient since children grow up. In fact, the job requires them to work to eliminate this authority. Finally, housewives' access to information is limited by their isolation and confinement to the home. They frequently must rely on their children or their husbands for information on such things as how to use computers, what the popular restaurants are, and what people are wearing to them, thus further increasing their dependence.

Selection, job choice, and tenure are handled differently in the domestic unit than they are in the industrial unit. Women are selected for the job, not on the basis of their housewifery or child-care skills, but on the basis of personal attributes unrelated to job requirements. Their economic support and their selection depend, to a large extent, on their attractiveness to the opposite sex. Thus their appearance plays an important role in gaining and maintaining their jobs. Furthermore, the assumption that any woman can perform the work means that there is less merit in having any particular woman carrying out these duties. Technological developments decrease creativity, increase triviality. There is little merit in making coffee that is already guaranteed to be good to the last drop. Feelings of competence do not arise from doing what any woman can do.

It is difficult to measure the degree to which women actually choose to marry. De

Beauvoir (1952: 405) argues that "she is led to prefer marriage to a career because of the economic advantages held by men." That the mothers of Grade 12 girls in Ontario are much less likely than their daughters to consider a mutually rewarding relationship with a man and having and rearing children very important suggests that experience creates awareness of the limits marriage and families place on women. That these mothers are also more likely to consider a career, a long-term job that would allow them to develop their skills and that would be personally rewarding, as very important further reinforces this suggestion (Porter, Porter, and Blishen, 1973: 116).

But even for those women who are fully aware of the job requirements when they marry, there is limited choice in terms of quitting if they do not like the work. Much more than a particular job is tied up in this decision. Given the nature of the job, women stay with it even if they know that they are not very good at it. And given that they are deserting their children if they leave, that the job opportunities available to them are poorly paid, and that their remarriage rates are low, the alternatives for women are severely restricted. They learn to live with their feelings of inadequacy. As a result, women are led toward "flexibility rather than single-mindedness, toward responsiveness rather than decisiveness, and toward the acceptance of the selves they live with as a bit inadequate" (Janeway, 1971: 87).

The specialization that is part of the industrial sector also leads directly to their feelings of inadequacy. Housewives remain generalists in a specialized society, and thus their work is less valuable. As is evident in *Crestwood Heights* (Seeley *et al.*, 1956), it is the specialist, not mother, who knows best. Women have the major responsibility for child-rearing but are not trained to carry out the task. Lopata's (1971: 374-75) American research indicates that women, especially those with higher education, lack confidence in their ability to perform at desired levels; the standards set by the professionals are so high. In her comparative study of married professional women and housewives, Birnbaum (in Bernard, 1975: 119) found that housewives experience some distress, have low self-esteem, and perceive themselves to be neither attractive nor especially competent. Professional women meanwhile tend to be unconventional, competitive, not self-sacrificing, to have high self-esteem, to feel attractive and personally competent. This suggests that the work itself contributes to self-conceptions regarding competency and confidence.

The value attached to work in the home does not alone account for the feelings of inadequacy and frustration. Komarovsky (1967: 49) argues that the middle-class housewives in her American study were disillusioned and depressed by the lack of recognition for their skills as housekeepers. The working-class wives, on the other hand, accepted housewifery without necessarily being satisfied homemakers.

> But their discontent is not caused by the low evaluation they place upon domesticity, stemming rather from other frustrations of housewifery. The esteem they attach to their role does not, then, ensure contentment in it. (Komarovsky, 1967: 49)

A more personal statement of similar sentiments comes from a Canadian working-class woman quoted by Luxton (1980: 12):

> It's looking after your family and what could be more important? You don't have anyone standing over you so you get to do what you want, sort of. But you don't get paid, so you're depen-

dent on your husband, and you have to be there all the time, and there's always something needs doing. I feel so confused because it could be so good and it never is.

The division between the domestic and industrial units has left women doing the more menial, repetitive, and boring tasks. So can the division of domestic labour in those cases in which husbands take over some of the more pleasant activities such as playing with the children. Their wives, like those in Luxton's (1983: 37) follow-up study of Flin Flon, are left to discipline and pick up after the children, to cook for the family, and to clean up the kitchen. Coolidge explains how such work affects the consciousness of the people performing it:

> There were thus both negative and positive reasons for woman to become small-minded. On the one hand, the sole occupation of her life consisted of exacting, repetitive, and ephemeral things; on the other, until there was an imperative call to other vocations outside, she could not develop the larger mind and become convinced of the futility of the conventional methods of housekeeping. The more conscientious the housewife was, the more petty she surely became, devoting herself to the elaboration of food, clothes, decoration, and needlework in the effort to be the perfectly correct feminine creature.... The cumulative effect of domesticity has been to produce scrappy-mindedness in women. (Quoted in Bernard, 1971: 76)

The work both requires and creates women who can deal with a multitude of small and menial tasks. Concentration and continuous devotion to one task are usually impossible, especially if children are present. The result is often mindless exhaustion. Many young wives say that this mental grey-out bothers them most in caring for home and children. " 'After a while your mind becomes

a blank,' they say 'you can't concentrate on anything. It's like sleepwalking' " (quoted in Friedan, 1968: 220).

Observed one of the housewives in Luxton's (1980: 196) study. "The worst thing about this job is the working conditions. I always feel so fractured because I always have to do several things at once. I feel so frazzled."

The American women in Lopata's (1971: 39) study considered patience to be the most important virtue of the ideal housewife. For the housewives of Crestwood Heights (Seeley *et al.*, 1956), patience and loving care for others were requirements of the job. In Kome's (1982: 26) study, 36 per cent of the women surveyed said that a "happy husband" was a "homemaker's greatest pleasure." Being housewives requires women to be more submissive and more patient, while preventing them from consistently developing their skills and abilities.

The work of men is often similarly restricting and mind-destroying, but at least they have regular hours when they do not have to work. They know relief is coming. In addition, they have greater choice if they want to leave the job. Although housewives, at least theoretically, are their own bosses during the day, this does not mean they are free to follow their own wishes. Women are free from constant supervision, but they are not free from the constant demands of children or their husband's requirements. In their study of a working-class Canadian community, Lorimer and Phillips (1971: 36) found that women were expected to do the housework and raise the children and that, while husbands varied somewhat in their standards, failure to carry out either of these responsibilities was considered very serious. Women can often decide whether to make the beds or do the dishes first, although even here children's naps and water supplies may set limits, but the very multitude of tasks performed by housewives requires an organized schedule that compels obedience. And the nature of the necessary tasks allows little time for creativity.

The extent to which children add to the burden of housewives is indicated by the fact that women are most satisfied with their marriages during the pre- and post-child-rearing stages (Feldman, 1965: 116-117). One Canadian woman describes the effects of staying at home to raise the children:

> Lack of self-worth goes along with this situation. All you have to offer at the end of the day are the dishes you washed, the pants you changed, and the flowers you saw on your walk. Meanwhile the father is growing more involved daily in his activities as the mother remains static and confined. (Nunes and White, 1972: 126)

For those who are successful in child-rearing, the job itself disappears. As Mitchell (1971: 109) explains, when children leave home women lose control over the major products of their labour, and the "mother's alienation can be much worse than that of a worker whose product is appropriated by the boss." Seeley *et al.* (1956: 181) explain that the women in Crestwood Heights are expected to give up their personal needs in order to provide for those of their children at the same time their efforts are directed toward eliminating this job, a separation that costs them dearly in terms of their feelings. The research repeatedly points to the distress women experience when they lose the job. Nowhere have the contradictions inherent in child-rearing been better expressed than by a Flin Flon woman.

> It's the perfect Catch 22. You get married cause you're having kids. And you set up house to care for your kids. But once you got kids, you got no time for your marriage and you can't keep a nice house. And you have those kids, God knows why, and there is no knowing how to raise them right. And you work and work and they grow up awful and lippy and you're embarrassed as hell that anyone might think they were your kids. And you fight with them and can't wait till they're gone and then you miss them like hell. My kids are the most important thing in my life. (Luxton, 1980: 92)

Isolation exacerbates many of the problems inherent in the housewife's work. The private home separates the housewife both from other women doing similar work and, more generally, from a range of adult contacts.

> Children and home may be an emotionally satisfying milieu but they are hardly mentally stimulating. Most of all, housewives suffer from social isolation — an isolation which a woman accustomed to contacts through her work feels even more acutely than one who has been born and bred a housewife. Their work does not naturally lead to social contacts as do other occupations or as it did in the old days when households were larger and work was done at the home which lent itself to communal activities. Their work does not provide them with the mental stimulus and emotional satisfaction which results from working in a team. (Myrdal and Klein, 1956: 146)

Little occupational solidarity or organization is possible. In addition, the isolation contributes to the invisibility of the work. A floor washed in the morning may be dirty again before any adult can admire it, and yet, dinners still have to be made and eaten, diapers changed and washed. The work itself has built-in controls that encourage resignation and submission, especially when social support mechanisms often found in other jobs may be missing. The isolation may also encourage the development of psychological stress symptoms. Both retired men and full-time housewives show high symptom rates for fainting, hand-trembling, inertia, nervous breakdowns, heart palpitations, and dizziness. Restriction to the home and social isolation may be critical factors in these symptoms (Oakley, 1974: 232).

The separation of the domestic unit from the industrial unit has also been accompanied by the division of "instrumental" from "expressive" functions. The home is a place for love and care, for women's work. The industrial sector is a place for rational behaviour, for men's work. Men are more likely to be loving and caring if their work encourages these characteristics. Women perform more rationally when the work allows for and demands rational behaviour.

Although the labours of love may often appear superior to those performed merely for a wage, the labours of love may in our society be debilitating. Care and love often mean submission to others, submission that is not often reciprocated. For women in the home, labours of love usually mean work without pay, work done for others and in response to others. Such work encourages the development of people who are passive, submissive, dependent, expressive, and concerned about their appearance.

Women's Work in the Labour Force and Women's Consciousness

The segregation of women into the domestic unit performing their isolated household chores ensures that their consciousness differs from that of men. To the extent that women are also segregated into particular female jobs in the labour force, they will tend to develop a consciousness that is different from that of men. This section examines the nature of women's paid jobs in relation to their ideas about themselves and others.[2]

Work in the industrial unit is an important source of feelings of usefulness and worth for many women (Weiss and Samuelson, 1958). Labour force participation has certain advantages over work in the home: it does take place outside the home; it usually involves some contact with other adults; it stops and starts; it may provide some objective evaluation standards based on performance; and it usually has a paycheque. These differences should not, however, be exaggerated.

The similarities between women's work in the domestic unit and in the industrial unit have already been outlined. In both units, women perform jobs that require little recognized skill and are dull, repetitious, demanding, supportive, and integrative. In both units, there is little training or opportunity for promotion. As a laundry worker explained, "I don't think there's such a thing there as promotion. If I'm taken off my job, I'm put out to do somebody else's. I mean I don't get no higher pay and I still have to work 40 hours a week" (Armstrong and Armstrong, 1983: 14). In the labour force, too, status may depend more on the men that women work for than on their own job performance (Status of Women, 1970: 190). Selection is frequently based on attractiveness rather than skill. In short, work outside the home does not usually provide a significant alternative in terms of the conditions and nature of the work for women. It thus has similar effects upon women's consciousness.

Women's work in the domestic unit places restraints on their labour force participation, restraints that contribute to the segregated nature of their participation and in turn to their consciousness. The demands of the work at home help create the vicious circle described earlier. The better pay and job opportunities available to men are justified on the basis of women's sporadic labour force participation, and the exhaustion resulting from carrying out two jobs often prevents women from performing their paid work at optimum levels. Their work for pay is supplementary, because of both their dual responsibilities and their lower pay. And their lower pay is then justified on the basis of sexual differences.

Since men have advantages in seeking employment, it makes more sense for their families to reside near their places of work, thus further reducing employment opportunities for women. Not only do some women quit low-paying jobs to follow their husbands to new jobs in new cities, they also take and avoid particular jobs to accommodate their husbands' wishes. One stenographer we interviewed was employed by a temporary-help agency, despite the strain of forever having to go to new work sites, so that she could be free when her husband had holidays. Another woman refused her employer's offer of further training when her husband complained, "Who'll make my supper?" (Armstrong and Armstrong, 1983: 75). In subordinating their labour force participation to the wishes and requirements of their husbands, not to mention the demands of their children, these women place in jeopardy their feelings of self-confidence, self-reliance, and independence. Women's work in both the domestic and the industrial units is downgraded further by the expectation that women, but not men, can do both. If a woman can perform both jobs at the same time, it is often held that neither can be very onerous or difficult.

While women's participation in the labour force is on occasion sporadic and supplementary, this is not necessarily a matter of choice. The economic needs of the family encourage many women to work at the same time as family responsibilities inhibit their full and constant participation in the labour force. In her *Pages of a Shop Diary*, Domanski (1971: 93) reports that the American women working in the factory returned to their jobs because they found it impossible to live on their husbands' salaries, but that they had initially defined this work as temporary. They soon came to realize, as one worker put it, "Who'm I kidding — I'll probably be here until I collect my pension." Marriage, Domanski reports, often appears as an escape from the drudgery of factory work, and thus may prevent women from organizing to improve their condition. Once women are married, the demands of two jobs may leave them little time to participate actively in organizing or union activities. This may explain why Gagnon found that 78 per cent of the women holding executive positions in a large Quebec union were unmarried (cited in White, 1980: 67). Work in the factory may stop at a fixed time, but this simply frees women to begin their never-ending domestic chores. Work that responds to the needs and demands of others, that is exhausting and unrewarding, cannot encourage the development of people who are creative, aggressive, adventurous, or competitive.

Agassi (1972: 235), in her study of American women working in factories, describes the work as "demanding, high-speed, mind-dulling, and nerve-racking." But, as we found in conducting the research for *A Working Majority*, it is not only factory work that affects the minds of women. In many ways, our conclusions are similar to those drawn from research reports on male workers.

Kohn's study of class and values is particularly useful in this regard. His findings indicate that

> Closely supervised men tend to emphasize extrinsic benefits that jobs provide rather than opportunities for intrinsic accomplishment, to have standards of morality keyed to the letter rather than the spirit of the law, to be distrustful, to be resistant to innovation and change, to lack self-confidence, and to be anxious. (Kohn, 1969: 166)

Kohn (1969: 82-84) also reports that the higher men's social status, as measured by occupation and education, "the more self-confidence and the less depreciation they express; the greater their sense of being in control of the forces that affect their lives; the less beset by anxiety they are; and the more independent they consider their ideas to be."

In talking with working-class women in Canada, we were depressed by the tight control exercised over them in the labour force, by the contradictions evident in their responses as they live myths that help get them through the day, and by the number of women who blame themselves for their ill health, low pay, and poor working conditions.

At the same time, we were impressed by the commitment and pride they bring to de-valued, low-paid work, by their organizational skills in juggling two jobs, by their awareness of the consequences of the new, micro-electronic technology, and by the resistance that sometimes bubbles up despite their sympathy for their employers, the burden of two jobs, and the realistic assessment of the large reserve of unemployed women waiting and willing to take their paid jobs (Armstrong and Armstrong, 1983).

Slotted into jobs at or near the bottom of the labour force ladder, where workers are, and are seen to be, easily replaceable, it would be surprising if women were any more rebellious, rebellion of any sort being dangerous to the worker. Moreover, the least productive jobs are the ones that are most open to elimination by technology and/or the least responsive to demands for higher pay. Finally, since women are paid less than men, it is not surprising that they see themselves and their work as inferior or subordinate to men and their work. The tendency to measure worth by level of pay, which is pervasive in our society, applies with special force to women, given the wide sex gap in pay.

Women's work in the labour force does not promote the development of aggressive, independent, competitive, self-directing people.

Notes

1. The most "feminine" women are the domestic servants, according to Terman and Miles (1936), whose definition of what is "feminine" corresponds closely to that attributed to clinicians.

2. For a much fuller discussion of this question, see Armstrong and Armstrong (1983: especially 125-214).

32

*Taking on the Double Day**

Meg Luxton

Canadian women's work is ghettoized in the home as domestic labour and in "women's jobs" in the paid labour force. Most married women end up in both ghettos — holding down two jobs and working a double day. At home, they work long hours at very difficult, highly responsible work that receives very little social recognition and is, of course, unpaid. Within the paid labour force, they face a series of discriminatory practices, the most important of which is the low wages most women receive (Connelly, 1978; Armstrong and Armstrong, 1978).

As a result, women working the double day carry an extraordinarily heavy load and the price they pay is enormous. They work long hours and have virtually no leisure time for themselves. They are subject to high levels of stress and they get paid about half of what men receive. Given this situation, why are women with children entering the paid labour force in ever increasing numbers?

Why do women take on this double day?

It is generally argued in the literature that married women take on paid work for two reasons. The primary one is economic: women do paid work because they need the money. The secondary reason is closely related to the first. Like other workers, married women derive independence, satisfaction, sociability, and a sense of pride from their paid jobs. More recently, investigators have begun to analyze the structural imperatives that underly the work patterns of Canadian women.

In *Last Hired, First Fired* Pat Connelly addresses these questions by arguing that women in the home constitute a reserve army of labour and, as part of that analysis, she considers "the pressures that push housewives into the paid labour force" (1978: 63). Connelly demonstrates the existence of underlying structural imperatives which constrain and mould women's decisions of whether or not to take on paid labour. For Connelly, "women's participation in wage labour is not a matter of immediate situational factors but rather of prestructured alternatives which direct the decisions that women are compelled to make." (1978: 76).

*Abridged from Meg Luxton, "Taking on the Double Day: Housewives as a Reserve Army of Labour," *Atlantis* 7, 1 (1981), pp. 12-22. Reprinted with permission of the publisher and the author.

Most studies of women's work in Canada have concentrated, as Connelly does, on the general category "women": "This view distinguishes women as members of a special group" (1978: 6). While such general studies are vitally important, it is also necessary that we begin to refine our analyses by distinguishing patterns specific to particular categories of women. We need to know how the large-scale "macro" social processes are translated into individual behaviour.

So, while we have studies which show that the percentage of married women in the paid labour force is steadily increasing, we do not yet know whether this means essentially the same thing for all married women or whether some women have significantly different experiences from women in other circumstances. For example, are there important differences between married women with young children and those with no dependent children, or between married women whose husbands do not contribute to their wives' and childrens' support and those whose husbands do?

Of particular interest are those women who have young children and whose husbands have steady incomes which they contribute to supporting their wives and children. Domestic labour for these women is at its most intense and demanding. This, plus the appalling lack of adequate child care, coupled with all the social pressures which assert that women should stay home with their preschool children, exerts enormous pressure on women to do domestic labour full-time and to remain out of the paid labour force. When they have husbands with regular incomes, the potential for them to be financially dependent is maximized. Therefore, it is particularly significant when these women take on paid labour. In addition, we need to know whether working-class women have significantly different experiences from middle-class women. How does women's class position both structure the alternatives available to them and affect the way they respond to the structural imperatives which impel their lives?

The Study

This study is based on a comparison of two groups of 20 married women. At the time of the study, all 40 women had been married for at least five years and had at least one preschool child at home. The first group of 20 were working class; that is, they were members of family-based households which depended, for the major portion of their income, on hourly wages earned by the men. The second group of 20 were (loosely defined) middle class; that is, they lived in family-based households which received the major portion of their income from the salaries earned by husbands in professional occupations or in business. All of these women had, for at least one year in the five years prior to the study, worked as full-time domestic labourers and had been financially dependent on their husbands. All of them had full-time paid jobs outside the home and in addition, retained primary responsibility for the domestic labour in their households.

It is important to stress at the outset the unique features of this case study.[1] Flin Flon, where the study was conducted, is a small, single industry, northern, working-class community. While there is a middle-class component to the town's population, it is relatively small, elite and in circumstances quite unlike those in which the majority of middle-class Canadians live. Therefore, as I have argued elsewhere, while the working-class households in Flin Flon are typical and rep-

resentative of working-class households elsewhere in Canada, the middle class is unique
and therefore cannot be considered typical
(Luxton, 1980).

Increasing Household Income

All of the women interviewed were married
to husbands who were earning a regular
wage or salary, which had been, at some
point in the five preceding years, sufficient
to support a non-earning wife. Nevertheless,
all the women maintained that their main
reason for taking on paid work was because
"we need the money." This raises a very difficult question of how "need" is determined.
In some cases need was apparently obvious.
The household was in debt, and the husband's earnings alone would not be sufficient to sustain the household and pay off
the debt. However, while the debts were indeed real, they had often been incurred for
different reasons.

Middle-class households obviously had
more disposable income than working-class
households and thus had access to a wider
range of social and material comforts. All of
the households, however, had an established
standard of living which was, by the mid
1970s, being visibly eroded by inflation. The
majority of these women, regardless of class,
took on paid jobs to acquire the income necessary to sustain their households' standards.

Their class position affected the types of
jobs these women got and how they experienced their paid work. Employment for
women in Flin Flon is severely limited, as it
is in most primary industry communities.
There were many more women wanting
paid work than there were jobs available.
What jobs there were, were mainly traditional
"working-class female jobs" — sales and clerical work. While most of the working-class
women resented the job ghettos and wished
they could break out of them, for the most
part they assumed that this was the only type
of work they could expect to get anywhere.
Eight of the middle-class women had jobs
that were slightly better paying, or were
higher status than most — teachers, administrative assistants, social workers. They
expressed relative satisfaction with their
work. In contrast, the rest of the middle-class
women were unable to find such jobs. They
ended up in low-paid, low-status jobs, ex-
pressing frustration and anger at their situation. They resented being unable to use their
education and training. They felt they had
been forced to take jobs "beneath my position." One middle-class woman pointed out
very forcefully that the "crummy job" she
had proved how desperately her household
needed the "pittance" she earned: "No one
would do this job for this pay unless she was
absolutely strapped." These differences are
illustrated more clearly when we consider
what impels women into the paid labour
force when their households are not in a
state of immediate economic crisis.

The majority of the middle-class women,
regardless of what type of job they had, maintained that, if they did not need the money,
they would prefer to stay at home. Fourteen
out of the 20 women interviewed, including
six who had "good" jobs, said that they were
working for money because they had to.
They argued that they had entered the paid
labour force when their households were in
an economic crisis and they insisted that they
intended to leave as soon as possible. Six
middle-class women, including four with
"crummy" jobs, said they were working outside the home because they preferred their
paid jobs to domestic labour and they maintained that they would keep their paid jobs

regardless of the economic situation of their households.

For the majority of working-class women, the exact opposite was the case. Thirteen of these women maintained that they had taken on paid work at a point when their households were not in crisis. They maintained that when their husbands had regular employment, the household was not seriously in debt and things were running smoothly, that was the time when it was easiest for them to take on paid work. These women made their decision to enter the paid labour force based on two assumptions. The first was that if their households were running smoothly, it was possible for them to take on the added stress of the double day. The second assumption was that while things might be good at the moment, disaster was to be expected in the future and so they took on paid work to build up a nest egg of security for the hard times they anticipated ahead.

One women described her understanding of this situation:

I'd take on a job either if we really needed the money real bad or if things is [sic] going good at home, then I'd get a job so we could save up a little extra. When my husband's having a rough time at work, then I like to be at home so I can take care of him. . . .

The different motivations that women have in taking on paid work may be related to the fact that proportionately, the amount that working-class women contributed to their household incomes was considerably greater than the amount contributed by middle-class women. Again it is important to reiterate here the point that the middle-class women of this study may not be typical. It would be useful to examine household incomes for women who hold professional jobs to see whether such income discrepancies

occur for their households as well. The average earnings of the working-class husbands was $11 375.00 and of the wives $5275.00. By taking on paid work, these women increased their household incomes by 32 per cent. In contrast, middle-class husbands earned an average of $29 568.00 while their wives earned an average $7456.00. Thus, while the middle-class women earned on an average 29 per cent more than the working-class women, their contribution increased their household incomes by only 20 per cent.

All of the working-class women felt that their earnings were an essential part of the household income and most of them expected that they would probably have paid jobs for most of their lives. Even those who anticipated leaving the paid labour force at various periods knew that such absences were only temporary and that what they were earning at the time was necessary.

It may be that there is a correlation between the type of increasing expenses a household is forced to offset and the women's decision to take on paid work.[2] In other words, when household expenses increase in those areas where it is possible for housewives to intensify their own labour, women may choose to work harder at home, rather than take on the double day. So, for example, when food and clothing costs increase, women may offset those expenses by shopping more carefully, making more from scratch and mending more often. However, when household expenses increase in areas where women cannot intensify their labour, they often have no choice but to earn money so that the household has the necessary finances to meet the increased costs. For example, when the cost of home heating increased dramatically in the mid 1970s, most women had no way of intensifying their domestic labour to meet increased oil costs. In one exceptional case, the family installed a wood-burning stove and the housewife added chopping wood and stoking the fire to her domestic labour. This is not an option readily available to most households who must instead find more money to pay the oil bills.

If the cost of work-related expenses is subtracted from the amount of money women earn, the result gives some indication of the real contribution women's earnings make to the household income. On an average, the earnings of working-class women increase their total household income by 34 per cent. In contrast, because their husbands' incomes are so much higher, the earnings of middle-class women, on an average, increase their household's income by just 16 per cent. The implication of these figures is that, proportionately, working-class women are able to make a larger economic contribution to the subsistence of their households. It may be that there is a correlation between the relative importance of a woman's economic contribution and the respect and value that she and her husband attribute to her paid work.

Reduced Domestic Labour

When a woman takes on paid work, she usually does not relinquish her domestic labour. However, the amount of time and energy she has available for domestic labour is sharply reduced. Various time budget studies have suggested that married women working at two jobs in fact do less domestic labour than full-time housewives. However, when their paid work time and their domestic labour time are added together, the woman doing both jobs puts in about 12 hours more than full-time housewives each week.[3]

In comparing the way time was allocated by the two groups of women, a number of interesting observations emerged. On an average, the working-class women worked about 2.4 hours more than full-time housewives on a typical work day and about the same amount of time on weekends. In other words, this group corresponds to the findings of comparative time budget studies by working about 12 hours more than full-time housewives each week. In contrast, the middle-class women worked about 3.7 hours more than full-time, middle-class housewives on a typical work day and they worked 2.2 hours more on weekends. Thus these women were putting in about 22.9 hours per week more than full-time housewives or 10.9 hours more than working-class women! . . .

All the middle-class women felt very strongly that they had to continue improving the quality of their houses through activities which required their own labour. Where working-class women recognized that they could not keep up their former standards, middle-class women felt compelled to do so.

The second factor which contributes to the increased labour time of middle-class women is the extent to which husbands contribute to domestic labour. Cross class time budget studies have shown that husbands rarely increase the amount of time they spend doing domestic labour when their wives take on paid work. In this case, the working-class men did not increase the amount of time they spent on domestic labour on work days but on weekends they did half an hour more, spread over two days. In contrast, with one notable exception, the middle-class men actually reduced the amount of time they spent on domestic labour when their wives took on paid work![4]

One of the requirements of professional and commercial work is that a considerable amount of entertaining and social life must go on within the family household. Wives of professional and business men subsidize their husbands' jobs by maintaining an appropriately furnished home, by producing acceptable social events such as dinner parties and by accompanying the husband to social occasions organized by others. This conspicuous consumption and display behaviour is an essential part of maintaining social status. Regardless of what the wives may be doing elsewhere, they are expected to continue playing hostess for their husbands.

In contrast, the majority of working-class households, regardless of whether or not the woman was employed outside the home, did very little entertaining at home. Most of their social activities occurred outside the home, and the fact that the women were earning money meant that it was possible for them to increase the amount of socializing they did. Several of these women noted that by taking on paid work they were able to spend more money on organized leisure activities and therefore were able to do more: "Before I had a job I couldn't afford to get a sitter and go drinking. Now I can get out at least once a week."

Conclusions

The case study that I have presented here is very small and the class-based comparisons I have drawn may not be typical for Canada as a whole. What the study does show is that while many women experience a similar process, the content of their experience may well be very different depending on their class background and current class position.

Notes

1. The research on which this paper is based was carried out in Flin Flon, Manitoba. An extended analysis of the working class material is presented in Meg Luxton *More Than a Labour of Love*. I have just begun to analyse the middle-class data and this is the first time I have presented it.

2. I would like to thank Pat Armstrong for suggesting this line of research.

3. See Luxton, 1980, chapter 6 for a discussion of time budget studies.

4. The exception to this pattern occurred in one household where the couple were profoundly influenced by feminism. In this case, the husband did almost half of the domestic labour and the woman estimated that she did about six hours a week more than the working-class women but about 4.9 hours less than other middle-class women. In this household, both the wife and husband believed that when the woman worked outside the home, the domestic labour should be shared by both of them. The husband argued that such a system was only "fair."

33

*Gender and the Value of Time**

Margrit Eichler

This paper starts from the basic premise that there is an intimate connection between power and the value of a person's time. Specifically, it develops Schwartz's proposition (1974: 843) that: "Waiting is patterned by the distribution of power in a social system." Schwartz concludes that power is "the ultimate determinant of delay, the main assertion being that the distribution of waiting time coincides with the distribution of power. This proposition turns on the assumption that power is related to the scarcity of goods and skills that an individual server possesses." (Schwartz, 1974: 867).

Schwartz identifies the relationship between servers and clients in respect to waiting as an instance of an "organized dependency relationship". He argues that "Delay is therefore longest when the client is more dependent on the relationship than the server; it is minimized, however, when the

server is the overcommitted member of an asymmetrical relationship." (Schwartz, 1974: 867-8). This insight can be put into a propositional format, as follows:

Proposition 1:

Within a relationship, the more powerful a person, the more control this person has over his or her own time as well as that of others. This results in minimal waiting time on the part of the powerful person, and maximal waiting on the part of the least powerful person.

In this approach, time itself is seen as the resource that is being wasted or gained. This analysis can be extended in at least two ways: it can be extended to the prime measure of value in our society, namely money, and it can be applied to specific groups with differential access to power, such as the sexes. Considering the first issue first, we find that although a monetary parallel is drawn by Schwartz, the connection between the value of the time of a person, his or her position in the social structure, and the value of time in monetary terms is not made. Schwartz suggests that "Time, like money, is valuable because it is necessary for the achievement of productive purposes; ends cannot be

---

*Abbreviated version of a paper presented at the International Conference "Time as a Human Resource," University of Saskatchewan, Saskatoon, 1985. The author would like to thank Linda Williams who served as a research assistant for this paper.

reached unless an appropriate amount of it is 'spent' or 'invested' on their behalf.'' (1974: 868)

Others have made the relationship explicit, but in cursory form. Balla (1978: 28) argues that economic success depends largely on the optimization of economic processes, that is, it is premised on economizing with scarce goods within a social system that is characterized by scarcity of time. And Zerubavel (1979: 88) suggests that the capitalist orientation to time ''as a scarce resource (implying both linearity and convertibility into monetary terms) is among the basic cultural constituents of modern social organization of time.''

The intimate connection between the value of time and money is perhaps best expressed in the popular saying that ''time is money''. If Schwartz is right in postulating that the value of time is socially patterned, and that the value differs systematically with one's power position, then we should also find that the value of time measured in money is socially patterned, and that its value as measured in money differs systematically according to one's power position. The person with the most power is thus able to command most money for his or her time, and the person with least power is able to command least money. In the following, we shall therefore address the questions under what circumstances time is money, whose time is money, and how much money time is worth.

Under What Circumstances is Time Money?

Implicit in this question is its antithesis: under what circumstances is time not money? If time were money under all circumstances, we would all be rich, and the longer we lived,

the richer we would be. In a sense that is true, if we consider life — that is, our personal time — as of value in itself. But our present concern is not with the intrinsic value of time, but with its socially constructed value, which can be expressed in terms of money, namely, as an economic value. All other values are disregarded here. Looking at the issue in this way, we note that elderly people in Canada are disproportionately poor, especially if they are female. The value of time is therefore certainly not determined by the sheer quantity available to a person, as measured through his or her lifespan.

Nor is all time money. When we sleep, barring a few exceptions, time is not worth money. When we are ''killing time'', it is not worth money. When we spend time with family or friends, generally our time is not worth any money (although the way we spend it may cost us money). Our time is worth money when we work for pay.

It seems, then, that time is money only when an economic transaction is involved. Therefore time spent with a prostitute is worth money, while time spent in sexual activity with one's lover is not worth money. The activity may be the same, but one is an economic transaction, the other is not. Similarly, talking with one's friend about personal problems is not worth money, while talking with one's psychiatrist about these same problems in worth money. Eating dinner with one's family is not worth money, while taking a client to dinner and maybe eating exactly the same dish is worth money. It is not the activity itself but the social context that determines whether time spent is worth money.

We have therefore answered our first question: time is worth money within the context of economic relationships. Economic relationships are relationships that produce a product which can be sold or bought for money. The potential money value is not inherent in the product or directly related to the time needed to produce it, but depends on the value attributed to it. A giant jigsaw puzzle may take a long time to complete, but generally the time spent on this activity is not worth any money, since the product of the time invested is not saleable. Similarly, trees have an inherent value but it is non-economic, and the time needed for them to grow makes no difference in terms of money, unless they can be sold for money. For Christmas tree farm operators, by contrast, the time required by trees to grow does indeed become economically valuable. If it can be reduced, profits can be increased (assuming that there is a market for increased production, of course). The statement that economic relationships are relationships that produce a product which can be sold or bought for money is therefore not tautological but indicates the essential arbitrariness of whether time spent producing something is worth money or not.

Whose Time is Money?

If we go back to the examples of transactions mentioned above and consider the participants — the prostitute and the client, the psychiatrist and the patient, the client and the host — it becomes apparent that it is only the time of one of the parties involved that is worth money. The client pays the psychiatrist for his or her time — but the psychiatrist does not pay the client for her or his time, the expense of which was probably greater than for the psychiatrist, since it was probably the client who needed to add travel time and possibly waiting time to the total

time expense, and not the psychiatrist. This is true for other client-practitioner relationships in the broadest sense possible. For instance, if we consider the student-professor relationship, students not only engage in activities similar to those of the professor — reading materials, observing and reflecting on natural, cultural and social phenomena — but they may even produce similar outputs, such as papers (which may or may not be published). In the first case it is seen as part of the professorial role for which the university pays money. In the second case, while it is also seen as part of the student role, there is the important difference that the student pays for this privilege. This becomes confused when a student has a scholarship: he or she is in effect paid for doing the same work for which another student must pay.

In general, it is the expert or server whose time is considered to be worth money, while that of the client is worth nothing. Moreover, the client has to pay, directly, as in the case of paying an electrician who does your wiring, or indirectly, through taxes, the garbage collector, professor, psychiatrist[1] or police officer.

Sometimes, it is difficult to determine just who is receiving a service if we look at the transaction from the outside without further knowledge about the context. In the case of the client dinner, client and host are eating the same meal. In the case of the student and the professor, both of them discuss the same topic, and they may even publish a paper together. It is only upon knowing the roles that people play that we will be able to predict who will be paid for the activity engaged in and who will pay.

Nor can we say that it is always the service that is being paid for. In some situations, it is indeed the product (output) that is being paid for, as is the case when employers pay for piecework, such as in the garment industry. In other cases, however, it is the time spent (input) which is paid for, as is generally the case with professionals and salaried employees such as doctors, lawyers, teachers, nurses, clerks, receptionists, and bank tellers. In cases in which time spent (input) is paid for, rather than the product, the service or product may or may not be received.

With respect to the question, "whose time is money?" we also find an essential arbitrariness: it is the time of someone presumed to provide a service because of his or her role within the context of an economic relationship that is worth money, rather than an activity or product itself. In other words, it is the social context that determines whose time has monetary value, rather than the fact that the value is an inherent characteristic of a person or activity.

How Much Money is Time Worth?

We have seen that it is the role a person plays within the context of an economic relationship, and the way this relationship is organized, that determines whether a person's time is worth money. There is therefore an essential element of arbitrariness in the way value is assigned to time. We find the same phenomenon with respect to the amount of money which is assigned to time. It is by no means the case that the same amount of time is considered to be worth the same amount of money. In fact, one of the premises of our society is that the time spent in the performance of some roles is more valuable than that spent on others. This is exemplified most dramatically in the fact that we have differential salary scales for different types of work.

For instance, in 1980, according to the Economic Council of Canada (1983: 88-89), men in the five highest paid occupations had the following average annual earnings:

Directors General	$59 131
Physicians and surgeons	57 273
Dentists	54 312
Judges and magistrates	50 791
Lawyers and notaries	38 380

By comparison, men in the five lowest paid occupations in that same year had the following average annual earnings:

Babysitters	$ 4 311
Waiters, hosts and stewards	6 677
Guides, hosts, stewards *et al.*	8 346
Other farm, horticulture, and animal husbandry	7 399
Inspecting and sampling, fabrication of textile products	12 311

These figures are based on combining a large set of categories of occupations into a smaller set. Had the analysis focused on the five highest and lowest paid occupations in the larger set, the earnings differential would certainly have been considerably higher, since some chairmen of boards and directors general command salaries in the hundreds of thousands of dollars.

We have therefore seen that time *per se* has no objective money value, but that it has a monetary value only within an economic relationship for a person presumed to perform a service for another person, and that the amount will vary systematically according to the role performed. If Schwartz's thesis on the relationship between the value of time and power is also applicable to the monetary value of time, then the more powerful the incumbent of a role, the more money the time should be worth. We are therefore now ready to formulate a second general proposition:

Proposition 2:

The more powerful the incumbent of a role, the more money his or her time will be worth within the context of economic relationships; the less powerful the incumbent of a role, the less money his or her time will be worth.

So far, we have only considered situations in which the time of one party to a client relationship (which includes, of course, the employer-employee relationship) is worth money, in which, in other words, there is an exchange of time against money. In such situations, one person renders a service (works), while the other person receives the product of the service. The time of the service-producer is worth money, that of the service-recipient has no monetary value within the parameters of that relationship. There are, however, some situations in which the time of one of the participants to a relationship may have a negative monetary value, that is, it carries costs for another person who is not receiving a service in return.

When Does Time Cost Money?

If the most powerful can command most money for their time, one would expect that it would be the least powerful who might not just carry a zero-value on their time, but possibly even a negative value. Searching for cases in which people's time costs money rather than earning them money, we find that this is the case, for example, with small children who need adult supervision. Small children constitute a cost for their parents or guardians for the time spent supervising them, without producing monetary value in return (other values, as noted above, are not being considered here). The same is true for people in institutions, such as prisoners,

mental hospitals, treatment centres, and the like. In such situations, time has no money value for the person who spends it under supervision,[2] but nevertheless the time so spent costs somebody money, often the tax-payer, who has to pay for the time of the staff and the other expenses associated with running an institution.

In the case of small children, their supervision costs money, if conducted within the framework of an institution (e.g. a daycare centre or a nursery school) or by a non-family member, such as a neighbourhood sitter. If small children are supervised by a family member, such as the mother, it costs time which could otherwise be employed earning money. The case of small children (or disabled adults living at home but needing constant assistance) indicates that the phenomenon under discussion goes beyond people who are inmates in institutions and includes people who are defined as dependents.

If we see dependency as a form of powerlessness (Eichler, 1973 and 1981), it permits us to look at the time expenditure of dependent people in relation to the economic value they derive (or fail to derive) from it. The extreme form of dependency is surely slavery. Although slaves were typically engaged in activities which gained money for their owners, the slaves themselves were not entitled to any recompense for their time expenditure, while the money needed to feed and house them (and to buy them in the first place) was seen as a cost to their owner.

Just as we have seen that it is a social convention which fixes the value of a particular role at a particular monetary level, so we find that when people are defined as dependents, the products of their time expenditure is seen as valueless in money terms (irrespective of whether a valuable product or service has been produced or performed), while their upkeep and/or supervision is seen as a cost. We can now formulate our third general proposition:

Proposition 3:

To the degree that people are perceived as dependent on somebody else (whether this is an institution, a person, or a group of persons) their time will carry a negative economic connotation, irrespective of their actual activity.

We have formulated three general propositions, which, if true, should be applicable to all populations. They should also shed light on the relationship of the sexes. In the following, the three general propositions will therefore be reformulated taking sex as a stratifying variable into account.

Gender and the Value of Time

Overall, women as a group are less powerful than men as a group. This statement has received sufficient attention in the recent past to obviate the need for an elaborate defence, and the literature supporting it is quite voluminous. (For a few Canadian examples see the Report of the Royal Commission on the Status of Women in Canada, 1970; Report of the Commission on Equality in Employment, 1984; Report of the Committee on Sexual Offences Against Children and Youth, 1984; Miles and Finn, 1982; Fitzgerald, Guberman and Wolfe, 1982; Brodie and Vickers, 1982; and Dumont, Jean, Lavigne and Stoddart, 1982).

The three general propositions concerning the value of time stated above should be applicable to women and men as a group. This implies a double modification: for one, the propositions need to be changed from the general to the specific by identifying two

particular parties which are in a differential power relationship. For the other, they need to be made applicable to groups rather than people within a given relationship, that is, on this score, the proposition changes from the specific to the general. As a consequence, the propositions would only apply in general, or with respect to average patterns, rather than with respect to all female-male situations.

The three propositions can, with these considerations in mind, be reformulated as follows:

Proposition 1a:

To the degree that men as a group are more powerful than women as a group, women will wait longer than men.

Proposition 2a:

To the degree that men are more powerful than women, women's time will be worth less money than men's time.

Proposition 3a:

To the degree that women are dependent on men, their time will carry a negative economic connotation.

Do Women Wait Longer than Men?

In order to answer this question properly, we would have to be able to draw on some comprehensive studies of the sex composition of line-ups, as well as have empirical information on the amount of time waited by sex in other contexts such as waiting rooms, at home, etc. Such information is, to my knowledge, not available for Canada. However, there are two other indicators which are useful in this context. Waiting *on* is a form of waiting *for*: "To wait on others and to be kept waiting exhibit the common element of subordination." (Schwartz, 1974: 858). It is therefore useful to look at the occupational structure and ask ourselves: what are the occupations in which people wait on others? Are women more likely to be within such occupations than men? We can also examine what happens within the home and ask ourselves: who waits upon whom in the home?

Looking at the occupational structure first, we can consider the sex composition of major occupations in Canada. Using the data in the Report of the Commission on Equality in Employment (1984: 63, table 5) and computing the female/male ratio[3] we find five occupations in which in 1981 women exceeded men: in the social sciences and related fields (1.1); teaching and related occupations (1.47); in medicine and health (3.46); clerical and related occupations (3.48); and service occupations (1.1).

These ratios tell us something about the sex composition of an occupation, but they do not tell us anything about the importance of such an occupation for each sex. This is found in another set of figures. In 1981, the highest participation of women in the labour force was in clerical and related occupations, with 35.1 per cent of all women in this sector. The second highest proportion of women were in service occupations, with 15.4 per cent of all women in this field. More than 50 per cent of all women in the labour force were in only two types of occupations. (The next highest female participation was in occupations in medicine and health, with 8.3 per cent of all women in this field, *ibid.*, p. 65.) Clerical and related occupations and service occupations, by definition, involve waiting upon other people. Only 6.8 per cent of all men in the labour force were in clerical and related positions in 1981, and 9.5 per cent were in service occupations (*ibid.*, p. 64). While this is a rather crude analysis, it

does nevertheless suggest that within the occupational structure women are more likely to wait upon other people than are men.

Considering the second possible indicator of the amount of waiting by sex, we can turn towards time budget studies. Here the evidence is very clear that in general, and irrespective of the labour force participation of women or the presence of children in the home, women do more of the housework than men, who tend to have more leisure time. (Meissner *et al.*, 1975; Clark and Harvey, 1976)

On both the indicator of occupational distribution and housework, it turns out that women do more waiting on other people than do men. Nevertheless, it would be a better test of the proposition if it could be supported by empirical data on direct waiting behaviours, rather than by using indirect indicators as has been done here. We can therefore consider the proposition as having been supported by the analysis, but not proven. In other words, the answer to the question whether women wait more than men is only a qualified yes.

Is Women's Time Worth Less Money than Men's Time?

This question is very simple to answer. There is abundant information available that documents that women and men *within the same occupations* are being paid differentially, with women receiving substantially less pay for the same amount of time worked within the same occupation. This pattern is, unfortunately, consistent over time and across different occupations, whether these are receiving high pay or low pay (cf. Economic Council of Canada, 1983).

Looking at the average income of women

Table 33.1 Average income of women and men in the six occupations with the highest male average employment income, 1981

	Average male income	Average female income
Physicians and surgeons	$59 834	$36 115
Dentists	58 128	40 510
Salespeople and traders, securities	46 718	18 375
General managers and other senior officials	46 160	24 915
Lawyers and notaries	40 978	23 935
Other managers (mines and oil wells)	40 506	19 303

and men in 1981 in the six occupations with the highest male average employment income, in which there were sufficient females to make the comparison,[4] we find that women earn substantially less, as seen in Table 33.1 (adapted from the report cited above, p. 74).

The answer to the question posed above is therefore clear: yes, on average, women's time is worth less than men's time.

Does Women's Time Carry a Negative Economic Connotation When They are Defined as Dependent on Men?

The major form of female dependence on men takes place within the framework of marriage, in which wives who do not have an independent income (housewives) are conceptualized as dependents of their husbands. While by now more than half of all Canadian wives are in the labour force, this is a change which is very recent (it occurred in the 1980s) and which signifies a major departure from previous patterns. It is therefore not particularly astonishing if we find definitions in flux.

Until about 1978, it would have been appropriate to state that in general a patriarchal model of the family underlay Canadian policies. A patriarchal model of the family has been defined by the following eight characteristics:

(1) Household and family are treated as congruent.

(2) The family is treated as the administrative unit.

(3) The father/husband is seen as responsible for the economic well-being of the family.

(4) The wife/mother is seen as responsible for the household and personal care of family members, especially child care.

(5) Conversely, the father/husband is *not* seen as responsible for the household and personal care of family members, especially child care.

(6) The wife/mother is *not* responsible for the economic well-being of the family.

(7) Society may give some financial assistance to the man who supports his dependents (wife and/or children), but is not responsible for the economic well-being of the family where there is a husband present and is not responsible for

the household and personal care of family members, especially child care, when there is a wife present.

(8) As a consequence of (1) and (7), a husband is equated with a father, and a wife is equated with a mother (see Eichler, 1984: 2-3).

What is most important in this model in our context is that the wife is defined as her husband's dependent, regardless of the value of the services she renders within the household. It is only since women have started in large numbers to withdraw from unpaid household work as their *sole* occupation (housework continues to be an important secondary occupation for the majority of women), that the economic value of their services has become somewhat more visible. With the majority of Canadian wives and mothers in the paid labour force, it becomes evident that some of the work that women have done, and still do within the home, has always been economically valuable. Today, some of the services previously rendered ostensibly for free within the household have to be purchased. It has also become more obvious, through greatly increased participation rates of women in the labour force, that a woman foregoes a salary if she spends her entire time in unpaid household work.

For as long as wives were defined as their husbands' dependents, their unpaid work was, by definition, valueless, and they were seen as an expense to their husbands rather than an asset, hence the spousal tax deduction, which still applies. Family law, however, has changed considerably since 1978, and the wife's potential contribution to her husband's assets through her *unpaid* work is now to some degree recognized in all provinces (cf. Eichler, 1983).

We can, then, answer our third question: yes, to the degree that women are defined as men's dependents, the value of their work will not only go unrecognized, but they will be seen as an economic expense rather than as an economic asset, irrespective of the real value of the work that is being performed by them.

Conclusion

What is particularly interesting is the realization that the monetary value of people's time is in no way inherent in particular activities, but depends on the power of their role. Since the value of time assigned to a person or activity is merely a social convention, it follows that we can alter that value by creating another social convention.

This approach presents a rather different view of the value of time than that suggested by the logic of market economics. Market economics assumes that there is an internal logic and dynamic in the market that fixes the monetary value of a person's time according to the inherent quality of a product and equal to its value as a commodity. However, we have seen that for slaves and housewives the product of their time has no monetary value (even though its replacement would cost money), due to their lack of power, which expresses itself in their being defined as dependents. It follows that when we cease to define people as dependents, or when the power position of a group of people changes, the value of their time will change, even though in some cases the use to which this time is being put may not have changed.

Notes

1. If the psychiatrist or medical doctor has opted out of the provincial health plan, the client pays both directly and indirectly, of course.

2. Nor has the time much intrinsic value for the person who is being supervised. Catkins (1970) has identified six ways in which patients in a rehabilitation institution used their time, which she classified as "passing time, waiting, doing time, making time, filling time, and killing time." While the institution she studied was certainly not a prison, nevertheless all of the modes of time usage noted are a reaction to being an inmate in an institution and constituted attempts to spend time so that it did not become an irritating void.

3. There are a total of 23 major occupations listed. For each, the female percentage was divided by the male percentage. Since there are more men than women in the labour force (in 1981, 7 152 205 men and 4 853 120 women — see report cited pp. 64/5 — that is, a female/male ratio of 0.68) the representation of women and men within a given occupation would be proportionate if the female/male ratio were 0.68. This is approximately the case for sales occupations with a ratio of 0.69, which translates into 9.5 per cent of all men and 9.6 per cent of all women in the labour force being in this occupation. When the female/male ratio exceed 1, the discrepancy is, therefore, very considerable. Since the sex segregation of occupations in Canada is quite high, all ratios (with the exception of sales occupations) were either quite low or above 1.

4. Two occupations, judges and magistrates as well as optometrists, were eliminated from the table because no female salary figures were provided due to the low number of female incumbents.

34

Women in
*Male-Dominated Professions**

Katherine Marshall

One of the most significant social trends in Canada over the past several decades has been the dramatic increase in the labour force participation of women. Concerns have been raised, however, that while the number of working women has increased, most are still employed in so-called women's occupations which are often characterized by poor pay and low status.

There is evidence, however, that in the period 1971-1981, women made substantial inroads into what have traditionally been male-dominated professional occupations. These professions are of particular interest because they are generally among the best paid occupations in Canada, and most carry high levels of social status.

For the purposes of this report, professional occupations were those in which 45 per cent or more of those employed in that

occupation in 1981 had at least a bachelor's degree. For comparability, the same occupations were considered professional in 1971. A profession was classified as male-dominated if 65 per cent or more of the people employed in it in 1971 were men. Overall, 46 occupational groups met the criterion for being professional; 34 of these were classified as male-dominated.

While women did make substantial gains in male-dominated professions in the 1970s, they were still significantly under-represented in these professions in 1981. As well, because these occupations often involve considerable commitment to the workforce and a demanding workload (elements not generally compatible with a woman's conventional family role), many women entering these fields had to adopt new patterns of behaviour. Women in male-dominated professions, for example, were more likely than women in other occupations to have never married, or if married, to have had fewer children or to be childless.

The total number of women employed in male-dominated professions in Canada rose

*Originally published in *Canadian Social Trends*, Winter 1987. Statistics Canada. Reprinted by permission.

Table 34.1 Women in non-male-dominated professions, 1971 and 1981

	Total number of women			Women as a % of total growth in profession 1971-1981	Women as a % of total employment in profession	
	1971	1981	Percentage increase 1971-1981		1971	1981
Psychologists	2 035	4 600	126.0	56.1	48.7	52.6
Social workers	7 230	21 020	190.7	68.8	55.4	63.5
Supervisors in library, museum and archival sciences	600	1 440	140.0	79.2	47.4	62.1
Librarians and archivists	6 120	13 575	121.8	84.2	77.2	80.9
Educational and vocational counsellors	1 690	3 050	80.5	92.5	35.8	49.3
Elementary and kindergarten teachers	140 500	152 335	8.4	60.6	83.9	81.5
Secondary school teachers	56 615	63 320	11.8	27.3	47.2	43.8
Postsecondary school teachers	5 730	4 445	−22.4	27.6	49.4	63.9
Teachers of exceptional students	4 420	15 315	246.5	71.0	75.0	72.1
Physiotherapists, occupational and other therapists	5 895	12 525	112.5	86.9	82.9	85.0
Dieticians and nutritionists	2 010	3 280	63.2	91.7	95.9	94.3
Translators and interpreters	1 395	4 340	211.1	64.4	57.1	61.9
Total	234 240	299 250	27.8	62.3	67.4	66.2

Source: Statistics Canada, Census of Canada.

Women in Non-Male-Dominated Professions

By far, the vast majority of professional women work in the 12 occupational groups that were not male-dominated. In 1981, 78% of professional women, compared with just 30% of male professionals, were employed in one of these occupations. In fact, in 1981, 62% of all professional women were in teaching-related positions; however, this proportion was down from 79% in 1971. The female component of non-male-dominated professions ranged from 94% of dieticians and nutritionists, to 44% of secondary school teachers.

Between 1971 and 1981, the representation of women increased in 8 of the 12 non-male-dominated professions and declined in the others. Overall, while female representation dropped in only 5 of the 46 professions, because declines occurred in the two largest female-dominated occupations, elementary and kindergarten, and secondary school teachers, the percentage of women in all professional occupations actually fell slightly from 43.1% in 1971 to 42.5% in 1981.

from 30 410 in 1971 to 83 340 in 1981; this increase accounted for 29 per cent of the overall growth in these occupations during this period. As a result, in 1981, women made up 19 per cent of all those employed in male-dominated professions, up from 11 per cent in 1971.

During the 1971-1981 period (Table 34.2), the proportional representation of women increased in all but one of the 34 professions identified as male-dominated. In addition, women accounted for the major share of the overall growth in employment in several of these occupations. In fact, women accounted for more than half of the total increase in employment in six of the 34 male-dominated professions. The largest increase occurred among pharmacists; women accounted for 78 per cent of total employment growth in this profession over the 1971-1981 period.

The other professions in which women made up more than half of total employment growth were university teaching and related occupations[1] (55 per cent), mathematicians, statisticians and actuaries (55 per cent), management occupations in the social sciences and related fields (54 per cent), optometrists (52 per cent), and chemists (51 per cent).

Women also accounted for more than 40 per cent of the total increase in employment among community college and vocational school teachers (45 per cent), university teachers[1] (44 per cent), sociologists, anthropologists and other social scientists (43 per cent), and administrators in teaching and related fields (41 per cent).

As a result of this growth, the proportional representation of women in many of these professions also increased dramatically. The percentage of all pharmacists who were women, for example, rose from 25 per cent in 1971 to 42 per cent in 1981. In the same period, women as a proportion of all those employed in university teaching and related occupations increased from 30 per cent to 46 per cent, while for management positions in the social sciences and related fields, the increase was from 34 per cent to 48 per cent.

The proportional representation of women among optometrists, veterinarians, and lawyers and notaries also rose by 10 percentage points or more. However, even with these increases, women still made up fewer than one in five people employed in these professions in 1981.

Women also accounted for one-third of the total growth in the number of physicians and surgeons, the single, largest male-dominated professional group. As a result, the percentage of doctors who were women increased from 11 per cent in 1971 to 17 per cent in 1981.

On the other hand, women accounted for less than 10 per cent of total employment growth in nine of the 34 male-dominated professions during the 1971-1981 period. Women made up only 4 per cent of the increase in the number of physicists, and just 8 per cent of the increase in management occupations in engineering and the natural sciences. As well, about 8 per cent of all employment growth in the various engineering professions in the 1971-1981 period was due to the increasing number of female engineers.

Because of these relatively slow growth rates, increases in the proportional representation of women in these professions were relatively small. In fact, the percentage of all physicists who were women actually fell slightly, from 6 per cent in 1971 to 5 per cent in 1981. This, however, was the only male-dominated profession in which the proportional representation of women declined.

The proportion of engineers who were

women did increase; however, in 1981, only 4 per cent of engineers, compared with 1 per cent in 1971, were women. At the same time, the proportion of female managers in engineering and the natural sciences increased from 3 per cent in 1971 to 7 per cent in 1981.

Younger women were responsible for much of the increase in female participation in male-dominated professions. For example, women aged 25-34 accounted for almost half of the overall increase in female employment in these professions during the 1971-1981 period. In this period, the number of women aged 25-34 in male-dominated professions increased 274 per cent. This compared with increases of 128 per cent for women in all other age groups and 57 per cent for men aged 25-34.

The relative growth in employment of younger women in male-dominated professions was particularly strong in the prestigious categories of doctors, judges and lawyers, and university professors. Over the 1971-1981 period, the increase in the number of 25- to 34-year-old women in these professions was actually slightly greater than that for men in the same age group. Yet, despite this growth, women still made up just 20 per cent of all doctors, judges, lawyers, and university teachers in 1981, and only 27 per cent of those aged 25-34.

Socio-Economic Characteristics of Women in Male-Dominated Professions

Many of the social and economic characteristics of women employed in male-dominated professions differ from those of both men working in these professions and women employed in other occupations.

Compared with women in other occupations, those in male-dominated professions had the most education, the highest employment rate, and the greatest income. For example, women aged 25 and over employed full-time in male-dominated professions earned an average of $24 100 in 1980, compared with $21 100 for other professional women and $13 400 for women in non-professional occupations.

The average employment income of women in male-dominated professions, however, was considerably below that of men in these occupations. The average earnings of women working full-time in male-dominated occupations were just 71 per cent of those of comparable men in 1980. Part of this difference is explained by the relatively high proportion of women in these professions who were in the younger age groups; these women tend to have less seniority and lower average employment income than the older age groups. Also, women aged 25-34 in these professions had average employment incomes that were only 77 per cent those of comparable men.

The family characteristics of women in male-dominated professions also differ from those of other groups. Women in these professions were the least likely of any occupational category, either male or female, to be in a husband-wife family. They were also more likely than other women to have never married. Among employed women aged 45 and over, for example, 22 per cent of those in male-dominated professions had never married, compared with 15 per cent of those in other professions and just 7 per cent of non-professionals. As well, women in male-dominated professions had fewer children at home than other women and were more likely than other women not to have had children at all.

Table 34.2 Women in male-dominated professions, 1971 and 1981

	Total number of women			Women as a % of total growth in profession 1971-1981	Women as a % of total employment in profession	
	1971	1981	Percentage increase 1971-1981	1971-1981	1971	1981
Management occupations, natural sciences and engineering	70	800	1 042.9	7.6	2.7	6.6
Management occupations, social sciences and related fields	760	3 805	400.7	54.2	33.8	48.2
Administrators in teaching and related fields	6 445	9 120	41.5	41.2	21.5	25.0
Chemists	895	1 975	120.7	50.8	11.8	20.4
Geologists	145	795	448.3	23.2	2.9	10.3
Physicists	45	65	44.4	4.0	5.6	5.0
Meteorologists	40	90	125.0	27.0	4.9	9.0
Agriculturists and related scientists	330	1 220	269.7	31.8	5.1	13.2
Biologists and related scientists	830	2 330	180.7	36.4	26.1	31.9
Architects	125	560	348.0	14.0	3.0	7.7
Chemical engineers	65	340	423.1	12.9	1.8	5.9
Civil engineers	235	980	317.0	6.9	1.1	3.0
Electrical engineers	205	1 000	387.8	6.7	1.3	3.7
Mechanical engineers	100	380	280.0	4.5	0.8	1.9
Metallurgical engineers	15	50	233.3	3.8	1.7	2.8
Mining engineers	20	105	425.0	5.9	0.9	2.9
Petroleum engineers	15	225	1 400.0	6.7	1.1	4.9

Nuclear engineers	—	40	—	6.9	—	4.8
Other architects and engineers	140	1 640	1 071.4	15.0	4.0	12.2
Mathematicians, statisticians and actuaries	1 010	2 070	105.0	55.9	25.0	34.7
Economists	640	2 570	301.6	28.8	11.0	20.5
Sociologists, anthropologists and related social scientists	170	540	217.6	42.5	33.0	39.0
Judges and magistrates	75	220	193.3	18.6	5.7	10.5
Lawyers and notaries	860	5 390	526.7	24.9	5.2	15.5
Ministers of religion	900	1 785	98.3	26.9	4.5	7.6
University teachers	5 190	9 785	88.5	43.7	19.7	26.5
Other university teaching and related occupations	1 525	6 170	304.6	55.0	30.3	45.8
Community college and vocational school teachers	3 280	13 770	319.8	45.3	33.0	41.6
Physicians and surgeons	3 150	7 255	130.3	33.4	10.7	17.4
Dentists	330	860	160.6	13.6	4.9	8.1
Veterinarians	75	605	706.7	30.2	4.3	17.2
Osteopaths and chiropractors	80	340	325.0	22.0	7.3	14.9
Pharmacists	2 540	6 090	139.8	78.3	25.3	41.8
Optometrists	105	365	247.6	52.0	6.7	17.7
Total	30 410	83 340	174.1	29.0	11.0	18.6

Source: Statistics Canada, Census of Canada.

Table 34.3 Selected family indicators, 1981

	Women			Men in male-dominated professions
	Male-dominated professions	Other professions	Non-professionals	
% never married				
– 25-44 years	24.8	19.6	13.1	—
– 45 years and over	22.0	15.4	7.4	—
% who were spouses in husband-wife families	61.9	69.1	71.4	80.0
% of spouses in husband-wife families with children at home	59.8	67.9	69.0	69.9
% employed full-time				
– spouses in husband-wife families with children under 19 at home	50.8	46.2	47.8	93.2
– spouses in husband-wife families without children	73.6	70.3	62.6	82.0

– not available

Source: Statistics Canada, 1981 Census of Canada.

Figure 34.1 Average 1980 Employment Income of Men and Women in Male-Dominated Professions, by Age

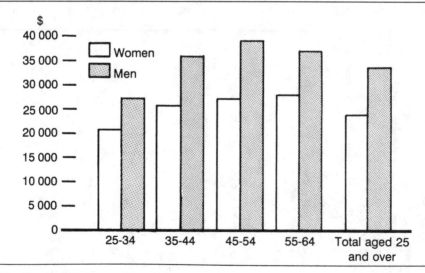

Source: Statistics Canada, 1981 Census of Canada.

The differences in family characteristics also extend to a comparison of women and men in male-dominated professions. Women in these occupations were much less likely than men to be a spouse in a husband-wife family. In 1981, 62 per cent of women in these occupations were married, compared with 80 per cent of men. As well, those women in male-dominated professions who were in husband-wife families were less likely than comparable men to have children: 60 per cent of married women, compared with 70 per cent of married men, home. In addition, only 51 pe sional women in husband-w children had full-time jobs, 93 per cent of similar men.

These figures indicate that it is still far easier for men to maintain both a professional career and a family. For many women, unlike men, the decision to pursue such a career may mean limiting marital or parental options.

Note

1. University teachers include tenured professors. University teaching and related occupations include non-tenured professors and lecturers, teaching and laboratory assistants, and other instructors.

Bibliography

Abella, Judge Rosalie
 1984 *Equality in Employment*. A Royal Commission report. Ottawa: Minister of Supply and Services.

Acheson, T. W.
 1969 "The Nature and Structure of York Commerce in the 1820's," *Canadian Historical Review* (December).

Adams, J. D. R. and J. Whalley
 1977 *The International Taxation of Multinational Enterprises in Developed Countries*. Westport, Ct.: Greenwood.

Agassi, Judith Buber
 1972 "Women Who Work in Factories," *Dissent*, (Winter): 234-40.

Aglietta, Michel
 1979 *A Theory of Capitalist Regulation*. London: New Left Books.

Aharoni, Y.
 1966 *The Foreign Investment Decision Process*. Boston: Division of Research, Graduate School of Business Administration, Harvard University.

Aitken, H. G. J.
 1959 "Defensive Expansionism: the State and Economic Growth in Canada." in H. G. J. Aitken (ed.), *The State and Economic Growth*. New York: Social Science Research Council, pp. 79-114.

Alford, R.
 1963 *Party and Society*. Chicago: Aldine.

Allingham, J. D.
 1967 "Class Regression: An Aspect of the Social Stratification Process," *American Sociological Review*, 32 (3): 442-9.

Amin, Samir
 1974 *Accumulation on a World Scale*. New York: Monthly Review Press, 2 vols.

Anderson, C. H.
 1974 *The Political Economy of Social Class*. Englewood Cliffs, N.J.: Prentice-Hall.

Apperson, G. L.
 1929 *English Proverbs and Proverbial Phrases*. London: J. M. Dent & Sons.

Archibald, W. Peter
 1978 *Social Psychology as Political Economy*. Toronto: McGraw-Hill Ryerson.

Armstrong, Pat
 1984 *Labour Pains: Women's Work in Crisis*. Toronto: The Women's Press.

Armstrong, Pat and Hugh Armstrong
 1983 *A Working Majority: What Women Must Do for Pay*. Ottawa: Supply and Services Canada for the Canadian Advisory Council on the Status of Women.

1984   *The Double Ghetto: Canadian Women and Their Segregated Work.* Revised edition.
[1978] Toronto: McClelland and Stewart.

Arnold, Stephen J. and James G. Barnes
1979   "Canadian and American National Character as a Basis for Market Segmentation," in J.
Sheth (ed.), *Research in Marketing.* Vol. 2, Greenwich, Conn: JAI Press, pp. 1-35.

Arnold, Stephen J. and Douglas J. Tigert
1974   "Canadians and Americans: A Comparative Analysis," *International Journal of Comparative Sociology,* 15: 68-83.

Aron, R.
1967   *The Industrial Society.* London: Weidenfeld and Nicholson.

Aronowitz, Stanley
1973   *False Promises.* New York: McGraw-Hill.

Arrighi, Giovanni
1978   *The Geometry of Imperialism.* London: New Left Books.

Ashley, C. A.
1957   "Concentration of Economic Power," *Canadian Journal of Economics and Political Science,* 23: 105-8.

Atwood, Margaret
1972   *Survival: A Thematic Guide to Canadian Literature.* Toronto: Anansi.

1984   *Second Words: Selected Critical Prose.* Boston: Beacon Press.

Avakumovic, Ivan
1978   *Socialism in Canada.* Toronto: McClelland and Stewart.

Babchuk, Nicholas and John N. Edwards
1965   "Voluntary Associations and the Integration Hypothesis," *Sociological Inquiry,* 35: 149-162.

Bachynski, M. P.
1973   "Science Policy in Canada," *Science Forum,* 31 (February) 19-27.

Baer, Doug, Edward Grabb and William Johnston
1990   "The Values of Canadians and Americans: A Critical Analysis and Reassessment," *Social Forces,* 68 (3), in press.

Bailyn, Bernard
1959   "Politics and Social Structure in Virginia," in James Morton Smith (ed.), *Seventeenth-Century America.* Published for the Institute of Early American History and Culture, Williamsburg, Virginia: University of North Carolina Press.

1968   "The Origins of American Politics," in D. Fleming and B. Bailyn (eds.), *Perspectives in American History,* 1:1.

Bairoch, Paul
1982   "International Industrialization Levels from 1750 to 1880," *Journal of European Economic History* 11:2 (Spring).

Balla, Balint
    1978   *Soziologie der Knappheit. Zum Verständnis individueller und gesellschaftlicher Mängelzustände*. Stuttgart: Ferdinand Enke.

Banks, J. A.
    1972   *The Sociology of Social Movements*. London: Macmillan.

Baran, P.A. and P. M. Sweezy
    1966   "Notes on the Theory of Imperialism," in *Problems of Economic Dynamics and Planning: Essays in Honour of Michal Kalecki*. New York: Pergamon Press.

Barker, Jane and Hazel Downing
    1980   "Word Processing and the Transformation of the Patriarchal Relations of Control in the Office," *Capital and Class*, 10 (Spring).

Barkin, David
    1981   "Internationalization of Capital: An Alternative Approach," *Latin American Perspectives*, 8 (3/4): 156-61.

Barnet, Richard J.
    1980   *The Lean Years*. New York: Simon & Schuster.

Barnet, Richard J. and Ronald E. Muller
    1974   *Global Reach*. New York: Simon & Schuster.

Barton, Allen H.
    1974   "Consensus and Conflict Among American Leaders," *Public Opinion Quarterly*, 38: 507-30.

Beard, Charles A. and Mary R. Beard
    1927   *The Rise of American Civilization.*. New York: Macmillan.

Beatles, The
    1969   *Abbey Road*.

Beauvoir, Simone de
    1952   *The Second Sex*. New York: Bantam.

Becker, Howard
    1957   "Current Sacred-Secular Theory and its Development," in H. Becker and A. Boskoff (eds.), *Modern Sociological Theory in Continuity and Change*. New York.

Bell, Daniel
    1973   *The Coming of Post-Industrial Society*. New York: Basic Books.

Bell, Daniel, ed.
    1963   *The Radical Right*. Garden City: Doubleday.

Bell, David V. J.
    1969   *"Nation and Non-Nation: A New Analysis of the Loyalists and the American Revolution."* Harvard University: unpublished Ph.D. dissertation.

Bell, David and Lorne Tepperman
    1979   *The Roots of Disunity: A Look at Canadian Political Culture*. Toronto: McClelland and Stewart.

Bennett, John W.
    1969   *Northern Plainsmen: Adaptive Strategy and Agrarian Life*. Chicago: Aldine.

Benokraitis, Nijole V. and Joe R. Feagin
   1978   *Affirmative Action and Equal Opportunity: Action, Inaction, Reaction.* Boulder, Colorado: Westview Press.

Bercovitch, Sacvan
   1981   "The Rites of Assent: Rhetoric, Ritual and the Ideology of American Consensus," in Sam B. Girgus (ed.), *The American Self: Myth, Ideology and Popular Culture.* Albuquerque: University of New Mexico Press, pp. 5-42.

Bercuson, David and Douglas Wertheimer
   1985   *A Trust Betrayed: The Keegstra Affair.* Toronto: Doubleday Canada Ltd.

Berger, Carl
   1970   *The Sense of Power: Studies in the Ideas of Canadian Imperialism 1867-1914.* Toronto: University of Toronto Press.

   1976   *The Writing of Canadian History.* Toronto: Oxford University Press.

Berger, Thomas R.
   1981   *Fragile Freedoms: Human Rights and Dissent in Canada.* Toronto: Clarke Irwin and Co.

Bergmann, Werner
   1983   "Das Problem der Zeit in der Soziologie. Ein Literaturüberblick zum Stand der 'zeitsoziologischen' Theorie und Forschung," *Kölner Zeitschrift für Soziologie und Sozialpsychologie,* 3: 462-504.

Berkowitz, S. D.
   1982   *An Introduction to Structural Analysis.* Toronto: Butterworths.

Berkowitz, S. D., Y. Kotowitz and L. Waverman, with B. Becker, R. Bradford, P. J. Carrington, J. Corman, and G. Heil.
   1976   *Enterprise Structure and Corporate Concentration.* Royal Commission on Corporate Concentration, Technical Study No. 17. Ottawa: Supply and Services Canada.

Berle, Adolph A. and Gardiner C. Means
   1967   *The Modern Corporation and Private Property.* New York: Harcourt, Brace and World.
   [1932]

Bernard, Jessie
   1971   *Women and the Public Interest.* Chicago: Aldine-Atherton.

   1973   *The Future of Marriage.* New York: Bantam Books.

   1975   *Women, Wives, Mothers.* Chicago: Aldine.

Berry, J. W., R. Kalin and D. M. Taylor
   1977   *Multiculturalism and Ethnic Attitudes in Canada.* Ottawa: Minister of Supply and Services Canada.

Bertaux, D.
   1977   *Destines personnels à structure de classe.* Paris: Presses Universitaires de France.

Bibby, Reginald W.
   1987   *Fragmented Gods: The Poverty and Potential of Religion in Canada.* Toronto: Irwin.

Bienvenue, R. M.
1985   "Colonial Status: The Case of Canadian Indians," in R. M. Bienvenue and J. Goldstein (eds.), *Ethnicity and Ethnic Relations in Canada.* 2nd edition. Toronto: Butterworths.

Bissell, Claude
1979   "The Place of Learning and the Arts in Canadian Life," in Richard A. Preston (ed.), *Perspectives on Revolution and Evolution.* Durham, N.C.: Duke University Press, pp. 180-212.

Black, Don and John Myles
1985   "Dependent Industrialization and the Canadian Class Structure: A Comparative Anlysis of Canada, the United States and Sweden." Working Paper No. 24. Comparative Project on Class Structure and Class Consciousness. Madison: University of Wisconsin. (Subsequently published in *Canadian Review of Sociology and Anthropology* 23:3, May 1986.)

Blanchard, François A.
1983   "A Statistical Study of the Agricultural Problems of the Province of New Brunswick," M.A. thesis, Cornell University, Ithaca.

Blanchard, Raoul
1935   *L'Est du Canada français.* Paris.

1936   "Etudes canadiennes," *Revue de géographie alpine*, XXV.

1937a   "Etudes canadiennes," *Revue de géographie alpine*, XXVI.

1937b   "Les Cantons de l'Est," *Revue de géographie alpine*, XXV.

1938   "Etudes canadiennnes," *Revue de géographie alpine*, XXVII.

Blau, P. M. and O. D. Duncan
1967   *The American Occupational Structure.* New York: Wiley.

Blishen, Bernard R.
1958   "The Construction and Use of an Occupational Class Scale," *Canadian Journal of Economics and Political Science*, XXIV (4): 519-25.

Blishen, B. and T. Atkinson
1981   "Regional and Status Differences in Canadian Values." Toronto: Institute of Behavioural Research, York University.

Blishen, B. and H. McRoberts
1976   "A Revised Socioeconomic Index for Occupation in Canada," *Canadian Review of Sociology and Anthropology*, 13 (1): 71-9.

Bliss, Michael
1974   *A Living Profit: Studies in the Social History of Canadian Business.* Toronto: McClelland and Stewart.

Bluestone, B. and B. Harrison
1982   *The Deindustrialization of America.* New York: Basic Books.

Blumer, Herbert
1948   "Public Opinion and Public Opinion Polling," *American Sociological Review*, XIII: 542-554. Reprinted in Herbert Blumer, *Symbolic Interactionism.* Englewood Cliffs, N.J.: Prentice-Hall, 1969: pp. 195-208.

Bodemann, Michael
  1984   "Elitism, Fragility and Commoditism: Three Themes in the Canadian Sociological Mythology," in S. D. Berkowitz (ed.), *Models and Myths in Canadian Sociology*. Toronto: Butterworths.

Booth, Alan
  1975   "Voluntary Association Affiliation and National Diversity," *Canadian Review of Sociology and Anthropology*, 12: 206-212.

Bosher, J. F.
  1972   "Governments and Private Interests in New France," in J. M. Bumsted (ed.), *Canadian History before Confederation*. Georgetown: Irwin Dorsey.

Bourgault, Pierre L.
  1972   *Innovation and the Structure of Canadian Industry*. Ottawa: Information Canada, Science Council of Canada.

Bourgeault, Ron
  1983a "The Indians, the Metis and the Fur Trade: Class, Sexism and Racism in the Transition from 'Communism' to Capitalism," *Studies in Political Economy*, 12 (Fall).

  1983b "The Development of Captialism and the Subjugation of Native Women in Northern Canada," *Alternate Routes*, 6.

Bourque, Gilles and Nicole Laurin-Frenette
  1972   "Social Classes and National Ideologies in Quebec, 1960-1970," in G. Teeple (ed.), *Capitalism and the National Question In Canada*. Toronto: University of Toronto Press.

Boverman, Inge K. *et al.*
  1970   "Sex Role Stereotypes and Clinical Judgements of Mental Health," *Journal of Consulting and Clinical Psychology*, 34 (6, February): 1-7.

Braverman, Harry
  1974   *Labour and Monopoly Capital*. New York: Monthly Press Review.

Brebner, J. B.
  1969   *The Neutral Yankees of Nova Scotia*. Toronto: McClelland and Stewart.
  [1937]

Brecher, I. and S. S. Reisman
  1957   *Canada - U. S. Economic Relations*. (Study done for the Royal Commission on Canada's Economic Prospects, Appendix D), Queen's Printer.

Brenner, Robert
  1977   "The Origins of Capitalist Development: A Critique of Neo-Smithian Marxism," *New Left Review*, 104: 25-92.

Breton, Raymond
  1972   "The Socio-Political Dynamics of the October Events," *Canadian Review of Sociology and Anthropology*, IX: 33-56.

Brewer, Anthony
  1980   *Marxist Theories of Imperialism*. Boston: Routledge & Kegan Paul.

Bridenbaugh, Carl
  1955   *Cities in Revolt*. New York: Capricorn.

Britton, N. H. and James M. Gilmour
  1978 *The Weakest Link, A Technological Perspective on Canadian Industrial Underdevelopment.* Ottawa.

Broadfoot, Barry
  1973 *Ten Lost Years, 1929-1939.* Toronto: Doubleday.

Brodie, M. Janine and Jill McCalla Vickers
  1982 *Canadian Women in Politics: An Overview.* CRIAW paper No. 2. Ottawa: Canadian Research Institute for the Advancement of Women.

Brooke, M. Z. and H. L. Remers
  1970 *The Strategy of Multinational Enterprise: Organisation and Finance.* New York: Elsevier.

Brookes, Ian
  1972 "The Physical Geography of the Atlantic Provinces," in A. Macpherson (ed.), *Studies in Canadian Geography: The Atlantic Provinces.* Toronto: University of Toronto Press, pp. 1-45.

Broude, Henry
  1959 "The Role of the State in American Economic Development," in H. Aitken (ed.), *The State and Economic Growth.* New York: Social Science Research Council.

Brown, Craig
  1966 "The Nationalism of the National Policy," in P. Russell (ed.), *Nationalism in Canada.* Toronto: McGraw Hill Ryerson.

Brown, J. J.
  1967 *Ideas in Exile, a History of Canadian Invention.* Toronto: McClelland and Stewart.

Brown, Russell M.
  (n.d.) "Telemachus and Oedipus: Images of Tradition and Authority in Canadian and American Fiction." Department of English, University of Toronto.

Brown, Wallace
  1965 *The King's Friends: The Composition and Motives of the American Loyalist Claimants.* Hanover, N.H.: University Press of New England.

Brym, Robert J.
  1978 *The Jewish Intelligentsia and Russian Marxism: A Sociological Study of Intellectual Radicalism and Ideological Divergence.* London: Macmillan.

  1979 "Political Conservatism in Atlantic Canada," in R. J. Brym and R. J. Sacouman (eds.), *Underdevelopment and Social Movements in Atlantic Canada.* Toronto: New Hogtown Press.

  1985 "The Canadian Capitalist Class, 1965-1985," in Robert J. Brym (ed.), *The Structures of the Canadian Capitalist Class.* Toronto: Garamond, pp. 1-20.

  1986 "Anglo-Canadian Society," *Current Sociology*, 34, 1.

  1988 "Foundations of Sociological Theory," in Lorne Tepperman and James Curtis (eds.), *Readings in Sociology: An Introduction.* Toronto: McGraw-Hill Ryerson.

  1989 "Canada," in T. Bottomore and R. Brym (eds.), *The Capitalist Class: An International Study.* Albany: State University of New York Press, pp. 177-206.

Brym, Robert J. and Barbara Neis
  1978   "Regional Factors in the Formation of the Fishermen's Protective Union of New-foundland," *Canadian Journal of Sociology,* 3: 391-407.

Buckley, Kenneth
  1974   *Capital Formation in Canada.* Toronto: Macmillan.

Bukharin, Nikolai
  1973   *Imperialism and World Economy.* New York: Monthly Review Press.

Bumsted, J. M., ed.
  1972   *Canadian History before Confederation.* Georgetown: Irwin Dorsey.

Burawoy, Michael
  1985   *The Politics of Production.* London: Verso.

Burnet, Jean
  1947   "Town-Country Relations and the Problem of Rural Leadership," *Canadian Journal of Economics and Political Science* 13: 395-409.

Butlin, N.
  1959   "Colonial Socialism in Australia, 1860-1900," in H. Aitken (ed.), *The State and Economic Growth.* New York: Social Science Research Council.

Callwood, June
  1981   *Portrait of Canada.* Garden City, N.Y.: Doubleday and Co.

Camilleri, Joseph
  1981   "The Advanced Capitalist State and the Contemporary World Crisis," *Science and Society,* 45: 130-58.

Campbell, Colin and George J. Szablowski
  1979   *The Superbureaucrats: Structure and Behaviour in Central Agencies.* Toronto: Macmillan.

Canada
  1937   *Report of the Royal Commission on Price Spreads.* Ottawa: King's Printer.

  1971   *Poverty in Canada: Report of the Special Senate Committee on Poverty.* Ottawa: Information Canada.

  1978   *Report on the Royal Commission on Corporate Concentration.* Ottawa: Minister of Supply Services.

Canadian Gallup Poll, The
  n.d.   "The Design of the Example." Toronto. mimeo.

Canadian Review Co.
  1922   *The Canadian Annual Review, 1921.* Toronto: Canadian Review Co.

Carchedi, Mino
  1977   *On the Economic Identification of Social Classes.* London: Routledge and Kegan Paul.

Cardinal, Harold
  1969   *The Unjust Society.* Edmonton: Hurtig.

Cardoso, F.H. and E. Faletto
  1979   *Dependency and Development in Latin America.* Los Angeles: University of California Press.

Careless, J. M. S.
  1954   "Frontierism, Metropolitanism, and Canadian History," *Canadian Historical Review*, 35 (1): 8-14.

Carroll, William K.
  1982   "The Canadian Corporate Elite: Financiers or Finance Capitalists?" *Studies in Political Economy*, 8: 89-114.

  1984   "The Individual, Class, and Corporate Power in Canada," *Canadian Journal of Sociology*, 9 (3): 245-68.

  1986   *Corporate Power and Canadian Capitalism.* Vancouver: University of British Columbia Press.

  1988   "The Political Economy of Canada," in James Curtis and Lorne Tepperman (eds.), *Understanding Canadian Society.* Toronto: McGraw-Hill Ryerson.

Carroll, William K., John Fox and Michael D. Ornstein
  1981   "Longitudinal Analysis of Directorate Interlocks," Paper presented at the annual meetings of the Canadian Sociology and Anthropology Association, Halifax, May.

  1982   "The Network of Directorate Interlocks Among the Largest Canadian Firms," *Canadian Review of Sociology and Anthropology*, 19 (1):44-69.

Castells, Manuel
  1980   *The Economic Crisis and American Society.* Princeton: Princeton University Press.

Catkins, Kathy
  1970   "Time: Perspectives, Marking and Styles of Usage," *Social Problems*: 487-501.

Caute, David
  1966   *The Left in Europe Since 1789.* New York: McGraw-Hill.

Caves, R. E.
  1982   *Multinational Enterprise and Economic Analysis.* Cambridge and New York: Cambridge University Press.

Census of Canada
  1911   Vol III. Ottawa: Dominion Bureau of Statistics.

  1931   Vol I. Ottawa: Dominion Bureau of Statistics.

  1931   Vol III. Ottawa: Dominion Bureau of Statistics.

  1931   Vol. VII. Ottawa: Dominion Bureau of Statistics, Table 49.

  1951   Vol. IV. Ottawa: Dominion Bureau of Statistics, Table 12.

  1951   Vol. X. Ottawa: Dominion Bureau of Statistics, pp. 145-46.

  1961   Vol. I. Ottawa: Dominion Bureau of Statistics, pp. 2-5, Table 36.

  1971   *Ethnic Groups by Age Groups.* (cat. 92-731).

  1971   *Labour Force and Individual Income* (cat. 94-709).

  1971   *Occupations.* (cat. no. 94-717).

  1971   *Religious Denominations by Age Groups.* (cat. 92-732).

Census of Manufacturing Industries in the Province of Quebec
   1934

Center for Applied Research in the Apostolate (CARA)
   1983a *Values Study: U.S. Percentages.* Washington, D.C.

   1983b *Values Study of Canada.* Code book. Washington, D.C.

Center for Settlement Studies
   1968 *Proceedings - Symposium on Resource Frontier Communities, Dec. 16, 1968.* Winnipeg: University of Manitoba.

Chambers, Ernest J., ed.
   1921 *The Canadian Parliamentary Guide, 1921.* Ottawa: Mortimer.

Chandler, Marsha A.
   1983 "The Politics of Public Enterprise," in J. Robert S. Prichard (ed.), *Crown Corporations in Canada.* Toronto: Butterworths, pp. 185-218.

Chapman, J. K.
   1976 "Henry Harvey Stuart (1873-1952): New Brunswick Reformer," *Acadiensis,* 5: 79-104.

Chilcote, R. and D. L. Johnson, eds.
   1983 *Theories of Development: Modes of Production or Dependency?* Beverly Hills: Sage Publications.

Chirot, Daniel
   1977 *Social Change in the Twentieth Century.* New York: Harcourt Brace Jovanovich.

Chodos, Robert
   1973 *The CPR: A Century of Corporate Welfare.* Toronto: James Lewis and Samuel.

Christian, William and Colin Campbell
   1983 *Political Parties and Ideologies in Canada,* 2nd ed. Toronto: McGraw-Hill Ryerson.

Clairmonte, Frederick
   1982 "Dynamics of Finance Capital," *Journal of Contemporary Asia,* 12 (2): 158-67.

Clark, Colin
   1960 *The Conditions of Economic Progress.* 3rd edition. London.

Clark, S. D.
   1939 In H. F. Angus (ed.) *Canada and Her Great Neighbor: Sociological Surveys of Opinions and Attitudes in Canada Concerning the United States.* Toronto: The Ryerson Press.

   1959a *Movements of Political Protest, 1640-1940.* Toronto: University of Toronto Press.

   1959b *The Canadian Manufacturers' Association.* Toronto: University of Toronto Press..

   1966 *The Suburban Society.* Toronto: University of Toronto Press.

   1968 *The Developing Canadian Community.* Toronto: University of Toronto Press.

   1975 "The Post Second World War Canadian Society," *Canadian Review of Sociology,* 12 (February): 25-32.

Clark, Susan and Andrew S. Harvey
   1976 "The Sexual Division of Labour: The Use of Time," *Atlantis,* 2 (1): 46-66.

Clement, Wallace

1975   *The Canadian Corporate Elite: Economic Power in Canada.* Toronto: McClelland and Stewart (The Carleton Library).

1977   *Continental Corporate Power: An Analysis of Economic Power.* Toronto: McClelland and Stewart.

1978   "A Political Economy of Regionalism in Canada," in D. Glenday *et al.* (eds.), *Modernization and the Canadian State.* Toronto: Macmillan, pp. 89-110.

1981   *Hardrock Mining: Industrial Relations and Technological Change at Inco.* Toronto: McClelland and Stewart.

1983   *Class, Power and Property: Essays on Canadian Society.* Toronto: Methuen.

1985   "Elites" in *The Canadian Encyclopedia*, Vol. I. Edmonton: Hurtig, pp. 562-563.

1986   *The Struggle to Organize: Resistance in Canada's Fishery.* Toronto: McClelland and Stewart.

Cohn, Werner

1976   "Jewish Outmarriage and Anomie: A Study in the Canadian Syndrome of Polarities," *Canadian Review of Sociology and Anthropology*, 13 (1): 90-105.

Coleman, James S.

1964   *Introduction to Mathematical Sociology.* New York: Free Press of Glencoe.

Colquette, R. D.

1957   *The First Fifty Years: A History of United Grain Growers Limited.* Winnipeg: The Public Press.

Connelly, Pat

1978   *Last Hired, First Fired: Women and the Canadian Work Force.* Toronto: The Canadian Women's Education Press.

Connolly, William E.

1969   *The Bias of Pluralism.* N.Y.: Atherton Press.

Converse, Philip E.

1964   "The Nature of Belief Systems in Mass Publics," in David E. Apter (ed.), *Ideology and Discontent.* London: Collier-Macmillan, pp. 206-261.

Courchene, T. J.

1970   "Interprovincial Migration and Economic Adjustment," *The Canadian Journal of Economics*, 3 (4): 550-576.

1974a   "Migration and the Maritimes," *Atlantic Canadian Economic Association Papers*, 3: 1-39.

1974b   *Migration, Income and Employment: Canada, 1965-1968.* Montreal: C. D. Howe Research Institute.

1976   "Alternative Regional Development Strategies in a Federal State," in *Regional Poverty and Change.* Ottawa: Canadian Council on Rural Development, pp.191-206.

1978   "Avenues of Adjustment: The Transfer System and Regional Disparities," in M. Walker (ed.), *Canadian Confederation at the Crossroads.* Vancouver: The Fraser Institute, pp.145-186.

Craven, Paul and Tom Traves
　　1979　"The Class Politics of the National Policy," *Journal of Canadian Studies*, 14:3 (Fall).

Crawford, Craig and James Curtis
　　1979　"English Canadian-American Differences in Value Orientations," *Studies in Comparative International Development*, 14: 23-44.

Creighton, Donald
　　1937　*The Commercial Empire of the St. Lawrence 1760-1850*. Toronto: Macmillan.

Crispo, John
　　1979　*Mandates for Canada*. Don Mills, Ontario: General Publishing Co.

Croll, D. A.
　　1971　*Poverty in Canada: Report of the Special Senate Committee on Poverty*. Ottawa: Queen's Printer.

Crysdale, Stewart
　　1968　"Family Kinship in Riverdale," in W. E. Mann (ed.), *Canada: A Sociological Profile*. Toronto: Copp Clark, pp. 106-14.

Cuneo, C. J. and J. E. Curtis
　　1975　"Social Ascription in the Educational and Occupational Attainment of Urban Canadians," *Canadian Review of Sociology and Anthropology*, 12 (1): 6-24.

Curtis, James
　　1971　"Voluntary Association Joining: A Cross-National Comparison," *American Sociological Review*, 36: 872-880.

Cypher, James M.
　　1979a　"The Internationalization of Capital and the Transformation of Social Formations: A Critique of the Monthly Review School," *Review of Radical Political Economics*, 11 (4): 33-49.

　　1979b　"The Transnational Challenge to the Corporate State," *Journal of Economic Issues*, 13: 513-42.

Dann, James
　　1979　"U.S. Hegemony Over the Three Worlds," *Review of Radical Political Economics*, 11 (4): 64-77.

Darroch, A. G.
　　1979　"Another Look at Ethnicity, Stratification and Social Mobility in Canada," *Canadian Journal of Sociology*, 4 (1): 1-25.

Davidson, P. E. and H. Anderson
　　1973　*Occupational Mobility in an American Community*. Stanford, California: Stanford University Press.

Davis, Arthur K.
　　1960　"Decline and Fall," *Monthly Review*, XII: 334-344.

　　1971　"Canadian Society and History as Hinterland versus Metropolis," in Richard J. Ossenberg (ed.), *Canadian Society: Pluralism, Change and Conflict*. Scarborough, Ontario: Prentice-Hall, pp. 6-32.

De Grass, Richard P.
1977   *Development of Monopolies in Canada from 1907-1913.* Master's thesis, University of Waterloo.

De Cormis, Anna
1983   "So Much for 'the American Way' in Auto and Steel," *Guardian (New York)*, 35 (32): 11.

Department of Labour
1984   *Information.* Ottawa, June 26.

Diamond, Sigmund
1972   "An Experiment in 'Feudalism'; French Canada in the 17th Century," in J. M. Bumsted (ed.), *Canadian History before Confederation.* Georgetown: Irwin Dorsey.

Dobb, Maurice
1963   *Studies in the Development of Capitalism.* New York: International Publishers.
[1947]

Domanski, Olga
1971   "Pages of a Shop Diary," in *Liberation Now*, pp. 88-94.

Dominion Bureau of Statistics
1969   *Estimates of Employees by Province and Industry 1961-1968.* (November, No. 8003-515).

Downes, Anthony
1972   "Up and Down With Ecology - The 'Issue-Attention Cycle'," *The Public Interest*, XVIII: 38-50.

Drache, D.
1970   "The Canadian Bourgeoisie and its National Consciousness," in Ian Lumsden (ed.), *Close the 49th Parallel etc.: The Americanization of Canada.* Toronto: University of Toronto Press: 3-25.

1983   "The Crisis of Canadian Political Economy: Dependency Theory Versus the New Orthodoxy," *Canadian Journal of Political and Social Theory*, 7 (3): 25-49.

Droucopoulos, Vassilis
1981   "The Non-American Challenge: A Report on the Size and Growth of the World's Largest Firms," *Capital and Class*, 14: 36-46.

Drummond, Ian
1962   "Canadian Life Insurance Companies and the Capital Market, 1890-1914," *Canadian Journal of Economics and Political Science*, 27: 204-24.

Dumont, Micheline, Michele Jean, Marie Lavigne and Jennifer Stoddart
1982   *L'Histoire des Femmes au Québec depuis quatre Siècles.* Montréal: Les Quinze.

Duncan, O. D., D. Featherman and B. Duncan
1972   *Socioeconomic Background and Achievement.* New York: Seminar.

Durkheim, Emile
1933   *The Division of Labor in Society.* Translated by George Simpson. New York: Free Press.
[1893]

1964   *The Division of Labor in Society.* 1st edition. New York: Free Press.
[1893]

1964   *The Rules of Sociological Method*. Edited by George Catlin. New York: Free Press.
[1895]

Easterbrook, W. T. and G. J. Aitken

    1956   *Canadian Economic History*. Toronto: Macmillan.

Economic Council of Canada

    1977   *Living Together: A Study of Regional Disparities*. Ottawa: Minister of Supply and Services Canada.

    1983   *On the Mend. Twentieth Annual Review 1983*. Ottawa: Minister of Supply and Services Canada.

Edwards, Meredith

    1981   *Financial Arrangements within Families*. [Canberra]: National Women's Advisory Council.

Eichler, Margrit

    1973   "Women as Personal Dependents: A Critique of Theories of the Stratification of the Sexes and an Alternative Approach," in M. Stephenson (ed.), *Women in Canada*. Toronto: New Press, pp. 38-55.

    1981   "Power, Dependency, Love and the Sexual Division of Labour. A Critique of the Decision-Making Approach to Family Power and an Alternative Approach with an Appendix: On Washing My Dirty Linen in Public," *Women's Studies International Quarterly*, 4 (2): 201-219.

    1983   *Families in Canada Today: Recent Changes and their Policy Consequences*. Toronto: Gage.

    1984   *The Connection between Paid and Unpaid Labour and Its Implication for Creating Equality for Women in Employment*. Paper prepared for the Royal Commission of Inquiry on Equality in Employment, 1984, forthcoming in vol. 2 of the Commission Report.

Eisenstadt, S. N.

    1952   "The Process of Absorption of New Immigrants in Israel," *Human Relations*, V, pp. 222-31.

    1954   "Social Mobility and Intergroup Leadership," *Transactions of the Second World Congress of Sociology*, II, pp. 218-30.

    1955   *The Absorption of Immigrants*. Glencoe, Ill.: Free Press.

Eldersveld, Samuel, Sonja Hubée-Boonzaaiger and Jan Kooiman

    1975   "Elite Perceptions of the Political Process in the Netherlands Looked at in Historical Perspective," in Mattei Dogan (ed.), *The Mandarins of Western Europe: The Political Role of Top Political Servants*. New York: Sage, pp. 129-61.

Engels, Friedrich

    1942   "Engels to Sorge," February 8, 1890, in Karl Marx and Friedrich Engels, *Selected Correspondence*. New York: International Publishers, pp. 466-468.

    1953   "Engels to Sorge," September 10, 1888, in Karl Marx and Friedrich Engels, *Letters to Americans*. New York: International Publishers, pp. 203-204.

Ernst, Joseph

    1976   "Political Economy and Reality: Problems in the Interpretation of the American Revolution," *Canadian Review of American Studies*, 7: 2 (Fall).

Esman, Milton J.
  1984 "Federalism and Modernization: Canada and the United States," *Publius: The Journal of Federalism*, 14 (Winter): 21-38.

Fallding, Harold
  1978 "Mainline Protestantism in Canada and the United States: An Overview," *Canadian Journal of Sociology*, 3: 141-160.

Fay, C. R.
  1928 *Great Britain: An Economic and Social Survey from Adam Smith to the Present Day.* London.

Feldman, H.
  1965 *Development of the Husband-Wife Relationship.* Ithaca: Department of Child Development and the Family.

Fennema, Meindert
  1982 *International Networks of Banks and Industry.* The Hague: Martinus Nijoff.

Fennema, Meindert and P. DeJong
  1978 "Internationale Vervlechting van Industire En Bankwezen," in A. Tevlings (ed.), *Herstrukturering van de Nederlandse Industrie.* Alphen a/d Rijn: Samson.

Fennema, Meindert and Huibert Schijf
  1979 "Analysing Interlocking Directorates: Theory and Methods," *Social Networks*, 1: 297-332.

Ferguson, George V.
  1960 "The English-Canadian Outlook," in Mason Wade (ed.), *Canadian Dualism.* Toronto: University of Toronto Press.

Field, F. W.
  1914 *Capital Investments in Canada.* Montreal.

Financial Post
  1979 *The Financial Post 500. Special Report.* June 16. Toronto.

  1986 *Survey of Industrials: The Financial Post Industry's 500.* Toronto.

Finnish Class Project
  1985 *Reality of Social Classes in Finland.* Tampere: University of Tampere.

Fitzgerald, Maureen, Connie Guberman and Margie Wolfe, eds.
  1982 *Still Ain't Satisfied! Canadian Feminism Today.* Toronto: The Women's Press.

Forbes, Ernest
  1983 *Aspects of Maritime Regionalism 1867-1927.* Ottawa

Forcese, D. and J. de Vries
  1977 "Occupations and Electoral Success in Canada: The 1974 Federal Election," *Canadian Review of Sociology and Anthropology*, 14.

Forrest, Anne
  1978 *Unions in the Collective Bargaining Process.* Toronto: Ontario Institute for Studies in Education.

Foster, William
  1968 "Canada First or Our New Nationality," Public Archives. Canada.
  [1871]

Fournier, Pierre
    1976   *The Quebec Establishment*. Montreal: Black Rose.

Fowke, Vernon C.
    1957   *The National Policy and the Wheat Economy*. Toronto: University of Toronto Press.

Fox, Bonnie
    1988   "Conceptualizing 'Patriarchy'," *Canadian Review of Sociology and Anthropology*, 25: 2 (May) 163-182.

Fox, Bonnie, ed.
    1980   *Hidden in the Household: Women's Domestic Labour Under Capitalism*. Toronto: The Women's Press.

Francis, Diane
    1986   *Controlling Interest*. Toronto: Macmillan.

Frank, Andre G.
    1966   "The Development of Underdevelopment," *Monthly Review* 18 (September).

    1969   *Capitalism and Underdevelopment in Latin America*. Revised and enlarged edition. New
    [1967] York: Modern Reader Paperbacks, Monthly Review Press.

    1979   *Dependent Accumulation and Underdevelopment*. New York: Monthly Review Press.

Frank, R. H.
    1967   *Distributional Consequences of Direct Foreign Investment*. New York: Academic Press.

Friedan, Betty
    1968   *The Feminine Mystique*. London: Penguin.

Frieden, Jeff
    1977   "The Trilateral Commission: Economics and Politics in the 1970s," *Monthly Review*, 29 (7): 1-18.

Friedenberg, Edgar Z.
    1980   *Deference to Authority*. White Plains, N.Y.: M.E. Sharpe, Inc.

Friedman, Jonathan
    1978   "Crises in Theory and Transformations of the World Economy," *Review*, 2: 131-46.

Frye, Northrop
    1982   *Divisions on a Ground: Essays on Canadian Culture*. Toronto: Anansi.

Fuentes, C.
    1963   *Whither Latin America?* New York: Monthly Review Press.

Galitzi, E. A.
    1929   "A Study of Assimilation Among the Roumanians in the United States," unpublished Ph.D. dissertation, Columbia University.

Galtung, J.
    1971   "A Structural Theory of Imperialism," *Journal of Peace Research*, 8: 81-114.

Garson, Barbara
    1975   *All the Livelong Day*. New York: Doubleday.

George, R.E.
    1970   *A Leader and a Laggard: Manufacturing Industry in Nova Scotia, Quebec and Ontario.* Toronto: University of Toronto Press.

Gérin, Léon
    1938   *Le type économique et social des Canadiens.* Montreal.

Gerschenkron, Alexander
    1962   *Economic Backwardness in Historical Perspective.* Cambridge, Mass.

Gibbins, R.
    1980   *Prairie Politics and Society: Regionalism in Decline.* Toronto: Butterworths.

    1982   *Regionalism: Territorial Politics in Canada and the United States.* Toronto: Butterworths.

Giddens, Anthony
    1973   *The Class Structure of Advanced Societies.* London: Hutchinson University Library.

    1978   *Durkheim.* London: Fontana.

    1980   *The Class Structure of Advanced Societies.* 2nd edition. London: Hutchinson.

Gillespie, Dair L.
    1972   "Who Has the Power?" in Hans Peter Dreitzel (ed.), *Family, Marriage and the Struggle of the Sexes.* New York: Macmillan, pp. 121-50.

Gillespie, W. Irwin
    1978   *In Search of Robin Hood.* Montreal: C. D. Howe Research Institute.

Glass, D. V., ed.
    1954   *Social Mobility in Britain.* London: Routledge and Kegan Paul.

Glazebrook, G. P. de T.
    1964   *A History of Transportation in Canada.* Vols 1 and 2. Toronto: Macmillan.

Glazier, Kenneth M.
    1972   "Canadian Investment in the United States: 'Putting Your Money Where Your Mouth Is'," *Journal of Contemporary Business*, 1 (Autumn): 61-66.

Goldfrank, Walter L.
    1977   "Who Rules the World? Class Formation at the International Level," *Quarterly Journal of Ideology*, 1 (2): 32-7.

Gonick, C. W.
    1970   "Poverty and Capitalism," in W. E. Mann (ed.), *Poverty and Social Policy in Canada.* Vancouver: Copp Clark, pp. 66-81.

Gonick, Cy
    1978   *Out of Work.* Toronto: James Lorimer.

Goodman, L. A.
    1972   "A General Model for the Analysis of Surveys," *American Journal of Sociology*, 77 (6): 1035-86.

Gordon, C. Wayne and Nicholas Babchuk
    1959   "Typology of Voluntary Associations," *American Sociological Review*, 24: 22-29.

Government of Canada
    1921   *Census of Canada.* Ottawa: The Queen's Printer. Vol. 5.

1931   *Census of Canada*. Ottawa: The Queen's Printer. Vol. 8.

1941   *Census of Canada*. Ottawa: The Queen's Printer. Vols. 4,7,8.

1972   *Foreign Direct Investment in Canada*. Ottawa.

Government of New Brunswick
1962   *Report of the Royal Commission on the New Brunswick Potato Industry*. Fredericton: The Queen's Printer.

Grabb, Edward G. and James Curtis
1988   "English Canadian-American Differences in Orientation Toward Social Control and Individual Rights," *Sociological Focus*, 21: 127-141.

Grant, George
1965   *Lament for a Nation, The Defeat of Canadian Nationalism*. Toronto: Macmillan.

1969   *Technology and Empire*. Toronto: House of Anansi.

Grant, J. W.
1937-   "Populations Shifts in the Maritime Provinces," *Dalhousie Review* 17: 283-94.
1938

Gray, James H.
1966   *The Winter Years*. Toronto.

Grayson, J. Paul and L. M. Grayson
1974   "The Social Base of Interwar Political Unrest in Urban Alberta," *Canadian Journal of Political Science* 7: 289-313.

Griffiths, Curt T., John F. Klein, and Simon N. Verdun-Jones
1980   *Criminal Justice in Canada*. Toronto: Butterworths.

Guindon, Hubert
1964   "Social Unrest, Social Class, and Quebec's Bureaucratic Revolution," *Queen's Quarterly*, LXXI.

1978   "The Modernization of Quebec and the Legitimacy of the Canadian State." in Daniel Glenday *et al.* (eds.), *Modernization and the Canadian State*. Toronto: Macmillan.

Gwyn, Richard
1984   *The 49th Paradox*. Toronto: Paperjacks.

Hagan, John and Jeffrey Leon
1978   "Philosophy and Sociology of Crime Control," in Harry M. Johnson (ed.), *Social System and Legal Process*. San Francisco: Jossey-Bass, pp. 181-208.

Haliburton, R. G.
1869   *The Men of the North and Their Place in History*. Montreal.

Hamburg, Morris
1970   *Statistical Analysis for Decision Making*. N.Y.: Harcourt, Brace and World.

Hammond, Bray
1967   "Banking in Canada Before Confederation, 1672-1867," in Easterbrook and Watkins (eds.), *Approaches to Canadian Economic History*. Toronto, pp. 127-168.

Hann, Russell
1975 *Farmers Confront Industrialism: Some Historical Perspectives on Ontario Agrarian Movements*. 3rd revised edition. Toronto.

1976 "Brain Workers and the Knights of Labor: E.E. Sheppard, Phillips Thompson and the Toronto News, 1883-1887," in Gregory Kealey and Peter Warrian (eds.), *Essays in Canadian Working Class History*. Toronto: McClelland.

Hänninen, Sakari and Leena Paldán
1983 *Rethinking Ideology: A Marxist Debate*. New York: International General.

Hansen, Marcus Lee
1961 *The Atlantic Migration*. New York: Harper Torchbooks.

Hardin, Herschel
1974 *A Nation Unaware: The Canadian Economic Culture*, Vancouver: J.J. Douglas.

Harrington, Michael
1972 *Socialism*. New York: Saturday Review Press.

Harris, R. C.
1967 *The Seigneurial System in Early Canada*. Madison.

Hartz, Louis
1955 *The Liberal Tradition in America*. New York: Harcourt Brace.

Hartz, Louis, ed.
1964 *The Founding of New Societies*. New York: Harcourt, Brace and World.

Harvey, David
1982 *The Limits to Capital*. Oxford: Basil Blackwell.

Hastings, Elizabeth H. and Philip K. Hastings, eds.
1982 *Index to International Public Opinion*, 1980-1981. Westport, Conn.: Greenwood Press.

Hawley, Jim
1979 "The Internationalization of Capital: Banks, Eurocurrency and the Instability of the World Monetary System," *Review of Radical Political Economics*, 11 (4): 78-90.

Haythorne, George V.
1938 "Agriculture and the Farm Worker in Eastern Canada." Harvard University: unpublished Ph.D. dissertation.

1941 *Land and Labour*. Toronto.

Head, Wilson, A.
1975 *The Black Presence in the Canadian Mosaic: A Study of Perception and the Practice of Discrimination Against Blacks in Metropolitan Toronto*. Ontario Human Rights Commission. Toronto: Queen's Printer.

Hedley, Max
1976 "Independent Commodity Production," *Canadian Review of Sociology and Anthropology*, 13: 413-21.

Heilbroner, R.
1959 *The Future as History*. New York: Harper.

Helmes-Hayes, Richard C.
  1986   "Images of Inequality in Pre-Porter Canadian Sociology." A paper presented at the annual meeting of the Ontario Anthropology and Sociology Association, Waterloo, Ontario.

Henripin, Jacques
  1968   *Tendances et Facteurs de la Fécondité au Canada.* Ottawa: Dominion Bureau of Statistics.

Henripin, Jacques and Yves Peron
  1972   "The Demographic Transition in the Province of Quebec," in D. V. Glass and Roger Revelle (eds.), *Population and Social Change.* London: Edward Arnold, pp. 213-31.

Henry, F.
  1978   "The Dynamics of Racism in Toronto," Toronto: York University, Department of Anthropology, mimeo.

Henry, Frances and Effie Ginzberg
  1985   *Who Gets the Work?: A Test of Racial Discrimination in Employment.* Toronto: Urban Alliance on Race Relations and the Social Planning Council.

Henry, Louis
  1961   "Some Data on Natural Fertility," in *Eugenics Quarterly*, 8 (June): 81-91.

Higley, John, Desley Deacon and Don Smart, with the collaboration of Robert C. Cushing, Gwen Moore and Jan Pakulski
  1979   *Elites in Australia.* London: Routledge and Kegan Paul.

Hilferding, Rudolf
  1970   *Le Capital financier.* Paris: Editions de Minuit.
  [1910]

  1981   *Finance Capital.* London: Routledge and Kegan Paul.

Hiller, Harry H.
  1976   *Canadian Society: A Sociological Analysis.* Scarborough, Ontario: Prentice-Hall Canada.

Hobsbawm, Eric
  1962   *The Age of Revolution: Europe 1789-1848.* London.

Hodge, R. W.
  1966   "Occupational Mobility as a Probability Process," *Demography*, 3 (1): 19-34.

Hoffman, Lois W.
  1960   "Effects of the Employment of Mothers on Parental Power Relations and the Division of Household Tasks," *Marriage and Family Living*, 22 (February): 392-95.

Hofstadter, Richard
  1951   *The American Political Tradition And The Men Who Made It.* New York.

Hofstede, Geert
  1984   *Culture's Consequences: International Differences in Work-Related Values.* Beverly Hills: Sage Publications.

Hogg, Peter
  1982   *The Canada Act, 1982.* Toronto: Carswell.

Holland, S.
  1976   *Capitalism Versus the Regions.* London: The MacMillan Press.

Horn, Michael
 1972   *The Dirty Thirties: Canadians in the Great Depression.* Toronto: Copp.

Horowitz, Gad
 1966   "Conservatism, Liberalism and Socialism in Canada: An Interpretation,"*Canadian Journal of Economics and Political Science*, 32: 143-60.

 1968   *Canadian Labour in Politics.* Toronto: University of Toronto Press.

Horowitz, Irving Louis
 1973   "The Hemispheric Connection: A Critique and Corrective to the Entrepreneurial Thesis of Development with Special Emphasis on the Canadian Case," *Queen's Quarterly*, 80 (Autumn): 327-59.

Howe, Gary N.
 1981   "Dependency Theory, Imperialism, and the Production of Surplus Value on a World Scale," *Latin American Perspectives*, 8 (3/4): 82-102.

Howe, Gary N. and A. Sica
 1980   "Political Economy, Imperialism, and the Problem of World System Theory," in S. G. McNall and G. N. Howe (eds.), *Current Perspectives in Social Theory*, Vol 1. Greenwich, Connecticut: JAL Press, pp. 235-86.

Hueglin, Thomas O.
 1984   "The End of Institutional Tidiness? Trends of Late Federalism in the United States and Canada." Kingston, Ont.: Department of Political Science, Queen's University.

Hughes, Everett C.
 1943   *French Canada in Transition.* Chicago: University of Chicago Press.

Hunter, Alfred A.
 1986   *Class Tells: On Social Inequality in Canda.* 2nd edition. Toronto: Butterworths.

Hurd, W. Burton
 1937a   "The Decline in the Canadian Birth-rate," *Canadian Journal of Economics and Political Science*, III.

 1937b   *Racial Origins and Nativity of the Canadian People.* Census monograph No. 4. Ottawa: Dominion Bureau of Statistics.

Hutcheson, John
 1973   "The Capitalist State in Canada," in R. Laxer (ed.), *(Canada) Ltd.* Toronto: McClelland and Stewart.

 1978   *Dominance and Dependency.* Toronto: McClelland and Stewart.

Hymer, Stephen
 1972   "The Internationalization of Capital," *Journal of Economic Issues*, 6 (1): 91-111.

Hyson, Ronald V. S.
 1972   "Factors which Prevent the Electoral Success of 'Third Parties' in the Maritime Provinces." M.A. thesis, McGill University, Montreal.

Innis, Harold A.
 1971   *A History of the Canadian Pacific Railway.* Toronto: University of Toronto Press.
 [1923]

Irving, John A.
1959   *The Social Credit Movement in Alberta.* Toronto: University of Toronto Press.

Iverson, N. and R. Matthews
1968   *Communities in Decline.* St. John's, Nfld.: Institute for Social and Economic Research, Memorial University of Newfoundland.

Jacobsen, Chanoch
1969   "Who Joins Farm Organizations?" *Journal of Cooperative Extension*, 7: 225-32.

Jahoda, Marie
1964   "Stereotype," in Julius Gould and William L. Kolb (eds.), *A Dictionary of the Social Sciences.* New York.

Janeway, Elizabeth
1971   *Man's World, Women's Place.* New York: Delta.

Johnson, Leo A.
1972   "The Development of Class in Canada in the Twentieth Century," in Gary Teeple (ed.), *Capitalism and the National Question in Canada.* Toronto: University of Toronto Press, pp. 141-84.

Jones, F. L.
1969   "Social Mobility and Industrial Society: A Thesis Re-examined," *Sociological Quarterly*, 10 (Summer): 292-305.

Jordan, Z. A.
1971   *Karl Marx: Economy, Class and Social Revolution.* London: Michael Joseph.

Kalbach, Warren E.
1970   *The Impact of Immigration on Canada's Population.* Ottawa: Dominion Bureau of Statistics, 1970.

Katznelson, Ira
1981   *City Trenches: Urban Politics and the Patterning of Class in the United States.* Chicago: University of Chicago Press.

Kavaler, Lucy
1960   *The Private World of High Society.* N.Y.: David McKay.

Kay, Geoffrey
1975   *Development and Underdevelopment: A Marxist Analysis.* New York: St. Martin's Press.

Kealey, Gregory S.
1982   *Dreaming of What Might Be: The Knights of Labour in Ontario, 1880-1900.* London.

Kendall, John C.
1974   "A Canadian Construction of Reality: Northern Images of the United States," *The American Review of Canadian Studies* 4 (Spring): 20-36.

Kerr, C. *et al.*
1960   *Industrialism and Industrial Man.* Cambridge: Harvard University Press.

King, W. L. Mackenzie
    1918   *Industry and Humanity*. Toronto: Macmillan.

Klein, John F., Jim R. Webb, and J. E. DiSanto
    1978   "Experience with Police and Attitudes Towards the Police," *Canadian Journal of Sociology*, 3 (4): 441-456.

Kohn, M.
    1969   *Class and Conformity*. Homewood: The Dorsey Press.

Kolko, Joyce
    1977   "Imperialism and the Crisis of Capitalism in the 1970s," *Journal of Contemporary Asia*, 7 (1): 9-21.

Komarovsky, Mirra
    1967   *Blue-Collar Marriage*. New York: Vintage.

Kome, Penney
    1982   *Somebody Has To Do It*. Toronto: McClelland and Stewart.

Kotz, David M.
    1978   *Bank Control of Large Corporations in the United States*. Berkeley: University of California Press.

Kresl, Peter Karl
    1982   "An Economics Perspective: Canada in the International Economy," in William Metcalf (ed.), *Understanding Canada*. New York: New York University Press, pp. 227-295.

Kroeber, A. L. and T. Parsons
    1958   "The Concepts of Culture and of Social System," *American Sociological Review*, XXIII (October).

Kubat, D. and D. Thornton
    1974   *A Statistical Profile of Canadian Society*. Toronto: McGraw-Hill Ryerson.

Kudrle, Robert T. and Theodore R. Marmor
    1981   "The Development of Welfare States in North America," in Peter Flora and Arnold J. Heidenheimer (eds.), *The Development of Welfare States in Europe and America*. New Brunswick, N.J.: Transaction Books, pp. 81-121.

Kuznets, Simon
    1969   *Modern Economic Growth: Rate Structure and Spread*. New Haven.

Laclau, E.
    1971   "Feudalism and Capitalism in Latin America," *New Left Review*, 67 (May-June): 19-38.

Lambert, Ronald D., Steven D. Brown, James E. Curtis, Barry J. Kay and John M. Wilson
    1986   *The 1984 Canadian National Election Study Codebook*. Waterloo, Ontario.

Lamontage, Maurice
    1969   "The Role of Government," in K. J. Rae and J. T. McLeod (eds.), *Business and Government in Canada*. Toronto: Methuen.

Landon, F.
    1967   *Western Ontario and the American Frontier*. Toronto: Macmillan.

Lapiere, R. T.
 1954   *A Theory of Social Control*. New York.

Larrain, Jorge
 1979   *The Concept of Ideology*. London: Hutchinson

Laski, H. J.
 1935   *The State in Theory and Practice*. London: Allen & Unwin.

Lautard, Hugh and Donald J. Loree
 1984   "Ethnic Stratification in Canada, 1931-1979," *Canadian Journal of Sociology*, 9: 333-44.

Laxer, Gordon
 1981   *The Social Origins of Canada's Branch Plant Economy*, 1837 to 1914. Doctoral dissertation, University of Toronto.

 1985a "Foreign Ownership and Myths About Canadian Development," *Canadian Review of Sociology and Anthropology*, 22: 3 (August).

 1985b "The Political Economy of Aborted Development," in Robert J. Brym (ed.), *The Structure of the Canadian Capitalist Class*. Toronto: Garamond.

Laxer, J.
 1970   *The Energy Poker Game: The Politics of the Continental Resource Deal*. Toronto: New Deal.

Laxer, J. and D. Jantzi
 1973   "The De-Industrialization of Ontario," in R. Laxer (ed.), *(Canada) Ltd*. Toronto: McClelland and Stewart.

Laxer, Robert, ed.
 1973   *(Canada) Ltd.: The Political Economy of Dependency*. Toronto: McClelland and Stewart.

League of Nations (Hilgerdt)
 1945   *Industrialisation and World Trade*. USA.

LeDuc, L., H. Clarke, J. Jenson and J. Pammett
 1974   "A National Sample Design," *Canadian Journal of Political Science*, 7 (4): 701-5.

Lemieux, O. A. *et al.*
 1934   "Factors in the Growth of Rural Population in Eastern Canada," *Proceedings of the Canadian Political Science Association*, VI, pp. 196-219.

LeNeveu, A. H.
 1931   "The Evolution and Present-Day Significance of the Canadian Occupational Structure." Census monograph (unpublished).

Lenin, V. I.
 1970   "Imperialism, the Highest Stage of Capitalism," in V. I. Lenin, *Selected Works*, Vol. 1.
 [1917] Moscow: Progress Publishers, pp. 667-768.

Letourneau, Firmin
 1952   *Histoire de l'Agriculture (Canada Français)* 2nd edition. Montreal.

Lévesque, René
 1968   *An Option for Quebec*. Toronto: McClelland and Stewart.

LeVine, Robert A. and Donald T. Campbell
  1972 *Ethnocentrism: Theories of Conflict, Ethnic Attitudes, and Group Behavior.* New York: John Wiley & Sons.

Levitt, Kari
  1970 *Silent Surrender: The Multinational Corporation in Canada.* Toronto: Macmillan.

Li, Peter S.
  1980 "Income Achievement and Adaptive Capacity: An Empirical Comparison of Chinese and Japanese in Canada," in K. Victor Ujimoto and Gordon Hirabayashi (eds.), *Visible Minorities and Multiculturalism: Asians in Canada.* Toronto: Butterworths.

  1986 "Race and Ethnic Relations," in Lorne Tepperman and R. Jack Richardson (eds.), *The Social World: An Introduction to Sociology.* Toronto: McGraw-Hill Ryerson.

Light, Ivan
  1972 *Ethnic Enterprise in America.* Berkeley: University of California Press.

Linteau, Paul-André *et al.*
  1983 *Quebec: A History 1867-1929.* Toronto

Lipset, Seymour Martin
  1950 *Agrarian Socialism: The Cooperative Commonwealth Federation in Saskatchewan.* Berkeley: University of California Press.

  1963a "The Value Patterns of Democracy: A Case Study in Comparative Analysis," *American Sociological Review*, 28: 515-531.

  1963b *The First New Nation: The United States in Historical and Comparative Perspective.* New York: Basic Books.

  1964 "Canada and the United States - A Comparative View," *Canadian Review of Sociology and Anthropology*, 1: 173-185.

  1965a "Revolution and Counterrevolution: The United States and Canada," in Thomas R. Ford (ed.), *The Revolutionary Theme in Contemporary America.* Lexington: University of Kentucky Press, pp. 21-64.

  1965b *Political Man.* Garden City, N.Y.: Doubleday.

  1967 *The First New Nation.* Garden City, N.Y.: Doubleday Anchor Books.

  1968a *Revolution and Counterrevolution.* New York: Basic Books.

  1968b *Agrarian Socialism: The Cooperative Commonwealth Federation in Saskatchewan.*
  [1950] Berkeley: University of California Press.

  1970 *Revolution and Counterrevolution.* Garden City, N.Y.: Anchor Books, 2nd edition.

  1976 "Radicalism in North America: A Comparative View of the Party Systems in Canada and the United States," *Transactions of the Royal Society of Canada*, 14 (Fourth Series), pp. 19-55.

  1977 "Why No Socialism in the United States?" in S. Bialer and S. Sluzar (eds.), *Sources of Contemporary Radicalism.* Vol. 1, Boulder, Colorado: Westview Press, pp. 31-149.

1979 "Value Differences, Absolute or Relative: the English Speaking Democracies," in *The First*
[1963] *New Nation: The United States in Historical Comparative Perspective*. Expanded paper-
back edition. New York: W.W. Norton, pp. 248-273 [New York: Basic Books].

1983 "Socialism in America," in P. Kurtz (ed.), *Sidney Hook: Philosopher of Democracy and Humanism*. Buffalo, N.Y.: Prometheus Books, pp. 47-63.

1985 "Canada and the United States: The Cultural Dimension," in Charles F. Doran and John H. Sigler (eds.), *Canada and the United States: Enduring Friendship, Persistent Stress*. Englewood Cliffs, N.J.: Prentice-Hall, pp. 109-160.

1986 "Historical Traditions and National Characteristics: A Comparative Analysis of Canada and the United States," *Canadian Journal of Sociology*, 11 (2): 113-155.

Lipset, S. M. and R. Bendix
1966 *Social Mobility in Industrial Society*. Berkeley: University of California Press.

Lipset, S. M. and J. H. M. Laslett, eds.
1974 *Failure of a Dream? Essays in the History of American Socialism*. Garden City, N.Y.: Doubleday Anchor Books.

Litt, Edgar
1970 *Ethnic Politics in America: Beyond Pluralism*. Glenview: Scott, Foresman.

Litvak, I. A. and C. J. Maule
1981 *The Canadian Multinationals*. Toronto: Butterworths.

Locke, John
1965 *Two Treatises on Government*. Edited by Peter Laslett. New York: Mentor Books.
[1690]

Lopata, Helena
1971 *Occupation: Housewife*. New York: Oxford University Press.

Lorimer, James and Myfanwy Phillips
1971 *Working People: Life in a Downtown City Neighbourhood*. Toronto: James Lewis & Samuel.

Lower, A. R. M.
1943 "Two Ways of Life: The Primary Antithesis of Canadian History," Canadian Historical Association, *Report*, 1-14.

1977 *Colony to Nation*. Toronto: McClelland and Stewart.

Lumsden, Ian
1970 "American Imperialism and Canadian Intellectuals," in Ian Lumsden (ed.), *Close the 49th Parallel etc.: The Americanization of Canada*. Toronto: University of Toronto Press, pp. 321-36.

Luxemburg, Rosa
1951 *The Accumulation of Capital*. New York: Monthly Review Press.

Luxton, Meg
1980 *More than a Labour of Love: Three Generations of Women's Work in the Home*. Toronto: The Canadian Women's Educational Press.

1983 "Two Hands for the Clock: Changing Patterns in the Gendered Division of Labour in the Home," *Studies in Political Economy*, 12 (Fall): 27-44.

MacLennan, Hugh
  1945 *Two Solitudes.* Toronto: Popular Library.

  1977 "A Society in Revolt," in Judith Webster (ed.), *Voices of Canada: An Introduction to Canadian Culture.* Burlington, Vt.: Association for Canadian Studies in the United States, pp. 29-30.

MacNutt, W. S.
  1963 *New Brunswick: A History: 1784-1867.* Toronto: Macmillan.

Macpherson, C. B.
  1962 *Democracy in Alberta: Social Credit and the Party System.* Toronto: University of Toronto
  [1953] Press.

  1977 *The Life and Times of Liberal Democracy.* Oxford.

Maizels, Alfred
  1963 *Industrial Growth and World Trade.* London

Mandel, E.
  1973 *Capitalism and Regional Disparities.* Toronto: New Hogtown Press.

Manzer, Ronald
  1974 *Canada: A Sociopolitical Report.* Toronto: McGraw-Hill Ryerson.

Marchak, Patricia
  1975 "Class, Regional and Institutional Sources of Social Conflict in B.C.," *British Columbia Studies*, No. 27 (Autumn).

Marcussen, Henrik and Jans Torp
  1982 *The Internationalization of Capital.* London: Zed Press.

Marsden, Lorna R. and Edward B. Harvey
  1979 *Fragile Federation: Social Change in Canada.* Toronto: McGraw-Hill Ryerson.

Marsh, Leonard C.
  1940 *Canadians In and Out of Work: A Survey of Economic Classes and Their Relations to the Labour Market.* Toronto: Oxford University Press.

Marshall, Herbert *et al.*
  1976 *Canadian-American Industry: A Study in International Investment.* Toronto: Macmillan.
  [1936]

Martindale, Don
  1960 *American Social Structure.* New York: Appleton, Century Crofts.

  1967 "The Sociology of National Character," *Annals of the American Academy of Political and Social Sciences*, 370

Marx, Karl
  1963 *The 18th Brumaire of Louis Bonaparte.* New York: International Publishers.
  [1852]

  1967 *Capital.* New York: International Publishers, 3 vols.

  1971 "Peasantry as a Class," in Teodor Shanin (ed.), *Peasants and Peasant Societies: Selected Readings.* Harmondsworth: Penguin, pp. 229-37.

  1973 *Grundrisse: Introduction to the Critique of Political Economy.* London: Pelican.
  [1939]

Marx, Karl and Friedrich Engels

1967 *The Communist Manifesto.* With an introduction by A. J. P. Taylor. Harmondsworth:
[1848] Penguin Books.

1968 *Selected Works.* New York: International Publishers.

Matthews, R.

1976 *There's No Better Place Than Here: Social Change in Three Newfoundland Communities.*
Toronto: Irwin Publishing.

1980 "Class Issues and the Role of the State in the Development of Canada's East Coast Fishery,"
Canadian Issues: Journal of the Association for Canadian Studies, 3 (1): 115-124.

1981 "Two Alternative Explanations of Regional Dependency in Canada," *Canadian Public
Policy*, 7: 268-283.

1983 *The Creation of Regional Dependency.* Toronto: University of Toronto Press.

Matthews, R. and J. C. Davis

1986a "The Comparative Influence of Region, Status, Class and Ethnicity on Canadian Attitudes
and Values," in R. J. Brym (ed.), *Regionalism in Canada.* Toronto: Irwin Publishing.

1986b "Is Regionalism Dead?: Confronting Recent Interpretations of Regionalism in Canada," in
J. Acheson and R. Berry (eds.), *Regionalism and National Identity.* Christchurch, N.Z.:
Association for Canadian Studies of Australia and New Zealand and University of Canter-
bury Press.

Matthiasson, J. S.

1970 *Resident Perception of Quality of Life in Resource Frontier Communities.* Winnipeg:
Center for Settlement Studies, University of Manitoba.

McClelland, D. C.

1961 *The Achieving Society.* Princeton, N. J.: Van Nostrand.

1969 *Motivating Economic Development.* New York: Free Press.

1971 "The Achievement Motive in Economic Growth," in P. Kilby (ed.), *Entrepreneurship and
Economic Development.* New York: Free Press, pp. 109-122.

McCormack, A. Ross

1977 *Reformers, Rebels and Revolutionaries: The Western Canadian Radical Movement 1899-
1919.* Toronto: University of Toronto Press.

McCrorie, James N.

1971 "Change and Paradox in Agrarian Social Movements: The Case of Saskatchewan," in
Richard Ossenberg (ed.), *Canadian Society: Pluralism, Change and Conflict.* Toronto:
Prentice-Hall, pp. 36-51.

McKercher, William R.

1983 *The U.S. Bill of Rights and the Canadian Charter of Rights and Freedoms.* Toronto:
Ontario Economic Council.

McKie, Craig

n.d. "An Ontario Industrial Elite: The Senior Executive in Manufacturing Industry." Unpublished doctoral dissertation, University of Toronto.

McLennan, J. L.

1929 *The Merger Movement in Canada Since 1880.* Master's thesis, Queen's University.

McLeod, J. T.

1976 "The Free Enterprise Dodo is No Phoenix," *Canadian Forum*, 56 (August): 6-13.

McMillan, Charles J.
  1978   "The Changing Competitive Environment of Canadian Business," *Journal of Canadian Studies* 13 (Spring): 38-48.

McNally, David
  1981   "Staple Theory as Commodity Fetishism: Marx, Innis and Canadian Political Economy," *Studies in Political Economy*, 6: 35-63.

McNaught, Kenneth
  1975   "Political Trials and the Canadian Political Tradition," in Martin L. Friedland (ed.), *Courts and Trials: A Multidisciplinary Approach*. Toronto: University of Toronto Press, pp. 137-161.

  1984   "Approaches to the Study of Canadian History," *The (Japanese) Annual Review of Canadian Studies, 5: 89-102*.

McRae, Kenneth
  1964   "The Structure of Canadian History," in Louis Hartz *et al.* (eds.), *The Founding of New Societies*. New York: Harcourt Brace.

McWhinney, Edward
  1982   *Canada and the Constitution, 1979-1982*. Toronto: University of Toronto Press.

Meissner, Martin *et al.*
  1975   "No Exit for Wives: Sexual Division of Labour and the Cumulation of Household Demands," *Canadian Review of Sociology and Anthropology*, 13 (4): 424-439.

Mellos, Koula
  1978   "Developments in Advanced Capitalist Ideology," *Canadian Journal of Political Science*, XI: 829-61.

Menshikov, S.
  1969   *Millionaires and Managers*. Moscow: Progress Publishers.

Mercer, John and Michael Goldberg
  1982   "Value Differences and Their Meaning for Urban Development in the U.S.A.," Working Paper No. 12, UBC Research in Land Economics, Vancouver, B.C.: Faculty of Commerce, University of British Columbia.

Merleman, M.
  1968   "On the Neo-elitist Critique of Community Power," *American Political Science Review*, 62: 451-60.

Merton, Robert K.
  1957   *Social Theory and Social Structure*. Glencoe, Ill.: The Free Press.

Michels, Robert
  1962   *Political Parties*. New York: Free Press.
  [1911]

Miles, Angela and Geraldine Finn, eds.
  1982   *Feminism in Canada: From Pressure to Politics*. Montreal: Black Rose.

Miliband, Robert
  1969   *The State in Capitalist Society*. London: Weidenfeld and Nicholson.

Mills, C. Wright
  1948   *The New Men of Power*. New York: Harcourt, Brace and World.

  1951   *White Collar: The American Middle Classes*. New York: Oxford University Press.

1956   *The Power Elite.* New York: Oxford University Press.

Mills, C. W. *et al.*
1950   *The Puerto Rican Journey.* New York: Harper and Bros.

Miner, Horace
1939   *St. Denis, A French-Canadian Parish.* Chicago: University of Chicago Press.

Mitchell, Juliet
1971   *Woman's Estate.* Harmondsworth: Penguin.

1972   "Marxism and Women's Liberation," *Social Praxis*, 1 (1): 23-33.

Moore, Barrington
1966   *Social Origins of Dictatorship and Democracy: Lord and Peasant in the Making of the Modern World.* Boston: Beacon.

Moore, Steve and Debi Wells
1975   *Imperialism and the National Question in Canada.* Toronto: privately published.

Moore, W. E.
1965   *The Impact of Industry.* Englewood Cliffs, N. J.: Prentice-Hall.

1979   *World Modernization: The Limits of Convergence.* New York: Elsevier.

Morgal, Janine and Gitte Vedel
1985   "Office Automation: The Case of Gender and Power," *Economic and Industrial Democracy*, 6.

Morton, W. L.
1978   *The Progressive Party in Canada.* Toronto: University of Toronto Press.
[1950]

Moss, John
1974   *Patterns of Isolation in English Canadian Fiction.* Toronto: McClelland and Stewart.

Myers, Gustavus
1972   *History of Canadian Wealth.* Toronto: Lorimer.
[1914]

Myles, John
1979   "Pensions, Power, and Profits: The Political Economy of Old Age Security in Canada." Saskatoon: Annual Meetings of the CISAA.

Myrdal, Alva and Viola Klein
1956   *Women's Two Roles.* London: Routledge and Kegan Paul.

Nabudere, D. W.
1977   *The Political Economy of Imperialism.* London: Zed Press Ltd.

1979   *Essays on the Theory and Practice of Imperialism.* London: Onyx Press Ltd.

Naegele, Kaspar D.
1964   "Further Reflections," in Bernard R. Blishen *et al.* (eds.), *Canadian Society*, rev. ed. Toronto: Macmillan.

National Opinion Research Center (NORC)
1953   "Jobs and Occupations: A Popular Evaluation," in R. Bendix and S. M. Lipset (eds.), *Class Status and Power.* Glencoe, Illinois: Free Press, pp. 411-26.

1985   *General Social Surveys, 1972-1985: Cumulative Codebook.* Chicago: University of Chicago.

Naylor, R. T.
  1972a "The Ideological Foundations of Social Democracy and Social Credit," in Gary Teeple (ed.), *Capitalism and National Question in Canada*. Toronto: University of Toronto Press, pp. 251-6.

  1972b "The Rise and Fall of the Third Commercial Empire of the St. Lawrence," in Gary Teeple (ed.), *Capitalism and the National Question in Canada*. Toronto: University of Toronto Press, pp. 1-41.

  1975 *The History of Canadian Business 1867-1914*. Toronto: Lorimer, 2 vols.

Neatby, H. Blair
  1972 *The Politics of Chaos: Canada in the Thirties*. Toronto: Macmillan.

Nelles, H. V.
  1974 *The Politics of Development, Forests, Mines and Hydro-electric Power in Ontario 1849-1946*. Toronto: Macmillan.

  1980 "Defensive Expansionism Revisited: Federalism, the State and Economic Nationalism in Canada, 1959-1979," *The (Japanese) Annual Review of Canadian Studies 2: 127-145*.

Nettle, J. P.
  1969 "Consensus or Elite Domination: The Case of Business," in R. Rose (ed.), *Studies in British Politics*. London: Macmillan.

Neufeld, E. P.
  1969 *A Global Corporation: A History of the International Development of Massey Ferguson Ltd*. Toronto: University of Toronto Press.

  1972 *The Financial System of Canada: Its Growth and Development*. New York.

Niosi, Jorge
  1978 *The Economy of Canada*. Montreal: Black Rose.

  1981 *Canadian Capitalism*. Toronto: Lorimer.

  1983 "The Canadian Bourgeoisie: Towards a Synthetical Approach," *Canadian Journal of Political and Social Theory*, 7 (3): 128-149.

  1985 *Canadian Multinationals*. Toronto: Garamond.

Nisbet, Robert
  1966 *The Sociological Tradition*. New York: Basic Books.

Nolan, Richard L. and Rodney E. Schneck
  1969 "Small Businessmen, Branch Managers, and Their Relative Susceptibility to Right-wing Extremism: An Empirical Test," *Canadian Journal of Political Science*, 2: 89-102.

Normandin, A. L.
  1936 *The Canadian Parliamentary Guide, 1936*. Ottawa: Syndicats d'oeuvres sociales limitée.

  1945 *The Canadian Parliamentary Guide, 1945*. Ottawa: Syndicats d'oeuvres sociales limitée.

Nunes, Maxine and Deanna White
  1972 *The Lace Ghetto*. Toronto: New Press.

Oakley, Ann
  1974 *The Sociology of Housework*. New York: Pantheon.

Oberschall, Anthony
  1973 *Social Conflict and Social Movements*. Englewood Cliffs, N.J.: Prentice-Hall.

O'Connor, James
   1970   "The Fiscal Crisis of the State," *Socialist Revolution*, No. 1 and 2.

Offe, Klaus
   1974   "Structural Problems of the Capitalist State," in Klaus von Beyme (ed.), *German Political Studies*. London: Sage, pp. 31-57.

Olsen, Dennis
   1980   *The State Elite*. Toronto: McClelland and Stewart.

Ornstein, Michael D.
   1981   "The Occupational Mobility of Men in Ontario," *Canadian Review of Sociology and Anthropology*, 18 (2): 183-215.

   1984   "Interlocking Directorates in Canada: Intercorporate or Class Alliance," *Administrative Science Quarterly*, 29: 210-231.

Ornstein, M. D., M. M. Stevenson and A. P. Williams
   1980   "Region, Class and Political Culture in Canada," *Canadian Journal of Political Science*, 13: 229-271.

Ossowski, Stanislaw
   1963   *Class Structure in the Social Consciousness*. London: Routledge and Kegan Paul.

Ouellet, Fernand
   1980a *Economic and Social History of Quebec 1760-1850*. Toronto.

   1980b *Lower Canada 1791-1840: Social Change and Nationalism*. Toronto.

Overbeek, Henk
   1980   "Finance Capital and the Crisis in Britain," *Capital and Class*, 2: 99-120.

Owaisi, Lateef and Zafar Bangash
   1978   *Visible Minorities in Mass Media Advertising*. Ottawa: Minister of Supply and Services.

Packer, Herbert
   1964   "Two Models of the Criminal Process," *University of Pennsylvania Law Review*, 113 (November): 1-68.

Palloix, Christian
   1975   "The Internationalization of Capital and the Circuit of Social Capital," in Hugo Redice (ed.), *International Firms and Modern Imperialism*. Markham: Penguin, pp. 63-88.

Palma, G.
   1978   "Dependency: A Formal Theory of Underdevelopment or a Methodology for the Analysis of Concrete Situations of Underdevelopment," *World Development*, 6: 881-924.

Palmer, Bryan D.
   1983   *Working-Class Experience*. Toronto: Butterworths.

Paltiel, Khayyan Z.
   1970   *Political Party Financing in Canada*. Toronto.

Panitch, Leo
   1981   "Dependency and Class in Canadian Political Economy," *Studies in Political Economy*, 6: 7-33.

Panitch, Leo, ed.
   1977   *The Canadian State: Political Economy and Political Power*. Toronto: University of Toronto Press.

Panitch, Leo and Reg Whitaker
1974   "The New Waffle: From Matthews to Marx," *Dimension*, 10, 1.

Park, Libbie and Frank Park
1973   *Anatomy of Big Business.* Toronto: Lewis and Samuel.
[1962]

Parsons, Talcott
1961   "An Outline of the Social System," in T. Parsons, E. Shils, K.D. Naegele, J.R. Pitts (eds.),
        Theories of Society. New York: The Free Press of Glencoe.

Parsons, Talcott and Neil Smelser
1957   *Economy and Society.* London: Routledge and Kegan Paul.

Pentland, H. C.
1981   *Labour and Capital in Canada 1650-1860.* Toronto: Lorimer.

Petersen, W.
1958   "A General Typology of Migration," *American Sociological Review*, XXIII, pp. 256-66.

Petras, James and Morris Morley
1982   "The New Cold War: Reagan's Policy Towards Europe and the Third World," *Studies in
        Political Economy*, 9: 5-44.

Pfeffer, Richard
1979   *Working for Capitalism.* New York: Columbia University Press.

Philbrook, T.
1966   *Fisherman, Logger, Merchant, Miner: Social Change and Industrialization in Three
        Newfoundland Communities.* Study No. 1, Newfoundland Institute for Social and
        Economic Research, St. John's.

Phillips, Anne
1977   "The Concept of Development," *Review of African Political Economy*, 8: 7-20.

Phillips, James
1980   "Renovation of the International Economic Order: Trilateralism, the IMF, and Jamaica,"
        in Holly Sklar (ed.), *Trilateralism: The Trilateral Commission and Elite Planning for World
        Management.* Boston: South End Press, pp. 468-91.

Phillips, Paul
1979   "The National Policy Revisited," *Journal of Canadian Studies*, 14: 3-13.

Piedalue, Gilles
1976   "Les Groupes financiers au Canada 1900-1930," *Revue d'Histoire de l'Amérique
        Française*, 30 (1): 3-34.

Pineo, P.
1977   "The Social Standing of Ethnic and Racial Groupings," *Canadian Review of Sociology and
        Anthropology*, 14 (May): 147-57.

Pineo, P. C. and J. Porter
1967   "Occupational Prestige in Canada," *Canadian Review of Sociology and Anthropology*, 4
        (2): 24-40.

Piven, A. and R. Cloward
1971   *Regulating the Poor.* New York: Pantheon Books.

Ponting, J. Rick

1984   "Conflict and Change in Indian/Non-Indian Relations in Canada: Comparison of 1976 and 1979 National Attitude Surveys," *Canadian Journal of Sociology*, IX (2): 137-158.

1987a *Profiles of Public Opinion on Canadian Natives and Native Issues: Module 1 - Constitutional Issues.* Calgary, Alta.: Research Report No. 87-01, Research Unit for Public Policy Studies, The University of Calgary.

1987b *Profiles of Public Opinion on Canadian Natives and Native Issues: Module 2 - Special Status and Self-Government.* Calgary, Alta.: Research Report No. 87-02, Research Unit for Public Policy Studies, The University of Calgary.

1987c "Notes for Remarks to the National Education Symposium," mimeo. Forthcoming as "Public Opinion and Social Action on Contemporary Native Issues," *Saskatchewan Federated Indian College Journal.*

1987d *Profiles of Public Opinion on Canadian Natives and Native Issues: Module 3 - Knowledge, Perceptions, and Sympathy.* Calgary, Alta.: Research Report No. 87-03, Research Unit for Public Policy Studies, The University of Calgary.

1988a *Profiles of Public Opinion on Canadian Natives and Native Issues: Module 4 - Native People, Finances, and Services.* Calgary, Alta.: Research Report No. 88-01, Research Unit for Public Policy Studies, The University of Calgary.

1988b *Profiles of Public Opinion on Canadian Natives and Native Issues: Module 5 - Land, Land Claims and Treaties.* Calgary, Alta.: Research Report No. 87-02, Research Unit for Public Policy Studies, The University of Calgary.

Porter, John

1965   *The Vertical Mosaic: An Analysis of Social Class and Power in Canada.* Toronto: University of Toronto Press.

1967   "Canadian Character in the Twentieth Century," *The Annals of the American Academy of Political and Social Science*, 370 (March).

1975   "Foreword," in Wallace Clement, *The Canadian Corporate Elite: An Analysis of Economic Power.* Toronto: McClelland and Stewart.

Porter, Marion R., John Porter and Bernard R. Blishen

1973   *Does Money Matter?* Toronto: York University Institute for Behavioural Research.

Portes, Alejandro and John Walton

1981   *Labor, Class, and the International System.* Toronto: Academic Press.

Poulantzas, Nicos

1973   "On Social Classes," *National Left Review*, 78 (March-April).

1974   "Internationalization of Capitalist Relations and the Nation-State," *Economy and Society*, 3: 145-79.

1977   "The New Middle Class," in Alan Hunt (ed.), *Class and Class Structure.* London: Lawrence and Wishart.

Presthus, Robert

1973   *Elite Accommodation in Canadian Politics.* Toronto: Macmillan.

1974   *Elites in the Policy Process.* London: Cambridge University Press.

1977   "Aspects of Political Culture and Legislative Behavior: United States and Canada," in Robert Presthus (ed.), *Cross-National Perspectives: United States and Canada.* Leiden: E. J. Brill, pp. 7-22.

Presthus, Robert and William V. Monopoli
1977 "Bureaucracy in the United States and Canada: Social, Attitudinal and Behavioral Variables," in Robert Presthus (ed.), *Cross-National Perspectives: United States and Canada.* Leiden: E. J. Brill, pp. 176-190.

Price, C. A.
1959 "Immigration and Group Settlement," in W. D. Borrie (ed.), *The Cultural Integration of Immigrants.* New York: UNESCO.

Priscepionka, Algimantas V. J.
1963 "Agriculture in the Maritime Provinces of Canada: Past and Present," M.A. thesis, University of California, Berkeley.

Przeworski, Adam
1977 "Proletariat into a Class," *Politics and Society,* 7 (4): 365-367.

Putnam, D. F.
1939 "Distribution of Agriculture in New Brunswick," *Public Affairs,* 3(1): 8-11.

Puxley, E.
1971 *Poverty in Montreal.* Montreal: Dawson College Press.

Pye, A. Kenneth
1982 "The Rights of Persons Accused of Crime under the Canadian Constitution: A Comparative Perspective," *Law and Contemporary Problems,* 45 (Autumn): 221-248.

Pye, Lucian W.
1964 "The Roots of Insurgency and the Commencement of Rebellions," in Harry Eckstein, (ed.) *Internal War: Problems and Approaches.* Westport, Ct.: Greenwood.

Redfield, Robert
1953 *The Primitive World and Its Transformations.* Ithaca, New York: Great Seal Books, Cornell University Press.

Reiter, Ester
1986 "Life in a Fast-Food Factory," in Craig Heron and Robert Storey (eds.), *On the Job: Confronting the Labour Process in Canada.* Montreal: McGill-Queen's University Press.

Report of the Commission on Equality in Employment
1984 *Equality in Employment.* Ottawa: Minister of Supply and Services.

Report of the Committee on Sexual Offences Against Children and Youths
1984 *Sexual Offences Against Children.* 2 vols. Ottawa: Minister of Supply and Services.

Report of the Royal Commission on the Status of Women in Canada
1970 Ottawa: Information Canada.

Resnick, Philip
1982 "The Maturing of Canadian Capitalism," *Our Generation,* 15 (3): 11-24.

Reynolds, Lloyd George
1935 *The British Immigrant: His Social and Economic Adjustment in Canada.* Toronto: Oxford University Press.

Richards, A. E.
1940 "Farmers' Cooperative Business Organizations in Canada, 1938-39," *The Economic Annalist,* 10 (1): 35-41.

Richards, John and Larry Pratt
  1979   *Prairie Capitalism: Power and Influence in the New West*. Toronto: McClelland and Stewart.

Richardson, R. Jack
  1982   "Merchants Against Industry: An Empirical Study," *Canadian Journal of Sociology*, 7: 279-96.

  1988   "'A Sacred Trust': The Trust Industry and Canadian Economic Structure," *Canadian Review of Sociology and Anthropology*, 25 (1): 1-22.

Richler, Mordecai
  1975   "Letter from Ottawa: The Sorry State of Canadian Nationalism," *Harper's*, 250 (June): 28-32.

Ridge, J. M.
  1973   "Three Generations," in J. M. Ridge (ed.), *Oxford Studies in Social Mobility: Working Papers*. London: Oxford University Press, pp. 47-71.

Rinehart, James
  1975   *The Tyranny of Work*. Toronto: Longman Canada.

Rioux, Marcel
  1965   "Conscience ethnique et conscience de classe au Québec," *Recherches Sociographiques*, 6 (January-April).

Robin, Martin
  1968   *Radical Politics and Canadian Labour*. Kingston.

Robinson, Ira M.
  1962   *New Industrial Towns on Canada's Resource Frontier*. Chicago: University of Chicago, Department of Geography, Research Paper no. 73.

Rocher, Guy
  1973   *Le Québec en mutation*. Montreal: Hurtubise.

Rogin, Michael Paul
  1967   *The Intellectuals and McCarthy: The Radical Specter*. Cambridge, Mass.: The MIT Press.

Rohmer, Richard
  1970   *The Green North*. Toronto: Maclean-Hunter Learning Matls..

Rose, Joseph B. and Gary N. Chaison
  1985   "The State of the Unions: United States and Canada," *Journal of Labor Research*, 6 (Winter): 97-111.

Rosenstone, Steven J., Roy L. Behr, and Edward H. Lazarus
  1984   *Third Parties in America: Citizen Response to Major Party Failure*. Princeton, N.J.: Princeton University Press.

Rostow, W. W.
  1971   *The Stages of Economic Growth*. Cambridge: Cambridge University Press.

Rowthorn, B.
  1975   "Imperialism in the 1970s - Unity or Rivalry?" in Hugo Radice (ed.), *International Firms and Modern Imperialism*. Markham, Ontario: Penguin, pp. 158-80.

Royal Commission on Bilingualism and Biculturalism
  1969   *Report*. Book 4. *The Cultural Contribution of the Other Ethnic Groups*. Ottawa: Queen's Printer.

Royal Commission on the Status of Women
  1970   *Report.* Ottawa: Information Canada.

Rumilly, R.
  1975   *Honore Mercier et son Temps.* Vol. 1. Montreal.

Rush, Gary B.
  1983   "State, Class and Capital: Demystifying the Westward Shift of Power," *Canadian Review of Sociology and Anthropology,* 20: 255-289.

Rustow, Dankwart
  1955   *The Politics of Compromise.* Princeton.

Ryder, N. B.
  1955   "The Interpretation of Origin Statistics," *Canadian Journal of Economics and Political Science,* 4: 466-79.

Sacouman, R. James
  1977   "Underdevelopment and the Structural Origins of Antigonish Movement Cooperative Associations in Eastern Nova Scotia," *Acadiensis* 7: 66-85.

  1979   "The Differing Origins, Organization, and Impact of Maritime and Prairie Co-operative Movements to 1940," in Robert Brym and R. J. Sacouman, *Underdevelopment and Social Movement in Atlantic Canada.* Toronto: New Hogtown Press.

Safarian, A. E.
  1969   *The Performance of Foreign-Owned Firms in Canada.* Washington, D.C.: National Planning Association.

Schattschneider, E. E.
  1960   *The Semisovereign People.* New York.

Schlesinger, Arthur M., Jr.
  1964   *Paths to the Present.* Boston: Houghton Mifflin.

Schmidt, Ray
  1981   "Canadian Political Economy: A Critique," *Studies in Political Economy,* 6: 65-92.

Schwartz, Barry
  1974   "Waiting, Exchange and Power: The Distribution of Time in Social Systems," *American Journal of Sociology,* 79 (4): 841-870.

Science Council of Canada
  1972   "Innovation in a Cold Climate: 'Impediments to Innovation'," in Abraham Rotstein and Gary Lax (eds.), *Independence: The Canadian Challenge.* Toronto: The Committee for an Independent Canada, pp. 120-131.

Scott, John
  1985   *Corporation, Classes and Capitalism.* 2nd edition. London: Hutchinson.

  1987   "Intercorporate Structure in Western Europe: A Comparative Historical Analysis," in Mark S. Mizruchi and Michael Schwartz (eds.), *Intercorporate Relations: The Structural Analysis of Business.* Cambridge: Cambridge University Press.

Seeley, John R., R. Alexander Sim and E. W. Loosley
  1956   *Crestwood Heights.* Toronto: University of Toronto Press.

Seidman, Ann and Phil O'Keefe
  1980   "The United States and South Africa in the Changing International Division of Labour," *Antipode,* 12 (2): 1-16.

Shortt, S. E. D.
   1972   "Social Change and Political Crisis in Rural Ontario: the Patrons of Industry, 1889-1896,"
          in Donald Swainson (ed.), *Oliver Mowat's Ontario*. Toronto: Macmillan.

Siegfried, André
   1966   *The Race Question in Canada*. Toronto: McClelland and Stewart.

Simeon, R.
   1979   "Regionalism and Canadian Political Institutions," in R. Schultz *et al.* (eds.), *The Canadian
          Political Process*. Toronto: Holt Rinehart & Winston, pp. 293-301.

Simmel, G.
   1955   *Conflict*. Glencoe, Ill.: Free Press.

Sinclair, Peter R.
   1973   "The Saskatchewan CCF: Ascent to Power and the Decline of Socialism," *Canadian
          Historical Review*, 54: 419-33.

   1975   "Class Structure and Populist Protest: The Case of Western Canada," *Canadian Journal of
          Sociology,* 1: 1-17.

Singelmann, Joachim
   1978   *From Agriculture to Services*. Beverly Hills: Sage.

Sklar, Holly, ed.
   1980   *Trilateralism: The Trilateral Commission and Elite Planning for World Management*.
          Boston: South End Press.

Smart, John
   1969   *The Patrons of Industry in Ontario*. M.A. thesis, Carleton University, Department of
          History.

Smigel, Erwin O.
   1969   *Wall Street Lawyer*. Bloomington: Indiana University Press.

Smiley, Donald V.
   1984   "Public Sector Politics, Modernization and Federalism: The Canadian and American
          Experiences," *Publius: The Journal of Federalism*, 14 (Winter): 52-59.

Smith, A. J. M.
   1979   "Evolution and Revolution as Aspects of English-Canadian and American Literature," in
          Richard A. Preston (ed.), *Perspectives on Evolution and Revolution*. Durham, N.C.: Duke
          University Press.

Smith, Denis
   1971   *Bleeding Hearts...Bleeding Country: Canada and the Quebec Crisis*. Edmonton: M.G.
          Hurtig.

Smith, Goldwin
   1971   *Canada and the Canadian Question*. Toronto: University of Toronto Press.

Sorokin, P. A.
   1964   *Basic Trends of Our Time*. New Haven: College and University Press.

Stacey, C. P.
   1940   *The Military Problems of Canada: A Survey of Defence Policies and Strategic Conditions
          Past and Present*. Toronto.

Stapells, H. G.
   1927   *The Recent Consolidation Movement in Canada*. Master's thesis, University of Toronto.

Statistical Abstracts of the U.S.
  1983   *Statistical Abstracts of the U.S. 1982-83.* 103rd edition.

Statistics Canada
  1970a   *Corporation Financial Statistics*, 1970. (cat. 61-207) Ottawa.

  1970b   *Manufacturing Industries of Canada: Geographical Distribution*, 1970. Ottawa.

  1972a   *Corporations and Labour Unions Returns Act, Part I: Corporations.* Ottawa.

  1972b   *Income Distribution by Size, 1972.* Ottawa.

  1978   "Structural Aspects of Domestic and Foreign Control in the Manufacturing, Mining and Forestry Industries, 1970-1972." Ottawa.

Stevens, G. R.
  1962   *Canadian National Railways.* Vol 2. Toronto.

Stewart, Walter
  1977   *Strike!* Toronto: McClelland and Stewart.

Supply and Services Canada
  1984   *Corporations and Labour Unions Return Act for 1983. Part I: Corporations.* CS61-21-1984, Ottawa.

Sutherland, Ronald
  1977   *The New Hero: Essays in Comparative Quebec/Canadian Literature.* Toronto: Macmillan.

  1982   "A Literary Perspective: The Development of a National Consciousness," in William Metcalfe (ed.), *Understanding Canada.* New York: New York University Press, pp. 401-414.

Svalastoga, K.
  1959   *Prestige, Class and Mobility.* Copenhagen: Gyldendal.

  1965   "Social Mobility: The Western European Model," *Acta Sociologica*, 9: 175-82.

Swartz, Donald
  1977   "The Politics of Reform," in Leo Panitch (ed.), *The Canadian State.* Toronto: University of Toronto Press.

Sweeny, Robert
  1980   *The Evolution of Financial Groups in Canada and the Capital Market Since the Second World War.* Master's thesis, Universite du Quebec a Montreal.

Sweezy, Paul
  1959   "The Theories of New Capitalism," *Monthly Review*, 11 (3 & 4) (July and August).

Swinton, Katherine
  1979   "Judicial Policy Making: American and Canadian Perspectives," *The Canadian Review of American Studies*, 10 (Spring): 89-94.

Szymanski, Albert
  1981   *The Logic of Imperialism.* New York: Praeger.

Tarasoff, Nadya
  1973   "Some Notes on 'Government Transfer Payments to Individuals'." Ottawa: Social Planning Council of Ottawa, November 28.

Tarnopolsky, Walter S.
  1982   "The Equality Rights," in W. S. Tarnopolsky and G. A. Beaudoin (eds.), *The Canadian Charter of Rights and Freedoms: Commentary.* Toronto: Carswell Co.

Task Force on the Structure of Canadian Industry
1968   *Foreign Ownership and the Structure of Canadian Industry (Watkins Report).* Ottawa: Privy Council Office.

Taylor, Charles
1965   "Nationalism and the Political Intelligentsia," *Queen's Quarterly*, 72 (Spring).

Taylor, J. G.
1979   *From Modernization to Modes of Production: A Critique of the Sociologies of Development and Underdevelopment.* Atlantic Highlands, N.J.: Humanities Press.

Taylor, Norman W.
1964   "The French-Canadian Industrial Entrepreneur and His Social Environment," in Marcel Rioux and Yves Martin (eds.), *French-Canadian Society*, Vol. 1. Toronto: The Carleton Library, McClelland and Stewart, pp. 271-95.

Tepperman, Lorne
1975   *Social Mobility in Canada.* Toronto: McGraw-Hill Ryerson.

1977   "Effects of the Demographic Transition Upon Access to the Toronto Elite," *Canadian Review of Sociology and Anthropology*, 14: 285-93.

1989   *Choices and Chances: Sociology for Everyday Life.* Toronto: Holt Rinehart Winston.

Terman, Lewis M. and C. C. Miles
1936   *Sex and Personality: Studies in Masculinity and Femininity.* New York: McGraw-Hill.

Therborn, Goran
1983   "Why Some Classes Are More Successful Than Others," *New Left Review*, 138: 37-55.

Thomas, W. I. and F. Znaniecki
1920   *The Polish Peasant in Europe and America.* Boston.

1958   *The Polish Peasant.* 2nd edition. New York.

Thompson, E. P.
1963   *The Making of the English Working Class.* Harmondsworth: Penguin.

Thompson, Grahame
1977   "The Relationship between the Financial and Industrial Sector in the United Kingdom Economy," *Economy and Society*, 6: 235-83.

Tilly, Charles
1976   *The Vendée.* Cambridge, Mass: Harvard University Press.
[1964]

Tilly, Charles *et al.*
1975   *The Rebellious Century, 1830-1930.* Cambridge, Mass: Harvard University Press.

Tocqueville, Alexis, de
1968   *De la démocratie en Amérique.* J. P. Mayer (ed.), abridged ed., Paris: Gallimard, Collection Idées.

Tonnies, Ferdinand
1963   *Community and Society.* Translated and edited by Charles Loomis. New York: Harper
[1887] Torchbook.

Troy, Leo and Leo Sheflin
1985   *Union Sourcebook.* West Orange, N.J.: IRDIS Publishers.

Trudeau, Pierre E.
1968   *Federalism and the French Canadians.* Toronto: Macmillan.

Trueman, Allan M.
  1975 "New Brunswick and the 1921 Federal Election." M.A. thesis, University of New Brunswick, Fredericton.

Truman, Tom
  1971 "A Critique of Seymour M. Lipset's Article, Value Differences, Absolute or Relative: The English-Speaking Democracies," *Canadian Journal of Political Science*, 4: 497-525.

Tugendhat, C.
  1973 *The Multinationals*. London: Penguin.

Tulchinsky, Gerald
  1972 "The Montreal Business Community, 1837-1853," in D. S. Macmillan (ed.), *Canadian Business History, Selected Studies*, 1497-1971. Toronto: McClelland.

Turner, F. J.
  1921 *The Frontier in American History*. New York: Henry Holt.

Underhill, Frank
  1960 *In Search of Canadian Liberalism*. Toronto: Macmillan.

  1964 *Image of Confederation*, Massey Lectures, Third Series. Toronto: C.B.C.

UNESCO
  1982 *Statistical Yearbook*, (1982). Paris: UNESCO.

United Nations
  1983 *World Economic Survey*, 1983 (supplement). New York: United Nations.

United States Department of the Interior
  1939 *The Structure of the American Economy*. Washington: United States Government Printing Office.

U.S. Arms Control and Disarmament Agency
  1982 *World Military Expenditures and Arms Transfers 1971-1980*. Washington, D.C.

U.S. News and World Report
  1984 "How Big is Government's Bite?" August 27, 1984:65.

Useem, Michael
  1984 *The Inner Circle*. New York: Oxford University Press.

Vallee, Frank G. and Donald R. Whyte
  1964 "Canadian Society: Trends and Perspectives," in Bernard R. Blishen *et al.* (eds.), *Canadian Society*, rev. ed. Toronto: Macmillan..

Vallee, Frank G. and Donald R. Whyte, eds.
  1971 *Canadian Society: Sociological Perspectives*. Third edition. Toronto: Macmillan.

Vallee, Frank G., Mildred Schwartz and Frank Darknell
  1957 "Ethnic Assimilation and Differentiation in Canada," *Canadian Journal of Economics and Political Science*, XXIII (4): 540-49.

Van Tyne, C. H.
  1959 *The Loyalists in the American Revolution*. Gloucester, Mass.: Peter Smith.

Viner, Jacob
  1975 *Canada's Balance of International Indebtedness 1900-1913*. Toronto: Macmillan.

Wade, Mason
  1968 *The French Canadians*, Vol. I. Toronto: Macmillan.

1974   "Québécois and Acadien," *Journal of Canadian Studies,* 2: 2 (May), 47-53.

Walker, Richard A.
1978   "Two Sources of Uneven Development Under Advanced Capitalism: Spatial Differentiation and Capital Mobility," *Review of Radical Political Economics*, 10 (3): 28-38.

Warner, W. L. *et al.*
1945   *The Social System of American Ethnic Groups.* New Haven, Conn.: Yale University Press.

Warren, Bill
1975   "How International is Capital?" in Hugo Radice (ed.), *International Firms and Modern Imperialism: Pioneer of Capitalism.* London: New Left Books.

1981   *Imperialism: Pioneer of Capitalism.* London: New Left Books.

Warriner, Charles K. and Jane E. Parther
1965   "Four Types of Voluntary Associations," *Sociological Inquiry*, 35: 138-48.

Watkins, Mel H.
1966   "The American System and Canada's National Policy," *Bulletin of the Canadian Association for American Studies.*

1970   "Preface" in Kari Levitt, *Silent Surrender.* Toronto: Macmillan of Canada, pp. ix-xvii.

1973   "Resources and Underdevelopment," in R. M. Laxer (ed.), *Canada Ltd.: The Political Economy of Dependency.* Toronto: McClelland and Stewart, pp. 107-126.

1975   "Economic Development in Canada," in I. Wallerstein (ed.), *World Inequality.* Montreal: Black Rose Books, pp. 72-96.

1977   "The Staple Theory Revisited," *Journal of Canadian Studies*, 12 (5): 83-95.

Watt, James
1967   "Anti-Catholicism in Ontario Politics: The Role of the Protestant Protective Association in the 1894 Election," *Ontario History,* LIX:1 (March).

Weaver, John Charles
1973   "Imperilled Dreams: Canadian Opposition to the American Empire, 1918-1930," Ph.D. dissertation, Department of History, Duke University.

Weber, Max
1947   *Social and Economic Organization.* Talcott Parsons (ed.) New York: Free Press.

1964   *The Theory of Social and Economic Organization.* Introduced and edited by Talcott Parsons. New York: Free Press.

1968   *Economy and Society.* New York: Bedminster Press.

Wechter, Dixon
1937   *The Saga of American Society: A Record of Social Aspiration, 1607-1937.* N.Y.: Charles Scribner's Sons.

Weeks, John
1981   "The Differences between Materialist Theory and Dependency Theory and Why They Matter," *Latin American Perspectives*, 8 (3/4): 118-123.

Weimann, Gabriel and Conrad Winn
1986   *Hate on Trial: The Zundel Affair, The Media, and the Public Opinion in Canada.* Oakville, Ontario: Mosaic Press.

Weinfeld, Morton
  1980   "The Jews of Quebec: Perceived Anti-Semitism, Segregation and Emigration," *Jewish Journal of Sociology*, 22: 1 June.

  1981   "The Development of Affirmative Action in Canada," *Canadian Ethnic Studies*, 13 (2): 23-39.

Weiss, R. S. and Nancy M. Samuelson
  1958   "Social Role of American Women: Their Contribution to a Sense of Usefulness and Importance," *Marriage and Family Living*, 20 (November): 358-66.

Westergaard, John and Henrietta Reisler
  1975   *Class in a Capitalist Society*. London: Heinemann.

Westin, Alan F.
  1983   "The United States Bill of Rights and the Canadian Charter: A Socio-Political Analysis," in William R. McKercher (ed.), *The U.S. Bill of Rights and the Canadian Charter of Rights and Freedoms*. Toronto: Ontario Economic Council, pp. 27-44.

Westley, William and Margaret Westley
  1971   *The Emerging Worker*. Montreal: McGill-Queen's University Press.

Whitaker, Reginald
  1977   "Images of the State in Canada," in L. Panitch (ed.), *The Canadian State: Political Economy and Political Power*. Toronto: University of Toronto Press.

White, Julie
  1980   *Women and Unions*. Ottawa: Supply and Services Canada for the Canadian Advisory Council on the Status of Women.

White, William H. Jr.
  1956   *The Organization Man*. New York.

Whyte, John D.
  1976   "Civil Liberties and the Courts," *Queen's Quarterly*, 83 (Winter): 655-663.

Wiener, Jonathan M.
  1975   "The Barrington Moore Thesis and Its Critics," *Theory and Society*, 2 (Fall).

Wigle, D. J. and Y. Mao
  1981   *Income Levels in Urban Canada, 1980*. Ottawa: Health and Welfare Canada.

Wilkins, Mira
  1969   *The Emergence of Multinational Enterprise: American Business Abroad from the Colonial Era to 1914*. Cambridge.

Williams, Glen
  1983   *Not for Export: Toward a Political Economy of Canada's Arrested Industrialization*. Toronto: McClelland and Stewart.

Williams, William A.
  1961   *Contours of American History*. Cleveland: World Publishing Co.

  1962   *The Tragedy of American Diplomacy*. New York: Dell.

  1969   *The Roots of the Modern American Empire*. New York.

Wilmott, Donald E.
  n.d.   *Organizations and Social Life of Farm Families in a Prairie Community*. Saskatoon:
  [1964] Centre for Community Studies, University of Saskatchewan.

Winn, Conrad
  1985 "Affirmative Action and Visible Minorities: Eight Premises in Quest of Evidence," *Canadian Public Policy*, 11 (4): 684-700.

Wolpe, H., ed.
  1980 *The Articulation of Modes of Production*. London: Routledge and Kegan Paul.

Wood, Louis A.
  1975 *A History of Farmers' Movements in Canada: The Origins and Development of Agrarian*
  [1924] *Protest*, 1872-1924. Toronto: University of Toronto Press.

Woodward, Calvin A.
  1976 *The History of New Brunswick Provincial Election Campaigns and Platforms*, 1886-1974. Toronto: Micromedia.

World Bank
  1983 *World Development Report 1983*. New York: Oxford University Press.

Wright, Erik Olin
  1976 "Class Boundaries in Advanced Capitalist Societies," *New Left Review*, 98: 3-42.

  1978 *Class, Crisis, and the State*. London: New Left Books.

Wright, Esther
  1955 *The Loyalists of New Brunswick*. Fredericton.

Wright, Jim F. C.
  1956 *Prairie Progress: Consumer Co-operation in Saskatchewan*. Saskatoon: Modern Press.

Young, Ruth C. and Olaf F. Larson
  1965 "The Contribution of Voluntary Organizations to Community Structure," *American Journal of Sociology*, 7: 178-186.

Young, Walter D.
  1969a *The Anatomy of a Party: The National CCF*, 1932-1961. Toronto: University of Toronto Press.

  1969b *Democracy and Discontent: Progressivism, Socialism and Social Credit in the Canadian West*. Toronto: McGraw-Hill Ryerson.

Younger, R. M.
  1970 *Australia and the Australians: A New Concise History*. New York.

Zakuta, Leo
  1964 *A Protest Movement Becalmed*. Toronto: University of Toronto Press..

Zelan, J. H., E. Freeman and A. H. Richardson
  1968 "Occupational Mobility of Spanish-American War Veterans and Their Sons," *Sociology and Social Research*, 52 (3): 211-23

Zerubavel, Eviatar
  1979 *Patterns of Time in Hospital Life: A Sociological Perspective*. Chicago: University of Chicago Press.